Jones & Bartlett
Student Edition

C Programming for Scientists and Engineers

With Applications

Rama N. Reddy • Carol A. Ziegler

JONES AND BARTLETT
PUBLISHERS
BOSTON TORONTO LONDON SINGAPORE NEW DELHI

World Headquarters
Jones and Bartlett Publishers
40 Tall Pine Drive
Sudbury, MA 01776
978-443-5000
info@jbpub.com
www.jbpub.com

Jones and Bartlett Publishers
Canada
6339 Ormindale Way
Mississauga, Ontario L5V 1J2
CANADA

Jones and Bartlett
Publishers International
Barb House, Barb Mews
London W6 7PA
UK

First Indian Edition 2010

Jones and Bartlett India Pvt. Ltd.
4262/3, Ansari Road, Daryaganj
New Delhi – 110 002
Tel. 011–4361 3900
info@jbpubindia.net
www.jbpubindia.com

ISBN : 978-93-80108-34-6

Printed and bound in India by Sanat Printers, Kundli - 131 028, Sonepat, Haryana.

This book is dedicated to:

Dr. Charles B. Cliett; Retired Chairman
Dr. Joe F. Thompson; Distinguished Professor, and my advisor
Aerospace Engineering, Mississippi State University

My Loving late brothers:
Mr. Rama Nanjunda Reddy
Dr. Rama Vrenkataswamy Reddy

Contents

Preface

C is a comprehensive procedural and modular programming language with built-in data types, standard control structures, and a rich collection of library functions, including input/output functions, mathematical functions, string manipulation functions, and dynamic storage allocation functions. *C Programming for Scientists and Engineers with Applications* uses the ANSI C standard.

The book is organized into 11 chapters. The syntax and semantic concepts, as well as the programming concepts, are introduced with sample code that has been tested for accuracy. This book also has programming hints and warnings. The complete solutions to science and engineering problems are provided at the end of each chapter, including a definition of each problem, the solution method, appropriate input data, and the pseudocode and/or flowcharts as appropriate. The code has been tested with sample input, and the output is provided after the code is executed with the given input. The sample problems, with complete solutions, presented at the end of each chapter are carefully chosen from science and engineering subjects such as chemistry, physics, mechanical engineering, electrical engineering, and mathematics.

This book is designed to teach C programming to engineering and science students with no prior programming experience. Chapter 1 explains the basic terminology relating to hardware, software, problem definition, and solution. The concept of modularization of solutions is introduced through structured charts, and the implementation of the solutions algorithm is demonstrated using flowcharts and/or pseudocode. The compilation of the source code into object code and the process of linking the object code with libraries to produce the executable code are also presented. This chapter may be covered in two to three lectures.

Chapter 2 presents the basic elements of C, starting with the character set, identifiers, declaration and definition of variables, arithmetic and arithmetic expressions, executable statements, and program structure. The early introduction of pointers in this chapter directs students' attention to this powerful feature of C. This chapter must be covered in detail. At the completion of this chapter, students should be able to write code and compile and execute simple problems. Some basic input and output statements that are presented in Chapter 3 need to be introduced here for the students to start programming.

Chapter 3 covers the details of the standard input/output and file input/output functions from the standard library. The format control strings for the input/output of `int`, `float`, `double`, and `char` data types are presented with all the necessary details. The sample programs at the end of the chapter will reinforce the format control string specification spacing for input and output. This chapter must be covered completely, and students should be assigned one or two programs with all of the input/output features.

Chapter 4 covers the control structures: sequence, selection, and repetition, which are the standard control structures of structured programming language. There are special control structures: case structure, which is implemented with the `switch` statement, and `else if` statements. The special looping control statements for loops and nested loops are presented. This chapter must be covered in depth. The sample programs at the end of this chapter use these control structures to reinforce the concepts.

Chapter 5 emphasizes modular programming using the powerful feature of functions. This chapter covers in detail the concepts of passing arguments by value and by pointers. The concepts of passing multiple arguments and returning multiple parameters are introduced with many examples. Passing arguments to parameters by pointer is a difficult concept for students to grasp and must be explained thoroughly. Students should write two programs to understand the concept of passing multiple arguments and parameters back and forth between calling functions and called functions. Several sample programs, with complete solutions, are presented at the end of the chapter to show the passing of arguments to function parameters by value and by pointer.

Chapter 6 introduces the concepts of scope of variables and storage classes, such as auto, which is the default; extern, which can be used across different files; static; and the register class, which defaults to the auto class. Complete solutions, with the code and sample output, are presented at the end of the chapter for single-file and multiple-file applications.

Chapter 7 presents one-dimensional arrays. The declaration, storage, input/output, and arithmetic manipulations are presented in detail. This chapter is important for science and engineering students and, therefore, must be covered in depth. The sample programs at the end of this chapter show engineering and science applications, as well as some sorting and search algorithms.

Chapter 8 presents multidimensional arrays. The declaration, storage, input/output, and arithmetic manipulations are presented in detail. This chapter covers both two-dimensional and three-dimensional arrays. The sample programs at the end of this chapter show the use of two-dimensional arrays in particular. The programs are complete, and the input and output are presented.

Chapter 9 covers character and string data types. The declaration and storage of character and string data types are presented. Input/output of character and string data are covered in depth. At the end of the chapter, there are sample programs, with complete code, including input and output. Sorting and search algorithms are presented. The extent to which this chapter should be covered depends on how much students will be expected to use character and string data types in future classes.

Chapter 10 addresses the concepts of pointers and dynamic pointers, with an emphasis on arrays and character strings. The concept of the pointer is introduced in Chapter 2. This chapter presents advanced uses—in particular, using dynamic pointers for arrays and strings. There are many examples at the end of the chapter, including sample programs using dynamic pointers. Students interested in this topic should be encouraged to look at the code and the input/output of the sample programs.

Chapter 11 covers structures: declaration of structures to set storage templates, and declaration and initialization of structure variables. The structure variable member operator and member dereference operator are presented. Input and output to structure variables using the member operator are given in detail. Arithmetic operations and passing and returning structure variables to functions are presented in depth. Nested and self-referential structures, with sample code, are also presented. The enumeration data type is provided at the end of this chapter.

The complete solutions to engineering and science problems at the end of each chapter, with the documentation, code, input, and output, has been run and tested. These are presented as examples for students to run, reinforcing the C language features and good programming habits.

Appendix A contains ASCII code, Appendix B contains the important functions of various standard libraries that the C language supports and a table of operator precedence, and Appendix C provides the complete answers to all of the review questions in the text by chapter and section.

Ancillaries

An online instructor's manual is provided, with a brief description of the material to be covered in the text by chapter and by section, and the answers to all of the review questions and exercises at the end of each chapter.

Acknowledgments

We would like to thank the following reviewers for their valuable suggestions: Mitchell Nielson, of Kansas State University, and Leonard Marino, of the University of San Diego.

We would also like to thank the following students for their help running the code in the text: David Yarbrough, Christopher Robinson, and Songul Cecen.

Finally, thank you to those at Jones and Bartlett who have helped us during the publication of this book, especially: Tim Anderson, Acquisitions Editor; Melissa Potter, Editorial Assistant; Amy Rose, Production Director; Ashlee Hazeltine, Production Assistant; and Andrea DeFronzo, Senior Marketing Manager.

CHAPTER 1

Introduction to Computers and Programming

Objectives

To understand the basic concepts of the hardware and software components of a computer system, program development, program compilation and execution in C, and the C program processing environment.

General purpose computers have become an important part of everyday life, particularly with the evolution of internet technology. Computers and computer programming are essential components in modern problem solving and in the technology of information transfer. A computer can store large volumes of data with fast access, perform complex computations at high speed, and accurately and efficiently share the resulting information. Solid-state electronics and integrated circuits [particularly very large scale integrated (VLSI) circuits], have revolutionized the computer industry, making it possible to build increasingly powerful computers with storage capacity and processing power at decreasing cost. Modern machines are compact, efficient, affordable, and indispensable in every area of research and applications used in industry, universities, medicine, music, entertainment, business, and communications, among others.

Computers are used in educational institutions for teaching, research, and administrative activities; in industry they are used for research, design, and manufacturing; in medical sciences for research, diagnosis, treatment, and record keeping; in aeronautics and space exploration for the design, control, and navigation of space vehicles; in the exploration of natural resources, for weather forecasting, film production, and in other such fields. Special types of computer systems are used for engineering analysis and design, to construct intelligent decision systems, to process natural language documents, to control production, and in the development of expert diagnostic systems, in speech recognition, image processing, and robotics.

Because computers and computer programs are widely used in mission critical applications, cost effectiveness, speed, and reliability are very important factors. The degree of reliability needed depends on the application. For applications such as space exploration, nuclear power production, defense, and medical technology, failure of computerized devices is not acceptable. A high degree of reliability of the entire system is critical and essential. The concept of reliability has led to the development of fault-tolerant computer systems. Such systems are designed not to fail (hardware or software) under any circumstances. A critical part of these systems is the reliable and failure-free computer program.

Computer users have little control over the speed and accuracy of the computers they are using. However, users who write their own programs can make decisions affecting the speed of processing by how they choose to have the computer store the data, how it is accessed, and the method used to solve the problem. For example, accessing data randomly is slower than accessing it sequentially and trial and error methods of solution are slower than using formulas. Program writers can also influence the accuracy of answers by the choice of formulas, the data storage formats, and the treatment of significant digits in numeric data. They can influence the reliability of answers by building checkpoints into the program.

1.1 Concept of Computers and Computer Systems

Computers are electromechanical devices that function semi-automatically and are capable of accepting instructions and data, performing computations, and manipulating data to produce useful results. The term *hardware* applies to the collection of all of the physical components that constitute a computer. *Software* is the collection of all of the programs that run on the hardware of the computer. Each program consists of a sequence of instructions, which directs the computer to input and manipulate data based on the solution algorithm to produce an answer to the problem and output the results. *Firmware* is the part of hardware that is permanently programmed; this type of built-in software is essential in order to activate (*boot*) the system.

A *computer system* consists of hardware, software, and firmware. Computers are categorized according to their size (memory and number of processors), functions, and areas of applications. With the revolution of internet technology, they are further classified according to design and function as general-purpose, server, workstation, web hosting, and network computers. *General-purpose computers* can run many different programming languages and solve many different types of problems. *Special-purpose computers* use a single programming language designed for a specific type of application.

General-purpose computers are broadly classified as mainframe, super, personal, and laptop based on physical size, memory size, word size, processing speed, number of peripheral devices supported, and network support. *Mainframe computers* are found in installations where there is high demand for computer power and a large amount of data to be processed. *Supercomputers* are extremely fast machines used primarily for complex and scientific computations. *Personal computers* (PCs) are found in homes, schools, libraries, businesses and other small installations, and in laboratories where there are limited amounts of data to process. Personal computers are used primarily for science and engineering applications, bookkeeping, writing, and personal use. The present generation of personal computers provides powerful computational capability. *Laptops* are small portable computers with capabilities similar to those of personal computers.

Servers and workstations are special purpose machines. *Servers* are large computer systems that store large varieties of programs and databases to provide service to the organizations and people using the internet. Servers are the backbone of the internet, which supports millions of users and many types of applications including email service and e-commerce. *Workstations* are capable of performing large computations. They can be configured based on the memory and processing needs to be stand-alone units with processing power and graphics capabilities, or they can be connected to other computers for special activities such as email and internet access.

Most current computers store and then process the instructions one at a time in a predetermined sequence and store intermediate results of computations. Advances in hardware technology have made it possible to approach the limit of electronic speed. Further speed increase will be attained by packaging electronic elements closer together so that the signals travel shorter distances. The electronic speed limits the amount of computing the computer can complete within a given period of time.

1.1.1 Hardware Components and Functions

The primary hardware components of a computer are the input/output devices, memory units (both primary and secondary), and processing units. The *central processing unit* (CPU) consists of the arithmetic-logic unit (ALU) and the control unit (CU). The block diagram of a typical system is shown in Figure 1.1. Large systems also have support hardware, which performs addi-

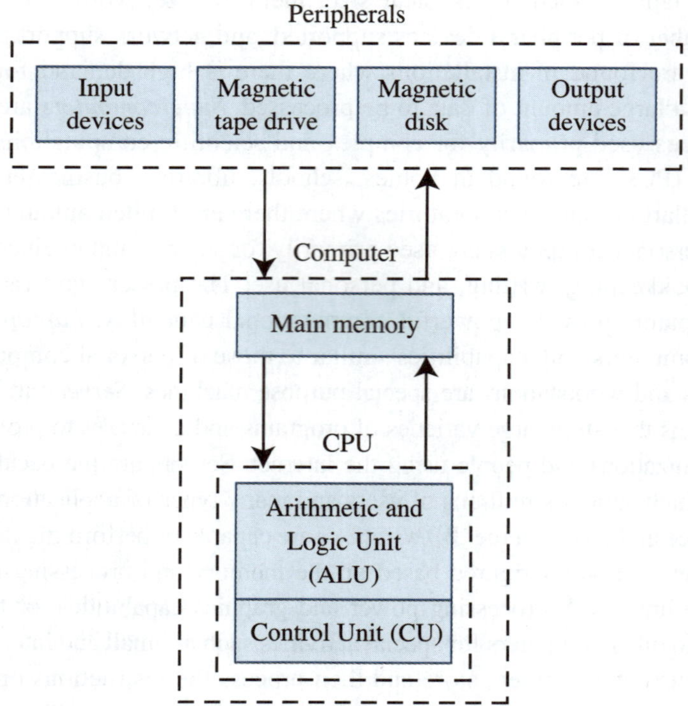

Figure 1.1 Block diagram of a computer

tional specialized functions such as graphic display, networking, image processing, or managing secondary storage. All of these are primarily electronic, consisting of digital logic gates and circuits that control and drive the mechanical processes.

Input/Output (I/O) Devices *Input devices* are used to input instructions and data into the computer, usually in character form. Some installations use optical scanners or magnetic scanner devices to read data on marked and printed paper and transmit it to the computer memory. For some purposes, punched card readers are used. Key entry devices, such as interactive terminals, are the most common form of input device used today. Instructions and data are typed at the keyboard and the characters are transmitted directly or indirectly to main memory. In recent hand-held computers, such as the palm pilot, touch pen input devices are used.

Output devices make the processed information available in the form of printouts, screen displays, graphics, sound and speech, or file output on a disk. The most common output devices are printers, displays, graphics terminals, and disk drives. A *printe*r prints on paper the output information that was stored in main memory. Some printers print characters one at a time like typewriters; others print one line at a time. Dot matrix printers are usually used for rough drafts. Higher quality output is produced by laser, chain, inkjet, and other special printers, such as those needed for desktop publishing. Large computer installations use line printers and higher speed laser printers. *Magnetic storage devices* such as tape drives and disk drives are used for both input and output. Although they are peripheral devices, they are part of the system. Magnetic storage devices provide secondary storage. They hold large volumes (gigabytes and terabytes) of data in very little space. Data values are coded in magnetic dots, representing zeros and ones. Magnetic devices are convenient, cost effective, and store information permanently, but the data stored on them can only be read by computers. These devices come in many different forms, with different access speeds and storage capacities.

Memory Devices *Memory devices* store both program instructions and data. The main memory, also called random access memory (RAM), is used for storing instructions currently being executed and data currently being processed. This is fast memory with microsecond to nanosecond speed. The *processor* communicates directly with the main memory, fetching instructions and fetching and storing data. Many of today's desktop personal computers have more RAM, which makes them more powerful, and have greater processing speeds and capabilities than the room size computers of only a few years ago.

Central Processing Unit The central processing unit (CPU) consists of the control unit and the arithmetic-logic unit. The *control unit* (CU) contains electronic circuitry that fetches the instructions from memory and decodes them. The decoded signals for the operation code and the operands are sent to the arithmetic-logic unit (ALU), directing it to carry out the arithmetic and logic operations. The CU stores the results of the arithmetic and logic operations in main memory. It also supervises the input and output of data. The details of input and output are usually handled by independent processors called input/output (I/O) processors.

The *arithmetic-logic unit* (ALU) contains the electronic circuitry that performs standard arithmetic operations and makes logic decisions by comparing values. The arithmetic circuits can add, subtract, multiply, and divide, using two numbers at a time. The result of such operations is numeric. The logic circuits can compare either numeric or character values. The output of the logic circuits is interpreted as a logical value of true or false. The logic circuits can also perform standard logical operations: selecting, testing, and altering logical values. In large mainframe and supercomputers, the ALU often contains coprocessors so that logic decisions may be made at the same time calculations are being carried out. *Coprocessors* are also very common in microcomputers, especially when using mathematically oriented languages. All computer instructions are based on these elementary operations of fetching, arithmetic, comparison, and storing.

1.1.2 Software Components and Functions

A *program* is a sequence of instructions written in a programming language that directs a computer in problem solving. The *software* in a computer system consists of programs written to support the basic operations of the system and programs written to carry out an application. There are several levels of software active at all times. Figure 1.2 shows some of these software systems and their hierarchy.

The software that controls the execution of an application program is called *system software*. The major system software components are the operating system and the programming language systems, which include utility programs and library routines. These programs keep the computer functioning efficiently and provide a comfortable environment for the user. They allow the user to access data in a variety of forms and to set up filing systems for data.

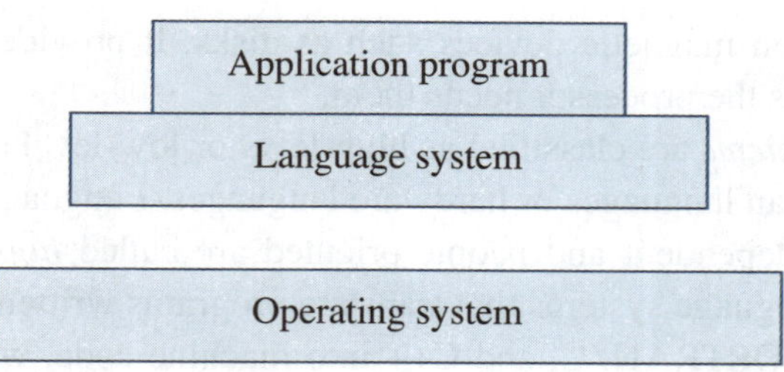

Figure 1.2 Application and system software

The *operating system* makes the system facilities available to the application programs and controls their use. It provides access to a variety of programming and debugging tools and provides an interface between the user and the computer hardware. It schedules program execution and directs traffic through the computer. The operating system manages all the system resources—allocating and deallocating memory, processor, devices, and files to a particular application program as they are needed. Operating systems have their own nonstandardized control languages. Instructions in these languages direct the computer to undertake tasks and make resources available to the tasks. Every programmer needs at least minimal knowledge of the control language of the computer being used.

System management is designed to balance processing and input/output, with the aim of providing reasonable minimum turnaround and maximum throughput. *Turnaround* is the amount of time elapsing between a request to the computer to execute a program and the availability of output. *Throughput* is measured by the number of jobs that are completed in a given time period.

With interactive systems, response time is also important. *Response time* is the time lapse between interactive input and output that indicates that the input has been received.

The operating system contains system utility programs and a system library. *System utility programs* are data management and device management system software. The data management software manages the formatting of the input/output. The device management software makes the devices available as though they are extensions of memory. The *system library* contains graphics packages, mathematics packages, statistics packages, database management routines, and data communication and networking software.

The *file management system,* which is part of the operating system, controls the storage and retrieval of records from program and data files, which are normally stored on magnetic devices such as disks. It provides instructions and data to memory as the processor needs them.

Language systems are classified as high-level or low-level depending on their similarity to human languages or hardware languages. Languages that are reasonably machine independent and people-oriented are called *high-level languages*. *Compilers* are language systems that translate programs written in high-level languages such as FORTRAN, C, and C++ into machine code, which the hardware can interpret and execute directly. Assembly language and other machine-oriented languages are called *low-level languages*. Programs written in assembly language are also assembled (translated) to machine code. Compilers that translate source code into particularly efficient machine code are called *optimizing compilers*.

Application software consists of programs written to analyze data and solve specific problems. Application programs produce output concerning the exterior world, while system programs produce output concerning the state of the computer system. Application programs may be written by users, but more often are written by professional programmers. Programmers may write a program to compute a payroll, for example, or to implement an automatic navigation system for an aircraft. When adequate application software can be purchased, programmers often modify it to their company's specific needs.

When an engineer uses a computer to process data, the engineer uses an input device to tell the operating system what application software to run. The application program requests data, calls on the system library for routines that decode the data, and converts it into a computer-usable format. The application program then processes the data, calling on the system library for standard mathematical routines and for routines that convert the results to a form the engineer can understand. It then calls on the file management system to store the results until the engineer needs them.

When an engineer writes his or her own application program, the program must be thoroughly tested on the computer before it can be used to process data. To do this, the engineer uses an input device to tell the operating system which compiler to run. The engineer has prepared a sequence of instructions in the programming language that are input as data to the computer and stored on a disk. The compiler checks the instructions one by one for spelling and syntax, translates them into a machine-usable format, and calls on the file management system to store the results until they are needed. Before finishing and returning control to the operating system, the computer sends error messages and program statistics to the engineer.

Before an engineer writes an application program and submits it to the computer it is necessary to design the input layout of the data, the output layout of the computational results, and to thoroughly think through the steps involved in processing the data.

1.1.3 Integration of Hardware and Software

Hardware cannot function by itself without software; software cannot function unless it has hardware to run on. Both are necessary to make a computer system work properly. Programs written in high-level languages go through several levels of translation and interpretation before the machine can execute them. Application programs written in C are translated by the compiler into a machine language that is then interpreted for execution by the digital logic gates and circuits.

1.1.4 Review Questions

1. A computer system consists of both ________________ and ________________.
2. Three major hardware components of a computer are ________________, ________________, and ________________.
3. A compiler translates a high-level language program to ________________.
4. The arithmetic-logic unit of a computer performs ________________ and ________________ operations.
5. Machine language instructions are fetched and decoded by the ________________ unit.
6. Input/output operations are controlled by the ________________ unit.
7. The input devices handle instructions and data in ________________ form.
8. Common secondary storage devices are ________________ and ________________.
9. Programs written to manipulate data and solve problems are called ________________ software.
10. The central processing unit consists of ________________, ________________, and ________________.
11. The program in a computer system that manages the computer resources is called an ________________ system.

12. Software programs permanently installed to control equipment are called ________________.

1.2 Modular Programming

Modularization is the process of breaking down a complex problem into easily solvable, manageable, and functional units. Modularization is based on the concept of "divide and conquer." For example, some problem solutions have the form:

1. Get data
2. Process data
3. Output results

Other problem solutions may have the form:

1. Set up a table
2. Put data in the table
3. Analyze the table
4. Output the results

The process of modularization would then call for more detailed descriptions as to where to get the data, how to validate it, how to process it, how to arrange it in a table, how to analyze it, and so forth.

To understand and analyze a complex problem may be difficult, but once the problem is subdivided into smaller understandable pieces called subproblems, it is easier to understand the original problem and design a process to solve it.

1.2.1 Modular Design

The first step in modular design is to divide the complex problem into major subproblems. Then the major subproblems are divided into further sub-problems until they are simple to solve. The problems and subproblems are called *modules*. Modules should be designed in such a way that they are *loosely coupled*. Loose coupling simply means that if a change is made in any of the modules it does not force change in other modules. There are two types of modules: functional modules and spatial modules. A module with a specific function or task to perform is called a *functional module*. If there is a repeated process in several places in the overall design, such a process can be made into a *module* and such a module can be used to replace the repeated process. It is called a *spatial module*. The C programming language provides the facility to represent these functional and spatial modules so that they are loosely coupled.

During the design process the user requirements are spelled out. A prototype of the design is developed and tested to see whether it meets the requirements. During the design process the designer must document the design and provide the capability for future updates. The design steps may be repeated several times before writing the application program, to eliminate any design flaws. If there are any design flaws in the solution algorithm, it may be too late to correct them when the final product is found to be functionally incorrect. Therefore, we cannot overstress the importance of the solution algorithm design process. This is the most crucial phase in the development of any software.

1.2.2 Structure Charts

A structure chart is a design tool that represents the functional and spatial modules of the algorithm and their relationship to one another. In a structure chart, the statement of the problem to be solved is represented in the form of a rectangular box at the top level. For example, in Figure 1.3 "Calculate the square root of a number" is the statement of the problem. The functions in the next level are represented in rectangular boxes horizontally from left to right in the order in which they are activated. If there is any function in the second level that needs to be further divided into subfunctions, they are represented in the next level. The functions at each level are represented from left to right and the further subdivision of the functions at each level is represented vertically.

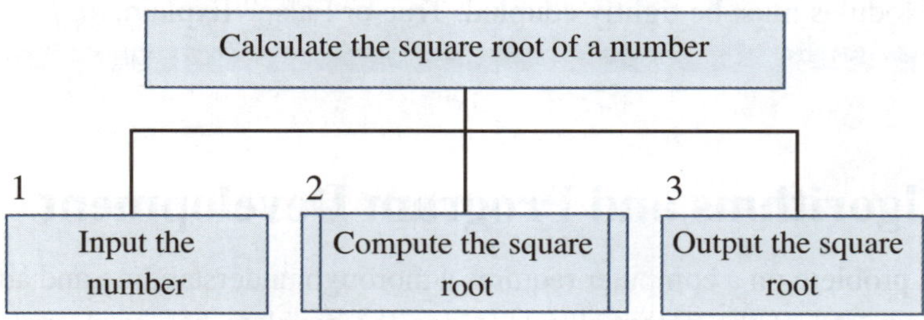

Figure 1.3 Structure chart

The structure chart represents the analysis of the problem of calculating the square root of a number. It also represents program modules. The module "Calculate the square root of a number" invokes the modules beneath it, passing data back and forth to them.

1.2.3 Functional Modules

Modules communicate with one another by passing information back and forth. In C, these modules receive numeric values and manipulate them, and the result is conveyed back to the invoking module. An invoking module is a function that calls another function. C provides the facility to write these modules as independent units of a program. These units can be compiled, debugged, and tested independently, then linked together into an executable program. Modules can be input modules, computational modules, or output modules. There are a number of functional modules available in C's rich library of functions such as `sqrt()` to compute a square root of a number or `max()` to compute a maximum of a set of values. There may also be functional modules written by other people that are available for use. Programmers write their own functional modules for specific problems and, in addition, they can use standard library functions and library functions written by other people, as they fit into their application. C is rich in library functions, which will be presented throughout the text. The list of all library functions is provided in Appendix B.

1.2.4 Review Questions

1. In modular design the large problem is divided into ________________.
2. What is the relationship between lower-level and higher-level modules in a hierarchy chart?
3. Modules must be tightly coupled. True or False? Explain.

1.3 Algorithms and Program Development

Solving a problem on a computer requires a thorough understanding and analysis of the problem and of the potential data. Once the problem has been analyzed, the detailed design of a solution can be developed. One of the steps in designing and developing a computerized solution to a problem is to develop an algorithm to solve the problem. At the same time, the algorithm must filter out inappropriate data.

1.3.1 Concept of an Algorithm

An *algorithm* is a procedure consisting of a finite number of precisely defined steps for solving a problem. Each step of an algorithm must be an unambiguous instruction which, when written in a computer language, can be executed by a computer. The order of the steps is critical, because most computers execute steps in the order in which they are presented. An algorithm must terminate whether or not the task is completely successfully executed. That is, it must recognize the end of the input data and when an answer is sufficiently accurate. Algorithms that monitor the weather, automatic teller machines, and nuclear reactors are continually active. These types of algorithms are apparent exceptions to the termination requirement. However, they idle as they continuously poll input devices and are normally reactivated as needed.

> *Programming Warning:* Every step in the algorithm must be clear and precise and the algorithm must terminate.

Programmers should choose an algorithm on the basis of efficiency, accuracy, reliability, and clarity. Algorithms should be efficient with respect to computational time, storage requirements, and response time. The degree of accuracy required is specified by the user. An algorithm is reliable when it consistently produces correct answers from valid data and rejects invalid data. Clarity means that an understandable programming style is used. Clarity should not be compromised. However, sometimes a compromise between the other factors is necessary. For example, efficiency may be sacrificed for the sake of a high degree of reliability.

The design of algorithms to solve simple problems can be straightforward, but design of algorithms for large, complex problems can be difficult and time consuming. Although this text can only deal with simple problems, the techniques we use are important in the design of algorithms for complex problems.

One common approach to large and complex problems is to use top-down design. Top-down design starts at the top of the structure chart with a general statement of the problem written in a precise, formal way to provide a high-level specification of the algorithm. This is divided into separate logical parts and a general specification for the solution of these parts is given. These parts correspond to major modules in the final algorithm. The parts are then further subdivided and specifications are drawn up. Finally the algorithm reaches a stage where the specification consists of computations, comparisons, and data access that can be programmed without further explanation.

An Example of a High-Level Problem Specification Calculate, in pounds, the total amount of steel required to build a pipeline to carry water.

The next step would be to divide the problem into logical parts as follows:

1. Input the pipeline dimensions
2. Check their validity
3. Calculate the cross-sectional area
4. Calculate the volume of steel
5. Calculate the weight
6. Output the weight

Each stage of the algorithm should be carefully checked before the algorithm is written in a computer programming language and again before it is tested on a computer. If the design is not proved correct at each stage, it may contain errors that make it necessary to start over. Careful validation during the design process leads to a more nearly correct solution.

1.3.2 Concept of Programs and Data

A *program* is a sequence of executable, unambiguous instructions written in a computer language. The computer can understand instructions of various types: *input/output* instructions to input data into the computer and output answers from it; *move* instructions to rearrange data; *arithmetic* instructions to perform calculations; *control* instructions to control selection and repetition of actions; *logic* instructions to help the computer make choices. These types of instructions are available in most programming languages. In C there are also instructions to control where data is stored in the computer memory.

Input refers to data sent to the computer processor from a file on an automatic storage device or from an outside source. Input may come from a keyboard or an automatic device such as a weather station.

Output refers to data sent out from the computer processor to automatic storage devices or to an outside device or a person. Output may be printed, displayed on a CRT screen, written on a tape, disk or diskette, plotted (rendered) on a graphic device, or used to control an automatic device.

The internal rearrangement of data, during which values are copied from one memory location to another, is achieved primarily through assignment instructions, which look like simple equations. For example, the C instruction

```
a = b;
```

does not mean that a and b are the same things, but rather that a is being assigned (given) the same value as b. In effect the value contained in the memory location named b is copied into the memory location named a. After the statement a = b is carried out by the computer the memory location a will contain the same value as the memory location b.

Arithmetic instructions consist of the basic arithmetic operations of addition, subtraction, multiplication, division, remainder, and exponentiation (raising to a power), as well as assigning the answer to a variable. Thus,

```
a = 2.5 + 6.5 / 3.25;
```

means that 4.5 is calculated as the value assigned to a. Arithmetic expressions are evaluated by the computer with the same operator precedence as they are evaluated in mathematics. In this example, the division is performed before the addition.

Control instructions are used to switch from one set of instructions to another depending on the logical comparison of data values. For example, the computer might choose between addition or subtraction depending on whether a number is positive or not.

```
if(x > 0)
   z = x + 5;
else
   z = x - 5;
```

Control instructions always involve the comparison of one value with another for equality or relative size. All comparisons result in an answer of true or false, which becomes the basis for a control decision. The logical comparisons are presented in Chapter 4.

Concept of Data The collection of related information to be processed by an application program such as temperatures to be averaged over a period of time is known as *data*. Data can be numeric, character, or logical. Numeric data can be written as decimal numbers, as integers, or in scientific notation. Numeric data values are treated as numeric values even though they are written as strings of digits and special characters. In C, character data values are written as characters inside a single quote as `'a'` or strings of characters inside double quotes as `"axbcd"`. While C does not have a data type specifically for logical data, integers are used to represent true and false. Zero is interpreted as false, and all other integers are interpreted as true.

NUMERIC DATA	CHARACTER STRING DATA
254	"JAMES MILLER"
−52.75	"LMNOP3476"
0.125	"LEEMAN BROTHERS"
+17.357	"+17.357"
0.32987653E02	"+=23765"

Data values are usually stored in a file on the disk. A *data file* is a repository to store data and contains a structured collection of data. Input data must be structured in a systematic way. Every program includes a description of the data structure so that the computer knows how to interpret it. If a program is to find its input data on a disk, the data must be keyed into a data file. Input data can also be keyed directly into an executing program. When data values are keyed directly, it is particularly important that the program validate the data before using it. In either case, the end of the input data must be recognizable. When data values are keyed directly, a special control character is used as an end symbol.

> *Programming Hint:* Check that input data is valid. Validation of input data is critical.

Data generated by the computer for output can be of many types: solutions to mathematical equations, numbers, pictures, graphs, textual material, or special symbols. Output data must be formatted properly for the output device by having appropriate vertical and horizontal spacing. Data must be in a usable form. Numbers printed or displayed should be arranged and labeled with headings, subheadings, and whatever other identification is helpful.

Output should be understandable, easy to use, and attractive. Good output is worth the time expended in designing and formatting it.

Programming Hint: Make output readable and visually attractive. Use titles and column headings. Align data. Output date and time in reports.

Example: Tabular output (columns labeled)

PARTS INVENTORY REPORT (11/17)

PART NAME	UNITS	UNIT COST	TOTAL COST OF UNITS
Bolts	50	0.50	25.00
Nails	500	0.01	5.00
Struts	200	0.10	20.00
…..	…….	……..	
Screws	400	0.05	20.00

Example: Interactive output (values labeled)

MATERIAL VOLUME

DIAMETER = 5	LENGTH = 10	VOLUME = 195.35
………………	………………	……………………
DIAMETER = 8	LENGTH = 14	VOLUME = 427.85

Not all values calculated by a program are part of the output data. Such values as counts, intermediate computational results, and logical values that control processing are *internal* data. Internal data also includes status flags for various pieces of equipment and for functions of the operating system.

To a computer, data consists of more than just numbers or character strings. A set of data values is identified as being of a particular data type, being written in a particular notation, being suitable for certain operations, and being given a name by which it can be identified. There also may be criteria for validity and attached units of measurement. For example, data representing the speed of a car would be numeric, be written with a decimal point, be called "speed" or "velocity," be in miles/hour or kilometers/hour, be used in arithmetic, or be used as output, and would not be a negative number. Data representing an identification number would be characters, written within double quotes, might be either alphabetic characters or digits, and could be used only for comparison and for output.

1.3.3 Procedure for Problem Analysis

To analyze a problem, besides writing a precise specification of the algorithm, the user should write precise specifications for the input and output data. These specifications should include initial conditions and boundary conditions, such as those associated with mathematical models and computational simulations, in addition to the equations or formulas to be used. Some problems do not have exact solutions. Such problems should be analyzed for ways of obtaining approximate solutions, determining the quality of these solutions and the degree of accuracy needed. Side effects, options, and possible disastrous cases must be considered. Once the problem is clearly understood and the associated side effects are resolved, programming can begin.

Problem Types and Solution Methods There are engineering and scientific type problems requiring solutions for which empirical equations have been derived with known and unknown variables. There are also problems for which closed-form solutions are known using appropriate formulas with known and unknown variables. There are other problems for which mathematical models have been developed in the form of a process to be followed using dependent and independent variables. All of these equations are solved by some appropriate numerical scheme.

There are three basic types of solutions. First, when a closed-form solution to a problem is known, the appropriate equations can be used in a program. Second, when no closed-form solutions are known, or when the mathematical solution involves trial and error, numerical methods can be used to approximate the solution. Third, some types of problems have so many independent variables that rather than a single answer, a variety of possible solutions is desirable. In addition, there are problems having more than one solution where it may be satisfactory to find any one solution rather than all of them.

Data Types The procedure for problem analysis includes analyzing categories of possible input data. In some cases the input values are external to the program, in other cases they are generated internally. When external data values are used, the input must be validated by the computer according to clearly defined specifications as the computer cannot guess the intent of the person entering the data. Data specification includes such requirements as the type of data expected (numeric or character), the form of the data (integer, real numbers, complex numbers, logical data, etc.), the size of the data (number of digits or characters), the arrangement of the data (lists, tables, records, etc.), and any restrictions on the range of the data values. For example, a set of measurements of the depth of water in a lake might be assumed to contain at least one measurement; be positive, real numbers rather than integers; be significant to two decimal places; and have a unit of measurement such as meters. Program documentation should state this and the algorithm should check that the data meets these conditions.

> *Design step*: Describe the input and output formats.

1.3.4 Solution Design Methodology

Once the problem has been clearly stated and analyzed, and the details of the data specified, the solution can be developed. This involves the actual design of the input, output, internal data, the development of an algorithm, and the development of test data for the algorithm. For example, the computer must know whether the data values consist of integers or real numbers and whether they are in normal decimal notation or scientific notation. It must know how many data values are expected and how to identify the end of the list of data values. If the algorithm includes a repeated calculation, assumed preconditions and postconditions must be recognized.

At the design stage, the algorithm can be represented by structure charts, pseudocode and/or flowcharts, or by other logic representation techniques. Consider the simple problem of calculating and printing the average depth of water in a lake with a set of sample depth measurements. The basic steps in the calculation are:

1. Input, validate, and add the data values one by one, counting the number of data values
2. Divide the sum of the data values by the number of data values
3. Print the average depth

The first of these steps includes repeated input, validation, and addition. The program instructions must include information about the variables to be added and incremented in the repetition loop, and how to detect the end of the data. The instruction to calculate the average and print the average follows the repetition loop. Step 1 will only work if there is an internal variable to use to accumulate the sum of the data values, and an internal variable to use as a counter. Both of these must be cleared before any data is processed. The precondition for Step 1 is that total = 0 and count = 0 where total and count are names for the internal variables. The precondition for Step 2 is that count > 0. Therefore there must be at least one positive data value.

The simplest pseudocode description of this algorithm is as follows:

```
initialize total and count
process positive data values in a set of data values
calculate average
print average
```

This could also be drawn as a flowchart as shown in Figure 1.4.

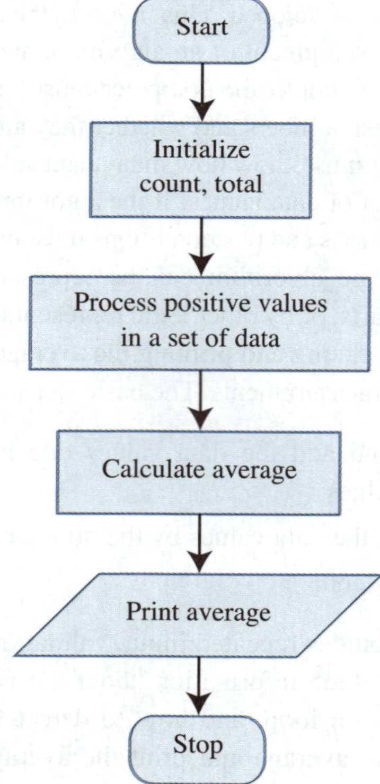

Figure 1.4 Flowchart to compute an average

In the flowchart in Figure 1.4, arrows indicate the flow of control while different shaped boxes are used for different types of operations. Unless there are many data values to be processed the same way, the flow of control is strictly from the top down.

The following is a pseudocode description of this algorithm that assumes there is at least one valid data value.

Algorithm

```
Initialize the total and the count to zero (This is necessary to meet the first
    precondition)
For each input data value greater than 0     (precondition: assume total ≥ 0, count ≥ 0
                                              every time a new data value is obtained)
  Add the data value to the total
  Add 1 to the count
End for
Divide the total by the count to get the average depth ( precondition; assume count > 0)
Print the average depth
Stop
```

> *Programming Hint:* Note that totals and count must always be initialized to zero to reflect the possibility that there may not be any data to process.

This can be drawn as a flowchart as shown in Figure 1.5.

The steps in the flowchart in Figure 1.5 can be described either in language or in mathematical notation. Note that we have not yet considered how to identify the end of the data or how to control the repetition.

The part of the pseudocode that is bracketed by `For` and `Endfor` processes the entire set of data values and can be drawn in flowchart form as shown in Figure 1.6.

Note that each data value is processed separately; therefore, there is a loop back to obtain the next data value. This construct enters at the top and exits at the bottom; but it exits only when there are no more data values to be processed.

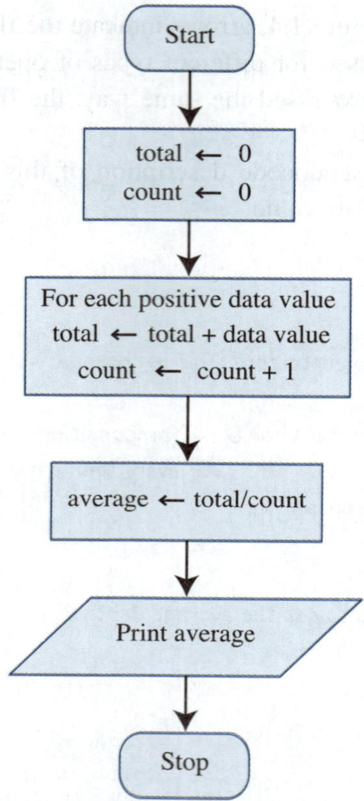

Figure 1.5 Flowchart to compute average

For each input data value > 0 the part of the pseudocode that is bracketed by `If` and `Endif` processes a single data value and can be drawn as shown in Figure 1.7.

Note that a positive value will be added to the total and the count will be incremented. However, nothing will be done if a data value is not positive. Put these `For...Endfor` and `If...Endif` constructs together with the preceding sequential flowchart and we obtain the flowchart of Figure 1.8.

Pseudocode *Pseudocode* is a semiformal description of the steps to be carried out by the computer, including steps that are to be repeated and decisions that are to be made. There is more than one way of writing an algorithm in pseudocode.

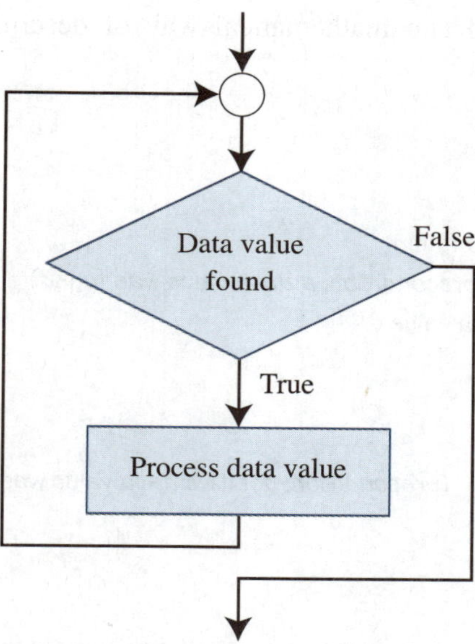

Figure 1.6 Flowchart for repetition

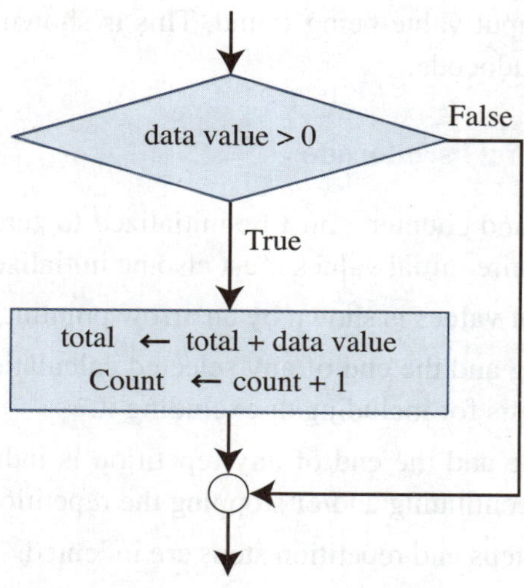

Figure 1.7 Flowchart for selective processing

Another more detailed and mathematical way of describing this algorithm in pseudocode would be:

```
total ← 0.0
count ← 0
For each input data value found
   If data value > 0      (precondition: a data value was found)
      total ← total + data value
      count ← count +1
   EndIf
Endfor
average ← total / count   (precondition: positive data value was found)
print average
Stop
```

Note that several assumptions have been made: that there is at least one positive measurement, that the measurement is a real number rather than an integer (total is initialized to 0.0 rather than 0), and that a measurement of 0 doesn't count.

The processing of a data value depends on the value being positive, which in turn depends on an input value being found. This is shown by the two levels of indentation in the pseudocode.

Convention for Writing Pseudocode

1. Summations and counters must be initialized to zero, and other variables that require initial values must also be initialized.
2. Assignment of values is shown by an arrow pointing to the left.
3. The beginning and the end of any selected calculation is indicated as well as the basis for including or excluding it.
4. The beginning and the end of any repetition is indicated, as well as the basis for continuing and/or stopping the repetition.
5. Conditional steps and repetition steps are indented.
6. Either words or arithmetic operations may be used for arithmetic.

7. The algorithm termination must be clearly indicated.

These conventions are demonstrated in the previous examples of pseudocode.

Flowchart A *flowchart* uses standard symbols to show different operations and the order of execution of the steps of the algorithm. Lines and arrows are used to show the flow of control. Figure 1.8 shows a flowchart for the problem of finding

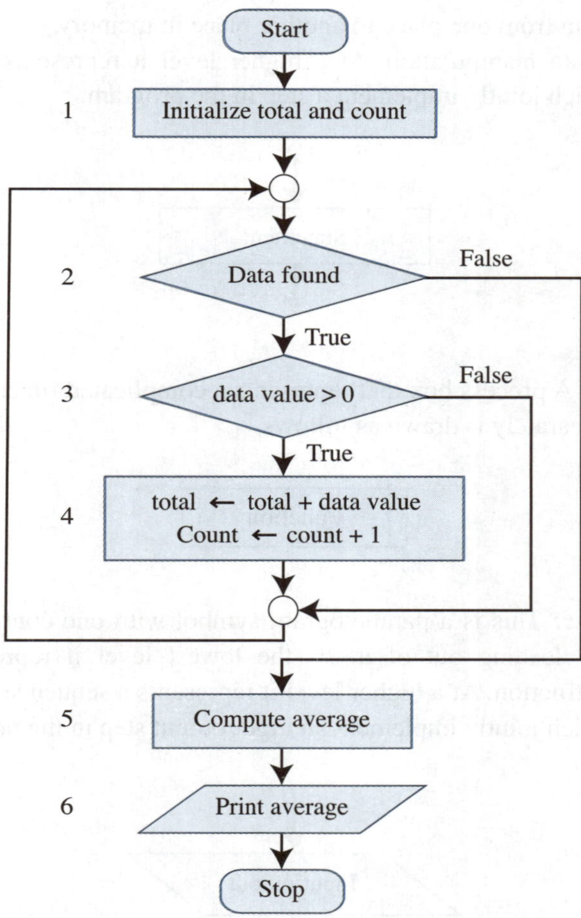

Figure 1.8 Flowchart to compute average depth

the average depth of water in a lake. Flowcharts help the programmer understand the flow of control in complex algorithms.

Standard Flowchart Symbols Each flowchart symbol represents part of an algorithm or program. When flowcharts are used in a structured way, symbols are grouped together to form a single-entry, single-exit structure.

Process box: This is a rectangle with one control line leading into it and one leading out of it. At the lowest level it represents a single instruction that computes, moves data from one place to another place in memory, or carries out some other type of data manipulation. At a higher level it represents a sequence of instructions, which jointly implement a step in the program.

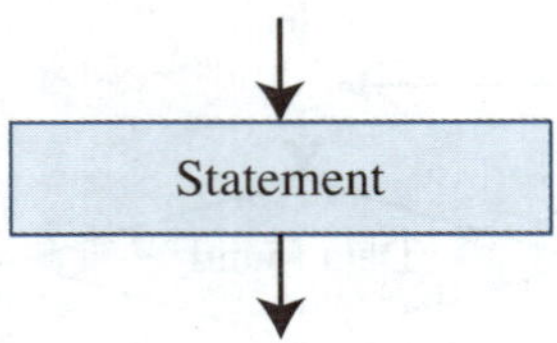

A function box: A process box that represents a complicated function that will be implemented separately is drawn as follows.

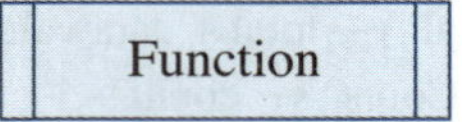

Input/output box: This is a parallelogram symbol with one control line leading into it and one leading out of it. At the lowest level it represents a single input/output instruction. At a higher level it represents a sequence of input/output instructions, which jointly implement an input/output step in the program.

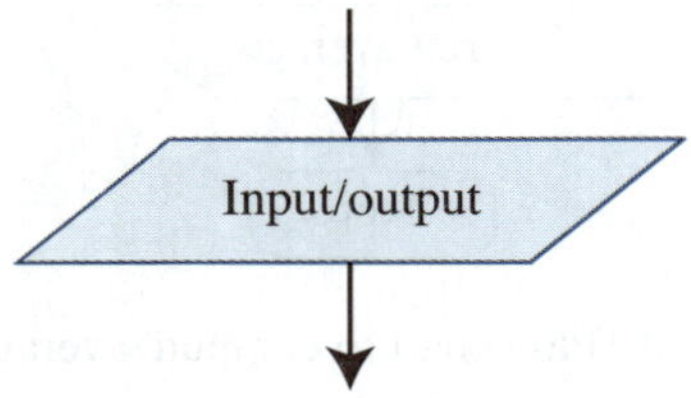

Decision box: A diamond-shaped symbol is used for the comparison of quantities for equality. The comparison generates a true or a false answer, which is the basis for a decision.

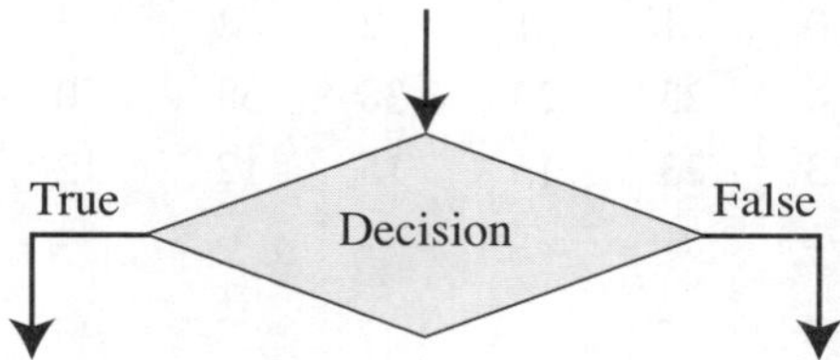

Execution follows either the path on the "true" branch or the path on the "false" branch, but not both paths.

Connector: A small circle is used as a connector symbol when two flow lines are to be coming together. Two lines are drawn into the circle and a single line is drawn out of it. A connector is also used when a flowchart is too large to fit on a single page or too complicated for all the lines to be drawn completely. In this case, the circle has only a single line in or a single line out and is labeled to show that parts of the flowchart are connected.

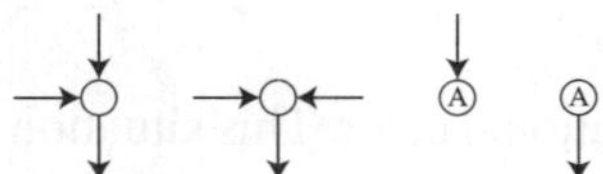

Flow lines: These lines are used to connect process boxes and decision symbols in the order of the logic and control flow of the program. An arrowhead is used to indicate the direction of the logic flow.

A flowchart that shows a step indicating input of data values must follow it with a check to determine whether the input attempt was successful. If the values are to be processed one at a time, they must be input one at a time. The flowchart loop indicates the processing of individual data values only when there are values. Note that the computer cannot identify the last data value. It can only detect the presence or absence of a data value.

Sample Test Data To test this analysis, we select a set of values, for example 23, 15, and 12 and work through the steps of the algorithm of Figure 1.8.

STEP		1	2	3	2	3	2	3	2	4	5
Count		0	0	1	1	2	2	3	3	3	3
Total		0	0	23	23	38	38	50	50	50	50
Data		-	23	23	15	15	12	12	-	-	-
Average	-	-	-	-	-	-	-	-	-	16.67	
Output	-	-	-	-	-	-	-	-	-	-	16.67

The algorithm is correct with this ordinary data. However, using extreme data may uncover errors—for example, if there are no positive data values.

STEP	1	2	4	5
Total	0	0	0	
Count	0	0	0	
Data	-	-	-	
Average	-	-	0/0	
Output	-	-	-	

This is a logical and computational error. This situation could be detected by checking the value of the count before computing the average, as shown in Figure 1.9.

At this stage of the design process, working with both words and a variety of diagrams provides more insight into the solution than either method would by itself. Errors found when working with the diagrams can be used to correct the specifications, which in turn leads to changes in the diagrams. This feedback and correction process should be repeated until the designer is satisfied that the solution is feasible with available computer resources. Any errors not found during the design phase can be very expensive to correct later on.

Structure Chart *Structure charts* were introduced in Section 1.2.2 as a way to show modularity. Since each step in an algorithm is a simple module, they can be used to represent an algorithm. The steps in Figure 1.10 are numbered for easy reference. The structure chart in Figure 1.10 corresponds to the levels of the

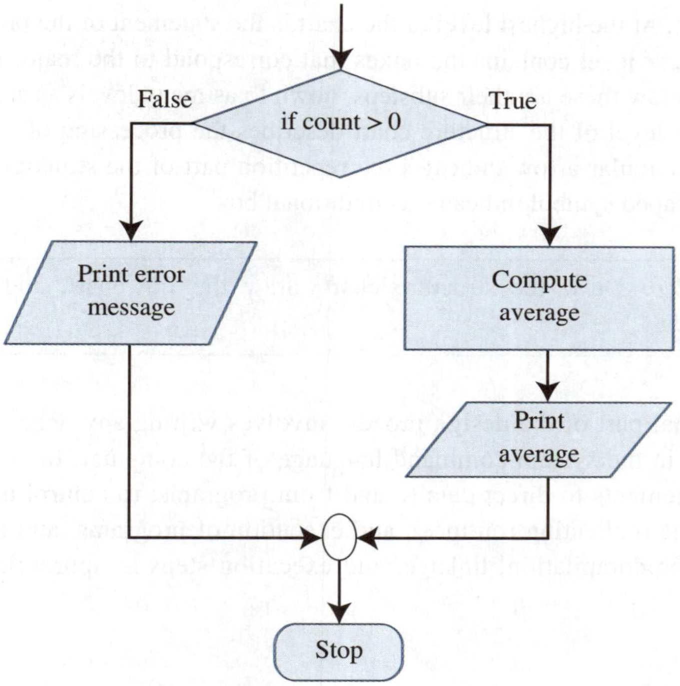

Figure 1.9 Branching structure

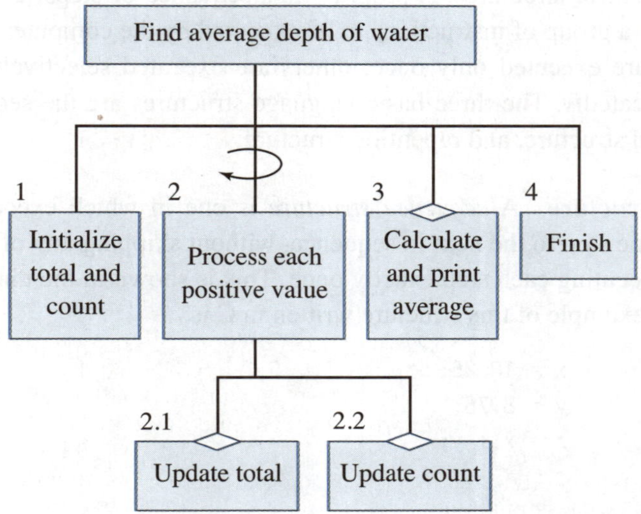

Figure 1.10 Structure chart to compute average depth

pseudocode. At the highest level of the chart is the statement of the problem solution. The next level contains the boxes that correspond to the major steps in the solution. Below these are their substeps, down to as many levels as are necessary. The bottom level of the structure chart describes the processing of a single data value. The circular arrow indicates the repetition part of the structure chart. The diamond shaped symbol indicates a conditional box.

Design Step: Draw the structure chart, draw the flowchart, and write the pseudocode.

The final part of the design process involves writing any necessary control statements in the system command language of the computer. In general, these will be statements to direct data to and from programs; to control the compilation, linkage (collecting routines), and execution of programs; and to save output from the compilation, linkage, and execution steps in appropriate files for later use.

1.3.5 Concept of Structured Programming

The development of algorithms in top-down methodology should use only the three basic control structures. A program is a sequence of steps; each step is an instruction or a group of instructions to be executed by the computer. Some of the instructions are executed only once; others are executed selectively; others are executed repeatedly. The three basic language structures are the sequence structure, selection structure, and repetition structure.

Sequence Structure A *sequence structure* is one in which execution control flows from one step to the next in sequence, without skipping any of the algorithmic steps, executing each step exactly once. This is shown in the diagram in Figure 1.11. An example of this structure written in C is:

```
stmt 1          x = 18.25;
stmt 2          y = 8.75;
stmt 3          z = x + y;
```

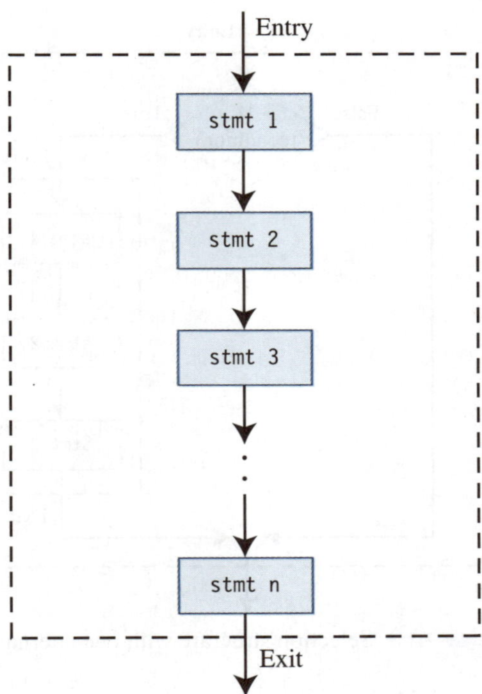

Figure 1.11 Sequence structure

Selection Structure The *selection structure* gives the computer a choice of executing one of a set of statements. Usually there are two alternative sequences, but in some cases only one sequence, and in some cases many. Exactly one alternative must be chosen, and executed only one time. C has special constructs for the selection structure. The diagrams for selection structure with one sequence and two alternative sequences are shown in Figure 1.12 and Figure 1.13 respectively. Notice that within the selection structure a sequence structure is embedded in one or more branches with the entries at the top and the exit at the bottom. The following examples of these structures show the general forms in pseudocode and a C equivalent.

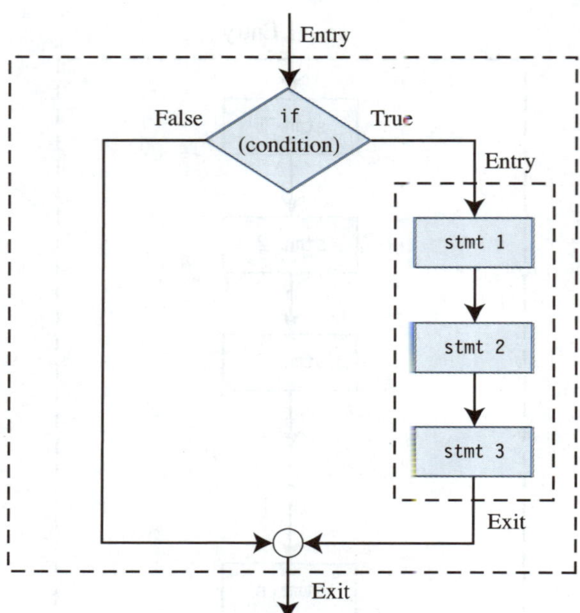

Figure 1.12 Selection structure with one alternative

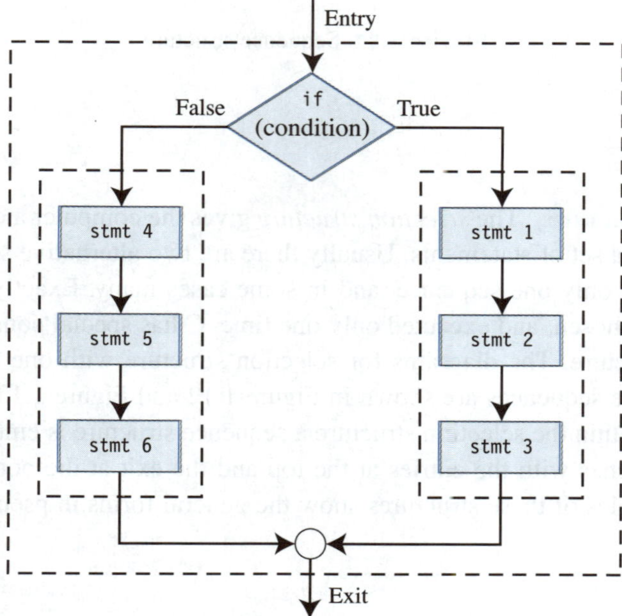

Figure 1.13 Selection structure with two alternatives

The pseudocode corresponding to each flowchart and an example of C code are as follows:

```
if condition                    if ( x > y )
   stmt 1                       {
   stmt 2                              x = -x;
   stmt 3                              w = x *5 - y / 2.0;
end if                                 p = 20 * x * w;
                                }

if (condition)                  if ( x >= 0 )
   stmt 1                       {
   stmt 2                              z = 5 * x;
   stmt 3                              w = y + z;
otherwise                              p = n * m;
    stmt 4                      }
    stmt 5                      else
    stmt 6                      {
end if                                 n = m * 5 - k * x;
                                       p = n - 5 * r - s / t;
                                       c = n + p;
                                }
```

Notice that in the second example there are two sequence structures: One embedded in the left branch and one in the right branch with an entry at the top and an exit at the bottom of each. The embedded sequences are contained between braces ("{" and "}") in the C code.

Selection structures may be stacked and nested depending on the logic of the algorithm. Symbols such as >=, =, *, +, /, −, etc., used in the C code will be explained later. However, their meaning should be obvious. Stacked and nested control structures will be discussed in detail in Chapter 4.

Repetition or Looping Structure The *repetition structure* contains one or more instructions that must be executed many times. A diagram for one form of this structure is shown in Figure 1.14. A pseudocode equivalent and C example follow. C has special constructs for the repetition structures.

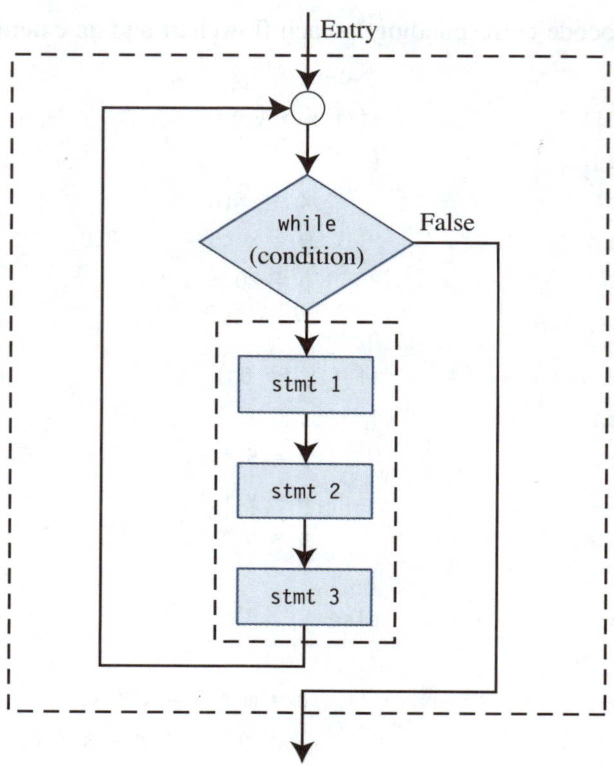

Figure 1.14 Repetition structure

The *while* and *do while* are the standard explicit repetition control structures in C. The basic difference between them is that the `while` construct begins by testing the condition as shown in Figure 1.14. The `do while` construct executes the subordinate sequence first and then tests the condition.

For condition	`while( count < 10)`
stmt 1	`{`
stmt 2	`scanf("%d", &num);`
stmt 3	`sum =  sum + num;`
End for	`count  = count + 1;`
	`}`

The detailed implementation of the input statement `scanf("%d", &num)` and the control structure `while(count < 10)` with their syntax and semantics will be explained in Chapters 3 and 4.

1.3.6 Review Questions

1. What is an algorithm?
2. What is a program?
3. Explain top-down design methodology.
4. Why is it important to validate algorithm design?
5. What does an assignment instruction do?
6. Name some different forms of computer output.
7. What are the fundamental types of instructions in any programming language?
8. What kind of data can computers process besides numbers?
9. Information supplied to an application program is called __________________.
10. Information produced by an application program is called __________________.
11. Data generated within a program that is not part of the output is called __________________ data.
12. What is data validation?
13. What is pseudocode used for?
14. What is a hierarchy chart used for?
15. What is a flowchart used for?
16. Why is the format of the output data important?
17. Why are reliability and efficiency important?
18. What are control instructions used for?

1.4 Program Processing

Once the design is complete, the computer program can be written. This consists of *source code* (data specification and instructions for the computer to interpret) and *documentation* (comments that document the code and the whole programming process as an aid to the programmer and other people who may need to read or alter the code). When the code appears to be error-free, it is submitted to the computer for compilation. The compiler not only converts the source code to object code, it checks for errors in grammar, spelling, and punctuation. Usually it is necessary to compile code several times, making corrections, before it compiles correctly. The resulting object code is linked to modules from the system library. Again there is a possibility of error if all of the modules are not linked properly. When a program finally links correctly, it is executed using input data and providing output data that then needs to be verified and validated. When consistently correct output is obtained, using all types of input data, the program is ready to be used. At that point the programmer finishes the documentation. The details of documentation standards in the C language will be discussed in Chapter 2.

1.4.1 Program Coding

Source code should be written and tested one module at a time, corresponding to the submodules of a complex hierarchy chart or flowchart. As it is written, comments are included in the source code, documenting the purpose of the module, the input and output variables, the formula used, and anything else that clarifies what is being written. When a module is finished, it should be carefully read and tested by hand, using representative data before being tested on the computer.

Implementation Step: Desk check the computer source code before compiling and executing it.

The C language includes input and output statements, arithmetic assignment statements, `if` structures, `while` structures, a statement to mark the end of the program—everything that has been included in the hierarchy chart, pseudocode, and flowchart examples.

Consider the simple example of finding the sum of the numbers from 1 through 100 by generating them and adding them. The pseudocode and the corresponding C source code would be as follows:

```
                              #include <stdio.h>
                              int main( )
                              {
                                int sum, number;
sum ← 0                         sum = 0;
number ← 1                      number = 1;
For number ≤ 100                while(number < 101)
                                {
  sum ← sum + number              sum = sum + number;
  number ← number + 1             number = number + 1;
Endfor
print sum                       }
                                printf("%d\n", sum);

                                return 0;
                              }
```

The C source code instructions outside the outer braces are instructions to the compiler. The outer braces enclose the C language equivalent of the pseudocode. The inner braces correspond to the indentation in the pseudocode; the beginning and then the end of the instructions that are to be repeated. Note that all of the instructions are necessary, if the sum were not cleared in the beginning, it might give a wrong answer. If the number was not started at 1, the code would not meet the specifications of summing numbers from 1 to 100. The summation takes place by adding each new value of a number to the accumulated sum. Then the number is incremented to the next value. The repetition is controlled by checking whether the current value of the number is < 101. If that check were missing, or if the number was not incremented, the repetition would never end. Whenever an algorithm contains repetition, the termination condition must be reachable. The details of this code will be discussed in the next chapter. For now it is enough to recognize its relationship to the examples given in discussing the design method.

1.4.2 Program Compilation

The first step in testing and debugging a program on the computer is *compilation*. During this process, the computer checks whether the program has syntax, punctuation, or spelling errors, that is, that it follows correct grammatical rules for C. If it appears to be all right, it is translated into machine code.

Note that the compilation process does not detect incorrect spelling of the names of library modules or other separately compiled modules. It also does not detect errors in the description of input and output data. And it does not detect errors in logic that lead to wrong answers, nonterminating repetitions, or impossible situations such as division by zero. Any mistakes in defining the lower-level modules of a complicated problem will not show up until later.

When the compiler detects an error, it identifies the location of the error and indicates what is wrong. It is up to the programmer to go back and fix the source code before compiling it again. Of course if any program logic is changed, it may be necessary to desk check the source code once more, using the sample data.

When the program compiles correctly, it produces object code and a list of the other modules needed. These are either stored for later use, or submitted to the linker in the program execution phase of the process. A program that compiles correctly does not need to be compiled again.

1.4.3 Program Execution

After the main program and any submodules have been written and compiled correctly, the resulting object modules are linked along with any mathematical or other library routines needed, and a single executable module is built. The process of building an executable module, or linking, is shown in Figure 1.15. The linkers and loaders of the operating system are responsible for building the executable module and executing it. If these system routines detect errors, corrections must be made to the appropriate source code module, any changed modules are recompiled, and the linking is repeated.

When the program is finally executed, the computer carries out the programmer's instructions in logical sequence, accepts the designated input, performs the required calculations, and produces output. The output includes messages indicating whether the execution contained errors and statistics about the computer resources used. When there are execution errors, the source code must be corrected and the program recompiled, re-linked, and re-executed. The programming

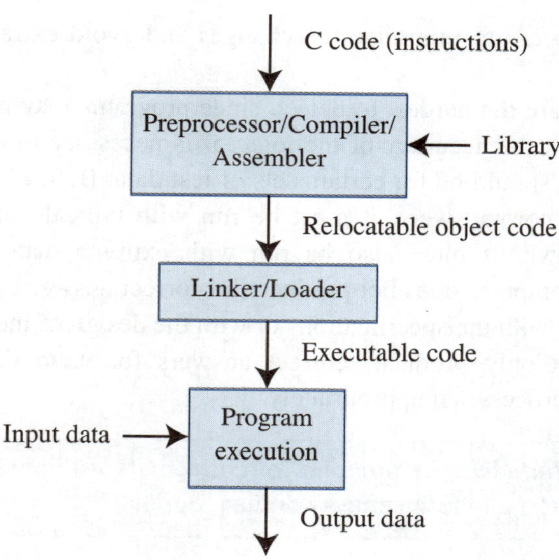

Figure 1.15 Program compilation and execution

is finished only when the program terminates normally, producing correct answers without any execution errors.

> *Program Warning:* Computers will not allow the linking and execution of programs with compilation errors.

1.4.4 Program Testing

Program development is almost never error-free. However, it would be better to develop a correct program than attempt to find errors in an already completed program by repeated recompilation, linking, and execution. Errors may be of many types, such as data specification, problem specification, program design errors, implementation errors, typing errors, logic errors, and data input errors. Errors are detected at different stages of the programming process. The errors in a program are called *bugs*, and the process of detecting and removing them is called *debugging*. It is desirable to detect any error as early as possible in the programming process to minimize the changes and avoid extra implementation cost and effort.

Logic errors are the hardest to detect, since programs may produce incorrect answers. To check the accuracy of the logic, it is necessary to know in advance what the answers should be for certain sets of test data. Before a program can be used to produce new answers, it must be run with typical data for which the answers are known. It must also be run with extreme data that has known answers. If the computer does not produce the correct answers, there is probably something wrong with the specifications or with the design of the program. A correct program not only produces correct answers for valid data, it diagnoses invalid data and processes it appropriately.

Programming Hint: Test the program for correctness using specially designed sets of data that test all the statements of the program.

Logic errors may be caused by careless copying of numbers, formulas, or data formats. Because it is very hard to find typographical errors, sometimes it is helpful to have another programmer look at the code. Explaining the code to someone else is also a good way of finding logic errors.

Some programming languages have built-in tools for testing, and some installations have system and software tools for testing for correctness. Use these aids whenever they are available. When they are not, build programs using extra output statements so that you can see what is happening at intermediate stages of processing.

Testing is a process intentionally designed to find errors in programs. This must be done systematically. Each module must be separately tested for errors and when the modules are put together, the results must be tested further. Any time a change is made, there is the possibility of introducing more errors. Not only must a program give correct answers to correct input, it should be able to detect incorrect input. It should also avoid giving incorrect answers for accurate but unusual input.

Testing procedures for large, complex systems are extensive and detailed. The test cases must be carefully designed to check the entire system. In general, the people testing the system should not be the same ones who design and implement it.

Programming Hint: Echo print input data until the computed results are accurate.

1.4.5 Program Documentation

Documentation, an important part of software development, should be carried out simultaneously with design. Documentation is used to keep track of the design process and to keep track of implementation and testing. It becomes part of the final system, to be used by the programmers who will maintain or modify the system. There are two types of documentation, system documentation and program documentation. *System documentation* includes functional descriptions, introductory manuals, reference manuals, installation manuals, user manuals, and so forth. *Program documentation* includes all phases of program development documents. It should include:

- Statement of the problem
- Glossary of input/output variables
- Description of each module of the program
- Error messages produced by the program and their causes
- Security measures to be incorporated in the program to protect the programs and data
- Test data to be used in program modification

Some of the program documentation is part of the source code of the program.

Programming Rule: Program code must be documented.

The total documentation package should include everything anyone who uses the system needs to know about the system. It should be organized according to the needs of the various people who deal with the system.

Once a programming project has been completed and proven useful, it takes on a life of its own, outliving the immediate need, the programming team, and the hardware. Therefore, modifications become inevitable.

Documentation may need to be changed any time changes are made to the program. Just as there are various versions of the source code on the computer, so there will be various versions of the documentation.

Programming Objective: Write easy-to-maintain source code and easy-to-understand documentation.

During the life of a production program, further modifications will be needed to meet changing situations and to correct previously undetected errors. All useful programs can be expected to evolve to meet changing circumstances.

1.4.6 Review Questions

1. What does a compiler do?
2. What does a linker do?
3. The language in which the program is written is called ________________ code.
4. The compilation process produces ________________ code.
5. What does a loader do?
6. List the types of errors according to developmental stages.
7. Give two reasons why documentation is important.
8. The process of locating and correcting errors is called ________________.
9. Why is it important to test a program with data that intentionally contains errors?

1.5 Program Processing Environment

There are two ways to look at a processing environment: as a computer system environment or as a programming environment. The system environment in which the program runs is characterized as single-user or single-job, time-sharing, multiprogramming, or multiprocessing. The programming environment is batch, interactive, or real-time.

1.5.1 Computer System Environment

A *single-job environment* is one in which only one program at a time can be loaded into the computer for execution. All the system resources in such an environment, such as disk, memory, and processor, are allocated to a single job. Once the job is completed, all the system resources are released.

Most mainframe computers and minicomputers and some microcomputers support a time-sharing environment. A *time-sharing environment* is one in which several users can have access to the computer at the same time, running different programs. Multiprogramming, multiprocessing, and parallel processing are all different forms of time-sharing environments.

In a *multiprogramming environment*, several executable programs can exist in memory at the same time, but only one program is active at any given instant. The programs that are loaded for execution will take turns using the time and resources available within the time limit allocated to each. In a *multiprocessing environment* there is more than one CPU, making it possible to execute several programs simultaneously. Alternately, several processors may be working on the same program at the same time. In a *parallel processing* environment, the program is partitioned into blocks that can be executed in parallel by different processors.

1.5.2 Programming Environment

Programming environments are designed for different user needs. In *batch processing*, programs are executed when it is convenient for the computer installation. Usually large amounts of data are involved and the actual time of execution is not critical. In *interactive processing*, programs are executed while the user waits online for the output. *Real-time processing* is used to directly control equipment.

Batch Processing In multiprogramming and multiprocessing environments, the batch processing mode is commonly used for program testing and for numeric applications. In *batch processing*, the operating system takes control of the program. The computer schedules and controls program execution. Several jobs may be entered through terminals, or loaded from disk files, and left to be executed when sufficient time is available.

Jobs submitted in a batch environment are stored on the disk (*spooled*) and scheduled by the operating system according to the priority of the job and the resources it needs. The output is spooled to the disk print file so that it can be printed once the program has terminated and the printer is available.

Batch processing is used when there are large amounts of data to process, or when time is not critical. The output usually consists of reports. Batch processing cannot be used when the user must interact with the program, processing transactions, correcting drawings, or directing choices. Batch processing is used, however, for updating an online transaction system when the transactions can be collected and processed at a single time, for example, at the end of the day.

Interactive Processing In *interactive processing*, the user is in communication with the computer system. Data values are entered through terminals and the user expects an immediate response from the system. Output design may differ from that sent to a printer. Interactive processing is primarily used for transaction processing, changing permanently stored data, and retrieving information.

Several interactive terminals can be connected to a large computer system, each one having access to the computer hardware and software resources. If there are several users at the same time, the CPU will share its time with all of them. There are various strategies for allocating time to a user. The operating system attempts to keep all the hardware operating as near capacity as possible without causing any user to wait very long. C is designed for both batch processing and interactive processing applications.

Real-time Processing In *real-time processing*, when a computer is used to directly control equipment, computer response must be as fast as data collection. Embedded computer systems are real-time systems. Examples include a computer onboard an aircraft that controls the autopilot, or computers that control nuclear reactor cooling systems, space shuttles, pacemakers, power fluctuations, and automobile ignition systems. Real-time systems are online systems that must respond immediately to changing needs. They have critical time constraints. Such systems are dedicated to single applications. C may be used for real-time applications in special hardware and software environments.

1.5.3 Review Questions

1. What is meant by time-sharing?
2. What is a batch-processing environment?
3. What is multiprogramming?
4. A multiprocessing system will have more than one what?
5. Why is real-time processing important?
6. Is interactive processing the same as real-time processing? Explain.
7. Why is programming for interactive processing different from programming for batch processing?

1.6 Samples of Algorithms

The following examples show the design and development of algorithmic procedures. These examples are chosen from engineering, science, and mathematics. Each step of the algorithm must perform a single function. Together, the steps must arrive at the desired solution. The algorithm must end. Each algorithm must have a single entry point and a single exit.

The most common complications in learning to design an algorithm are the need to detect data which would cause problems in a formula, the need to anticipate that data may be missing, the need to count data, and the accumulation of totals. All of these except totals and counting of totals are shown in the following examples. The use of totals and counting have already been introduced in this chapter.

1.6.1 Resistance and Voltage of a Parallel Circuit

This example includes data validation.

Problem Compute the effective resistance and voltage of an electrical circuit containing three resistances connected in parallel, with the current and resistance as input data.

Data Three positive values for resistances, and a positive value for current (ohms).

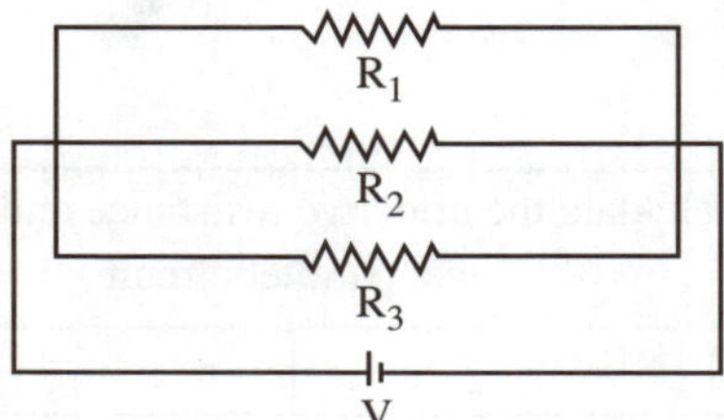

Method The formula for the resistance R of a parallel circuit with resistances R_1, R_2, and R_3 and the voltage V assuming a current of I is as follows:

$$1/R = 1/R_1 + 1/R_2 + 1/R_3$$

Solved for the effective resistance R, this is

$$R = 1/(1/R_1 + 1/R_2 + 1/R_3)$$

The voltage is computed from the following formula:

$$V = I \times R$$

Algorithm in Pseudocode

```
Input R1, R2, R3, and I the resistances and current respectively
Check that they are positive
If so, compute the effective resistance:
   R ← 1/(1/R1 + 1/R2 + 1/R3)
Compute the voltage using
   V ← I × R
Output R and V, labeled
Stop
```

The algorithm is shown as a structure chart in Figure 1.16. The algorithm is also shown as a flowchart in Figure 1.17. The structure chart and the flowchart show the input of the resistances and current, and the output of computed effective resistance and the computed voltage.

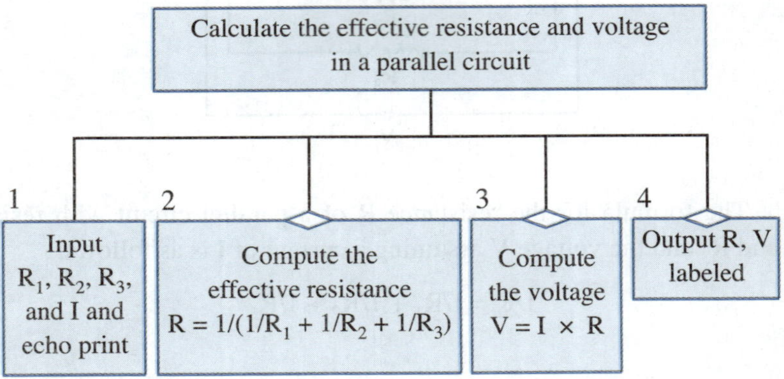

Figure 1.16 Structure chart to compute the voltage of a parallel circuit

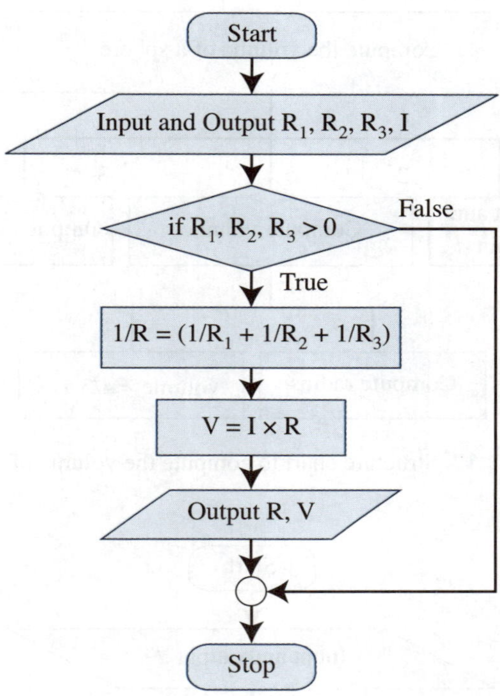

Figure 1.17 Flowchart to compute the voltage of a parallel circuit

1.6.2 Volume of a Sphere

The second part of this example introduces the use of a counter to control data input.

Problem Write an algorithm to compute the volume of a sphere of diameter *d*. Output the diameter and the volume.

Method The volume of a sphere of diameter *d* is given by the formula:

$$r = d / 2$$
$$\text{volume} = 4/3\ \pi\ r^3$$

Data A positive real number is representing the diameter in inches.

The algorithm is shown as a structure chart in Figure 1.18. The algorithm is shown as a flowchart in Figure 1.19. The input is the diameter of the sphere and the output is the computed volume. The algorithm shows the calculation of volume for one sphere.

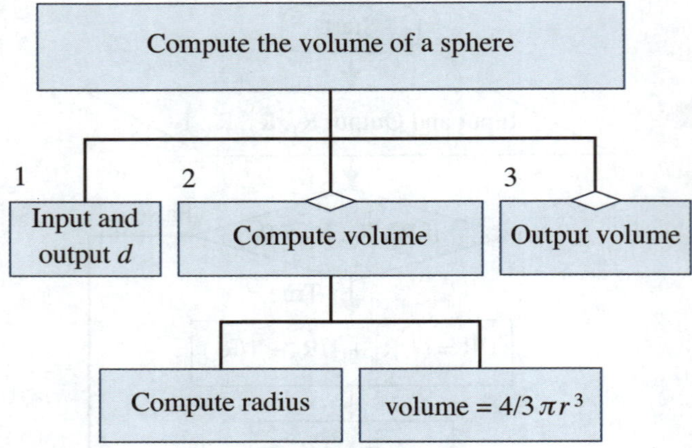

Figure 1.18 Structure chart to compute the volume of a sphere

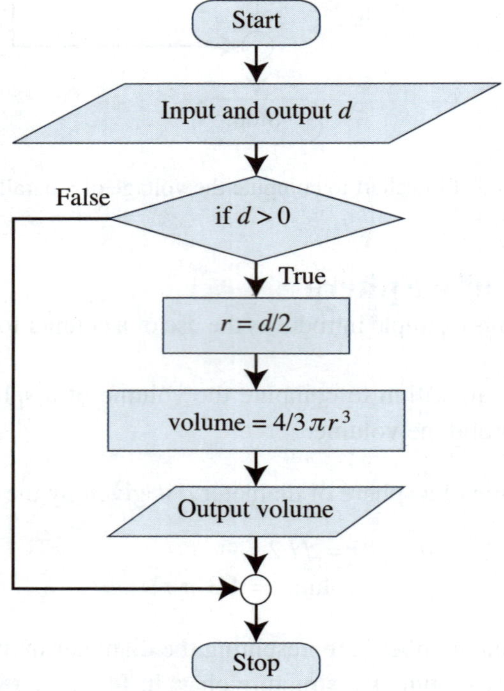

Figure 1.19 Flowchart to compute the volume of a sphere

Algorithm in Pseudocode

```
Input and output diameter d
If d > 0
    Compute the radius
      r ← d / 2
    Compute the volume
      Volume ← 4/3 π r³
    Output the volume
End if
Stop
```

The preceding algorithm computes the volume for one sphere of diameter *d*. The following algorithm shows the computation of the volumes of several spheres with different diameters.

If the volume is to be calculated for 10 spheres, the algorithm is as shown in the structure chart of Figure 1.20 and the flowchart of Figure 1.21.

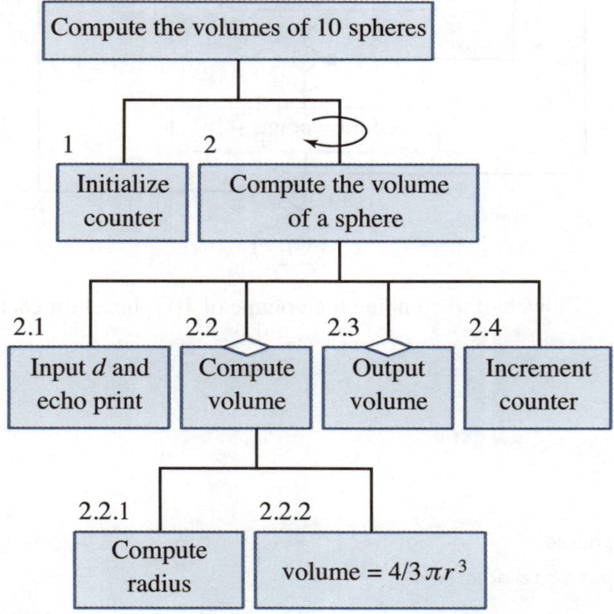

Figure 1.20 Structure chart to compute the volume of 10 spheres of different diameter

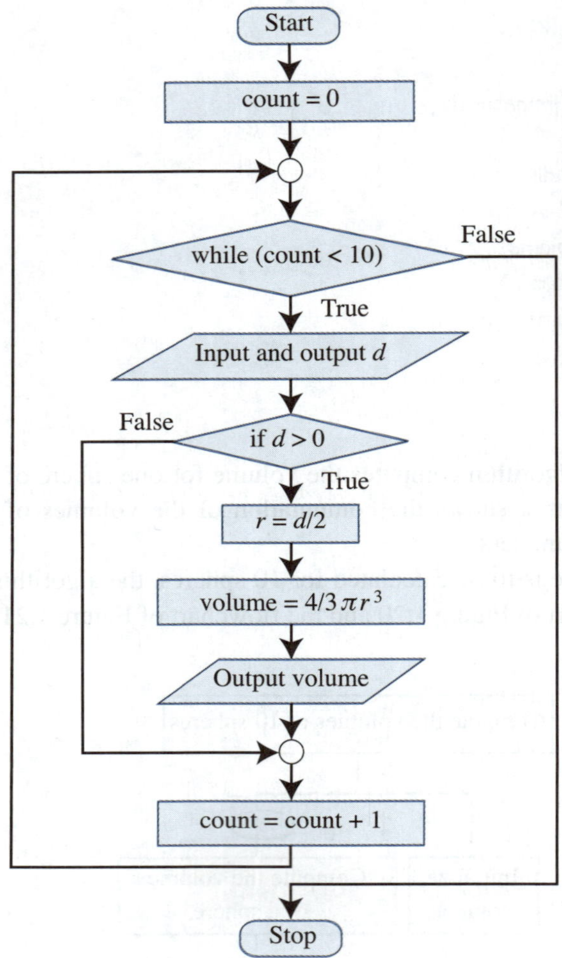

Figure 1.21 Flowchart to compute the volume of 10 spheres for each diameter

Algorithm in Pseudocode

Count = 0
For each of 10 spheres
  Input and output the diameter d

```
If d > 0
   Compute the radius
     r ← d / 2
   Compute the volume
     Volume ← 4/3 π r³
     Output the volume
  End if
  Count = Count + 1
End for
Stop
```

The curved arrow in the structure chart shows that the calculation of volume is repeated for spheres of different input diameters.

This algorithm assumes that there are 10 data values. If there are fewer than 10 data values, an error check must be incorporated in the algorithm to output an error message stating that there are fewer than 10 data values. The error message must be in the exit from the while loop. Then the algorithm will be robust, meaning that it is fail-safe.

1.6.3 Square Root Approximation

This example introduces the use of an iterative formula in a repetition structure controlled by a predetermined limit.

Problem Write an algorithm to compute the square root of x by using the Newton–Raphson formula:

$$s_{k+1} = (s_k + x/s_k)/2 \qquad k \geq 1$$
$$s_1 = x/2 \qquad x > 0$$

This formula is based on the fact that

$$\text{if } s_k = \sqrt{x}$$

then $s_k^2 = x$ and $s_{k+1} = (\sqrt{x} + x/\sqrt{x})/2 = (\sqrt{x^2} + x)/(2\sqrt{x}) = \sqrt{x}$

Data A positive real value for x and a constant specifying the required accuracy.

Method The iterative solution of the problem assumes that given the value of x, the value s_1 is calculated. Then the formula for s_{k+1} is used repeatedly until sufficient accuracy has been obtained. For $k = 1$ $s_2 = (s_1 + x/s_1)/2$

$$k = 2 \quad s_3 = (s_2 + x/s_2)/2$$

....

$$k = n \quad s_{n+1} = (s_n + x/s_n)/2$$

This process will continue until the difference between s_k and s_{k-1} is less than, or equal to, a predetermined value. When this happens, s_k is accepted as the square root of x. Note that the computer must be given explicit instructions about when to stop an iterative approximation, otherwise the calculations would continue indefinitely without ever providing an answer.

Algorithm in Pseudocode

```
Input the value of x > 0
Initialize limit
     limit ← 0.0001
Calculate s1
     s0 ← x
     s1 ← x / 2
     k ← 1
while( |sk − sk−1| > limit )
     sk+1 ← (sk + x /sk) / 2
     k ← k + 1
End while
```

Output x and s_k as the square root of x, labeled.

The algorithm is shown as a structure chart in Figure 1.22. The algorithm is shown as a flowchart in Figure 1.23. Later we will see that it is not necessary to have all the different s values available at the same time. It is possible to write this algorithm using only two names, for example s_k and s_{knext}.

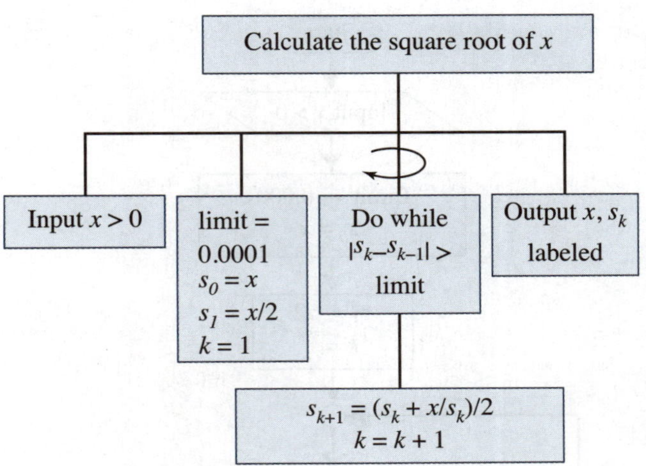

Figure 1.22 Structure chart to compute the square root of a number

Wherever possible an algorithm should be hand-checked before a computer program is written. Assume that

$$x = 25.0$$

Then

$$s_0 = 25.0$$
$$s_1 = 25.0/2 = 12.5$$
$$s_2 = (12.5 + 25.0/12.5)/2 = 7.25$$
$$s_3 = (7.25 + 25.0/7.25)/2 = 5.349\ldots$$
$$s_4 = (5.349 + 25.0/5.349)/2 = 5.0113\ldots$$

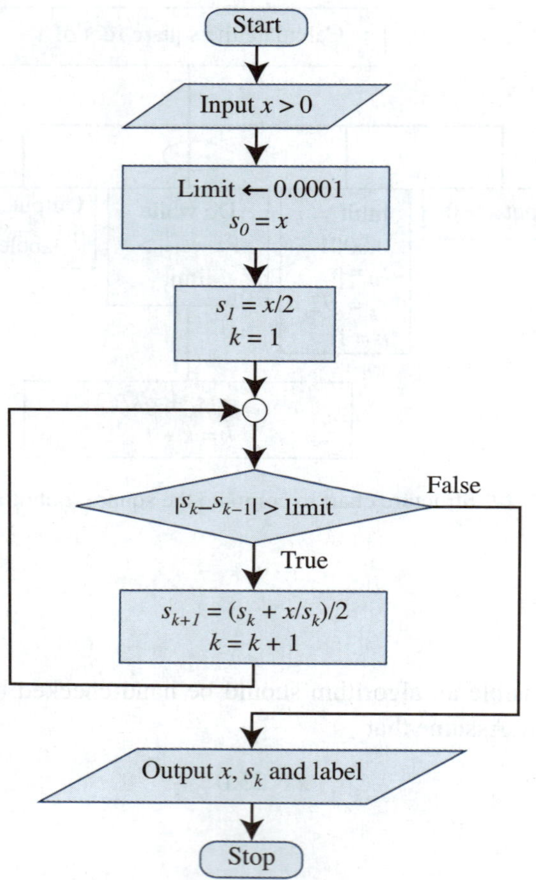

Figure 1.23 Flowchart to compute the square root of a number

The calculated value appears to be converging to 5.0, the correct square root. The computer iteration will stop when two successive values of *s* differ by less than a predetermined amount, in this case 0.0001.

1.6.4 Total Pressure of Gaseous Mixture

This example introduces a repetition construct controlled by an input value that gives the number of data values. The data values are validated, and if found to be invalid, an error message is printed and the process is terminated.

Problem Write an algorithm to compute the total pressure given the partial pressures of perfect gases by using Dalton's law of partial pressures of perfect gases. The law states that the pressure exerted by a mixture of perfect gases is the sum of the partial pressures of the gases.

Data Positive integers to specify the number of components of perfect gases in the mixture and positive real values to specify partial pressures of the perfect gas components in the mixture.

Method Given the partial pressures of the perfect gases A, B, C, …., N as p_A, $p_B, p_C, \ldots, p_N$, the total pressure is computed as follows:

Total pressure = partial pressure of gas A + partial pressure of gas B + partial pressure of gas C + ⋯ + partial pressure of gas N

$$p = p_A + p_B + p_C + \cdots + p_N$$

The structure chart is shown in Figure 1.24 and the flowchart is shown in Figure 1.25.

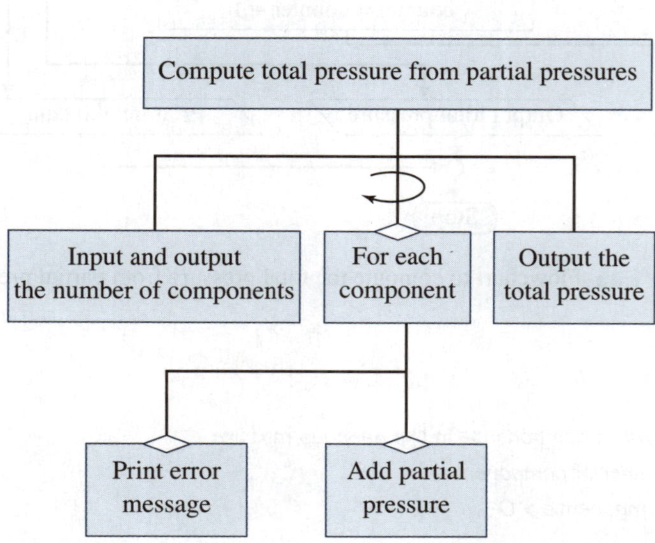

Figure 1.24 Structure chart to compute the total pressure from partial pressures

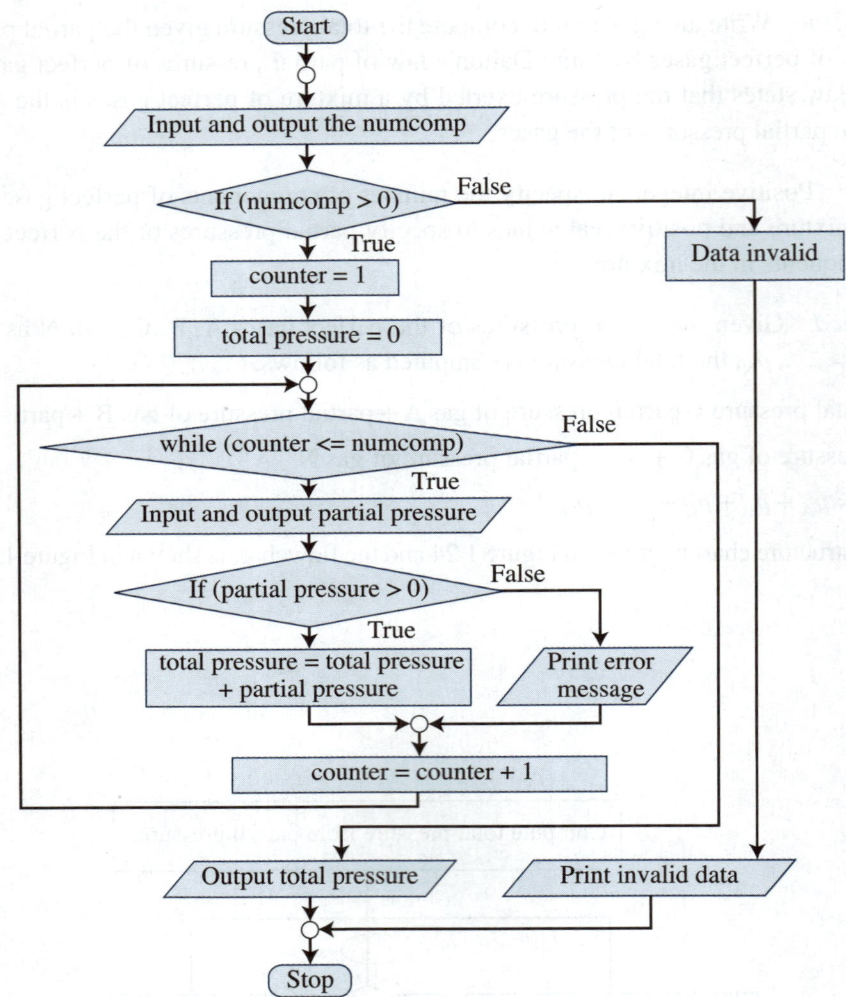

Figure 1.25 Flowchart to compute the total pressure from partial pressures

Algorithm in Pseudocode

Input the number of components in the gaseous mixture
Output the number of components
If number of components > 0
    counter = 1
    total pressure = 0

```
    For each component
      Input and output the partial pressure
      If partial pressure > 0
        total pressure = total pressure + partial pressure
      Else
        Print error message
      End if
        counter = counter + 1
    End for
      Output the total pressure
Else
      Output message "Invalid Data"
End if
Stop
```

1.6.5 Mass Flow Rate of Air Through Pipes

This example introduces a repetition construct controlled by the use of a known final value. Two variables range through a set of values.

Problem Write an algorithm to compute the mass flow rate of air in a pipe diameter $d = 5, 10, 15, 20, \ldots, 50$ inches at pressures of $p = 50, 60, 70, \ldots, 100$ psi and a temperature of T degrees. Barometric pressure is p_b psi and velocity is V ft/sec. Compute the number of pounds of air per second flowing through the pipe.

Data Input positive real numbers to specify the universal gas constant, the velocity of the air, and the temperature.

Method Given different diameters, different pressures, universal gas constant, temperature of air, and velocity of air, compute the density of air from the following formula:

$$\gamma = \frac{p}{rt}$$

Where: γ is the density of air,

p is the absolute pressure,

r is the universal gas constant, which is 53.3ft/R, and

t is the absolute temperature in degree Kelvin.

The mass flow rate is computed from the equation

$$w = \gamma q$$

Where: q is the flow rate in cubic feet per second and q is given by the equation

$$q = av$$

Where: a is the cross sectional area of the pipe in square feet, and

v is the velocity in ft/sec

Notice that the units must be converted.

The structure chart is shown in Figure 1.26 and the flowchart is shown in Figure 1.27.

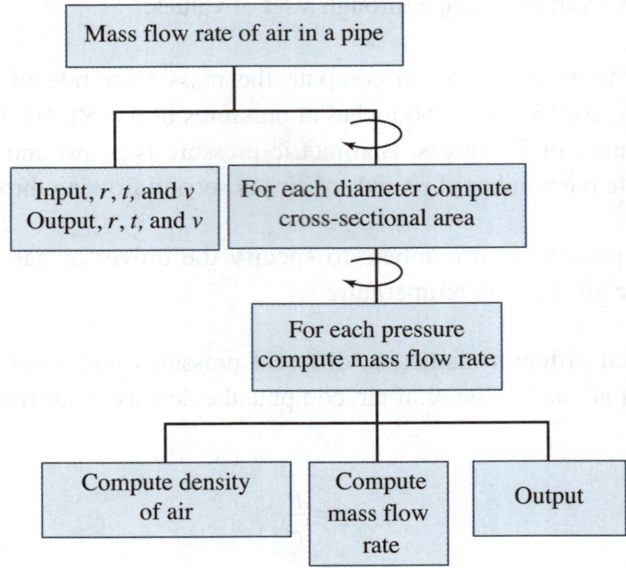

Figure 1.26 Structure chart to compute the mass flow rate of air in a pipe

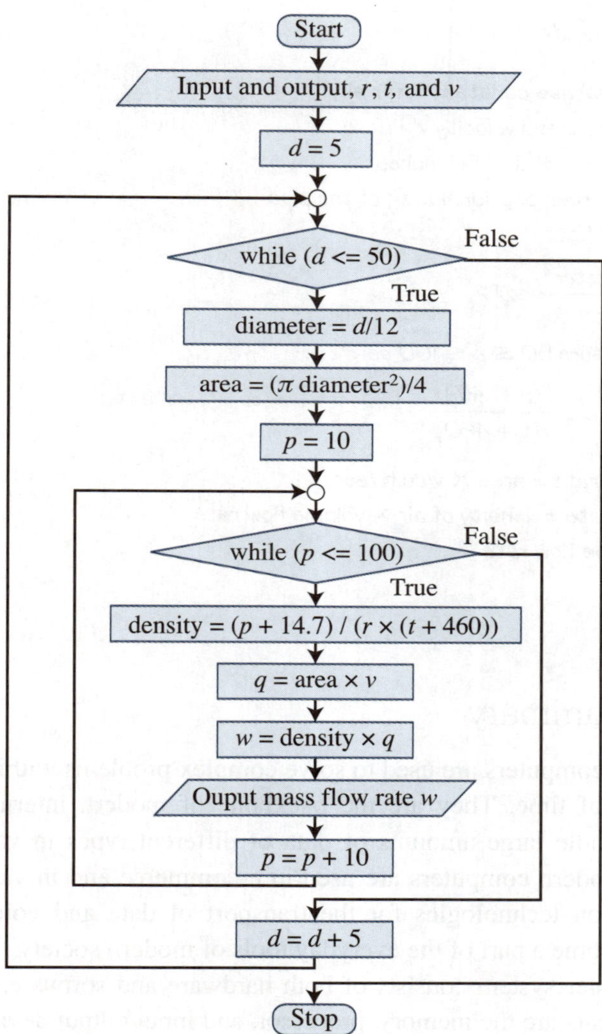

Figure 1.27 Flowchart to compute the mass flow rate of air in a pipe

Algorithm in Pseudocode

```
Input the universal gas constant R for air,
      temperature t and velocity v
For each diameter 5 ≤ d ≤ 50 inches
   Calculate the cross sectional area of the pipe
   diameter = d / 12.0
```

$$\text{area} = \frac{\pi \ \text{diameter}^2}{4} \text{ sq ft}$$

```
   For each pressure 50 ≤ p ≤ 100 psi
```

$$\text{density of air} = \frac{(p + 14.7)}{r(t + 460)}$$

```
      volume flow rate = area × v cu.ft/sec
      mass flow rate = density of air × volume flow rate
      Output mass flow rate
   End for
End for
```

Chapter Summary

- Modern computers are used to solve complex problems within a reasonable amount of time. They are the backbone of modern internet technology. They handle large amounts of data of different types in various applications. Modern computers are used in e-commerce and in various telecommunication technologies for the transport of data and voice. Computers have become a part of the everyday tools of modern society.
- A computer system consists of both hardware and software. The hardware components are the memory, processor, and input/output devices (peripheral devices such as disk drives, tape drives, mouse, light-pulse magnetic character readers, optical character readers, graphic display devices, and plotters and printers). The input devices transmit the information to be processed into the computer. Output devices return the processed information from the computer system to the outside world. The processor performs the arithmetic and logic operations on the information stored in memory under the command of the control unit.

- The main software component is the operating system, which manages all the system resources and provides an environment for the user to communicate with the computer. Other software modules include the system utilities, file management software, assemblers, and compilers. The most frequently used application software modules include word processors, spreadsheets, database applications, and presentation software.
- Programs written to solve various types of problems in different areas of engineering and science are known as application software. These programs are written in high-level languages, compiled, debugged to eliminate errors, linked with library routines, and executed.
- Solving problems on a computer involves several steps. The first step is to describe the data and the problem. The next step is to divide the problem into subproblems. The subproblems are divided further into understandable and manageable units. This process, called modularization, is the major design step. It involves various design aids such as pseudocode, structure charts, and flowcharts. The other steps are implementation, testing, production use, and maintenance. The design step also includes design of data formats for input/output, an algorithm, test data, and testing procedure. Documentation is written at each step. These steps are repeated until a program is obtained that reliably produces correct results.
- An application program may run in a batch environment or an interactive environment. The environment may be single-job, time-sharing, multiprogramming, multiprocessing, or real-time.

Exercises

1. Write an algorithm to compute the volume of a cylinder with diameter d and height h and print the diameter, height, and the volume.
2. Write an algorithm to compute the volume of water in cubic feet, flowing through a pipe of diameter d in feet, with a velocity of v feet per second. The formula to compute the volume flow rate per second is given by:

   $r = d/2$

   area $= \pi \times r^2$, and

   volume $=$ area $\times v$

The algorithm should print d, v, and volume, labeling the output.

3. Write an algorithm to compute the distance s fallen by an object in free fall. The formula is:

$$s = s_0 + v_0 t + \frac{1}{2} a t^2$$

where s_0 is the initial position in feet, v_0 is the initial downward velocity in ft/sec, t is the time in seconds, and a is 32.2 ft/sec². The input values are s_0 and v_0. The output values are s and t where $t = 0$, 5, 10, 15, 20,…, 100.

4. Write an algorithm to compute the compression stress on a rectangular steel column of width w and depth d subject to a compression load of p tons for $p = 10, 20, 30, \ldots, 50$. It should print the cross-sectional dimensions of the column, the cross-sectional area, the load, and the compression stress. Validate w and d as positive numbers.

   area = $w \times d$, and
   stress = p/area

5. Write an algorithm to compute the area of a triangle given the three sides of the triangle as a, b, and c. Use the following formula to compute the area.

$$s = \frac{1}{2}(a + b + c)$$
$$\text{area} = \sqrt{s \cdot (s-a) \cdot (s-b) \cdot (s-c)}$$

   The algorithm should check that a, b, and c are each $< s$, and should print the sides and the area of the triangle, labeled.

6. Write an algorithm to compute the distance covered in 25 min, 50 min, 75 min, 100 min, 125 min, and 150 min, if a car is traveling at a speed of 80 miles per hour. Stop at 500 miles. It should print the time t and the distance traveled for each value of t.

7. Write an algorithm to generate the sum of the Fibonacci numbers between 1 and 100. Print the numbers and their sum. The formula for computing Fibonacci numbers is:

$$\text{fib}_n = \text{fib}_{n-1} + \text{fib}_{n-2}$$
$$\text{fib}_1 = \text{fib}_2 = 1$$

8. Write an algorithm to input a set of integer numbers, count and sum the positive numbers, and also count and sum the negative numbers. It should then print the count and sum of all positive numbers and the count and sum of all negative numbers.

9. Write an algorithm to compute the minimum diameter needed for a pipe to carry 2.22 N/s of air with minimum velocity of v m/s? The air is at t°C and under the absolute pressure of p. Given the following formulas

$$\gamma_{\text{air}} = \frac{p}{rt},$$

$w = 2.22$ N/s $= \gamma q$, therefore, $q = 2.22/\gamma$

Where w is weight flow rate
γ is specific weight for air

$$\text{minimum area } a = \frac{q}{\text{minimum velocity}}, \text{ and}$$

$$\text{minimum diameter} = \sqrt{(4 \times \text{area}) / \pi}$$

10. Write an algorithm to compute the kinetic energy of different disks of mass $m = 10$ to 100 kg in increments of 10 and the radius $r = 10$ to 50 cm in increments of 10. The disks rotate at a speed of 500 rpm. The kinetic energy is computed from the formula:

$$k = \frac{i\omega^2}{2}$$

where i is the moment of inertia of a uniform disk given by the formula:

$$i = \frac{mr^2}{2}.$$

Where r is the radius of the disk in meters
m is the mass of the disk in kg

The angular velocity is computed as follows:

$$\omega = \frac{500 \text{ rev}}{60 \text{ sec}} \times \frac{2\pi}{1 \text{ rev}}.$$

The algorithm must output the results in the form of a table as shown.

```
mass = 10
radius  10   kinetic energy = xx.xx joules
.............................................
radius  50   kinetic energy = xx.xx joules

mass = 20
radius  10   kinetic energy = xx.xx joules
.............................................
radius  50   kinetic energy = xx.xx joules

mass = 100
radius  10   kinetic energy = xx.xx joules
.............................................
radius  50   kinetic energy = xx.xx joules
```

CHAPTER 2

Basic Elements of the C Programming Language

Objective

To learn the syntax and semantics of the C language. To learn the logical and physical structure of programs and the types of data that can be processed.

C is a versatile, flexible, and powerful programming language that was designed and developed in 1972. C incorporated many of the ideas of its ancestral languages BCPL and B. BCPL (Basic Combined Programming Language) was developed in 1967 by Martin Richards. BCPL was a typeless (no data types) language using machine words and machine addresses. In 1970, Ken Thompson developed a programming language called B. B was also a typeless language, and was used for the development of the UNIX operating system. C differs from its predecessors in being strongly typed. C strictly enforces data types such as integer, floating-point, and character.

Dennis Ritchie and Brian W. Kernighan developed the language and also wrote a historic book, *"The C Programming Language,"* published by Prentice Hall. This traditional C was used until 1983. Various enhancements that were made to the original language led to nonstandard features and some ambiguous language constructs. In 1983, the American National Standard Institute (ANSI) formed a committee to standardize the language to make it unambiguous and machine independent. The ANSI standard was published in 1989. Programs written in ANSI C are easily transportable from one computer platform to another. The language presented in this book is ANSI C.

The power of the language lies in the use of pointers to manipulate single variables, array variables, and structure variables. Pointers and dynamic storage are the most powerful features of C. C has a rich collection of run-time libraries to support input/output functions, mathematical functions, string functions, and dynamic storage functions. There are software packages for scientific computing and visualization. There are application packages to manipulate data structures such as linked lists, pointer stacks and queues, binary tree manipulations, sorting, and searching.

The C programming language has been extensively used in the past two decades to develop system software such as operating systems (memory, processor, device, job, process, and file schedulers), utility software (editors, assemblers, compilers, linkers, and loaders), application software (word processors, spreadsheets, and presentation developers), and database software packages. The application software for industrial product development and manufacturing, banking transactions, travel planning and scheduling, energy exploration and distribution, and small and medium business needs is often written in C.

C has some of the mathematical features of FORTRAN 77; the first language developed for scientific and engineering applications. In addition, C has features such as pointers, function libraries, and dynamic storage for the manipulation of arrays and character strings, making it even more suitable than FORTRAN for scientific and engineering applications.

2.1 Introduction to C

The important features of C are:

1. Data type declarations and definitions that eliminate ambiguities associated with undeclared and undefined variables. This forces the programmer to think about the use and range of values for each variable at the beginning of the coding process, which reduces the number of errors in the program.
2. Standard control structures that make the program control flow top-down. This makes the program easier to read and update.

3. Functions to implement the modularity in programs. This makes the program logic simpler and the physical structure of the program easier to understand, read, and update. The programmer does not have to figure out all of the details at the same time, but can isolate complicated details and postpone work on them.
4. Derived data types such as arrays, character strings, and structures are available to handle complex data types. This makes it possible to store sets of data in the computer so that they can be processed repeatedly without reentering them.
5. Powerful features of the language include pointers, pointer variables, and dynamic storage. These make it possible for the programmer to utilize storage efficiently.

2.1.1 Structured Language

C is a structured programming language. In structured programming only three basic control structures are needed to design and develop programs. C has the three basic control structures of sequence, selection, and repetition. Each control structure is entered at the top and exited at the bottom. Use of these basic control structures fits well with top-down algorithm development.

The sequence structure corresponds to the modules in a single level of a structure chart that have the same parent module. The selection structure and repetition structure each correspond to a parent module and its submodules. In the hierarchy chart, shown in Figure 1.10, boxes 1, 2, 3, and 4 would be implemented using a sequence structure, as would boxes 2.1 and 2.2. In the pseudocode, statements and control structures that form a sequence structure follow each other with the same level of indentation.

The circular arrow above box 2 in Figure 1.10 shows that boxes 2, 2.1, and 2.2 would be implemented as a repetition structure. In the pseudocode, this is a `For...Endfor` construct. The diamond connectors of boxes 2.1, 2.2, and 3 indicate that boxes 2.1, 2.2, and 3 would be implemented as selection structures. The arrow connector is at a higher level in the hierarchy chart than the diamond connectors of 2.1 and 2.2, so the selection structure is subordinate to the repetition structure and physically contained with it. This is shown in the ordering and indentation of items in the pseudocode and the nesting of structures in the corresponding flowchart.

The function is the fourth control structure in C. The function corresponds to the topmost general level of a structure chart and, in effect, encompasses the entire chart as the body of the function. Functions can also be shown as boxes that connect separate structure charts and indicate a transfer of process from one to another. For example, to find the average depth of water in a lake, the two structure charts of Figure 2.1 might be used.

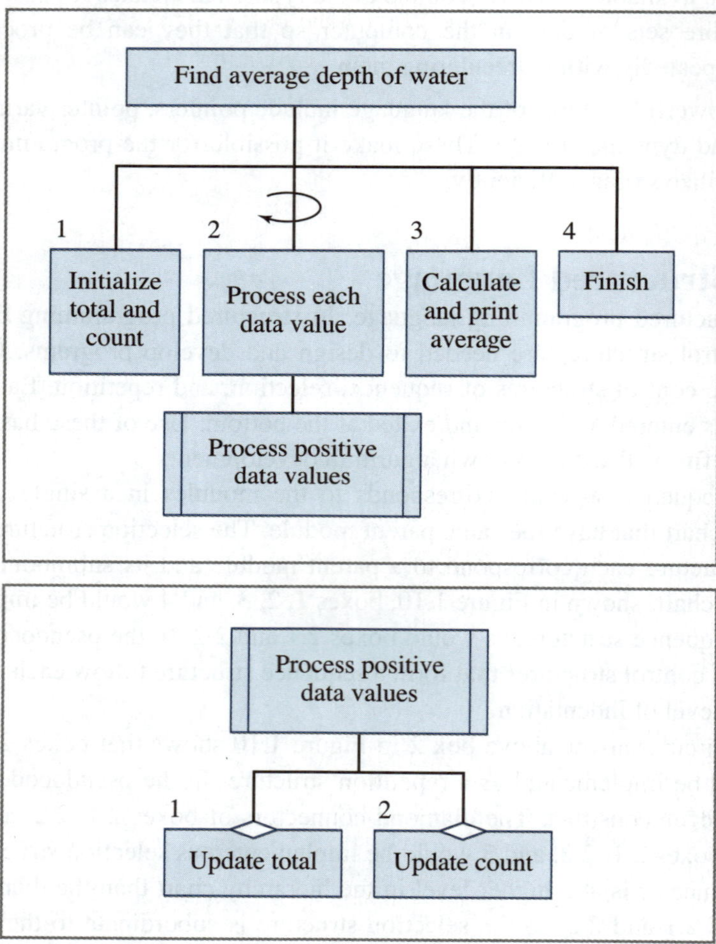

Figure 2.1 Structure chart to compute average depth

Using more than one structure chart (or flowchart, or pseudocode) modularizes the design process making it easier to develop, test, and debug the design. It also makes it easier to implement as C language statements and control structures. The algorithm as shown in Figure 2.1 would be implemented using two functions: the main function to find the average depth of water, and a subfunction to process a single positive data value.

Top-down solution algorithms using the basic control structures have clear logic structure, and are easy to follow and understand. Programs written using basic control structures and top-down solution algorithms are more reliable and easier to maintain than unstructured programs.

2.1.2 Procedural Language

Any complex logic modules resulting from the modular design process can be implemented as separate procedures. In C, these procedures are called functions. A function is a piece of program code written to perform a single specific task. Like control structures, it has one entry and one exit. The top module of a structure chart is implemented in C as a procedure known as the `main` function of the C program. The main function starts with the function name `main` and a statement block as shown.

```
int main( )
{
    statement block

    return 0;
}
```

There must always be a `main` function in C. Program execution starts at the beginning of the `main` function and stops at the end. It is customary, but not necessary, to have the `main` function as the first function in a C program. Anyone looking at the program code would probably want to read the `main` function first to find out what the program does. However, the physical layout of the functions is also significant in the C programming language.

A `main` function may invoke other functions that are part of the C program and refer to functions that are not part of it. However every function must be both declared and defined. A function is declared by writing a prototype of the function interface. Declaring a function gives it a name and says something about the data it needs as input and produces as output. Defining a function says what it does with the input data to produce the output data. This is done by writing a C programming language implementation of the function. If a function is defined ahead of the `main` function, the definition also serves as the function declaration. If a function is defined after the `main` function, it must be declared ahead of the `main` function or inside the `main` function block, if the function is invoked by `main`.

For example, as noted, the hierarchy chart of Figure 2.1 would be implemented as two functions. The function to implement the process to find the average depth of water would be the `main` function because it describes the entire problem and uses external data as input, produces external output, and is only invoked once. The function that processes a single positive data value should be given an appropriate name such as `compute`. It is not a `main` function as it takes as input a data value that has already been read and validated as positive, and is invoked many times, once for each positive data value. The function `compute` would then have to be both declared and defined using one of the following physical layouts:

```
function declaration compute
int main( )
{
......
    return 0;
}

function definition compute
```

or

```
function definition compute
int main( )
{
......
    return 0;
}
```

or

```
int main( )
{
function declaration compute
..........
    return 0;
}
```

```
function definition compute
```

A function declaration is a prototype consisting of the return type, the function name, and the parameter type list.

For example,

```
int round(float);
```

In this prototype of a rounding function the return type is `int`, the function name is `round`, and the single parameter is of type `float`. The return type is the type of the value calculated by the function. The function rounds a real number to the nearest integer.

The implementation of a function definition starts with a function header that is an example of the prototype consisting of the return type; function name; and the formal arguments, called parameters, enclosed within parentheses. This is followed by the function body enclosed in braces, consisting of a statement block that ends with a return statement.

This is the implementation of the function named `round`.

```
int round(float x)        x is declared to be the name of the parameter
{
    int y;                y is declared to be the name of the result
    y = (int) (x + 0.5);
    return(y);
}
```

The parameters are used to transmit values to a function. The return statement is used to return the result calculated by the function. Note that a `main` function is a function that need not have parameters and returns a zero.

Every function other than the `main` function is activated by being called from another function. The computed value of the function is then returned to the calling function. The details of function declaration, function definition, and function call will be presented in Chapter 5.

2.1.3 Statically Typed Language

In C, the data types of variables and functions must be declared. There are basic or built-in data types. The basic or built-in data types are integer (`int`), floating-point (`float`), double precision (`double`), and character (`char`). The basic or built-in data types are not enough to represent data for applications with complicated data types such as lists, tables, vectors, matrices, and records of mixed data types. In C, arrays, character strings, and structures are derived data types derived from the basic data types `int`, `float`, `double`, and `char`; vectors and arrays are homogeneous data aggregates of numeric and character types; character strings are homogeneous aggregates of characters; and structures are nonhomogeneous data aggregates of more than one type. These complex data types are presented in detail in Chapters 7, 8, and 9.

2.1.4 Review Questions

1. Indicate whether the following statements are true (T) or false (F).
   a. C is a structured programming language because you can build programs with it.
   b. In C there are three basic types of control structures.
   c. A control structure tells the computer what kind of data to use.
   d. In C every variable must be declared with a data type.
   e. Some data cannot be represented by variables of type `int`, `float`, `double`, or `char`.
   f. In C the `main` procedure must be the first function in the program.
2. Answer the following questions:
   a. The three basic control structures in C are ________, ________, and ________.
   b. C is a strongly ________ language.
   c. The derived data types in C are ________, ________, and ________.

d. In C the procedures are called ________________.

e. In C there is always a ________________ function.

2.2 Constants and Variables

There are constants and variables for every data type. Constants are values that are not usually named. In C, constants are values such as literal numbers (e.g., 735, 680.56) or character strings (e.g., `"company"`). Variables are similar to variables in algebraic expressions and mathematical formulas. The variables have names (e.g., `volume`, `price`) and can have different values at different times. Names such as `pi`, `zero`, and `g` can be used as constants, but they must be identified as such by declaring them type `const` and assigning them the values indicated by their names. For readability, the names of constants are generally written using capital letters (e.g., `PI`, `ZERO`, `G`). When names are used for constants and variables, the programmer must assign values to these constant and variable names before they are used in calculations or as output. In C, a constant or a variable is *undefined* until a value is assigned. A variable with a given name can have only one value assigned at a time. A name declared as a constant must not have its value changed. Both names and assigned values must be written according to the rules of the C language.

2.2.1 Character Set

The C language, like any other language, has a finite set of symbols called the *character set*. The C character set consists of all the uppercase and lowercase alphabetical characters of the English language, numeric digits of the decimal number system, all of the arithmetic operators, all of the relational operators, all of the grouping and separation characters, and some special characters.

Alphabetic Characters These are the 26 uppercase and 26 lowercase letters of the English alphabet:

A B C D E F G H I J K L M N O P Q R S T U V W X Y Z
a b c d e f g h i j k l m n o p q r s t u v w x y z

Numeric Characters These are the numeric digits of the decimal number system:

0 1 2 3 4 5 6 7 8 9

The decimal point can also be used in numbers, but a comma cannot.

Some Special Characters

arithmetic operators	+ - * / %
relational operators	< > == <= >=
assignment operator	=
grouping symbols	( ) { } [ ]
punctuation symbols	, . ‘ “ : ;
blank space	represented as b̸ for blank
underscore	_
logic operators	&& || !

Note that a blank space is, in fact, recognized as a symbol by the computer.

For other specific operations these symbols are used in combination. These special operation symbols will be shown when they are used in the following sections and chapters.

The characters from the character set are used to construct symbolic names to represent many real-world entities besides constants and variables. C has its own syntactic rules for the construction of names.

For alphabetizing character string data such as identification numbers, addresses, or names, an order known as the collating sequence is assigned to these symbols. In the collating sequence, the blank space precedes the alphabetic characters, and the alphabetic characters are in alphabetical order with the uppercase alphabet preceding the lowercase alphabet.

2.2.2 Identifiers

Identifiers are the symbolic names that represent various quantities such as function names, variable names, constant names, array names, character string names, structure tag names, and so on. According to the ANSI standard:

- An identifier must consist of 1 to 31 characters with no embedded blank spaces.
- The first character must be either an alphabetic character or an underscore. Normally the underscore as the first character is not recommended, because it looks odd.
- The other characters can be alphabetic or numeric or the underscore.
- No special characters are allowed in the identifier names.

> *Program Warning:* Identifiers with more than 31 characters may be acceptable but the ANSI standard requires the first 31 characters to be unique.

Note that in identifiers, the uppercase letters are distinguished from the lowercase letters. For example the name `BALANCE` is different from `balance`. C has many reserved words, which must not be used as identifiers.

VALID IDENTIFIERS	INVALID IDENTIFIERS	COMMENT
`stress`	`5identity`	first character cannot be a digit
`velocity`	`axcl dig`	blank space not allowed
`balance`	`con*st`	illegal character
`maximum_value`	`any,value`	illegal character
`total_count`	`while`	reserved word
`xal245c20`	`struct`	reserved word

It is possible to write long names for identifiers provided that the first 31 characters are unique. If an identifier name has more than one word, the words can be separated by an underscore character. For example, the quantity "compression stress" can be written as `compression_stress`. It is important to write meaningful names for identifiers. Writing meaningful names is self-documenting and easy for other programmers to understand. Names that are similar or differ by one character should not be used because they are not only confusing and too close to distinguish, but also may lead to errors in the code.

> *Programming Hint:* Make it a practice to write meaningful names for the identifiers.

Declaration of Variables and Constants All variables and named constants in C must appear in declaration statements. The declaration of a variable instructs the computer to do the following: allocate storage for the variable or constant, and associate the name of the variable or constant with the allocated storage. A declaration is also the definition of the variable or constant if it assigns a value. A constant must be defined at the same time it is declared. In C, the storage associated with a variable or constant is called a *storage cell*. A storage cell can be one byte, two bytes, four bytes, or eight bytes depending on the declared data type. In C the number of bytes allocated can be queried by using the `sizeof( )` operator. The use of the `sizeof( )` operator is explained in the next section.

2.2.3 Built-in Data Types

C has four data types built into the language. The built-in or basic data types are `int`, `float`, `double`, and `char`.

Data Type `int`: Integers are numbers having one or more digits and possibly a sign, but no comma or decimal point. The `int` data type is used to declare integer variables and constants. They are allocated storage space that can hold integer numbers. On some computers the storage allocated for the `int` data type will default to four bytes and on some other machines will default to two bytes. The machines with four byte default storage can be overridden by requesting two bytes of storage for the variable by defining the variable's data type as `short int` or `short`. The following examples show the definition of integer variables and constants. The machines with two-byte default storage can be overridden by requesting four bytes of storage for the variable by defining the variable's data type as `long int` or `long`. Note that in most programming environments `int` and `long int` variables are four bytes long. The header file `limits.h` defines certain constants and is shown in Table 2.1. The constants shown in the table specify the range of integers for a specific machine (IBM PC).

Table 2.1 Constants defined by `limits.h` for an IBM PC computer

Constant	Type	Storage	Value on IBM PC
CHAR_MIN	char	1 byte	−128
CHAR_MAX	char	1 byte	127
SHRT_MIN	short int	2 bytes	−32768
SHRT_MAX	short int	2 bytes	32767
INT_MIN	int	4 bytes	−2147483648
INT_MAX	int	4 bytes	2147483647
LONG_MIN	long int	4 bytes	−2147483648
LONG_MAX	long int	4 bytes	2147483647

Large computer system:

```
int  count;                    the default storage is four bytes
const int ZERO = 0;

short int  count;              the short storage is two bytes
or
short  count;
```

Personal computer system:

```
int  count;                    the default is two bytes
const int ZERO = 0;

long int  count;               the long storage is four bytes
or
long  count;
```

These declaration statements are for storing signed integer numbers. Notice that each declaration ends with a semicolon. Every statement in C ends with a semicolon with the exception of the control statements.

In C, one can store unsigned integer numbers. The declaration of unsigned integer numbers is as follows:

Large computer system:

```
unsigned int  var1, var2;           the storage is four bytes

unsigned short int  var1, var2;     the storage is two bytes
or
unsigned short  var1, var2;
```

Personal computer system:

```
unsigned int  var1, var2;           the storage is four bytes

unsigned long int  var1, var2;      the long store is four bytes
or
unsigned long  var1, var2;
```

If several variables need to be declared as integers, they can all be declared in one statement by separating the variables with commas. The following example shows such a declaration.

```
int count, value, item;
```

Notice that the variables `count`, `value`, and `item` are all declared as integer variables in one statement. As a matter of style some prefer to declare each variable in a separate line:

```
int count;
int value;
int item;
```

When variables and constants are declared separately, they can have separate documentation such as:

```
const int G = 32;     /*  gravity in ft/sec²  */
```

The data type `int` should be used for variables that are assigned integer values, such as variables representing counters, number of units, number of items, loop counters, loop index, array subscript, etc.

Data Type `float`: `float` is a data type for real numbers. Real numbers may be written in either of two forms; as one or more digits, a decimal point, and possibly a sign, or in scientific notation. The following are real numbers:

5.0
−0.017
3.7E15
−6.2E-8
+.023E+1

Variables or constants declared with a `float` data type are allocated four bytes of storage and used to store real numbers in a scientific form. When the letter E is used in a numeric literal, the number is a real number. The letter E stands for exponent. The number following the letter E is an exponent of 10 and it must be an integer. Therefore:

−0.6873E03	means	-0.6873×10^{03}
0.5634E−04	means	0.5634×10^{-04}

The following example shows the declaration of float variables and constants.

```
float load;
float area;
float stress;
const float PI = 3.141593; /* seven significant digits */
```

The three variable declarations can be combined into one statement as follows:

```
float load, area, stress;
```

Variables `load`, `area`, and `stress` are floating point variables that hold values limited to 7 decimal digits. There is an exact binary equivalent for 0.5 and 0.25 but not for 0.1. Therefore, float values may be approximate rather than exact.

41.23 is stored as approximately $.4123000 \times 10^2$

.00004123 is stored as approximately $.4123000 \times 10^{-4}$

2.0/3.0 is stored as approximately $.6666666 \times 10^0$

2.0 * 7.754321 is stored as approximately 15.50864 or $.1550864 \times 10^2$

Engineering and science applications deal with decimal numbers. In some engineering and science applications the number of digits is important for precision. The `float` variables only hold seven decimal digits, the last of which may be inexact. For higher precision the `float` data type is not sufficient.

Data Type `double`: When engineering and science applications require higher precision, data type `double` must be used. Data type `double` is also required by some of the library functions. A variable declared with data type `double` will be allocated eight bytes of storage, which can hold up to fifteen decimal digits, the last of which may be inexact.

The declaration of double-precision variables is as follows:

```
double atomic_number, planets_distance;
```

Variables `atomic_number` and `planets_distance` are allocated eight bytes of storage each. Most of the time high-precision values are represented in scientific notation. For example a number 123.456789 is represented in scientific notation as 1.23456789E02.

A named constant of data type `double` should be defined when it is declared.

```
const double PI = 3.141592653742; /* thirteen significant digits */
```

Data Type char: The data type `char` is allocated one byte of storage. A single byte of storage can hold one character.

The declaration of a character variable is as follows:

```
char ch1, ch2, ch3;
```

Each of the variables `ch1`, `ch2`, and `ch3` is allocated one byte of storage. A named constant of data type `char` should be defined when it is declared.

```
const char comma = ',';
```

In C, a character constant must be enclosed in single quotes. Note that `"ABC"` is a character string, not a single character, and cannot be assigned to a variable or constant of type `char`. Similarly, `"A"` is a character string whereas `'A'` is a single character.

Character Code in ASCII In computer memory a character is stored internally in coded form as a decimal integer. For example character 'A' has an internal numeric code of 65 in ASCII. Decimal digits also have an internal code in ASCII. For example decimal digit '5' stored as a character has an internal numeric code of 53 in ASCII.

When a variable is declared as a character variable using the data type `char` and such a variable is assigned a value it is internally stored with the numeric code for each character in whatever coding system is used by the computer. The following example shows such a declaration and the assignment of a character.

```
char  var1, var2;

var1 = 'X';
var2 = '7';
```

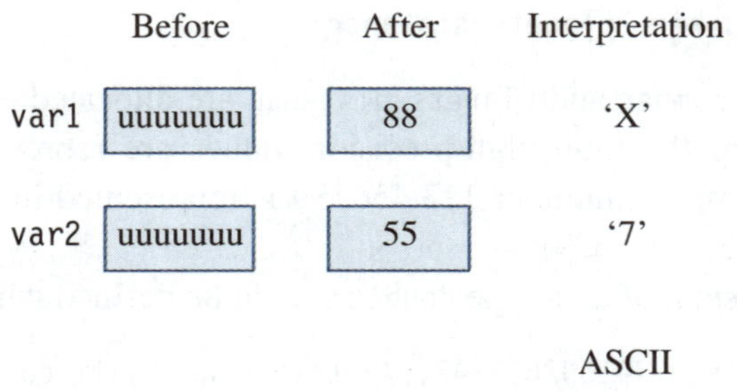

	Before	After	Interpretation
var1	uuuuuuu	88	'X'
var2	uuuuuuu	55	'7'

ASCII

Notice that uuuuuuu are used to indicate that the memory content is undefined when a variable is declared.

Table 2.2 ASCII and EBCDIC codes for special characters

Character	Interpretation	ASCII
`'\a'`	bell	7
`'\b'`	back space	8
`'\f'`	form feed	12
`'\n'`	new line	10
`'\t'`	tab	9
`'\0'`	null character	0
`'\\'`	\(backslash)	92
`'\''`	'(single quote)	39

Special Character Codes There are codes for some special characters that perform certain operations. Table 2.2 shows these special characters, their codes in ASCII, and the operations they perform.

Initialization of Variables Variables must be initialized before they are used in calculations or as output. Variables used for summations and counters are normally initialized when they are declared. The following examples show the initialization of variables in declaration statements. A variable is not defined until it has been initialized.

```
int  count = 0, sum = 0;

float  time = 0.0, velocity = 2175.36;
```

Notice that the integer variables `count` and `sum` both are initialized to 0. The real variable `time` is initialized to 0.0 and `velocity` is initialized to 2175.36. Initializing them defines the variables `count`, `sum`, `time`, and `velocity`.

2.2.4 Derived Data Types

There are many applications requiring more complex data types, where the built-in data types are not enough to represent the data. For example vectors, matrices, or lists may be needed. In C, complex data of homogeneous type can be stored in arrays. Arrays are derived data types derived from the basic data types `int`, `float`, `double`, and `char`.

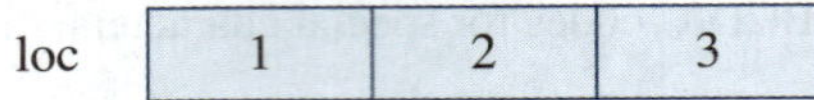

For example: `int loc[ ] = {1, 2, 3};` is a one-dimensional array named `loc` representing a position in three-dimensional space.

Arrays are presented in detail in Chapters 7 and 8.

Character strings are the data type derived from the basic data type `char` and the derived data type array.

digits	'0'	'1'	'2'	'3'	'4'	'5'	'6'	'7'	'8'	'9'	'\0'

For example: `char digits[ ] = {'0', '1', '2', '3', '4', '5', '6', '7', '8', '9', '\0' };` is a one-dimensional array with 11 elements; each of which is the character representation of a digit except the last one. The last one is the null character. This makes the array into a character string. Character strings are presented in detail in Chapter 9.

Structures are derived data types formed from the basic data types `int`, `float`, `double`, and the derived data types string and array. The members of the structure can be `int`, `float`, `double`, `char`, `array`, or `string` type variables. For example:

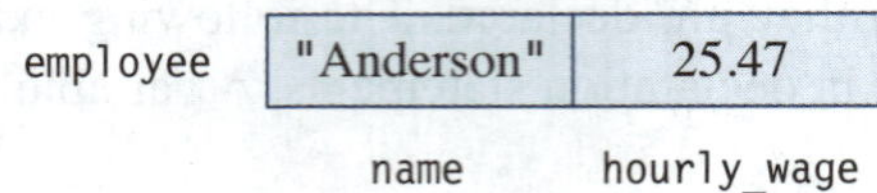

is a structure composed of the structure variable `employee` with a member `name`, which is a character string, and a member `hourly_wage`, which is of the data type `float`. Structures are presented in Chapter 11.

2.2.5 Pointer and Pointer Variables

A pointer is a powerful feature incorporated in C that allows the programmer to manipulate data using the memory address of a variable. In C, like any other programming language, when a variable is declared it is allocated storage space in memory and such storage space is identified by a unique number called a memory address. The value of a pointer is simply a memory address of a variable. The *pointer variable* points to the data value at the address stored in the pointer variable. A variable that contains an address is called a pointer variable. Naming a pointer variable follows the same identifier rules as naming a regular variable. The data type of the pointer variable is the same as the data type of the variable it points to. An asterisk (*) is used to show that it is a pointer variable. For example if the data type of a variable is `float` then the data type of a variable that points to it is `float *`. The following code shows the declaration of a variable and a pointer variable.

`float   var1 = 460.5;`	declaration and definition of a variable `var1`
`float  *ptrvar1;`	declaration of a pointer variable `ptrvar1`

The data type of the variable `var1` is `float`, whereas the data type of the pointer variable `ptrvar1` is `float *` indicating that `ptrvar1` will contain the address of a float variable. The names show the intended relationship of the two variables. However the pointer variable does not point to the other variable until the address of the other variable is assigned to it. Storage of four bytes is allocated to variable `var1` in memory and, say the memory address of this storage is 5000. Note that 5000 is the first byte location of the four bytes allocated to variable `var1`. The intention behind this declaration is to access the memory address of the variable `var1`, which is 5000, and store it in the pointer variable `ptrvar1`. This is accomplished by using a special operator called the address operator (&) provided in C. The following diagram shows how `var1` and `ptrvar1` are related.

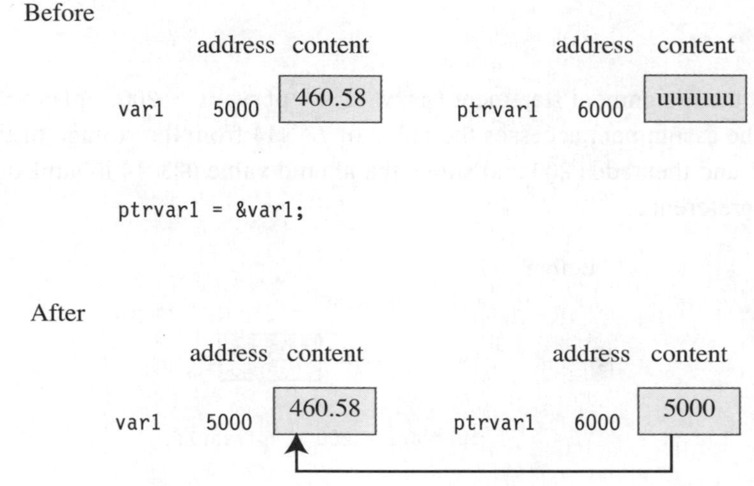

Notice that 5000 is the memory location (address) of the variable `var1` and 6000 is the memory location (address) of the pointer variable `ptrvar1`. Executing the assignment places the address of `var1` in the storage of `ptrvar1`.

Now the value for the variable `var1` may be accessed by the variable name `var1` or through the pointer variable `ptrvar1`. To access the value of `var1` through the pointer `ptrvar1` a dereference operator (*) must be used. The following code shows the use of the dereference operator.

Before

	address	
var1	5000	460.58

```
*ptrvar1 = 723.14;
```

After

	address	
var1	5000	723.14

```
ptrvar1 = &var1;
*ptrvar1 = 723.14;
```

is equivalent to

```
var1 = 723.14;
```

Similarly the assignment statement `*ptrvar1 = *ptrvar1 + 200;` `*ptrvar1` on the right of the assignment accesses the value of `723.14` from the storage of the variable `var1` and then adds `200` and stores the altered value `923.14` in `var1` using the pointer dereference.

Before

	address	
var1	5000	723.14

```
*ptrvar1 = 200 + *ptrvar1;
```

After

	address	
`var1`	5000	923.14

2.2.6 Review Questions

1. Indicate whether the following statements are true (T) or false (F).
   a. Every variable in C must be declared.
   b. A variable declared with data type `double` will be allocated four bytes of storage.
   c. Derived data types are derived from basic or built-in data types.
   d. A structure data type is a homogeneous data type.
   e. An array is a heterogeneous data type.
   f. Variables in C can be initialized when they are declared.
   g. Named constants in C must be declared just like any other named variables.
2. Answer the following questions:
   a. Declare the following variables as integer variables.

      ```
      iter, counter
      i, j, k
      max, min, ival, imax, jmax
      ```

   b. Declare and initialize the following variables to the values specified.

      `maxcount` to 50, `icount` to 20, `kvalue` to 100

   c. Declare the following variables as floating-point variables.

      ```
      balance, energy, power, voltage, current, acidity, phvalue
      ```

   d. Declare the following variables as double-precision variables.

      ```
      atomic-number, refractive-index, specific-gravity, density
      ```

   e. Declare the following variables as character variables.

      ```
      code, basic_colors, student_status, depth_code.
      ```

f. Declare and define the following constants, giving them the obvious values.

```
three, plus, e, gravity
```

3. Answer the following questions
   a. In C the built-in data types are ________________
   ________________, ________________, ________________,
   and ________________.
   b. In C the derived data types are ________________,
   ________________, and ________________.

2.3 Arithmetic Operations and Expressions

Engineering and scientific computing involves arithmetic operations and arithmetic expressions. Arithmetic operations can be performed on numeric data of type `int`, `float`, and `double`, which have the usual arithmetic operations built into the language. Millions of arithmetic operations are performed every day in engineering and scientific calculations. Computers are designed to perform them very quickly.

2.3.1 Arithmetic Operators and Operations

The basic arithmetic operations are expressed in C using the following symbols:

addition	+
subtraction	−
multiplication	*
division	/
remainder	%

Each of these has multiple meanings depending on the declared types of the operands.

Exponentiation is performed in C by using the function `pow(double, double)`, from the math library. The addition and subtraction symbols can be used with either one operand a unary plus (e.g., +245), a unary minus (e.g., −12), or two operands (to indicate addition or subtraction). Unary operators should be separated by parentheses so that two operators do not immediately follow each other. The following examples show the use of the operators.

	Expression	**Value**
Unary plus:	+(+15)	15
Addition operation:		
	8 + 5	13
	−8 + 15	7
	18 + (−25)	−7
	−15 + (−18)	−33
	18.54 + 3.21	21.75
	−0.124 + 1.23	1.106
Unary minus:		
	−(−10)	10
	−23.321	−23.321
Subtraction operation:		
	12 − 8	4
	−16 − 7	−23
	8 − (−6)	14
	−5.67 − 2.43	−8.10
	9.98 − 6.33	3.65
Multiplication operation:		
	8 * 4	32
	6 * (− 4)	−24
	2.5 * 3	7.5
Division operation:		
	16/2	8
	20/(−4)	−5
	−50/5	−10
	14/5	2 not 2.8
	6.6/2.0	3.3

> *Programming warning:* Division of an integer by an integer produces an integer.

When both operands are integers, the result of division is an integer. This may lead to undesirable results in computations involving integer division. The result of an integer division is an integer where the fractional part is not rounded but is truncated. If a division expression has two operands as integers, to keep the fractional part you must cast one or both the integers to either `float` or `double` as shown in the following examples. `(float)7/4` or `(float)7/(float)4` or `7/(float)4` will give the result 1.75. But float(7/4) will give the result 1.0. Preceding the number by a data type converts the number to that type.

Either or both of the numbers can be made real by adding a decimal point as shown in the following example:

`7.0/4` or `7/4.0` or `7.0/4.0` will give the result 1.75

Remainder Operation	Value	Mathematics
8 % 3	2	8 / 3 = 2 R 2
16 % 2	0	16 / 2 = 8 R 0
15 % 4	3	15 / 4 = 3 R 3
(−8) % 3	−2	−8 / 3 = −2 R −2

Notice that the remainder operation is restricted to the integer data type. The R stands for remainder. This operator is also called a modulo operator and reads as "8 mod 3."

Exponentiation Operation The *pow* function from the math library is used for exponentiation. The arguments must be of data type `double`. The general expression is as follows:

a^b `pow((double) a, (double) b)`

Expression	Operation	Value
5^2	`pow((double) 5, (double) 2)`	25.0
$(-5)^2$	`pow((double) -5, (double) 2)`	25.0
$2^{.5}$	`pow((double) 2, (double)(.5))`	1.414
$2^{-0.5}$	`pow((double)2, (double)(-.5))`	0.707

If the base *a* and the exponent *b* are declared as double precision variables, then the pow function call is as follows:

```
    double x, y;
x^y pow(x, y);
```

Notice that the exponentiation operation is restricted to the `double` data type.

Table 2.3 Data type of mixed mode arithmetic

		operand2		
		int	float	double
operand1	int	int	float	double
	float	float	float	double
	double	double	double	double

Mode of Arithmetic Results If the two operands of an arithmetic operation are of the `int` data type the result is an `int` value. If the two operands are `float` the result is `float`. If the two operands are of the same data type the result is the same data type as the operands. If the two operands are mixed, (e.g., one operand is `int` and the other is `float`, the arithmetic is known as *mixed-mode* arithmetic) and the result has the `float` data type. Table 2.3 shows the data type of the result when mixed-mode arithmetic is involved. The following examples show mixed-mode operations:

Expression	**Result**
16 + 2.0	18.0
15 − 12.5	2.5
15 / 3.5	4.285728
15.0 / 2	7.5

Programming Warning: When doing mixed-mode arithmetic, be careful about the integer division operation. Make sure to cast one of the operands in such an operation to data type `float` or `double` or the decimal digits will be lost.

When arithmetic is performed using both integer and floating-point operands, the computer has to change the integer operand to a floating-point number before performing the arithmetic, for example

15 + 6.0	becomes	15.0 + 6.0	with the result	21.0
18.5 / 2	becomes	18.5 / 2.0	with the result	9.25
12.25 * 2	becomes	12.25 * 2.0	with the result	24.50

When a double-precision value is used in a mixed-mode operation with an integer or single-precision value, the integer or single-precision value is converted to double-precision before the operation is performed. The result is a double-precision value that has no more accuracy than the less accurate of the two operands.

2.3.2 Arithmetic Expressions

In engineering and scientific applications it is very common to use arithmetic expressions that include constants as well as variables. An expression can be used in a C program wherever a value of the same type can be used. The examples show arithmetic expressions and the results for the following variable declarations.

```
int    a, b, c, d;
float  x, y, z, w;
```

C Expression	Result
`5 + 6 * 8 / 2`	integer constant
`3.0 + 5 * 2.5 + 6.0 / 2`	floating-point constant
`a + b * c – d / c`	integer value
`x – y * z + w / 2`	floating-point value
`a * x – b / y + w / c`	floating-point value

2.3.3 Assignment Statement

The assignment statement is the fundamental statement in most computer programming languages, including C. In C the equal sign (=) is used in the assignment statement. This symbol does not have the same meaning that it does in algebraic expressions. The meaning of this symbol in C is like its meaning in mathematical formulas. It indicates that the value computed from the expression on the right of the equal sign is to be assigned to the variable on the left (or stored in the memory location allocated to the variable on the left side of the equal sign). The following examples show the assignment statement:

```
area = (3.141593 * d * d) / 4.0;
```

means calculate $\frac{\pi d^2}{4}$ and assign the result to area.

That is, find the area of a circle by multiplying π times the diameter squared and dividing by 4. π has seven digits because values of data type `float` are stored with seven digits.

Since in an assignment statement the value computed for the expression on the right of the equal sign is assigned to the variable on the left, assignment statements such as the following are meaningful:

		Before		After
`float a = 10;` `a = a + 5.2;`	a	10.00	a	15.20

The computer executes the assignment statement by getting the current value from memory cell a, which is 10.00, adding 5.2 to it, and storing the result back in memory cell a, replacing the value 10.00 with the new value, 15.20. In doing this, the computer writes the new value over the old value contained in the memory cell a; the old value is erased.

The expression on the right side of an assignment statement may be of any appropriate type and may be a constant, another variable that has already been given a value, or a valid C expression that is to be evaluated. The left side must be a variable or a dereferenced pointer to a variable. The following are examples of valid assignment statements:

Assignment Statement	**Comments**
`factor = 12.65;`	assuming factor is `float`, it takes the value12.65
`a = e;`	*a* is given the same value as *e*
`x = 'c';`	assuming *x* is a character variable, it takes 'c' as its value
`s = t * r * l;`	using the values of *t*, *r*, and *l*, *t* * *r* * *l* is calculated and the result is stored in *s*
`x = x / 5 + x * y - x / z;`	the previous value of *x* is replaced by a value calculated using *y*, *z*, and the previous value of *x*
`*ptrw = 27.5;`	the previous value of the variable pointed to by `ptrw` is replaced by 27.5

Each assignment statement is carried out in three steps:

1. The computer evaluates the expression on the right side of the equal sign.
2. If the result is not of the same data type as the variable on the left side, it is converted to the data type of that variable.

3. The computer assigns the resulting value to the variable on the left side. In effect, the value is stored in the memory cell allocated to that variable, except that with the pointer variable, one level of indirection is used.

When an integer value is assigned to a `float` variable, it is converted to a `float` value having a fractional part of .0 before being stored. When a `float` value is assigned to an `int` variable, the fractional part of the value is discarded before the value is stored.

> *Programming Warning:* The computer does not round floating-point values assigned to integer variables. The fractional parts are truncated.

```
int a, b, c;
float x, y, z;
```

For these variable declarations, the expressions and the calculated values and the values assigned are shown as follows:

Assignment Statement	Calculated Value	Value Assigned
`a = 15 / 2;`	7	7
`b = -28.0 / 3.2;`	−8.75	−8
`c = 3 * 4 * 1.2;`	14.4	14
`y = 2 / 5;`	0	0.0
`x = 4.5 * (1/2);`	0	0.0
`z = 4.5 * 2.3 / 1.5;`	6.9	6.9

Notice that this last value may be 6.9 or 6.899998 depending on whether the multiplication or division is carried out first. In this case, the multiplication is carried out first before the division. Since multiplication and division have the same order of precedence, and operations of equal precedence are performed left to right, the value assigned is 6.9.

2.3.4 Order of Evaluations

The order of evaluation of operations in arithmetic expressions depends on the precedence of the operations. This precedence is:

highest	( )
	+ − unary
	pow( )
	* and / and % left to right
lowest	+ and −

This order is called the hierarchy of operators. Operations of the same precedence are performed left to right. If one of the operands includes an operation of higher precedence, the higher precedence operation is performed first just as in arithmetic. Therefore the following are equivalent:

$a + b + c$	$(a + b) + c$
$a - b - c$	$(a - b) - c$
$a + b - c$	$(a + b) - c$
$a / b / d$	$(a / b) / d$
$a / b * c$	$(a / b) * c$
$-a * b$	$(-a) * b$
$a + b * c$	$a + (b * c)$

The following calculations show the order of precedence:

12 / 3 * 2 + 4 − 8 * 2 + 6 / 3
is 4 * 2 + 4 − 8 * 2 + 6 / 3
is 8 + 4 − 8 * 2 + 6 / 3
is 12 − 8 * 2 + 6 / 3
is 12 − 16 + 6 / 3
is − 4 + 6 / 3
is − 4 + 2
is − 2

This example shows the step-by-step evaluation of an arithmetic expression.

The following example shows the details of the step-by-step evaluation of an algebraic expression.

	$a - b\,c + g \div k + f\,e^2 - x\,y \div z$	algebraic expression
	`a - b * c + g / k + f * e * e - x * y / z`	C expression
Step 1	$a - r1 + g / k + f * e * e - x * y / z$	where $r1 = b * c$
Step 2	$r2 + g / k + f * e * e - x * y / z$	where $r2 = a - r1$

Step 3	$r2 + r3 + f * e * e - x * y / z$	where $r3 = g / k$
Step 4	$r4 + f * e * e - x * y / z$	where $r4 = r2 + r3$
Step 5 + 6	$r4 + r5 - x * y / z$	where $r5 = f * e * e$
Step 7	$r6 - x * y / z$	where $r6 = r4 + r5$
Step 8	$r6 - r7 / z$	where $r7 = x * y$
Step 9	$r6 + r8$	where $r8 = r7 / z$
Step 10	$r9$	where $r9 = r6 + r8$

$r1, r2,...,r8$ are the intermediate results calculated by the computer before it reaches the final result $r8$. Notice that the calculations are carried out in the order of precedence, comparing two operators at a time, from left to right, the multiplication and the division are done before addition and subtraction. At each step, the computer uses the current values of the variables to calculate the new value. If the types don't match, it converts the value to the type needed to carry out the operation.

This is shown in the following example:

```
int a, b;
float x, y, z;

a = 4;
b = 2;
x = 5.0;
y = 4.5;
z = 2.0;
```

	`a + b * x - b * a - y / z`	C expression
Step 1	`a + 10.0 - b * a - y / z`	value of `b` is converted to `float` 2.0 * 5.0 is computed
Step 2	`14.0 - b * a - y / z`	value of `a` is converted to `float` 4.0 + 10.0 is computed
Step3	`14.0 - 8 - y / z`	`b * a` is evaluated as integer
Step 4	`6.0 - y / z`	8 is converted to `float` 14.0 − 8.0 is computed
Step 5	`6.0 - 2.25`	4.5 / 2.0 is computed
Step 6	`3.75`	6.0 − 2.25 is computed

The final result of the computation is a `float` value of 3.75.

2.3.5 Use of Parentheses

The examples shown in the previous section are based on the hierarchy of operations when there are no parentheses in the expression. In some algebraic expressions in C, parentheses are necessary to retain the meaning of the expression. The following examples show the use of parentheses:

The algebraic expression $\frac{w+x}{a+b}$ becomes the C expression `(w + x) / (a + b)`

Parentheses are generally necessary when an algebraic expression has fractions or exponents. The nonparenthesized C expression `w + x / a + b` is equivalent to $w+\frac{x}{a}+b$.

Several possible ways of parenthesizing C expressions and their algebraic equivalence are shown as follows:

Algebraic Expression	C Expression
$\frac{w+x}{a+b}$	`(w + x) / (a + b)`
$w+\frac{x}{(a+b)}$	`w + x / ( a + b)`
$\frac{(w+x)}{a}+b$	`(w + x) / a + b`
$w+\frac{x}{a}+b$	`w + x / a + b`

> *Programming Hint:* Use extra parentheses when there is any doubt as to how the expression will be evaluated.

The general rule is to place the numerator and denominator of a fraction in parentheses if they are not positive numbers or simple variables. When parentheses are used in an algebraic expression, they are also needed in the equivalent C expression.

The hierarchy of operations shows that when an expression contains parentheses the parenthesized subexpressions must be evaluated first. When there are nested parentheses, the expression inside the inner parentheses is evaluated first, according to the hierarchical order of the operators, resulting in the removal of the inner parentheses. Then, the innermost remaining expression is evaluated and its parentheses removed, and so on, until there are no parentheses left and the remaining parentheses-free expression can be evaluated.

The following example shows the evaluation of an algebraic expression containing nested parentheses:

$$\frac{s+t}{w+x+\dfrac{y+z}{a+b}}$$ algebraic expression

`(s + t) / ( w + x + (y + z) / (a + b))` C expression

Step 4	$r1 / (r2 + r3 / r4)$	where $r1 = s + t$ $r2 = w + x$ $r3 = y + z$ $r4 = a + b$
Step 5	$r1 / (r2 + r5)$	where $r5 = r3 / r4$
Step 6	$r1 / r6$	where $r6 = r2 + r5$
Step 7	$r7$	where $r7 = r1 / r6$

In this example, all the parentheses shown in the C expression are necessary to retain the meaning of the algebraic expression. As each of the parentheses is evaluated, the operations are performed according to the hierarchical precedence of operations. Whenever there are nested parentheses, the inner parentheses are evaluated before they can be used as an operand.

> *Programming Warning:* Proper nesting of parentheses is essential for correct computation.

2.3.6 Special Operators

Assignment with Arithmetic Operators In C an assignment operator may be combined with the arithmetic operators to form new accumulation operations. For example, the assignment operator (=) may be combined with the addition operator (+) as (+=) to form a summation operator. The following examples show the use of these special operators. For example, to sum the values of x the assignment statements are needed.

`sum = 0;` to initialize the sum

`sum = sum + x;` within a loop with new values of x

The variable sum appears on both sides of an assignment statement sum = sum + x. In such an arithmetic expression the assignment symbol (=) and the addition symbol (+) can be combined into one operator as (+=) and the expression sum = sum + x may be written as sum += x.

```
Summation Operation
sum = 0;
for each x
   sum += x;   /* calculates Σ x */
end for
```

It increments the sum by an amount of x using different values of x.

Similarly other arithmetic operators may be combined with the assignment symbol and the expressions may be written as follows.

variable = variable * x is equivalent to variable *= x product operation.

Similarly,

variable = variable − x is equivalent to variable −= x decrement operation,

variable = variable / x is equivalent to variable /= x fractional operation, and

variable = variable % x is equivalent to variable %= x remainder operation.

Notice that these special operators can only be used in assignment statements where otherwise the same variable must appear on both sides of the assignment symbol. They operate on a variable to change its value.

When the increment is an expression other than a scalar value (for example, sum = sum + x * y) then parentheses must be used as follows:

`sum = sum + x * y ;` is equivalent to `sum += (x * y);`

Unary Increment ++ and Decrement −− Operators In C to increment a variable by 1, a (++) operator may be used; and to decrement a variable by 1 a (−−) operator may be used. These operators are used for counters that need to be incremented or decremented by 1. For example, to increment a variable *x* by 1, an assignment may be written as *x* = *x* + 1 or *x* += 1 or *x*++. Similarly, a decrement operator may be used to decrement a variable by writing *x*−−. The following examples show the use of these operators. If the increment operator appears in front of a variable it is called preincrement (++*x*), if the operator appears after the variable (*x*++) it is called postincrement. The following examples show other uses of the increment and decrement operators.

Preincrement is effective in the expression in which it is used, which means the variable preceded by the (++) symbol is incremented before the expression is evaluated. The following example shows the use of the preincrement.

		Before		After
`x = 10;`	*x*	uuuuuu	*x*	10
`y = ++x;`	*x*	10	*x*	11
	y	uuuuuu	*y*	11

Notice that *x* is incremented before its value is assigned to *y*.

Postincrement is not effective in the expression in which it is used, which means the expression is evaluated first before the increment operator is applied. The following example shows the use of the postincrement.

		Before		After
`x = 10;`	*x*	uuuuuu	*x*	10
`y = x++;`	*y*	uuuuuu	*y*	10
	x	10	*x*	11

Notice that the value of *x* is assigned to *y* before it is incremented.

Predecrement is effective in the expression in which it is used. The following example shows the use of the predecrement.

		Before		After
`x = 10;`	*x*	uuuuuu	*x*	10
`y = --x;`	*x*	10	*x*	9
	y	uuuuuu	*y*	9

Notice that the value of *x* is decremented before it is assigned to *y*.

Postdecrement is not effective in the expression in which it is used. The following example shows the use of the postdecrement.

		Before		After
`x = 10;`	*x*	uuuuuu	*x*	10
`y = x--;`	*y*	uuuuuu	*y*	10
	x	10	*x*	9

Notice that the value *x* is assigned to *y* before *x* is decremented.

Cast Operator In C a cast operator may be used to convert a value to another data type after accessing the value without changing the data type in storage. Since C is a statically typed language the data type of the declared variable can not be altered by using a cast operator. For example, to convert the value of a variable with data type `int` to the data type `float` and vice versa follows:

```
int var1;
float var2;
```

`(float) var1;` changes the `int` data type value fetched from the storage of `var1` to the `float` data type without changing the data type of `var1` or the value stored in `var1`

`(int) var2;` changes the `float` data type value fetched from the storage of `var2` to the `int` data type without changing the data type of `var2` or the value stored in `var2`

Notice that a cast operator is a data type written with parentheses. These changes happen outside the variable's storage in the expressions in which the cast is used. The original declared data type will not change and the value in storage will not change. An `int` value may be changed to `float` by the use of mixed-mode arithmetic, for example, `var1 + 0.0` or `1.0 * var1`, but a `float` value can only be changed to `int` by using the cast operator.

`sizeof` Operator The storage for a variable is allocated in bytes. One byte of storage is required to store a character. In C, the number of bytes of storage allocated to a variable depends on the data type of the variable. At run-time the `sizeof` operator determines the number of bytes of storage allocated for a particular variable or a data type. The `sizeof` operator may also be used to determine the storage allocated for the basic data types of a specific computer. The following examples show the use of the `sizeof` operator.

To determine the default number of bytes allocated for an `int` variable on a computer:

```
int  var, varsize;

varsize = sizeof(int);
```

or

```
varsize = sizeof(var);
```

Both statements will assign the same value, which is four, to `varsize` on most computers.

To determine the default number of bytes allocated for a `float` variable on a computer:

```
float var;
int varsize;

varsize = sizeof(float);
```

or

```
varsize = sizeof(var);
```

Both statements will assign the same value, which is four, to `varsize` on all computers.

To determine the default number of bytes allocated for a `double` variable:

```
double var;
int varsize;

varsize = sizeof(double);
```

or

```
varsize = sizeof(var);
```

Both statements will assign the same value, which is eight, to `varsize` on many computers.

To determine the number of bytes allocated for a `char` variable:

```
char var;
int varsize;

varsize = sizeof(char);
```

or

```
varsize = sizeof(var);
```

Both statements will assign the same value, which is one, to `varsize`.

2.3.7 Accuracy of Computation

That the computer produces a numeric answer does not guarantee that the answer is correct and accurate. Certainly, if incorrect data are provided to a computer, the answer will be incorrect. However, there are some types of numeric errors that are not found until the accuracy of the answer is analyzed.

These errors can be classified as caused by:

- Nonsignificant digits in the computer form of input data
- Inexactness of computer representation of real numbers
- Adjustment of computational results to fit computer storage

For example, if measurements are made with a gauge that can be read to the nearest hundredth of an inch, a measurement of .06 may represent any value from .055 to .065. The measurement is inexact to begin with. But in the computer it will be stored as .06000000 or .05999999, either of which is misleading as the original number was not accurate to seven significant digits.

A little thought would indicate that

$$\begin{aligned}(1.0 / 3.0) * 3.0 &= 0.3333333 * 3.0 \\ &= 0.9999999 \\ &\neq 1.0\end{aligned}$$

when calculated by a computer, because the order of operations requires the division to be performed first, and computers can only store seven significant digits for real numbers. Expressions that are equivalent in algebra are not necessarily equivalent when evaluated by a computer.

This same inaccuracy arises with calculations such as

(1.0 / 10.0) * 10.0, which is not 1.0

which can be calculated exactly with paper and pencil. Since most computers use binary rather than decimal numbers, values such as 0.1 can only be approximated. Therefore, choices between alternatives that are based on a comparison of real numbers, should consider them equal if they differ by less than some small margin of error (e.g., if $(x - y) < 0.0001$).

The inaccuracy that arises with integer calculations has already been discussed, for example, that

(1 / 2) * 2 is 0, and

1 / 2 * 2 is 0,

but 2 * 1 / 2 is 1.

Similarly inaccuracies due to loss of significance, arise in scientific calculations when the original values are inexact. For example, if 0.42598 and −0.42406 are each accurate to five decimal places, their sum 0.00192 is also accurate to five decimal places, but has only three significant digits rather than the original five. If the original values were each approximate rather than exact, the sum has only two significant nonzero digits. Once values are inaccurate, further computation increases the inaccuracy. The order of the variables in the expression can also affect the accuracy.

2.3.8 C Libraries and Functions

C has a rich collection of libraries. These libraries contain predefined functions that programmers can use. The code has already been written and tested for correctness and accuracy. The C library functions are grouped according to their functionality and use. Function prototypes for each of the groups is stored in a separate file called a header file. To access the groups of functions contained in these libraries the programmer must include the header files in the program by using the `#include` statement. The `#include` statement is a *preprocessor directive*. There are header files for input and output functions, character string manipulation functions, mathematical functions, memory allocation functions, and other miscellaneous functions. As with all function declarations the header files must precede the main function. The linker/loader then knows what function implementations to load.

The header files, the detailed descriptions of the preprocessor directives, and most of the common functions are presented in Appendix B.

2.3.9 Review Questions

1. Indicate whether the following statements are true (T) or false (F).
   a. The order of precedence of arithmetic operators is important in the evaluation of a C expression.
   b. Parentheses have the lowest order of precedence in evaluating a C expression.
   c. The order of evaluation of the arithmetic operators is that division and/or multiplication is performed before addition and/or subtraction.
   d. The order of evaluation of an expression with parentheses is the same as the order of evaluation of a nonparenthesized expression.
   e. When an algebraic expression is divided by another algebraic expression you must enclose each of the expressions with parentheses.
   f. When an arithmetic operation involves a mixed data type, the simple data type is converted to the more complex data type, the arithmetic is carried out, and the result has the more complex data type.
   g. C has a large collection of library functions.

2. Write the equivalent C expression for each of the following algebraic expressions:
   a. $x + y / z + wp$
   b. $(x + y) \div w + r - s$
   c. $8(a + b) \div 6f - kn$
   d. $-a + bc\ (-d) * g$
   e. $(1 / 3)\ bh + (1/4)\ kn$
3. Given the values of the following `int` variables: $x = 4, y = 5, z = 6,$ and $w = 2$, compute the value of each of the following expressions:
   a. $x + y * z / w$
   b. $(x + y) / z + w$
   c. $(x + y * z) / w$
   d. $(x + y) / (z + w)$
   e. $(x + y) + z / w$
4. Given the values of the following `float` variables: $a = 4.5$, $b = 5.0$, $c = 6.5$, and $d = 2.5$, compute the value of each of the following expressions:
   a. $a + b / c * d$
   b. $(a + b) / c + d$
   c. $(a + b * c) / d$
   d. $(a + c) /(b + d)$
   e. $(a + b) + c / d$
5. Given the following algebraic expressions, write the equivalent C expressions
   a. $(w + x) / (y + 2) + xt$
   b. $ax + bx - cx + d$
   c. $(a + b + c) \div (d + e - (f + g) \div (1 + j))$
   d. volume = length · width · height
   e. force = mass · acceleration
6. Given the values of the `int` variables $a = 10$, $b = 6$ and `float` variables $x = 10.5$, $y = 12.0$, and $w = 8.5$, determine the value computed

and the value stored in each of the following assignment statements. The variables *s*, *t*, and *r* are type `int`, and *l* and *m* are type `float`.

a. `s = a – b * 5 – x / 2 + y;`

b. `t = a * x + b – y / 2;`

c. `r = a / 2 + x + y;`

d. `l = a * 5 + b / 2 + x – y + w;`

e. `m = x + a / 2 + b – y * 5;`

7. Write the C assignment statements for each of the following equations used in engineering applications, where *p* is pressure, *v* is volume, *m* is moles, *R* is the universal gas constant, and *t* is temperature:

a. $p = (mRt)/v$

b. $p1 = (p2v2)/v1$

c. From the equation $pv = mRt$, write a C statement to calculate the mass, given *p*, *v*, *R*, and *t*.

d. Given the formula $a = 4\pi r^2$ for the surface area of a sphere, write a C statement to calculate the radius of the sphere given the surface area.

e. The moment of inertia of a disk about its fixed axis of rotation is given by $a = 0.5mr^2$. Write a C statement to calculate the mass given *a* and *r*.

f. The state equation for an ideal gas is given by the formula $p = \rho Rt$, where *p* is absolute pressure, ρ is mass density, *t* is absolute temperature, and *R* is the universal gas constant. Write a C statement to find the pressure for gases at 100° Celsius.

g. The pressure loss in a pipe carrying water is given by:

$$h = \frac{flv}{d^2 g}.$$

Where *f* is the friction coefficient, *l* is length, *v* is velocity, *d* is diameter, and *g* is gravitational acceleration. Write a C statement to calculate *h*.

h. The discharge over a rectangular weir is given by:

$$q = k\sqrt{2g\,lh^{3/2}}.$$

Write a C statement to calculate *q*.

i. The effective resistance of a parallel circuit with five parallel resistances is given by:

$$r = \frac{1}{\frac{1}{R1} + \frac{1}{R2} + \frac{1}{R3} + \frac{1}{R4} + \frac{1}{R5}}$$

Write this as a C statement to calculate the effective resistance R.

2.4 Overview of Implementation

Since C is a procedural language, the basic units of the program are the functions. In a C program there is always a function called `main`. The execution of a C program starts with the `main` function, which invokes other functions. In C every function must be declared before it is defined by its C code implementation. The function declaration is called a *function prototype*. If the function implementation appears before `main`, the implementation header serves as a prototype. In such cases there is no need for a separate function prototype. If the implementation appears after `main`, then a function prototype is required.

Note that placing the implementation before `main` is not common and is not encouraged. In ANSI C, for every function there must be a prototype and an implementation. The detailed discussion of prototypes and implementations is presented in Chapter 5.

Every implementation contains a body that is a sequential control structure within braces. The sequential control structure is a sequence of data declarations, executable statements, and subordinate repetition and selection control structures. Each repetition and selection control structure must also contain a body that is itself a sequence. The braces that delineate a body may be omitted if the body contains only one item (declaration, statement, or substructure.) The semicolon (;) is used to separate items in a sequence that do not themselves have bodies.

2.4.1 Formatting of Statements

In C there are two types of statements: comment statements and program statements.

Comment Statement A *comment statement* starts with /* and ends with */. A comment statement can also continue into two or more lines. Comments are not compiled or executed. They are used for program documentation and program internal documentation. They are used for documentation of the main program as well as documentation of functions. All through this text every program is documented. The following examples show sample documentation.

Single line comment statement: /* This is a C program */
Multiple line comment statement: /* This program computes the average of ten integer numbers and prints the average */

Notice that a multiple line comment statement starts with a (/*) and continues into the next line then ends with a (*/). Everything between (/*) and (*/) is part of the comment.

ANSI C also supports single-line comments delimited using //.

Program Statements Program statements are *free format*; this means blank spaces can be inserted between variables, operators, reserved words, and parentheses for readability and clarity of the code. Any statement can continue into two or more lines. A *program statement* can start in any position on a line and end on the same line or end on the next line. The following examples show a program statement.

```
    a = b + c - d * e / f;
or  a = b + c
    - d * e / f;
```

Notice that the second statement is split between two lines; this is perfectly valid as long as it ends with a semicolon. For statements that are very long, it may be necessary to continue into the next line. The line may be split at the end of a variable or an operator, but not in the middle of a variable name.

Notice that blank spaces are provided between the operators and the operands, so that the code is clear and easy to read. We highly recommend the use of spaces for clarity and self-documentation.

> *Program warning:* Do not split any variable name when a statement is split into two lines.

2.4.2 Formatting of a Program

A well designed program has separate sections for documentation, declarations, definitions, and program statements. These are stored in the program file. Data is stored in a data file. There must be external names for the program file and the data file that are known to the operating system. Control statements that are used to compile, link, load, and execute a program refer to the external names of the program and data files. Control statements are not part of a program.

A large program may have several program files, each containing several functions. It is the job of the linker to find all the functions, as well as the library functions needed, and combine them to form executable code. In a C program the main program is the function definition consisting of the header `int main( )` followed by a body of instructions. When the code is compiled the closing braces at the end of the sequence indicate the physical end of the main function. When the code is executed, the `return` statement indicates the end of the execution. The `return` statement is always the last statement in the body of the `main` function. The functions following the `main` function are compiled separately.

Every C program has the following general form:

```
documentation describing the entire program
preprocessor directives
defined constants        /* optional, to be explained later */
global variables         /* not recommended, to be explained later */
function prototypes

int main ( )
{
    declarations of variables and constants
    . . .
    executable statements
    . . .
    return 0;
}

function implementations
```

The `main` function starts with the word `main` with left and right parentheses following it. The variable definitions and executable statements are all included within the body of the main program. The `main` function is the top-level module in the structure chart. `main` is a function with return type `int`. The function returns 0 to indicate that it has terminated successfully.

Both the implementation of the `main` function and subordinate function definitions start with function headers followed by the bodies of the functions enclosed in braces. The structure of a subordinate function is as follows:

```
documentation describing the function
external variables    /* not recommended, to be explained later */
return type   function name(parameter list)
{
    declarations of variables
    . . .
    executable statements
    . . .
    return;
}
```

2.4.3 Data Design

A program should be designed with sufficient data validation to prevent the program from crashing when input data is missing or incorrect, and when internal variables might cause a mathematically impossible situation such as division by 0, or an impossible engineering situation such as a negative physical measurement. That is, a program must compute correct answers when given correct data, and avoid giving misleading answers when the data is inappropriate, and diagnose invalid data. In programs handling large amounts of data, the program must format output pages correctly (putting titles and totals in appropriate places), and detect the ends of output pages as well as the end of input data.

The design phase of the program is the time to also design the test data. To test the algorithm of Figure 1.8 and the related pseudocode and flowchart forms that compute the average of a set of positive numbers, we would want several sets of test data. One would consist of numbers easily used in a desk calculation, e.g., 8.5, 11.5, 13.9. Their total is 33.9 so their average is 11.3. Working step-by-step through the flowchart, pseudocode, or hierarchy chart (better yet, all three) with these values should give this answer. When the C program code is written, compiled, and executed, these data values should give the same answer.

We should also try sets of data values that have extreme values. What happens if the data is 3.4, −7.6, 0, and 14? The answer should be 8.7 if the negative and zero values are simply ignored. If either of them is handled incorrectly, the answer will be different. Another kind of extreme situation is a data set with only one value or with none at all. Does the algorithm handle these correctly? If an input mistake is made such as miskeying a number so that it has a comma rather than a period, or an "E" instead of a "3", the input function will catch the error and inform the program. The handling of that kind of situation is discussed in Chapter 3.

2.4.4 Review Questions

1. Indicate whether the following statements are true (T) or false (F).
   a. The procedures in C are called functions.
   b. Every C program must have a function called `main`.
   c. Every function in C is a block structure; the body of the block structure starts with a left brace and ends with a right brace.
   d. A function need not have a function header.
   e. A function declaration is called a function prototype.
   f. In C every statement terminates with a semicolon.
   g. Program statements in C are free formatted.
   h. In C, comment statements are executable statements.
2. Answer the following questions:
   a. A comment statement starts with ______________ and ends with ______________.
   b. The main program header is ______________.
   c. The function header must not end with ______________.
   d. Write a function header for a function that returns an integer variable, with the function name `addsub` with no parameters.
   e. Write a comment statement with the following comment: "I am learning C programming fundamentals in this chapter."

2.5 First Complete Programs

The following sample programs illustrate the use of arithmetic operators and operations. Their output follows the source code. The standard input and output statements are used; which will be explained in detail in Chapter 3. The form of the input and output shown is for the interactive programs so that you can try these programs on your computer. The line numbers are for reference and explanation only; do not consider these as part of the program.

2.5.1 Sample C Program

Problem Add two integer numbers and output the numbers and the sum.

```
/*****************************************************/
/*                                                   */
/*      THIS IS THE FIRST COMPLETE C PROGRAM         */
/*                                                   */
/*****************************************************/

1  #include <stdio.h>
2  int main( )
3  {
4     int x, y, sum;
5     x = 5;
6     y = 6;
7     sum = x + y;
8     printf("x = %d    y = %d    sum = %d\n", x, y, sum);
9     return 0;
10 }
```

The output is as follows:

```
x = 5    y = 6    sum = 11
```

Statement 1: `#include<stdio.h>` is a preprocessor directive, which causes all of the input and output functions contained in the `stdio.h` library to be included in the linked code.

Statement 2: `int main( )` is the `main` function header.

Statement 3: Left brace, by itself for style and readability, indicates the beginning of a sequence of declarations and instructions in the body of the function.

Statement 4: Declaration of integer variables *x*, *y*, and sum. This allocates required storage of the default number of bytes for each of these variables.

Statements 5–6: Defines the variables *x*, *y*. The assignment statements assign a scalar value 5 to the variable *x* and assigns a scalar value of 6 to variable *y*.

Statement 7: Assignment statement assigns the calculated value to the variable sum after evaluation of the right-side expression by adding the values of x to y.

Statement 8: Output statement prints the values of the variables x, y, and sum stored in the memory. The output function `printf` is the key word for standard output, which will be explained in detail in the next chapter. The output is shown following the program code.

Statement 9: `main` returns 0 indicating termination after successful execution.

Statement 10: Right brace, by itself for style and readability, indicates the end of the body of the function.

2.5.2 Slope of a Straight Line

Problem Write a program to calculate the slope of a line, given the data for coordinates of the end points of the line.

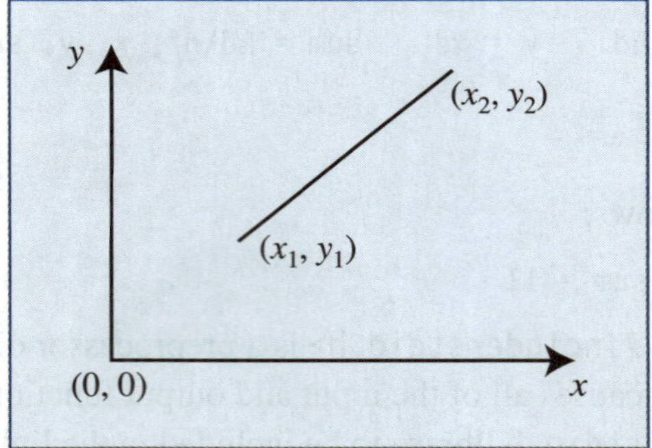

Method The slope of a line is given by the formula $m = \dfrac{y_2 - y_1}{x_2 - x_1}$.

To calculate the slope of the line, the coordinate, the values of the two end points of the line, must be known. This program inputs the coordinate values for the two end points of the line. The value computed for the slope of the line is printed. The output shows the input coordinate end points and the calculated value for the slope.

Data Four real numbers representing coordinates x_1, y_1 and x_2, y_2.

Pseudocode

Input the values for the coordinate end points (x_1, y_1) and (x_2, y_2)
Compute the slope of the line:
  slope $\leftarrow (y_2 - y_1) / (x_2 - x_1)$
Output the coordinates and the slope
End

Program

```
/*********************************************************/
/*                                                       */
/*          Calculation of the Slope of a Line          */
/*                                                       */
/*********************************************************/
/*                                                       */
/*    Input Variables:                                   */
/*                                                       */
/*        x1, y1 - coordinates of point1                 */
/*        x2, y2 - coordinates of point2                 */
/*                                                       */
/*    Computed Variables:                                */
/*                                                       */
/*        slope - slope of the line                      */
/*                                                       */
/*    Output Variables:                                  */
/*                                                       */
/*        x1, y1 - coordinates of point1                 */
/*        x2, y2 - coordinates of point2                 */
/*        slope  - slope of the line                     */
/*                                                       */
/*                                                       */
/*********************************************************/

#include <stdio.h>
int main( )
{
    float x1, y1, x2, y2;
    float slope;
    printf("Input the Coordinate Points of the Line:\n");
```

```
7      scanf("%f  %f  %f  %f", &x1, &y1, &x2, &y2);

8      printf("Coordinates of Point1: x1 = %5.2f  y1 = %5.2f\n",
                x1, y1);
9      printf("Coordinates of Point2: x2 = %5.2f y2 = %5.2f\n",
                x2, y2);
10     if (x1 != x2)
11     {
12         slope = (y2 – y1) / (x2 – x1);
13         printf("Slope of the Line:  %5.2f\n", slope);
14     }
15     else
16         printf("line is vertical\n");

17     return 0;
18 }
```

Interactive Input and Output

```
Input the Coordinate Points of the Line:
3.00       4.00        16.00       18.00
Coordinates of Point1: x1 =  3.00   y1 =  4.00
Coordinates of Point2: x2 = 16.00   y2 = 18.00
Slope of the Line:  1.08
```

Statement 1: Includes the header file `stdio.h` for the input and output library functions. This is in one of the C libraries and must be included to use the input function `scanf( )` and output function `printf( )`. These functions are presented with details of implementation in Chapter 3.

Statement 2: `main` function header.

Statement 3: Left brace indicating the beginning of the `main` function block.

Statement 4: Declaration of integer variables x_1, y_1, x_2, and y_2.

Statement 5: Declaration of floating-point variable `slope`.

Statement 6: Output statement that simply prompts the user for input of data.

Statement 7: Input statement, consisting of the format control field with four control specifications to input four numbers for the four variables of the two coordinate points. The input statement will be presented along with implementation details in Chapter 3.

Statement 8: Output statement to print the text enclosed within the double quotes, inserting the coordinate values for the first point. The `\n` within the double quotes is the line feed character.

Statement 9: Output statement to print the text enclosed within the double quotes, inserting the coordinate values for the second point. The `\n` within the double quotes is the line feed character.

Statement 10: An `if` statement to check whether the line is a vertical line. The logic operator != stands for "not equal."

Statement 11: Left brace indicating the beginning of the selection block.

Statement 12: Computes the slope of the line.

Statement 13: Output statement to print the text enclosed within the double quotes inserting the value of the slope of the line. The `\n` within the double quotes is the line feed character.

Statement 14: Left brace indicating the end of the selection block.

Statement 15: An `else` clause in the selection statement.

Statement 16: Output statement to print a message with a line feed character `\n`.

Statement 17: `return` statement returns 0 for the successful completion of the `main` function.

Statement 18: Right brace indicating the end of the `main` function block.

Run from an interactive terminal, the computer prompts the user to input the data for the two coordinate end points. The values for the points are entered on the keyboard, followed by a carriage return. The output is displayed on the terminal screen.

2.5.3 Compression Stress in a Steel Column

Problem Compute the compression stress in a steel column of diameter d inches subject to the compression load of p pounds.

Data Two positive integers representing p and d.

Method The formula for the compression stress is given as follows:

$$\text{area} = \pi d^2 / 4$$

$$f = p / \text{area}$$

Where: *p* is the compression load in pounds,
area is the cross-sectional area of the steel column in square inches, and
f is the compression stress in pounds per square inch.

Pseudocode

Input the compression load p, and the diameter d
If data is valid
Compute the area
area ← π d²/4
Compute the compression stress
f ← p / area
Output the compression load p, diameter of column d, and the compression stress f
End

Program

```
/*****************************************************/
/*                                                   */
/*  Compute the Compression Stress in a Steel Column */
/*                                                   */
/*****************************************************/
/*                                                   */
/*    Defined constants:                             */
/*                                                   */
/*        PI     - 3.141593                          */
/*                                                   */
/*    Input Variables:                               */
/*                                                   */
/*        p      -  Compression  Load                */
/*        diam   -  Diameter of the Steel Column     */
/*                                                   */
/*    Computed Variables:                            */
/*                                                   */
/*        area   -  Cross sectional area of the      */
/*                  steel column                     */
/*        stress -  Compression Stress               */
/*                                                   */
/*    Output Variables:                              */
/*                                                   */
/*        p   -  Compression Load                    */
```

```
/*        diam   - Diameter of the Steel Column        */
/*        stress - Compression Stress                  */
/*                                                     */
/******************************************************/

#include <stdio.h>

int main( )
{
   const float  PI = 3.141593;
   float  area, stress;
   int diam, p;

   printf("Input the Compression Load");
   printf(" and Diameter of the Column:\n");

   scanf("%d    %d", &p, &diam);

   if( p > 0 && diam > 0)
   {
      printf("\n\nCompression Load: %d pounds\n", p);
      printf("Diameter of  the Steel Column: %2d inches\n",
             diam);

      area = PI * ( (diam * diam) / 4.0);
      stress = p / area;
      printf("Compression Stress: %7.2f pounds per square inch\n",
             stress);
   }

   return 0;
}
```

Interactive Input and Output

```
Input the Compression Load and Diameter of the Column:
200000  12

Compression Load:  200000 pounds
Diameter of the Steel Column: 12 inches
Compression Stress: 1768.39 pounds per square inch
```

Notice that, for clarity, there are two output statements for the input prompt. A program is easier to read and debug if the statements are short and are listed one per line.

2.5.4 Set of Simultaneous Equations

Problem Solve a set of simultaneous equations:

$$ax + by = c$$

$$dx + ey = f$$

where a, b, c, d, e, and f are the input values.

Data Six real numbers.

Method The formulas for the solution are:

$$x = \frac{ce - bf}{ae - bd}$$

$$y = \frac{af - cd}{ae - bd}.$$

Output all the input values a, b, c, d, e, and f and the computed values for x and y.

Pseudocode

```
Input the values for a, b, c, d, e, f
Output the values of a, b, c, d, e, f
Calculate the denominator
denom = (ae – bd)
if denom ≠ 0        This test is necessary to prevent an arithmetic error
   Calculate the value of x and y
   x = (ce – bf) / denom
   y = (af – cd) / denom
   Output the values of x and y
end if
end
```

Program

```
/*****************************************************/
/*                                                   */
/*    Solution to a Set of Simultaneous Equations    */
/*                                                   */
/*****************************************************/
/*                                                   */
/*   Input Values:                                   */
/*                                                   */
/*       a, b, c, d, e, and f  -  the coefficients   */
/*                                                   */
/*   Computed Variables:                             */
/*                                                   */
/*       x and y -  the solution                     */
/*                                                   */
/*   Output Variables:                               */
/*                                                   */
/*       x and y -  the solution                     */
/*                                                   */
/*****************************************************/

#include <stdio.h>

int main( )
{
    float a, b, c, d, e, f;
    float  denom, x, y;

    printf("Input the Values for the constants: \n");
    scanf("%f  %f  %f  %f  %f  %f",&a, &b, &c, &d, &e, &f);

    printf("\nGiven: ");
    printf("a = %4.2f b = %4.2f c = %4.2f d = %4.2f e = %4.2f");
    printf(" f = %4.2f\n", a, b, c, d, e, f);

    denom = a * e - b * d;
```

```
    if( denom != 0.0)
    {
        x = (c * e - b * f) / denom;
        y = ( a * f - c * d) / denom;
        printf(" x = %4.2f     y = %5.2f\n", x, y);
    }

    return 0;
}
```

Input and Output

```
Input the Values for the Constants:
2.5  1.6  3.2  5.4  6.2  4.6

Given: a = 2.50  b = 1.60  c = 3.20  d = 5.40  e = 6.20  f = 4.60
x = 1.82    y = -0.84
```

2.5.5 Area of a Scalene Triangle

Problem Compute the area of a scalene triangle given the sides of the triangle.

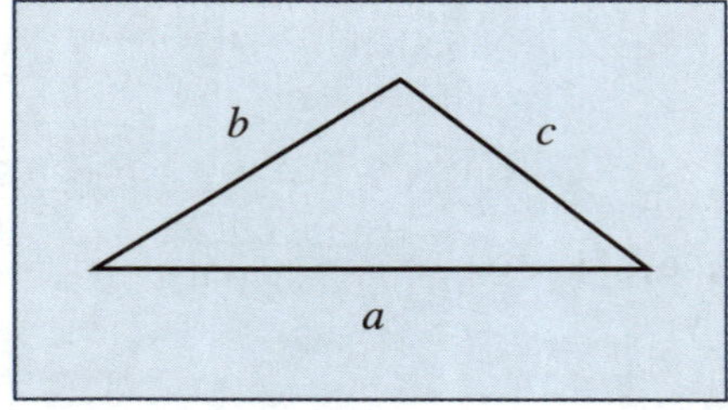

Data Three positive integers.

Method Given the sides a, b, and c of the scalene triangle, the area is computed from the following equations.

$$\text{area} = (s\,(s - a)\,(s - b)\,(s - c))^{1/2}$$

where $s = (a + b + c) / 2$.

Pseudocode

```
Input the values for the sides a, b, and c of the triangle
Output the sides of the triangle a, b, and c
If( a > 0 and b > 0 and c > 0)
   Compute the value of s from the formula
      s ← (a + b + c)/2
   If(s > a and s > b and s > c)
      Compute the area from the formula
         area ← (s (s – a) (s – b) ( s- c))^1/2
        Output the area of the triangle
   End if
End if
End
```

Note: The tests are necessary to determine whether the three input values can be the sides of a triangle.

Program

```
/*******************************************************/
/*                                                     */
/*          Area of a Scalene Triangle                 */
/*                                                     */
/*******************************************************/
/*                                                     */
/*    Input Variables:                                 */
/*                                                     */
/*        a, b, and c – sides of a scalene triangle    */
/*                                                     */
/*    Computed Variables:                              */
/*                                                     */
/*        s      –   half the sum of the sides         */
/*        area   –   area of the scalene triangle      */
/*                                                     */
/*    Output Variables:                                */
/*                                                     */
```

```
/*    area   -   area of the triangle                    */
/*                                                       */
/*********************************************************/

#include <stdio.h>
#include <math.h>
int main( )
{
    int  a, b, c;
    float s, area;

    printf("Input integer values for the Sides:\n");
    scanf("%d     %d    %d", &a, &b, &c);
    printf("\nThe Sides of the Triangle: %d  %d  %d\n",
           a, b, c);

    if(a > 0 && b > 0 && c > 0)
    {
        s = (a + b + c) / 2.0;
        if( s > a && s > b && s > c)
        {
            area = sqrt(s * (s - a) * (s - b) * (s - c));
            printf("The Area of the Triangle: %5.2f\n",
                   area);
        }
    }

    return 0;
}
```

Input and Output

```
Input integer values for the Sides:
12  14  16

The Sides of the Triangle: 12  14  16
The Area of the Triangle: 81.33
```

2.5.6 Volume of a Sphere

Problem Compute the volume of a sphere of radius *r*.

Data Radius *r.*

Method Given the radius *r*, the volume of the sphere is computed from the formula

$$\text{volume} = 4/3\pi r^3.$$

Pseudocode

```
Input the value of r
If r > 0
Compute the volume

volume = 4/3π r³

Output the volume
Stop
```

Note: The test is necessary to make sure that the radius *r* is positive.

Program

```
/*****************************************************/
/*                                                   */
/*         Volume of a Sphere                        */
/*                                                   */
/*****************************************************/
/*                                                   */
/*   Defined Constants:                              */
/*                                                   */
/*       PI    - 3.141593                            */
/*                                                   */
/*   Input Variables:                                */
/*                                                   */
/*       radius - radius of a sphere                 */
```

```
/*                                                       */
/*    Computed Variables:                                */
/*                                                       */
/*        volume - volume of the sphere                  */
/*                                                       */
/*    Output Variables:                                  */
/*                                                       */
/*        radius - radius of the sphere                  */
/*        volume - volume of the sphere                  */
/*                                                       */
/*********************************************************/

#include <stdio.h>
int main( )
{
    const float PI = 3.141593;
    float radius, volume;

    printf("Input a real value for the radius:\n");
    scanf("%f", &radius);
    printf("\nThe radius of sphere is: %6.2f inches\n", radius);
    if(radius > 0)
    {
        volume = 4.0/3.0 * PI * radius * radius * radius;
    }
    printf("The volume of sphere is: %6.2f cubic inches\n", volume);

    return 0;
}
```

Input and Output

```
Input a real value for the radius:
4.0

The radius of the sphere is:   4.00 inches
The volume of the sphere is: 268.08 cubic inches
```

Chapter Summary

C is a structured, procedural, and strongly typed programming language. C has the capability to manipulate integer and floating-point numeric data. Scientific and engineering computations use integers and floating-point numbers in both single-precision and double-precision. These are available in C. C also has the capability of deriving new data types. In a C program every variable must be declared.

Declaration of integer variables:

```
int var1, var2,. . .,varn;
```

In large computer systems the default storage allocated for an integer variable is four bytes. In such systems to allocate two bytes of storage the definition is as follows:

```
short int var1, var2,. . .,varn;
or   short  var1, var2,. . . varn;
```

In personal computer systems the default storage allocated for an integer variable is two bytes. In such systems, to allocate four bytes of storage, the declaration is as follows:

```
long int var1, var2,..,varn;
or long  var1, var2,. . .,varn;
```

Declaration of floating-point variables is:

```
float  var1, var2,... ,varn;
```

The storage allocated for floating-point variables and constants is four bytes.

Declaration of double-precision variables is:

```
double  var1, var2,...,varn;
```

The storage allocated for double-precision variables and constants is eight bytes.

Declaration of character variables is:

```
char var1, var2,. . .,varn;
```

Note that the actual memory needed for the various data types may very well be system dependent. Also, allocating storage does not erase whatever was previously stored in that location. For results to be meaningful, constants and variables must be defined as well as declared. This may be done through input, within the declaration, or by an assignment statement.

The basic executable statement is an assignment statement. The assignment statement is interpreted in three steps: calculating the value of the expression on the right, converting it to the proper type, and storing it in the variable on the left, directly or indirectly.

Variables must be given names; constants may be given names. The names in a programming language are called identifiers. An identifier starts with a letter of the alphabet, may contain letters, digits, and the underscore character. Meaningful names should be used to represent variables in the program. Arithmetic operators and operations are used to perform the numerical computations in science and engineering problems.

C has a rich collection of library functions, consisting of input/output functions, mathematical functions, string manipulation functions, memory allocation functions, standard library functions, and other miscellaneous functions. These functions have prototypes organized and stored in header files. The programmer must include the appropriate header file to use these functions. For example to use input and output functions write the following statement:

```
#include <stdio.h>
```

Every C program must have a function called `main()`. Every function including the `main` function is block structured. This means the instructions following the function header must be enclosed in braces, starting with a left brace and ending with a right brace. The body of the function is a sequence of declarations, control structures, and executable statements ending with a return. Comments should be used to make the code more readable.

Exercises

1. Write a program to convert Fahrenheit temperature to Celsius temperature for one input value. Output both the Fahrenheit and the Celsius values. The conversion formula is:

$$c = \frac{5(f - 32)}{9}$$

2. Write a program to compute the internal volume of a rectangular water tank of internal length l, width w, and height h.

3. Write a program to evaluate the polynomial

$$f(x) = x^3 + 5x^2 + 10x + 15$$

4. Write a program to compute the distance between the points $p_1(x_1, y_1)$ and $p_2(x_2, y_2)$ given the coordinates (x_1, y_1) and (x_2, y_2).

$$\text{Distance} = \sqrt{(x_2 - x_1)^2 + (y_2 - y_1)^2}$$

5. Write a program to calculate the volume flow rate in cubic feet per second of water flowing through a pipe of diameter d in inches and a velocity of v feet per second. The formula for the flow rate is given by:

$$q = \text{area} * \text{velocity}$$

where area $= \pi d^2/4$ in square feet.

6. Write a program to calculate the x and y coordinates of a point at a distance r from the origin at an angle θ to the x-axis as shown in the following figure.

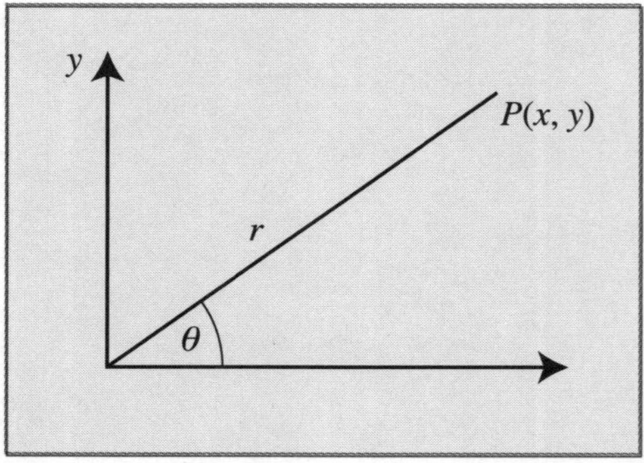

The trignometric functions are as follows:

$$x = r \cos \theta$$

$$y = r \sin \theta.$$

7. Write a program that calculates the two solutions of the equation $ax^2 + bx + c = 0$, given a, b, and c. The solutions are given by

$$x_1 = \frac{-b \pm \sqrt{b^2 - 4ac}}{2a}.$$

CHAPTER 3

Input and Output

Objectives

To learn the use of the instructions that move data in and out of the computer memory. To learn the design of readable data.

Input means providing the information or data the program needs for computation, and output means displaying, printing, or writing to a data file the computed results or the data the program produces. C provides various functions to input the data to the program and various functions to output the data from a program. The following sections present these functions.

3.1 Input and Output Functions

In C, data input and data output are accomplished by using built-in library functions. The input/output functions in C fall into two groups. The first group of functions uses a format string and accepts a variable number of arguments. The input and output are controlled by the format. We have already seen such functions as `scanf( )` and `printf( )`. If a file is being used, the functions are `fscanf( )` and `fprintf( )`. The number of arguments is controlled by the number of input and output variable formats. The second group of functions uses preformatted data with a fixed number of items in a predetermined order; these include `getchar( )`, `putchar( )`, `getc( )`, `fgetc( )`, `putc( )`, `fputc( )`, `gets( )`, `fgets( )`, `puts( )`, `fputs( )`, etc. In these functions the number of arguments and the order of the arguments can not be changed. This group of functions will be discussed in Chapter 9.

There are many header files in the C language and they are listed in Appendix D. The header file `stdio.h` contains prototypes of all the functions needed to perform the input and output operations in a C program. To access the input and output functions within the program, the header file must be included in the program by using the `#include <stdio.h>` directive at the beginning of the program. Before execution, all of the input and output library functions will be linked to the code.

Formatted input and output function calls consist of a function name, followed by a list of items separated by commas, enclosed in parentheses, and terminated with a semicolon. The following statement shows the general form of an input or output function call:

```
function-name(item1, item2, item3,......, itemn);
```

The input and output can be standard input and output or file input and output. The standard input is keyboard input; standard output is either a monitor display or printed output. File input is from a data file previously stored on a diskette, disk drive, or on a magnetic tape. File output is output to be written to a data file created on a diskette, disk drive, or magnetic tape. The concepts of standard input and output, and file input and output, will be discussed in detail in the following sections.

3.1.1 Formatted Input and Output Functions

The input and output functions presented in this chapter, allow the programmer to control the spacing of data. Each of these functions has the general form

```
function-name("format control string", var 1, var 2, ...,  var n);
```

The format control string is a character string consisting of text with embedded format control fields. Each format control field specifies a data type of a variable specified in the input/output argument list. It may also specify the number of positions occupied by the data values that is the field width. There is one format control field for each of the remaining arguments of the function call. Number, order, and type in the control fields and variables specified as arguments must match.

The simplest input/output does not specify field width, but allows the computer to use a default field width. This is practical when the programmer does not know what size to expect. On output, the computer uses a default field width and left justifies numbers if the field width is not specified. If it is specified, the computer right justifies output values within the fields. By omitting the field width, the programmer can align output on the left. By specifying a field width the programmer can align output on the right or align decimal points. When computer values are only accurate to a certain number of decimal places, or as in the case of money, are meaningless beyond a certain number of decimal places, field width should be specified so that the number of fractional digits printed can be controlled.

In the following sections, standard input and output are presented followed by file input and output. When data is input from a file, or output to a file, there are additional functions that must be called. These will be discussed in Section 3.2.

3.1.2 Standard Input Function

The standard library function used to input data from a keyboard is `scanf( )`, which takes a list of items called arguments separated by commas. The first item of the function is a format control string which, like all other character strings, is enclosed in double quotation marks. The rest of the arguments are the addresses of the input variables. This function can be called to input numeric, character, or character string data. The general form of the input function call is as follows:

```
scanf("format string", &var1, &var2,....., &varn);
```

Remember that the address of `var1` is `&var1`, the address of `var2` is `&var2`, and so forth. In this context the "&" symbol is an *address operator*, which transmits the address of the variable to the input function so that the computer knows where to store the input value.

> *Programming Rule:* The addresses of the input variables must be specified in the `scanf( )` function.

When the `scanf( )` function is executed, input is expected from the keyboard. Program execution will wait for the input of values. The programmer is expected to enter one value for each of the variables specified in the call to the `scanf( )` function.

Input of Integer Numbers Integer numbers are whole numbers without any decimal point or fractional digits. They must not contain commas but they may be either signed or unsigned. The following example shows the input of integer numbers to three variables:

```
int var1, var2, var3;                             /* declaration */

scanf("%d  %d  %d", &var1, &var2, &var3);         /*input function call */
```

This statement contains the format control string "%d %d %d", which contains three control fields spaced with one space. Each "%d" is a control field for a single integer number. Each of the three control fields corresponds to an address of a variable in the list. When the `scanf( )` function is called, the computer waits for the user to enter three integer data values separated by one or more blank spaces. The data can be entered in any one of the following ways:

```
+58  87  -12      or      +58      or      +58  87      or      +58
                          87               -12                  87 -12
                          -12
```

The numbers are stored in the variables as follows:

var1	var2	var3
58	87	-12

Notice that there is flexibility in entering the data.

Input of Real Numbers with Data Type `float` or `double` Real numbers are numbers with decimal points whether or not there are fractional digits. In C real numbers may contain at most 15 digits. Numbers with seven or fewer digits may be input as values of `float` variables. Numbers with more than seven digits should be input as values of `double` variables. The following example shows the input of floating-point data.

```
float var1, var2, var3;        /* declaration */
```

or

```
double var1, var2,var3;

scanf("%f  %f  %f", &var1, &var2, &var3);   /* input function call */
```

This statement contains the format control string "%f %f %f", which contains three control fields spaced for readability. Each %f is a control field for a single real number. Each of the three control fields corresponds to an address variable in the argument list. When the scanf( ) function is called, the computer waits for the user to enter three decimal data values separated by one or more blank spaces.

When numbers are represented in scientific notation, the input format control field %e may be used. The following code shows the input of real numbers using the %e format specification.

```
float  var1, var2, var3;

scanf("%e  %e  %e", &var1, &var2, &var3);
```

The input data is entered as follows:

```
1.24765E02    -0.0004532E06      653482.789E-04
```

These numbers are interpreted as follows:

```
124.765      -453.2      65.3482789
```

These numbers are stored in the storage allocated to var1, var2, and var3 as follows:

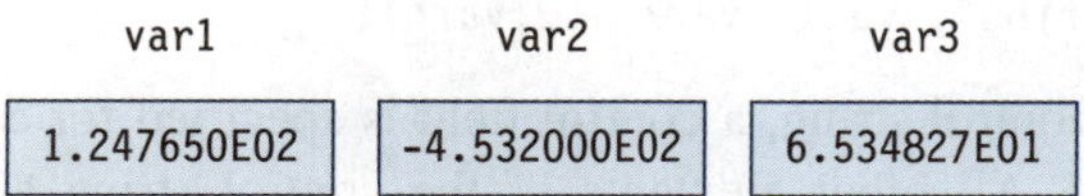

Notice that the decimal point is shifted to the right if the exponent is positive and to the left if the exponent is negative. The exponent is the number following the letter "E" when representing the numbers in scientific notation.

Values of more than one data type may be input with a single statement.

```
int  var1;
float  var2, var3;
double  var4;

scanf("%d    %f    %f    %e", &var1, &var2, &var3, &var4);
```

The data can be entered as follows:

```
18 -43.00 26.765 1.2345678E-03 or

18                  or     18                   or     18 -43.00
-43.00                     -43.00 26.765               26.765 1.2345678E-03
26.765                     1.2345678E-03
1.2345678E-03
```

The numbers are stored in the variables as follows:

var1	var2	var3	var4
18	-43.00000	26.76500	1.2345678E-03

Notice that there is flexibility in entering the data.

3.1.3 Standard Output Function

The `printf( )` function is used to output data to a monitor or to a printer. The first argument of the `printf( )` function must be a format control string. Following the format control string the other arguments are the variables to be printed, separated by commas. The `printf( )` function is used to output numeric, character, or character string data. The general `printf( )` function call is as follows:

```
printf("format string", var1, var2,...,varn);
```

Within the format control string, a control field is specified for each of the variables to be printed. All other elements of the control string are displayed or printed with the data.

Note that the values of the variables are passed to the output function, not their addresses.

Output of Integer Numbers Integer numbers are output as whole numbers with no decimal point or decimal digits. The following example shows the output of three integer numbers.

```
int var1, var2, var3;
```

Assume the following numbers are in the storage for the variables `var1`, `var2`, and `var3`.

var1	var2	var3
587	9756	-65

```
printf("%d%d%d", var1, var2, var3);
```

The output of this function call appears as follows:

```
5879756-65
```

Notice that there are no spaces between the numbers 587, 9756, and −65 in the output, because there are no spaces provided between the control fields within the format control string. It is hard to read this output, without having any knowledge of what is contained in the storage.

> *Programming Hint:* Numbers must be separated for readability and clarity.

The following print statement specifies output with spaces between the numbers.

```
printf("%d    %d    %d", var1, var2, var3);
```

The output of this function call appears as follows:

```
587    9756    -65
```

Notice that there are four spaces between each of the numbers 587, 9756, and −65 in the output, because there are four spaces between each of the string control fields specified within the format control string.

The following example shows the use of text in an output function call to label the output values.

```
printf("var1: %d    var2: %d    var3: %d", var1, var2, var3);
```

The output of this statement appears as follows:

```
var1: 587    var2: 9756    var3: -65
```

Notice that the format control string is printed with each control field replaced by a number. This is a very easy way to label output.

Numbers can be printed on separate lines as follows:

```
printf("var1:  %d\nvar2: %d\nvar3: %d\n", var1, var2, var3);
```

The output of this statement appears as follows:

```
var1: 587
var2: 756
var3: -65
```

The new line character \n shifts the output of each number with the associated text string to the next line. The numbers are printed left justified.

Output of Real Numbers Real numbers are output with a decimal point, whether or not there are fractional digits. In C real numbers are stored as the values of either `float` or `double` variables. The following example shows the output of real variables.

```
float var1, var2, var3;
```

Assume the following decimal numbers are in the storage:

var1	var2	var3
-234.5600	78.16300	9567.050

```
printf("%f%f%f", var1, var2, var3);
```

The output of this statement appears as follows:

```
-234.56000078.1630009567.050000
```

Notice that there are no spaces between the numbers −234.560000, 78.163000, and 9567.050000 in the output, because there are no spaces between the control string fields. The number of fractional digits printed by default is six. If a number has more than six fractional digits, the sixth digit will be rounded automatically for output. Note that this output can be misleading as the value may not contain six significant fractional digits.

```
printf("%f  %f  %f", var1, var2, var3);
```

The output of this statement appears as follows:

```
-234.560000  78.163000  9567.050000
```

Notice that there are two spaces between each of the numbers 234.560000, 78.163000, and 567.050000 in the output, because there are two spaces between each of the control fields.

Numbers can be printed on separate lines as follows:

```
printf("%f\n%f\n%f\n", var1, var2, var3);
```

The output of this function call appears as follows:

```
-234.560000
78.163000
9567.050000
```

Notice that the new line character \n shifts the output of each number to the next line. The numbers are printed left justified. The following program shows the input of integer numbers that are then output with different format control specifications:

```
#include <stdio.h>
int main( )
{
    int  a, b, c,  d;

    printf("Enter four integer numbers:\n");
    scanf("%d %d %d %d", &a, &b, &c, &d);
    printf("Output without spaces:\n");
    printf("%d%d%d%d\n\n", a, b, c, d);
    printf("Output with four spaces:\n");
    printf("%d    %d    %d    %d\n\n", a, b, c, d);

    return 0;

}
```

The input and output of this program is as follows:

```
Enter four integer numbers:
 9563 786  123987  34586

Output without spaces:
 956378612398734586
```

```
Output with four spaces:
9563    786    123987    34586
```

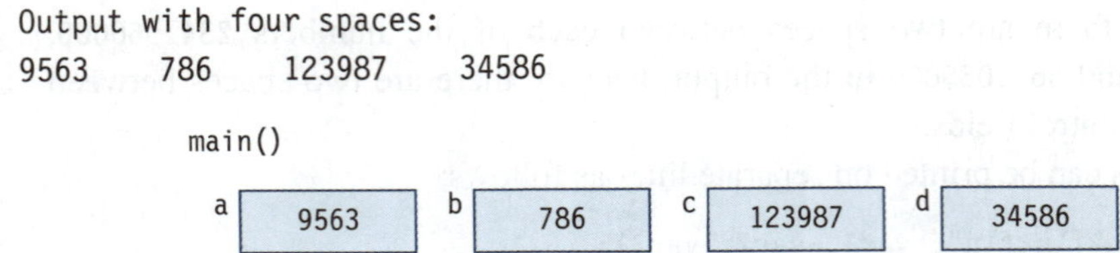

3.1.4 Review Questions

1. Indicate whether the following statements are true or false.
   a. Formatted input and output requires a format control string.
   b. The format control field specification to input and output `double` numbers is `%d`.
   c. The format control field specification to input and output whole numbers is `%f`.
   d. When printing real numbers, if the number of fractional digits is not specified, the number of fractional digits printed defaults to six.
   e. Any text within the format control field will be printed in the output, with the output value.
2. Write the input statements to input values
   a. of appropriate types for the following variables: `ID_num`, `count`, `cost`, `weight`, and `average`.
   b. of daily temperatures, for a week's readings.
   c. from the data stream 123.4567.8901 when each real value has one digit to the right of the decimal point.
3. Write an output statement to output values for the following:
   a. The radius and diameter of a circle with appropriate labels.
   b. Five purchases, in a column, with a line drawn underneath, then the total.
   c. The real values of *x*, *y*, and *z* with one blank space between them.
4. What output format control field always works for each of the following:
   a. a cost less than $1,000,000
   b. a real number between −1 and 1

c. any value of type `long int`

d. any value of type `short int`

e. any integer between −9999999 and 9999999

3.2 File Input and Output

Instead of using a keyboard to input data to a program and a monitor to display the results generated by the program, data can be read from a data file, and results generated by the program can be written to a data file. Data files used for input and output are stored on a disk, which is an external mass storage device. The disadvantage of using keyboard input is that every time the program is executed the data must be reentered. If for some reason the program terminates during execution, then the input data needs to be entered from the beginning. This is good for testing a program but is inefficient if data is to be used more than once. It is also time-consuming to enter large volumes of data from the keyboard. Once data files have been created, every time the program is executed there is no need to reenter the data, as input data is read directly from one data file and output data is written to another data file. Both files can be reused. Most application programs use data files for input and output.

The following sections show how data files are created and used for input and output. There are three important modes in which the data files can be used. These are read `(r)`, write `(w)`, and append `(a)`. There are other modes not commonly used, which can be found in a C manual. The read, write, and append modes will be explained in Section 3.2.2.

3.2.1 Declaration of File Pointers

A data file has both an external and an internal name. The external name is unique to the file and identifies it to the operating system. The internal name is unique within a program. It is the job of the operating system to associate an external name with an internal name, making an actual file available to a program.

An internal name for a file takes the form of a file pointer. It is a variable that is declared to be a pointer to a file. The file pointer is declared as follows:

```
FILE   *fptr;
```

`FILE` is a keyword for the file pointer type, and it must be in capital letters. `fptr` is a file pointer that is a programmer-given pointer variable name. The asterisk (*)

indicates that `fptr` is a pointer variable. This declaration declares `fptr` as a file pointer. The program only uses the file pointer `fptr`, and not the external file name. The file pointer declared in the program space is connected to the external data file by using a file `open` statement. The file `open` statement will be discussed in detail in Section 3.2.2.

If several file pointers are needed they can be declared in one statement as follows:

```
FILE  *inptr, *outptr;
```

The two pointer variables `inptr` and `outptr` are declared in the same declaration statement. The file pointer `inptr` would be used to reference the input file and file pointer `outptr`, to reference the output file.

> *Warning:* Do not use an external file name in any place other than the `open` statement. Once the external file is opened all references to the file must be made through the file pointer.

3.2.2 open and close Statements

Data files normally stored on the disk have a file name with the `dat` extension. Files with this extension are external to any program. The internal file pointer declared within the program, and the external files on the disk, are connected logically and physically by using an `open` statement. Once the external file and the internal file pointer are connected, the connection will remain in effect until either the file is closed or the program is terminated. After the file is opened for input or for output, the program can communicate with the file on the disk through the file pointer. Note that if the file is already open and the program attempts to open it again then the file `open` statement, when executed, will return a `null` value. The file can be closed explicitly by using an `fclose` statement. Once the file is closed it is disconnected from the program. If it has been disconnected, it can be reconnected and opened again.

open Statement For a program to communicate with an external file through the internal file pointer, the internal file pointer must be connected to the external file by means of an `fopen` statement. The general form of the `fopen` statement to connect the external data file name, for example "myfile.dat", on the disk to the internal file pointer fptr declared within the program is as follows:

```
FILE   *fptr;

fptr = fopen("myfile.dat", mode);
```

Where fopen is a function call that returns a link to the external file, fptr is the declared file pointer, and mode is simply the way the file is to be used. There are three common modes of operation, they are: read (r), write (w), and append (a). In read mode the file is opened for data input, in write mode the file is opened to receive output, and in append mode the file is opened for adding data to the end of the file. Opening the file for modes r or w positions the file at the beginning. Opening the file for mode a positions the file at the end.

An fopen( ) function call using read mode must reference an existing file. If the file does not exist or the file is already opened the function will return a null pointer rather than a pointer to the file. The program must then check whether the file has been opened successfully.

In the write mode, if the file already exists, its contents will be erased and over-written from the beginning of the file. If the file does not exist it will be created and written from the beginning of the file. If the file is already open, the function will return a null value rather than a pointer to the file and the file will be unavailable.

In append mode, if the file exists the new data will be added to the end of the existing data. If the file does not exist the file will be created and the data will be written starting at the beginning of the file. If the file is already open, the function will return a null pointer rather than a pointer to the file.

The open statements for different modes of input and output operations are as follows:

`fptr = fopen("myfile.dat" , "r");`	Reads if the file exists, error if the file does not exist.
`fptr = fopen("myfile.dat" , "w");`	Writes to the file from beginning if the file exists. Creates a new file and writes to the file from the beginning if the file does not exist.

`fptr = fopen("myfile.dat" , "a");`	Appends to the end of the file if the file exists. Creates and writes to the new file if the file does not exist.
`fptr = fopen("myfile.dat" , "r+");`	Opens file for reading and writing if the file exists, error if the file does not exist.
`fptr = fopen("myfile.dat" , "w+");`	Opens a new file for reading and writing if the file exists. Creates a new file if the file does not exist.
`fptr = fopen("myfile.dat" , "a+");`	Opens the file for reading and writing at the end of the file if the file exists. Creates a new file if the file does not exist.
`fptr = fopen("myfile.dat" , "wb");`	Opens the binary file for writing.
`fptr = fopen("myfile.dat" , "r+b");`	Opens the binary file for reading and writing.

The fopen function requires two arguments: a character string, which is the external name of the data file, and a character string, which indicates the use of the file.

Once the file is opened in any of these modes the program can communicate with the data file on the disk through the pointer fptr. When the file is no longer being used, it should be disconnected by using an fclose statement.

close Statement The fclose statement logically disconnects the file from the program. The general form of the fclose( ) function is as follows:

```
fclose(file pointer);
```

If the file pointer is `fptr`, the `fclose` statement is:

```
fclose(fptr);
```

After this function is executed the data file will be disconnected from the program and becomes available for reuse.

3.2.3 Input from a Data File

The input from a data file is obtained by calling the library function `fscanf( )` in the program. The general form of the function call is:

```
fscanf(file pointer, "format control string", &var1, &var2,....,&varn);
```

The first argument must be the file pointer already connected to a file by an `fopen` statement. The second argument must be the format control string that specifies the input data format with an individual control field corresponding to each of the variables. The remaining arguments are the addresses of variables. If there is not enough data in the file the `fscanf` function returns a special EOF (end-of-file) flag. The following examples show input from a data file.

Input of Numbers The following numbers contained in a data file `myfile1.dat`,

```
231 5647 72.034 -2349.13957E02
```

are to be input into the variables `var1`, `var2`, `var3`, and `var4`.

The following code shows the input.

```
FILE  *inptr;

int var1, var2;
float var3;
double var4;

inptr = fopen("myfile1.dat", "r");

fscanf(inptr, "%d  %d  %f  %e", &var1, &var2, &var3,
      &var4);
```

Before:

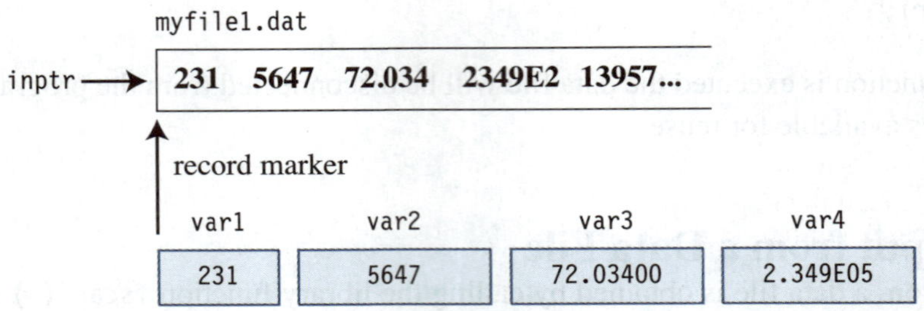

After:

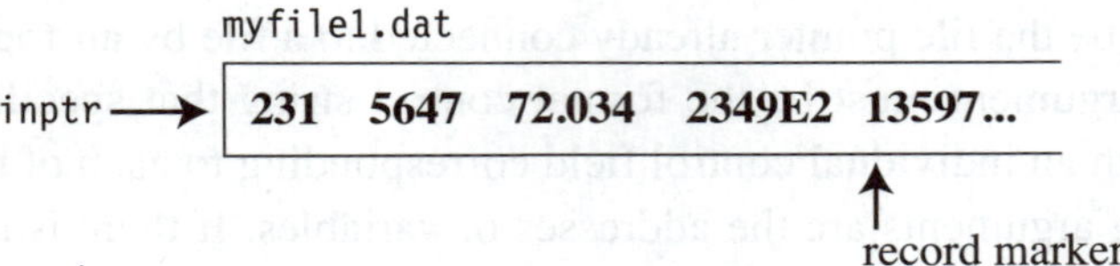

Notice that once the file pointer is connected to the external file through the `open` statement, the program communicates with the external file only through the file pointer. In the input statement the file pointer `inptr` is specified as the first argument. The values are read from the data file "`myfile1.data`," connected through the internal file pointer `inptr`. The data values are stored in the memory allocated for the variables as shown.

Concept of Record and Record Marker The amount of data read by an input statement is called an input record, also the amount of data written by an output statement is called an output record. Every time a record is read by an input statement from a data file or a record is written by an output statement to a data file, the record marker is moved to the beginning of the next record. Initially the record marker is set to the first record in the beginning of the file. After the first record has been read for the first `fscanf` statement, the record marker is moved to the beginning of the next record in the file to be read by another `fscanf` statement. This will continue until all the input is read from the data file or all the output is written to the data file. When all the data is read or written the record marker will be pointing to a special character at the end of the data file called the EOF marker.

Failsafe Input of Numbers The following decimal numbers contained in a data file `myfile2.dat`,

695.23 23.5647 0.2034 2349.7658

are to be input into the variables `var1`, `var2`, `var3`, and `var4`.

The following code shows the input.

```
FILE  *inptr;

float var1, var2, var3, var4;

inptr = fopen("myfile2.dat", "r");

if(inptr)
{
    fscanf(inptr, "%f  %f", &var1, &var2);
    fscanf(inptr, "%f  %f", &var3, &var4);
}
else
{
    printf("file myfile2.dat not available\n");
}
```

Notice that if the file is opened successfully for input, `inptr` is a pointer to the file that is interpreted as "true," otherwise `inptr` is a null pointer that is interpreted as "false." The data is read from the input file and stored in the variables `var1`, `var2`, `var3`, and `var4`. If the file is not successfully opened for input then an error message is displayed on the screen.

3.2.4 Output to a Data File

Output to a data file uses a function call to the `fprintf( )` library function. The general form of the function call is:

```
fprintf(file pointer, "format control string", var1, var2,....,varn);
```

The first argument must be the output file pointer; the next, the format control string; and the remaining arguments, a list of variables. The following examples show output to a data file.

Output of Numbers The format control field for the output of integer numbers is %d. To space the individual data values in the output, blank spaces must be provided within the format control field. The following examples show the output of integer numbers. The numbers in storage are as follows:

var1	var2	var3	var4
65438	87.63900	.2561670	-1032

The statements needed to output these numbers into a data file `myfile3.dat` are as follows:

```
int  var1, var4;
float var2, var3

FILE  *outptr;

outptr = fopen("myfile3.dat", "w");

fprintf(outptr,"%d  %f  %f  %d", var1, var2, var3, var4);
```

The output statement uses the format control field `"%d  %f  %f  %d"`, which specifies the types of numbers to be written to the output file. There are four control fields within the format control string that correspond to four variables specified in the output statement. The output written to the output data file `myfile3.dat` is as follows:

Before:

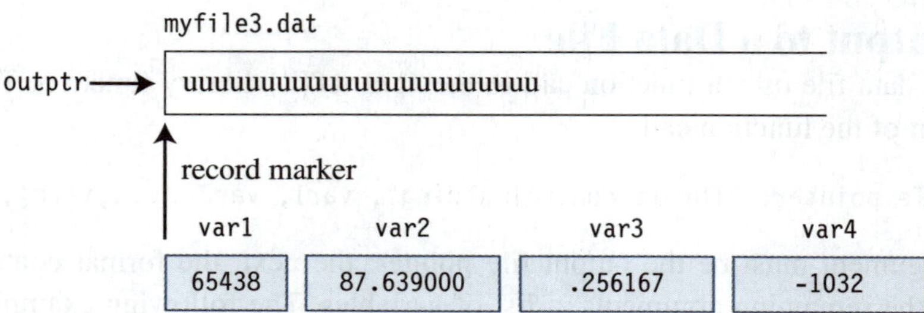

After:

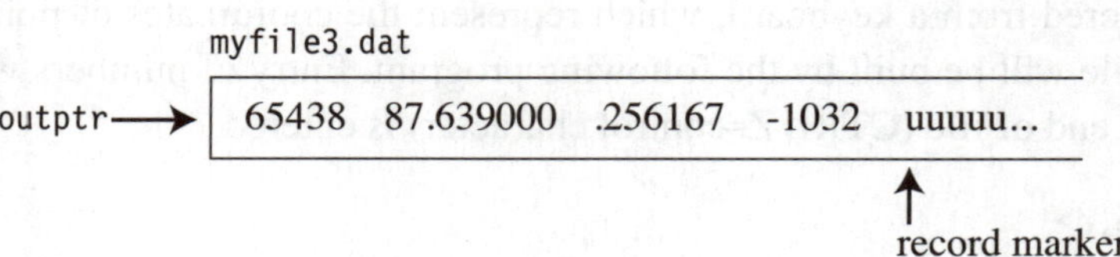

Notice that the numbers written to the output data file have two spaces between them. These spaces correspond to the spaces provided in the format control string. After the numbers have been written, the record marker points to the next available data items, ready for another `fprintf` statement.

Failsafe Output of Numbers The following decimal numbers are to be written to the beginning of a file `myfile5.dat`:

The statements needed are as follows:

```
int  var1, var2, var3, var4;

FILE  *outptr;

outptr = fopen("myfile5.dat", "w");

if(outptr)
{
   fprintf(outptr,"%f   %f   %f   %f", var1, var2, var3, var4);
}
else
{
   printf("file myfile5.dat not available");
}
```

The error message will be displayed on the standard output device if the file is already opened or if it cannot be found.

Building a Data File Assume that a file `graph.dat` is to be created from pairs of real numbers entered from a keyboard, which represent the coordinates of points on a graph; the file will be built by the following program. Entry of numbers will continue until an end of file (CTRL Z–control character) is entered.

```
#include <stdio.h>
int main( )
{
   float  x, y;
   FILE *graphptr;

   graphptr = fopen("graph.dat", "w");

   if(graphptr)
   {
      while(scanf("%f  %f", &x, &y))
      {
         fprintf(graphptr, "%f  %f", x, y);
      }
      fclose((graphptr));
   }
   else
      printf("File <graph.dat> is not available");

   return 0;
}
```

If the data already exists and more data is being added to it, the file would be opened for `a` (append) rather than `w` (write).

Listing a Data File The following program includes the display of a message if the data file cannot be opened successfully. Assuming that a file `myfile.dat` contains many real values representing the coordinates of a point on a graph (pairs of real numbers) separated by spaces, the entire file will be read and printed by the following program:

```
#include <stdio.h>
```

```
int main( )
{
   float  x, y;
   FILE *fptr;

   fptr = fopen("myfile.dat", "r");

   if(fptr)
   {
      printf("      x        y\n");
      while ((fscanf(fptr, "%f  %f", &x, &y)) != EOF)
         printf("%f     %f\n", x, y);
      fclose(fptr);
   }
   else
      printf("File <myfile.dat> not available \n");

   return 0;
}
```

When the data file is successfully opened for input, the data is read until the EOF marker is found. When EOF is found, the condition `!= EOF` will be false and the `while` loop terminates.

Notice that if the data file cannot be opened successfully then the following error message will be displayed on the monitor.

```
File <myfile.dat> not available
```

3.2.5 Review Questions

1. Indicate whether the following statements are true or false.
   a. Data files are stored external to the program.
   b. In C a file pointer must be declared using the keyword `FILE`.
   c. The file pointer declared within the program must be connected to the external data file by using a read or write statement.
   d. There are four basic modes in which a data file can be opened; they are the read (`r`), write (`w`), append (`a`), and substitute (`s`) modes.

e. A data file opened for input must be in `w` mode.

f. When a file is opened in `a` mode the contents of the file are read then rewritten.

g. Every file must be opened before it is used.

h. `fopen` is the keyword used to open a data file.

i. `close` is the keyword used to close the data file.

2. Write the following C statements and show the results, where `inptr` and `outptr` are the input and output file pointers.

   a. An input statement to input the following integer numbers from a data file into the following variables: `value1`, `const1`, `pressure`, `velocity`, and `projection`.

      `manyval.dat`

876	-3489	235692	-432	1290...

   b. An input statement to input the following real numbers from a data file into the following variables: `minval`, `variance1`, `stress`, and `load`.

      `maxval.dat`

123.564	458.3245	657.540	0.5423...

3. Write the following C statements and show the result, where `inptr` and `outptr` are the input and output file pointers.

   a. An output statement to write the following integer numbers into a data file from the following variables: `value1`, `const1`, `pressure`, `velocity`, and `projection`.

value1	const1	pressure	velocity	projection
876	-3489	235692	-432	1290

b. Write an output statement to output the following real numbers into a data file. Use the following variables: `minval`, `variancel`, `stress`, and `load`.

minval	variancel	stress	load
123.564	458.3245	657.540	0.5423000

4. Write all the statements needed to obtain the *x*, *y*, and *z* coordinates of point *p*1 and point *p*2 from a data file.

3.3 Field Width Specification

Within the format control string, the width for each of the control fields can be specified for both the input and output variables. The specification of the number of characters to output the data is very important when uniform output needs to be displayed or written to the data file. The following examples and program segments show the input and output format field width specifications.

3.3.1 Input Field Width Specification

The general form of the field width specification is as follows:

`%nd` for integer numbers, `n` must be a numeric literal specifying the number of positions for digits and signs, e.g., `%7d`, `%10d`.

`%nf` for real numbers, n must be a numeric literal specifying the total number of digits, decimal point position, and sign position, e.g., `%10f`, `%6f`.

The following examples show input with control field width specification.

Input of Integer Numbers The following numbers are to be input into the variables `var1`, `var2`, and `var3`:

7865−5134690487

The code to input these numbers is as follows:

```
int var1, var2, var3;
```

```
scanf("%4d %5d %6d", &var1, &var2, &var3);

printf("%d    %d    %d", var1, var2, var3);
```

The numbers can be entered with one space as follows:

7865 –5134 690487

The spaces in the `scanf` format control specification directs the computer to skip the spaces between the data values, then pick up the number of characters specified by the field width.

Notice that the first four non-blank characters are read as the value of `var1`, the next five are read as the value of `var2`, and the last six are read as the value of `var3`.

The output will appear with four blank spaces between the numbers as follows:

```
7865    -5134    690487
```

The spaces in the `printf` format control field direct the computer to output an equal number of spaces between the data values.

Notice that the first four characters are printed as the value of `var1`, the next five characters are printed as the value of `var2`, and the last six characters are printed as the value of `var3` with four blank spaces between the numbers as specified in the format control field.

Input of Real Numbers The following numbers are to be input into the variables; `var1`, `var2`, `var3`.

78.654–5.1348690.4878

The code to input these numbers is as follows:

```
float var1, var2, var3;

scanf("%6f  %7f  %8f", &var1, &var2, &var3);

printf("%f    %f    %f", var1, var2, var3);
```

The numbers can be entered as follows:

78.654 –5.1348 690.4878

The output will appear as follows:

```
78.654000    -5.134800    690.487800
```

Notice that the first six non-blank characters are read as the value of `var1`, the next seven are read as the value of `var2`, and the last eight are read as the value of `var3`. The decimal point and the negative sign are included as part of the number. Also notice that the output is spaced because control fields are spaced in the output format control string by four spaces. Notice that there are six digits printed in the output to the right of the decimal point, the default number of digits.

3.3.2 Output Field Width Specification

The general form of the field width specification is as follows:

`%nd` For integer numbers, `n` must be a numeric literal specifying the number of digits, plus one for the sign, plus the number of leading blanks desired.

`%n.mf` For real numbers, `n` must be a numeric literal specifying the field width, which includes the total number of digits, plus one for the decimal point, plus one for the sign, plus the number of leading blanks desired, and `m` must be a numeric literal specifying the number of digits to be printed to the right of the decimal point.

The following examples show output with control field width specification.

Output of Integer Numbers The variables: `var1`, `var2`, `var3` have values 7865, −5134, and 690487 respectively.

var1	var2	var3
7865	-5134	690487

The code to output these numbers from storage in three different ways is as follows:

```
int var1, var2, var3;

printf("%d\n%d\n%d\n\n", var1, var2, var3);

printf("%6d\n%6d\n%6d\n\n", var1, var2, var3);

printf("%8d\n%8d\n%8d\n\n", var1, var2, var3);
```

The output corresponding to the three `printf` statements appears as follows:

```
7865
-5134
690487

  7865
 -5134
690487

    7865
   -5134
  690487
```

Notice that when field widths are not specified the output is left justified. The output is right justified when the field width is specified. Extra positions to the left are filled with blanks. When the specified field width is too small for all the digits, the `printf` function provides the extra spaces required to print the number.

Output of Real Numbers The variables: `var1`, `var2`, and `var3` have values 78.653, −513.4236, and 69048.72 respectively.

var1	var2	var3
78.653	-513.4236	69048.72

The code to output these numbers from storage in three different ways is as follows:

```
float var1, var2, var3;

printf("%f\n%f\n%f\n\n", var1, var2, var3);

printf("%9.3f\n%9.3f\n%9.3f\n\n", var1, var2, var3);

printf("%10.3f\n%10.3f\n%10.3f\n\n", var1, var2, var3);
```

The output will appear as follows:

```
78.653000
-513.423600
69048.720000

   78.653
 -513.424       the number -513.4236 is rounded
69048.720

    78.653
  -513.424      the number -513.4236 is rounded
 69048.720
```

Notice that, in the first case, when the field widths are not specified, the output is left justified. In the second case, the output is right justified with a field width based on the number with the largest number of whole and fractional digits. In the third case, the output is right justified in a larger field.

3.3.3 Review Questions

1. Indicate whether the following statements are true or false.
   a. Field widths can be specified in an input control string.
   b. Field widths must be specified in an output control string.
   c. The field width specification for input of a real number indicates where the decimal point is in the data.

d. The field width specification for the input of a real number is the total number of digits plus any decimal point or sign.
e. If the field width is not specified for the output of integer numbers they are printed right justified.
f. If the field width is not specified for the output of real numbers they are printed with decimal points aligned.
g. When the field width is specified for integer numbers they are printed right justified within the specified field width.
h. When the field width is specified for real numbers space must be provided for six fractional digits.
i. If the number of fractional digits is not specified in the field width, the default number of fractional digits printed is six.
j. If the field width is not specified when printing integer or fractional numbers, the numbers are printed left justified.
k. If the field width is specified when printing integer or real numbers, the numbers are printed with the decimal points aligned.
l. When a field width is specified, if the number to be printed has more whole digits than the number of spaces provided in the field width, C will provide the extra spaces needed to print the number.

2. Write the following C statements and show the output of the data.
   a. An input statement to read the following integers:

      `23522   5678   9876543  -2350`

      - with appropriate field width, no spaces between the control fields, and data without spaces
      - with appropriate field width, two spaces between the control fields, and data without spaces
      - with appropriate field width, no spaces between the control fields, and two spaces between the data values
      - with the same field width specification for all data items

   b. An input statement to read the following real numbers:

      `123.456      -432.76      987.098   0.0345`

      - with appropriate field width, no spaces between the control fields, and data without spaces

- with appropriate field width, two spaces between the control fields, and data without spaces
- with appropriate field width, no spaces between the control fields, and two spaces between the data values
- with the same field width specification for all data items

3. Write the following C statements and show the results.

   a. An output statement to write the following integers:

   ```
   23522    5678    9876543   -2350
   ```

   - with field width specification left aligned on separate lines using the new line character `\n`.
   - with field width specifications right aligned on separate lines using the new line character `\n`.
   - with field width specified as 10 on separate lines using the new line character `\n`.

   b. An output statement to write the following real numbers:

   ```
   123.456       -432.76       987.098    0.0345
   ```

   - with minimum field width specifications left aligned on separate lines using the new line character `\n`.
   - with field width specification right aligned on separate lines using the new line character `\n`.
   - with the field width specification decimal point aligned on separate lines

3.4 Input and Output of Characters

Characters in ASCII are represented internally in memory by numbers. The ASCII code for the characters is given in Appendix A.

The declaration of a character variable allocates one byte of memory. One byte of memory can hold decimal numbers in the range 0 to 255. Since ASCII character codes range from 0 to 127, one byte of storage is enough to store any character in the ASCII code. Character variables are declared as follows:

```
char ch1, ch2, ch3;
```

3.4.1 Standard Input and Output

The standard input of characters is from a keyboard, and the standard output is to a monitor or to a printer. The following sections show the standard input and output of character data.

Input of Character Data The input function `scanf` is used to input characters from a keyboard. The input statement to input characters into the character variables `ch1`, `ch2`, and `ch3` is as follows:

```
scanf("%c%c%c",&ch1, &ch2, &ch3);
```

Notice that the format specifier `%c` is used in the format control string, because the variables `ch1`, `ch2`, and `ch3` are declared as `char` variables. The address of the character variables must be specified in the input statement.

When the characters XYZ are entered they are stored in ASCII as decimal codes as follows:

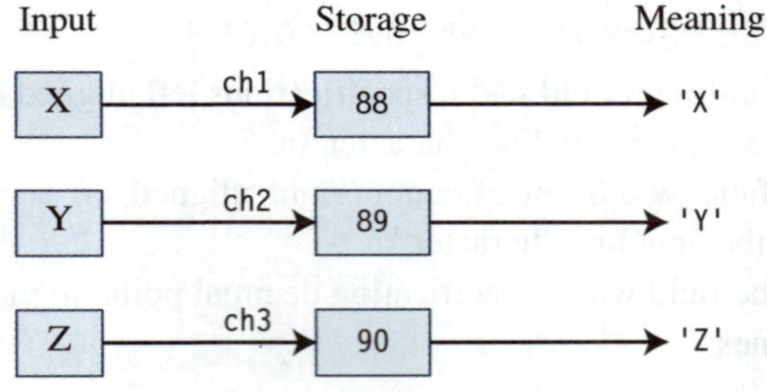

There are no blanks between the characters XYZ as they are typed so no blanks are used between specifications in the format.

Output of Character Data The output function `printf` can be used to output characters to a monitor or to a printer. The output statement to output the characters to the screen from the variables `ch1`, `ch2`, and `ch3` is as follows:

```
printf("%c  %c  %c",ch1, ch2, ch3);
```

Notice that the format specifier `%c` is used in the format control string, because the variables `ch1`, `ch2`, and `ch3` are declared as `char` variables. To display or print characters you must use the `%c` format specifier.

The output appears on the screen as follows:

```
X  Y  Z
```

If the format specifier is %d rather than %c, the output will appear as the ASCII decimal number code as follows:

```
printf("%d  %d  %d", ch1, ch2, ch3);
```

The output is as follows:

```
88  89  90
```

Notice that the format specifier %c understands the decimal number as an ASCII character code, and the format specifier %d simply prints the decimal numbers, which are the internal representations of the characters.

3.4.2 File Input and Output

Character data stored in a file on a disk can be input into the program. Data from a program can be written to a data file on an external storage device. The following examples show the input and output of character data.

Input of Character Data from a Data File The statements needed to input character data from a data file are as follows:

```
FILE   *inptr;

inptr = fopen("myfile7.dat", "r");

char  ch1, ch2, ch3, ch4;

fscanf(inptr,"%c%c%c%c", &ch1, &ch2, &ch3, &ch4);
```

The data read from the data file is as follows:

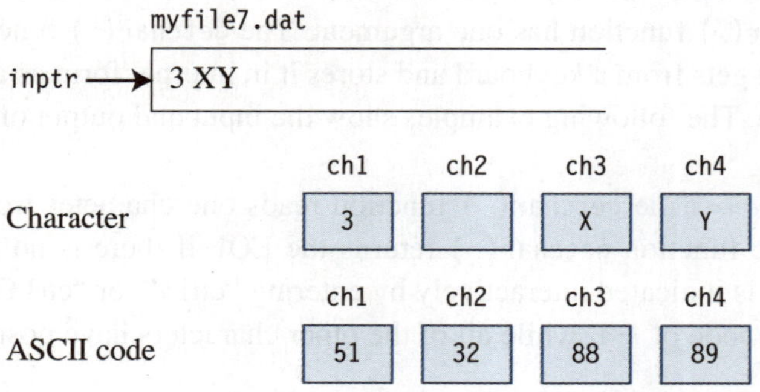

This data is read from the data file `myfile7.dat` and stored in the variables `ch1`, `ch2`, `ch3`, and `ch4` as shown. In the data file there is a blank space between the character `3` and the character `X`. Digits read using `%c` specification are stored as characters. The ASCII code is also stored for a blank space.

Output of Character Data to a Data File The statements needed to output character data to a data file are as follows:

```
char ch1='3', ch2=' ', ch3='X', ch4='Y';

FILE   *outptr;

outptr = fopen("myfile8.dat", "w");

fprintf(outptr,"%c%c%c%c", ch1, ch2, ch3, ch4);
```

The data contained in character variables `ch1`, `ch2`, `ch3`, and `ch4` is written to a data file `myfile8.dat` as follows:

```
                 myfile8.dat
outptr ──────► | 3 XY
```

3.4.3 Unformatted Input and Output

`getchar( )` and `putchar( )` are the unformatted library functions for the input and output of characters from standard input and output devices. The `getchar( )` function gets a single character from the keyboard, and the `putchar( )` function places a single character in an output buffer, which will be displayed when the enter key is pressed on the keyboard. The `getchar( )` function has no arguments, and the `putchar( )` function has one argument. The `getchar( )` function returns the value that it gets from a keyboard and stores it in internal form as an integer in the ASCII code. The following examples show the input and output of characters.

`getchar` *Function* The `getchar( )` function reads one character from the standard input. The function `getchar( )` returns the EOF if there is no character to read. The EOF is indicated interactively by entering “ctrl Z” or “ctrl C”. The EOF has a character code of −1, while all of the other characters have positive character codes. The following example shows the input of a character using the `getchar( )` function.

```
char ch;          97   meaning a
getchar( );       ch
```

Enter the character `a`, it is stored in `ch` as `97`, because the ASCII code for character `a` is 97. The `getchar( )` function converts the character to ASCII and returns the corresponding ASCII code.

`putchar` *Function* The following example shows the output of a character using the `putchar( )` function.

```
char ch;          88   meaning X
putchar(ch);      ch
```

The `char` variable `ch` contains the ASCII code for character `X` as shown. This output statement displays the character `X` on the CRT screen as shown.

The following example shows the input and output of the following string of characters.

Input string: `COMPUTERS ARE ELECTRONIC`

```
char ch;

while(( ch = getchar( )) != '\n')
     putchar(ch);
```

When this code is executed it asks for the input from the keyboard. Then the characters shown above are entered from the keyboard one after the other. After all the characters are entered, the carriage return is entered. The output of the characters entered is displayed on the screen as follows;

Output string: `COMPUTERS ARE ELECTRONIC`

In C, an assignment such as `ch = getchar( )` has a value, the same value that is being assigned.

When the character data is entered the `getchar( )` function inputs the characters one by one into the variable `ch` and then the output function `putchar( )` writes the character contained in the variable `ch` to an output buffer. When the "enter key" is pushed the characters contained in the buffer are displayed as shown. The enter key carriage return indicates an end-of-file.

`Getchar( )` and `putchar( )` are the basic character input/output functions in the C language. Since everything typed on a keyboard or displayed on a monitor or printed on paper is in the form of characters that are readable by people, the computer does all input and output character-by-character. However if these were the only input and output functions available to the programmer, every programmer would have to develop numeric input/output routines in order to be able to process numbers.

If the stream contained the characters −234 preceded by a blank, the programmer would have to determine that the number is negative and then accumulate its value by using the iterative formula as follows:

$$-1(10 * (10 * (0 + 2) + 3) + 4)$$

The algorithm for this is as follows:

```
For each leading blank
   Ignore it
End for

value = 0
if next character is a minus sign
   sign = -1
else
   sign = 1

For each digit
   value = 10 * value + digit
End for

value = value * sign
```

For every programmer to develop a private library of input/output functions, or to rewrite them every time a program is written, is an unnecessary duplication of effort. For this reason the library `<stdio.h>` was developed as part of the C programming environment.

3.4.4 Review Questions

1. Indicate whether the following statements are true or false.
   a. The `getchar( )` function returns a value that must be assigned to a character variable to save for further use.
   b. The `getchar( )` function expects input from a data file.
   c. The `getchar( )` function requires an argument.
   d. The `getchar( )` function does not return a value when "ctrl Z" is pressed.
   e. The `putchar( )` function requires an argument.
   f. The `putchar( )` function displays a character on the screen.
2. Write the following C statements.
   a. Write the code to input characters using the `getchar( )` function and write the characters to a data file `chfileout.dat`.
   b. Write the code to input characters from a data file and display them on a screen using the `putchar( )` function.
3. Write C statements to input `time1` and `time2`, each in the format `hh:mm` and calculate the elapsed time from `time1` to `time2`.
4. Write C statements for the following to input from a file `myfilein.dat` and output to a file `myfileout.dat`.

   `myfilein.dat`

COMPUTER TECHNOLOGY TELECOMMUNICATION LINK

3.5 Sample Programs

The following programs show the use of standard input and output and file input and output. The problems are chosen from engineering and science applications.

3.5.1 Conversion from Polar to Cartesian Coordinates

Problem Given the polar coordinates of a point, generate and print the Cartesian coordinates.

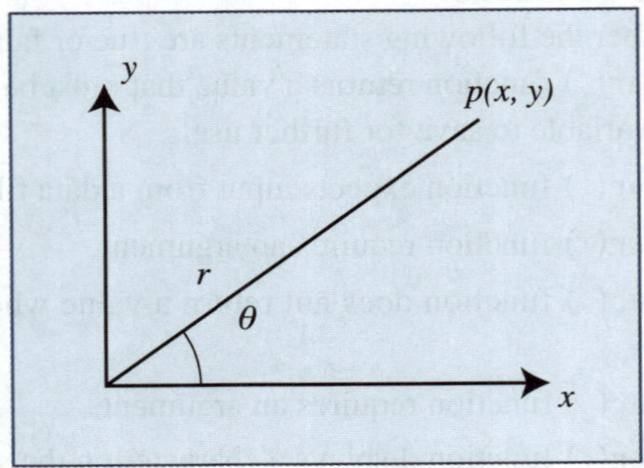

Method An angle a in degrees is converted to radians by the formula

$$\theta = \frac{\pi a}{180}$$

Given the radius r and the angle a in degrees, the Cartesian coordinates are calculated as follows:

$$x = r \cos \theta$$

$$y = r \sin \theta$$

Data The data consists of `float` values for radius r and the angle θ in degrees.

Pseudocode

Input the radius r and the angle θ of a point, $0 \leq \theta \leq 360$
Output the radius and the angle
Calculate the x and y coordinates

x ← r × cos θ
y ← r × sin θ

Output the value of x and y to two decimal places
End

Program

```
/*******************************************************/
/*                                                     */
/*     Calculation of Cartesian Coordinates from       */
/*     Polar Coordinates                               */
/*                                                     */
/*******************************************************/
/*                                                     */
/*    Defined Constants:                               */
/*        PI      - 3.141593                           */
/*                                                     */
/*    Input Variables:                                 */
/*      radius – distance of the point from the origin */
/*      angle  – angle from the positive x axis        */
/*              in degrees                             */
/*                                                     */
/*    Computed Variables:                              */
/*      theta – angle in radians                       */
/*      x     – x coordinate of the point P            */
/*      y     – y coordinate of the point P            */
/*                                                     */
/*    Output Variables:                                */
/*      x     – x coordinate of the point P            */
/*      y     – y coordinate of the point P            */
/*                                                     */
/*******************************************************/
#include <stdio.h>
# include <math.h>
```

```
int main( )
{
    const float PI = 3.141593;
    float  radius, theta, x, y, angle;

    printf("Enter the radius in inches and the angle in degrees:\n");
    scanf("%f %f",&radius,&angle);
    printf("\nRadius = %5.2f  Angle = %5.2f\n", radius,
          angle);

    theta = PI * angle / 180.0;
    x = radius * cos(theta);
    y = radius * sin(theta);

    printf("x = %5.2f  y = %5.2f\n", x, y);

    return 0;
}
```

Input and Output

```
Enter the radius in inches and the angle in degrees:
4.0 45.0

Radius =  4.00  Angle = 45.00
X =  2.83  y =  2.83
```

3.5.2 Cost of a Steel Cage

Problem Write a program to compute the amount of steel in pounds and the total cost of the steel to build a submersible steel cage. Input the number of identical steel rods, the diameter in inches, the length in feet, the density of the steel, and the cost per pound. Output the number of rods, their diameter, length, and cost per pound. Then output the pounds of steel required and the total cost of the steel.

Method Given the number of rods, n; length, l (ft.); the diameter, d (in.); the cost/pound; and the density; calculate the following:

$$d = \frac{d}{12} \text{ (converts } d \text{ from inches to feet)}$$

$$\text{area} = \frac{\pi d^2}{4} \text{ (in square feet)}$$

$$\text{volume} = \text{number of rods} \times \text{length} \times \text{area} \quad \text{(in cubic feet)}$$

$$\text{weight} = \text{volume} \times \text{density} \quad \text{(in pounds)}$$

$$\text{total cost} = \text{weight} \times \text{cost per pound}$$

Data Data consists of one integer number and three real numbers accurate to two decimal places.

Pseudocode

Input the number of rods, diameter, length, density, cost per pound of steel

Output the number of rods, diameter, length, density, and cost per pound of steel

Convert the diameter from inches to feet

$$d \leftarrow \frac{d}{12}$$

Calculate the cross sectional area

$$\text{area} \leftarrow \frac{\pi d^2}{4}$$

Calculate the volume

$$\text{volume} \leftarrow n \times l \times \text{area}$$

Calculate the weight

$$\text{weight} = \text{volume} \times \text{density}$$

Calculate the total_cost

Total_cost = weight × cost

End

Program

```
/**************************************************/
/*                                                */
/*    Computation of Amount of Steel and the Cost to */
/*    Build a Submersible Cage                    */
/*                                                */
/**************************************************/
/*                                                */
/*    Defined Constants:                          */
/*         DENSITY  - 441.48 pounds/ cubic feet   */
/*         PI       - 3.141593                    */
/*                                                */
/*    Input Variables:                            */
/*        numrod      - Number of steel rods      */
/*        diameter    - Diameter of the steel rods */
/*        length      - Length of the steel rods  */
/*        cost        - Cost per pound of steel   */
/*                                                */
/*    Computed Variables:                         */
/*        area        - Cross sectional area of rods */
/*        volume      - Total volume of steel     */
/*        weight      - Total weight of steel     */
/*        total_cost - Total cost of steel        */
/*                                                */
/*    Output Variables:                           */
/*        weight      - Total weight of steel     */
/*        total_cost - Total cost of steel        */
/*                                                */
/**************************************************/

#include <stdio.h>
```

```
int main( )
{
    const float PI = 3.141593;
    const float DENSITY = 441.48;

    int numrod;
    float diameter,length, cost, area, weight, volume,
          total_cost;

    printf("Input number of rods, diameter, length, and cost:\n");
    scanf("%d  %f  %f   %f", &numrod, &diameter, &length,
          &cost);

    printf("\nNumber of rods =%5d\n", numrod);
    printf("Diameter of rods =%6.2f\n", diameter);
    printf("Length of rods =%6.2f\n", length);
    printf("Cost per pound of steel =%6.2f\n\n", cost);

    diameter = diameter / 12.0;
    area = PI * diameter * diameter / 4.0;
    volume = numrod * area * length;
    weight = volume * DENSITY;
    total_cost = weight * cost;

    printf("Total weight of steel=%10.2f pounds\n", weight);
    printf("Total cost = $%8.2f\n", total_cost);

    return 0;
}
```

Input and Output

```
Input number of rods, diameter, length, and cost:
500 3.0 12.0 0.5

Number of rods =  500
Diameter of rods =  3.00
```

```
Length of rods = 12.00
Cost per pound of steel =  0.50

Total weight of steel = 130026.62 pounds
Total cost = $65013.31
```

3.5.3 Convection Heat Transfer

Problem Calculate the heat transfer through a metal plate of length l and width w (given in centimeters). Air is blowing at temperature t_1°C over a metal plate maintained at temperature t_2°C. The convection heat transfer coefficient is 28 W/m²°C.

Method From Newton's law of cooling, the heat transfer is given by the formula

$$q = h\,A\,(t_w - t_\infty)$$

Where q is the heat transfer in kilowatts or Btu/hour,

h is the convection heat transfer coefficient in watts/meter²°C,

a is the area of the plate in meters²,

t_{plate} is the plate temperature, and

t_{air} is the air temperature.

Data Five real numbers accurate to two decimal places representing l, w, t_{air}, t_{plate}, and heat transfer coefficient.

Pseudocode

```
Input the dimensions of the plate l and w
Input the air and plate temperatures t_air and t_plate
Input the convection heat transfer coefficient h
Output all the input variables
Convert the dimensions of the plate from centimeters to meters

    l ← l / 100.0;
    w ← w / 100.0;

Compute the area of the plate in square meters

    a ← l * w;
```

Compute the heat transfer in watts

$$q = h * a * (t_{plate} - t_{air})$$

Convert to kilowatts and Btu/hour

Output the heat transfer value.

End

Program

```
/*******************************************************/
/*                                                     */
/*   Computation of Heat Transfer Through a Plate      */
/*                                                     */
/*******************************************************/
/*                                                     */
/*   Constant:                                         */
/*      HCOF = 3411.87 - heat transfer coefficient     */
/*                                                     */
/*   Input Variables:                                  */
/*      length - plate length in centimeters           */
/*      width  - plate width in centimeters            */
/*      tplate - Plate temperature degree centigrade   */
/*      tair   - air temperature, centigrade           */
/*                                                     */
/*   Input Coefficient:                                */
/*      hcnvc  - convection heat-heat transfer         */
/*               coefficient                           */
/*                                                     */
/*   Working Variables:                                */
/*      area   - Area of the plate in meters           */
/*                                                     */
/*                                                     */
/*   Computed Variables:                               */
/*      qheat   -  Heat transfer in kw or Btu/h        */
/*                                                     */
/*   Output Variables:                                 */
/*      qheat   -  Heat transfer in kw or Btu/h        */
/*                                                     */
/*******************************************************/
```

```
#include <stdio.h>

int main( )
{
    const float HCOF = 3411.87;
    float  length, width, tplate, tair;
    float  hcnvc, area, qheat;

    printf("Input the length and width of the plate:\n");
    scanf("%f %f", &length, &width);
    printf("Input the temperatures of the plate and");
    printf(" the air in degrees centigrade:\n");
    scanf("%f %f", &tplate, &tair);
    printf("Input the convection heat transfer coefficient:\n");
    scanf("%f", &hcnvc);
    printf("\nLength = %6.2f    Width = %6.2f\n",
            length, width);
    printf("Temperature of plate = %6.2f Temperature of air = %6.2f\n",
            tplate, tair);
    printf("Heat transfer coefficient = %6.2f\n\n", hcnvc);

    length = length / 100.0;
    width = width / 100.0;

    area = length * width;
    qheat = (hcnvc * area * (tplate - tair))/1000;
    printf("\nHeat transfer = %5.2f in kW/hour\n", qheat);
    qheat = qheat * HCOF;
    printf("Heat transfer = %8.2f in Btu/hour\n", qheat);

    return 0;

}
```

Input and Output

```
Input the length and width of the plate:
200.0 100.0
Input the temperatures of the plate and the air in degrees centigrade:
400.0 30.0
Input the convection heat transfer coefficient:
25.0

Length = 200.00     Width = 100.00
Temperature of plate = 400.00 Temperature of air =  30.00
Heat transfer coefficient =  25.00

Heat transfer = 18.50 in kW/hour
Heat transfer = 63119.60 in Btu/hour
```

3.5.4 Air Conditioners Sales Report

Problem Write a program to input the sales data for a "COOL YOUR HOME" engineering company. The input record consists of salesman ID, the number of units sold, and the cost per unit. Compute the total sales and the commission paid to each salesman; the commission rate is 12% on the sales per week. Compute the total sales per week by all salesmen and the total commission paid to all salesmen.

Method

sales = number of units × cost per unit

commission = sales × commission rate

total sales = total sales + sales

total commission = total commission + commission

Data Input the two digit id, sales, and cost per unit.

Pseudocode

```
total_sales = 0.0;
total_commission = 0.0;
```

```
for each salesman
   input id, units, cost
   output id, units, cost
   sales ← units * cost
   commission = sales * 0.12
   total_sales = total_sales + sales
   total_commission = total_commission + commission
end for
output total_sales
output total_commission
stop
```

Program

```
/*********************************************************/
/*                                                       */
/*    Computation of Sales and Commission for            */
/*             Air Conditioners                          */
/*                                                       */
/*********************************************************/
/*                                                       */
/*    Input Variables:                                   */
/*        id       - salesman identification             */
/*        units    - units sold by each salesman         */
/*        cost     - cost per unit                       */
/*                                                       */
/*    Computed Variables:                                */
/*        sales    - sales per week by each salesman     */
/*        commission - commission paid to each salesman */
/*        total_sales - Weekly total sales               */
/*        total_commission - Weekly total commission     */
/*                                                       */
/*    Output Variables:                                  */
/*        sales    - sales per week by each salesman     */
/*        commission - commission paid to each salesman */
/*        total_sales - Weekly total sales               */
/*        total_commission - Weekly total commission     */
/*                                                       */
/*********************************************************/
```

```
#include <stdio.h>

int main( )
{
    FILE *inptr, *outptr;

    const float commission_rate = 0.12;
    int id, units;
    float cost, sales, commission, total_sales = 0.0,
          total_commission = 0.0;

    inptr = fopen("salesin.dat", "r");
    outptr = fopen("salesout.dat", "w");

    if(inptr)
    {
        fprintf(outptr,"id    units_sold  cost_per_unit");
        fprintf(outptr,"    sales      commission\n");

        while((fscanf(inptr,"%d  %d  %f", &id, &units, &cost))!= EOF)
        {
           sales = units * cost;
           commission = sales * commission_rate;
           total_sales += sales;
           total_commission += commission;

           fprintf(outptr,"%d    %d         %8.2f       %8.2f"
                   "    %7.2f\n", id, units, cost, sales,
                   commission);
        }
        fclose(inptr);
        fprintf(outptr,"\nTotal sales = %9.2f\n", total_sales);
        fprintf(outptr,"Total commission = %8.2f\n",
                total_commission);
    }
```

```
    fclose(outptr);
    return 0;
}
```

Input and Output

Input data file `salesin.dat`

```
17563  15  1245.56
59324  25  1567.95
65098  10  2050.76
45981  16  1850.67
```

Output data file `salesout.dat`

```
id     units_sold  cost-per-unit     sales       commission
17563     15           1245.56     18683.40       2242.01
59324     25           1567.95     39198.75       4703.05
65098     10           2050.76     20507.60       2460.91
45981     16           1850.67     29610.72       3553.29

Total sales = 108000.47
Total commission = 12960.06
```

3.5.5 Wavelength of an Electron

Problem Write a program to compute the wavelength λ of an electron at velocities of 20%, 30%,...,100% speed of light (considered as a particle) given the mass, *m*, in kilograms and velocity, *v*, in meters per second. This program uses scientific data in E format.

Method The equation (De Broglie's equation) to compute the wavelength λ of a particle is as follows:

$$\lambda = \frac{h}{mv}$$

Where λ is the wave length in meters,

h is Plank's constant 6.626×10^{-34} (kg m^2/s^2)(s),

v is velocity meters/s, and

m is in kilograms.

Data The data numbers for mass, Plank's constant, and velocity are double precision.

Pseudocode

```
Defined constants mass of the electron and velocity of light
output the mass of the electron
for each percentage of the velocity of light
   compute the velocity of the electron as a percentage of the velocity of light
      velocity of electron = percentage velocity of light
   compute the wavelength of the electron
      wavelength = Plank's constant /(mass of the electron * velocity of the electron)
   output the velocity and the wavelength
end for
stop
```

Program

```
/*********************************************************/
/*                                                       */
/*       Compute the Wavelength of an Electron           */
/*                                                       */
/*********************************************************/
/*                                                       */
/*    Constants:                                         */
/*       H  - Plank's constant = 6.626 x 10-34 kg m2/s2  */
/*       VEL_LIGHT  = 2.998 x 108  m/s                   */
/*       mass  - mass of the electron in kilograms       */
/*                                                       */
/*    Input Variables:                                   */
```

```
/*                                                   */
/*          -none-                                   */
/*                                                   */
/*    Computed Variables:                            */
/*        velocity - velocity of electron in m/s     */
/*        wavelength - wavelength of the electron in m  */
/*                                                   */
/*    Output Variables:                              */
/*        wavelength - wavelength of the electron in m  */
/*                                                   */
/*****************************************************/

#include <stdio.h>

int main( )
{
    const double H = 6.626E-34;
    const double VEL_LIGHT = 2.998E8;
    double mass = 9.109E-31;
    int light;
    double velocity, wavelength;

    printf("Plank's constant = %e\n", H);
    printf("Mass of the electron = %e kg\n\n", mass);

    for(light = 20; light <=100; light += 10)
    {
        velocity = (light / 100.0 )* VEL_LIGHT;
        wavelength = H / (velocity * mass);
        printf("Velocity = %e m/s    Wavelength = %e m\n",
                velocity, wavelength);
    }

    return 0;
}
```

Output

```
Plank's constant = 6.626000E-34
Mass of the electron = 9.109000E-31 kg

Velocity = 5.996000e+07 m/s    Wavelength = 1.213163e-11 m
Velocity = 8.994000e+07 m/s    Wavelength = 8.087752e-12 m
Velocity = 1.199200e+08 m/s    Wavelength = 6.065814e-12 m
Velocity = 1.499000e+08 m/s    Wavelength = 4.852651e-12 m
Velocity = 1.798800e+08 m/s    Wavelength = 4.043876e-12 m
Velocity = 2.098600e+08 m/s    Wavelength = 3.466180e-12 m
Velocity = 2.398400e+08 m/s    Wavelength = 3.032907e-12 m
Velocity = 2.698200e+08 m/s    Wavelength = 2.695917e-12 m
Velocity = 2.998000e+08 m/s    Wavelength = 2.426326e-12 m
```

Notice that a `for` statement is used for computing the various velocities. The velocity of light is incremented by 10% by using += 10 in the `for` loop. The `for` loop is discussed in detail in Chapter 4.

Chapter Summary

Input and output in C is performed using library functions that have prototypes stored in the header file `stdio.h`. The header file `stdio.h` must be included in the program in order to use the input and output functions. To include the header file the following statement must be used.

```
#include <stdio.h>
```

Standard Input and Output The standard input function is `scanf( )`. The `scanf( )` statement is used to enter data from the keyboard. The form of the standard input statement is

```
scanf("format control string", &var1, &var2, &var3,...,&varn);
```

The following format specifiers are used to input integer numbers, floating-point numbers, and character data:

`%d` for input of an integer number,

`%f` for input of a real number,

`%e` for input of a number in scientific notation, and

`%c` for input of a character.

The following input statements show the input of integer numbers, floating-point numbers in fixed format and scientific notation, scientific data, and character data:

```
scanf("%d  %d  %d", &var1, &var2, &var3);
```

Where var1, var2, and var3 are integer variables.

```
scanf("%f  %f  %f", &var1, &var2, &var3);
```

Where var1, var2, and var3 are floating-point variables.

```
scanf("%e  %e  %e", &var1, &var2, &var3);
```

Where var1, var2, and var3 are in scientific notation.

```
scanf("%c  %c  %c", &var1, &var2, &var3);
```

Where var1, var2, and var3 are character variables.

The following statement shows the specification of field width for the input of real numbers.

```
scanf("%5f%7f", &var1, &var2);
```

The input numbers are entered as continuous numbers; for example numbers 123.4 and 5456.78 can be entered as 123.45456.78. The field width specified will pick the correct number of digits, for example the field width `%5f` will pick the first five characters including the decimal point and `%7f` will pick the next seven characters including the decimal point.

The standard output function is `printf( )`. The `printf( )` statement is used to display output data on a CRT screen or print output data on a printer. The form of the standard output statement is

```
printf("format control string", var1, var2, var3,...,varn);
```

The following format specifiers are used to output the integer numbers, floating-point numbers, and character data, separated by blank spaces for readability

`%d or %nd` For output of integer number.

`%f or %n.mf`	For output of real numbers in fixed format, `n` is the total number of columns to print including integer digits, decimal point, and decimal digits. Whereas `m` is the total number of decimal digits to be printed.
`%e or %n.me`	For output of real numbers in scientific notation. `n` is the total number of columns to print including integer digits, decimal point, the letter e, the exponents, and decimal digits. Whereas `m` is the total number of decimal digits to be printed.
`%c`	For output of characters.

In the `scanf( )` function, the arguments are the addresses of variables. In the `printf( )` function, the arguments are the values of variables.

- Numbers are printed left justified, when the field width is not specified in the format specification. If the field width is specified, a number is printed right justified, with blank fill within the specified field width.
- When printing a real number the format field width must include space for the sign, the whole digits, the decimal point, and the fractional digits.
- If field widths are underspecified the functions will provide the extra spaces required to print the numbers.
- When printing real numbers without a field width, the number of fractional digits printed will default to six.
- When printing real numbers with field width specified, the number of fractional digits required must be explicitly specified.
- When printing real numbers in scientific notation with field width specified, the number of fractional digits required may be specified.

Any text included within a format control string will be printed exactly as it appears within the format control string. The format control string serves as a template for output, with the values of the variables replacing the format specifications.

File Input and Output Input of data to a program can be from a data file stored on disk. Output of data can be from a program to a data file created on a disk. Data files on a disk are made available to a program, by declaring file pointers in the program space and opening the files with an open statement. The declaration of file pointers and open statements is as follows.

```
FILE  *inptr, *outptr;

inptr = fopen("myfilein.dat", "r");

outptr = fopen("myfileout.dat", "w");
```

The pointer type used in the declaration is `FILE` in capital letters. Here `inptr` is an input file pointer and `outptr` is an output file pointer. In the open statement `fopen` is a reserved word that is used to open a file in C. The data file name with the data extension is given as a character string within double quotes. The mode of operation of the file is provided as the second argument, also a character string. The mode `r` is used for the input file, the mode `w` is used for the output file, and mode `a` is used for appending to a file.

`fopen` is a function that returns a pointer to the data file if it is available, or a `null` pointer if it is not. The input and output statements are nearly the same as standard input and output statements with the following modifications:

File Input Instead of using `scanf( )` use `fscanf( )`, the function name for input from a data file. The first argument must be an input file pointer. The form of the input statement for file input is as follows:

```
fscanf(inptr, "format control string", &var1, &var2, &var3, ... ,&varn);
```

Notice that the first argument is an input file pointer `inptr`, the second argument is a format control string enclosed within double quotes as in standard input, followed by the addresses of the variables as in standard input.

File Output Instead of using `printf( )` use `fprintf( )`, the function name for output to a data file. The first argument must be an output file pointer. The form of the output statement for file output is as follows:

```
fprintf(outptr, "format control string", var1, var2, var3, ... ,varn);
```

Notice that the first argument is an output file pointer `outptr`, the second argument is a format control string enclosed within double quotes as in standard output, followed by the variables as in standard output.

Exercises

1. Write a program to input the item number, quantity, and unit cost for two machine parts to assemble a machine unit. Print a report showing the input data and the total cost for each item, overall total quantity, and overall total cost. Titles and labels must be printed and the output must be aligned appropriately.

2. Write a program to compute the diameter in centimeters of a steel rod, an aluminum rod, and a copper rod, which can withstand a particular compression load. The allowable compression stress of steel, aluminum, and copper is 25,000 lbs/m^2, 15,000 lbs/m^2, and 20,000 lbs/m^2, respectively.

$$\text{area of rod} = \frac{\text{compression load}}{\text{allowable compression stress}}$$

$$\text{area} = \pi r^2 \text{ where diameter } d = 2r$$

Input the compression load. Print the type of material, load, allowable stress, and diameter. Use formatted output with field width specifications that align the output.

3. Write a program to compute the range of a projectile given the velocity and the angle at which the projectile is fired. The range is computed from the equation

$$R = v^2 \sin(2\theta) / g$$

where 2θ is in radians, and

$g = 32.2$ ft/sec^2 is the gravitational constant.

Compute the range for a velocity of 1000 ft/sec at angle α (degrees) for a value of α found in an input file. Print the velocity V, the angle θ in radians, and the range R. Write the title and label the output.

4. Write a program to compute the pressure of water at depths of 50, 100, and 150 ft. The weight density (d) of water is 62.4 lbs/ft^3. The formula for the pressure is given by

$$p = \text{density} * \text{depth lbs/ft}^2.$$

Print the output as a table showing the depth and the pressure. Use the formatted output with two decimal digits and label the output columns.

5. Write a program to determine the power input to a motor and the power output of the motor in horsepower. Determine also the efficiency, given that the motor requires 15 amps of current to lift a ton of weight at a rate of 50 ft/min. It is plugged into a 220 volt line.

   The power input is given by the formula:

$$\text{power\_input} = IV \text{ in watts}$$

$$\text{power\_input} = \frac{IV}{1000} * 1.34 \text{ in hp}$$

   where I is the current in amps and

   V is the voltage in volts.

   The power output is given by the formula:

$$\text{power\_output} = \frac{\text{FV}}{33000} \text{ in hp.}$$

   Where F is the weight to be lifted in pound force, and

   V is the velocity in ft/min.

   The efficiency is given by the formula:

$$\text{Efficiency} = \frac{\text{power output}}{\text{power input}} \times 100.$$

6. Write a program to compute the discharge rate of water through a venturi meter having a pipe diameter of d_p cms and a throat diameter of d_t cms, if the difference of the liquid height in the monometer tube is h cms.

Cross sectional area of pipe:

$$\text{pipe-area} = \frac{\pi d_p^2}{4}.$$

Cross sectional area of throat:

$$\text{throat-area} = \frac{\pi d_t^2}{4}.$$

Ratio of area of pipe to area of throat:

$$\text{ratio} = \frac{\text{pipe-area}}{\text{throat-area}}.$$

The discharge rate is given by the formula

$$Q = 25\pi\sqrt{\frac{2\times 980\times h}{\text{ratio}^2 - 1}}\ \text{cm}^3/\text{sec}$$

7. Write a program to compute the resulting focal length f of two thin lenses of focal length f_1 and f_2 placed in contact. The resulting focal length is derived from the formula

$$\frac{1}{f} = \frac{1}{f_1} + \frac{1}{f_2}.$$

The formula for the resulting focal length derived from the given formula is

$$f = \frac{f_1 f_2}{f_1 + f_2}.$$

Obtain f_1 and f_2 from standard input. Print f_1, f_2, and f labeled.

8. Write a program to estimate the cost of building an industrial plant with three buildings. Each building has the floor area of x square feet and it costs y dollars per square foot. The cost per square foot for each building is different. Each building is equipped with machinery. The total cost of machinery in each building is c, which is different for each building. Compute the cost for each building including the cost of the machinery. Compute the overall cost to build the industrial plant. Label the output.

CHAPTER 4

Control Structures

Objectives

To understand the logic sequence in which the program statements are executed. To learn to use the sequence, selection, and repetition structures.

The concept of structured programming was developed in the 1960s to eliminate the use of types of statements that made it difficult to follow the flow of control in a program. The sequence in which the statements in a program are executed should always be from the top to the bottom of a program structure. In structured programming languages, such as C, there are language features to implement the three basic control structures; the sequence structure, the selection structure, and the repetition structure. These three control structures are sufficient to write any complex program. Each of these control structures has an entry at the top and an exit at the bottom of the structure. Algorithms, which use basic control structures, have clear top-down structure and logic. Programs written using only the corresponding language features are easier to understand, are more reliable, and are easier to maintain.

The development of algorithms using top-down methodology corresponds to coding using the three basic control structures. A program is a sequence of steps where each step is an instruction or a group of instructions to be executed by the computer. Some of the instructions are executed only once; some are executed selectively based on a precondition; others are executed repeatedly based on a precondition.

A *sequence structure* is a basic control structure in which the statements are executed one after the other in the order in which they appear within the program. Sequence structures may appear as a sequence of statements or of other structures or they may be nested inside a selection or a repetition structure.

A *selection structure* is one in which there are one, two, or more options. A selection structure with one option is a simple selection structure with only one sequence to be chosen or to be omitted, and a selection structure with two options has two sequences to choose between. The choice of the selection is based on a question imposed by the program logic. There is a special selection structure that allows for more than two options. This structure, called a *case structure*, may be implemented in C several different ways.

A *repetition structure* repeats the execution of a sequence of statements zero or more times. This type of control structure is used to process several data records, or generate a set of data. In C these control structures can be implemented several different ways.

A sequence structure is a block or sequence of executable statements in a C program. The statements in a sequence structure are executed one after another in the order in which they appear in a program. The statements in a sequence structure may be simple executable statements or other control structures such as selection and repetition structures, as shown in Figure 4.1.

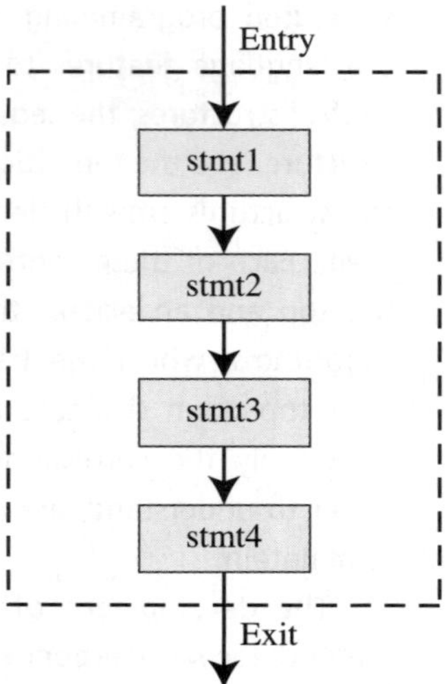

Figure 4.1 Sequence structure

The pseudocode for the sequence structure shown in Figure 4.1 is as follows:

```
stmt 1
stmt 2
stmt 3
stmt 4
```

In C an equivalent sequence of statements may appear as follows:

```
{
   c = 3.141593 * r * r;     /* area of circle */
   diag = r + r;             /* diagonal of inscribed square */
   s = 2 * r * r;            /* area inside square */
   a = c - s;                /* area not covered by square */
}
```

Given a circle of radius 1.0; statement `c = 3.141593 * r * r` assigns the value of 3.141593 to the variable `c`, `diag = r + r` assigns value 2 to the variable `diag`, `s = 2 * r * r` evaluates the expression and assigns the resulting value of 2 to variable `s`. The use of braces holds the statements together as a logical sequence.

A selection or a repetition structure or a function call may be embedded in a sequence structure, still maintaining the top-down flow of program control. Figure 4.2 shows such embedded structures.

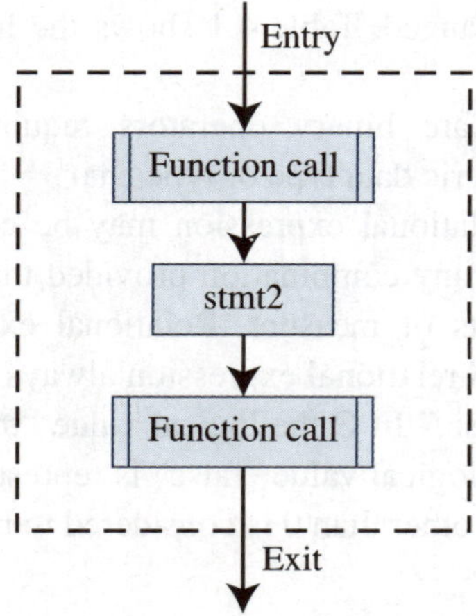

Figure 4.2 Sequence structure with embedded function calls

An example of C code that corresponds to the flowchart is as follows:

```
{
    scanf("%d   %d", &x, &y);
    area =  x * y;
    printf("%d", area);
}
```

When a sequence structure containing more than one statement is nested in another control structure, it is written as a block, using braces.

4.1 Relational and Logical Operations

Logical operators are used in formulating logical expressions. Logical expressions consist of logical operators and logical operands. The logical operands may be logical constants or relational expressions or integers representing true and false. The operands are evaluated before the logical operation is performed. The result of a logical operation is a logical value of either "true" or "false." Logical expressions are used in compound conditions.

4.1.1 Relational Operators and Relational Expressions

Relational operators are used to compare two values to control selection or repetition. Some of these relational symbols are written slightly differently in C. For example; the symbol for "less than or equal to" (≤) is written in C in the form <= but the meaning is not changed. Table 4.1 shows the list of relational operators used in C.

Relational operators are binary operators requiring two operands. The operands may be any numeric data type or type `char`.

The operands of a relational expression may be constants, variables, valid arithmetic expressions, or any combination provided that the operands have values having the same units of measure. Relational expressions are sometimes referred to as conditions. A relational expression always evaluates to either a logical value of "true" or "false." In C the logical value "true" is represented by the integer value of 1 and the logical value "false" is represented by the integer value of 0. In general, any value other than 0 is considered to be "true" in C.

Table 4.1 Relational Operators

Symbol	Meaning	Expression	Meaning
`>`	greater than	`operand1 > operand2`	is `operand1` greater than `operand2`?
`>=`	greater than or equal to	`operand1 >= operand2`	is `operand1` greater than or equal to `operand2`?
`<`	less than	`operand1 < operand2`	is `operand1` less than `operand2`?
`<=`	less than or equal to	`operand1 <= operand2`	is `operand1` less than or equal to `operand2`?
`==`	equal to	`operand1 == operand2`	is `operand1` equal to `operand2`?
`!=`	not equal to	`operand1 != operand2`	is `operand1` not equal to `operand2`?

Warning: When a double symbol is used for relational operations, (==, >=, <=, or !=) there must not be any space between the two characters.

Appropriate Comparisons	Inappropriate Comparisons
`area >= 0`	`area > length`
`sin(x) < sin(y)`	`ht == voltage`
`a + b > c`	`vol < 0`
`measurement != 27.4`	`3.5 != "A"`

Relational Expressions Relational expressions may be used to compare constants, variables, and valid arithmetic expressions for their equality or inequality, as in the following examples:

```
  5 > 10        evaluates to 0, false
8.5 < 12.6      evaluates to 1, true
```

Notice that 5, 10, `8.5`, and `12.6` are all scalar constants.

```
a = 10;
b = 5;
a > b           evaluates to 1, true
a >= b          evaluates to 1, true
a == b          evaluates to 0, false
```

Notice that a and b are variables.

```
a = 5;
b = 6;
c = 3;
d = 8;
a * b > c + d     evaluates to 1, true
b / c > a         evaluates to 0, false
```

Notice that a * b, c + d, and b/c are arithmetic expressions. When arithmetic expressions are used in a relational expression, the arithmetic expressions are evaluated first, and then the relational expression is evaluated. Avoid the comparison for equality of arithmetic expressions producing real numbers because real numbers may not be stored accurately in the computer.

> *Programming Hint:* When real numbers are compared, it is better to compare for approximate equality of the two operands.

The following example shows the comparison of two floating-point numbers:

```
float a;
a = 1.0 / 3.0;
a = 3 * a;
if(fabs(a - 1.0) < 0.0001) /* is approximately equal */
```

rather than

```
if(a == 1.0)
```

Relational expressions may be used in arithmetic. The following example determines which is the largest of two numbers:

```
big = a * ( a > b) + b * (b > a) + a * ( a == b);
```

The relational operations evaluate to true or false, which are represented by 1 or 0, respectively, and can be used in arithmetic.

4.1.2 Logical Operators and Logical Expressions

In C there are three logical operators. The logical operators are && (AND), || (OR), and ! (NOT). The logical operators && and || are binary operators requiring two operands and ! is a unary operator requiring only one operand. The order of evaluation of the logical operators are as follows: ! is evaluated first, followed by the && operator, and then by the || operator in a parentheses-free expression. If there are parentheses then the expression inside the parentheses is evaluated first. The operands of a logical expression must have logical values. The following tables show the results of logical operators &&, ||, and !.

&& Operator: The result of the && operation is true only if both operands are true, otherwise it is false. The following table shows the result of the && operation.

var1	var2	var1 && var2
false	false	false
false	true	false
true	false	false
true	true	true

a && b is the C code way of saying that a and b are both true, a claim about a and b that may be true or may be false. For example (x > 0 && y > 0) claims that x and y are both positive.

|| Operator: The result of the || operation is "true" if one of the operands is true or both operands are true, otherwise it is false. The following table shows the result of the || operation.

var1	var2	var1 || var2
false	false	false
false	true	true
true	false	true
true	true	true

a || b is the C code way of saying that a and b are not both false, but at least one of them is true. For example (x > y || x > z) claims that x is not the smallest of the three numbers.

! Operator: The result of the ! operation is false if the operand is true, true if the operand is false.

var1	!var1
false	true
true	false

`!errflag` is the C code way of saying that there was no error in the operation that set the flag. Notice that ! is a unary operator that operates on only one operand.

Logical Expressions The result of a logical expression is a logical value. Relational expressions may be used as the operands of logical expressions. The following example shows the evaluation of a logical expression.

```
int  a = 5,  b = 6, c = 3, d = 10;

a > b && c < d
false && true
     false
```

Notice that the relational expression `a > b` yields a logical value of false and the relational expression `c < d` yields a logical value of true. These values are used to evaluate the logical expression containing the && operator, the result of this logical expression is false.

```
int  a = 5,  b = 6, c = 3, d = 10;

a > b || c < d
false || true
     true
```

Notice that the relational expression `a > b` gives a logical value of false and the relational expression `c < d` gives a logical value of true. These values are used to evaluate the logical expression containing the || operator, the result of this logical expression is true.

```
int  a = 5, b = 6;

!(a > b)
!false
 true
```

Notice that the relational expression `a > b` gives a logical value of false and this value is used to evaluate the logical expression containing the `!` operator. The result of this logical expression is true. In a parentheses-free expression, a relational operator has higher priority than a logical operator.

Given the following logical values and relational expressions, the logical expressions are evaluated as follows:

`expr1` = true, `expr2` = false, `expr3` = false, and `expr4` = true

`expr1 && expr2`	is false
`expr1 || expr3`	is true
`expr1 || expr2 && expr4`	is true
`expr2 || expr1 && expr4`	is true
`!(expr1 && expr4)`	is false
`!expr1 && expr4`	is false
`expr1 && (expr2 || expr3)`	is false
`expr1 && !(expr2 || expr3)`	is true

The following expressions show the precedence of the operators. They are equivalent for all values of the expression. Therefore the parentheses are not needed.

`expr1 || (expr2 && expr3)`	and	`expr1 || expr2 && expr3`
`expr1 || !expr2 && expr4`	and	`expr1 || ((!expr2) && expr4)`
`expr3 && (!expr4)`	and	`expr3 && !expr4`
`(!expr2) || expr3`	and	`!expr2 || expr3`
`expr1 && expr2 || expr3`	and	`(expr1 && expr2) || expr3`

Parentheses may be used to change the order of the evaluation of the logical expressions. The following examples show the use of parentheses:

`expr1 && ( expr2 || expr3)`	in this expression `expr2 || expr3` is evaluated first and then `&&` is evaluated.
`!(expr1 || expr2 || expr3)`	in this expression the expression `expr1 || expr2 || expr3` is evaluated first and then `!` is evaluated.

With the previous values, the following expression is evaluated as follows:

```
!(expr1 || expr2 && (expr3 || expr4))
!(expr1 || expr2 && true)
!(expr1 || false)
!(true)
false
```

> *Programming Hint:* Use parentheses in logical expression for clarity and to avoid execution errors.

The order of precedence of operators in a logical expression is: the parentheses, arithmetic operators, relational operators, and logical operators.

Highest	parenthesized expressions
	arithmetic operations
	relational operations
	logical operations
Lowest	assignment

Given the values for the following variables, evaluate the following expression containing the arithmetic, relational, and logical operator.

```
a = 10, b = 5, c = 6, and d = 2,

!(a + b > c * d) && c * d < a + d
!(15 > 12 )&& 12 < 12
!true && false
false && false
false
```

The relational expressions and logical expressions are used to make logical choices in the selection and looping structures. The following sections show the use of the relational and logical expressions.

4.1.3 Review Questions

1. Indicate whether the following statements are true or false.
   a. In an && operation, if the first operand is true the result is true.

b. In an `&&` operation, if the first operand is false the result is false.

c. In an `||` operation, if the first operand is true the result is true.

d. In an `&&` operation, if both operands are true the result is true.

e. In an `||` operation, if the first operand is false the result is false.

f. In the evaluation of a logical expression, `!` has priority over the `&&` and `||` operations.

g. In the evaluation of a logical expression, parentheses have higher priority than logical operators.

h. In the evaluation of a logical expression, arithmetic operators have higher priority than relational and logical operators.

i. In the evaluation of a relational expression, relational operators have lower priority than logical operators.

2. Given the following logical values, `expr1` = true, `expr2` = false, `expr3` = true, `expr4` = false, evaluate the following logical expressions.

   a. `expr1 && expr2 || expr3`

   b. `expr1 || expr2 && expr3`

   c. `!expr2 && expr1 || expr4`

   d. `!expr2 && (expr1 || expr3)`

   e. `!(expr1 && expr3) || expr1`

3. Given the following values for the variables, `a = 10`, `b = 5`, `c = 12`, and `d = 8`, evaluate the following relational and logical expressions.

   a. `a > b || b < c && d > b`

   b. `!(a < b && c > d) || c < d`

   c. `a <= b || !b < c && d > a`

   d. `a > c && !d < c || (a > b && b < d)`

4. Given the following values for the variables, `a = 10`, `b = 15`, `c = 10`, and `d = 25`, evaluate the following relational expressions.

   a. `a >= c`

   b. `b < d`

   c. `a * b / 2 >= c + d / 5 + 2`

   d. `a – b <= c + d – 4`

4.2 Selection Structures

Each sequence and selection structure can be implemented in C as a block of code with an entrance at the top and an exit at the bottom. The control flow is from top to bottom. After the execution of either the sequence block or the selection block, the execution continues according to the flow control.

4.2.1 Two-Way Selection Structures

The *selection structure* gives the computer a choice of executing at most one of a set of statements. A question with a true or false answer is asked. Each answer leads to a block of code containing zero or more instructions. For example,

<u>to print only positive values:</u>

```
if(x > 0)
    printf("%f\n", x);
```

or

```
if(x > 0)
{
    printf("%f\n", x);
}
```

<u>to sum and count positive values:</u>

```
if(x > 0)
{
    sum = sum + x;
    cnt = cnt + 1:
}
```

<u>to print one pair of values if they are equal, both if they are unequal:</u>

```
if(fabs(x - y) < 0.00001)
    printf("%f\n", x);
else
    printf("%f    %f\n"), x, y);
```

or

```
if(fabs(x - y) < 0.00001)
{
    printf("%f\n", x);
}
else
{
    printf("%f    %f\n", x, y);
}
```

to solve the quadratic equation $ax^2 + bx + c = 0$, assuming the roots are real:

```
if(a == 0)
{
    if(b != 0)
    {
        x1 = -c / b;        /* solution to bx + c = 0 */
    }
}
else        /* solution to ax² + c = 0 and ax² + bx + c = 0 */
{
    d = sqrt(b * b – 4.0 * a * c);
    x1 = (-b + d) / (2.0 * a);
    x2 = (-b – d) / ( 2.0 * a);
}
```

The following examples of these structures show the general forms in pseudocode and the equivalent C code. Figure 4.3 shows selecting or bypassing a sequence, the situation where no action is to be taken if the condition is false.

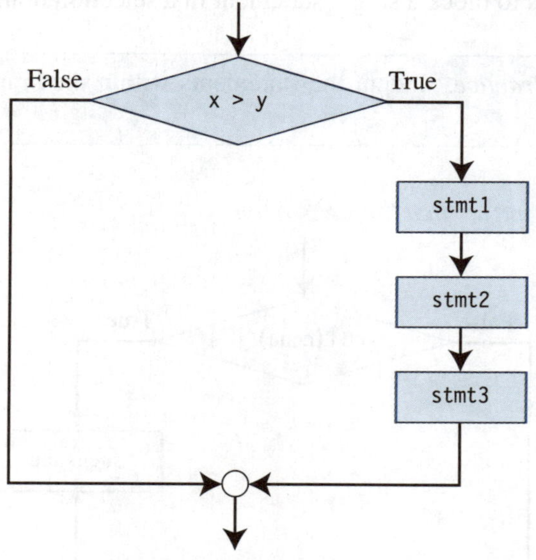

Figure 4.3 Two-way selection branching structure

One Statement in a Single Branch Single statement in one branch of selection structure—an `if` structure

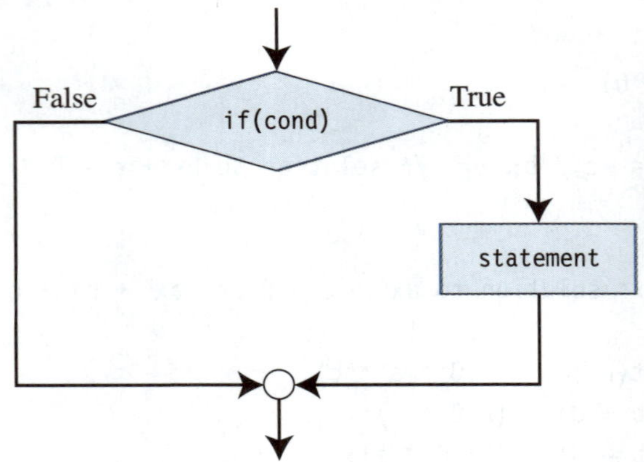

The form of the C code is as follows:

```
if(condition)
   statement;        /* single statement  */
```

Notice in this structure there is only one statement in the true branch. There is no need to use braces to block a single statement in a selection branch.

> *Programming Practice:* Indent the statements within the branches of a selection structure.

Two or More Statements in a Single Branch

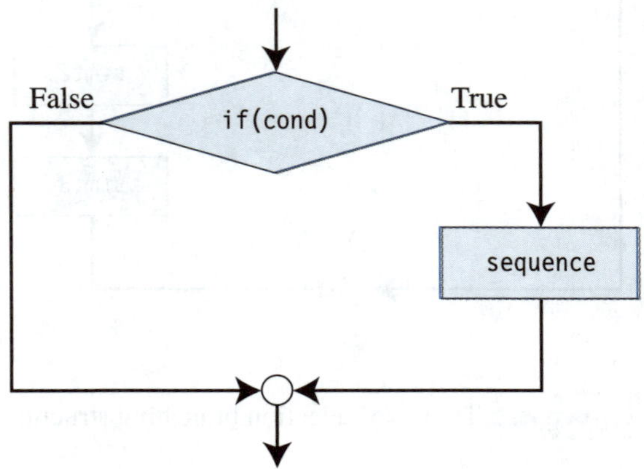

The C code is as follows:

```
if(cond)
{
    sequence   /* sequence block */
}
```

Programming Rule: When there are two or more statements in any conditional branch they must be enclosed with a pair of braces.

Notice in the flowchart of Figure 4.3 there are three statements in the true branch. This sequence structure is written as a block, which is a set of left and right braces enclosing the three statements. If there is only one statement on the true branch, the braces are not needed.

The general form of the branching statement uses the reserved word *if* followed by left parentheses followed by a condition or relational expression followed by right parentheses. The general form of a conditional branching header is:

```
if(condition or relational expression)
```

Programming Error: There is no semicolon at the end of the selection header. Programmers must pay attention to this potential error.

Figure 4.4 shows a selection structure with a sequence on each branch. It is also possible to write a selection structure with a `null` true branch and a sequence on the false branch. These selection structures may be stacked and nested depending on the logic of the algorithm. Problems with complex solutions may require stacked and nested control structures.

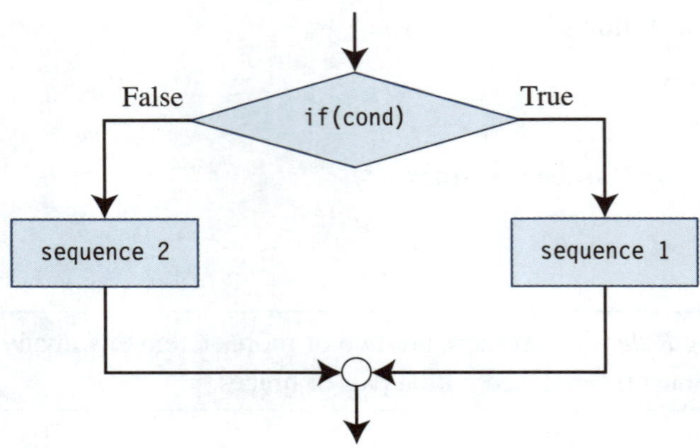

Figure 4.4 General two-way selection branching structure

One or More Statements in Each Branch—an `if-else` *Structure* The C code has the form

```
if(condition)
{
    sequence 1
}
else
{
    sequence 2
}
```

The execution sequence of this code is as follows:

- If the condition is true, sequence 1 is executed and sequence 2 in the false branch is skipped.
- If the condition is false, sequence 2 is executed and sequence 1 in the true branch is skipped.

Notice that the braces are used to block the sequences in both branches, because there is more than one statement in each sequence. The following example shows the selection structure with a single statement in each of the true and false branches.

Single Statement in Each Branch—an `if-else` *Structure*

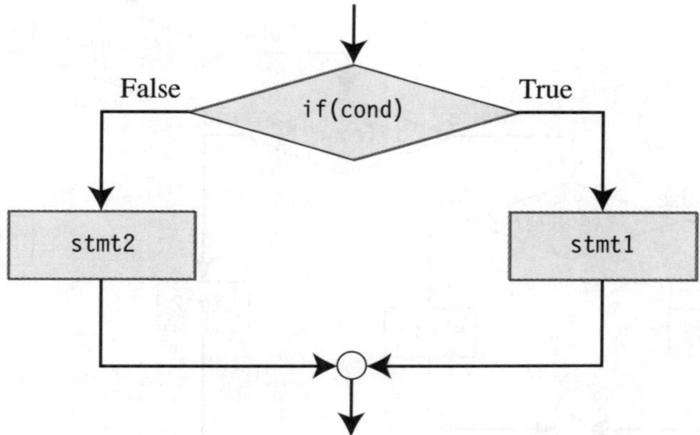

The pseudocode is as follows:

```
if(condition)
  stmt1;
else
  stmt2;
```

The execution sequence of this code is as follows:

- If the condition is true, statement `stmt1` is executed and statement `stmt2` in the `else` clause is skipped.
- If the condition is false, statement `stmt2` is executed and statement `stmt1` in the true branch is skipped.

A case structure is a selection structure with more than two branches written as nested selection structures as `if...else if...else if...else if...else`.

The C code for the control structure shown in Figure 4.5 has the form:

```
if(cond1)
    stmt1;
else if(cond2)
    stmt2;
else if(cond3)
    stmt3;
else
    stmt4;
```

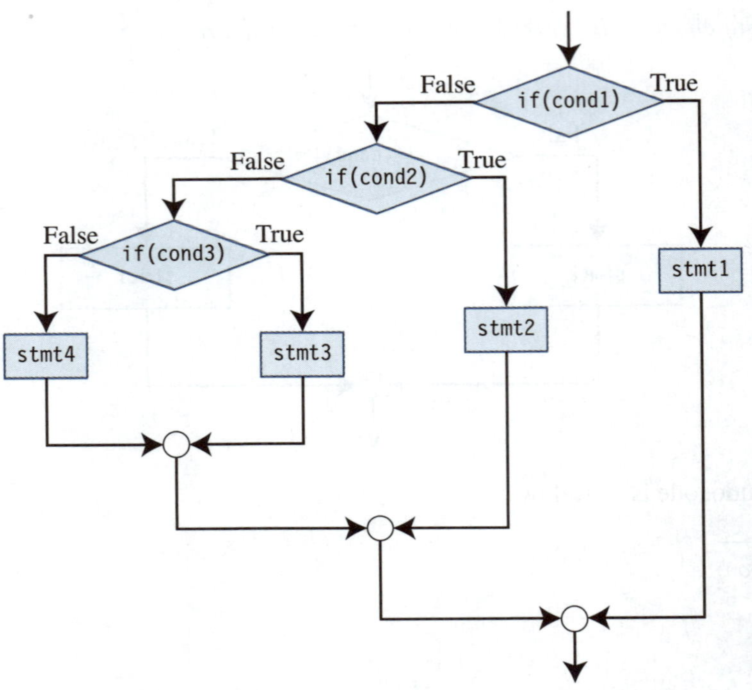

Figure 4.5 Nested selection branching structure

The flowchart in Figure 4.5 illustrates a case structure.

For example, if data contains three measurements *x*, *y*, and *z* that must be positive, then the data can be validated by the following code:

```
if(x <= 0)
   printf("Invalid value for x");
else if(y <= 0)
   printf("Invalid value for y");
else if (z <= 0)
   printf("Invalid value for z");
else
   printf("The values are:", func(x, y, x));
```

Exactly one of the four statements will be executed regardless of the number of conditions that may be true.

Notice that the default is the `else` clause. If all the conditions are false it automatically defaults to the `else` clause. If there is more than one sequence statement in any of the branches, the sequence must be blocked with braces.

Another way to validate the data values, *x*, *y*, and *z* (values representing the sides of a rectangular solid), and print the volume is shown in the following C code and corresponding flowchart:

```
if( x > 0)
{
   if(y > 0)
   {
      if(z > 0)
         printf("volume is: %f", x * y * z);
      else
         printf("Invalid value for z");
   }
   else
      printf("Invalid value for y");
}
else
   printf("Invalid value for x");
```

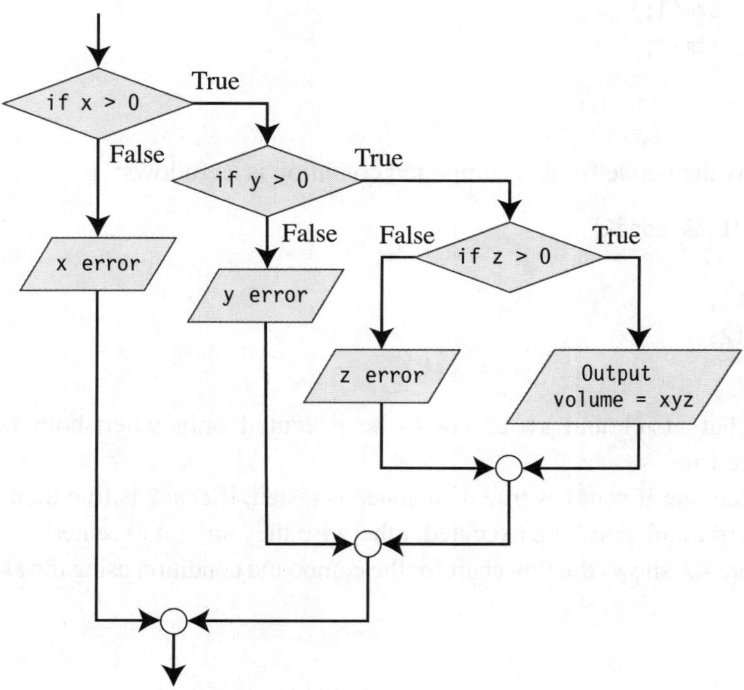

Note that this validation code does not detect all invalid values, but whether or not there is an invalid value.

> *Programming Practice:* Always have a default `else` clause in a multiselection.

4.2.2 Compound Conditions

Compound conditions are used when two or more conditions need to be tested to make a logical choice. Instead of nested simple conditions, a compound condition is simpler to code and implement.

&& Condition Consider the case that two conditions must be met for processing to take place. The following example shows the implementation of this compound condition.

```
if(cond1)
{
    if (cond2)
    {
        stmt1;
        stmt2;
    }
}
```

The equivalent code for this compound condition is as follows:

```
if( cond1 && cond2)
{
    stmt1;
    stmt2;
}
```

Notice that `stmt1` and `stmt2` are to be executed only when both `cond1` and `cond2` are true.

Notice that if `cond1` is true then `cond2` is tested, if `cond2` is true then the statements `stmt1` and `stmt2` are executed, otherwise they are not executed.

Figure 4.6 shows the flowchart for the compound condition using the && operator.

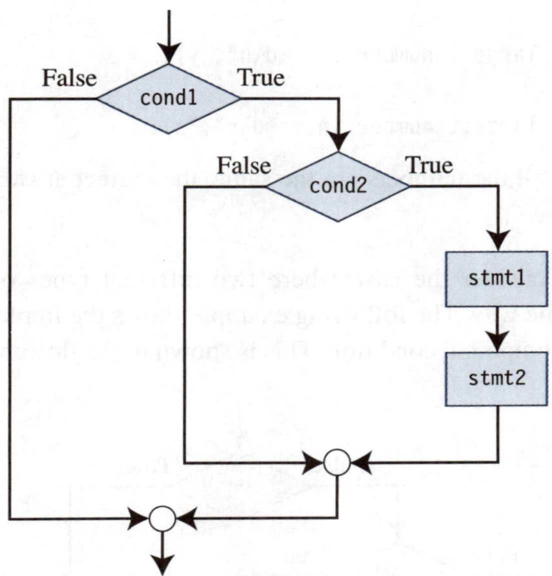

Figure 4.6 Flowchart of a compound condition

To validate three measurements *x*, *y*, and *z* as positive values, a compound condition must be used in a single structure.

```
if( x > 0 && y > 0 && z > 0)
{
    printf("%f\n", func(x,y,z));
}
else
{
    printf("invalid data");
}
```

To determine which of the numbers *x*, *y*, or *z* is the largest, assume that *x* is; that is, that $x > y$ and $x > z$. If this is not so, then either *y* or *z* is the largest and it is only necessary to compare *y* and *z*.

```
if ( x > y &&  x > z)
    printf("The largest number is: %d\n", x);
```

```
else if (y > z)
    printf("The largest number is: %d\n", y);
else
    printf("The largest number is : %d\n", z);
```

Note that even if all the numbers are the same, the correct answer will be printed by the default case.

|| Condition Consider the case where two different types of data are to be processed the same way. The following example shows the implementation of the || operator in a compound condition. This is shown in the flowchart in Figure 4.7.

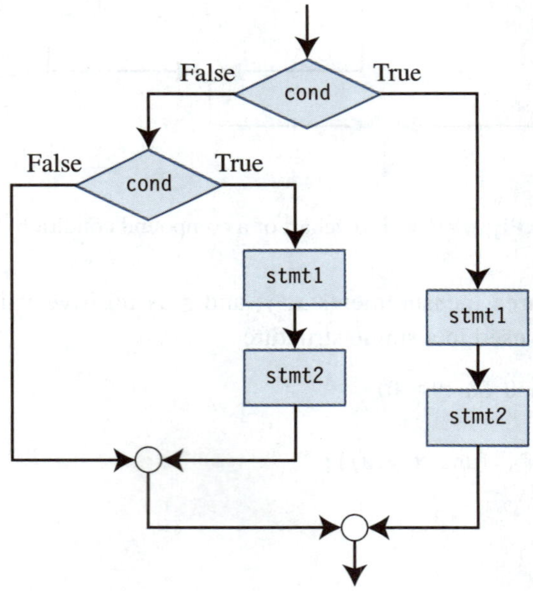

Figure 4.7 Flowchart of a compound condition

The code with the simple conditions is:

```
if(cond1)
{
    stmt1;
    stmt2;
}
else if(cond2)
```

```
{
    stmt1;
    stmt2;
}
```

Since the two embedded sequences contain the same statements, this can also be written as:

```
if(cond1 || cond2)
{
    stmt1;
    stmt2;
}
```

As an example consider the solution of the quadratic equation $ax^2 + bx + c = 0$. If $a = 0$ or $b^2 - 4ac < 0$, then the formula for solving the equation for real roots cannot be used. The following code would be used to solve the equation.

```
if(a == 0 || (b * b – 4 * a * c ) < 0)
{
    printf("This is not a solvable equation");
}
else
{
    d = sqrt(b * b - 4 * a * c);
    x1 = (-b + d) / (2 * a);
    x2 = (-b – d) / (2 * a);
}
```

Compound logical expressions can be used. In the following example, a senior student is eligible for a scholarship if he or she has a grade point average of at least 3.5. The same scholarship can be awarded to a junior student who has a grade point average of at least 3.75.

```
If( ((level == senior )&& (GPA >Bplus) || (level == junior) && (GPA >
   Aminus)) )
{
   printf("student-id : %d  is eligible for a scholarship\n", std_id);
}
```

In this example `level` and `GPA` are variables while `junior`, `senior`, `Aminus`, and `Bplus` are constants.

4.2.3 Multiway Structures

There is a special statement equivalent to the `if-else...if-else...if-...-else`. This can be used when all of the conditions check for values of the same variable, and those values may be 1, 2, 3, etc. This is usually used with assigned codes. The structure is called a case structure. In C it can be implemented by a `switch` statement.

The following example shows the use of `if-else` to implement a case structure:

```
int student_code;

scanf("%d", &student_code);

printf("Student code = %d\n", student_code);
if (student_code == 1)
{
    printf("The student is a freshman.\n");
}
else if (student_code == 2)
{
    printf("The student is a sophomore.\n");
}
else if (student_code == 3)
{
    printf("The student is a junior.\n");
}
else if (student_code == 4)
{
    printf("The student is a senior.\n");
}
else
{
    printf("The student is unclassified.\n");
}
```

If the `student_code` matches the code specified in a conditional branch, only statements in the corresponding branch are executed. If the `student_code` does not match 1, 2, 3, or 4, it automatically executes the `else` branch by default. If there is only one statement in each selection branch there is no need to use braces to block a single statement.

Switch Statement The `switch` statement can also be used to implement a case structure. The general form of the `switch` statement is as follows:

```
switch(expression)
{
  case # or char:
    stmt1;
    break;
  case # or char:
    stmt2;
    break;
}
```

The expression is expected to evaluate to one of a predetermined set of values. The value of the expression is used as follows:

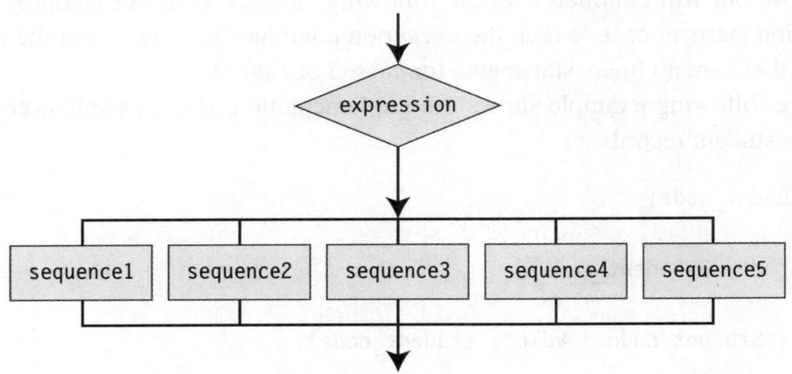


```
switch(expression)

{
   case 1:
     sequence1
     break;
```

```
    case 2:
      sequence2
      break;
    case 3:
      sequence3
      break;
    case 4:
      sequence4
      break;
    default:
      sequence5
}
```

In this structure the expression may have a numeric value of 1, 2, 3, or 4; then `sequence1` is executed for `case 1`, `sequence2` executed for `case 2`, and so on. If the numeric value of the expression is other than 1, 2, 3, or 4 then `sequence5` is executed, which is, of course, the default case. The `break` statement is a special language statement that transfers the control to the end of the structure. This statement is needed to exit out of the switch structure once a specific case is executed. If there is no break statement, then the execution will not terminate from a specific case but will continue with the following case, as well. For example, if the execution starts at `case 3` then the execution continues to `case 4` and the default case if there are no break statements for `case 3` or `case 4`.

The following example shows the implementation of the switch structure to process student records

```
int student_code;

scanf("%d", &student_code);

printf("Student code = %d\n", student_code);

switch(student_code)
{
case 1:
    printf("The student is a freshman.\n");
    break;
```

```
case 2:
    printf("The student is a sophomore.\n");
    break;
case 3:
    printf("The student is a junior.\n");
    break;
case 4:
    printf("The student is a senior.\n");
    break;
default:
    printf("The student is unclassified.\n");
}
```

The valid values of the expression `student_code` are 1, 2, 3, and 4. Any other value will result in the default case. It is important to note that the switch statement only works with `int` and `char` data types. The controlling expression must evaluate to an integer constant or a specific character value, such as 'a', in order to implement the case. The case code must be an integer constant or character (`char`) constant. The following code shows evaluation of a logical case:

```
int a, b;

scanf("%d %d", &a, &b);

switch((a-b)>0)
{
      case 0:
          printf("This is case 1: a is less than or equal to b");
          break;
      case 1:
          printf("This is case 2: a is greater than b");
          break;
}
```

Note that distinguishing between less than and equal to in this case is not possible without further conditional statements, such as `if-else` statements. This is because the logical statement generates a binary response. Only two case codes are valid for this type of statement, 0 or 1. In most instances, the `if-else` statement would be preferable to implement logical decisions.

A variation in the use of the switch statement is where two or more cases can be checked at one time, provided they require the same actions. The following example shows such a switch structure.

```
switch(expression)
{
case 1:
    printf("This is case 1: %d\n", expression);
    break;
case 2:
case 3:
    printf("This is case 2 or case 3: %d\n", expression);
    break;
default:
    printf("This is the default: %d\n", expression);
}
```

Notice that because `case 2` does not have a break statement, under `case 2` or `case 3` the same set of statements is executed. This is a convenient structure if similar data sets need to be processed with the same set of program statements.

The case structure can be used to check for multiple matches as shown in the following example, where a count is used to indicate how many matches are found.

```
int count=0;
if(a==b)
    count += 1;
if(b==c)
    count += 1;
if(a==c)
    count += 1;

switch(count)
{
case 0:
```

```
        printf("If abc is a triangle, it is scalene.");
        break;
    case 1:
        printf("If abc is a triangle, it is isosceles.");
        break;
    case 3:
        printf("If abc is a triangle, it is equilateral.");
        break;
    default:
        printf("This is impossible.");
}
```

In this sequence, the `if` statements test all of the conditions and determine the value of count. The switch case structure uses the value of the count to distinguish between none of the sides being equal, one pair of sides being equal (any pair), and all three sides being equal. Note that the default case is not actually necessary in this code, but it is included here to demonstrate this point. One of the case values will be satisfied by the initial test.

4.2.4 Review Questions

1. Indicate whether the following statements are true or false.
   a. A relational expression assigns values to the operands, which make it true.
   b. When a relational operator has two characters such as >= or <= or != there should not be any spaces between them.
   c. In a relational expression with arithmetic operations, arithmetic operations are performed before the relational operations.
   d. A relational expression may compare operands of any data type.
   e. Relational expressions are used to make logical choices in branching control structures.
   f. Relational expressions evaluate to 0 or 1.
   g. Relational expressions are also called conditions.

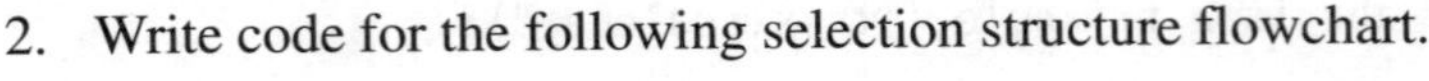

2. Write code for the following selection structure flowchart.

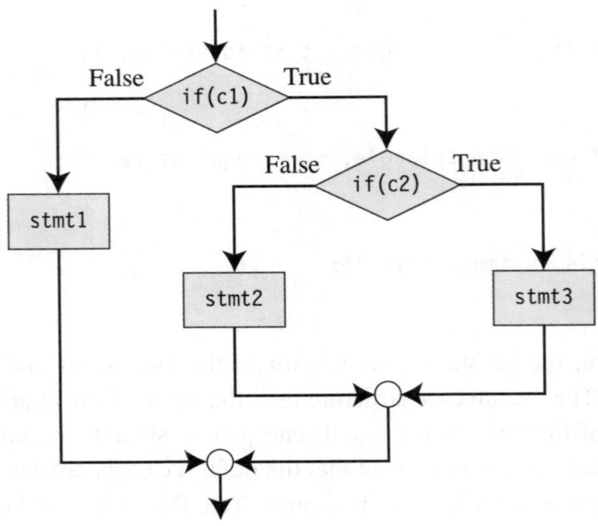

3. Write the flowcharts and the code for the selection structures for the following statements.
   a. If *x* is greater than 25, add 20 to *y*.
   b. If *z* is less than 15, add *x* to *y*.
   c. If *n* is 40, input values to *l*, *m*, and *r*.
   d. If *p* is greater than or equal to *r*, increment *r* by 1.
4. Write the segment of C code for the following:
   a. If the compression stress is greater than 50,000, execute the following code.

```
printf("stress = %8d\n", stress);
printf("This stress is greater 50000\n");
```

   b. If the number of cars sold per month by XYZ Motor Company is greater than 10,000, add a 5% bonus to employees' monthly paychecks.
   c. If the monthly sales of an employee exceeds $50,000, award a 10% bonus, if it exceeds $100,000 award a 15% bonus, if it exceeds $150,000, award a 20% bonus. If it is less than $10,000 there will be no bonus.

5. Write the C code for the following:
   a. The computed roots of a quadratic $ax^2 + bx + c = 0$ are given by the formulas

$$x_1 = \frac{-b + \sqrt{b^2 - 4ac}}{2a} \qquad x_2 = \frac{-b - \sqrt{b^2 - 4ac}}{2a}.$$

   These formulas cannot be used if the value of a is 0, and the answers are complex if the value of $b^2 - 4ac$ is negative. Print the two real roots if they exist; otherwise print appropriate messages.
   b. If the salesman of a Farm Equipment Company sells $100,000 or more, his commission is 25%. If he sells less than $100,000, his commission is 15%. Print the amount of sales and the commission.
   c. The formula for the area of any triangle is:

$$\text{Area} = \sqrt{s(s-a)(s-b)(s-c)}$$

$$\text{Where } s = \frac{a+b+c}{2}.$$

   Given the sides a, b, and c of a triangle, determine whether it is a right triangle. Print the sides and the area. A triangle is a right triangle if $c^2 = a^2 + b^2$ where c is the longest side.

4.3 Repetition Structures

The repetition control structure is used to execute one or more instructions zero or more times. A repetition structure is also called a looping structure. There are two types of loops: iterative loops and conditional loops. The iterative loops, which are controlled by counting, are `for` loops. These call for a block of instructions to be executed a predetermined number of times. The conditional loops, which are controlled by the value of a condition, are `while` and `do while` loops. These call for a block of instructions to be executed repeatedly, as long as the condition is true. The looping structures may be stacked or nested depending on the complexity of the algorithm. In the following sections conditional loops are presented in detail.

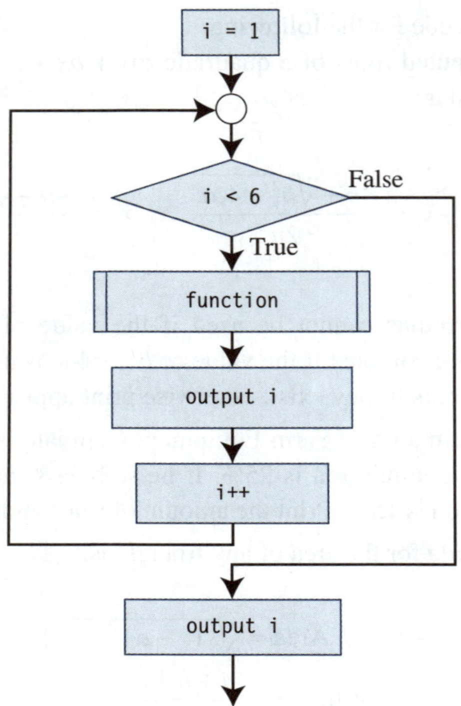

Figure 4.8 Flowchart of a `for` loop

4.3.1 Iterative Loops

Iterative loops, also called counting loops, use the keyword `for` in C. These loop control structures are used to control processing of a known number of data values, to assign index numbers to data or output, or to generate a set of equally spaced numbers.

The flowchart shown in Figure 4.8 might control the numbering of five lines or five pages of output. Or it might control the processing of five data values.

In C, the initialization of the count, the testing of the count, and the increment of the count before it is retested, are all part of the loop header. The C form of this `for` loop is

```
for(i = 1; i < 6; i++)
```

`for` is the keyword and `i` is the loop control variable. The first item specified inside the parentheses `i = 1` initializes the loop variable `i` to a value 1, the second item `i < 6` is a relational expression to control the execution of the loop, as long as the condition is true the loop will continue to execute. The last item `i++` increments the loop variable. In the case of a `for` loop the initialization, relational condition, and the increment of the loop variable are done in one statement. Figure 4.8 shows the flowchart for the loop.

The code corresponding to the flowchart in Figure 4.8 is as follows:

```
for(i = 1; i < 6; i++)
{
    funcall( );
    printf("i = %d\n", i);
}
printf("i = %d\n", i);
```

The output is as follows:

```
i = 1
i = 2
i = 3
i = 4
i = 5
i = 6
```

When the value of `i` is 6 the loop terminates without printing the value 6. It is printed by the output statement following the loop. This is an increment loop where the loop variable `i` is incremented until the loop terminates. But the loop can be a decrement loop where the loop variable is decremented. The following example shows a decrement `for` loop.

```
for(i = 4; i >= 0; i--)
{
    funcall( );
    printf("i = %d\n", i);
}
printf("i = %d\n", i);
```

The output is as follows:

```
i = 4
i = 3
i = 2
i = 1
i = 0
i = -1
```

Notice the loop starts with the value of the loop variable `i` equal to 4 , and the value of the loop variable is decremented by 1 until it is −1 when the repetition condition fails. The index variable may be incremented or decremented by any amount provided the termination condition will occur.

4.3.2 Nested Iterative Loops

The `for` loops may be nested. For example, the printing of 3 sets of 40 values each would be controlled by the nested repetition structures of Figure 4.9. In this example, the indices are output just to show what is happening as the loop is executing.

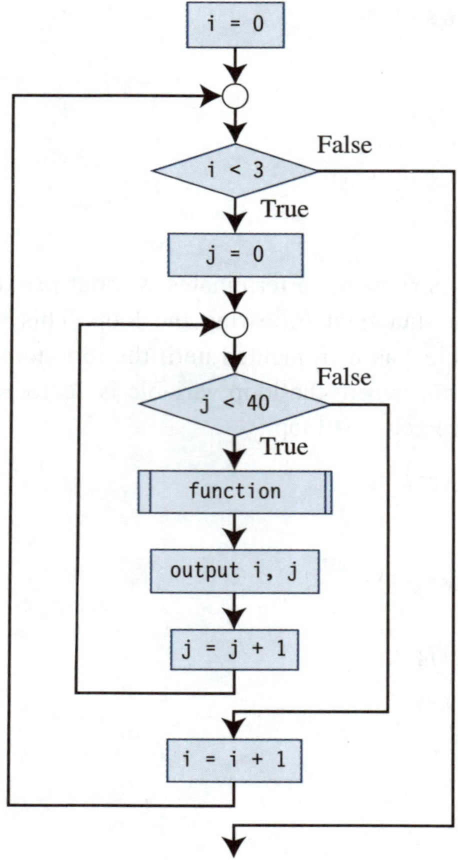

Figure 4.9 Flowchart of nested `for` loops

```
for(i = 0; i < 3; i++)
{
    for(j = 0; j < 40; j++)
    {
        funcall( );
        printf("i = %d    j = %d\n", i, j);
    }
    printf("\n");
}
```

The output is as follows:

```
i = 0    j = 0
i = 0    j = 1
i = 0    j = 2
i = 0    j = 3
.   .   .   .
i = 0    j = 39

i = 1    j = 0
i = 1    j = 1
i = 1    j = 2
i = 1    j = 3
.   .   .   .
i = 1    j = 39

i = 2    j = 0
i = 2    j = 1
i = 2    j = 2
i = 2    j = 3
.   .   .   .
i = 2    j = 39
```

Notice that for every time the `i` loop is executed, the `j` loop is executed 40 times. This is shown in the output. When a loop is nested inside another loop it must be totally nested. In addition, the inner loop variable must be distinct from the outer loop variable. Figure 4.10 shows the proper nesting of `for` loops.

Notice that because the outer loop has loop variable `i`, the inner loops cannot use `i` as the loop control variable. The first inner loop variable is `j`, the loops contained inside this `j` loop cannot use `i` or `j` as loop control variables. The `k` loops

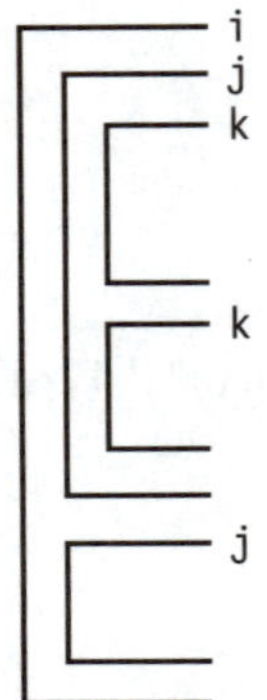

Figure 4.10 Proper nesting of `for` loops

are distinct, because they are not one inside the other. The second `j` loop inside the `i` loop is also distinct, because this `j` loop is not inside the other `j` loop.

> ***Warning:*** Do not reuse an active loop variable.

4.3.3 Conditional Loops

Conditional loops are loops controlled by an expected event. It may be a flag indicating the end of the input data, a value indicating that an approximation is of sufficient accuracy, the finding of a specific data value, or an internal variable reaching a limit. Whatever variable is being tested for the termination condition must have an initial value. The keyword `while` implies that processing is to continue and the termination condition has not been met.

The following code corresponds to the flowchart of the conditional looping structure shown in Figure 4.11. Notice that the entry to the structure is at the top and the exit is at the bottom.

```
float  r, a;
const float PI = 3.141593;


scanf("%f", &r);
while(r != 0)                                      /* while(condition) */
{                                                  /* {                */
     a = PI * r * r;                               /*      stmt 1;     */
     printf ("radius = %f  area = %f\n", r, a);    /*      stmt 2;     */
     scanf("%f",&r); /* enter 0 to terminate */    /*      stmt 3;     */
}                                                  /* }                */
```

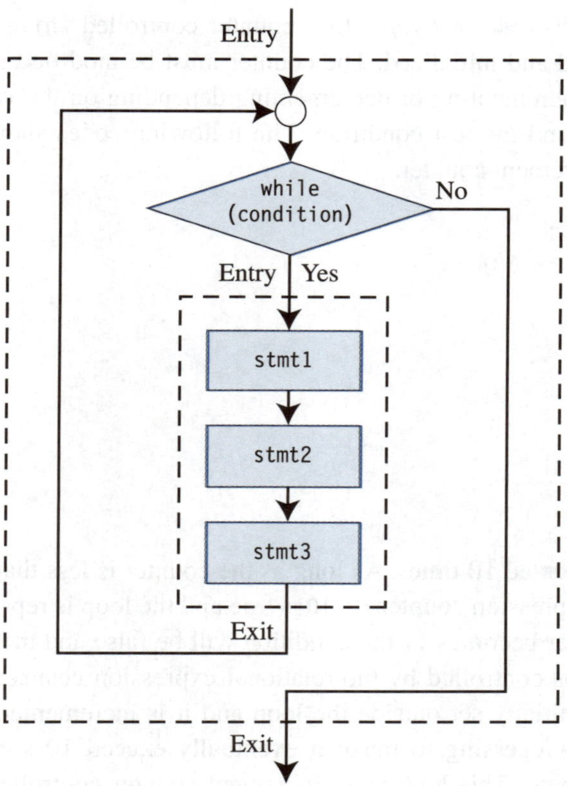

Figure 4.11 Conditional structure

This example shows a loop that terminates when the radius is 0.

> ***Programmer Warning:*** The loop termination condition must be such that the loop will, in fact, terminate.

`While` ***Loops*** A `while` loop is an explicit conditional loop used to process one or more statements repetitively. The loop is controlled by an explicit relational expression. In a `while` loop the condition is tested at the beginning of the loop. If the condition is true the statement or statements belonging to the loop are executed, otherwise the loop terminates. If the condition is false to begin with, the loop may not be executed at all. There are three different ways the `while` loop can be controlled. `While` loops can be controlled by a counter or other computer generated value, by an input value, or by a flag such as an end-of-file.

Counter Controlled **while** *Loop* In a counter controlled `while` loop, a counter must be declared and initialized. The counter must be modified at the end of the loop by either incrementing or decrementing depending on the value set initially for the counter and the test condition. The following codes show the increment counter and decrement counter.

```
int counter = 1;
while( counter <= 10)
{
    stmt 1;
    stmt 2;
      .
    stmt n;
    counter++;
}
```

This loop is executed 10 times. As long as the counter is less than or equal to 10, the relational expression counter `<= 10` is true and the loop is repeatedly executed. When the counter becomes 11 the condition will be false and the loop will terminate. The loop is controlled by the relational expression `counter <= 10`. Notice the counter is initially set outside the loop and it is incremented inside the loop after the other processing to make it eventually exceed 10 so that the loop is forced to terminate. This loop is an increment counter controlled loop. The following code shows the decrement counter controlled loop, where the counter is set to the number of times the loop is to execute, and inside the loop the counter decremented to reach the termination condition.

```
int counter = 10;

while( counter >= 1)
{
    stmt 1;
    stmt 2;
      .
    stmt n;
    counter--;
}
```

Notice that the counter is initially set to 10 outside the loop and the relational expression `counter >= 1` is evaluated to be true while the value of the counter is greater than or equal to 1. The counter is decremented inside the loop to reach the termination value of 0, which makes the relational expression evaluate to false. Counter controlled `while` loops are simple to implement if the number of data values to be processed is known. Note that this `while` loop corresponds more directly to the flowchart than the `for` loop does.

Data Value Controlled **`while`** *Loop* A data value controlled `while` loop is controlled by an input value, which is not part of the data but acts as an end marker. This type of loop requires one input to initiate the loop. The loop starts with one set of data; then after the data is processed, the next value is input before the loop is repeated. When the termination value (also called sentinel value) is read, the loop will terminate. The following example shows a data value controlled `while` loop with 999 as the sentinel value.

```
int  num;
scanf("%d", &num); /*enter 999 to terminate*/
while(num != 999)
{
    stmt 1;
    stmt 2;
     . . .
    stmt n;
    scanf("%d", &num);
}
```

As long as the data values are not equal to 999 the relational expression `num != 999` is true and the loop is executed. When the value 999 is read, the relational expression will be false, the processing is complete, and the loop will terminate. However, if the 999 is part of the data, then processing will terminate too soon.

If the sentinel value is of a data type that does not match the input format then the loop can be controlled by the value returned by the input statement. The following example shows a loop terminated when a character other than a blank, digit, or sign is read.

```
int  num;

while(scanf("%d", &num) > 0)
{
    stmt 1;
    stmt 2;
    . . .
    stmt n;
}
```

Flag Controlled (EOF) `while` Loop The end of a data file is marked by the sentinel value EOF. When the data is read from a data file, the EOF marker can be checked in the `while` statements. The following example shows the use of the EOF marker to terminate the loop.

```
int  num;
    .
    .
while((fscanf(inptr, "%d", &num)) != EOF)
{
    stmt 1;
    stmt 2;
      .
    stmt n;
}
```

Notice that the loop is controlled by the value returned by the input function. The loop is repeated as long as the data is read from the data file. Once the EOF is read the `while` loop terminates. If there is no data in the file, the body of the loop is not executed at all. This is the way to input data if the number of data values contained in the file is not known. It should be included as part of the loop control any time data is read from a file as there may be an error in the data count or the termination sentinel value may be missing. For interactive input, either "ctrl D" or "ctrl Z" sets the EOF condition, depending on the operating system. (Make sure that both the keys are pressed simultaneously.) Also, most compilers will auto-

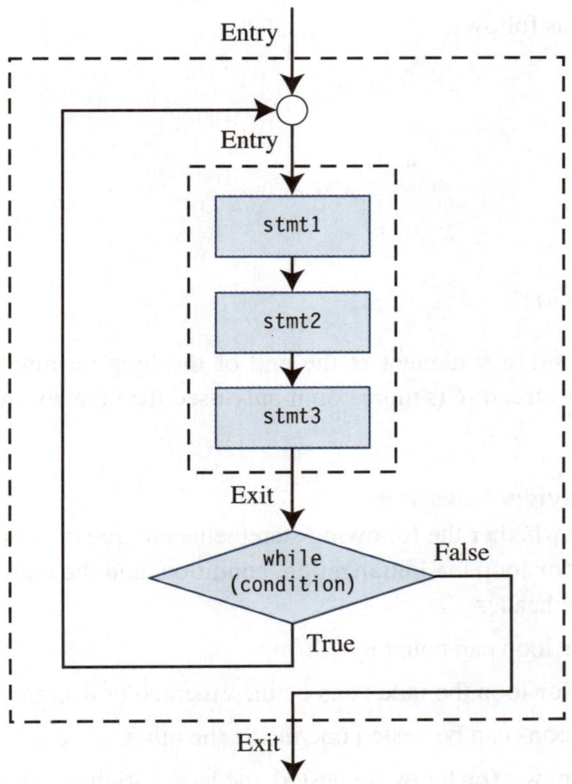

Figure 4.12 Repetition structure

matically set this condition if a new line (enter key) is used as the last entry in the data input file.

`do while` ***Loop*** A `do while` loop is a conditional loop, in which the condition is a relational expression that is tested only at the end of the loop, therefore the loop is executed at least once.

A `do while` loop is shown in Figure 4.12. Notice that the condition is tested at the end of the loop. If the condition is true, control will go back to the beginning of the loop, otherwise the loop terminates. It is guaranteed that the loop is executed at least once.

The code is as follows:

```
do
{
    stmt 1;
    stmt 2;
    stmt 3;
}
while (condition);
```

Notice that the `while` statement at the end of the loop terminates with a semicolon. The `while` structure is more commonly used than the `do while`.

4.3.4 Review Questions

1. Indicate whether the following statements are true or false.
   a. In a `for` loop the initialization, condition, and the increment are all in the header.
   b. A `for` loop can count by 10.
   c. In a `for` loop the index can be incremented or decremented.
   d. `for` loops can be nested one inside the other.
   e. When two `for` loops are nested, the loop variables must be distinct.
   f. In a `for` loop statement, more than one variable can be initialized, by using a comma (`,`) operator.
2. What is the error in each of the following examples?
   a. `for(i = 0; i < 10; i++);`
   b. `for(i = 10; i < 0; i++)`
   c. `for(i = 0; i < 10; i--)`
   d. `for(i = 0; i < 10, i++)`
   e.
   ```
   for(i = 0; i < 10; i++)
       for(i = 0; i < 10; i++)
   ```
   f.
   ```
   for(i = 0; i < 10; i++)
      for(j = 0; j < 8; j++)
         for(i = 0; i < 5; i++)
   ```
3. What is printed in the following simple `for` loops?

a.
```
for(i = 0; i < 4; i++)
    printf("Inside for loop i = %d\n", i);
printf("Outside for loop i = %d\n", i);
```

b.
```
for(i = 5; i > 0; i–)
    printf("i = %d\n", i);
printf("Outside for loop i = %d\n", i);
```

c.
```
for(i = 0, sum = 0; i < 4; i++)
{
    sum += i;
     printf("Inside loop i = %d\n", i);
}
printf("Outside loop i = %d\n", i);
printf("Sum = %d\n", sum);
```

4. What is printed in the following nested for loops?

a.
```
for(i = 0; i < 2; i++)
    for(j = 0; j < 3; j++)
    printf("i = %d   j = %d\n", i, j);
```

b.
```
for(i = 0; i < 2; i++)
{
    printf("i = %d \n", i);
          for(j = 0;  j < 3;  j++)
    {
       printf("   j = %d \n", j);
    }
    printf("Outside j = %d \n", j);
}
printf("Outside i = %d \n", i);
```

4.4 Stacking and Nesting of Control Structures

In complex applications the control flow will have several sequence, branching, and looping structures. These control structures may be stacked and/or nested depending on the program logic. These are presented in the following sections.

4.4.1 Control Structure Stacking

The following examples show the stacking of control structures. In Figure 4.13 the sequence structure is stacked ahead of the selection structure, which in turn, is stacked ahead of the looping structure. The dotted lines show each structure distinctly. All the dotted boxes together form a sequence structure. The control flow is top-down. The control enters at the top and exits at the bottom of each structure. The program logic totally dictates the formation of such a stacked control structure.

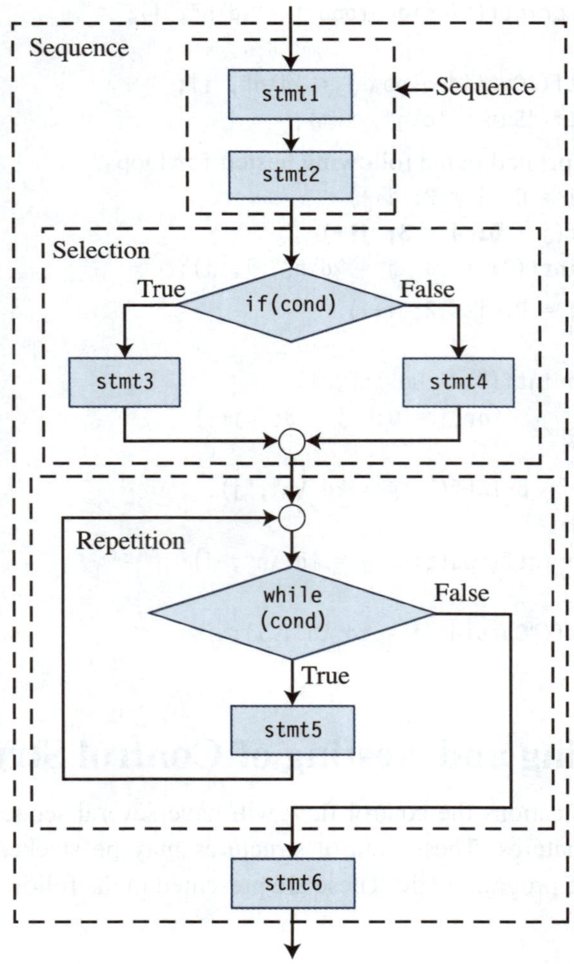

Figure 4.13 Stacked control structure

4.4.2 Nested Control Structures

Control structures can be nested one inside the other. As we have seen, a selection structure may be nested inside another selection structure. A looping structure may be nested inside another looping structure. A selection structure may also be nested inside a looping structure. And a looping structure may also be nested inside a selection structure. The degree of nesting of control structures depends on the program logic and the problem being solved. Many examples have already been given. Structures may be nested or stacked, but they must not overlap.

Nested Selection Structures The following example that finds the largest of three unequal numbers, shows one way of nesting selection structures. Figure 4.14 shows nested selection control structures. There are two selection structures inside a selection structure.

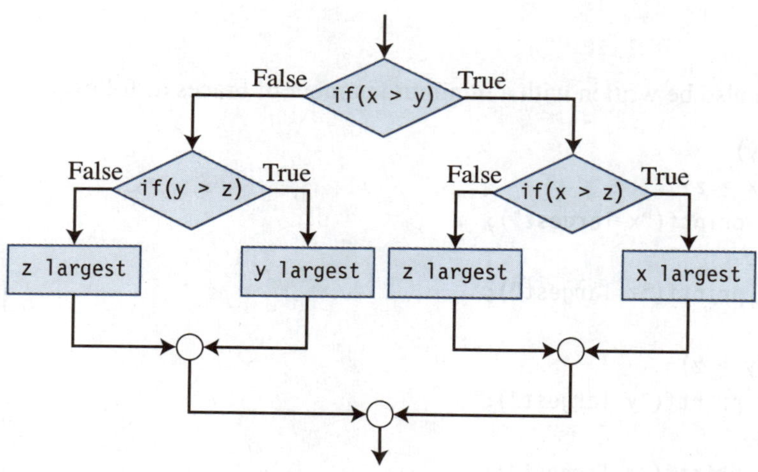

Figure 4.14 Nested selection structure

The code for these structures is as follows:

```
if(x > y)
{
    if (x > z)
    {
       printf("x largest");
    }
```

```
        else
        {
            printf("z largest");
        }
        else
        {
            if(y > z)
            {
                printf("y largest");
            }
            else
            {
                printf("z largest");
            }
        }
}
```

This can also be written with a minimum number of braces as follows:

```
if(x > y)
    if(x > z)
        printf("x largest");
    else
        printf("z largest");
else
    if(y > z)
        printf("y largest");
    else
        printf("z largest");
```

The block of statements following `if` or `else` can either be a single statement, a single selection, a repetition structure, or a sequence of one or more statements enclosed in braces. Essentially, a single selection or repetition structure functions as a statement.

Special Case of a Nested Selection Structure When there are no statements on one branch, as shown in Figure 4.15 of a nested selection structure, the code must indicate this. This may be done either of three ways.

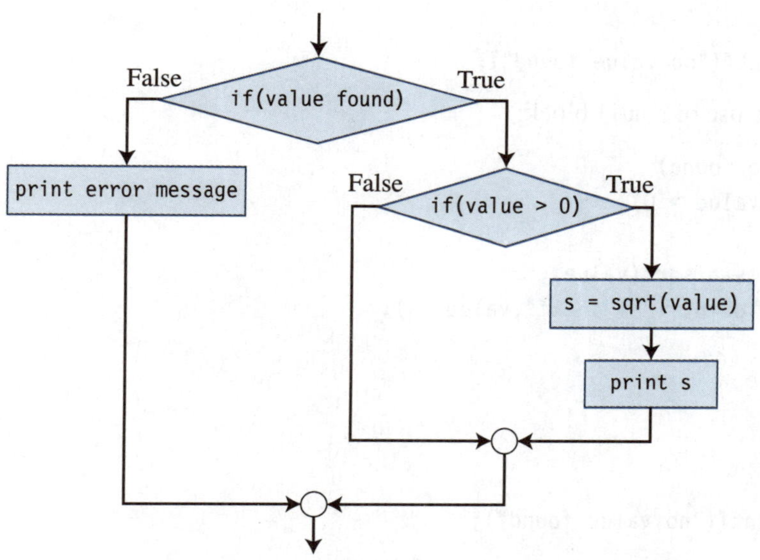

Figure 4.15 Nested selection structure

By the use of braces as follows:

```
if(value found)
{
    if(value > 0)
    {
        s = sqrt(value);
        printf("%f  %f", value ,s);
    }
}
else
    printf("no value found");
```

or by the use of a `null` `else` statement as follows:

```
if(value found)
    if(value > 0)
    {
        s = sqrt(value);
        printf("%f    %f", value, s);
    }
    else;
```

```
else
   printf("no value found");
```

or by the use of a `null` block:

```
if(value found)
   if(value > 0)
   {
      s = sqrt(value);
      printf("%f     %f",value, s);
   }
   else
   {
   }
else
   printf("no value found");
```

In the first version, since the embedded selection structure is an `if...end` not an `if...else...`, the extra set of braces is needed so that the computer knows with which `if` the `else` belongs. In the second and third versions, that problem is avoided by making both of the selection structures of the form `if...else...` even though the inner `else` has no body of code. Notice that either a semicolon after the first `else` or empty braces indicate a `null` branch.

Nested Selection Structure Inside a `while` Loop Assume candidates A and B are running for office. As the precinct results come in, the votes for each candidate are totaled, also the total number of votes are summed. Assume there are 100 precincts.

The C code for the flowchart in Figure 4.16 is as follows:

```
int totvote = 0, atot = 0, btot = 0, a, b;
int num_precincts = 1;              /*precincts counter*/
while(num_precincts <= 100)         /*Total number of precincts*/
{
   printf("Enter the number of votes for a and b");
   printf(" for precinct %d:", num_precincts);
   scanf("%d   %d", &a, &b);
   totvote = totvote + a + b;
   atot  = atot + a;
   btot = btot + b;
   if(atot > btot)
```

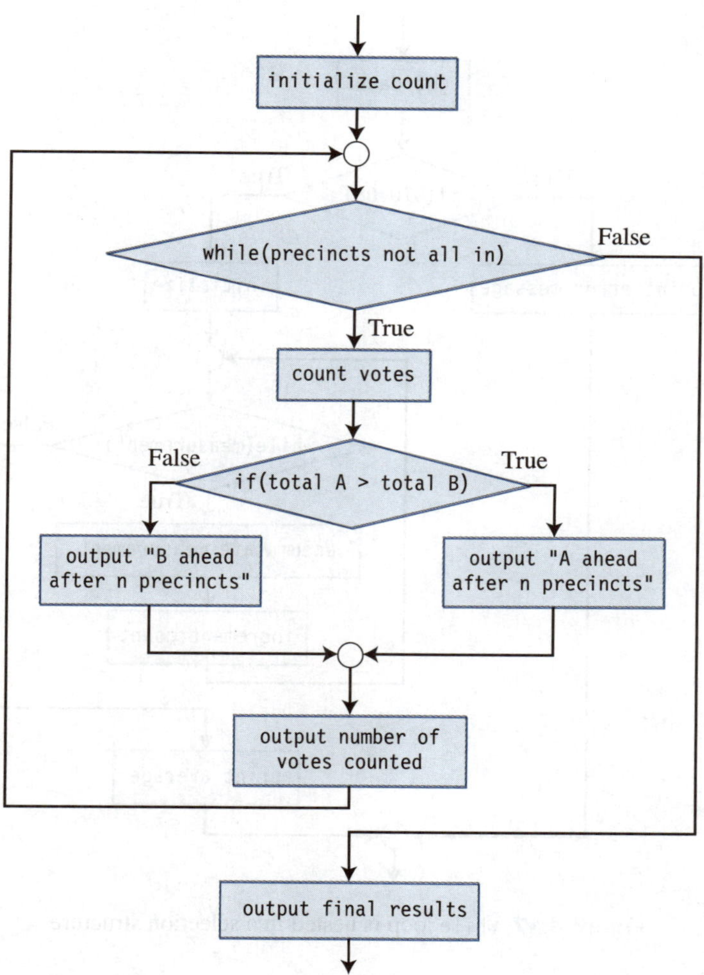

Figure 4.16 Selection nested inside a `while` loop

```
        printf("\na ahead with %d precincts reporting\n",
                num_precincts);
    else
        printf("\nb ahead with %d precincts reporting\n",
                num_precincts);
    num_precincts = num_precincts + 1;
}
printf("\na:  %d votes b:  % d  final count\n" atot, btot);
```

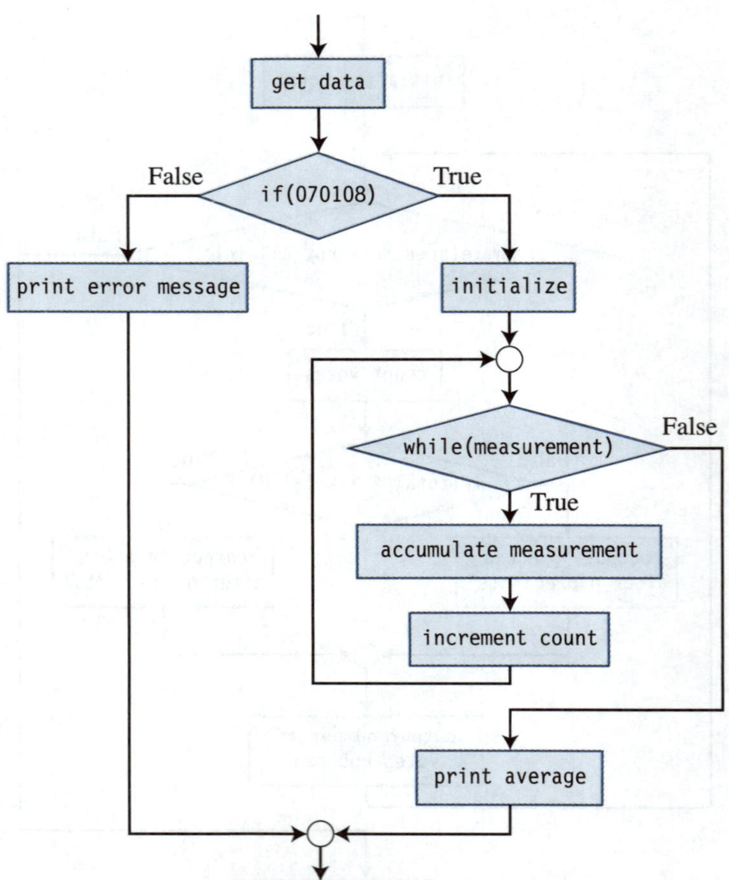

Figure 4.17 `while` loop is nested in a selection structure

`while` *Structure Nested inside a Selection Structure* The C code for the flowchart shown in Figure 4.17 is as follows:

```
fscanf(inptr, "%f", &date_measured);
if(date_measured = 070108)
{
    int count = 0;
    float total = 0;
```

```
    while(fscanf(inptr, "%f", &measurement) != EOF)
    {
        total = total + measurement;
        count = count + 1;
    }
    printf("average of measurements is: %f",
            (total/count));
}
else
    printf("not correct data");
```

Notice that `inptr` is the input file pointer for the data file containing the date and the measurement data.

4.4.3 Review Questions

1. Indicate whether the following statements are true or false.
   a. The nesting and stacking of control structures depends on the logic of the program.
   b. A selection structure may not be nested inside a `do while` structure.
   c. A `while` loop can be nested inside a nested selection structure.
   d. Structures can at most be nested three deep.
2. Draw a flowchart to determine whether three values could represent the sides of a triangle. Determine also whether the triangle is equilateral, isosceles, or scalene, and whether it is a right triangle.

4.5 Sample Problems and Programs

These problems are selected from engineering and science applications. The sample programs show the use of the various control structures. In some of the solutions the input data is interactive, and so identified where it is applicable.

4.5.1 Impedance and Inductance of an Electrical Coil

Problem Write a program to compute the impedance Z and the inductance L of an electrical coil, given the voltage V, current I (amps), resistance R (ohms), and frequency F (cycles/second) for six different circuits.

This example demonstrates the use of repetition controlled by a counter. The coil is in the following AC circuit:

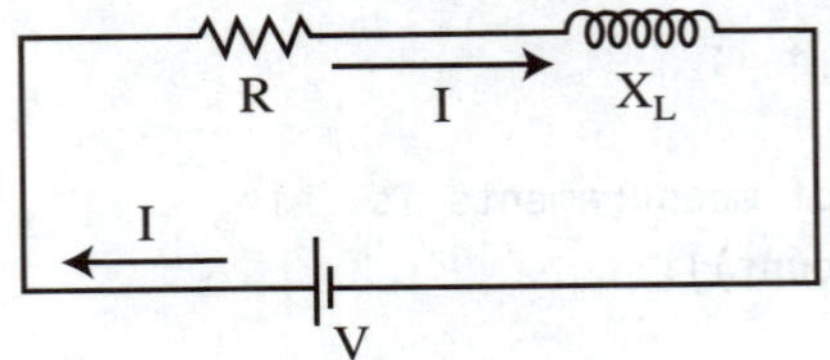

Data Input voltage (volts), current (amps), resistance (ohms), and frequency (cycles/second).

Method

$$Z = \frac{V}{I}$$

$$Z^2 = X_L^2 + R^2$$

$$X_L = \sqrt{Z^2 - R^2}$$

$$X_L = 2\pi f L$$

$$L = \frac{X_L}{2\pi f}$$

where L is the inductance of the coil,
X_L is the reactance, and
Z is the impedance.

Pseudocode

For each of six sets of values
Input voltage, current, resistance, and frequency
Calculate the impedance

$Z \leftarrow V/I$

Calculate the reactance

$X_L = \sqrt{Z^2 - R^2}$

Calculate the inductance

$L = X_L / (2.0 \times \pi \times f)$

Output the voltage, current, inductance, reactance
End for
Stop

Program

```
/*****************************************************/
/*                                                   */
/*  Inductance of a coil in a resistance and reactance */
/*  AC circuit for six sets of values                */
/*                                                   */
/*****************************************************/
/*                                                   */
/*    Constants:                                     */
/*                                                   */
/*        PI = 3.141593                              */
/*                                                   */
/*    Input Variables:                               */
/*                                                   */
/*        voltage      - voltage (volts)             */
/*        current      - current (amps)              */
/*        resistance   - resistance (ohms)           */
/*        frequency    - frequency (cycles/second)   */
/*                                                   */
/*    Computed Variables:                            */
/*                                                   */
/*       impdnc    - impedance                       */
/*       indctn    - inductance                      */
/*       rectnc    - reactance                       */
/*                                                   */
/*    Output Variables                               */
/*                                                   */
/*       impdnc    - impedance                       */
```

```
/*      indctn    -  inductance                           */
/*      rectnc    -  reactance                            */
/*                                                        */
/*********************************************************/

#include <stdio.h>
#include <math.h>
int main( )
{
    int  i;
    float voltage, current, resistance, frequency;
    float impdnc, indctn, rectnc;

    const float  PI = 3.141593;

    /*  input six sets of values  */

    printf("INPUT                          OUTPUT\n");
    for(i = 0; i < 6; i++)
    {
        scanf("%f  %f  %f  %f", &voltage, &current,
               &resistance, &frequency);

        impdnc = voltage / current;
        rectnc = sqrt(impdnc * impdnc - resistance *
                     resistance);
        indctn = rectnc / (2.0 * PI * frequency);

        printf("                            ");
        printf("%5.2f  %5.2f  %5.2f"  %5.2f\n", voltage, current, rectnc,
               indctn);
    }
    return 0;

}
```

Input and Output

```
INPUT                           OUTPUT
120. 12. 8. 50.
                                120.00  12.00   6.00   0.02
250. 14. 7. 50.
                                250.00  14.00  16.43   0.05
150. 16. 9. 50.
                                150.00  16.00  2.62   0.01
100. 10. 5. 50.
                                100.00  10.00   8.66   0.03
220. 12. 8. 50.
                                220.00  12.00  16.50   0.05
300. 19. 9. 50.
                                300.00  19.00  12.97   0.04
```

4.5.2 Altitude of a Projectile

Problem Write a program to determine the maximum height to which a projectile will travel if atmospheric resistance is neglected, for different initial velocities. This example demonstrates the use of repetition controlled by a terminating limit.

Method The mass of the projectile is m, initial velocity is v_0 m/sec, last initial velocity is v_f ft/sec.

From equations of motion:

$$w = mg, \quad \Sigma Fz = maz.$$

Applying these equations for the projectile results in the following equations:

$$-mg = ma_c \text{ gives } a_c = -g$$

Initial conditions: $s_0 = 0 \quad v_0 = v$

Final conditions: $s_f = h \quad v_f = 0$

From Kinematics: $v_f^2 = v_0^2 + 2a_c(s_f - s_0)$

$$0 = v^2 + 2a_c(h - 0)$$

$$2a_c h = -v^2$$

$$h = \frac{-v^2}{2a_c}$$

Data Real values of initial velocity at 50, 100, 150, and 200 ft/sec.
Real value of gravitational acceleration is 32.2 ft/sec².

Pseudocode

```
For each initial velocity
    Height ← − (initial velocity * initial velocity) / (2.0 * acceleration)
    Output the initial velocity and height
End for
Stop
```

Program

```
/********************************************************/
/*                                                      */
/*    Determination of the Maximum Height of a          */
/*    Projectile Fired with an Initial Velocity         */
/*                                                      */
/********************************************************/
/*                                                      */
/*  Constants:                                          */
/*    GRAV_ACCEL = 32.2 ft/sec² gravitational           */
/*               - acceleration                         */
/*                                                      */
/*  Input Variables:                                    */
/*                                                      */
/*    initvel  -  initial velocity of firing ft/sec²    */
/*                                                      */
/*  Computed Variables:                                 */
```

```
/*    height   -  height the projectile reaches             */
/*                                                          */
/*  Output Variables:                                       */
/*                                                          */
/*    initvel  -  initial velocity of firing ft/sec²        */
/*    height   -  height the projectile reaches             */
/*                                                          */
/**********************************************************/

#include <stdio.h>

int main( )
{
    const float GRAV_ACCEL = 32.2;
    float initvel,height;

    printf("Initial Velocity    Height\n\n");
    initvel = 50;
    while(initvel <= 200)
    {
        height = - (initvel * initvel) /
                  (2.0 * GRAV_ACCEL);
        printf("%6.2f             %8.2f\n",
               initvel, -1.0 * height);
        initvel += 50;
    }
    return 0;
}
```

Output

```
  Initial Velocity    Height
     50.00             38.82
    100.00            155.28
    150.00            349.38
    200.00            621.12
```

4.5.3 Shear Stress of a Metallic Member

Problem Write a program to compute and print a table of torsion shear stresses for circular rods having various torsion loads at various offsets. This example demonstrates the use of nested repetitions.

Data

diameter: 5 and 6 inches
load: 1000 and 12,000 pounds
offset: 10, 15, and 20

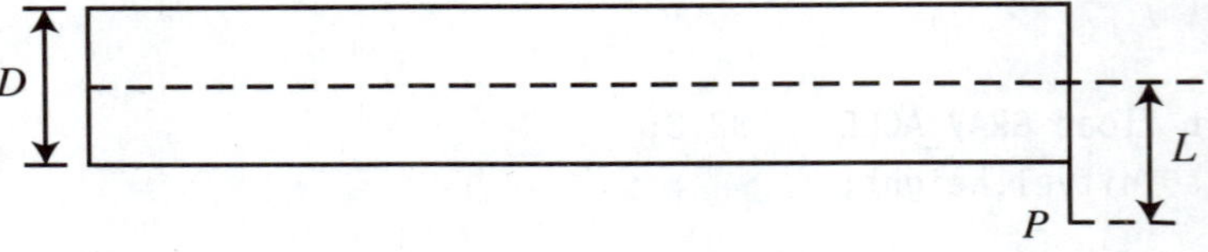

Method

Let D = diameter of the rod
P = torsion load in pounds
L = offset

The torsion shear stress is given by the formula

$$T_s = \frac{16PL}{\pi D^3}$$

Pseudocode

```
For each diameter of the rod
  Output the diameter of the rod
  For each load
    Output the load
    For each offset
      Shear stress ← (16 × Torsion load × Length offset) / (π × diameter × diameter ×
                     diameter)
```

```
      output shear stress
    End for
  End for
End for
Stop
```

Program

```
/******************************************************/
/*                                                    */
/*      Print a Table of Torsion Shear Stress         */
/*                                                    */
/******************************************************/
/*                                                    */
/*   Constants:                                       */
/*                                                    */
/*     PI = 3.141593                                  */
/*                                                    */
/*   Input Variables:                                 */
/*                                                    */
/*     diameter      -  diameter of rod               */
/*     torsion_load  -  torsion load                  */
/*                      applied (pounds)              */
/*     length_offset -  load offset length (inches)   */
/*                                                    */
/*   Computed Variables:                              */
/*                                                    */
/*     shear_stress - shear stress                    */
/*                    pounds/square inch              */
/*                                                    */
/*   Output Variables:                                */
/*                                                    */
/*     shear_stress - shear stress                    */
/*                    pounds/square inch              */
/*                                                    */
/******************************************************/
```

```
#include <stdio.h>

int main( )
{
    const float  PI = 3.141593;
    int  diameter, torsion_load, length_offset;
    float shear_stress;
    int page = 0;

    for(diameter = 5; diameter < 7; diameter++)
    {
        page = page + 1;
        printf("                                                ");
        printf("                                         %d\n", page);
        printf("\n                                 Diameter of Rod: %d\n",
                diameter);
        printf("                                   __________________ \n");

        for(torsion_load = 10000; torsion_load <= 12000;
            torsion_load += 2000)
        {
            printf("\nTorsion load is: %d\n", torsion_load);
            printf("\n    Length Offset                      Torsion");
            printf(" Shear Stress\n");
            printf("     ________________                ______");
            printf("_______________\n");

             /*  computation of torsion shear stress */

            for(length_offset = 10; length_offset <= 20;
                length_offset += 5)
            {
                shear_stress = (16.0 * torsion_load *
                length_offset) /( PI * diameter * diameter
                * diameter);
                printf("      %d", length_offset);
                printf("                                   %8.2f\n",
                       shear_stress);
            }
```

```
        }
    }

    return 0;

}
```

Output

1

```
                     Diameter of Rod: 5

Torsion Load is: 10000

    Length Offset              Torsion Shear Stress
         10                         4074.37
         15                         6111.55
         20                         8148.73

Torsion Load is: 12000

    Length Offset              Torsion Shear Stress
         10                         4889.24
         15                         7333.86
         20                         9778.48
```

2

```
                     Diameter of Rod: 6

Torsion Load is: 10000

    Length Offset              Torsion Shear Stress
         10                         2357.85
         15                         3536.78
         20                         4715.70
```

```
Torsion Load is: 12000

       Length Offset                Torsion Shear Stress
            10                            2829.42
            15                            4244.13
            20                            5658.84
```

4.5.4 Table of Periods of a Pendulum

Problem Write a program to compute the periods of a simple pendulum for arm lengths starting at 12 inches and reaching a period of less than or equal to 3.45. This program uses a repetition controlled by a terminating limit.

Data The arm length L in feet varies from 1 to n.

Method The formula to compute the period is

$$T = 2\pi\sqrt{\frac{L}{g}}$$

where $g = 32.2$ ft/sec2.

T is the period of the pendulum in seconds to be computed.
L is the arm length of the pendulum in feet.

Pseudocode

```
L ← 1
Calculate pendulum period
While period ≤ 3.45
   Calculate pendulum period
   Output length and period
   L = L + 1
End while
Stop
```

Program

```
/*******************************************************/
/*                                                     */
/*   Print a Table of Pendulum Length and Period       */
/*                                                     */
/*******************************************************/
/*                                                     */
/*   Constants:                                        */
/*                                                     */
/*       PI = 3.141593                                 */
/*       GRAVITY = 32.2 ft/sec *sec                    */
/*                                                     */
/*   Input variables                                   */
/*                                                     */
/*       length - length of pendulum arm (feet)        */
/*                                                     */
/*   Computed Variables:                               */
/*                                                     */
/*       period   - period of pendulum (seconds)       */
/*       constant - 2PI                                */
/*                                                     */
/*   Output Variables:                                 */
/*                                                     */
/*       period   - period of pendulum (seconds)       */
/*                                                     */
/*******************************************************/

#include <stdio.h>
#include <math.h>

int main( )
{
    FILE *fptrout;
    const float GRAVITY = 32.2;
    const float PI = 3.141593;
```

```
    float length, period, constant;

    fptrout = fopen("pend.dat", "w");

    constant = 2.0 * PI;
    length = 1.0;
    period = constant * sqrt(length / GRAVITY);
    fprintf(fptrout, "                    OUTPUT\n");
    fprintf(fptrout, "         length              ");
    fprintf(fptrout, "period\n");
    fprintf(fptrout, "         ______              ");
    fprintf(fptrout, "______\n");

    while(period <= 3.45)
    {
        fprintf(fptrout,"        %2.0f.                 %5.2f\n",
                length, period);
        length += 1.0;
        period = constant * sqrt(length / GRAVITY);
    }

    return 0;
}
```

```
               OUTPUT
     Length              period
        1.                1.11
        2.                1.57
        3.                1.92
        4.                2.21
        5.                2.48
        6.                2.71
        7.                2.93
        8.                3.13
        9.                3.32
```

4.5.5 Compression Stress and Strain in Steel Rods

Problem Write a program to compute the stress and strain in steel rods of different diameters D varying from 2 inches to 5 inches with increments of 1.0 subject to compression load P varying from 50,000 to 100,000 pounds per square inch in increments of 25,000. The modulus of elasticity Es for steel is 30×10^6 lb/in^2. This program uses nested iterative repetition loops and writes the output to a file.

Method The compression stress is computed from the formula:

$$\sigma_C = \frac{P}{\text{area}}.$$

Where σ_c = compression stress in lb/in^2

P = compression load

area = cross-sectional area of steel rods given by the formula

$$\frac{\pi d^2}{4}$$

d = the diameter of the steel rod.

The compression strain is computed from the formula:

$$\varepsilon = \frac{\sigma_c}{Es}$$

Where σ_c = compression stress in lbs/in^2

ε = the strain (nondimensional)

Es = the modulus of elasticity of steel in lb/in^2.

Data Real values of load of 50,000, 75,000, and 100,000 pounds.

Real values of diameter 2.0, 3.0, 4.0, and 5.0 inches.

Pseudocode

```
For each load
  Output the load with label
  For each diameter
    area ← (3.141593 * d * d) / 4.0
    stress ← p / area
    strain ← stress / Es

    output the diameter, stress, strain
  End for
End for
Stop
```

Program

```
/**********************************************************/
/*                                                        */
/*    Stress and Strain in Steel Rods under               */
/*          Compression Loading                           */
/*                                                        */
/**********************************************************/
/*                                                        */
/*    Constants:                                          */
/*                                                        */
/*        PI = 3.141593                                   */
/*                                                        */
/*        ES = 30 x 10⁶(lb/in²)                           */
/*                                                        */
/*    Input variables                                     */
/*                                                        */
/*        load     - compression load (pounds)            */
/*        diameter - diameter of steel rods(inches)       */
/*                                                        */
/*    Working Variables:                                  */
/*                                                        */
/*        area     - cross sectional area (sq-in)         */
```

```
/*                                                             */
/*    Computed Variables:                                      */
/*                                                             */
/*        stress   - compression stress (lb/in²)              */
/*        strain   - nondimensional                            */
/*                                                             */
/*    Output Variables:                                        */
/*                                                             */
/*        load     - compression load (pounds)                 */
/*        diameter - diameter of steel rods(inches)            */
/*        stress   - compression stress (lb/in²)              */
/*        strain   - nondimensional                            */
/*                                                             */
/***************************************************************/

#include <stdio.h>
FILE  *outptr;

int main( )
{
    const  float PI = 3.141593;
    const  float ES = 30000000;
    float  load, diameter, area, stress, strain;

    outptr = fopen("fileout.dat", "w");

    for(load = 50000; load <= 100000; load += 25000)
    {
        fprintf(outptr,"\nCompression Load = %10.2f\n\n",
               load);
        fprintf(outptr,"Diameter          Stress           Strain\n");
        for(diameter = 2.0; diameter <= 5.0; diameter += 1.0)
        {
            area = (PI * diameter * diameter) / 4.0;
            stress = load / area;
            strain = stress / ES;
            fprintf(outptr,"%5.2f             %8.2f         %8.6f\n",
                  diameter, stress, strain);
```

```
            }
        }
        fprintf(outptr, "\n");
        return 0;
}
```

Output Data File `"fileout.dat"`

```
Compression Load =    50000.00

Diameter              Stress           Strain
  2.0               15915.49          0.000531
  3.0                7073.55          0.000236
  4.0                3978.87          0.000133
  5.0                2546.48          0.000085

Compression Load =    75000.00

Diameter              Stress           Strain
  2.0               23873.24          0.000796
  3.0               10610.33          0.000354
  4.0                5968.31          0.000199
  5.0                3819.72          0.000127

Compression Load =   100000.00

Diameter              Stress           Strain
  2.0               31830.98          0.001061
  3.0               14147.10          0.000472
  4.0                7957.75          0.000265
  5.0                5092.96          0.000170
```

4.5.6 Types of Triangles

Problem Write a program to determine whether, for each set of integers in a file, they can be lengths of the sides of a triangle. If so, determine whether it is a scalene triangle and if it is a scalene triangle determine whether it is a right triangle. This example demonstrates the use of nested selection structures, `while` loops, and also file input and output.

Method Given the sides of the triangle *a*, *b*, and *c*, determine if *a*, *b*, and *c* form a triangle by comparing them to make sure that the sum of any two sides is larger than the third side. If the sides form a triangle, determine whether the triangle is scalene by checking whether all the lengths are different. If it is scalene then determine whether the triangle is a right triangle by determining whether the square of the hypotenuse equals the sum of the squares of the other two sides. The logic for this method is demonstrated by the flowchart in Figure 4.18.

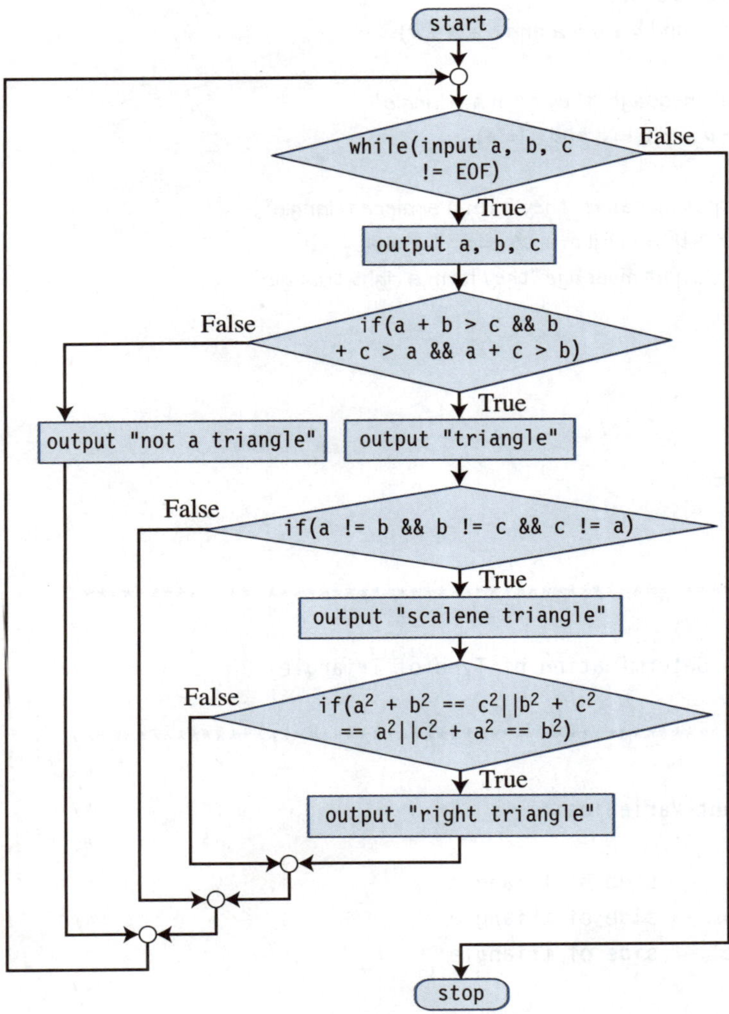

Figure 4.18 Flowchart for triangles

Data Sets of integer numbers 3, 4, 5, etc.

Pseudocode

```
For each set of data in a file
{
  Input sides a, b, c
  Output sides a, b, c
  If(a + b > c and b + c > a and c + a > b)
  {
    Output message "they form a triangle"
    If(a != b and b != c and c != a)
    {
      Output message "they form a scalene triangle"
      If(a² + b² == c² || b² + c² == a² || c² + a² == b²)
          Output message "they form a right triangle"
    }
  }
}
End for
Stop
```

Program

```
/**********************************************************/
/*                                                        */
/*        Determination of Type of Triangle               */
/*                                                        */
/**********************************************************/
/*                                                        */
/*    Input Variables:                                    */
/*                                                        */
/*      a  -  side of triangle                            */
/*      b  -  side of triangle                            */
/*      c  -  side of triangle                            */
/*                                                        */
/*    Output Messages:                                    */
```

```
/*          This is a triangle                            */
/*          This is not a triangle                        */
/*          This is a scalene triangle                    */
/*          This is a right triangle                      */
/*                                                        */
/*********************************************************/

#include<stdio.h>
FILE  *inptr, *outptr;

int main( )
{
    int  a, b, c;

    inptr = fopen("trianglein.dat", "r");
    outptr = fopen("triangleout.dat", "w");

    while((fscanf(inptr,"%d  %d  %d", &a, &b, &c))
            != EOF)
    {
        fprintf(outptr,"\n%2d  %2d  %2d\n", a, b, c);
        if(a + b > c && b + c > a && c + a > b)
        {
            fprintf(outptr, "This is a triangle\n");
            if(a != b && b != c && c != a)
            {
                fprintf(outptr, "This is a");
                fprintf(outptr," scalene triangle\n");
                if(a * a + b * b == c * c || b * b + c * c
                   == a * a || c * c + a * a == b * b)
                {
                    fprintf(outptr, "This is a");
                    fprintf(outptr," right triangle\n");
                }
            }
        }
```

```
            else
            {
                fprintf(outptr, "This is not a triangle\n");
            }
        }
        return 0;
}
```

Input File "trianglein.dat"

```
10  12  15
 2   3   7
 3   4   5
 6   9   5
 6   6   6
 6   8  10
 7   7   9
```

Output File "triangleout.dat"

```
10  12  15
This is a triangle
This is a scalene triangle

 2   3   7
This is not a triangle

 3   4   5
This is a triangle
This is a scalene triangle
This is a right triangle

 6   9   5
This is a triangle
This is a scalene triangle

 6   6   6
This is a triangle
```

```
 6  8 10
This is a triangle
This is a scalene triangle
This is a right triangle
 7  7  9
This is a triangle
```

Note that the input data was designed to include all possibilities.

Chapter Summary

C has three basic control structures for the control of the execution sequence of program statements. The basic control structures are sequence, selection, and repetition. The sequence structure is a sequence of statements executed one after the other.

Selection Structures

Selection structures use relational expressions called conditions. The relational expressions use relational operators and numeric or character operands. They produce the logical values of either true or false. Based on the logical value, a selection of a statement or a block of statements is made. Logical operators may be used to combine simple conditions to make compound conditions.

- When a single selection is to be made, a single branch `if` control structure is used.
- When two alternatives are available, a two branch `if ... else` control structure is used
- When more than two alternatives are available, an `if ... else if ... else if ... else if ... else` control structure is used.
- There is a special selection structure to select from several predetermined values of the same expression. This is a `switch( )` control structure. A `break` statement is used in the switch control structure to prevent the selection of more than one alternative.
- Selection structures can be nested inside each other.

Repetition Structures

There are several repetition control structures. There are conditional loops and iterative loops. The explicit loops are the `while` loop and the `do while` loop. In a `while` loop the condition is tested in the beginning of the loop, whereas in the `do while` loop the condition is tested at the end of the loop. In a `while` loop if the condition is false the first time, the loop is not executed, whereas in the `do while` loop if the condition fails the first time, the loop has already been executed once. A `while` loop can be controlled by a counter, by a limiting or terminal value, or by a flag. A `do while` loop can be controlled similarly.

Iterative loops are called `for` loops. Repetition structures can be nested inside each other or inside a selection structure. When `for` loops are nested, the loop variables must be distinct.

Control structures can be stacked or they can be nested depending on the logic of the program. Stacked control structures are executed one after the other. Nested control structures are executed in a top-down fashion with the inner structure being exited before the outer structure is exited. Sequence, selection, and repetition structures may be nested inside each other.

Exercises

1. A 3000 pound vehicle traveling on a road at 100 ft/sec requires a force of $F = ma$ ($m = 3000$) to stop, where $a = (v_i^2 - v_o^2) / (2d)$, ($v_o = 100$, $v_i = 0$). Write a program to calculate the retarding force needed to stop the car at distances $d = 20, 30, 40, 50, \ldots, 100$ ft. Output the values of d and F.

2. Write a program to compute the pressure per square inch at the bottom of a reservoir, if the depth of water increases from 50, 60, 70, . . ., 150 feet. The formula for computing the pressure is

$$\text{pressure} = \frac{62.4 \times \text{depth}}{144}$$

$$\text{pressure} = 0.43333333 \times \text{depth}.$$

Print the output in the form of a table as shown.

Depth in feet	**Pressure in psi**
50	21.67

3. Write a program to compute the power loss in a transmission line with a resistance of 0.05 ohms/mile. Compute the power loss if 500 kW of power is transmitted from a power generating station to cities at distances of 20, 30, 40, 50, ...,100 miles at 100 V and 200 V.

   The current i is calculated from:

$$i = \frac{\text{power tranmitted in watts}}{\text{volts transmitted}}.$$

   The total resistance R is computed from the equation:

$$R = r \times \text{miles}$$

   where r is the resistance per mile.

   The power loss is computed from the equation:

$$\text{Power loss} = i^2 \times R.$$

4. Write a program to estimate the shear stress and total angle of twist of a thin walled circular cylinder shown below. A steel tube is .8 ft long and is transmitting a torque of 100, 200, 300,..., 1000 N.m. The material constants are $E = 24 \times 10^{10}$ N/ft^2 and $\nu = 0.25$.

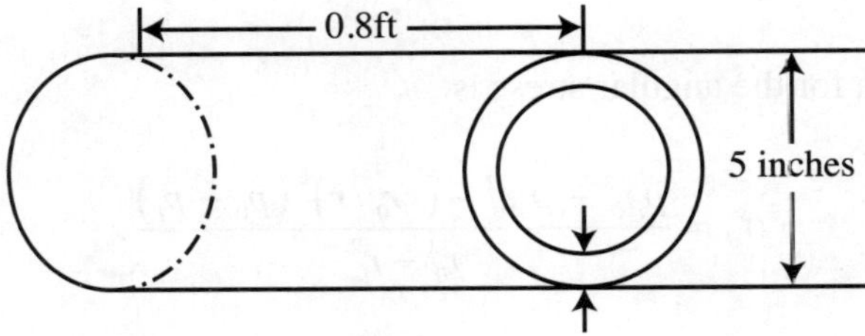

   thickness $t = 0.25$ inches.

   The mean radius $r = (5.0 - 0.25) / 2 = 2.375$ inches.

   The mean area $a_m = \pi r^2$.

   The torsion shear stress is computed from the formula:

$$\tau = \frac{T}{2a_m t}$$

Where T = the torque N.m
a_m = mean area of cross-section
t = the thickness of the circular section

The angle of twist is computed from the formula:

$$\theta = \frac{\pi(1+v)TLr}{Ea_m^2 t}.$$

Where L = the length of the steel member
E = modulus of elasticity
r = the mean radius

5. Write a program to compute the stress distribution in a cylinder with an inner diameter D_i and outer diameter of D_o with inside pressure p_i and the outside pressure p_o.

The formula for the radial stress is

$$\sigma_\tau = \frac{p_i r_i^2 - p_0 r_0^2 + (r_i r_0 / r)^2 (p_0 - p_i)}{r_0^2 - r_i^2}.$$

The formula for the angular stress is

$$\sigma_\theta = \frac{p_i r_i^2 - p_0 r_0^2 - (r_i r_0 / r)^2 (p_0 - p_i)}{r_0^2 - r_i^2}.$$

Vary the inside pressure from 4000 pounds/square inch to 10,000 pounds/square inch in increments of 1000 pounds. Print the stresses in columns as shown. Assume the outside pressure is 0. The radius r varies from r_i to r_0.

Internal Pressure   Radial Stress   Angular Stress

6. Write a program to read measurements from a file and print them 6 per line, numbering the lines, with 10 lines per page, numbering the pages. There should be a title on the first page and column headings on every page. Do not number a line if there are no measurements to print in it. Do not number a page and print column headings if there are no measurements to print on it.

7. Write a program to print all of the numbers from a file that should contain only positive measurements. Print appropriate error messages if the file header is not 070503 followed by an integer that tells how many measurements are in the file, or if the measurements are not all positive.

CHAPTER 5

Modular Design and Functions

Objective

To divide and subdivide the problem into logical modules. The modules are written in C as manageable and meaningful units called functions.

The concept of modular programming was introduced in Chapters 1 and 2. Large and complex engineering and scientific problems require many lines of code to solve them. It is difficult for a programmer to write the code of a long program as a single unit or to debug and maintain a long program as a single unit. It is easier to find logic and execution errors in short modules. When a group of programmers works on a program, they work on separate modules, which are then integrated. As we have seen, a program can be modularized by using design tools such as hierarchy charts, flowcharts, pseudocode, and control structures to implement a program as functional modules. C has the built-in capability for modules to be coded as independent functions. These functions are logical pieces of code, which can be compiled, executed, and tested separately for their correctness and functionality. Once functions are written and tested they can be integrated incrementally into an existing program.

5.1 Introduction to Modular Programming

Present day projects in engineering and science are too large and complex to implement as single large programs. First of all it is difficult to analyze the problem as a whole. The problem should be divided into smaller problems along logical lines and the smaller problems analyzed in order to understand the big picture of the entire problem. The project can be easily managed if it is divided into specific tasks and further divided into subtasks that can be easily understood and programmed. Also, computations that are repeated in several places in a program can be identified as subtasks. Tasks and subtasks are represented as boxes in hierarchy charts at the solution design step of program development. Tasks and subtasks are defined as the functional units of the program. A functional unit is one that does a particular computation or moves specific data. Modular programs have the following advantages:

- Smaller modules are easier to understand and maintain.
- Separate modules can be tested independently before the entire program is written and executed.
- Different programmers can write different modules.
- Modules can be modified or replaced by new modules to tune the program to the needs of a new application without changing the rest of the program.
- Repeated code can be replaced by a function call.
- A modularized program is simpler and easier to read, understand, and maintain because each module only does one specific task.
- Independent modules are modules that interface with the rest of the program only through data that is explicitly passed to them or returned from them. Independent modules are easier to debug.

Programming hint: Design a program so that the modules are independent.

5.1.1 Design of Modular Programs

In modular design the top module implements the functional description of the program. For example to design a circular reinforced concrete tank of diameter (d) and height (h) with the wall thickness (t), define the top module as:

Design a circular reinforced concrete water tank.

The design can be decomposed into steps that are functional modules:

- Obtain the capacity of the water tank in cubic feet
- Compute the dimensions based on the assumption that the height (h) of the tank is twice the diameter (d) of the tank
- Estimate the quantity of materials
- Estimate the cost
- Finish the design

The materials can be further decomposed into two modules:

- Steel
- Concrete

The concrete can be further decomposed into two more modules:

- Cement
- Sand

The cost can be decomposed into two modules:

- Materials cost
- Labor cost

The relationship between various components and their instructions is shown diagrammatically in Figure 5.1. The hierarchical nature of the diagram in Figure 5.1 shows the generality of the modules at higher levels and the greater details in the modules at the lower levels. Notice that the general module that computes materials is further divided into two modules, steel and concrete, and the module concrete is further divided into detailed instructions in modules cement and sand. Also the module cost is divided into more detailed instructions: materials cost and labor cost.

At this stage it is possible to determine what information each module needs from the module above it, and what information each module can provide to the one above it. Each module can also be categorized as computational, input, or output. Table 5.1 shows the data flow between modules and the type of each module for the modules of Figure 5.1.

From the table it becomes clear that module 3.2 must calculate the amount of concrete needed before calling on module 3.2.1 and 3.2.2 to calculate the amount of cement and sand. Also, module 4.1 must have a way to look up the costs of materials and module 4.2 must have a formula for estimating the amount of labor involved and information on current wages.

There are two approaches commonly used in the implementation of modular programs. The *top-down* approach would be to start at the top of the diagram and

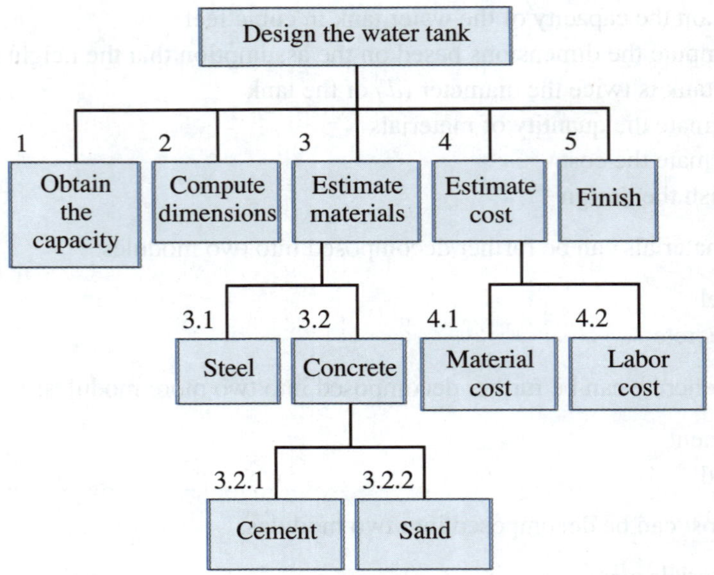

Figure 5.1 Structure chart for the design of a water tank

Table 5.1 Flow of Data Between Modules

Module	Type	Needs to Know	Provides
1	input	——	capacity of tank
2	computation	capacity of tank	dimensions of tank
3	computation	dimensions of tank	estimate of materials
4	computation	estimate of materials	estimate of cost
5	output	estimate of cost	——
3.1	computation	dimensions of tank	estimate of steel
3.2	computation	dimensions of tank	estimate of concrete
4.1	computation	estimate of materials	cost of materials
4.2	computation	estimate of materials	cost of labor
3.2.1	computation	estimate of concrete	estimate of cement
3.2.2	computation	estimate of concrete	estimate of sand

implement the main module first, then those on the next level and so forth, leaving the details to last. The *bottom-up* approach would be to start with little details such as computing the amount of cement. When the modules to estimate the amount of cement and sand had been written, the programmer would write their parent module that estimates the amount of concrete. Programming would start at the lowest level and move up the chart.

The advantage of top-down programming is that it focuses on analyzing the overall problem correctly, leaving the details until later. One disadvantage is that in order to test and debug a higher level module, it is necessary to write dummy versions of the functions it calls. Another disadvantage is the assumption that the problem is solvable when that is not known until the lower modules containing the computations have been implemented.

The advantage of bottom-up programming is that the little sticky details are worked out first before the whole puzzle is put together. The disadvantage is that it is necessary to write a dummy version of the calling program, called a driver, in order to test and debug each module.

The modular design process consists of the following steps:

- Define the problem clearly without any ambiguities.
- Select the simplest and most efficient solution algorithm.
- Identify the major tasks and subtasks to be performed to as many levels as seems necessary.
- Draw the structure chart to show the relationship between different tasks and subtasks.
- Determine what data each module needs and what result it provides.
- Draw the flowcharts to show the logic involved in each module.
- Review the design for accuracy and completeness of the specifications and, if necessary, revise the design.

Each module shown in the structure chart may be implemented by a control structure or function, depending on its complexity.

After dividing a problem into functional modules, the programmer should:

- Identify the way the data values are obtained and stored.
- Identify the formulas and equations to process the data.
- Identify any processing and formatting to output the results.
- Design the flow of data between modules.

A program normally is divided into three parts as follows:

- Data input—from a standard input device or file input from a data file
- Processing—computations
- Data output—to a standard output device such as a monitor or file output to a data file

At the same time the program is designed, the programmer should design input data to test it. If the input data consists of distinct categories of information, input should occur within the modules that need the information. For instance in the previous example, only module 2 needs to know the capacity of the tank; only module 3.2.1 needs information on various types of cement; only module 4.1 needs a catalog of supply costs; and only module 4.2 needs information on prevailing wages. This information can be built into the program. However, if the program is to be used over a period of time, this information will change, so it is better to treat it as external input to specific modules.

5.1.2 Functional Modules in C

C has the instructions necessary for writing modular programs. In C, every program is a hierarchy of functions. The top-level module called `main()` is a function. Data may be explicitly passed from a calling function to a lower level function through the argument/parameter list. This is a list of variables and addresses enclosed in parentheses following the name of the function. For example `sqrt(x)` calls a function from the mathematics library, passing one value to it through the argument list `(x)`. Inside the library function, `(x)` is called the parameter list. Data may also be passed from a lower level function back to the function calling it. A function in C may return a single value to the calling program through a `return` statement, or it may return several values to the calling program through addresses in the argument/parameter list. The `sqrt()` library function returns a single value, while the `scanf()` library function may return several values. If data is being returned through the argument/parameter list, the `return` statement can be used to return a status code or, optionally, it need not return a value. The details of the transfer of data between functions will be discussed in the following sections of this chapter.

As an example of the difference between these two ways to transfer data, consider a function `largest(x, y, z)` that determines the largest of three values. The three values must be passed to the function from the calling routine. There is only one value to return, so it should be returned to the calling routine through a `return` statement. However, a function that determines the largest and smallest of a set of three values has to return two values. This would be done through two addresses in the argument/parameter list of the calling and the called functions, for example `minmax(x, y, z, &max, &min)`.

A function that returns a single value through its `return` statement is called a pure function. A function that returns values through its argument/parameter list is sometimes called a procedure or subroutine in other languages, but in C it is also called a function.

As another example, consider a function to find, input, and validate a set of data. A set of values cannot be returned through the `return` statement, so they would be returned through the argument/parameter list, while the `return` statement would be used to indicate whether the input is successful. The `scanf()` function and other standard input functions do exactly that. A standard output function such as `printf()` is a pure function in that it does not return values through its parameters, but returns a value through its `return` statement, which indicates whether output has been successful.

In C, pure functions and subroutine-type functions can be written to replace frequently repeated code in a large program, provided that the repeated code meets the requirements of a functional module: entry at the top, exit at the bottom, and carries out a single task.

The advantage of using functions in modular programs is that any change made in a specific function that does not affect the argument/parameter list, is effectively isolated to that function. This prevents unwanted and hard-to-detect side effects. Only the function modified needs to be recompiled. Separately compiled, debugged, and recompiled functions are linked together by the computer to produce an executable program.

5.1.3 Review Questions

1. Indicate whether the following statements are true or false.
   a. Modular programming is a methodology to understand and implement solutions to complex problems.
   b. In the modular approach a large problem is divided into input, calculation, and output.
   c. A subproblem is simply a specific task performed in a program.

   d. In C, subproblems can be represented as functions.
   e. In C, subproblems cannot be represented as control structures.
   f. Modules at the same level can pass data back and forth.
2. What does the top module in a structure chart represent?
3. What is the relationship between the modules at the same level?
4. What is the relationship between modules at a lower level and the modules above them?
5. What is a modular program?
6. What is a pure function in C?
7. What is a subroutine-like function in C?

5.2 Functions

A function is a separate unit of a C program that has a prototype and an implementation containing a header with a block of executable code. A function is written to perform a specific task. In C the execution of the program always starts at the beginning of a function called `main`. The `main` function is a special function in that its name is a reserved word and it is called by the operating system. It is also called a driver function in that it controls the rest of the processing. In C when the execution of a `main` function is successfully completed, the program is complete and processing is terminated.

5.2.1 Function Declaration

In C every programmer function must be declared except `main`. The declaration of a function is called a function prototype. The terms "function declaration" and "function prototype" are used interchangeably. The function prototype indicates the return data type, the function name, and in parentheses, the data types of the parameters. These must match the data types of the arguments in the function call. The names of the parameters in the function prototype are optional. Names are specified only for documentation. The general form of a function prototype is as follows:

return-data-type function-name(list of parameter data-types);

An example written in C code is as follows:

```
int funcsort(int, float, int, double, char);
```

where return-data-type is `int`
function-name is `funcsort`
parameter-data types are `int, float, int, double, char`

A prototype must end with a semicolon.

If a function returns a value through a `return` statement, the data type of the value returned by the function must be specified as the first item in the prototype.

If the return type is not specified as the first item in the prototype the return-data-type defaults to `int`.

The following prototypes are equivalent:

```
funcsort(int, float, int, double, char);
```

and

```
int funcsort(int, float, int, double, char);
```

> *Programming Hint:* Do not depend on a default `return` data type. Always specify the `return` data type. If there is no return data type specify `void`.

If a function does not return any value through a `return` statement the return-data-type must be specified as `void`. This will only happen with functions that cannot fail and do not need to return either a value or a status flag.

The following statement declares a function that does not return a value through a `return` statement.

```
void funcsort(int, float, char, double);
```

If there is a possibility of error in the function, declare the function to be of type `int` rather than `void` so that an error code can be returned.

A function name can be any valid identifier. Parameters in the prototype must specify the data types of the arguments passed by the calling function to the function being declared. The order and the number of parameters must match the order and number of arguments passed to the function. In the function prototypes, variable names may be specified, but are optional. If one chooses to specify names, they do not have to be the same names as the arguments, but can be dummy names. These names should prompt the programmer as to the meaning of the arguments.

The following prototype shows the specification of dummy variable names:

```
int funcsort(int input_int, float length_in_ft, double height_in_ft,
                   char site_id);
```

The variable names `input_int`, `length_in_ft`, `height_in_ft`, and `site_id` are dummy names and are optional. The specification of names in the prototype is one way to document function code.

It is standard practice to declare functions at the beginning of the program and implement them after the main function.

5.2.2 Function Definition

Every nonlibrary function must be implemented. A function implementation starts with a function header followed by the function body. The function body consists of statements enclosed between left and right braces. The general form of the function header is as follows:

return-data-type function-name(list of parameters with their data types)

An example written in C code is as follows:

```
int  funcsort(int id_num, float cost, double quantity, char
order_status)
```

A function header must match the function prototype as follows:

- The return-data-type must match
- The function-name must match
- The number, data types, and order of the parameters must match

The only difference is that

- In a prototype there is no need to specify the names of the parameters, only their data types. Specification of names is optional, and they are dummy names, whereas in a function header, in addition to the specification of data types, the local names of the variables must be specified. This declares and defines the parameter variables.
- A prototype ends with a semicolon, whereas a function header does not end with a semicolon as it is followed by the function body in braces.
- A prototype does not define any variables, whereas a function header declares local names for the parameter variables.

The following example shows a function header and function body:

```
int funcsort(int var1, float var2, double var3, char var4)
{
    int result;

    result = ...;

    return result;
}
```

Notice that the return-data-type is `int`, the function-name is `funcsort`, the function parameters are `var1`, `var2`, `var3`, and `var4`. The variables `var1`, `var2`, `var3`, and `var4` are declared in the function header, are initialized by the calling routine at the time of the call, and must not be declared again. This function returns an integer value computed within the function `funcsort` for the variable `result`. The type of this variable matches the return data type.

A Simple Function The simplest function one can write in C is a function that does not return any value through the return statement and does not have any arguments or parameters. Such functions can be used to output character string constants, such as printing messages, headings, and subheadings. The following sample code shows such a function:

```
void print_titles( )
{
   printf("Materials Inventory of ABC Company\n\n");
   printf("Items     Unit-Cost       Total_Cost\n");
   printf("_____     _________       _________\n");

   return;
}
```

This function is called with a null list of arguments, as

```
print_titles( );
```

Notice that this function has return type `void`, meaning that this function will not return any value through its return statement; and there is a null parameter list because the function does not need any information from the calling function. A function such as this may be called anywhere in a program where titles need to be printed in the output.

A More Complex Function A function may return a value through its return statement yet not require arguments and parameters. All the data required in the function is locally generated in the function and a return value is generated in the function and returned to the calling program. The following example shows such a function definition for computing and returning area:

```
float  circle_area( )
{
    const float PI = 3.141593;
    float diameter, area;

    scanf("%f", &diameter);
    area = 0;
    if(diameter > 0)
        area = (PI * diameter * diameter) / 4.0;
    return area;
}
```

Notice that in this function all the required data is provided locally in the function and the function does not receive any arguments and does not have any parameters. The function returns a real value, in this case the area, to the calling function or zero is returned if the area cannot be calculated.

When a function with no arguments and parameters is called, the function name must be followed by parentheses with a null argument list. The following example shows such a call to function `circle_area`:

```
A = circle_area ( );
```

> *Programming Rule:* A function without arguments and parameters must be called with a null argument list.

A function in general returns a value through a return statement calculated from arguments passed to the function parameters. In C arguments are passed to the function parameters in two different ways. They are either passed by value or passed by pointer. These are presented with details of use and implementation in the following sections.

A modularized C program consists of a sequence of function definitions. Function definitions may not be nested.

> *Programming Rule:* The definition of a function inside another function is not legal.

The following example illustrates the form of a C program:

```
#include <stdio.h>                   /* directives */
float compute_area(float);           /* function declaration */

int main( )                          /* definition of function main */
{                                    /* left brace */
    float r, area;                   /*  variable declaration */
    inputf(&r);                      /*  function call (not defined in this
                                         example)*/
    area = compute_area( r);         /*  area = return value of function
                                         call */
    outputf(area);                   /*  function call (not defined in this
                                         example) */

  return 0;
}

float compute_area( float radius) /* function definition */
{
    const float PI = 3.141593;  /* constant and variable declarations */
    float area;
    area = PI * radius * radius;
    return area;
}
```

Notice that the `main` function and the `compute_area` subfunction are similar in that each is defined by a function header followed by a block of code containing variable definitions, computations, and a return statement. Each has a declared data type and a parameter list. The two functions differ in that `main` has a name assigned by the C language and therefore does not need to be declared. Also, `main` has a parameter list that is optional.

A function name appears in at least three different situations:

- Function call
- Function prototype
- Function implementation

The arguments in a function call, in the prototype, and in the implementation header must match as to number, order, and data type.

5.2.3 Scope of Names

In C every name has a scope, that is, the name is known and recognized within a particular section of the program. A name is global if its scope is the entire program. In the previous example, `main` and `compute_area` are global names. A name is local if its scope is a single function of a program. In the example, `r`, `area`, `radius`, and `PI` are local names. If a name is known to several functions, but not to all the functions, it is said to be "global to" those functions where it is known. In the example, `area` is not global—rather there are two variables named `area`, one local to `main` and the other local to `compute_area`.

Whether a name is local or global depends on where it is declared. If a name is declared ahead of all of the function definitions, including `main( )`, then it is global. Any function can access a name that is global to it. It can also access local names. But a function cannot access a name that is neither global to it or local.

```
int  MAX;
FILE  *inptr;
int  gooddata(int,  int,  float);

int main( )    /*  MAX, inptr, gooddata are global  */
{
  . . .
}
```

If a name is declared partway down a sequence of function definitions, it is "global to" the functions that follow it.

```
void funcaccurate(float,  float,  float);  /* funcaccurate is global */
int main( )
{
  . . .
}

const float limit = 0.0001;   /* limit is global to funcaccurate */
                              /* can not be accessed by main */
void funcaccurate(float  x,  float  y,  float  z)
{
   . . .
}
```

If a name is declared in the body of a function, its scope is local.

```
int funcinit(int);   /*  funcinit is global */
int main( )
{
    int var;         /*   var is local to main    */
    . . .            /*   and cannot be accessed by funcinit   */
}

int funcinit(int x)  /*   x is local to funcinit    */
{
    int  var1;       /*   var1 is local to funcinit    */
       . . .         /*   and cannot be accessed by main */
}
```

Scope applies to the names of variables, files, functions, and anything that is programmer named. In C scope is static because it depends on the physical placement of prototypes, declarations, and implementations in the code.

> *Programming Hint:* Limit the use of global names to files, constants, and functions.

Function Calling Functions may be declared inside other function implementations. If a function prototype is before the `main` function, the function has global scope in that the `main` and all functions defined after it can call it. If a function prototype is inside the `main`, only the `main` can call the function. In general if a function prototype is inside another function implementation only that function can call the function declared inside it.

The following examples show the scope of the functions with respect to the function calls.

Example 1:

```
int  func1( .....);          /*  prototype of func1   */

int main( )
{
    float val1, val2;
    float func2(...);        /*  prototype of func2   */
```

```
    val1 =  func1(.. );        /* func1 can be called, because it is
                                  global  */
    val2 = func2(..);          /* func2 can be called because it is local
                                  to main  */
}

int func1(.... )               /*  implementation of func1  */
{
     int  val3;
     val3 = func2(..);         /* error cannot be called because it is
                                  local to main */
     return val3;
}

float func2(....... )          /*  implementation of func2  */
{
    float val4;
    val4 = func1(..);          /* func1 can be called because it is
                                  declared global */
    return val4;
}
```

Note that even when function prototypes are local, the function implementation must sequentially follow the `main` function. In effect, a program is a library of function implementations. The functions are declared only where they are needed.

Example 2:

```
int func1(.  .  . );          /*  prototype of func1 */
int main( )
{
    int val1, val2;
    val1 =  func1(. . .);     /* can be called, because it is global  */
    val2 =  func2(. . .);     /* error cannot be called because it is
                              /* declared after main and is only global to
                                 func1. */
    return 0;
}

int  func2(.  .  .);          /*  prototype of func2  */
int  func1(.  .  .);          /*  implementation of func1  */
{
```

```
    int val;
    val = func2(. . .);     /*  can be called because it is declared
                                before func1 */
    return val;
}

int func2(....... )          /* implementation of func2  */
{
    int val3;
    val3 = func1(..);        /*  can be called because it is global to
    return val3;             /*  func2, but not a good idea, because of
}                            /*  the possibility of an endless loop */
```

Warning: If functions call each other there must be a way to terminate the calls.

Mechanism of Function Calls The structure chart in Figure 5.2 shows the hierarchy of functional modules. The C code that follows shows the mechanism of the function calls for a program to calculate the cost of building a concrete tank of length *l*, width *w*, height *h*, and thickness *t*.

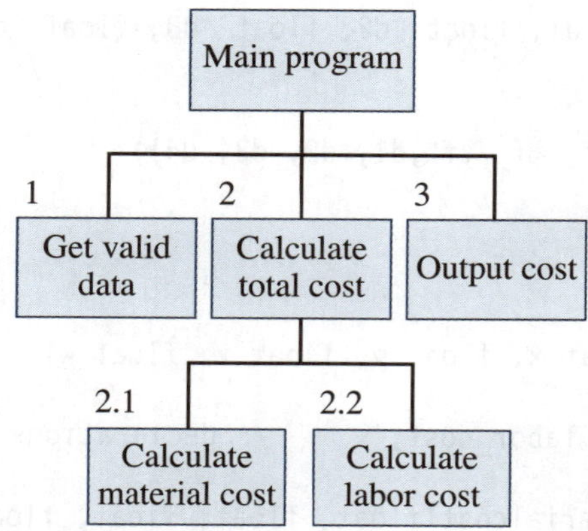

Figure 5.2 Structure chart of functional modules

Notice that the `main` program calls the functions numbered 1, 2, and 3. The function numbered 2 calls the functions numbered 2.1 and 2.2.

```
#include <stdio.h>                /*  I/O function prototypes  */

int main( )          Execution starts /* main function implementation */
{
   float  l, w, t, h, cost;  /* declarations */
   int flag;

   int  get_data(float *, float *, float*, float *);   /* function
                                                           prototypes */
   float calc_cost(float, float, float, float);
   void output_cost(float);
                                        /* executable code */
   flag = get_data(&l, &w, &t, &h);    /* call for input */

   if(flag == 1)
   {
      cost = calc_cost(l,w, t, h);  /* call for calculation */
      output_cost(cost);            /* call for output */
   }

   return 0;
}                                       Execution terminates

int get_data(float *d1, float *d2, float *d3, float *d4) /* function  */
{                                                  /* implementations */
   int flag = 0;
   if(scanf("%f  %f  %f  %f",d1, d2, d3, d4))
      flag = 1;
   return flag;
}

float calc_cost(float x, float y, float z, float w)
{
   float mat_cost, labor_cost;        /* declarations */

   float  calc_materialcost(float, float, float, float); /*function */
   float calc_labor(float);                             /* prototypes */
                                                    /* executable code */
   mat_cost = calc_materialcost(x, y, z, w);       /* function calls */
```

```
    labor_cost = calc_labor(mat_cost);

    return  (mat_cost + labor_cost);
}

float calc_materialcost(float x, float y, float z, float w)
{
    float outervol, innervol, volume, costcft, matcost;

    scanf("%f",&costcft);
    outervol = x * y * z;
    innervol = (x - (2 * w)) * ( y - (2 * w))- (z - (2 * w));
    volume = outervol - innervol;
    matcost = volume * costcft;

    return matcost;
}

float calc_labor(float costmat)
{
    float costlabor;

    costlabor = .60 * costmat;
    return costlabor;
}

void output_cost(float cost)
{
    printf("Total cost: %10.2f", cost);
    return;
}
```

The execution starts at main, which calls get_data. Control is passed to get_data. After it is executed, control returns to main to the next statement following the call, which is a call to calc_cost. Control is passed to calc_cost. It calls calc_materialcost. After calc_materialcost is executed the control is passed back to calc_cost to the next statement following the call, which is a call to calc_labor. After calc_labor, the control is passed back to calc_cost, which passes control back to main. Then main calls output_cost passing control to output_cost. After output_cost is executed, control is returned to main. After main completes its execution the program terminates.

Notice that get_data, calc_cost, and output_cost are available to main because they are declared in main. The functions calc_materialcost and calc_labor are not available to main, but they are available to calc_cost because they are declared inside the implementation of calc_cost. If a function is called by one other function, it should be declared within the calling function. This helps avoid errors.

Programming Hint: Functions should only be global when they are part of a function library being developed by the programmer.

5.2.4 return Statement

A return statement at the end of a function, when executed, returns control to the calling function. If a function returns a single value, it should be returned through the return statement. If the function does not return a value through the return statement, then the return statement is optional; in such a case, the right brace identifies the end of the function causing control to return to the calling program. It is always better to include a return statement at the end of the function whether or not a value is returned through it.

Programming Hint: It is good programming practice to include a return statement as the last statement within the function body.

A function should have only one return statement. If a function cannot carry out its task and is returning a status flag then the status flag should be initialized at the beginning of the function. For example, if the function has several selection control structures to check the data validity, each call may take a different processing path. The following example shows this.

```
int quadratic(float a, float b, float c) /* print solution to ax² + bx
                                             + c = 0*/
{
    int flag;
    float sqval;
    float x1,  x2;

    flag = 2;                   /* assume two real solutions */
```

```
    if( a == 0)                      /* not a quadratic equation */
        flag = 0;
    else if( b * b < (4 * a * c))    /* no real solutions */
        flag = -1;
    else if(b * b == (4 * a * c))    /* one solution */
    {
        x1 = -b /(2 * a);
        printf("x1 = %f", x1);
        flag = 1;
    }
    else
    {                                /* two solutions */
        sqval = (b * b – (4 * a * c));
        x1 = ( -b + sqrt (sqval)) / (2*a);
        x2 = ( -b – sqrt (sqval)) / (2*a);
        printf("x1 = %f     x2 = %f", x1, x2);

    }
    return flag;
}
```

Notice that there is a single `return` and a flag that indicates the state of the computation. The C language allows more than one `return` statement, which would have slightly simplified the program logic but would have violated the modular principle of one entry and one exit for each module.

5.2.5 Review Questions

1. Indicate whether the following statements are true or false.
   a. A function declaration is only used to establish the scope of the function.
   b. A function declaration is called a function prototype.
   c. The data types of the arguments passed to the function must be specified in the parameter list of the function prototype.
   d. If a return data type is not specified in the function prototype no data can be returned.
   e. If there is no return data type it defaults to void.

f. In C every nonlibrary function must be implemented by the programmer.
g. The first statement in a function implementation is called a function header.
h. The function header is a duplicate of the function prototype.
i. The function prototype must terminate with a semicolon, whereas the function header must not terminate with a semicolon.
j. The last statement in a function implementation should be a return statement.
k. A return statement, when executed, will return the control to the calling function.
l. The specification of variable names in the function header is optional; if specified, they can be dummy names.

2. Write the following C code:
   a. Write a prototype for a function named *manipulate*, with two integer data types and one floating-point data type as parameters, which returns a floating-point value.
   b. Write a function header for the function declared in 2a (two integer data types and one floating-point data type as parameters and returning a floating-point value). Assume the following variable names: `var1`, `var2`, and `var3`.
   c. Write a prototype for a function named *compute*, with two double data types and one integer data type as parameters, which does not return any value.
   d. Write a function header as in 2c (two double data types and one integer data type as parameters and not returning any value). Assume the following variable names: `var1`, `var2`, and `var3`.
3. Answer the following questions.
   a. What are the errors in the following function prototypes?

```
int func1(int, float)
void func2(x, y, z);
func3(int, float, double)
```

   b. What are the errors in the following function headers?

```
int func1(int, float);
void func2(x, y, z)
func3(int a, float b, double c)
```

c. Which function or functions in the following code can call func1( ). Why? Which can call func2( )?

```
int func1(int, float);
int main( )
{
    void  func2(float, double);
    ......
    return 0;
}

void func2(float x, double y)
{
    ......
}
void func1(int a, float b)
{
    ......
}
```

d. Which function or functions in the following code can call func1( ) and func2( ). Why?

```
int main( )
{
    void  func2( float, double);
    ......
    return 0;
}

int func1(int, float);

void func2(float x, double y)
{
    ......
}
void func1(int a, float b)
{
    ......
}
```

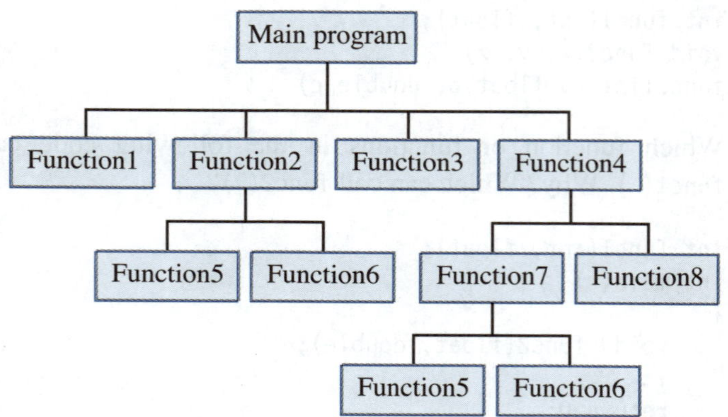

Figure 5.3 Structure chart with 10 functions

4. Given the structure chart in Figure 5.3 give the order of execution of the functions. What functions could be declared in each module?

5.3 Computation Functions

A calling function is a function that is calling (invoking) another function. A called function is a function called (invoked) by another function. For example, if `main` calls (invokes) a function `func1` then `main` is the calling function and `func1` is the called function. The communication between the calling function and the called function is through the argument parameter list and the value returned. The items of information passed to the called function by the calling function are called arguments. The places in the called function receiving the items of information are called formal parameters. The list of arguments must match the list of parameters as to their data types, order, and number.

5.3.1 Passing Arguments by Value

When arguments are passed to the function parameters by value, the names of the variables are specified in the argument list, separated by commas. The data types of the parameters must match the data types of the arguments. When arguments are passed to the function by value, the values of the arguments are copied into temporary storage locations associated with the parameters. The parameters can only access the copies. Any changes to the parameters in the function change only the copies and not the arguments. This is to protect the arguments from inadvertent changes. The parameters are local to the function and the function header serves as their declaration. Once control exits outside of the function, the temporary storage created for the copies will disappear. The following example shows the passing of arguments to parameters by value.

```
int funcsum(int, int, int);  /* function prototype */
int main( )
{
    int var1, var2, var3, sum;              /* storage for variables */
    var1 = 10;
    var2 = 20;
    var3 = 30;
    sum = funcsum(var1, var2, var3);        /* function call transfers
                                               values */
    printf("var1 = %d  var2 = %d  var3 = %d  sum = %d\n",
    var1, var2, var3, sum);

    return 0;
}

int funcsum(int varx, int vary, int varz) /* function implementation */
{
                                          /* sets up storage for copies */
    int sum1;                             /* storage for local variable */
    sum1 = varx +  vary + varz;

    return sum1;                          /* function returns value  */
}
```

Output: `var1 = 10  var2 = 20  var3 = 30  sum = 60`

Figure 5.4 shows the storage of variables in the `main` function and the function `funcsum`. After the function `funcsum` has been executed the variables, `varx`, `vary`, `varz`, copied into the function parameters disappear and the value of `sum1` is assigned to the sum in the `main` program. The following example shows what happens if the values of the parameters are changed in the function `funcsum`.

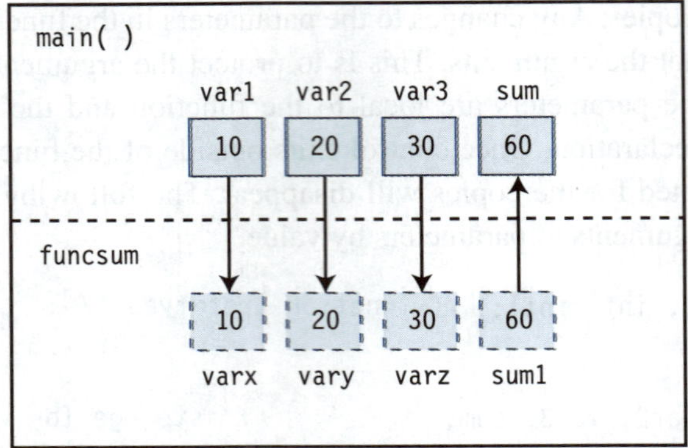

Figure 5.4 Storage allocation in main and funcsum

```
int  funcsum(int, int, int);
int main( )
{
    int var1,  var2, var3, sum;
    var1 = 10;
    var2 = 20;
    var3 = 30;
    sum = funcsum(var1, var2, var3);
    printf("var1= %d  var2 = %d  var3 = %d  sum = %d\n",
                var1, var2, var3, sum);
    printf("sum = %d\n", var1 + var2 + var3);

    return 0;
}

int  funcsum(int  varx, int  vary,  int varz)
{
    int sum1;
    varx += 10;                         /* varx is now 20 */
    vary += 15;                         /* vary is now 35 */
    varz += 20;                         /* varz is now 50 */
    sum1 = varx +  vary + varz;
    return sum1;
}
```

Output: var1 = 10 var2 = 20 var3 = 30 sum = 105

sum = 60

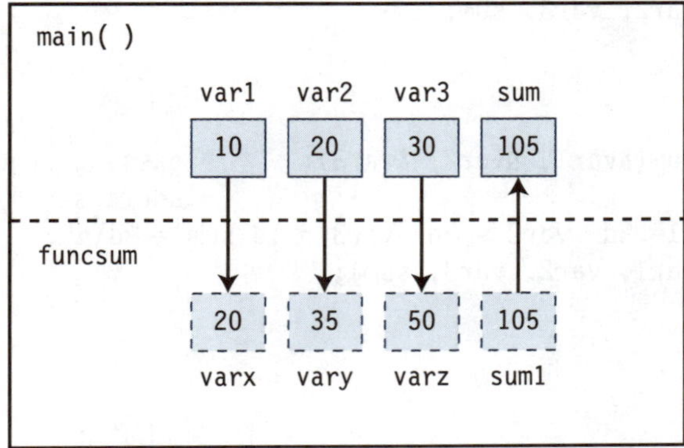

Figure 5.5 Storage allocation in `main` and `funcsum`

Figure 5.5 shows the state of variables in the `main` program and the function `funcsum` after changing the parameters in the function `funcsum`.

Notice that when the values of the parameters in the function `funcsum` have changed; only the copies are changed and not the variables in the main program. Once the execution of the function `funcsum` is completed the function parameters are destroyed and the temporary storage created for the copies is destroyed. Also, the `sum1` declared as a local variable in the function is destroyed. The value to be returned by the function is copied from temporary storage before the function terminates its execution.

> *Programming Hint:* Pass the arguments to the function by value if they are not intended to be changed in the function.

5.3.2 Passing Arguments by Pointer

The arguments from the calling function may be passed to the called function as pointers. A pointer is simply an address of a variable. Pointers, the addresses of variables, are passed as arguments instead of the variables themselves as we have done in passing by value. This is done by preceding each argument name with an address operator (&).

```
int  funcsum(int   *,  int   *,  int   *); /* declaring parameters to
                                              be pointers */

int main( )
{
```

```
    int var1, var2, var3, sum;
    var1 = 10;
    var2 = 20;
    var3 = 30;
    sum = funcsum(&var1, &var2, &var3);      /* passing arguments as
                                                 addresses */
    printf("var1= %d  var2 = %d  var3 = %d sum = %d\n",
              var1, var2, var3, sum);

    return 0;
}

int  funcsum(int  *varx, int  *vary,  int *varz) /* define parameters */
{                                                 /* as specific pointers  */
    int sum1;

    sum1 = *varx +  *vary + *varz;  /*  accessing values through
                                         pointers */

    return sum1;
}
```

Output: `var1 = 10  var2 = 20  var3 = 30  sum = 60`

Figure 5.6 shows the state of variables and their memory address in the `main` program. The addresses of the variables `var1`, `var2`, and `var3` are passed as arguments. Since the arguments of the function call in the `main` program are addresses, the function prototype must declare the parameters as pointer data types. The parameter data types are `int *`, `int *`, and `int *` in the function prototype. In the function header the data types must match the data types in the prototype. Therefore the data type of the parameters in the function header is `int *`, `int *`, and `int *`, which matches the data type specified in the prototype.

We have already seen call-by-pointer in the use of standard input functions. When a function is to return a value through the argument list it must be given an address to which it will return the value. We have already seen this with the use of the library input routines. For instance,

```
int a, b, errflg;
..................
errflg = scanf("%d   %d", &a, &b);
```

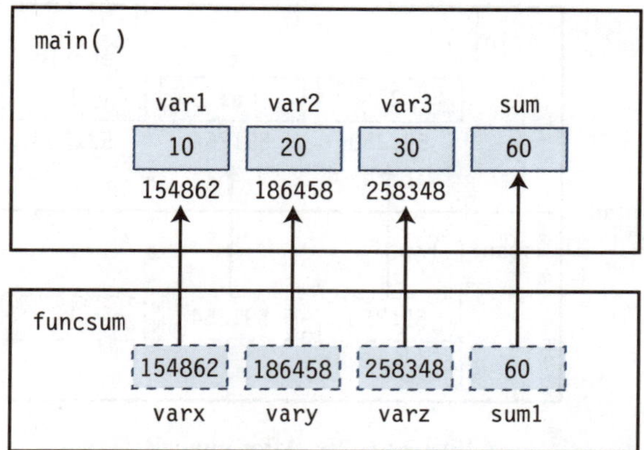

Figure 5.6 Storage allocation in `main` and `funcsum`

involves the passing of the address of the variables `a` and `b` when the library input routine is called. The input routine reads the data and places the value in the program storage for `a` and `b` and returns control to the program as shown in Figures 5.7a and 5.7b, assuming the data values are 27 and 63, respectively.

Notice that the addresses passed to the input function are used to tell it where to place the input data. The status flag used for the function return is set in the function and a copy of it is passed back to the calling routine. The status flag has a value of 1 when the input is successful.

The function to output the solutions of a quadratic equation in Section 5.2.4 can be altered to return the solutions rather than output them. Since the return

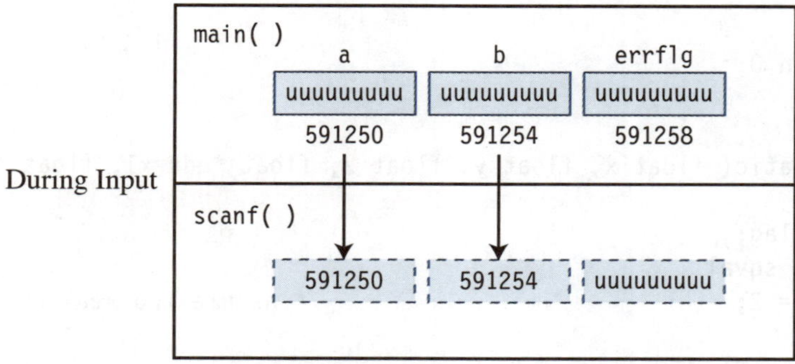

Figure 5.7a During input

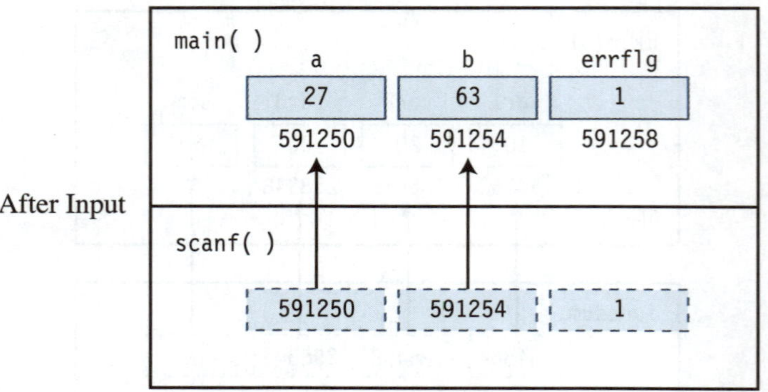

Figure 5.7b After input

statement can only return one value and is being used for a status code, the solutions to the equation can be returned to the calling program by passing addresses for them as follows:

```
int quadratic(float, float, float, float *, float *);

int main( )
{
    float a, b, c, x1, x2;
    int status;
    .  .  .  .  .
    status = quadratic(a, b, c, &x1, &x2);

    .  .  .  .
    return 0;
}

int quadratic( float x, float y, float z, float *addrx1, float *addrx2)
{
    int flag;
    float sqval
    flag = 2;                               /* assume two real answers */

    if(x == 0)
        flag = 0;                           /* not a quadratic equation */
```

```
    else if(y * y < 4 * x * z)
        flag = -1;                           /* answers are complex */
    else if( y * y == 4.0 * x * z)
    {
        flag = 1;                            /* one real answer */
        *addrx1 = - y / (2.0 * x);
    }
    else                                     /* two real answers */
    {
        sqval = (b * b - (4 * a * c));
        *addrx1 = (-y + sqrt(sqval) / (2.0 * x));
        *addrx2 = (-y - sqrt(sqval) / (2.0 * x));
    }
    return flag;
}
```

In this example, a, b, and c are passed by value while addresses are passed for x1 and x2 so that values may be returned. This is shown in Figure 5.8 for the quadratic equation $x^2 + 5x + 4 = 0$.

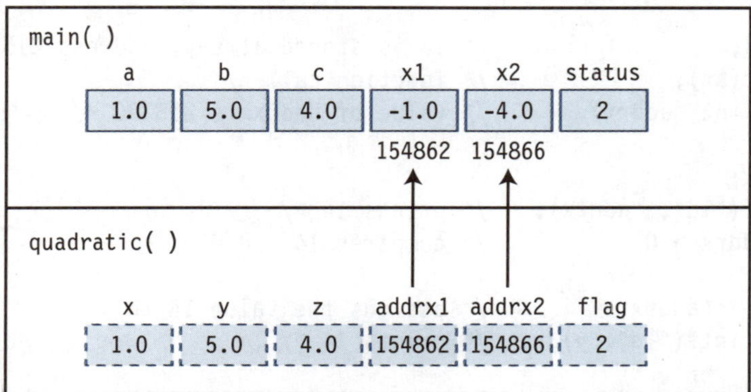

Figure 5.8 Solution to quadratic equation

Dereferencing of Pointers In call-by-pointer, a function receives pointers through its parameters. The pointers are the addresses of the arguments being passed to the parameters. To access the data contained in these pointers they must be dereferenced. The dereference operator asterisk (*) must be used in front of the pointer variable to access the value contained in that variable. In the function

```
int funcsum(int *varx, int *vary, int *varz)
{
    int sum;
    sum = *varx + *vary + * varz;
    return sum;
}
```

the variables varx, vary, and varz are dereferenced by placing an asterisk (*) in front of them. The value of pointer varx is an address and its content is *varx, which is, say, 10. The value of pointer vary is an address and its content is *vary, which is, say, 20. Finally, the value of varz is an address and its content is *varz, which is, say, 30. In the assignment statement sum = *varx + *vary + *varz, *varx is replaced by 10, *vary is replaced by 20, and *varz is replaced by 30. The result assigned to the variable sum is 60. The asterisk (*) tells the computer to use the value as an address, find that address, and pick up (or store) the value there.

If the address variable is dereferenced in an output statement, on the right side of an assignment statement, or anywhere a value is needed, the value at that address is picked up and used.

```
int x = 14;                    /* 14 is stored at say, address 215390 */
. . . func(&x);                /* function call */
int func( int *addrx)          /* value of addrx is 215390 */
{
    int  y;
    printf("%d", *addrx);      /* prints 14 */
    if(*addrx > 0)             /* compares 14 and 0 */
    {
        y = *addrx;            /* assigns the value 14 to y */
        printf("%d", y);       /* prints 14 */
    }
    return 0;
}
```

If the address variable is dereferenced on the left side of an assignment statement or anywhere an address is needed for storing, a value is stored in the storage of the argument in the function call.

```
int  x, y;
x = 14;                        /* 14 is stored at say, address 215390 */
y = 27;                        /* 27 is stored at say, address 215394 */
...func(&x, &y);               /* function call */
```

```
int func( int *addrx, int *addry)    /* addrx has  value 215390 */
{                                    /* addry has value 215394 */
    int  z;
    scanf("%d  %d", addrx, &z);      /* values are input for x and z,
                                        addrx has not changed, but x is no
                                        longer 14 */

    *addry = z;                      /* the value of z is stored in y,
                                        addry has not changed but y is no
                                        longer 27 */
    return 0;
}
```

Dereferencing a pointer tells the computer where to pick up or store a value.

If the values pointed to by the pointer variables are changed in the function, the changes are reflected in the arguments. The following program shows how changes in the parameters in the function will change the corresponding argument values in the `main` function. This was not the case in passing by value. Passing the arguments by pointers causes side effects in the arguments if the parameters in the function are dereferenced. The following program shows such side effects.

In the following code the parameters are changed in the function `funcsum`:

```
int  funcsum(int  *, int  *, int  *);

int main( )
{
    int var1, var2, var3, sum;

    var1 = 10;
    var2 = 20;
    var3 = 30;

    sum = funcsum(&var1, &var2, &var3);

    printf("var1= %d  var2 = %d  var3 = %d sum = %d\n",
                 var1, var2, var3, sum);
    printf("sum = %d\n", var1 + var2 + var3);

    return 0;
}
```

```
int  funcsum(int  *varx, int  *vary,  int *varz)
{
    int sum1;
    *varx += 10;
    *vary += 15;
    *varz += 20;
    sum1 = *varx +  *vary + *varz;
    return sum1;
}
```

Output: `var1 = 20  var2 = 35  var3 = 50  sum = 105`

`sum = 105`

Figure 5.9 shows the status of the variables after they are changed in the function. When arguments are passed as pointers to the function parameters, the function has the right to access the storage locations of the arguments used in the calling function. Any changes made through the function parameters will be reflected in the arguments of the `main` program. In this code the pointers `varx`, `vary`, and `varz` are dereferenced and their values are changed. The statements `*varx += 10`, `*vary += 15`, and `*varz += 20` changed the value of `var1` from 10 to 20, `var2` from 20 to 35, and `var3` from 30 to 50 in the function.

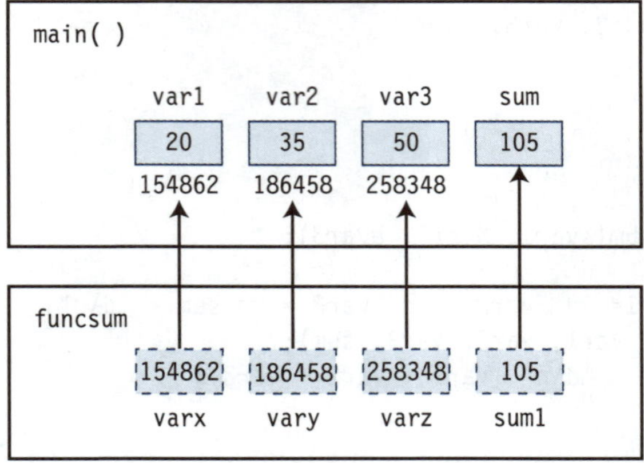

Figure 5.9 Storage allocation in `main` and `funcsum`

> *Programming warning:* If the arguments are passed to the function parameters as pointers, any changes to those pointers in the function will be reflected in the arguments of the calling function.

Passing by Value Versus Passing by Pointer It is important to know when to pass by value and when to pass by pointer. Functions are normally written to perform a specific task and return a single value to the calling program. With functions that use parameters in computations and do not alter their values it is always best to use call-by-value. A function that returns a single value by means of a `return` statement may be used in the following ways.

- As an expression on the right side of an assignment statement to save the value returned for further use in the program.

```
int  sum;
sum = func(arg1, arg2, agr3);
```

- As an expression in an arithmetic expression.

```
a = b * c - func(arg1, arg2, arg3) * m / n;
```

- As an expression to be evaluated and printed.

```
printf("Value returned = %d\n", func(arg1, arg2, arg3));
```

- As an argument in another function call as follows:

```
value = funcx(func(arg1, arg2, arg3));
```

In this case the argument to `funcx()` is the value returned by a call to the function `func(arg1, arg2, arg3)`. In other words a simple call may be used anywhere an expression of the same type may be used.

A function may need to return more than one value. This can only be done by using parameters that are pointer variables. Functions may pass some arguments by value and some by pointer. Constants such as PI and literals such as 1.75 and 'A' may only be passed by value. It is important to use pass-by-pointer only for arguments that are intentionally being changed.

5.3.3 Review Questions

1. Indicate whether the following statements are true or false.
   a. When variables are passed by value, the variable name must be specified in the argument list.
   b. When variables are passed by pointer, the address of the variable name must be specified in the argument list.
   c. Passing arguments to function parameters by value prevents the function from changing the values of arguments.
   d. Parameters are local variables with their own storage.
   e. In the function, when passing by pointer, the arguments in permanent storage in the calling function can be changed.
   f. Passing an argument by pointer passes the address of the variable specified.
   g. When a pointer is passed to a function, if the function alters the value of the parameter, then it points to something different.
   h. If a function is written to compute a single value from the parameters, it is always better to pass the arguments by value.
2. Write a function declaration for each nonlibrary function in the following segments of code.
   a.

```
int main( )
{
     int x, y, z, sum;
     sum = func(x, y, z);
     printf("sum = %d\n", sum);

     return 0;
}

int func(int a, int b, int c)
{
     int sum1;
     sum1 = a + b + c;
     return sum1;
}
```

b.
```
int main( )
  {
      float x, y, z, sum;
      sum = func(&x, &y, &z);
      printf("sum = %f\n", sum);

      return 0;
  }

  float func(float *a, float *b, float *c)
  {
      float sum1;
      sum1 = *a + *b + *c;
      return sum1;
  }
```

3. Write a function declaration and definition for each nonlibrary function in the following segment of code.

a.
```
int main( )
  {
      int num1, num2, num3, largest_num;

      largest_num = funclargest( num1, num2, num3);
      printf("The largest number is: %d\n", largest_num);

      return 0;
  }
```

b.
```
int main( )

  {
      int num1, num2, num3, minnum, maxnum;

      funcminmax( num1, num2, num3, &minnum, &maxnum);
      printf("The largest number is: %d\n", maxnum);
      printf("The smallest number is: %d\n", minnum);

      return 0;
  }
```

5.4 Input and Output Functions

The input and output functions discussed in Chapter 3 return status flags because there is always the possibility that the input/output (I/O) has failed. A file may not be open, there may not be any further data, a printer may not be online, or the data may be of the wrong type. Therefore, it is important to always check the condition of these flags to make sure that the I/O was successful. If output was not successful, then the user needs that information. If input was not successful, then there are no data values to be processed. Checking the status of the input is an important part of data validation. In addition, when a separate function is written to get input and validate it, the function should return its own status flag. Since error conditions may arise in the course of input or output, the return statement should be used to return a status indicator, usually a one when no errors have been found and a zero when an error is found.

5.4.1 Input Using Functions

Data can be obtained by a function and returned to the calling function for processing. This separates data editing and validation from the processing. To send input data through the function parameters, the storage addresses of the arguments in the function call are needed. The following example shows the standard input of data in a function and its transmission back to the main program where it is stored and printed.

Standard Input

```
void  funcinput(int  *, int *, float *, float *);
int main( )
{
    int var1, var2;
    float  var3, var4;

    funcinput(&var1, &var2, &var3, &var4);
    printf("var1 = %d  var2 = %d  var3 = %f  var4 = %f\n",
            var1, var2, var3, var4);

    return 0;
}

void funcinput(int  *varx, int *vary, float *varz, float  * varw)
{
    scanf("%d  %d  %f  %f", varx, vary, varz, varw);
    return;
}
```

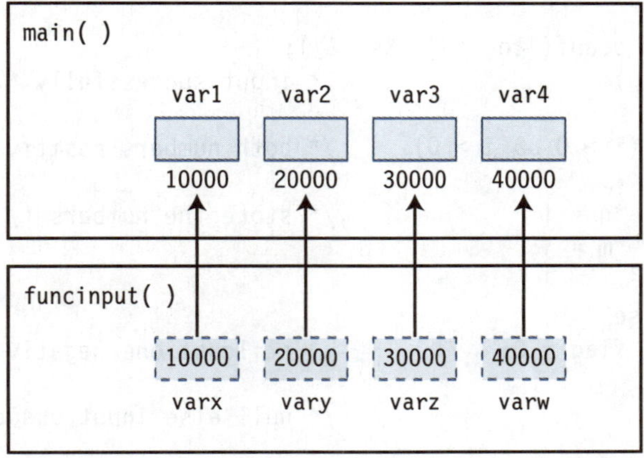

Figure 5.10 Passing pointers to function

Notice that the addresses are sent from the `main` program to the function as shown in Figure 5.10. In the function, `varx`, `vary`, `varz`, and `varw` have the addresses of the variables declared in the `main` program. Any values that are input via the addresses in `varx`, `vary`, `varz`, and `varw` are actually stored in the main program in `var1`, `var2`, `var3`, and `var4`. The address operator "&" is not needed in the call to `scanf` since `varx`, `vary`, and `varz` are already the addresses for the input data.

Validating Input A function written to obtain valid input for processing should use call-by-pointer so that the input can be returned through the argument/parameter list, and the return statement used for a status flag. The following function prompts the user to input a pair of positive numbers and returns a flag indicating whether or not valid data is being returned.

```
int get_pos_nums(int *n, int *m)
{
    int  i, j, flag;

    flag = printf("\n enter two positive numbers");

    if(flag)                        /* prompt displays successfully */
```

```
    {
        flag = scanf("%d  %d", &i, &j);
        if(flag)                    /* input successfully */
        {
            if(i > 0 && j > 0)      /* both numbers positive */
            {
                *n = i;             /* store the numbers */
                *m = j;
            }
            else
                flag = 0;           /* at least one negative input */
        }
        else;                       /* null else input unsuccessful */
    }
    else;                           /* null else prompt unsuccessful */
    return flag;
}
```

If the library output routine `printf()` is successful, it returns 1; if it fails, it returns 0. If the library input routine `scanf()` is successful, it returns 1; if it fails, it returns 0. The variables `i` and `j` are local to the function because there is no point in returning invalid values. Valid values are returned through assignment through the parameter address variables.

The function could try repeatedly to obtain a pair of positive values and return either valid data or an error flag if none is found.

```
int get_pos_nums(int * n, int *m)
{
    int  i, j, flag;

    flag = printf("\n enter two positive numbers");

    if(flag)            /* prompt successful */
    {
        i = 0;
        j = 0;
        flag = scanf("%d  %d", &i, &j);
        while(flag && (i <= 0 || j <= 0))
        {
            printf("\n enter two positive numbers");
            flag = scanf("%d  %d", &i, &j);
        }
        if(flag)        /* input successful and numbers positive */
```

```
        {
          *n = i;
          *m = j;
        }
        return flag;
    }
}
```

The body of the while loop is repeated until either the input fails or a pair of positive numbers are found. The if statement that follows determines which situation occurred. If the input failed, the flag was set to 0 by the input statement. If a pair of positive numbers was found, the flag was set to 1 by the input statement, and it is only necessary to return the numbers. The flag must also be returned.

Input from a File Declared Local to main Assume the input data is coming from a data file stored on the disk. If the file is declared inside the main function then the file name becomes local to main. The following program shows how to declare a file as local and input the data from such a file in a function.

```
int funcinput(FILE *, int  *, int *, float *, float *);

int main( )
{
    FILE  *inptr;
    int var1, var2;
    float  var3, var4;
    inptr = fopen("myfilex.dat", "r");

    if(funcinput(inptr, &var1, &var2, &var3, &var4));
        printf("var1 = %d  var2 = %d  var3 = %f  var4 = %f\n",
                              var1, var2, var3, var4);

    else
        printf("Error in input \in");
    fclose(inptr);

    return 0;
}
```

```
int funcinput(FILE *dataptr, int *varx, int *vary, float *varz,
           float *varw)
{
   int flag = 0;
   if(fscanf(dataptr, "%d  %d  %f  %f", varx, vary, varz, varw)
            != EOF)
      flag = 1;
   return flag;
}
```

Notice that the file pointer is declared local to the main function where it is opened. Since the file pointer is declared local to the main function it must be passed to the input function like any other pointer. The pointer type must be specified in the function prototype and in the function header. In the function header the local file pointer name must be specified. The same name must be used in the input statement. If the data input is being controlled by the main then the file pointer should be declared and the file should be opened in the main function.

Input From a Data File Declared Local to a Function Instead of declaring the file pointer inside the main it can be declared and opened within the function in which the data is input. The following code shows such input.

```
int  funcinput(int  *,  int  *,  float  *,  float  *);

int main( )
{
   int var1, var2, flag;
   float  var3, var4;
   flag = funcinput(&var1, &var2, &var3, &var4);
   if(flag)
      printf("var1 = %d  var2 = %d  var3 = %f  var4 = %f\n",
            var1, var2,var3, var4);
   else
      printf("Error in input\n");

   return 0;
}

int funcinput(int  *varx,  int  *vary, float  *varz, float  *varw)
{
   int  flag  = 0;
   FILE  *inptr;

   inptr = fopen("myfilex.dat","r");
```

```
    if(fscanf(inptr, "%d  %d  %f  %f", varx, vary, varz, varw) != EOF)
        flag = 1;

    return flag;
}
```

Notice that the file pointer is locally declared within the function `funcinput` and opened and used inside the function. One use for this would be to open a file and verify that it is the correct file before processing it. This function cannot be called a second time as it would be an error to try to open a file that is already opened.

> *Program Warning:* Do not open a file inside a function if the function is called more than once.

5.4.2 Output Using Functions

A function is usually used for output when the output formatting is elaborate and would clutter the `main` function. As was mentioned in the early sections of this chapter, the simplest output function one can write is to output messages in the form of character string constants. The messages may be report titles, headings subheadings, tables, or error messages. When data is printed by an output function, the data is passed to the function from the calling function. Since the data is only printed and it is not changed in the output function it is best to pass the data by value rather than by pointers if there is only a small amount of data. If passed by value, the arguments are secure and the parameters do not have to be dereferenced. Otherwise, if passed by pointer, they have to be dereferenced in the function and the arguments are not protected.

Standard Output from a Function The following example shows an output function receiving several variables that are printed on the printer or displayed on the monitor. The values to be printed are passed as arguments by value to the output function parameters. They are printed in the output function. The values are not changed in the function, they are simply printed or displayed or written to an output file.

```
void funcoutput(int, int, float,  float);

int main( )
{
    int var1, var2, var3, var4;
```

```
    funcoutput(var1, var2, var3, var4);

    return 0;
}

void funcoutput(int varx, int vary, float varz, float varw)
{
    printf("varx = %d  vary = %d  varz = %f  varw = %f\n",
                  varx, vary, varz, varw);
    return;
}
```

The storage of var1, var2, var3, and var4 in main has the values as shown in Figure 5.11.

Notice that values of the arguments var1, var2, var3, and var4 are copied into parameters in the function headers varx, vary, varz, and varw. When the control is returned to the main program the function parameters and the copies created are destroyed.

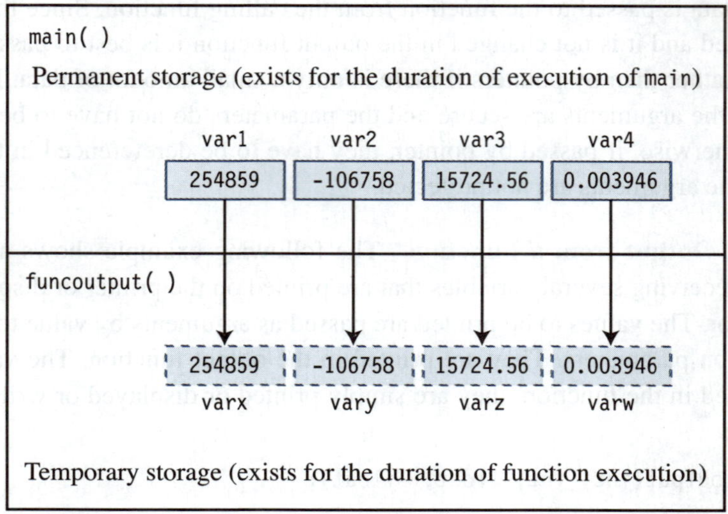

Figure 5.11 Passing arguments by value

Output to a Data File Declared Global Assume the output data is written to a data file stored on the disk. If the file is declared ahead of the `main` function then the file becomes global to the entire program. The following example shows how to declare a file as global and output the data to such a file in a function.

```
FILE  *outptr;
void  funcoutput(int  , int , float , float );

int main( )
{
    int var1, var2;
    float  var3, var4;
    outptr = fopen("myfiley.dat", "w");
    funcoutput(var1, var2, var3, var4);

    return 0;
}

void funcoutput(int varx, int vary, float varz, float  varw)
{
    fprintf(outptr, "%d  %d  %f  %f", varx, vary, varz, varw);

    return;
}
```

Notice that in this case the file pointer is declared global, and the file is opened in the `main` function. Since the file pointer is declared global, several output functions can access the file pointer and write data to the data file "`myfiley.dat`."

Output to a Data File Declared Local to `main` Assume the output data is written to a data file stored on the disk. If the file is declared inside the `main` function then the file pointer becomes local to `main`. The following example shows how to declare a file as local and output data from a function.

```
void  funcoutput(FILE *, int, int, float, float );

int main( )
{
    FILE  *outptr;

    int var1, var2;
    float  var3, var4;
```

```
    outptr = fopen("myfilexy.dat", "w");

    if (outptr ! = NULL)
    {
        funcoutput(outptr, var1, var2, var3, var4);

        fclose(outptr);
    }

    return 0;
}

void funcoutput(FILE  *fileptr, int  varx, int vary, float varz,
                      float  varw)
{
    fprintf(fileptr, "%d  %d  %f  %f", varx, vary, varz, varw);

    return;
}
```

Notice that in this case the file pointer is declared local to the `main` function and the file is opened in it. Since the file pointer is declared local to `main`, the function cannot access the file pointer. The file pointer must be passed to the function like any other pointer. The pointer type must be specified in the function prototype and in the function header. In the function header the local file pointer name must be specified. That name can be any name. The same name must be used in the output statement.

Output to a Data File Declared Local to a Function Instead of declaring the file pointer ahead of the `main` function or inside the `main` function, it can be declared and opened within the function in which the data is output. The following code shows such file output.

```
int  funcoutput(int, int, float, float);

int main( )
{
    int var1, var2, flag;
    float  var3, var4;

    flag = funcoutput(var1, var2, var3, var4);

    return 0;
}
```

```
int funcoutput(int  varx,  int  vary, float  varz, float  varw)
{
    FILE  *outptr;
    int flag = 0;

    outptr = fopen("myfiley.dat","r");

    if (outptr != NULL)
    {
        fprintf(outptr, "%d  %d  %f  %f", varx, vary, varz,
                        varw);
        flag = 1;
    }

    fclose(outptr);

    return flag;
}
```

Notice that the file pointer is locally declared within the function `funcoutput` and opened and used inside the function. This output function can only be called once as once a file is open, it cannot be opened again. One use for this would be to write header information to a file before using it for output. In a later chapter we will see that there are ways of setting up a flag to indicate whether or not a file has been opened that will allow input and output functions to be called more than once.

5.4.3 Review Questions

1. Indicate whether the following statements are true or false.
    a. When multiple values are to be returned from a function to the calling program, they cannot be returned through the `return` statement.
    b. Multiple values may be returned from a function to a calling program through the parameters.
    c. The arguments must pass the addresses of variables that are to be changed by the function called.
    d. Data input using a function can only be passed back to the main program through pointers.

e. A calling function must declare the variables and send the addresses through arguments to the parameters of the input function to receive the input data values from a function.

f. To print the data in an output function the calling program may send the data to the output function by value.

g. If a file is declared global and opened in `main`, the input function can access the data from the data file.

h. If a file is declared and opened in the `main` function, the file pointer can be accessed by a called function.

i. A file pointer may not be declared and opened in a function.

2. Write the following C code:

   a. Write a `main` function and an input function to input the lengths of the sides of a triangle and transmit the data to the `main` function.

   b. Write a function to input a five digit salesman ID and weekly sales, and transmit the data to the `main` function.

   c. Write an output function to output the salesman ID, weekly sales, and weekly commission.

5.5 Recursive Functions

A recursive function is a function that calls itself. In C, recursive functions are declared and defined the same way nonrecursive functions are declared and defined. The parent function that invokes the recursive function transfers control to the recursive function; after the recursive function terminates, control is returned back to the calling function. Certain real-world processes are recursive. Most iterative formulas can be programmed using recursive functions, although it may not be efficient to do so. For example, factorial is recursive, and generation of Fibonacci numbers is recursive.

5.5.1 Concept of Recursion

Recursion occurs when a function repeatedly calls itself until a termination condition occurs. The termination condition in a recursive function is called a base condition. Every recursive function must have a base condition, otherwise the recursion will not terminate.

The classic mathematical example of recursion is n factorial, written as $n!$, meaning the product of the integers from 1 through n. Four factorial is $1 \times 2 \times 3 \times 4$, which is 24 in value. The general case $n!$ is defined mathematically as follows:

$$n! = \begin{cases} 1 & \text{for } n = 1 \quad \text{base condition} \\ n(n-1)! & \text{for } n > 1 \quad \text{recursive formula} \end{cases}$$

This is a recursive definition as the factorial symbol (!) appears on the right side, as well as the left side, of the formula. Every recursive definition has at least two parts, one to define the function in terms of itself, and the other, without the self-reference, is the base condition. A recursive function is declared and defined like a regular function in C, but the base case must precede the self-reference call within the function. The recursive function declaration and definition to compute the factorial of n is as follows:

Declaration:

```
int  fact(int);          /* declaration or prototype */
```

Definition:

```
int  fact(int n)
{
   if( n == 1)             /*  base case */
     return 1;
   else
     return(n * fact(n - 1)); /* self-reference */
}
```

In $n = 1$ this function returns 1. If $n = 2$ or greater the function calls itself.

The variable n counts down as the function is called repeatedly. Notice that the termination condition (`n == 1`) is checked ahead of the recursive call. The base case (termination condition) will eventually become true and control will be returned back to the function that invoked the recursive function.

The activation of the recursive function involves keeping more than one copy of the function information in memory at the same time. Figure 5.11 shows the contents of memory if the function is invoked as `fact(3)`.

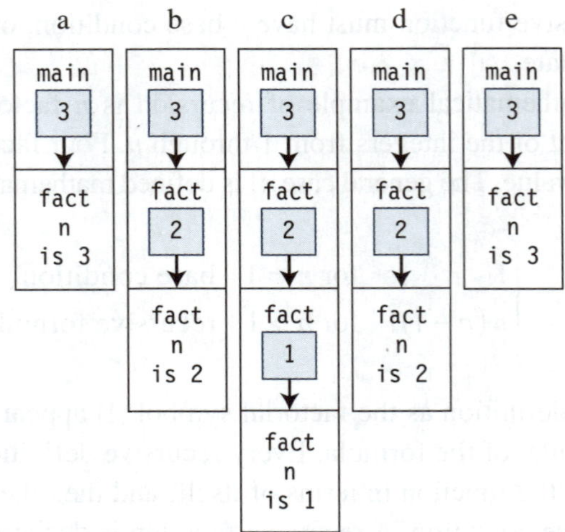

Figure 5.12 Recursive function stack operation

Figure 5.12a shows the memory status after the function is called for the first time. The dummy argument *n* refers back to the value 3 in the main program. After the second call, shown in 5.12b, the argument *n* refers to a value for $n - 1$ in the first call of the function. At that time *n* was 3, so the new value of *n* is 2 and in the last call, *n* is 1.

When *n* is 1, the function is exited returning the value 1. Control returns to the next operation after the function was invoked. Since the function was invoked in an expression, control returns to the multiplication, which could not be completed until the value of the factorial was known. When *n* is 2, the expression

$$n * \text{fact}(n - 1) \text{ has the value } 2 * \text{fact}(1)$$

When *n* is 1, the value 1 is returned to the previous call where the multiplication can be completed. This continues until finally control returns to the main program, returning the value 6. The arguments are calculated on the recursive descent and the values are returned on the recursive ascent, as shown here:

n is 3	↓	first call	↑ returns 3 * 2 = 6
n is 2	↓	second call	↑ returns 2 * 1 = 2
n is 1	↓	third call	↑ returns 1

There are more efficient, nonrecursive ways of computing a factorial. But since recursion involves a totally different way of looking at a calculation, a simple example is easier to follow than a complex one.

The following code shows the `main` program and the factorial function and the result of execution of the program.

```
#include <stdio.h>

int fact(int);

int main( )
{
    int   n, factn;

    scanf("%d", &n);
    factn = fact(n);
    printf("n = %d    factn = %d\n", n, factn);

    return 0;
}

int fact(int n)
{
    if(n == 1)
        return 1;
    else
        return(n * fact(n - 1));
}
```

Notice that in the function `fact`, `n = 3` returns 6. The base case is the condition when `n == 1`, it returns 1, otherwise it calls the recursive function `fact` to continue. Since every time the function is called, its argument is a smaller positive number, eventually it will be called with 1 as the argument. The recursive computations are shown in Figure 5.11. Several examples of recursive functions are presented in Chapter 6.

5.5.2 Relationship Between Iteration and Recursion

Most iterative formulas can be programmed using recursive functions. The base condition corresponds to the initialization of the repetition, and the recursive formula corresponds to the repetition. For example, if 10 numbers are to be read from a file and added, they must be read in the order: num1, num2, num3, ..., num10. Using iteration, this might be written as

```
sum = 0
count = 1
while count <= 10
   sum = sum + input
   increment count
end while
```

Written as a formula for recursion, this would be

$$\text{sum} = \begin{cases} \text{input} & \text{count} = 1 \\ \text{sum}(\text{count} - 1) + \text{input} & 1 < \text{count} <= 10 \end{cases}$$

called as sum(10)

The function call would expand as follows:

```
sum(10)
sum(9) + input 10
sum(8) + input 9 + input 10
sum(7) + input 8 + input 9 + input 10
.............................................
sum(1) + input 2 + ........+ input 10
input 1 + input 2 + input 3 +.............+ input 10
```

The 10 numbers will be read from the file in the correct order because an arithmetic expression is evaluated from left to right, so the 10th number would not actually be read until `sum(9)` had been evaluated. The sum would expand as indicated, and be evaluated from left to right.

This is an example of "left recursion." The preceding factorial example used "right recursion." The value `fact(n)` could have been calculated by either left recursion or right recursion, using the formulas below.

$$\text{Left recursion} \quad n! = \begin{cases} 1 & \text{for } n = 1 \\ (n-1)!\,n & \text{for } n > 1 \end{cases}$$

$$\text{Right recursion} \quad n! = \begin{cases} 1 & \text{for } n > 1 \\ n(n-1)! & \text{for } n > 1 \end{cases}$$

Both of these are accurate because (using 5! as the example) ((((1) × 2) × 3) × 4) × 5 is equal to 5 × (4 × (3 × (2 × (1)))).

5.5.3 Review Questions

1. Indicate whether the following questions are true or false.
   a. A recursive function must return ultimately to the function that called the recursive function.
   b. A recursive function must have a base case.
   c. A recursive function must have a recursive step.
2. Write a recursive function that computes the first *n* Fibonacci numbers: 1, 1, 2, 3, 5, 8, 12. . . .
3. Write a recursive function that computes the combination of *n* things taken *k* at a time.

$$C(n,k) = \begin{cases} 1 & n = 1 \\ 1 & k = 1 \\ C(n-1,\ k-1) + C(n-1,\ k) & n > 1,\ 1 < k \le n \end{cases}$$

5.6 Sample Programs

The examples presented in this section are chosen from science, engineering, and mathematics to illustrate the concepts of modular programming, the use of functions, and the integration of functions into an executable program. The `main` function and the subfunctions are documented. In some sample programs the output includes the input data values; where they are included they are identified.

5.6.1 Rocket Motor Thrust

Problem Write a `main` function and two subfunctions to compute the average thrust of a rocket motor, given the weight of the rocket and its average velocity during the burning of the first stage (time interval *t*). This example demonstrates call-by-value.

Method

main program:

```
input the weight, velocity, and the time
output weight, velocity, time
```

```
    call funcforce( )     /* function call */
    call functhrust( )
output force and thrust
stop
```

`funcforce( )`: function to compute the total force.

Compute the total force from the formula

$$f = \frac{wv}{gt}$$

where w is the weight of the rocket in pounds,
v is the average velocity of the rocket in feet/second,
t is the time interval in seconds, and
g is the gravitational acceleration in feet/sec^2.

`functhrust( )`: function to compute the total thrust.

$$t = w + f$$

where t is the total thrust,
w is the weight of the rocket, and
f is the total force.

Data Input data

weight of the rocket
velocity of the rocket
time

Pseudocode

```
main( )
input the weight, velocity, time
output weight, velocity, time
   force ← funcforce( )
   thrust ← functhrust( )
   output force, thrust
stop
```

funcforce( )
compute the force from the formula
f ← (w × v) / (G × t)
return f

functhrust( )
compute the thrust from the formula
t ← w + f
return t

Program

```
/*********************************************************/
/*                                                       */
/*  Computation of Thrust of a Rocket Motor Under        */
/*        Gravitation and Acceleration                   */
/*                                                       */
/*********************************************************/
/*                                                       */
/*    Input Variables:                                   */
/*                                                       */
/*       weight    - weight of the rocket (pounds)       */
/*       velocity  - velocity of the rocket(feet/second)*/
/*       time      - duration of the thrust (seconds)    */
/*                                                       */
/*    Computed Variables:                                */
/*                                                       */
/*       force      - force due to acceleration (pounds)*/
/*       thrust     - total thrust due to acceleration   */
/*                    and weight (pounds)                */
/*                                                       */
/*    Output Variables:                                  */
/*                                                       */
/*       force      - force due to acceleration (pounds)*/
/*       thrust     - total thrust due to acceleration   */
/*                    and weight (pounds)                */
/*                                                       */
/*    Functions:                                         */
/*                                                       */
/*       funcforce  - function to compute the force      */
/*       functhrust - function to compute the thrust     */
/*                                                       */
/*********************************************************/
```

```
#include <stdio.h>

float  funcforce(float, float, float);
float  functhrust(float, float);

int main( )
{
    float weight, velocity, time;
    float force, thrust;

    printf("INPUT DATA\n");
    scanf("%f  %f  %f", &weight, &velocity, &time);

    printf("\nOUTPUT DATA\n");
    printf("Weight = %7.2f\n", weight);
    printf("Velocity = %7.2f\n",velocity);
    printf("Time = %5.2f\n\n", time);

    force = funcforce(weight, velocity, time);
    thrust = functhrust(weight, force);

    printf("Force due to acceleration = %8.2f\n", force);
    printf("Total thrust due to acceleration = %8.2f\n",
            thrust);

    return 0;
}


/*****************************************************/
/*                                                   */
/*   Function to Compute the Force on the Rocket     */
/*                                                   */
/*****************************************************/
/*                                                   */
/*   Constants:                                      */
/*                                                   */
/*      G = 32.2 ft/sec² – gravitational acceleration */
/*                                                   */
/*   Input Parameters:                               */
/*                                                   */
/*      weight1    – weight of the rocket (pounds)   */
/*      velocity1  – velocity of the rocket(feet/second)*/
```

```
/*        time1      - duration of the thrust (seconds)   */
/*                                                         */
/*    Return Variable:                                     */
/*                                                         */
/*         force    - force of the rocket motor            */
/*                                                         */
/*********************************************************/

float funcforce(float weight1, float velocity1, float time1)
{
    const float G = 32.2;
    float force;

    force = (weight1 * velocity1)/( G * time1);

    return force;
}

/*********************************************************/
/*                                                       */
/*   Function to Compute the Thrust on the Rocket        */
/*                                                       */
/*********************************************************/
/*                                                       */
/*    Input Parameters:                                  */
/*                                                       */
/*      weight1   - weight of the rocket (pounds)        */
/*      force1    - force on the rocket (pounds)         */
/*                                                       */
/*    Return Variable:                                   */
/*                                                       */
/*      thrust1  - thrust on the rocket motor            */
/*                                                       */
/*********************************************************/

float functhrust(float weight1, float force1)
{
    float thrust1;

    thrust1 = weight1 + force1;

    return thrust1;
}
```

Input and Output

```
INPUT DATA
5000.0 2000.0 10.0

OUTPUT DATA
Weight = 5000.00
Velocity = 2000.00
Time = 10.00

Force due to acceleration = 31055.90
Total thrust due to acceleration = 36055.90
```

There are two functions in this program, one to compute the force of the rocket motor and the other to compute the thrust of the rocket motor. These functions return single values and the values are stored in the variables `force` and `thrust` in the `main` program. Notice that the value returned from the `funcforce` is used in the function `functhrust` to compute the thrust. These functions pass the arguments by value and compute single values that are returned through the `return` statements.

5.6.2 Current in Series Circuit

Problem Write a program to compute the current in an AC circuit that has three resistances in series, and then, compute the voltage drop across the resistances. This example demonstrates several calls to a single function and the use of an expression as an argument.

Method Input the voltage V and the resistances R1, R2, and R3. Write two functions, one for computing the voltage drops across each resistance and another to output the current and the voltage drops in the circuit.

$$\text{effective resistance } R = R1 + R2 + R3 \text{ (ohms)}$$

$$\text{current } I = \frac{V}{R} \text{ (amps)}$$

$$\text{Voltage drop across R1} \quad V1 = IR1$$

$$\text{Voltage drop across R2} \quad V2 = IR2$$

Voltage drop across R3 V3 = IR3

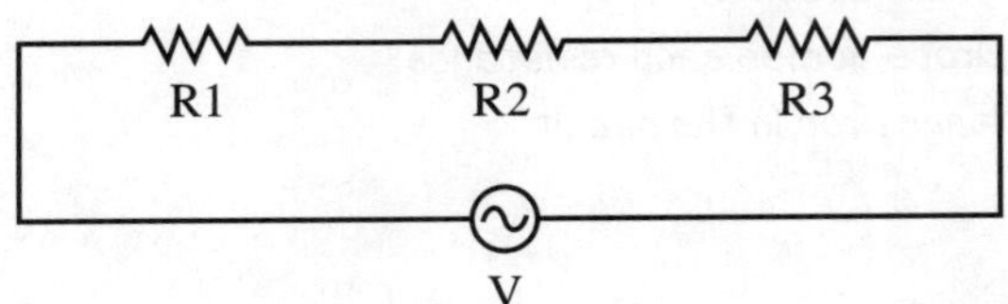

Data Input the values for voltage *v*, resistances *r*1, *r*2, and *r*3.

Pseudocode

```
main: program
  input voltage v, resistances r1, r2, r3
  funccurrent( )
  funcvoltdrop( )
  funcvoltdrop( )
  funcvoltdrop( )
  funcoutput( )
stop
function: funccurrent
  calculate the effective resistance

    r ← r1 + r2 + r3

  calculate the current

    i ← v / r

  end funccurrent

function: funcvoltdrop
  calculate voltage drop across a resistance

    v ← i * r

  end funcvoltdrop
```

function: funcoutput
  print the current in the circuit
  print the voltage drops across each resistance
  print the total voltage drop in the circuit
end funcoutput

There are three functions in this algorithm: The first function computes the current in the circuit, the second function computes the voltage drop across a single resistance, and the third function outputs the results of the computations.

Program

```
/***********************************************************/
/*                                                         */
/*     Compute the Current and Voltage Drop in an         */
/*                AC Series Circuit                        */
/*                                                         */
/***********************************************************/
/*                                                         */
/*    Input Variables:                                     */
/*                                                         */
/*        voltage  -  voltage of circuit (volts)           */
/*        res1, res2, res3 - resistances in series(ohms)  */
/*                                                         */
/*    Computed variables:                                  */
/*                                                         */
/*        current  -  current in the circuit               */
/*        volt1, volt2, volt3 - voltage drops across       */
/*                              each resistance            */
/*                                                         */
/*    Output variables:                                    */
/*                                                         */
/*        current  -  current in the circuit               */
/*        volt1, volt2, volt3 - voltage drops across       */
/*                              each resistance            */
/*                                                         */
/*    Functions called:                                    */
/*                                                         */
/*        funccurrent - function to compute the current    */
/*        funcvoltdrop - function to compute the voltage  */
/*                       drop                              */
```

```
/*        funcoutput  - function to output the results   */
/*                                                       */
/*********************************************************/

#include <stdio.h>

float funccurrent(float,  float,  float,  float);
float funcvoltdrop(float, float);
void funcoutput(float,  float,  float,  float,  float);

int main( )
{
    float  voltage, res1, res2, res3, current, volt1,
           volt2, volt3;
    printf("INPUT DATA\n");
    scanf("%f  %f  %f  %f", &voltage, &res1, &res2, &res3);
    current = funccurrent(voltage, res1, res2, res3);
    volt1 = funcvoltdrop(current, res1);
    volt2 = funcvoltdrop(current, res2);
    volt3 = funcvoltdrop(current, res3);

    funcoutput(current,volt1, volt2, volt3,
            volt1 + volt2 + volt3);

    return 0;
}


/*********************************************************/
/*                                                       */
/*     Function to Calculate the Current in the Circuit  */
/*                                                       */
/*********************************************************/
/*                                                       */
/*    Input Parameters:                                  */
/*        voltage1   -  voltage v in the circuit         */
/*        res1   -  resistance r1 in the circuit         */
/*        res2   -  resistance r2 in the circuit         */
/*        res3   -  resistance r3 in the circuit         */
/*                                                       */
/*    Local Variables:                                   */
/*       totres      -  total resistance of the circuit  */
/*       circurrent   -  current in the circuit          */
/*                                                       */
```

```
/*   Called by:                                             */
/*       main                                               */
/*                                                          */
/*   Return Variable:                                       */
/*      circurrent   -  current in the circuit              */
/*                                                          */
/************************************************************/

float funccurrent(float voltage1,  float res11,
                  float  res22,  float  res33)
{
    float  totres, circurrent;

    totres = res11 + res22 + res33;
    circurrent = voltage1 / totres;

    return circurrent;
}


/************************************************************/
/*                                                          */
/*      Function Computes the Voltage Drop Across a         */
/*               Resistance                                 */
/*                                                          */
/************************************************************/
/*                                                          */
/*   Input Parameters:                                      */
/*       current1  -  current in the circuit                */
/*       res       -  resistance in the circuit             */
/*                                                          */
/*   Output Parameters:                                     */
/*       none                                               */
/*                                                          */
/*   Local Variable:                                        */
/*       volt - voltage drop across resistance              */
/*                                                          */
/*   Called by:                                             */
/*       main                                               */
/*                                                          */
/*   Return Variable:                                       */
/*       volt  -  voltage drop across resistance            */
/*                                                          */
/************************************************************/
```

```
float funcvoltdrop(float current1, float res)

{
    float volt;
    volt = current1 * res;

    return volt;
}


/********************************************************/
/*                                                      */
/*          Function to Output the Results              */
/*                                                      */
/********************************************************/
/*                                                      */
/*   Input Parameters:                                  */
/*       current1 - current in the circuit              */
/*       volt11   - voltage drop across resistance r1   */
/*       volt22   - voltage drop across resistance r2   */
/*       volt33   - voltage drop across resistance r3   */
/*       totvolt  - total voltage drop across the       */
/*                     circuit                          */
/*                                                      */
/*   Called by:                                         */
/*       main                                           */
/*                                                      */
/*   Return Variable:                                   */
/*       none                                           */
/*                                                      */
/********************************************************/

void funccoutput(float current1, float volt11,float volt22,
            float volt33,float  totvolt)
{
    printf("\n                          OUTPUT DATA\n");
    printf("      Current in the circuit = %4.2f\n", current1);
    printf("      Voltage drop across resistance r1 = %6.2f\n",
           volt11);
    printf("      Voltage drop across resistance r2 = %6.2f\n",
           volt22);
    printf("      Voltage drop across resistance r3 = %6.2f\n",
           volt33);
```

```
printf("        Total voltage drop across circuit = %6.2f\n",
            totvolt);
return;
}
```

Input and Output

```
INPUT DATA
200. 50. 100. 150.

                    OUTPUT DATA
        Current in the circuit = 0.67
        Voltage drop across resistance r1 =  33.33
        Voltage drop across resistance r2 =  66.67
        Voltage drop across resistance r3 = 100.00
        Total voltage drop across circuit = 200.00
```

This program has a `main` function and three subfunctions. The `main` calls the subfunctions. The input data is in the `main`. Function `funccurrent` computes the current in the circuit and returns the value computed to the `main` function through the `return` statement. Function `funcvoltdrop` computes the voltage drop across each of the resistances one at a time, and returns each voltage drop to the `main` function through the `return` statement. Function `funcoutput` prints the results computed by `funcvoltdrop` and their sum.

5.6.3 Square Root Function

Problem Write a square root function that returns an error flag when a negative argument is passed to it. Write a `main` program to test the function. This example demonstrates call-by-value, call-by-pointer, and the return of a status flag.

Method The Newton–Raphson method of computing the square root is used. If the argument is negative, the function returns a flag. The algorithm is presented in Chapter 1, Section 1.6.3.

Data Input a real number for which a square root is required.

Pseudocode

```
main function:
   number of inputs
   for each input number
```

```
      invoke the function: numsqrt( )
    if it has a square root
      output the number, square root
    else
      print number and a message: "no real square root"
    end for
stop

function numsqrt:
compute the square root of num
if num < 0
    signal an error by returning an error flag
else if num == 0
    square root is 0
else
    x0 ← x
    x1 ← x / 2.0
    do while |x0 – x1| > 0.0001
      x0 ← x1
      x1 ← (x0 + x/x0) / 2.0
    end do
    square root = x1

    return success flag;
end numsqrt
```

Program

```
/******************************************************/
/*                                                    */
/*     Compute the Square Root of a Number            */
/*                                                    */
/******************************************************/
/*                                                    */
/*    Input Variables:                                */
/*                                                    */
/*      num   – number                                */
/*                                                    */
/*    Computer variables:                             */
```

```
/*                                                     */
/*      sqroot  - square root of the number num        */
/*                                                     */
/*   Output variables:                                 */
/*                                                     */
/*      numsqroot  - square root of the number num     */
/*                                                     */
/*   Functions called:                                 */
/*                                                     */
/*      numsqrt  - function to compute the             */
/*                 square root                         */
/*                                                     */
/*******************************************************/

#include <stdio.h>
#include <stdlib.h>

int numsqrt(float, float  *);

int main( )
{
    int flag, count;
    float num, sqroot;

    printf("How many numbers to calculate?\n");
    scanf ("%d", &count);
    printf("Input Data     Number     Square Root\n");

    while(count != 0)
    {
        scanf("%f", &num);
        flag = numsqrt(num, &sqroot);
        if(flag == 0)
        {
            printf("                %6.2f      Negative number, ",
                   num);
            printf("                            no real square root\n");
        }
        else
        {
            printf("                %6.2f      %6.2f\n",
                   num, sqroot);
        }
```

```
        count--;
    }

    return 0;
}

/*****************************************************/
/*                                                   */
/*          Approximation of Square Root Using       */
/*            Newton-Raphson Method                  */
/*                                                   */
/*****************************************************/
/*                                                   */
/*    Input Parameters:                              */
/*        num1 - real, number whose square root      */
/*                is required                        */
/*                                                   */
/*    Output Parameters:                             */
/*        sqroot - square root of num1               */
/*                                                   */
/*    Local Variables:                               */
/*        flag - set 0 if input is negative          */
/*                1 otherwise                        */
/*        sqroot0 - temporary variable to hold the   */
/*                  approximate square root value    */
/*        sqroot1 - required accuracy of square root */
/*                                                   */
/*****************************************************/

int numsqrt(float num1, float *sqroot)
{
    int flag = 1;
    float sqroot0, error;
    if(num1 < 0)
    {
        flag = 0;
    }
    else if(num1 == 0)
        *sqroot = 0;
    else
    {
        error = .0001;
        sqroot0 = num1;
```

```
        *sqroot = num1 / 2.0;

        do
        {
            sqroot0 = *sqroot;
            *sqroot = (sqroot0 + (num1 / sqroot0))/ 2.0;
        }while((abs(*sqroot - sqroot0)) > error);

    }
    return flag;
}
```

Input and Output

```
How many numbers to calculate?
5

Input Data        Number       Square Root
25.00
                   25.00          5.00
677.00
                  677.00         26.02
-16.00
                  -16.00         Negative number,
                                 no real square root
625.00
                  625.00         25.00
0.00
                    0.00          0.00
```

To thoroughly test this program, the data must include both positive and negative numbers as well as a 0.00.

Chapter Summary

C uses program units called functions to implement modularity. A function is block structured. The body of a function begins with a left brace ({) and ends with a right brace (}).

- Every function in C must be prototyped. The declaration of a function is called a function prototype. The computer uses a function prototype to check that the arguments and corresponding parameters match with respect to data type, order, and number. The general form of the function prototype is:

data-type-returned function-name(list of data types of the parameters);

data-type-returned may be: `int`, `float`, `double`, `char`, or `void`.

function-name: any name that describes what the function does and is a valid identifier.

data types of parameters: must correspond to list of data-types of arguments.

A function prototype must precede any call to the function.

- Every function must be implemented. The actual code of the function is contained in the function implementation. The general form of a function implementation is:

```
data-type-returned function-name(list of typed parameters)
{
    body of the function

    return value;
}
```

- If a function returns a value through the `return` statement, the function header and the function prototype must specify the data type of the value the function is returning.
- If a function does not return a value through the `return` statement, then the function data type in the function header and prototype must be specified as `void`.
- A function should have a `return` statement as its last statement.

The simplest function one can write in C is to print headings and subheadings, or to initialize a process. Such functions will not return any value through the `return` statement, so there is no need to specify the return data type. For such functions the return data type is specified as `void`. Also there is no need to specify the parameters so the parameter list is an empty set of parentheses.

A function may return more than one value. When a function returns more than one value, they are returned through the parameters rather than the `return` statement. Any time a function returns more than one value through the parameters, the addresses of the variables receiving the values must be specified in the argument list of the calling function.

The communication between the calling function and the called function is through the arguments and parameters and through the `return` statement. Values can be passed between functions in two different ways:

- By value—in this case the arguments are copied into temporary locations and the function parameters access copies.
- By pointer—in this case the memory addresses of the arguments are passed to the function parameters and the function parameters access the values by dereferencing the addresses or using the addresses to store values.
- An input function normally receives memory addresses from the calling function so that the function can return the input values to the calling function by storing them directly into the argument addresses.
- An output function normally receives the data from the calling function by value. The data is passed by value so that the data is protected and cannot be altered.
- A function may receive some arguments by value and others by pointer.
- A return statement passes a value.

Recursive functions can be written in C. A recursive function is a function that calls itself. A recursive function is called by a parent function the first time, after which the function calls itself. A recursive function ultimately must return the control to the parent function under a specific condition. The specific condition is called a base condition. Several recursive functions are presented in this chapter and in later chapters.

Exercises

1. Write a `main` function and the subfunctions that computes the tip speed of a propeller whose shaft speed S varies from 1000 to 10,000 rpm in increments of 1000. Pass the diameter D of the propeller to the function from the `main`.

- A function to compute the angular velocity in rad/sec for tip speed S of a propeller from the formula

$$\omega = \frac{2\pi S}{60}$$

- A function to output the tip speed and the angular velocity.

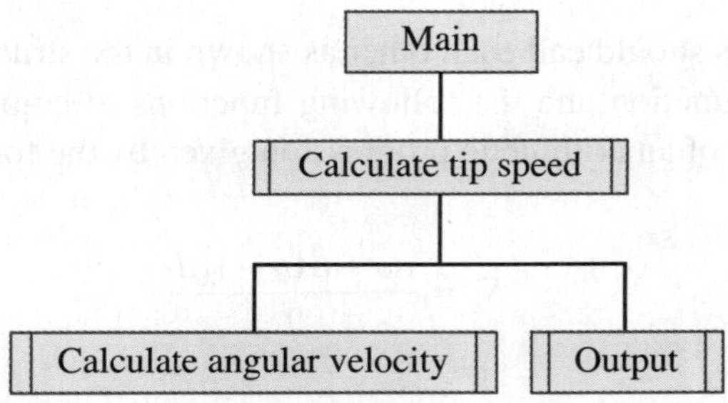

2. Write a `main` function and the following functions to compute the stress and strain in a steel rod of diameter D (inches) and length L (inches) subject to the compression loads P of 10,000 to 1,000,000 pounds in increments of 100,000 pounds. The modulus of elasticity E for steel is 30×10^6.
   - A function to compute the stress from the formulas

$$\text{stress } f = \frac{P}{A}$$

   where $A = \pi D^2 / 4.0$
   - A function to compute the strain from the formulas

$$\text{elongated or shortened length } \Delta L = \frac{fL}{E}$$

$$\text{strain } e = \frac{\Delta L}{L} = \frac{f}{E}$$

- A function to output the stress and strain at different loads of P.

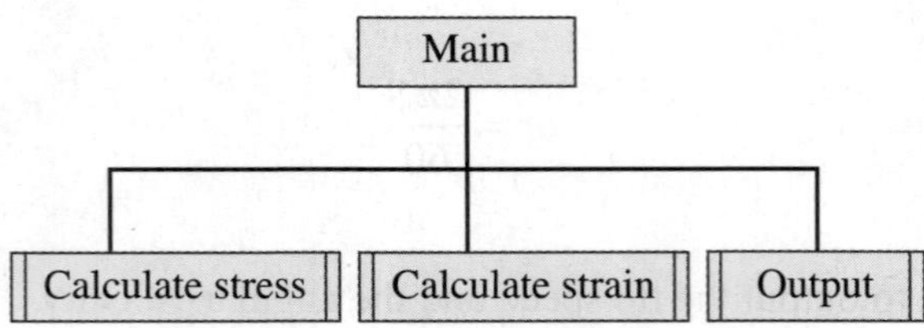

The functions should call each other as shown in the structure chart.

3. Write a `main` function and the following functions to compute and print the sum of n terms of an arithmetic progression given by the formula

$$S_n = \frac{na + n(n-1)d}{2}$$

where a is the first term of the progression,
d is the common difference, and
n is the number of terms in the sum.

When applied to a sum-of-years depreciation problem both a and d are taken to be 1. Use a function to print the numbers from 10 to 100 by 10's as column headings for values of n.

- A function to compute S_n from 10 to 1000 in increments of 10.
- A function to print the computed values of S_n in the form of a table, 10 per line.

The functions should call each other as shown in the structure chart. Note that each value is printed as it is calculated. Therefore, the output will need to keep track of how many values it has printed to use the line feed character after every 10th value.

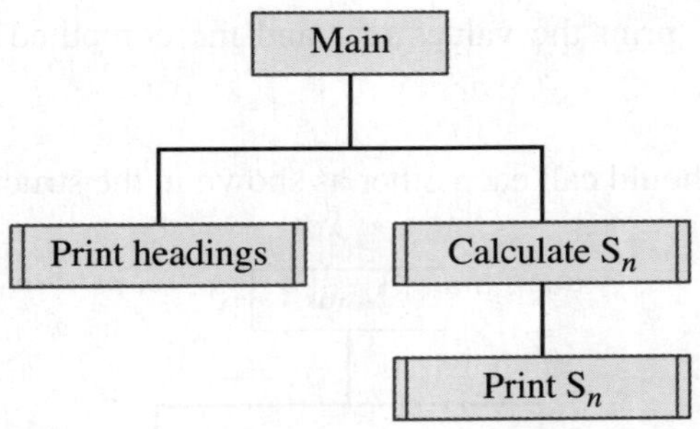

4. Write a `main` function and the following functions to compute the velocity at various time intervals of a body sliding down a slope with an initial velocity v_0. If initial velocity $v_0 = 5$ and acceleration $a = 20.5t + 9.75$.

   Acceleration a as derivative of velocity with respect to time is given by

$$a = \frac{dv}{dt} \quad \text{at } t = 0$$

therefore,

$$\int_5^v dv = \int_0^t a\,dt$$

$$= \int_0^t (20.5t + 9.75)\,dt$$

therefore,

$$v - 5 = \frac{20.5}{2} t^2 + 9.75t$$

therefore,

$$v = 10.25t^2 + 9.75t + 5$$

- A function to compute v from the preceding formula with $t = 0.5$ to 10.0 by increments of 0.5.

- A function to print the values of t and the computed value of v two pairs per line.

The functions should call each other as shown in the structure chart.

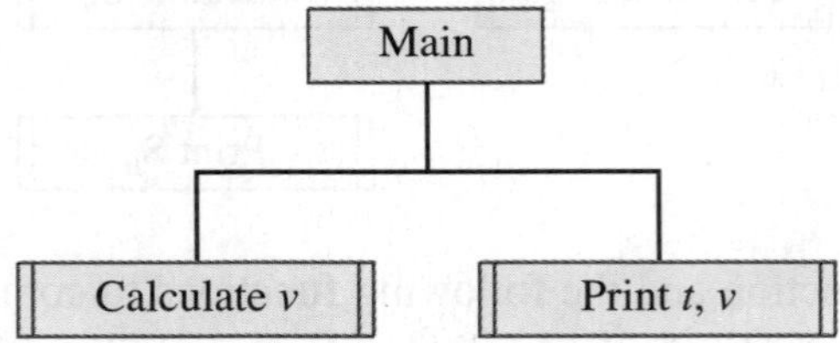

5. Write a `main` function and subfunctions to compute and print the mass of a balloon inflated to V cu ft, at P pounds of pressure, at a temperature of T degrees. A function reads the input values for the pressure P, volume V, and temperature T from a file `datex.dat`. The formula relating the variables is:

$$PV = 0.42M\,(T + 460)$$

$$M = \frac{PV}{0.42\,(T + 460)}$$

- A function to compute M from the preceding formula.
- A function to print the values of P, V, T, and M.

The functions should be called as shown in the structure chart.

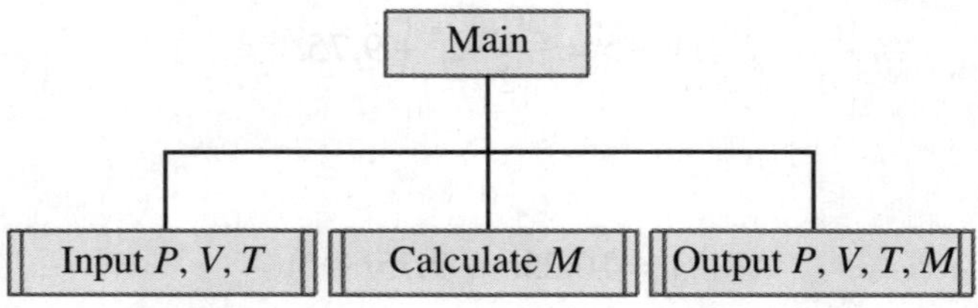

6. Write a `main` function and subfunctions to compute and print the retarding force required to stop a train of weight m lbs traveling at velocity V miles/sec

within a distance of 300, 400, 500, and 600 feet. Input the mass m and velocity V in the `main` program.

- A function to compute the retarding force as follows:
  The formula for acceleration is given by

$$a = \frac{V_f^2 - V_0^2}{2d}$$

where a is the acceleration,
V_f is final velocity,
V_0 is the initial velocity, and
d is the distance.

Retarding force $F = ma$

- A function to print the distance and the retarding force with labels.

These functions should call each other as shown in the structure chart.

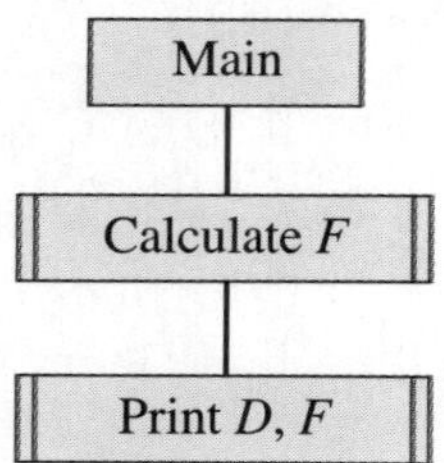

7. Write a `main` function and subfunctions to compute the amount of steel and concrete required for the construction of a series of cooling tanks for a power plant. The dimensions of each tank (length `l`, width `w`, and height `h`) are the input to the `main` program. The wall thickness is t_w and the floor thickness is t_f. The ratio of steel to concrete is 1:4.

   - A function to compute the amount of steel.
   - A function to compute the amount of concrete required to construct each tank.
   - A function to print the amount of steel and amount of concrete for each tank.

The functions should call each other as shown in the structure chart.

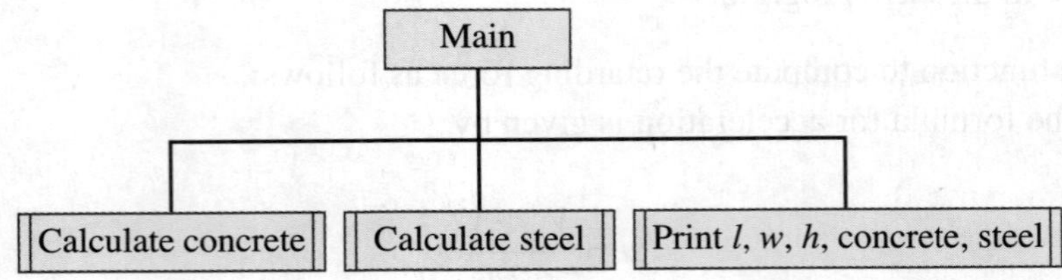

CHAPTER 6

Storage Classes

Objective

To understand the existence, nonexistence, accessibility, and suspension of memory allocated for the variables declared global and local to functions.

Memory must be allocated by the computer for all variables declared in a program. Depending on the location of the variable declaration, the storage for the variable may continue to exist or cease to exist during program execution when the variable is no longer used. On the basis of where the variables are declared, the storage allocated for each variable is classified by the compiler as belonging to the `auto`, `extern`, `static`, or `register` storage class. The storage for variables declared in a function exists whenever the function is executed. If the function is not executed, storage for the variables does not exist. This may be overridden by explicitly declaring the storage class. The location of the declaration and the storage class to which a variable belongs determines where in the program the storage for the variable is accessible and where it is not accessible. The storage class determines which part of the program can access the storage for a variable and which part of the program cannot access the storage for a variable.

6.1 Scope of Variables

The scope of a variable is defined as that part of a program where the name of the variable is known and its storage can be accessed. This depends on where in the program it is declared. If a variable is declared ahead of the definition of the `main` and all other functions it has global scope. Global scope means the `main` and all the functions can reference the variable name and can access its storage. If a variable is declared inside the `main`, it is local to the `main`; it has local scope and it can be referenced and accessed by that name only inside the `main`.

6.1.1 Block Structure

The variables declared in a C program have block scope. A block is a collection of statements enclosed between left and right braces. All functions are block structures in C. A variable may be declared outside or inside a block. If a variable is declared outside a block and another variable with the same name is declared inside a block, the name will reference the one inside the block rather than the one declared outside the block while the block is being executed. The variable declared outside is suspended until execution of the block finishes, but it still exists. The following examples show the scope of variables in a block structure.

Example 1

```
#include <stdio.h>

int main( )
{
    int  a = 10;
    printf("a = %d\n", a);        /* 1 */
     {
      int b = 5;
      printf("b = %d\n", b);      /* 2 */
      b = b + 15;
      printf("b = %d\n", b);      /* 3 */
      {
         int c  = 40;
         printf("c = %d\n", c); /* 4 */
      }
      b = b + 4;
      printf("b = %d\n", b);      /* 5 */
    }
    a = a + 15;
    printf("a = %d\n", a);        /* 6 */

    return 0;
}
```

The numbered lines with `printf( )` are executed in the following order with the following effect on storage allocation:

1 a exists with value 10,

2, 3 a and b exist with values 10 and 5 (line 2) 10 and 20 (line 3),

4 a, b, and c exist with values 10, 20, 40,

5 a and b exist with values 10 and 24, c is nonexistent, and

6 a exists with value 25, b and c are nonexistent.

The output is as follows:

```
a = 10
b = 5
b = 20
c = 40
b = 24
a = 25
```

When all the variables of the preceding example are given the same name, the effect is as follows:

Example 2

```
#include <stdio.h>

  int main( )
  {
     int  x = 10;
     printf("x = %d\n", x);            /* 1 */
     {
        int x = 5;                     /* this is a new x */
        printf("x = %d\n", x);         /* 2 */
        x = x + 15;
        printf("x = %d\n", x);         /* 3 */
        {
           int  x = 40;                /* this is a new x */
           printf("x = %d\n", x);      /* 4 */
        }
        x = x + 4;                     /* only the 2nd x is accessible */
        printf("x = %d\n", x);         /* 5 */
     }
     x = x + 15;                       /* only the 1st x is accessible */
     printf("x = %d\n", x);            /* 6 */

     return 0;
     }
```

The numbered lines with `printf( )` are executed in the following order with the following effect on storage:

1 1st x exists with value 10,

2 1st x exists but is suspended, 2nd x exists with value 5,

3 1st x exists but is suspended, 2nd x exists with value 20,

4 1st and 2nd x exist but are suspended, 3rd x exists with value 40,

5 1st x exists but is suspended, 2nd x is reactivated with value 24, 3rd x is non-existent, and

6 1st x is reactivated with value 25, 2nd and 3rd x are nonexistent.

The output is as follows:

```
x = 10
x = 5
x = 20
x = 40
x = 24
x = 25
```

> *Programming Warning:* No two variables declared in the same block may have the same name. It is poor programming practice to reuse a name in a single function.

6.1.2 Global Scope and Block Scope

A function is a block, as it has a collection of statements enclosed between left and right braces. If a variable is declared outside and ahead of the definition of any function or functions it has global scope with respect to those functions. All the functions following the declaration can reference the name and have access to the storage of such variables. On the other hand if the variable is declared inside a function it has local scope. A variable with local scope can only be referenced and accessed by the local name by the function in which the variable is declared. Since `main` is a function, a variable declared outside and ahead of the `main` is global to `main` and the functions that follow `main`. A variable declared inside the main is local to main and only main can reference and access that variable by the local name.

Variables declared as global can be seen and accessed by the main and all other functions that follow the main. The problem with global variables is that they may be easily altered in any function because of their accessibility in the entire program. It is always better to declare variables local to a function so that no other function can reference and access those local variables and alter them. Local variables are strictly controlled by their local scope and outside the local scope they are not accessible unless they are passed as arguments. The following examples show the global and local scope of names.

> *Programming Hint:* Using local variables protects them from unintentional changes because the local variables are referenced by name only within the block in which they are declared.

Example 1

```
#include <stdio.h>
void func1(void);        /* func1 is global */
void func2(void);        /* func2 is global */
void func3(void);        /* func3 is global */

int main( )
{
   int  x = 20;
   printf("In main x = %d\n", x);     /* 1 */
   func1( );
   x = x + 10;
   printf("In main x = %d\n", x);     /* 2 */
   func2( );
   x = x + 40;
   printf("In main x = %d\n", x);     /* 3 */
   func3( );

   return 0;
}
```

scope of 1st x

```
int  x;
void func1(void)
{
   x = 5;
   printf("In func1 x = %d\n", x); /* 4 */
   return;
}

void func2(void)
{
   int x = 0;
   printf("In func2 x = %d\n", x); /* 5 */
   x = 50;
   printf("In func2 x = %d\n", x); /* 6 */
   return;
}

void func3(void)
{
  printf("In func3 x = %d\n", x);   /* 7 */
  return;
}
```

scope of 2nd x

scope of 3rd x

The numbered lines are executed in the following order of the `printf( )` statements with the following effect on storage allocation:

1 1st x exists with value 20,

4 1st x exists but is suspended, 2nd x exists with value 5,

2 1st x is reactivated with value 30, 2nd x exists but is suspended (see section on storage classes),

5 1st x and 2nd x exist but are suspended, 3rd x exists with value 0,

6 1st x and 2nd x exist but are suspended, 3rd x exists with value 50,

3 1st x is reactivated with value 70, 2nd x exists but is suspended, 3rd x is nonexistent, and

7 1st x exists but is suspended, 2nd x is reactivated with value 5, 3rd x is nonexistent.

Note when control leaves a block by means of a function call, local variables are suspended rather than becoming nonexistent. When control returns to the calling block, variables local to the function become nonexistent, but variables global to the function are suspended everywhere they are not global.

The output is as follows:

```
In main x = 20
In func1 x = 5
In main x = 30
In func2 x = 0
In func2 x = 50
In main x = 70
In func3 x = 5
```

Notice that the variable x declared in main is local to main. The variable x declared after main but before func1 is global to func1, func2, and func3. The variable x declared inside func2 is local to func2. The variable x declared in func2 will override the variable x declared before func1. In effect, main and func2 each have their own variable x, while func1 and func3 share a variable x.

> *Programming Hint:* Confusion can be avoided by using different variable names in different functions and avoiding global variables.

6.1.3 Scope of Access

When variables are declared with local scope, they can be accessed by a different name outside that scope by passing their values or addresses as arguments. The following example differs from the example of Section 6.1.2 in that each function call passes the variable x by value to a function that picks it up under the local name y. The print statements have been altered to print both x and y.

```
#include <stdio.h>
void func1(int);
void func2(int);
void func3(int);

int main( )
{
    int x = 20, y = 9;

    printf("In main x = %d   y = %d\n", x, y);     /*  1  */
    func1(x);
    x = x + 10;
    printf("In main x = %d   y = %d\n", x, y);     /*  2  */
    func2(x);
    x = x + 40;
    printf("In main x = %d   y = %d\n", x, y);     /*  3  */
    func3(x);
```

```
    return 0;
}


int x;
void func1(int y)
{
    x = 5;
    printf("In func1 x = %d   y = %d\n", x, y);    /* 4 */
    return;
}

void func2(int y)
{
    int x = 0;
    printf("In func2 x = %d   y = %d\n", x, y);    /* 5 */
    x = 50;
    printf("In func2 x = %d   y = %d\n", x, y);    /* 6 */

    return;
}

void func3(int y)
{
    printf("In func3 x = %d   y = %d\n", x, y);    /* 7 */
    return;
}
```

The scope and value of the variables are as follows:

	1st x	1st y	2nd x	2nd y	3rd x	3rd y	4th y
Line 1	20	9	/	/	/	/	/
Line 4	20	9	5	20	/	/	/
Line 2	30	9	5	/	/	/	/
Line 5	30	9	5	/	0	30	/
Line 6	30	9	5	/	50	30	/
Line 3	70	9	5	/	/	/	/
Line 7	70	9	5	/	/	/	70

The variables that exist but are suspended are shown in shaded boxes. The value of the first *x* is accessible in `func1`, `func2`, and `func3` under another name because it is passed to those functions. Note that variables can only be passed as arguments when they are active.

6.1.4 Review Questions

1. Indicate whether the following statements are true or false.
   a. Any variable declared before the `main` function is global to the `main` and to all other functions that follow the `main`.
   b. If a variable is declared before a function and a variable with the same name is declared inside, then inside the function, the one declared inside has precedence over the one declared outside the function.
   c. Any variable declared inside a block is local to the block.
   d. It is safer to declare variables global rather than local.
   e. A function is block structured. Therefore, any variable declared inside a function is local to the function.
2. Answer the following questions.
   a. What is printed by the following code?

```
#include <stdio.h>
int main( )
{
     int x = 5;
     printf("x = %d\n", x);
     {
          x = x + 10;
          printf("x = %d\n", x);
          {
               int x = 25;
               printf("x = %d\n", x);
          }
          x = x + 15;
          printf("x = %d\n", x);
     }
     x = x + 20;
     printf("x = %d\n", x);

     return 0;
}
```

b. What is printed by the following code?

```
#include <stdio.h>
void func1(void );
int x = 10;

int main( )
{
    printf("In main x = %d\n", x);
    x = x + 15;
    printf("In main x = %d\n", x);
    func1( );
    x = x + 10;
    printf("In main x = %d\n", x);

    return 0;
}

void  func1(void)
{
    printf("In func1 x = %d\n", x);
    x = x + 10;
    printf("In func1 x = %d\n", x);
    {
        int x = 5;
        printf("In func1 x = %d\n", x);
    }
    x = x + 10;
    printf("In func1 x = %d\n", x);

    return;
}
```

3. Find and explain three errors in the following code.

```
#include <stdio.h>

int a = 5;

void func1(void);
void func2(int);
```

```
int main( )
{
      int  b = 8;

      printf("a = %d\n", a);
      func1( );
      func2(b);

      return 0;
}

void func1(void)
{
      int a;
      printf("a = %d\n", a);
      printf("c = %d\n", c);
      return;
}

void func2(void)
{
      printf("b = %d\n", b);
      return;
}
```

6.2 Storage Classes in a Single File

Variables are classified by storage classes according to their declarations and where in the program the variables are declared. There are four storage classes: `auto`, `extern`, `static`, and `register`. All storage classes except `extern` have file scope. This means they are only accessible in the program file in which they are declared. The `extern` storage class is accessible across files and might be used when building a library of programs. When a variable is declared with an explicit storage class the general form of the declaration statement is:

storage-class data-type variable-name;

Notice that the storage class must be specified first and then data type followed by a variable name. The following examples show the proper declaration of variables.

```
auto int x;
extern int Y;
static int Z;
register int W;
```

6.2.1 Storage Class auto

Storage class auto is the default storage class. All local variables declared inside a block are of the auto storage class. The explicit declaration of an auto storage class variable is as follows:

```
auto int x;
```

which, is the same as: `int x;`

An auto storage class variable need not be given a value when it is declared. However such a variable must be given a value before its value is used. An auto variable may be given a value in a declaration statement or through an assignment statement or through an input statement. The following examples show the declaration and use of auto class variables.

```
#include <stdio.h>
int  func1(int,  int);
int main( )
{
    int  x = 10, y = 5, z;
    z = func1(x, y);
    printf("x = %d   y = %d    z = %d\n", x, y, z);

    return 0;
}

int func1(int a, int b)
{
    int c;

    c = a + b;

    return c;
}
```

main( )

x	y	z
10	5	15

func1( )

c
15

The output from this program is:

```
x = 10    y = 5    z = 15
```

Notice that the variables x, y, and z in the main are local variables and are auto storage class variables by default. Their storage is local to main; they exist in the storage space of the main program, x and y are given values in the declaration, z is given a value by an assignment statement, and a and b are declared in the function header and given values when the function is called. The variable c declared in func1 is an auto storage class variable that is local to func1, and exists in the storage space of func1. This is why x, y, and z can only be accessed in main and must be passed as parameters to func1. It also explains why main cannot access the computed value of c directly, but it must be returned by func1.

6.2.2 Storage Class extern

The extern storage class is used primarily to access functions that have been declared and implemented in another source code file, and to access tables that are stored in separate files.

Any variable declared global to the entire program or declared outside any function or functions is an extern storage class variable. An extern storage class variable is automatically defined when it is declared and given a default value of zero, provided that it is not declared as having the class extern. When it is specifically declared as extern, no storage is assigned and no value is assigned. The following examples show the definition and declaration of extern storage class variables.

```
#include <stdio.h>

void  func1(void);
void  func2(void);

int main( )
{
    int  x = 5;               /*  local auto class variable declaration  */
    printf("In main x = %d\n", x);  /* 1 */
    func1( );
    x = x  + 5;
    printf("In main x = %d\n", x);  /* 2 */
```

```
    func2( );
    x = x + 5;
    printf("In main x = %d\n", x);  /* 3 */

    return 0;
}

int x;                     /* extern storage class variable definition */
void func1(void)
{
    printf("In func1 x = %d\n", x); /* 4 */
    x = 15;
    printf("In func1 x = %d\n", x);
    x = x + 10;
    printf("In func1 x = %d\n", x);
}

void func2(void)
{
    x = x + 20;
    printf("In func2 x = %d\n", x); /* 5 */
    x = x + 15;
    printf("In func2 x = %d\n", x);
}
```

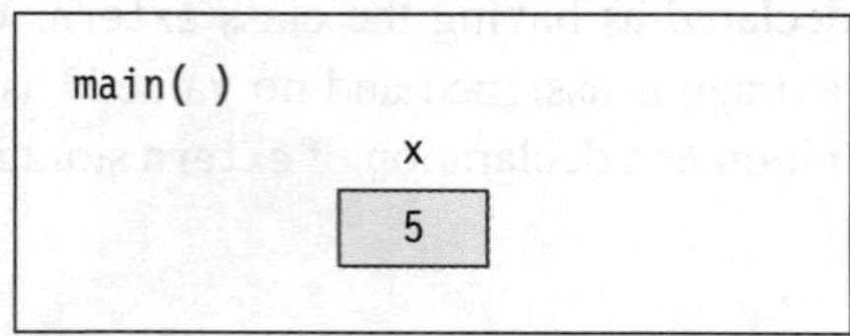

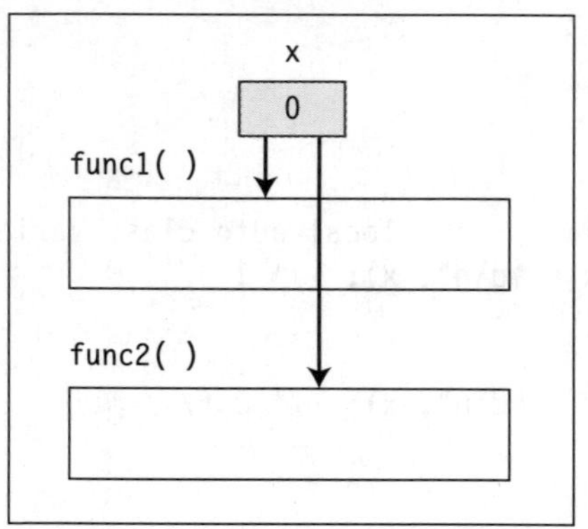

The numbered lines are executed in the following order with the following effect on storage allocation.

1 1st x exists with value 5, 2nd x is suspended,
4 1st x exists but is suspended, 2nd x activated with default value of 0,
2 1st x is reactivated with value 10, 2nd x exists but is suspended,
5 1st x exists but is suspended, 2nd x is reactivated with value 60, and
3 1st x is reactivated with value 15, 2nd x exists but is suspended.

The output is as follows:

```
In main x = 5
In func1 x = 0 /* extern variables are automatically initialized to 0 */
In func1 x = 15
In func1 x = 25
In main x = 10
In func2 x = 45
In func2 x = 60
In main x = 15
```

Notice that the variable `x` defined outside `func1` and `func2` is an `extern` class variable. The functions `func1` and `func2` can access this variable. The scope of the `extern` variable `x` is `func1` and `func2`. The `main` program can not access the `extern` variable `x` defined before `func1`. The `main` program has a local variable `x`, and can only access the local variable `x`. The output shows the sequence in which the `printf()` statements are executed. For the `main` program to access the `extern` variable `x` defined before the `func1`, the variable `x` must be declared in the `main` program as an `extern` variable.

The following program segment shows the declaration of `x` in `main` as an `extern` variable and the output shows how the `main` program can access the `extern` variable even though it is not within its scope. In fact, the C code for the `main` program could be in a different file than the code for `func1` and `func2`.

```
#include <stdio.h>

void  func1(void);
void  func2(void);

int main( )
```

```
{
    extern int  x;
    x = 5;
    printf("In main x = %d\n", x);
    func1( );
    x = x + 5;
    printf("In main x = %d\n", x);
    func2( );
    x = x + 5;
    printf("In main x = %d\n", x);

    return 0;
}

int  x;
void func1(void)
{
    printf("In func1 x = %d\n", x);
    x = 15;
    printf("In func1 x = %d\n", x);
    x = x + 10;
    printf("In func1 x = %d\n", x);
}
void func2(void)
{
    x = 20;
    printf("In func2 x = %d\n", x);
    x = x + 15;
    printf("In func2 x = %d\n", x);
}
```

The output is as follows:

```
In main x = 5
In func1 x = 5
In func1 x = 15
In func1 x = 25
In main x = 30
In func2 x = 20
In func2 x = 35
In main x = 40
```

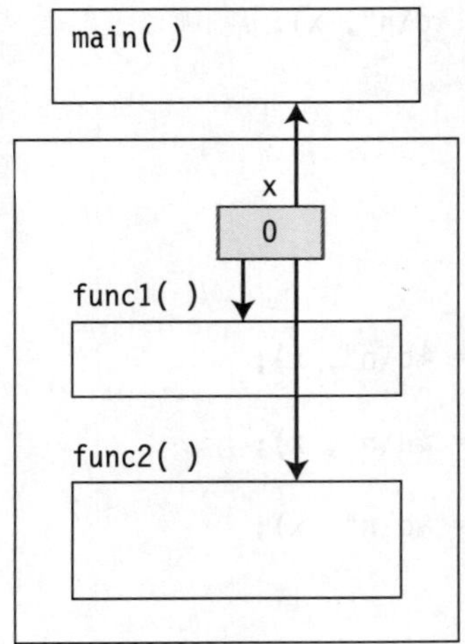

Notice that the `main` function can access the `extern` variable defined ahead of the function `func1`, because the `extern` variable `x` is declared in `main` as `extern`. The output shows the sequence in which the `print()` statements are executed.

An `auto` variable with the same name as an `extern` variable has precedence, within its scope, over the extern variable. An `auto` variable with the same name as the `extern` variable overrides the `extern` variable. The following program segment shows the `extern` variable and an `auto` variable and the output.

```
#include <stdio.h>

void  func1(void);
void  func2(void);

int main( )
{
    extern int  x;
    x = 5;
    printf("In main x = %d\n", x);
    func1( );
    x = x  + 5;
    printf("In main x = %d\n", x);
    func2( );
    x = x + 5;
```

```
    printf("In main x = %d\n", x);

    return 0;
}

int  x;
void func1(void)
{
    printf("In func1 x = %d\n", x);
    x = 15;
    printf("In func1 x = %d\n", x);
    x = x + 15;
    printf("In func1 x = %d\n", x);
}

void func2(void)
{
    int  x = 10;
    printf("In func2 x = %d\n", x);
    x = x + 15;
    printf("In func2 x = %d\n", x);
}
```

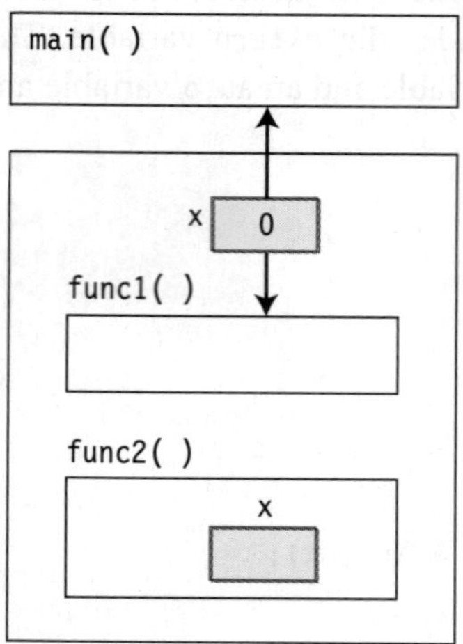

The output is as follows:

```
In main x = 5
In func1 x = 5
In func1 x = 15
```

```
In func1 x = 30
In main x = 35
In func2 x = 10
In func2 x = 25
In main x = 40
```

Notice that the declaration of x in func2 is local to func2, as it is an auto variable that overrides the extern variable defined ahead of func1 and declared as extern in main.

Functions themselves have the default storage class extern. Functions that are declared ahead of the main function are global to all of the functions of a program and therefore can be called by any of them. However, if a function is declared anywhere other than ahead of the main function, it is only accessible where it is global or local, unless it is explicitly declared extern.

6.2.3 Storage Class static

Variables declared as static are used for accumulators, counters, and summations. A static variable is defined when it is declared and is automatically initialized to zero unless another value is specified. Unlike an auto variable it does not cease to exist outside its scope, but becomes inaccessible, retaining its value until it is accessible again. Because the storage of a static variable retain the updated value every time it is changed, it is effective for the entire duration of the program execution. The following code segments show the use of static variables.

static Variable Local to a Function:

```
#include <stdio.h>
int func1(int  );
int main( )
{
    int i, sum;                              /* 1 */
    for (i = 0; i < 3; i++)
    {
        sum = func1(i);
        printf("In main sum = %d\n", sum); /* 2 */
    }

    return 0;
}

int func1(int  k)                       /* this function accumulates a sum */
{
    static  int  sumk ;
```

```
    sumk += k;                                    /* 3 */
    printf("In func1 sumk = %d\n", sumk);
    return sumk;
}
```

The numbered lines are executed in the following order with the following effect on storage allocation:

1 `i, sum` exists, `sumk` is nonexistent;

3 `i, sum` exists but are suspended, `sumk` exists with default value 0;

2 `i, sum` are reactivated, `sumk` exists but is suspended;

3 `i, sum` are suspended, `sumk` is reactivated; and

2 `i, sum` are reactivated, `sumk` exists but is suspended.

The output is as follows:

```
In func1 sumk = 0
In main sum = 0
In func1 sumk = 1
In main sum = 1
In func1 sumk = 3
In main sum = 3
```

Notice that `sumk` is automatically initialized to zero in the function when it is declared. It is updated using the values of `i`. Since it is a `static` variable it will stay updated until the program terminates. The effect is to calculate ((0 + 0) + 1) + 2.

`static` Variable Global to Several Functions

```
#include <stdio.h>

int func1();
int func2();

int main( )
{
    int i, sum;                                   /* 1 */
    for (i = 0; i < 3; i++)
    {
        sum = func1( );
        printf("In main sum = %d\n", sum);    /* 2 */
        sum  = func2( );
        printf("In main sum = %d\n", sum);    /* 3 */
    }
```

```
    return 0;
}

static  int  sumk = 2;
int func1()
{
    sumk += 5;
    printf("In func1 sumk = %d\n", sumk);     /* 4 */
    return sumk;
}

int func2()
{
    sumk += 10;
    printf("In func2 sumk = %d\n", sumk);     /* 5 */
    return sumk;
}
```

The numbered lines are executed in the following order with the following effect on storage allocation.

1 `i` and `sum` exist, `sumk` is nonexistent;

4 `i` and `sum` are suspended, `sumk` exists;

2 `i` and `sum` are reactivated, `sumk` exists but is suspended;

5 `i` and `sum` exist but are suspended, `sumk` is reactivated; and

3 `i` and `sum` are reactivated, `sumk` exists but is suspended.

The output is as follows:

```
In func1 sumk = 7
In main sum = 7
In func2 sumk = 17
In main sum = 17
In func1 sumk = 22
In main sum = 22
In func2 sumk = 32
In main sum = 32
In func1 sumk = 37
In main sum = 37
In func2 sumk = 47
In main sum = 47
```

Notice that sumk is a static variable declared outside and ahead of the functions func1 and func2 and initialized to 2. The static variable is global to func1 and func2. The output shows the updated values of the static global variable sumk. Notice that sumk is updated every time it is changed until the program terminates.

static variables are used to accumulate, to tally an activity of a function, or to retain memory of a prior activation. For example, by using a static variable to indicate whether a file has been opened or not, references to a file can be localized to a single function. The following function inputs data from a file, one value at a time.

```
int get_data(float *x)
{
    static  FILE *inptr;
    static  int ready;
    float  y;
    int  flag;

    if(!ready)
    {
        inptr = fopen("filein.dat", "r");
        ready = 1;
    }

    flag = fscanf(inptr, "%f", &y);
    if(flag)
        *x = y;
    else
    {
        fclose(inptr);
        ready = 0;
    }
    return flag;
}
```

This is the only routine that performs any operation on the file "filein.dat," so if the data file is changed in any way, this is the only function that needs to be modified, The static variable ready has a default value of zero the first time the function is called, so the file is opened. The variable ready is then given the value one so that the function will not attempt to open the file on subsequent calls. However, when all of the data has been read and the input function fails, not only does this function return a flag indicating that, it also closes the file and resets ready to zero so that the file can be processed again from the beginning. The file pointer is also a static variable as it is given a value when the data file is opened and needs to retain that value between calls. The variables `y` and `flag` do not need to be `static` as they are initialized before they are used.

6.2.4 Storage Class `register`

There is a set of general purpose processor registers within the central processing unit of a computer. The access speed of a register is much faster than that of memory. A programmer may request these registers as storage for variables such as counters and accumulators that are used frequently, for computational efficiency. But the compiler has the privilege of honoring the request or not honoring the request. If the registers are all assigned at the time the request is made, then the compiler will not assign a register to the variable requesting the register. It will automatically assign the storage class `auto`. `Register` storage class defaults to `auto` storage class if a register cannot be assigned to the variable. In general a `register` class variable is declared as follows.

```
{
    register int count;

}
```

The `register` storage class variables are local to the functions and the local blocks. Their scope follows the same rules as `auto` variables. The `register` storage class is only needed when a brute force algorithm is being used and there are many cases to check. In general, it is better to avoid that kind of algorithm.

The following table shows the scope, initialization, retention status, speed of access, and declaration of the `auto`, `extern`, `static`, and `register` storage classes.

	Scope	Initialization	Retains value between function calls	Speed of access	Declaration
`auto`	local	explicit	no	normal	default class in block
`extern`	global	0 default	yes	normal	default class outside all blocks
`static`	local/global	0 / explicit	yes	normal	explicit
`register`	local/global	explicit	no	fast	explicit

An `extern` class variable can be referenced ahead of its definition by explicit declaration, whereas a `static` class variable cannot be referenced ahead of its definition. An `extern` variable can be referenced across files whereas a `static` variable cannot be referenced across files.

6.2.5 Review Questions

1. Indicate whether the following statements are true or false.
   a. The `auto` storage class is the default storage class.
   b. An `auto` variable is automatically initialized to zero when it is declared.
   c. An `extern` storage class variable requires both definition and declaration.
   d. An `extern` storage class variable is not initialized when it is declared.
   e. All global variables are `extern` class variables.
   f. A `static` variable is defined automatically when it is declared.
   g. A `static` variable may be global to several functions or local to a specific function.
   h. A `register` class variable defaults to `auto` class if a register is not available at the time the request is made.
2. Answer the following questions.
   a. What is printed by executing the following code?

```
#include <stdio.h>

int  x = 5;

float func1( int, float);

int main( )
{
     int  a = 10;
     float  b = 12.5, c;

     c = func1(a, b);
     printf("a= %d  b = %f  c = %f\n",a, b, c);
     printf("x = %d\n", x);

     return 0;
}
```

```
float func1(int a1, float b1)
{
    int  x = 10;

    x = x + (int)(a1 * b1);
    printf("x = %d\n", x);

   return (a1 * b1);
}
```

b. What is printed by executing the following code?

```
#include <stdio.h>
int  x = 5;

float func1( int, float);
float func2(int );

int main( )
{
    int  a = 10;
    float  b = 12.5, c;

    c = func1(a, b);
    printf("a= %d  b = %f  c = %f\n", a, b, c);
    printf("x = %d\n", x);
    c = func2(a);
    printf(" c = %f\n", c);

    return 0;
}

float  w;
float func1(int a1, float b1)
{
    x = x + a1 + (int)b1;
    printf("x = %d\n", x);
    w = w + 5.0;
    return(x + w);
}

float func2(int a2)
{
    float  w = 6.5;
```

```
        x = x + a2 +(int)w;
        printf("x = %d\n", x);
        w = w + 5.0;
        return(x + w);
    }
```

c. What is printed by executing the following code?

```
#include <stdio.h>

int func1( void);
int func2(void);

int main( )
{
    int  a, b, i;

    for(i = 0; i < 4; i++)
    {
       a = func1( );
       printf("a = %d\n", a);
       b = func2( );
       printf("b = %d\n", b);
    }

    return 0;
}

int func1(void)
{
    static  int  x;

    x = x + 2;

    return x;
}

int func2(void)
{
    int  x = 10;

    x = x + 5;

    return x;
}
```

6.3 Storage Classes in Multiple Files

Only the extern storage class variables can be made visible across different files. A variable defined in one file can be made visible in another file by declaring it there.

6.3.1 Storage Class Extern

An extern storage class variable has multiple file scope. This means an extern storage class variable defined in one file can be made visible and accessed in another file by explicitly declaring such a variable in another file. For example, if an extern variable is defined in program file A, it can be made visible and accessed in program file B by explicitly declaring it in file B. An extern variable is automatically initialized to zero when it is declared. The following code segment shows access of an extern variable across files.

File A:

```
#include <stdio.h>

void func1(void);
void func2(void);

int main( )
{
    extern int a;                       /* a is made visible */
    func1( );
    a = a + 5;
    printf("In main a = %d\n", a);
    func2( );
    a = a + 25;
    printf("In main a = %d\n", a);

    return 0;

}

int   a;                                /* a is declared and defined */
void func1(void)
{
    a = 15;
    printf("In func1 a = %d\n", a);

    return;
}
```

File B:

```
extern int  a;                          /* a is made visible */
void func2(void)
{
    a = a + 10;
    printf("In func2 a = %d\n", a);

    return;
}
```

The output is as follows:

```
In func1 a = 15
In main a = 20
In func2 a = 30
In main a = 55
```

Note that in C multiple files can be compiled and linked using the command line of the computer. The program execution always begins in the file where the `main` function is located. Also, if you are using a windows-driven compiler (such as DEV-C++ 4.9.9.2), each of the C source files must be included in a Project file in order for the `extern` class variables to cross file boundaries. Once a Project is assembled, the program can be executed by compiling and running the Project. Notice that the extern variable a is defined in File A before the `func1` definition. It is global to `func1`; therefore, it is visible inside `func1`, assigned a value of 15, and it is printed inside `func1`. The variable, `a`, is not visible in `main` so it must be declared `extern` inside `main` to make it accessible. It is changed in `main` and printed. The variable a defined in File A is declared in File B as an `extern` variable. It must be declared `extern` to avoid allocating storage for it in file B. `Func2` in File B can access the variable a defined in File A. The output of a inside `func2` shows that it is accessible in File B.

File A:

```
#include <stdio.h>

void  func1(void);
void func2(void);

int main( )
{
    extern  int  a;
    extern  int  b;
    func1( );
```

```
    a = a + 5;
    b = b + 12;
    printf("In main a = %d\n", a);
    printf("In main b = %d\n", b);
    func2( );
    a = a + 25;
    b = b + 15;
    printf("In main a = %d\n", a);
    printf("In main b = %d\n", b);

    return 0;

}

int   a;
void func1(void)
{
    extern int  b;
    a = 15;
    b = b + 10;
    printf("In func1 a = %d\n", a);
    printf("In func1 b = %d\n", b);
    return;
}
```

File B:

```
int b = 10;
extern int  a;
void func2(void)
{
    a = a + 10;
    b = b + 5;
    printf("In func2 a = %d\n", a);
    printf("In func2 b = %d\n", b);
    return;
}
```

The output is as follows:

```
In func1 a = 15
In func1 b = 20
In main a = 20
In main b = 32
In func2 a = 30
In func2 b = 37
```

```
In main a = 55
In main b = 52
```

Notice that a is defined in File A and b is defined in File B. The extern variable a defined in File A is made visible in File B by declaring a as an extern variable. The variable b defined in File B is made visible in File A by declaring b as an extern variable in File A; within the main and func1. The following code shows that the variable b defined in File B can be declared in File A as a global extern variable.

File A:

```
#include <stdio.h>
void func1(void);
void func2(void);

extern  int  b;
int main( )
{
    extern  int  a;
    func1( );
    a = a + 5;
    b = b + 12;
    printf("In main a = %d\n", a);
    printf("In main b = %d\n", b);
    func2( );
    a = a + 25;
    b = b + 15;
    printf("In main a = %d\n", a);
    printf("In main b = %d\n", b);

    return 0;
}



int   a;
void func1(void)
{
    a = 15;
    b = b + 10;
    printf("In func1 a = %d\n", a);
    printf("In func1 b = %d\n", b);

    return;
}
```

File B:

```
int b = 10;
extern int  a;
void func2(void)
{
    a = a + 10;
    b = b + 5;
    printf("In func2 a = %d\n", a);
    printf("In func2 b = %d\n", b);

    return;
}
```

The output is as follows:

```
In func1 a = 15
In func1 b = 20
In main a = 20
In main b = 32
In func2 a = 30
In func2 b = 37
In main a = 55
In main b = 52
```

6.3.2 Review Questions

1. Indicate whether the following statements are true or false.
   a. `auto` variables are visible across files.
   b. `static` variables are not visible across files.
   c. `static` variables have file scope.
   d. `extern` variables are not visible across files.
   e. `extern` variables defined in one file may be accessed in another file.
   f. A `static` variable defined in one file may not be declared in another file.
2. What is printed by executing the following code?

   FILE A:

   ```
   #include <stdio.h>

   void func1(void);
   ```

```
int main( )
{
    extern int  x;

    x = x + 10;
    printf("In main x = %d\n", x);

    func1( );
    x = x + 5;
    printf("In main x = %d\n", x);
    return 0;
}
```

FILE B:

```
int  x;
void func1(void)
{
    x = x + 5;
    printf("In func1 x = %d\n", x);
    return;
}
```

3. What is printed by executing the following code?

FILE A:

```
#include <stdio.h>
void func1(void);

int  y;
int main( )
{
    extern int  x;
    y = y + 15;
    x = x + 10;
    printf("In main y = %d\n", y);
    printf("In main x = %d\n", x);

    func1( );
    x = x + 5;
    y = y + 20;
    printf("In main x = %d\n", x);
```

```
    printf("In main y = %d\n", y);

    return 0;

}
```

FILE B:

```
extern int y;
int  x;

void func1( void)
{
    y = y + 15;
    x = x + 5;
    printf("In func1 x = %d\n", x);
    printf("In func1 y = %d\n", y);
    return;
}
```

6.4 Sample Programs

The sample programs presented show the use of storage classes. These programs have been executed and the output is provided at the end of each program. The programs have been selected from science and engineering applications.

6.4.1 Flow Through Pipes

Problem Write a program to compute the flow rate of water through different pipes, given the number of pipes and the diameter in feet and velocity in feet per second for each. The `main` function performs the input and output, the `main` invokes the computation function that is in a file of scientific functions. `Extern` storage class variables are used to pass data between the two files.

Method The formula for the flow rate is:

$$q = a \times v$$

Where q is the flow rate in cubic feet,

a is the cross sectional area of the pipe in square feet, and

v is the velocity of water flowing through the pipe in feet per second.

The cross sectional area of the pipe is computed as follows:

$$a = \pi d^2 / 4.0$$

Where d is the diameter of the pipe in feet.

Data

The input data is: diameter d in feet

velocity v in feet/sec

Pseudocode

FILE A

main

Call funcinput( )

Call funccomput( )

Call funcoutput( )

Stop

funcinput:

Input the diameter and velocity

funcoutput:

Output the diameter and velocity

Output the flow rate

FILE B: Requires access to variables named diameter and velocity, provides access to variable named flowrate.

funccomput:

Compute the cross sectional area of the pipe

$a = \pi\ d^2 / 4.0;$

Compute the flow rate in cubic feet per second

$q = a \times v$

where q is the flow rate in cubic feet per second.

Program

FILE proga.c

```
/**********************************************************/
/*                                                        */
/*    Main Program: Compute the Flow Rate in Pipes        */
/*                                                        */
/**********************************************************/
/*                                                        */
/*    Defined Constants:                                  */
/*       NUMPIPS - Number of pipes                        */
/*                                                        */
/*    Input Variables:                                    */
/*       diameter - diameter of pipe in feet              */
/*       velocity - velocity of water in feet per sec     */
/*                                                        */
/*    Working Variables:                                  */
/*       count - counter control variable to control loop */
/*       flag -  flag to indicate the input status        */
/*                                                        */
/*    Computed Variables:                                 */
/*       flowrate -  flow rate in cubic feet per sec      */
/*                                                        */
/*    Output Variables:                                   */
/*       diameter - diameter of pipe in feet              */
/*       velocity - velocity of water in feet per sec     */
/*                                                        */
/*    Extern Variables:                                   */
/*       flowrate -  flow rate in cubic feet per sec      */
/*                                                        */
/*    Functions Called:                                   */
/*       funcinput( )                                     */
/*       funccompute( )                                   */
/*       funcoutput( )                                    */
/*                                                        */
/**********************************************************/
```

```
#include <stdio.h>

#define NUMPIPS  5

int funcinput( );
void funcoutput( );
int funccompute( );

FILE  *inptr, *outptr;

float  diameter, velocity;

int main( )
{
    int   count = 0;
    int  flag;
    inptr = fopen("flowin.dat", "r");
    outptr = fopen("flowout.dat", "w");
    while(count < NUMPIPS)
    {
        flag = funcinput( );
        if(flag)
        {
            funccompute( );
            funcoutput( );
        }
        count++;
    }

    return 0;
}

/************************************************************/
/*                                                          */
/*    funcinput: Input the Data                             */
/*                                                          */
/************************************************************/
/*                                                          */
/*    Input Variables:                                      */
/*        diameter - diameter of pipe in feet               */
/*        velocity - velocity of water in feet per sec      */
/*    Returns status of input                               */
/*                                                          */
/************************************************************/
```

```
int funcinput( )
{
    int flag = 1;

    fscanf(inptr,"%f  %f", &diameter, &velocity);
    if(diameter <= 0 || velocity <= 0)
      flag = 0;
    return flag;
}

/*******************************************************/
/*                                                     */
/*    funcoutput: Output the Data                      */
/*                                                     */
/*******************************************************/
/*                                                     */
/*    Output Variables:                                */
/*        diameter - diameter of pipe in feet          */
/*        velocity - velocity of water in feet per sec */
/*        flowrate -  flow rate in cubic feet per sec  */
/*                                                     */
/*                                                     */
/*******************************************************/
void funcoutput( )
{
    extern float flowrate;
    fprintf(outptr,"Diameter: %6.2f feet", diameter);
    fprintf(outptr,"   Velocity: %6.2f ft/sec\n",velocity);
    fprintf(outptr,"Flow Rate: %8.2f cft per sec\n\n",
            flowrate);

    return;
}
```

FILE: progb.c

```
/*******************************************************/
/*                                                     */
/*    funccompute: Computes the Flow Rate              */
/*                                                     */
/*******************************************************/
/*                                                     */
/*    Constant:                                        */
```

```
/*         PI = 3.141593                                       */
/*                                                             */
/*    Extern Variables:                                        */
/*         diameter - diameter of pipe in feet                 */
/*         velocity - velocity of water in feet per sec        */
/*                                                             */
/*    Local Variables:                                         */
/*         - none -                                            */
/*                                                             */
/*    Computed Variables:                                      */
/*         flowrate -  flow rate in cubic feet per sec         */
/*                                                             */
/*                                                             */
/***************************************************************/
extern float diameter, velocity, flowrate, area;
const float PI = 3.141593;
void funccompute(void)
{
   area = PI*((diameter/12.0) * (diameter/12.0))/4.0;
   flowrate = area * velocity;

   return;
}
```

Input and Output

```
=====================
INPUT FILE:  "flowin.dat"
1.0   50.0
0.5   25.0
0.71  36.7
0.88  80.0
1.33  40.0

OUTPUT FILE:  "flowout.dat"
Diameter:  1.00 feet   Velocity:   50.00 ft/sec
Flow Rate:   39.27 cft per sec

Diameter:   .50 feet   Velocity:   25.00 ft/sec
Flow Rate:    4.91 cft per sec

Diameter:   .71 feet   Velocity:   36.70 ft/sec
Flow Rate:   14.53 cft per sec
```

```
Diameter:   .88 feet   Velocity:  80.00 ft/sec
Flow Rate:   48.66 cft per sec

Diameter:  1.33 feet   Velocity:  40.00 ft/sec
Flow Rate:   55.57 cft per sec
```

Notice in this program diameter and velocity are global in `FILE: proga.c` and are declared as `extern` class variables in `FILE: progb.c`. The variables diameter and velocity are accessible in `FILE: progb.c`. Also, notice that the flow rate is defined as global in `FILE: proga.b` and is declared as `extern` class variables in `FILE: progb.a`, and is accessible in `FILE: progb.a`. Note that this is not a safe way to pass data values because the computation function could easily change the value of diameter and velocity.

All function names are of storage class `extern`. They do not have to be explicitly declared `extern` outside the file where they are defined because the computer will automatically look through all the linked files to find the functions. If the program is run in a windows-driven compiler (like DEV-C++ 4.9.9.2), the separate programs, `proga.c` and `progb.c` would be included as parts of a Project. The Project would then be compiled and run to execute the programs together.

6.4.2 Water Pressure

Problem Write a program to compute the average depth and pressure of water in a lake. Input the depth of water in feet at different locations in the lake. Put this function in a separate file. Write a function in another separate file to compute the pressure at different depths of water. Write functions to compute the sum of all the depths and the sum of all the pressures. These functions must be in the same file as the `main` program. Compute the average depth and the average pressure in the `main` program. Write a function in another separate file to output the depth, pressure, average depth, and the average pressure. Use `static` variables to accumulate the sums. Only the `main` program knows the identity of the input and output files.

Method Formula for calculation of pressure at the bottom of the lake is given by

$$p = \rho g d$$

Where p is the pressure in pounds per square inch,
ρ is the mass density of water (mass per unit volume),
g is the gravitational acceleration (32 feet/sec^2), and
d is the depth of water in feet.

Since ρ and g are constants

$$\gamma = \rho\, g$$

and γ is the specific weight of water as 62.4 lbs/ft^3

$$\rho = \gamma / g \text{ lbs sec}^2/\text{ft}^4$$

Substituting this in the formula for pressure gives

$$p = 62.4 \times d \text{ lbs/ft}^2$$

$$p = 0.4333333 \times d \text{ lbs/in}^2$$

`File1` contains routines unique to this program. `File2` contains 10 routines. `File3` contains scientific computations that are shareable. The `main` function tells the I/O routines where to find the data and place the output.

Pseudocode

```
main program: (file1)
  for each depth
     call funcinput( )
     call funcpressure( )
     output the depth and pressure
      sumdepth = funcsumdepth( )
      sumpressure = funcsumpress( )
  end for
  averagedepth = sumdepth / numval
  averagepressur = sumpressure / numval
  call funcoutput( )
stop
```

funcsumdepth: (file1)

sumdepth ← sumdepth + depth

rerturn sumdepth

funcsumpress(file1)

sumpressure ← sumpressure + pressure

return sumpressure

funcinput: (file2)

input depth

funcpressure: (file3)

pressure ← .4333333 × depth

return

funcoutput: (file4)

print avgdepth, avgpressure

return

Program

main program: proga.c

```
/**********************************************************/
/*                                                        */
/*    Main Program: Computation of Pressure               */
/*                                                        */
/**********************************************************/
/*                                                        */
/*    Defined Constants:                                  */
/*         count  - number of data values for depth       */
/*                                                        */
/*   Input Variables:                                     */
/*         depth - depth of water in feet                 */
/*                                                        */
/*   Computed Variables:                                  */
/*         pressure - pressure in psi at different depths */
/*         avgdepth - average depth of water              */
```

```
/*          avgpressure – average pressure                    */
/*                                                            */
/*      Output Variables:                                     */
/*          depth – depth of water in feet                    */
/*          pressure – pressure in psi at different depths */
/*          avgdepth – average depth of water                 */
/*          avgpressure – average pressure                    */
/*                                                            */
/*      Functions Called:                                     */
/*          funcinput – function to input data                */
/*          funcoutput – function to output data              */
/*          funccompute – function to compute pressure        */
/*          funcsumdepth – computes sum of the depths         */
/*          funcsumpress – computes sum of the pressures      */
/*                                                            */
/*      Values Returned:                                      */
/*          sumdepth – sum of the depths                      */
/*          sumpressure – sum of the pressures                */
/*                                                            */
/************************************************************/

#include <stdio.h>
#define NUMVAL 5
int   funcinput(FILE *, float *);
float funcpressure (float);
float funcsumdepth(float );
float funcsumpress(float);

void  funcoutput(FILE *,float, float);

int main( )
{
    FILE  *inptr, *outptr;
    int  flag, count = 1;
    float  depth, pressure, sumdepth, sumpressure;
    float  avgdepth, avgpressure;

    inptr = fopen("depth.dat", "r");
    outptr = fopen("pressur.dat", "w");

    flag = 1;
    while(count <= NUMVAL && flag)
```

```
{
    flag = funcinput(inptr, &depth);
    if (flag)
    {
        pressure = funcpressure(depth);
        fprintf(outptr,"Depth: %6.2f    Pressure: %6.2f\n",
                depth, pressure);
        sumdepth = funcsumdepth(depth);
        sumpressure = funcsumpress(pressure);
    }
    count++;
}
avgdepth = sumdepth / NUMVAL;
avgpressure = sumpressure / NUMVAL;
funcoutput(outptr, depth, pressure);

return 0;

}
```

funcsumdepth: proga.c

```
/*****************************************************/
/*                                                   */
/*    funcsumdepth: Computes the Sum of the Depths   */
/*                                                   */
/*****************************************************/
/*                                                   */
/*   Input Parameters:                               */
/*       depth1 -  depth of water                    */
/*                                                   */
/*   Static local Variables:                         */
/*       sumdepth1 -  sum of the depths              */
/*                                                   */
/*****************************************************/
float  funcsumdepth(float depth1)
{
   static float  sumdepth1;

   sumdepth1 += depth1;

   return sumdepth1;
}
```

funcsumpress: proga.c

```
/*********************************************************/
/*                                                       */
/*    funcsumpress: Computes the Sum of the Pressures    */
/*                                                       */
/*********************************************************/
/*                                                       */
/*   Input parameters:                                   */
/*       pressure1 - Pressure of water                   */
/*                                                       */
/*   Static local Variables:                             */
/*       sumpres1 -  sum of the pressures                */
/*                                                       */
/*********************************************************/
float  funcsumpress(float pressure1)
{
   static float  sumpres1;

   sumpres1 += pressure1;

   return sumpres1;
}
```

funcinput: progb.c

```
/*********************************************************/
/*                                                       */
/*    funcinput: Input the Depth Data                    */
/*                                                       */
/*********************************************************/
/*                                                       */
/*    Input Parameters:                                  */
/*        inptr1 - input file pointer                    */
/*        depth1 - depth of water                        */
/*                                                       */
/*********************************************************/
#include <stdio.h>

int funcinput(FILE *inptr1, float *depth1)
{
   int flag;
```

```
    flag = fscanf(inptr1, "%f", depth1);

    return flag;
}
```

funcpressure: progc.c

```
/*****************************************************/
/*                                                   */
/*    funccompute: Computes the Pressure             */
/*                                                   */
/*****************************************************/
/*    Input Parameters:                              */
/*       depth1  - depth of water                    */
/*                                                   */
/*    Computed Variable:                             */
/*       pressure - pressure of water at certain depth  */
/*                                                   */
/*****************************************************/

float funcpressure(float depth1)
{
    float pressure;

    pressure = 0.4333 * depth1;

    return pressure;
}
```

funcoutput: progd.c

```
/*****************************************************/
/*                                                   */
/*    funcoutput: Output Average Depth and Pressure  */
/*                                                   */
/*****************************************************/
/*                                                   */
/*    Input Parameters:                              */
/*        outptr1      - output file pointer         */
/*        avgdepth1    - average depth               */
/*        avgpressure1 - average pressure           */
/*                                                   */
/*****************************************************/
#include <stdio.h>

void funcoutput(FILE *outptr1, float avgdepth1,
```

```
                  float avgpressure1)
{
    fprintf(outptr1,"Average Depth: %6.2f\n", avgdepth1);
    fprintf(outptr1,"Average Pressure: %6.2f\n",
           avgpressure1);

    return;
}
```

Input file: "depth.dat"

```
100.65
280.43
540.65
376.23
458.94
```

Output file: "pressure.dat"

```
Depth: 100.65    Pressure:   43.61
Depth: 280.43    Pressure:  121.51
Depth: 540.65    Pressure:  234.26
Depth: 376.23    Pressure:  163.02
Depth: 458.94    Pressure:  198.86

Average Depth: 458.94
Average Pressure: 198.86
```

Note that the functions that compute sums use `static` variables for the sums.

Chapter Summary

Variables are stored along with the code that contains the declaration. C is a block-structured language and a variable declared outside a block is global to all other blocks that are nested inside that block or stacked after that block. A variable declared inside a block is local to the block, and such a variable can not be accessed outside the block. Local variables with the same name as global variables have precedence within their scope over the global variables.

There are four storage classes: `auto`, `extern`, `static`, and `register`. If a storage class specification is included in the variable declaration, the storage class must precede the data type of the variable. The general form of the declaration of a variable with storage class specification is as follows:

storage-class data-type variable;

example: `auto int x;`

```
extern  float  y;
static  float  w;
register  int p;
```

Storage class `auto`**:** Storage class `auto` is the default storage class for any variable declared inside a block. An `auto` variable is not automatically initialized when it is declared. An `auto` variable must be initialized before its value is used. This can be done by initializing it in the declaration or by an explicit assignment or through input. `Auto` variables are not accessible outside a file. `Auto` variables are accessible only within the block and the file in which they are declared, because storage for them is allocated along with the code for the block. When the block is exited they cease to exist.

Storage class `extern`**:** Variables declared outside all blocks are by default `extern` storage class. When an `extern` variable is declared it is also defined automatically by assigning a default value of zero unless it is explicitly declared `extern`. An `extern` variable is accessible in the block or blocks that follow the declaration. An `extern` variable is not accessible outside the scope of its declaration. However it can be made accessible by explicitly declaring it as an `extern` class variable in those functions where it is not global.

An `extern` class variable has file scope, but it can be made accessible across different files. Its actual storage allocation is connected with the file in which it is global rather than being explicitly identified as an `extern` variable. Therefore a variable declared as `extern` in one file must appear outside all blocks in exactly one other file. Functions also belong to the `extern` class, therefore no two functions may have the same name.

Storage class `static`**:** Local variables declared with a `static` storage class are automatically defined with an initial value of zero if they are not explicitly initialized. These are used in functions that are called more than once where they must be initialized only once and then are updated every time after that. `Static` variables exist for the duration of the program execution even when they are not accessible.

Storage class `register`**:** Variables declared as `register` storage class are allocated a general purpose processor register by the compiler. If a register is not available, a variable declared with `register` storage class is automatically changed to `auto` storage class. The compiler has the choice of allocating a register or not allocating a register for a `register` storage class variable. When a variable is used continuously, declaring it `register` may increase execution speed.

Exercises

1. Write a `main` function to input a set of numbers and find their average. Use a function to sum and count these numbers. The function should use `static` variables for the sum and count.
2. Write a `main` function to input 20 integers in the range of 1 to 6. Write a function to count the number of times the numbers 2 and 5 occur. The function should declare `static` variables `count2` and `count5`. Check the data validity in the `main` function.
3. Write a `main` function that calls `funcodd` if an integer input value is odd and `funceven` if it is even. `funcodd` should print out the odd integers and whether each is the 1st, 2nd, 3rd, etc., odd integer found. `funceven` should do the same for the even integers.
4. Write a `main` function and the following functions.
   a. Write a function in an input/output file to input monthly rain gauge values and temperatures from a data file. Check data validity.
   b. Write a function to compute the sum of its arguments using a static variable for the sum. This function must be in the same file as the `main` function. Use it to calculate both the sum of the rain gauge values and the sum of the temperatures.
   c. Write a function to output the sum and average rain gauge measurement and the sum and average temperatures. This must be in the same file as the input function.

CHAPTER 7

One-Dimensional Arrays

Objectives

To store and manipulate data aggregates of homogeneous type. In science and engineering they are vectors in the form of lists.

There are many applications in science and engineering that require complex data types. The simple built-in data types `int`, `float`, `double`, and `char` presented in Chapter 2 are inadequate for complex applications. In C one can derive data types such as arrays from the basic data types. A one-dimensional array is used to store a collection of homogeneous data that can be arranged as a list. Scientific and engineering data in the form of vectors is stored and manipulated using arrays. For example, a one-dimensional array can be used to store the height of the path of a missile or a projectile at different points in time, the flight path of a space shuttle, or pressure at different depths in water. A set of one-dimensional arrays may be used to store the temperature at different locations on a heated metal plate and so on. The data may or may not be independent of its position in the list.

Some of the operations performed on data, such as sorting, searching, and partitioning require that the entire list of data be in memory. Data in the form of a list in memory can be accessed much faster than data in a file, particularly if it must be scanned repeatedly.

7.1 One-Dimensional Arrays

A one-dimensional array is a named sequence of memory locations that is used to store a list. The named memory locations of an array are called the *elements* of the array. Each element of an array is identified by a unique number called the array *subscript* or array *index*. The "array subscript" and the "array index" are synonymous. The following example shows the named array x that has five named elements.

```
x[0]
x[1]
x[2]
x[3]
x[4]
```

Input/output operations, arithmetic, and logic operations performed on single variables can also be performed on elements of the array x.

Numeric data in the form of lists can be stored in one-dimensional arrays. In C, character data may be stored in an array as a string of individual characters. Character strings, stored as arrays, are presented in detail in Chapter 9.

Mathematically, a subscripted variable is used to indicate the different elements of homogeneous data. For example, the first measurement of pressure at a certain depth of water is represented as p_0. In C, the subscript starts at zero and must be an integer. For example, the pressure at 10 different measured depths can be represented as follows:

$$p_d \qquad d = 0, 1, 2, 3, 4, 5, 6, 7, 8, 9$$

which represent the measured pressures $p_0, p_1, \ldots, p_9$. Another example, a projectile fired at time $t = 0$ with the altitude h_0 having at time $t = 1$ the altitude h_1 and so on, can be represented as $h_0, h_1, \ldots, h_9$. The velocities computed at altitudes h_0, h_1,

…, h_9 are represented as v_0, v_1,…, v_9. Each value of the subscript is used to identify corresponding values of altitude and velocity.

Under certain cases subscripts may have meaning other than that of ordering and identifying array elements. If the altitude and velocity of a projectile are being calculated for zero minutes, one minute, two minutes, etc., after it is fired, then the subscript accurately represents time as well as order. Notice that each value of h_t must be measured in the same unit and represent the same physical element, the altitude of the projectile. In a similar way, each value of v_t represents the same physical element and is measured in the same unit, for example, miles per second.

If there is any natural order to the values, an order given by time or distance, or a desired output order such as that of cost, it should be the basis of storage. Many sorting and searching methods and algorithms have been developed for changing the order of data.

7.1.1 Subscripts and Subscripted Variables

The name of a one-dimensional array can be used by itself, or with a subscript as a subscripted variable. The name by itself, for example pressure *p*, represents the whole array. Used as a subscripted variable, for example p_4, it represents a single element of the pressure array. In C, since the subscripts start at zero, the subscript represents the offset of each element with respect to the beginning of the array, for example the element p_4 is the fifth element, which is offset by four from the beginning of the array *p*.

p_3 names the fourth element of the array *p*, which is offset by three

d_i names the i + first element of the array *d*, which is offset by i

These are abstract notations until numeric values are assigned to *i* and to the specific array elements referenced.

In C there are two ways to represent subscripted variables. The components of an abstract array a written mathematically as

$$a_i \qquad i = 0 \text{ to } 9$$

can be represented as

```
a0, a1, a2, a3, a4, a5, a6, a7, a8, a9
```

which are 10 different variables, related in the programmer's mind because of their similar names, but unrelated in the computer. This form is often convenient for arrays with a small number of elements. The coefficients of a quadratic equation could be called, c1, c2, and c3 rather than *a*, *b*, and *c*; but variables named this way are not truly subscripted. a_i cannot represent them, but is itself just another variable. If truly subscripted as

```
a[0], a[1], a[2], a[3], a[4], a[5], a[6], a[7], a[8], a[9]
```

then a is the collective name of the 10 elements, each one of which is identified by a unique subscript or index. Any one of them can be represented by `a[i]` provided `i` has a value from 0 through 9. Using a variable or an expression as a subscript and changing its value provides a convenient and systematic way of accessing the array elements. The elements of an array in C can be accessed in order by using `for` loops. The following example shows the use of a `for` loop to initialize the elements of the array a to zero.

```
int  i, a[5]; /* array a's declaration */

for(i = 0; i < 5; i++)
{
    a[i] = 0;
}
```

is equivalent to

```
a[0] = 0;
a[1] = 0;
a[2] = 0;
a[3] = 0;
a[4] = 0;
```

array storage

a[0]	0
a[1]	0
a[2]	0
a[3]	0
a[4]	0

An array subscript may be a constant, a variable, or an expression provided it has an integer value. The following are legitimate subscripted variables:

Algebraic form	**C form**
a_5	`a[5]`
x_i	`x[i]`
w_{n+1}	`w[n+1]`
z_{3j+5}	`z[3 * j + 5]`

7.1.2 Declaration of Arrays

In C, an array must be declared in order to allocate storage. The declaration of an array does not define an array, but simply allocates compile time storage. An array will be defined only when values are assigned to the array elements. The general form of an array declaration is as follows:

element-data-type array-name[number of elements];

An example of the C form is:

```
int a[10];
```

Here the element-data-type is `int`, the array-name is a, and the number of elements is 10. The array-name a can be 1 to 31 characters subject to the rules of naming identifiers in C.

The array size 10 specified in square brackets `[10]` is not part of the name. Declaring the size of the array a as 10, specifies that storage is to be allocated for 10 elements and each element is `int` data type and is allocated two or four bytes of storage depending on the computer. Throughout this chapter we assume the storage allocated for each element of the array is four bytes. Notice that the index varies from 0 to 9, which is one less than the declared size of the array, which is 10.

```
a[0]
a[1]
a[2]
a[3]
a[4]
a[5]
a[6]
a[7]
a[8]
a[9]
```

The arrays `pressure`, `temperature`, and `velocity` may be declared as follows:

```
float pressure[100];
float temperature[200];
float velocity[300];
```

Also arrays of the same data type can be declared in a single statement as follows:

```
float pressure[100], temperature[200], velocity[300];
int count[1000], constant[500];
```

Notice that the arrays `pressure`, `temperature`, and `velocity` declared in one statement, are all of data type `float` but have different array sizes. The arrays `count` and `constant` are both of data type `int` with different array sizes. The choice to declare an array either by a single statement for each array of the same data type or a single statement for several array variables of the same data type is the programmer's choice.

Arrays and single variables of the same data type can be declared in the same declaration statement. The following example shows such a declaration:

```
int value, constant, velocity[100];
```

Notice that `value` and `constant` are single scalar variables and `velocity` is an array variable. The storage for the variables `value` and `constant` and the array `velocity` is allocated at compile time. If the size of the array needs to be changed, the program must be recompiled. The amount of storage allocated to an array cannot be changed during execution. If the amount of storage needed is unknown, but there is known maximum such as, at most, 31 days in a month or 80 characters in an input line, an array should be declared with the maximum size. It is not necessary to use all elements of an array.

> *Programming Hint:* It is useful to specify an array size larger than necessary to anticipate the future needs of storage for applications.

If the size of a data array is not known at the time the program is written and debugged or if the size may change over the life of the program, a symbolic size should be defined as follows.

```
#define SIZE  5
```

This is a directive to the compiler to replace a particular name `SIZE` with the constant value 5. Then the name is used anywhere in the program that the array size is needed. This provides a simple way to change the size of the array everywhere in the program by changing only one statement.

7.1.3 Initialization of Arrays

An array is defined when values are stored in its cells. There are three different ways array elements can be initialized.

Array Initialization in the Declaration

```
int a[5] = {2, 6, 3, 8, 4};
```

Notice that the array a is initialized with five values enclosed within a pair of braces and separated by commas. The element a[0] is assigned the value 2, element a[1] is assigned the value 6, and so on.

If the number of values listed is less than the number of elements of the array, zeroes are assigned to the elements that do not have values listed in the initialization. The following initializations are equivalent.

```
int  a[5] = {2, 6, 3};
int  a[5] = {2, 6, 3, 0, 0};
```

If the number of values listed within the braces is more than the size of the array an error will occur. The following initialization will cause an error:

```
int a[5] = {2, 6, 3, 8, 4, 9, 10};
```

This will cause an error because seven values cannot be stored in an array that has five elements.

> *Program warning:* Initializing an array with more values than the size of the array will cause a compiler error.

When the size of the array is not specified in a declaration with initialization, the size is determined by the number of values listed in the initialization. The following example shows such a case:

```
int a[ ] = {2, 6, 3, 8, 4, 9, 10, 16, 20 ,34};
```

Notice that there is no size specified but 10 values are listed. The size of the array a is now determined to be 10. The array index should not exceed 9 and the index varies from 0 to 9. Storage is still allocated at compile time because the compiler can determine the number of elements in the array from the list of values.

> *Programming Hint:* For small arrays, initialization in the declaration is practical, but for large arrays it is not practical.

Initialization in the declaration is recommended for debugging and testing program code for correctness.

Array Initialization by Assignment Values can be assigned to individual elements of the array after the array is declared as follows:

```
int  a[5];

a[0] = 13;
a[1] = 25;
a[2] = 42;
a[3] = 12;
a[4] = 16;
```

array storage

a[0]	13
a[1]	25
a[2]	42
a[3]	12
a[4]	16

The value 13 is stored in the element a[0], value 25 is stored in element a[1], and so on. This is shown in the diagram with a storage cell for each element. An element of an array must be initialized before it is used. An error will occur if a subscript is too large for the array.

Array Initialization Using for Loops When all the elements have the same initial value, for example all the values are to be set to zero or all the values are to be set to 100.55, then a `for` loop can be used to initialize the values. The following code shows such an initialization:

```
int  i, cons[10];
float  temp[100];

for(i = 0; i < 10; i++)
{
    cons[i] = 0;
}
```

```
for(i = 0; i < 100; i++)
{
   temp[i] = 100.55;
}
```

Notice that each element of the array `cons` is initialized to zero and each element of the array `temp` is initialized to 100.55. A `for` loop can also be used to initialize an array with input data. The subscript must not be out of bounds. An array type `char` is declared and accessed like any other array, for example:

```
char  grade[5] = {'A', 'B', 'C', 'D', 'F'};
char  student[25];
```

Type `char` will be discussed in Chapter 9.

> *Programming Hint:* Use a `for` loop to initialize the elements of an array if all the elements have the same initial values.

7.1.4 Review Questions

1. Indicate whether the following statements are true or false.
   a. Arrays are used to store data aggregates of different data types.
   b. In C the array index starts with one.
   c. After arrays are declared the storage size can be changed.
   d. When an array is initialized with more values than the size of the array the compiler will ignore the extra values.
   e. The number of bytes allocated for each element of an array depends on the data type of the declared array.
   f. Only one array variable can be declared in one statement.
   g. Single variables and array variables of the same data type can be declared in the same statement.
2. For an array `float x[5]` indicate which of the following uses an incorrect subscript and why?
   a. `x[0]`
   b. `x[5]`
   c. `x[0,0]`
   d. `int j = 9`
      `.......x[j / 2]`
   e. `int x = 3`
      `.......x[x]`

f. `x[3 < y]`

3. Answer the following:
   a. Write declaration statements for the following subscripted variables.

      float x_i $i = 0$ through 99

      integer x_n $n = 0$ to 9

      double $value_k$ $k = 0$ to 199

   b. Show the storage allocated for the following array declarations.

      ```
      float x[5];
      double y[5];
      int w[10];
      ```

   c. Show the C code and storage for the following arrays.

      Declare and initialize the integer array `a[5]` with values 2, 5, 7, 1, and 3.

      Declare and initialize the float array `x[5]` with values 6.4, 5.8, 3.2, 4.9, and 2.4.

      Declare and initialize the double array `y[5]` with values 1.2245, 18.493827, and 12456965.

7.2 Input of One-Dimensional Arrays

In C, for large amounts of data, initialization and assignment of data to individual array elements is not practical. The practical way to assign data to a large array is either through input or through computation. The input of data can be accomplished any of three ways: using the array index, using the array pointer, or using a dynamic pointer. Input into an array using array pointers and dynamic pointers is presented in detail in Chapter 10.

7.2.1 Array Input

The following code shows input of numeric data using an array index. A `for` loop is used to index the elements of the array and the address of each element must be specified in the input statement.

Standard Input

```
#define SIZE 5
int i, a[SIZE];

for(i = 0; i < SIZE; i++)
```

```
{
    scanf("%d", &a[i]);
}
```

The data entered from the terminal keyboard and stored in the memory allocated for the array is as follows:

45 56 76 93 15

Notice that when the numbers are entered from the keyboard, 45 is stored in a[0], 56 is stored in a[1], and so on.

a[0]	45
a[1]	56
a[2]	76
a[3]	93
a[4]	15

Input from a Data File "myfilein.data"

```
#define  SIZE  5
FILE  *inptr;
int  i, a[SIZE];

inptr = fopen("myfilein.dat", "r");

for(i = 0; i < SIZE; i++)
{
    fscanf(inptr, "%d", &a[i]);
}
```

The data is read from a data file "myfilein.dat" stored in the memory allocated for the array as shown.

myfilein.dat

inptr ⟶ 45 56 76 93 15

Notice that the integer data value 45 read from the data file "myfilein.dat" is stored in a[0], 56 is stored in a[1], and so on. Similarly the input into a one-dimensional array of data type float or double may be input from a standard input device or from a data file.

7.2.2 Input of Parallel Arrays

Parallel arrays are arrays of the same size that contain related data such as the *x* and *y* coordinates of a set of points. Data can be input into parallel arrays in several ways depending on the order of the data values. The *x*, *y* coordinates of five points on a plane are stored as a list of *x* values and a list of *y* values. Input data to each array using a separate `for` loop for each array when the data is in order by array. The following example shows this.

```
#define ARR 5
int  i;
int  x[ARR], y[ARR];

for(i = 0; i< ARR; i++)
{
    scanf("%d", &x[i]);
}

for(i = 0; i< ARR; i++)
{
    scanf("%d", &y[i] );
}
```

The data for array `x` and array `y` are entered as follows:

```
12  18  25  65  87

25  65  76  80  98
```

Notice that two separate `for` loops are used for the array `x` and the array `y`. The data for the entire array `x` must be entered first from the keyboard and the data for the entire array `y` must be entered next.

If the data is entered as *x*, *y* pairs instead of using two separate `for` loops for the array `x` and array `y`, only one `for` loop is needed. The following `for` loop shows this.

```
#define ARR 5
int  i;
int  x[ARR], y[ARR];

for(i = 0; i< ARR; i++)
{
   scanf("%d    %d", &x[i], &y[i]);
}
```

The data for array x and array y are entered as follows:

```
12      25
18      65
25      76
65      80
87      98
```

Notice that the values for the array x and array y are entered as pairs, each pair representing a single coordinate point. The data value for each element of array x and the data value for the corresponding element of the array y are stored simultaneously.

7.2.3 Review Questions

1. Indicate whether the following statements are true or false.
   a. An array index can be used to input into a one-dimensional array.
   b. The compiler will generate an error message if the `for` loop that initializes the elements of the array has an index outside the range of the array dimension.
2. Write C code to input the following integer numbers from a data file `"filearrayin.dat"` to an array `a[5]`.

   `filearrayin.dat`

856 539 231 657 -125

3. Write an `input` loop to input the following real numbers through a standard keyboard to an array `a[5]` in reverse order.

   234.45   87.679   34.7612   276.5467   −231.546

4. Write an `input` loop to input integer numbers from the keyboard into two arrays, `x` and `y`. Pairs of data values are given for `x` and `y`.

   Data values are as follows:

   ```
   12      18
   16      19
   34      65
   76      96
   -54     45
   ```

7.3 Output of One-Dimensional Arrays

Assume an array contains values that are to be either displayed on a standard output device such as a CRT screen, printed on a printer, or written to a file on a disk. One-dimensional arrays are usually displayed or printed, either horizontally on a line or vertically in a column. A one-dimensional array can be written using an array index, an array pointer, or a dynamic pointer. The output of one-dimensional arrays using array pointers and dynamic pointers is presented in detail in Chapter 10.

7.3.1 Array Output

The following code shows the output of a one-dimensional array using an index. The storage with the array elements is shown as follows:

a[0]	12
a[1]	13
a[2]	25
a[3]	16
a[4]	43

Standard Output of Integers

```
#define N  5
int  i;
int  a[N] = {12, 13, 25, 16, 43};

for(i = 0; i < N; i++)
{
    printf("%d    ", a[i]);
}
printf("\n");
```

The output of the array elements will appear on a line with four blank spaces between each element as shown:

```
12    13    25    16    43
```

The elements of an array can be printed vertically in a column, as is done by the following code.

```
#define N  5
int  i;
int  a[N] = {12, 13, 25, 16, 43};

for(i = 0; i < N; i++)
{
   printf("%d\n", a[i]);
}
```

```
12
13
25
16
43
```

Output to a Data File "myfileout.data"

```
#define A  5
FILE  *outptr;
int  i;
int  a[A] = {12, 13, 25, 16, 43};

outptr = fopen("myfileout.dat", "w");

for(i = 0; i < A; i++)
    fprintf(outptr,"%d    ", a[i]);
```

The output of the array elements will be written to a data file "myfileout.dat" on a line with four blank spaces between each element as shown:

```
              myfileout.dat
outptr ──→ │ 12    13    25    16    43
```

Notice that the integer number 12 is from the storage of element a[0], 13 is from the storage of element a[1], and so on, are written horizontally along a line to a data file "myfileout.dat".

7.3.2 Output of Parallel Arrays

Several one-dimensional arrays may be printed either on separate lines or in columns. The following examples show the output of multiple arrays. The output of each array is printed horizontally.

```
#define  N  5
int i;
int  x[N] = {10, 15, 18, 45, 62};
int  y[N] = {26, 45, 53, 98, 70};

printf("Array x: ");
for(i = 0; i < N; i++)
{
    printf("%d    ", x[i]);
}

printf("\n\n");

printf("Array y: ");
for(i = 0; i < N; i++)
{
    printf("%d    ", y[i]);
}
printf("\n");
```

The output is as follows:

```
Array x: 10    15    18    45    62

Array y: 26    45    53    98    70
```

Notice that array `x` is printed first and then array `y` is printed on a separate line because there are two explicit `for` loops with an output statement between them, which forces a new line.

The arrays may be printed side-by-side vertically in columns using one `for` loop.

```
#define  N  5
int i;
int  x[N] = {10, 15, 18, 45, 62};
int  y[N] = {26, 45, 53, 98, 70};
```

```
printf("     Array x    Array y\n");
for(i = 0; i < N; i++)
{
   printf("%d        %d        %d\n", i + 1, x[i], y[i]);
}
```

The code above produces the following output:

```
       Array x     Array y
1        10          26
2        15          45
3        18          53
4        45          98
5        62          70
```

Notice that the corresponding elements of arrays x and y are printed side-by-side and the lines are numbered. Depending on the application, one can choose to print on a line horizontally or vertically in columns.

Note that the data may be written to a data file one array at a time or as pairs of corresponding elements.

7.3.3 Review Questions

1. Indicate whether the following statements are true or false.
   a. The output of an array can be controlled by a `for` loop.
   b. An array can be printed across the page as a line of values.
   c. An array can be printed along the length of the page.
   d. An index can be printed along with the values.
2. Given the following array show the output for the following output statements.

```
#define ASIZE  5
int  a[ASIZE] = {23, 43, 65, 67, 87};
```

a.
```
for(i = 0; i < ASIZE; i++)
{
     printf("%d   %d\n", i, a[i]);
}
```

b.
```
for(i = ASIZE - 1; i >= 0; i--)
{
      printf("%d    %d\n", i, a[i]);
}
```

3. Given the following arrays show the output for the following output statements.

```
#define  N  5
int  a[N] = {23, 43, 65, 67, 87};
int  b[N] = {86, 67, 43, 65, 59};
```

a.
```
for(i = 0; i < N; i++)
{
      printf("%d    %d    %d\n",  i,  a[i],  b[i]);
}
```

b.
```
for(i = N - 1; i >= 0; i--)
{
     for( j = 0; j < N; j++)
     {
          printf("%3d    ", a[i]+ b[j]);
     }
     printf("\n");
}
```

4. Write an output loop or loops to print the arrays `a[5]` and `b[5]` as follows:

```
int  a[5] = {56,  65,  34, 78, 97};

float  b[5] = {12.345, 43.567, 54.762, 79.635, 89.124};

element  1          2        3       4       5
a        56         65       34      78      97
b        12.345  43.567  54.762  79.635  89.124
```

5. Write an output loop or loops to print the arrays `a[5]` and `b[5]` as follows:

```
int  a[5] = {56,  65,  34, 78, 97};
float  b[5] = {12.345, 43.567, 54.762, 79.635, 89.124};
```

```
element   array a   array b
1.          56       12.345
2.          65       43.567
3.          34       54.762
4.          78       79.635
5.          97       89.124
```

7.4 Manipulation of Arrays

Any operation that can be performed on individual variables can be performed on the elements of an array. Array elements of type `int`, `float`, and `double` can be used in arithmetic calculations and logic comparisons just as single variables are. In C, arithmetic and logic operations are performed on individual elements by explicitly specifying the index of the element.

7.4.1 Array Assignment

The elements of a one-dimensional array may be manipulated by using the array index. They can be accessed individually by specifying the index of a specific element, or sequentially starting from the beginning index or from the end index of the array using a `for` loop. The values of the elements of one array are assigned to another array using a `for` loop. There is no assignment operation for arrays. The array elements must be copied individually from one array to another array. When numeric arrays are copied, if the data type of the source array does not match the data type of the destination array, data type conversion will occur for each element. The data values of the source array are converted to the data type of the destination array without changing the data type of the source array. The data conversion rules are the same as those presented in Chapter 2 for single variables. The following code shows the assignment of the elements of array `a` to array `b`.

```
#define  SIZE  5
int  i;
float a[SIZE], b[SIZE];
for(i = 0; i < SIZE; i++)
{
```

```
    b[i] = a[i];
}
```

Notice that the arrays must have the same number of elements. The values contained in the array a and the array b before the assignment and after the assignment are as follows:

Before

a[0]	12.75	b[0]	uuuuuuuuu
a[1]	18.34	b[1]	uuuuuuuuu
a[2]	9.85	b[2]	uuuuuuuuu
a[3]	23.78	b[3]	uuuuuuuuu
a[4]	16.96	b[4]	uuuuuuuuu

After

a[0]	12.75	b[0]	12.75
a[1]	18.34	b[1]	18.34
a[2]	9.85	b[2]	9.85
a[3]	23.78	b[3]	23.78
a[4]	16.96	b[4]	16.96

Notice that the values in the array b are replaced by the corresponding values of the array a. The values of the array a are not altered. Only values of the target array b, which is on the left side of the assignment symbol, are altered.

The array a can be copied into the array b in reverse order. The following code shows such a copy.

```
#define SIZE  5
int  i;
int  a[SIZE], b[SIZE];

for(i = 0; i < SIZE; i++)
{
    b[SIZE - 1 - i] = a[i];
}
```

Before

a[0]	12.75	b[0]	uuuuuuuuu
a[1]	18.34	b[1]	uuuuuuuuu
a[2]	9.85	b[2]	uuuuuuuuu
a[3]	23.78	b[3]	uuuuuuuuu
a[4]	16.96	b[4]	uuuuuuuuu

After

a[0]	12.75	b[0]	16.96
a[1]	18.34	b[1]	23.78
a[2]	9.85	b[2]	9.85
a[3]	23.78	b[3]	18.34
a[4]	16.96	b[4]	12.75

Notice that the elements of the array `a` are stored in the array `b` in reverse order.

When it is necessary to exchange the values of elements between two arrays of the same size a temporary variable is used. This is accomplished by using the `for` loop as follows:

```
#define  SIZE  5
int  i;
float  x[SIZE], y[SIZE], temp;

for(i = 0; i < SIZE; i++)
{
   temp = x[i];
   x[i] = y[i];
   y[i] = temp;
}
```

This swap operation is the basis of a simple but not very efficient method of sorting an array to arrange the values in ascending order called an *insertion sort*. The smallest element is located at position `a[k]` and placed in the position `a[0]` while the element originally in position `a[0]` is put in position `a[k]`. Then the second smallest element is located at position `k` (a new `k`) and placed in the position `a[1]` by swapping it with the element in a[1]. Each time through the array, the smallest remaining element is placed in position, until the whole array has been sorted. This in shown in the following example:

```
#define SIZE  5
int  i, j, k;
float  a[SIZE], temp;

for( j = 0; j < SIZE - 1; j++)
{
     temp = a[j];
     k = j;

/* find jth smallest number */

     for( i = j + 1; i < SIZE; i++)
     {
          if(a[i] < temp)
          {
               temp = a[i];
               k = i;
          }
     }
     a[k] = a[j];
     a[j] = temp;
}
```

Another common programming situation is moving some of the elements of a list down one position in order to insert a new element. In this example, assume that the element a[k] is to be placed at position a[j], j < k, by moving the elements a[j], a[j + 1],..., a[k-1] down one position to leave an empty storage location at a[j].

```
#define SIZE  5
int  i, j = 0, k = 4, SIZE = 5;
int a[SIZE], temp;

temp = a[k];
for( i = k; i > j; i--)
{
     a[i] = a[i-1];
}
a[j] = temp;
```

Lists of numbers are sorted when they must be in order by value. They are also sorted for some statistical operations such as finding the median value. At the end of this chapter several sorting and searching algorithms are presented.

7.4.2 Array Arithmetic

Arithmetic operations such as addition, subtraction, multiplication, and division can be performed on the elements of an array using a `for` loop to vary the subscript. Subscripted array variables may be used in arithmetic expressions. The following segments of code show the use of arrays in arithmetic expressions and their results.

Addition of a Scalar Constant to the Elements of an Array

```
#define SIZE  5
int i;
int a[SIZE];

for(i = 0; i < SIZE; i++)
{
    a[i] = a[i] + 5;
}
```

	Before		After
a[0]	12	a[0]	17
a[1]	18	a[1]	23
a[2]	9	a[2]	14
a[3]	23	a[3]	28
a[4]	16	a[4]	21

Similarly, subtraction, multiplication, and division operations can be performed on array elements with a scalar constant.

Arithmetic operations of adding, subtracting, multiplying, and dividing can be applied to the elements of two arrays and the result can be stored in another array. The following code segments show such operations.

Element-by-element addition of array a to array b with the result stored in array c is shown here.

```
#define SIZE  5
int  i;
int a[SIZE], b[SIZE], c[SIZE];

for(i = 0; i < SIZE; i++)
{
    c[i] = a[i] + b[i];
}
```

a[0]	12
a[1]	18
a[2]	9
a[3]	23
a[4]	16

b[0]	6
b[1]	9
b[2]	4
b[3]	11
b[4]	8

c[0]	18
c[1]	27
c[2]	13
c[3]	34
c[4]	24

Similarly, two arrays may be subtracted, multiplied, or divided, element-by-element.

Summation of Array Elements Summing array elements is a very common operation used, for example, to compute the averages in scientific and engineering applications. The following code segments show the summation of elements of an array.

```
#define SIZE  5
int  i;
int  a[SIZE];
int sum;

sum = 0;
for(i = 0; i < SIZE; i++)
{
    sum += a[i];
}
printf("Sum is: %d", sum);
```

a[0]	12
a[1]	18
a[2]	9
a[3]	23
a[4]	16

Using the data above, the resulting sum is printed as follows:

```
Sum is: 78
```

> *Program Warning:* When array elements are accessed outside the range of the index, the compiler will not give a warning. The programmer is responsible for using proper index values to avoid a run-time error.

Inner Product of Two Vectors If *x* and *y* are two vectors, then their inner product is defined mathematically as

$$x \cdot y = \sum_{i=1}^{n} x_i y_i$$

The following code computes this equation for vectors of length n.

```
int  i, n;
float sum = 0;

for(i = 0; i < n; i++)
{
    sum += x[i] * y[i];
}
```

7.4.3 Review Questions

1. Indicate whether the following statements are true or false.
   a. When an array of elements with float numbers is added to an array of elements with integer numbers, the resulting numbers are stored as float numbers.
   b. Arrays must be of the same numeric data type if their elements are in the same arithmetic expression.
   c. Array elements can be accessed sequentially from the beginning of the array or from the end of the array.
   d. Arithmetic operations may be performed on arrays, element-by-element, by using the array index.
2. Given the following arrays, show the result of the following arithmetic operations.

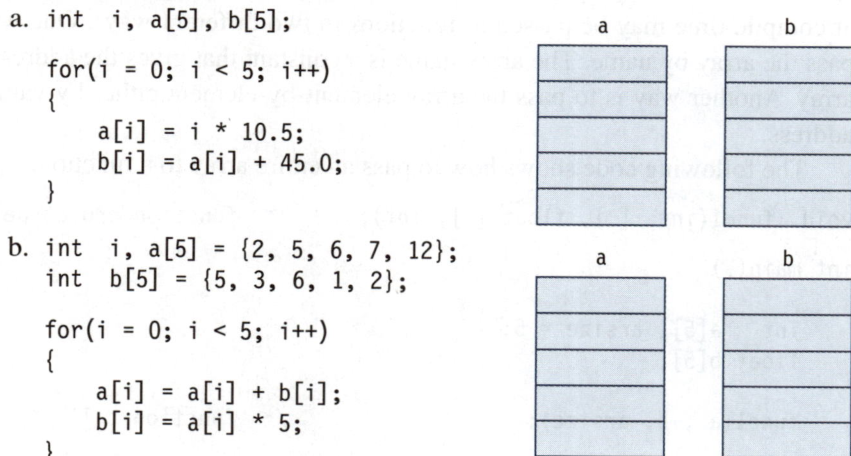

a.
```
int  i, a[5], b[5];

for(i = 0; i < 5; i++)
{
    a[i] = i * 10.5;
    b[i] = a[i] + 45.0;
}
```

b.
```
int  i, a[5] = {2, 5, 6, 7, 12};
int  b[5] = {5, 3, 6, 1, 2};

for(i = 0; i < 5; i++)
{
    a[i] = a[i] + b[i];
    b[i] = a[i] * 5;
}
```

c.
```
int  i, a[5] = {2, 5, 6, 7, 12};
int  b[5] = {5, 3, 6, 1, 2};

for(i = 0; i < 5; i++)
{
    a[i] = a[i] + b[3];
    b[i] = a[i] * b[2];
}
```

a	b

3. Given the following arrays show the results of the following arithmetic operations.

```
int  a[5] = { 6, 9, 5, 4, 25};
float b[5] = {12.5, 6.4, 3.4, 2.6, 1.5};

a[i] = a[i] / 4; i = 0, ...4
b[i] = b[i] / 2; i = 0, ...4
a[i] = a[i] + b[i]; i = 0, ...4
a[i] = a[i] – b[i]; i = 0, ...4
```

7.5 Passing Arrays to Functions

Arrays may be passed to functions. An array may be passed to a function as a whole or element-by-element. The following sections show both ways of passing an array.

7.5.1 Passing Fixed-Size Arrays

A one-dimensional array declared and defined in a `main` program or other function at compile time may be passed to functions in two different ways. One way is to pass the array by name. The array name is a constant that gives the address of the array. Another way is to pass the array element-by-element either by value or by address.

The following code shows how to pass an entire array to a function:

```
void  func1(int  [ ], float [ ], int);     /*  function prototype  */

int main( )
{
   int  a[5], arsize = 5;
   float b[5];
   . . .
   func1(a , b, arsize);                    /*  function call  */
```

```
    . . .
    return 0;
}

void func1(int   p[ ], float  q[ ], int n) /*  function header  */
{
    . . .
    return;
}
```

Notice that in the function prototype the data type is followed by square brackets, which indicate that an array is passed as an argument to the function `func1`.

Variable names must be specified in the function header. The variable names specified in the function header are local to the function. The function header has the following form.

```
void func1(int p[ ],  float q[ ], int n);
```

The square brackets indicate that p and q are array names. The argument passed to the function is an array name. Because only names are passed, a function may handle different size arrays at different times based on the declared size of the array. Therefore, the size of the array should be passed along with the name. An input or output function may be used for several different arrays having different sizes. The following example programs show the manipulation of arrays in functions.

Input of an Array in a Function

```
#include <stdio.h>
#define ARSIZE  5

void funcinput(int a[ ], int n);

int main( )
{
    int  i, x[ARSIZE];

    funcinput(x, ARSIZE);

    for(i = 0; i < ARSIZE; i++)
        printf("%d        ", x[i]);

    return 0;
}
```

```
/* array input using array index  */

void funcinput(int y[ ], int n)
{
    int  i;

    for(i = 0; i < n; i++)
        scanf("%d", &y[i]);

    return;
}
```

Notice that the array x declared in the main function has the actual storage, and the dummy array a in the function prototype and the array y in the function header do not have their own storage. The variable y specified in the function header will receive the address of the beginning of the array x from the main program. The address is passed by value, but the values stored in the array are not passed. In effect, y has access to the storage of x declared in the main program because the address of the array x becomes the address of the dummy array y in the function call. The elements of the array are changed by the function but the address is not altered.

Output of an Array in a Function

```
#include <stdio.h>
#define ARSIZE  5
void funcoutput(int a[ ], int n);

int main( )
{
    int x[ARSIZE];

    funcoutput(x, ARSIZE);

    return 0;
}

void funcoutput(int y[ ], int n)
{
    int  i;

    for(i = 0; i < n; i++)
        printf("%d     ", y[i]);

    return;
}
```

Manipulation of Arrays in a Function The following code shows the manipulation of arrays in a function. A function may receive the names of two arrays, perform some arithmetic operations, and store the result in another array. The resulting array, passed back to the calling program through the argument/parameter list as a return statement, can only return a single value, not an array.

Because the arrays are passed by name they are manipulated in the functions as though they were actually located in the function.

> *Program Warning:* The resulting array can not be returned through the return statement, but must be returned through a parameter.

```
#include <stdio.h>
#define  ARSIZE  5

void funcompute(int a[ ], int b[ ], int c[ ], int n);

int main( )
{
    int  i, x[ARSIZE], y[ARSIZE], z[ARSIZE];

    for(i = 0; i < ARSIZE; i++)
      scanf("%d  %d", &x[i],& y[i]);

    funcompute(x, y, z, ARSIZE);

    for(i = 0; i < ARSIZE; i++)
      printf("%d  %d  %d\n", x[i], y[i], z[i]);

    return 0;
}

void funcompute(int p[ ], int r[], int s[ ], int n)
{
    int  i;

    for(i = 0; i < n; i++)
        s[i] = p[i] + r[i];
    return;
}
```

Notice that the function receives the addresses of the beginning of arrays x, y, and z through the parameter arrays p, r, and s. In the function arrays p and r are added element-by-element and the result is assigned to the elements of array s. When the function returns control to the main program, the array z already contains the values assigned to the array s.

7.5.2 Passing Array Elements

Arrays can be passed to functions element-by-element either by value or by address, like scalar variables. When an element of an array is passed to a function from the calling program, the index of the element must be specified. The following code shows the passing of array elements by value and by address.

When array elements are passed to the function by value they are copied into temporary storage and the function parameter can only access the value in temporary storage. The following code shows array elements of an array passed by value and of array b passed by address a. The subfunction adds the elements of the two arrays plus two, one-by-one and returns the sums to the array b.

```
#include <stdio.h>
#define ARSIZE  5

void funcscalar(int,  int *);

int main( )
{
    int   i;
    int a[]= {1, 2, 3, 4, 5};
    int b[] = {6, 7, 8, 9, 10};

    for(i = 0; i < ARSIZE; i++)
        funcscalar(a[i], &b[i]);

    for(i = 0; i < ARSIZE; i++)
        printf("%d          %d\n", a[i], b[i]);

    return 0;
}

void funcscalar(int  x,  int  *y)
{
    x = x + 2;
    *y = x + *y;
    return;
}
```

Before (function call)

a[0]	1	b[0]	6
a[1]	2	b[1]	7
a[2]	3	b[2]	8
a[3]	4	b[3]	9
a[4]	5	b[4]	10

After (function call)

a[0]	1	b[0]	9
a[1]	2	b[1]	11
a[2]	3	b[2]	13
a[3]	4	b[3]	15
a[4]	5	b[4]	17

Notice that in the function call the elements of array a are passed by value as though they were scalars. The elements of array a are copied into temporary storage and the contents of the temporary storage is accessed in the function. If elements of array a are changed in the function, the original values of the elements of array a will not change because they are passed by value. This protects the original arrays but is inefficient for large arrays as the function must be called many times. The elements of array b are passed by address; therefore, changing the values in the function changes them in the original array.

Program Warning: Pass array elements by value to protect the array against changes in a function.

7.5.3 Review Questions

1. Indicate whether the following statements are true or false.
   a. Arrays may be passed to a function by means of an array name `func(arra)` or as an array with brackets `func(arra[ ])`.
   b. When arrays are passed by array name, they are passed by value.
   c. When arrays are passed to a function element-by-element, they are passed by value.

d. When an array is passed to a function by name, the parameter in the function must have brackets.

e. When arrays are passed to a function element-by-element, the parameter in the function must be a pointer.

f. When arrays are passed by array name to a function, if the array values are changed in the function they are changed in the calling routine.

2. Write a function to multiply two arrays element-by-element, store the result in another array, and return that array to the calling program. Do not pass individual elements.
3. Write a function to receive an array containing real numbers, sum the numbers, and return the sum to the calling program. Do not pass individual array elements.
4. Write a driver that passes the elements of two arrays, x and y, to a function that compares the values for equality. If a pair is equal, print the value and a message in the calling program.

7.6 Sample Programs

The following sample programs illustrate the use of one-dimensional arrays. Problems are selected from science and engineering applications that use arrays. Also the sample programs show sorting and searching methods. These programs have been executed and the results of computation are presented with the code.

7.6.1 Reynolds Numbers

Problem Write a program to compute and build a table of the Reynolds numbers at flow velocities varying from 100 to 1000 ft/s at increments of 100 given the following formula. This example shows the construction and output of an array.

$$Re = \rho\, v\, l \,/\, \mu$$

Where Re is the Reynolds number that is nondimensional,

ρ is the density of air in slug/ft^3,

v is the flow velocity in ft/sec,

l is the characteristic length in ft., and

μ is the viscosity of the air in slug/ft.sec.

Method

Define the constants ρ and μ for air.

Vary the velocity from 100 to 1000 in increments of 100.

Calculate the Reynolds number for each velocity.

Store the velocity and the Reynolds number in one-dimensional arrays.

Data

Density ρ of air 2.33×10^{-3} slug/ft^3

Viscosity μ for air 3.8×10^{-7} slug/ft.sec.

Velocity varies from 100 to 1000 at increments of 100

Pseudocode

```
density ρ and viscosity μ for air are defined constants
for each velocity from 100 to 1000 in increments of 100
   reynolds = (density * velocity * length) / viscosity
   reynoldsnum[i] = reynolds
end
for each velocity from 100 to 1000 in increments of 100
   Output velocity, reynoldsnum[i]
end
stop
```

Program

```
/*********************************************************/
/*                                                       */
/* Compute the Reynolds Numbers for Different Velocities */
/* of Fluid Flow over a Circular Cylinder                */
/*                                                       */
/*********************************************************/
/*                                                       */
/*    Constants:                                         */
/*        density   = 2.33 × 10^-3 slug/ft               */
/*        viscosity  = 3.8 × 10^-7 slug/(ft.sec)         */
/*                                                       */
/*    Input Variables:                                   */
```

```
/*                                                        */
/*        length = diameter of circular cylinder in ft    */
/*                                                        */
/*    Computed variables:                                 */
/*        velocity - velocity ft/sec                      */
/*        reynoldsnum - Reynolds number                   */
/*                                                        */
/*    Output Variables:                                   */
/*                                                        */
/*        velocity    - velocity ft/sec                   */
/*        reynoldsnum - Reynolds number                   */
/*                                                        */
/*    Functions called:                                   */
/*                                                        */
/*         -none-                                         */
/*                                                        */
/*********************************************************/
#include <stdio.h>
# define ARSIZE  10
int main( )
{
    int i;
    const float density = 2.33E-03;
    const float viscosity = 3.8E-07;
    float length;
    float velocity, reynoldsnum[ARSIZE];

    printf("Input the diameter of cylinder as length in ft:");
    scanf("%f", &length);
    velocity  = 100.00;
    i = 0;
    while(velocity <= 1000)
    {
        reynoldsnum[i] = (density * velocity* length)/ viscosity;
        velocity = velocity + 100;
        i++;
    }

    printf("\n\nindex    velocity     Reynolds number\n");
    velocity = 100.00;
    for(i = 0; i < ARSIZE; i++)
    {
        printf("%5d.   %8.2f    %14.2f\n",i+1, velocity,
                reynoldsnum[i]);
```

```
        velocity += 100;
    }

    return 0;
}
```

Input and Output

```
Input the diameter of cylinder as length in ft: 0.025

index     velocity      Reynolds number
   1.     100.00           15328.95
   2.     200.00           30657.90
   3.     300.00           45986.84
   4.     400.00           61315.79
   5.     500.00           76644.74
   6.     600.00           91973.69
   7.     700.00          107302.64
   8.     800.00          122631.59
   9.     900.00          137960.53
  10.    1000.00          153289.48
```

7.6.2 Stress and Strain

Problem Compute the stress and strain in steel columns subject to compression loads varying from 10,000 pounds to 100,000 pounds in increments of 10,000 pounds. The diameter of the column is input in inches. The modulus of elasticity for steel is $E = 30 \times 10^6$ psi. Store the load, stress, and strain in parallel one-dimensional arrays. Output the load, stress, and strain arrays in the form of a table. This example shows the construction and output of parallel arrays. The formulas for the stress and strain are as follows:

The stress is given by the formula: $\sigma = p/(\pi d^2/4)$

The strain is given by the formula: $\varepsilon = \sigma/E$

Where σ is the stress in pounds/in^2,

ε is the strain which is nondimensional,

p is the load in pounds,

d is the diameter in inches, and

E is the modulus of elasticity in pounds/in^2.

Data

Defined constant modulus of elasticity $E = 30 \times 10^6$ psi
Diameter of the column
Compression load

Pseudocode

```
constant E = 30e06
constant pi = 3.141593
input diameter
area = (pi * (diameter * diameter)) / 4
for load p = 10,000 to 100,000 increment by 10,000
  stress = load / area
  strain = stress / E
end
for i = 1 to 10
   output load, stress, strain
end
stop
```

Program

```
/*******************************************************/
/*                                                     */
/*   Compute the Stress and Strain for a Steel Column  */
/*   Subject to Compression Load                       */
/*                                                     */
/*******************************************************/
/*                                                     */
/*    Constants:                                       */
/*       modulus of elasticity (E)= 30 × 10^6 lbs/in^2 */
/*       PI = 3.141593                                 */
/*                                                     */
/*    Input Variables:                                 */
/*       diameter = diameter of the column in inches   */
/*                                                     */
/*    Computed variables:                              */
/*       stress – compression stress in pounds/in^2    */
/*       strain compression strain non dimensional     */
```

```
/*                                                         */
/*   Output Variables:                                     */
/*       stress - compression stress in lbs/in²            */
/*       strain compression strain non dimensional         */
/*                                                         */
/*   Functions called:                                     */
/*                                                         */
/*         -none-                                          */
/*                                                         */
/***********************************************************/
#include <stdio.h>
#define SIZE 10

int main( )
{
    int i;
    const float PI = 3.141593;
    const float E = 30E06;
    float diameter, area, load, stress[SIZE], strain[SIZE];

    printf("Enter the diameter (inches): ");
    scanf("%f", &diameter);

    area = PI * (diameter * diameter) / 4.0;
    load = 10000.00;
    for(i = 0; i < SIZE; i++)
    {
        stress[i] = load / area;
        strain[i] = stress[i] / E;
        load += 10000.00;
    }

    printf("\ncolumn diameter: %6.2f\n", diameter);
    printf("  index      compload      stress       strain\n");

    load = 10000.00;
    for(i = 0; i < SIZE; i++)
    {
        printf("  %d.   %10.2f   %9.2f   %12.8f\n",
               i, load, stress[i], strain[i]);
        load += 10000.00;
    }

    return 0;
}
```

Output

```
Enter the diameter (inches): 4

column diameter: 4.00
index      compload       stress       strain
  0.       10000.00       795.77     0.00002653
  1.       20000.00      1591.55     0.00005305
  2.       30000.00      2387.32     0.00007958
  3.       40000.00      3183.10     0.00010610
  4.       50000.00      3978.87     0.00013263
  5.       60000.00      4774.65     0.00015915
  6.       70000.00      5570.42     0.00018568
  7.       80000.00      6366.20     0.00021221
  8.       90000.00      7161.97     0.00023873
  9.      100000.00      7957.75     0.00026526
```

7.6.3 Standard Deviation

Problem Given the measurements of a certain scientific experiment, compute the mean and the standard deviation of the recorded experimental values. Print the experimental values that are outside one standard deviation of the mean. This example shows the use of functions to process an array.

Method Compute the sum of the squares of the values

$$\sum_{i=1}^{n} x_i^2$$

Compute the square of the sum of the values

$$\left(\sum_{i=1}^{n} x_i\right)^2$$

and the mean

$$\frac{1}{n}\sum_{i=1}^{n} x_i$$

The formula for standard deviation is as follows:

$$\text{Standard deviation} = \sqrt{\frac{\sum_{i=1}^{n} x_i^2 - \frac{1}{n}\left(\sum_{i=1}^{n} x_i\right)^2}{n-1}}$$

Data

Ten real measured data values

Pseudocode

```
main:
   input the measured data values into an array
   call funcmean
   call the funcstdev
   print the mean and standard deviation
   print the values outside the standard deviation
Stop

Function funcmean:
   sum the data values
   mean = sum of the data values / number of values
End

Function funcstdev:
Compute the sum of the squares of the values, and the sum of the values
Compute the square of the sum of the values
Compute the mean
Compute the standard deviation
Return the mean and the standard deviation
```

Program

```
/********************************************************/
/*                                                      */
/*    Main: Standard Deviation and Extreme Values       */
/*                                                      */
/********************************************************/
/*                                                      */
/*    Input Variables:                                  */
/*        expdata[ARSIZE] - Experimental data           */
/*                                                      */
/*    Output Variables:                                 */
/*        stdev            - standard deviation         */
/*        expdata          - extreme values             */
/*        mean             - mean value                 */
/*                                                      */
/*    Functions Called:                                 */
/*        funcmean         - function to compute the mean */
/*        funcstdv         - function to compute standard */
/*                           deviation                  */
/*                                                      */
/********************************************************/
#include <stdio.h>
#include <math.h>

#define ARSIZE  10

float funcmean(float [ ], int);
float funcstdev(float[ ] , int);

int main( )
{
    int i;
    float expdata[ARSIZE], mean, stdev;

    printf("Input ten data elements\n");
    for(i = 0; i < ARSIZE; i++)
        scanf("%f",&expdata[i]);

    mean = funcmean(expdata, ARSIZE);
    printf("mean = %5.2f\n", mean);

    stdev = funcstdev(expdata, ARSIZE);
    printf("standard deviation = %5.2f\n", stdev);

    printf("The extreme values:\n");
    for(i = 0; i < ARSIZE; i++)
```

```
    {
        if(fabs(expdata[i]- mean) > stdev)
            printf("%8.2f\n", expdata[i]);
    }

    return 0;
}

/***********************************************************************/
/*                                                                     */
/*    Function: funcmean – Computes the Mean                           */
/*                                                                     */
/***********************************************************************/
/*                                                                     */
/*    Input Parameters:                                                */
/*        expdata1[n]- Experimental data                               */
/*        n          – number of data values                           */
/*                                                                     */
/*    Local Variables:                                                 */
/*        mean       – mean value                                      */
/*        sum        – sum of data values                              */
/*                                                                     */
/*    Return value:                                                    */
/*        mean       – mean value                                      */
/*                                                                     */
/*    Functions Called: none                                           */
/*                                                                     */
/***********************************************************************/
float funcmean (float expdata1[ ], int n)
{
   int  i;
   float  sum = 0, mean;

   for(i = 0; i < n; i++)
       sum += expdata1[i];

   mean = sum / n;

   return mean;
}

/***********************************************************************/
/*                                                                     */
/*    Function: funcstdev - Computes the Standard                      */
/*                          Deviation                                  */
/*                                                                     */
/***********************************************************************/
```

```
/*    Input Parameters:                                             */
/*        expdata1[n]- Experimental data                            */
/*        n          - number of data values                        */
/*                                                                  */
/*    Local Variables:                                              */
/*        sumsqr     - sum of the squares of the data values        */
/*        sqrsum     - square of the sum of the data values         */
/*        stdev      - standard deviation                           */
/*                                                                  */
/*    Return value:                                                 */
/*        stdev      - standard deviation                           */
/*                                                                  */
/*    Functions Called: none                                        */
/*                                                                  */
/********************************************************************/

float funcstdev(float expdata1[ ], int n)
{
    int i;

    float sum = 0, sumsqr = 0, sqrsum, stdev;

    for(i = 0; i < n; i++)
    {
        sum += expdata1[i];
        sumsqr += expdata1[i] * expdata1[i];
    }
    sqrsum = sum * sum;

    stdev = sqrt((sumsqr - (sqrsum / n))/(n - 1));

    return stdev;
}
```

Input and Output

```
Input ten data values
12.0 5.0 2.0 19.0 7.0 11.0 6.0 8.0 10.0 9.0

mean =  8.90
standard deviation =  4.63

The extreme values:
    2.00
   19.00
```

7.6.4 Maximum and Minimum Values

Problem Write a program to locate and print the maximum and the minimum values of real data stored in an array. Use a function to find the maximum and minimum values. This example shows the use of a function to process an array using call by name and address. Since the function returns two values, the maximum and minimum must be passed by address.

Method

Input the values into an array
Assume the first value is the maximum and the minimum
For each value of the array:
    If the value is less than the minimum value, update the minimum value
    If the value is greater than the maximum value, update the maximum value
End `for`
Output the maximum and the minimum values
Stop

Data

List of integer numbers.

Pseudocode

```
main:
  Input the array a having n elements
  Call maxmin(n, a, amax, amin)
  Print amax and amin
  Stop

function maxmin:
amax ← a[0]
amin ← a[0]
for each array element i
if a[i] > amax
amax ← a[i]
else if a[i] < amin
```

```
amin ← a[i]
end for
return
end
```

Program

```
/********************************************************/
/*                                                      */
/*  Main: Determine the Maximum and the Minimum         */
/*                                                      */
/********************************************************/
/*                                                      */
/*    Constants:                                        */
/*                                                      */
/*        n  -  array size                              */
/*                                                      */
/*    Input Variables:                                  */
/*                                                      */
/*        number - array data values                    */
/*                                                      */
/*    Output Variables:                                 */
/*                                                      */
/*        amax - maximum value                          */
/*        amin - minimum value                          */
/*                                                      */
/*    Functions called:                                 */
/*                                                      */
/*        maxmin - determines maximum and minimum       */
/*                                                      */
/********************************************************/
#include <stdio.h>
# define  N  10
void maxmin(int, float [ ], float *, float *);

int main( )
{
    int  i;
    float  number[N], amax, amin;
    printf("Enter the Numbers:\n");
    for(i = 0 ; i < N; i++)
        scanf("%f", &number[i]);
```

```
    maxmin(N, number, &amax, &amin);

    printf("Maximum value = %5.2f\nMinimum value = %5.2f",
          amax, amin);

    return 0;
}

/*****************************************************/
/*                                                   */
/*    Determine the Maximum and the Minimum          */
/*                                                   */
/*****************************************************/
/*                                                   */
/*  Input Parameters:                                */
/*                                                   */
/*      number[count]   - array of real numbers      */
/*      count           - size of array              */
/*                                                   */
/*  Computed Variables:                              */
/*                                                   */
/*      amax1 - maximum value                        */
/*      amin1 - minimum value                        */
/*                                                   */
/*  Output parameters:                               */
/*                                                   */
/*      amax1 - maximum value                        */
/*      amin1 - minimum value                        */
/*                                                   */
/*                                                   */
/*****************************************************/
void maxmin(int count,float number1[ ],float *amax2,
            float *amin2)
{
    int i;

    *amax2 = number1[0];
    *amin2 = number1[0];
    for( i = 1 ; i < count; i++)
    {
        if(number1[i] > *amax2)
            *amax2 = number1[i];
        else if(number1[i] < *amin2)
            *amin2 = number1[i];
    }
```

```
    return;
}
```

Input and Output

```
Input the Numbers:
1.2 2.3 8.5 9.4 0.02 6.5 3.9 7.4 8.3 5.2

Maximum value =  9.40
Minimum value =  0.02
```

7.6.5 Sorting

Many applications require data to be arranged and organized in some particular order. Rearranging an array to put the data in ascending or descending order is called sorting. There are two types of sorting methods: insertion sorts, where each data value is placed in its proper position with respect to the sorted values already inserted into the array; and exchange sorts, where all the data values to be sorted are read into the array, and then the values are moved around until they are in the proper order. There are many different exchange sorting methods, such as selection sort, bubble sort, shell sort, radix sort, quick sort, quicker sort, and heap sort. These sorting methods can be found in any data structures book.

Sorts differ in the amount of storage required and the number of comparisons made. There is no one best sort for all types of data. The method that is best for a particular application depends on the original order of the data and the amount of storage space available. Usually the space and time complexity of the sorting algorithm must be analyzed and studied and a trade-off must be made. Often sorting software is available in the computer library.

Two sorting algorithms are presented in this section, they are the selection sort and the bubble sort. They are examples of exchange sorts.

Selection Sort

Problem Sort a one-dimensional array in ascending order using the selection sort.

Method A selection sort compares all the elements in a downward pass first to find the smallest element and place it in the first position in the array, then in a downward pass to find the next smallest element and place it in the second position in the array, and so forth. As each element is compared with the elements below it, each candidate for the smallest element is placed in the element position for the current pass by swapping it with the element in that position.

This method was already shown in Section 7.4.1. This example shows the use of functions to input the data, sort it, and print it.

Pseudocode

```
main:
  call funcinput( ) to input the array a
  call funcsort( ) to sort the array a
  call funcoutput( ) to print the sorted array a
  stop

funcinput:
  for each element i
    input a value into array element a[i]
  end
  return

funcsort:
  for each element i from 0 to n – 1
    for each element j from i + 1 to n
      if a[i] > a[j]
        Call funcswap to swap a[i] and a[j]
      end
    end
  end
  return

funcoutput:
  for each element i
    output a[i]
  end
  return
```

Flowchart The flowchart for the `main` function and function sort are shown in Figure 7.1. Notice the special symbol in the flowchart for the `main` program that indicates a function call.

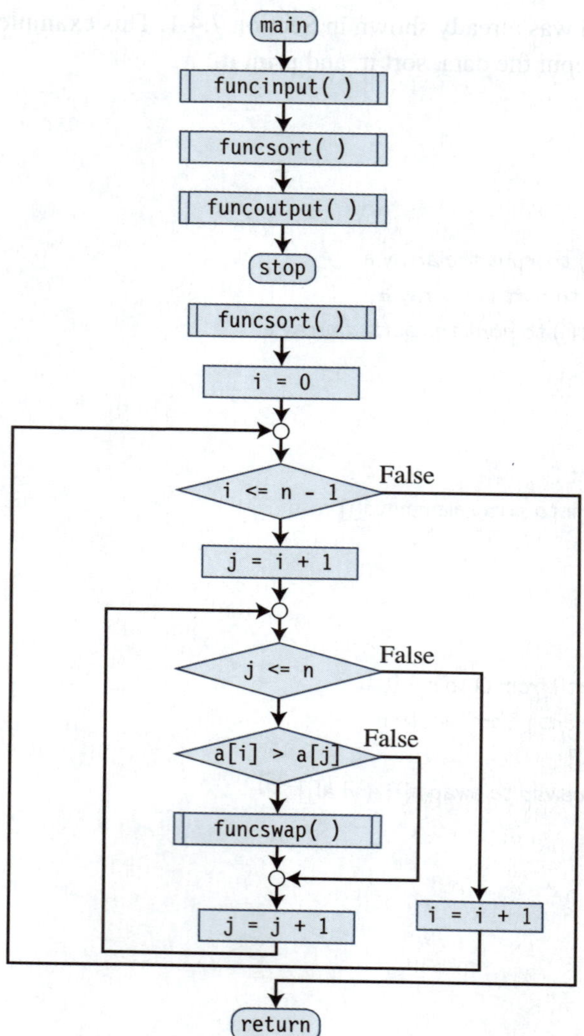

Figure 7.1 Flowchart for selection sort

This time let us assume that only a maximum size of the array is known in advance rather than the exact size.

Besides the functions called in the `main` function, the following function is needed.

```
funcswap:
    atemp ← a[i]
```

```
a[i] ← a[j]
a[j] ← atemp
return
```

If the inequality a[i] > a[j] is reversed to a[i] < a[j] the array a is sorted in descending order.

Program

```
/**********************************************************/
/*                                                        */
/*    Main: Selection Sort                                */
/*        Sort an Array of Numbers in Ascending Order     */
/*                                                        */
/**********************************************************/
/*                                                        */
/*    Defined Constants:                                  */
/*        ARMAX    - maximum size of the array            */
/*                                                        */
/*    Input Variables:                                    */
/*        number    - input value being sorted            */
/*                                                        */
/*    Output Parameters:                                  */
/*        numelm    - number of elements in the array     */
/*        array[numelm] - the array of values             */
/*                                                        */
/*    Function Called:                                    */
/*        funcinput - input the array to be sorted        */
/*        funcsort  - sort the array                      */
/*        funcswap  - swap the elements of the array      */
/*        funcoutput-  print the sorted array             */
/*                                                        */
/**********************************************************/
#include <stdio.h>
#define ARSIZE  10

int funcinput(float  [ ], int);
void funcsort(float  [ ], int);
void funcoutput(float  [ ], int);

int main( )
{
    int numelm;
    float  array[ARSIZE];
```

```
    numelm = funcinput(array, ARSIZE);
    funcsort(array, numelm);
    funcoutput(array, numelm);

    return 0;
}

/*****************************************************************/
/*                                                               */
/*   Function: funcinput                                         */
/*       Input the Data to be Sorted into an Array               */
/*                                                               */
/*****************************************************************/
/*                                                               */
/*   Output parameters:                                          */
/*       array1[count]        - array of real numbers            */
/*       count                - size of array                    */
/*                                                               */
/*****************************************************************/
int funcinput(float  array1[ ], int n)
{
    FILE  *inptr;
    int  count = 0;
    float value;

    inptr = fopen("sortdata.dat", "r");
    while((fscanf(inptr, "%f", &value))!=EOF && count < n)
    {
        array1[count]= value;
        count++;
    }
    fclose(inptr);

    return count;
}

/*****************************************************************/
/*                                                               */
/*   funcsort:  Sort the Array                                   */
/*                                                               */
/*****************************************************************/
/*                                                               */
/*   Input Parameters:                                           */
/*       array1[numelm1]  -  real array to be sorted             */
/*       numelm1 - number of elements in the array               */
```

```
/*                                                      */
/*   Output parameters:                                 */
/*       array1[numelm1]  -  sorted array               */
/*                                                      */
/*   Functions Called:                                  */
/*       funcswap - exchanges two array elements        */
/*                                                      */
/********************************************************/
void funcsort(float  array1[ ], int numelm1)
{
   void funcswap(float [ ], int, int);

   int  i, j;

   for(i = 0; i < numelm1 - 1; i++)
   {
      for(j = i + 1; j < numelm1; j++)
      {
         if (array1[i] > array1[j])
            funcswap(array1,i,j);
      }
   }

   return;
}

/********************************************************/
/*                                                      */
/*   funcswap: Swap the Elements with Index i and j     */
/*                                                      */
/********************************************************/
/*                                                      */
/*   Input Parameters:                                  */
/*       array1[ ] -  real array to be sorted           */
/*       i         - index of the element to be swapped */
/*       j         - index of the element to be swapped */
/*                                                      */
/*   Output Parameters:                                 */
/*       array1[ ] - the array with elements            */
/*                   i and j swapped                    */
/*                                                      */
/********************************************************/
void funcswap(float  array1[ ], int i, int j)
{
   float  arrtemp;
```

```
    arrtemp = array1[i];
    array1[i] = array1[j];
    array1[j] = arrtemp;

    return;
}

/*******************************************************/
/*                                                     */
/*    funcoutput:  Output the Sorted Array             */
/*                                                     */
/*******************************************************/
/*                                                     */
/*    Input Parameters:                                */
/*        array1[numelm1]  -  sorted array             */
/*        numelm1          - number of elements        */
/*                                                     */
/*******************************************************/
void funcoutput(float array1[ ], int numelm1)
{
    FILE  *outptr;
    outptr = fopen( "output.dat", "w" );
    int  i;

    for(i = 0; i < numelm1; i++)
        fprintf( outptr, "%6.2f ", array1[i]);

    return;
}

INPUT FILE: sortdata.dat
=======================
14.00 .50 -7.00 45.00 6.30

OUTPUT FILE: output.dat
======================
 -7.00     .50    6.30   14.00   45.00
```

Bubble Sort This is an exchange sort. In this sort, the elements of the array are compared from the bottom to the top. When any two adjacent elements are out of order, they are exchanged. This results in the largest element floating to the top when the array is to be sorted in descending order, or the smallest element moving to the top when the array is to be sorted in ascending order. In the next pass the next largest (descending order) or next smallest (ascending order) moves into its proper sorted position. The following example shows the result of the two passes needed to sort a short list in descending order.

ORIGINAL LIST	EXCHANGE			AFTER PASS 1	EXCHANGE	AFTER PASS 2
9	.	.	15	15	.	15
15	.	.	9	9	12	12
8	.	12	.	12	9	9
7	12	8	.	8	.	8
12	7	.	.	7	.	7

The basic bubble sort would use four passes to sort an array of five elements, whether or not all the passes were needed. An optimized bubble sort checks whether more passes are needed.

The pseudocode and the flowchart for the basic bubble sort and the optimized bubble sort are presented. In the basic bubble sort all the passes are used whether the list at some point is sorted or not. In the optimized bubble sort a conditional test is performed at the end of every pass to see if any exchange has occurred. If no exchange occurred during the latest pass, the list is already in sorted order and the sort is complete. This is a minor modification to the basic bubble sort. The flowchart for the bubble sort is given in Figure 7.2.

If the original list is arranged in the worst possible order, then $(n - 1)$ passes are needed to sort a list containing n elements. Each pass of a regular bubble sort involves $n - 1$ comparisons of values. This is a total of $(n - 1) \cdot (n - 1) = n^2 - 2n + 1$ comparisons. If the sort is optimized, then there are $n - 1$ comparisons in the first pass, $n - 2$ comparisons in the second pass, $n - 3$ comparisons in the third pass, etc., for a total of $(n - 1) + (n - 2) + (n - 3) + \cdots + 2 + 1 = n(n - 1)/2 = (n^2 - n)/2$ comparisons. Whether the bubble sort is optimized or not, the number of comparisons is roughly proportional to n^2. The bubble sort is said to be of the order of n^2.

Pseudocode

```
funcbubblesort:
  for each index i from 1 to n
      for each index j from n - 1 to i
          if a[j] > a[j-1]
              temp ← a[j]
```

```
            a[j] ← a[j-1]
            a[j-1] ← temp
         end if
      end for
   end for
```

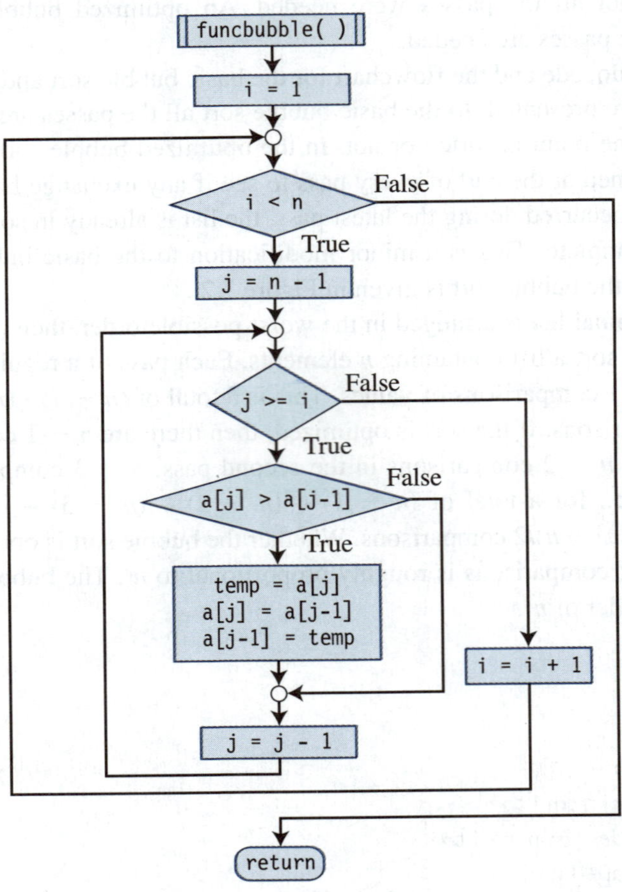

Figure 7.2 Flowchart for the bubble sort

Program

```
/*******************************************************/
/*                                                     */
/*    main: Bubble Sort                                */
/*        Sort a Set of Numbers into Ascending Order   */
/*                                                     */
/*******************************************************/
/*                                                     */
/*    Defined Constants:                               */
/*        ARSIZE  - maximum array size                 */
/*                                                     */
/*    Input Variables:                                 */
/*        array[ARSIZE]  -  array of values to be sorted */
/*                                                     */
/*    Output Variables:                                */
/*        array[ARSIZE]  -  array of values sorted     */
/*                                                     */
/*    Functions Called:                                */
/*        funcbubble: bubble sort in descending order  */
/*                                                     */
/*******************************************************/
#include <stdio.h>
#define  ARSIZE  10

void  funcbubble(float  [ ], int n);

int main( )
{
    float  array[ARSIZE];
    int i;

    printf("Enter ten values to be sorted:\n");
    for(i = 0; i < ARSIZE; i++)
        scanf("%f", &array[i]);

    funcbubble(array, ARSIZE);

    printf("\nSorted Array:\n");
    for(i = 0; i < ARSIZE; i++)
        printf("%5.2f    ", array[i]);
    printf("\n");

    return 0;

}
```

```
/*****************************************************/
/*                                                   */
/*    funcbubble: Bubble Sort                        */
/*                                                   */
/*****************************************************/
/*                                                   */
/*    Local Variables:                               */
/*      temp        - storage to hold array1 element */
/*                                                   */
/*    Input/Output Parameters:                       */
/*      array1[n]  - array                           */
/*      n           - size of array                  */
/*                                                   */
/*****************************************************/
void  funcbubble(float array1[ ], int n)
{
     float temp;
     int  i, j;

     for (i = 1; i < n; i++)
     {
          for(j = n - 1; j >= i; j--)
          {
               if(array1[j] > array1[j - 1])
               {
                  temp = array1[j];
                  array1[j] = array1[j - 1];
                  array1[j - 1] = temp;
               }
          }
     }
     return;
}
```

Input and Output

```
=================
Enter ten values to be sorted:
12.0 56.0 76.0 98.0 34.5 65.3 76.2 81.5 95.7 86.9

Sorted Array:
98.00 95.70 86.90 81.50 76.20 76.00 65.30 56.00 34.50 12.00
```

Optimized Bubble Sort

Pseudocode

Function funcoptbubble(optimized bubble sort)

```
  set flag to false
  i ← 1
  while( i <= n and not flag)
   set flag to true
   for each element j from n - 1 to i
      if array[j] > array[j – 1]
         temp ← array[j]
         array[j] ← array[j-1]
         array[j – 1] ← temp
         flag ← false
      endif
   end for
   i ← i + 1
  end while
  return
End
```

The flowchart for the optimized bubble sort is shown in Figure 7.3.

Program

```
/*******************************************************/
/*                                                     */
/*    main: Optimized Bubble Sort                      */
/*        Sort a Set of Numbers into Ascending Order   */
/*                                                     */
/*******************************************************/
/*                                                     */
/*    Defined Constants:                               */
/*        ARSIZE  - maximum array size                 */
/*                                                     */
/*    Input Variables:                                 */
/*        array[ARSIZE]  -  array of values to be sorted */
/*                                                     */
/*    Output Variables:                                */
/*        array[ARSIZE]  -  array of values sorted     */
/*                                                     */
/*    Functions Called:                                */
/*        funcoptbubble: bubble sort in descending order */
/*                                                     */
```

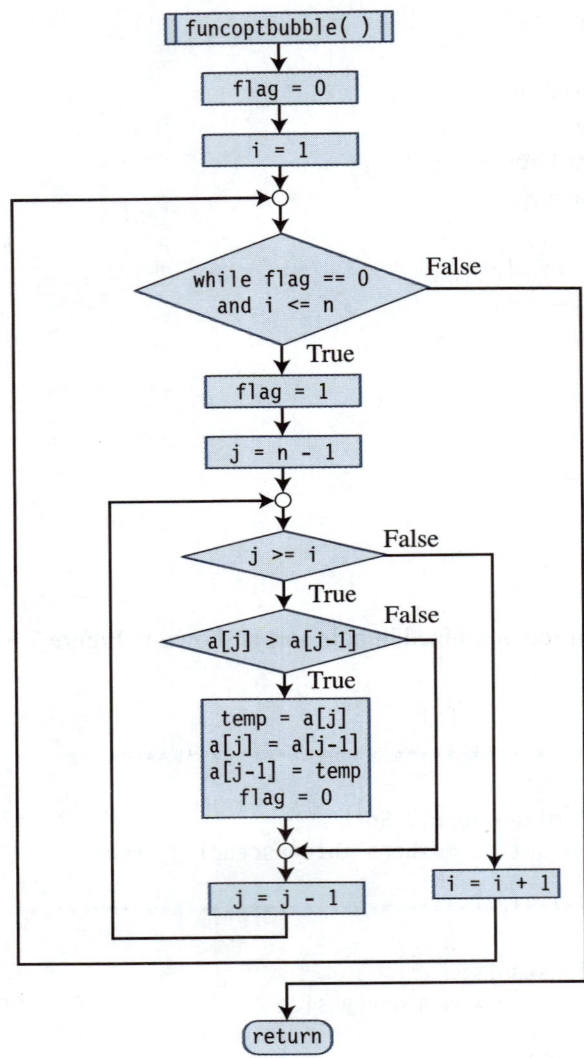

Figure 7.3 Flowchart for the optimized bubble sort

```
/*************************************************************/
#include <stdio.h>
#define  ARSIZE  5
void  funcoptbubble(float  [ ], int n);
int main( )
{
    float  array[ARSIZE];
```

```
    int i;
    printf("Enter five values to be sorted:\n");
    for(i = 0; i < ARSIZE; i++)
        scanf("%f", &array[i]);

    funcoptbubble(array,ARSIZE);
        printf("Sorted array:\n");
    for(i = 0; i < ARSIZE; i++)
        printf("%5.2f    ", array[i]);

    return 0;
}
/*****************************************************/
/*                                                   */
/* funcoptbubble:  Optimized Bubble Sort             */
/*                                                   */
/*****************************************************/
/*                                                   */
/*    Input/Output Parameters:                       */
/*        array1[n]  -  array                        */
/*        n          -  size of array                */
/*                                                   */
/*****************************************************/
void  funcoptbubble(float array1[ ], int n)
{
    int  i = 1, j,flag = 0;
    float  temp;

    while(!flag && i <= n)
    {
        flag = 1;     /*  assume already sorted */
        for(j = n - 1; j >= i; j--)
        {
            if(array1[j] > array1[j - 1])
            {
               temp = array1[j];
               array1[j] = array1[j - 1];
               array1[j - 1] = temp;
               flag = 0;          /*  indicate not already sorted */
            }
        }
        i++;
    }
    return;
}
```

Input and Output

```
Enter five values to be sorted:
34.5 12.5 67.3 89.4 19.4

Sorted array:
89.40    67.30    34.50    19.40    12.50
```

7.6.6 Searching

When it is necessary to look up a value in a list in order to access associated data, a search is needed. The search method depends on whether the list to be searched is sorted or unsorted. A linear search must be used if the list is not sorted. If the list is sorted, either a linear search or a binary search may be used to search for a specific value. A binary search is much faster than a linear search.

Linear Search The linear search is a sequential search until the required value is found. If the value is the first entry in the array, only one comparison is required; if the value is the tenth entry in the array, then ten comparisons are required; if the value is the last entry in the array, all the elements of the array need to be compared. If the value is not an entry in the array, the entire array must be searched. The linear search algorithm returns the location where the value is found, the value −1 if it is not found.

Pseudocode

```
main:
input the array
input the element to be found
call the function funcsearch
output the result of the search
stop

funcsearch:
   i ← 0
   set location to −1
   while i < n and location < 0
```

```
    if array1[i] = item-to-find
      set location to i
    else
      i ← i + 1
    end if
  end while
  return the location
  end
```

In the worst possible case, a linear search of an array containing *n* elements requires *n* comparisons. The best case requires one comparison. On the average, $(n + 1)/2$ comparisons are required to access any element with equal probability of accessing every element. The linear search is said to be of order of *n*.

Program

```
/*************************************************************/
/*                                                           */
/*    main: Linear Search                                    */
/*                                                           */
/*************************************************************/
/*                                                           */
/*    Defined Constants:                                     */
/*        ARSIZE          -  array size searched             */
/*    Input Variables:                                       */
/*        array[ARSIZE]   - the array of values to be        */
/*                          searched                         */
/*        value           - value to be found                */
/*                                                           */
/*    Output Variables:                                      */
/*        value           - value to be found                */
/*        location        - location of the value to be found */
/*        array[location] -  value found                     */
/*                                                           */
/*    Functions Called:                                      */
/*        funcsearch( )   - linear search                    */
/*                                                           */
/*************************************************************/
```

```
#include <stdio.h>

#define ARSIZE  5

int  funcsearch(float [ ], float, int n);

int main( )
{
    float array[ARSIZE], value;
    int flag, location, i;

    printf( "Enter the values for the array: \n" );
    for(i = 0; i < ARSIZE; i++)
        scanf("%f", &array[i]);

    printf( "Enter the value to be found: \n" );
    scanf("%f", &value);

    location = funcsearch(array, value, ARSIZE);

    if(location >= 0)
        printf("\n%4.1f is found in position %d",
                  array[location], location + 1);
    else
        printf("\n%4.1f is not found\n", value);

    return 0;
}

/*********************************************************/
/*                                                       */
/*    funcsearch: Linear Search                          */
/*                                                       */
/*********************************************************/
/*                                                       */
/*    Input Parameters:                                  */
/*        array1[n]     - the array of values to be      */
/*                          searched                     */
/*        value1        - value to be found              */
/*        n             - size of array                  */
/*                                                       */
/*    Output Parameters:                                 */
/*        location      - position of the value found    */
/*                                                       */
/*    Return variables:                                  */
/*        flag          - success flag                   */
/*                                                       */
/*********************************************************/
```

```
int funcsearch(float array1[ ], float value1, int n)
{
    int i, location = -1;
    for(i = 0; i < n; i++)
    {
        if(array1[i] == value1)
        {

             location = i;
             i = n;
        }
    }
return location;
}
```

Input and Output

```
=================
Enter the values for the array:
23.5 65.7 78.4 15.6 47.8

Enter the value to be found:
15.6

15.6 is found in position 4

Enter the values for the array:
23.5 65.7 78.4 15.6 47.8

Enter the value to be found:
56.7

56.7 is not found
```

Binary Search On the average, the linear search requires searching half of the list to locate an item in the list. This is very inefficient for sorted lists. A binary search is more efficient for sorted lists than a linear search. A binary search uses a probing procedure to look at the middle element of the list and determines which half the desired element is in. Then it looks at the middle element of that half to determine which quarter of the list contains the desired element. By repeatedly halving the search list, the element can be located very quickly.

Suppose we want the number 55 in the following list:

SORTED LIST	PROBE 1	PROBE 2	PROBE 3	PROBE 4
12	First			
18				
25				
36				
44				
49				
50	- 49 -	First	50	
60			Last	First
78		78		
80				
96				
98	Last	Last		

In the worst possible case, a binary search of a sorted array containing *n* elements requires $\log_2 n + 1$ comparisons. An average case requires $\log_2 n$ comparisons. Therefore the binary search is of the order of $\log_2 n$. The flowchart is shown in Figure 7.4.

Pseudocode

main:

```
   input the sorted array
   input the element to be searched
   call funcbinary( )
   if found
      output the location found
   else
      output a message
   stop
```

funcbinary:

```
   position ← −1
   first ← 0
```

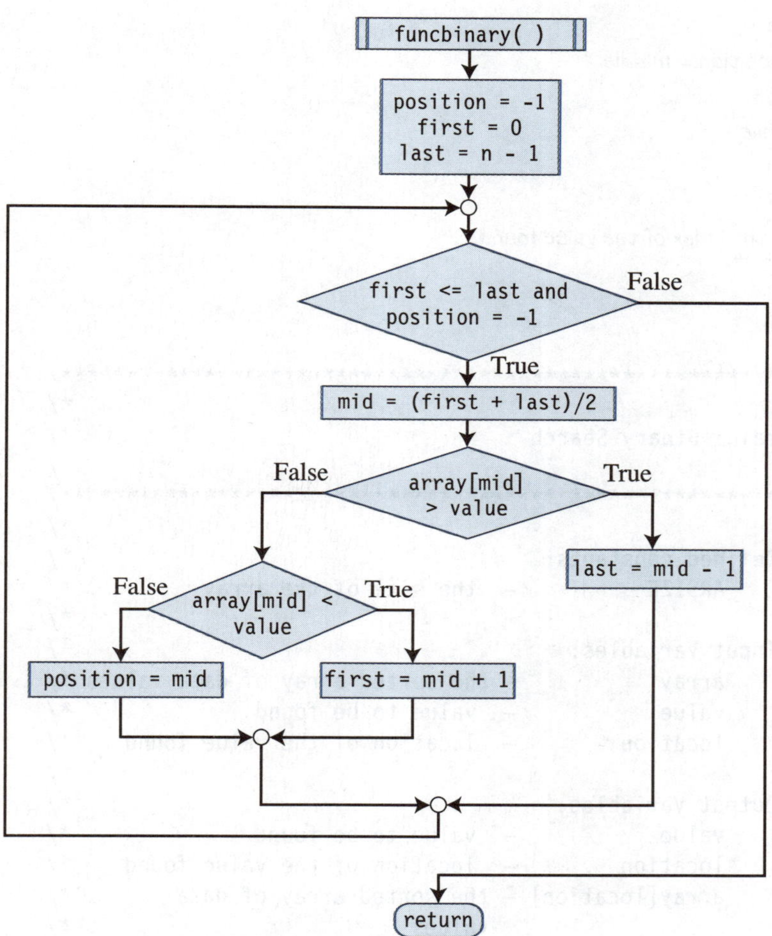

Figure 7.4 Flowchart for binary search

```
last ← n − 1
while first <= last and position = −1
   middle ← (first + last) / 2
   if(array[middle] > value)
      last ← middle − 1
   else if (array[middle] < value)
      first ← middle + 1
```

```
    else
        position = middle
    end if
  end while
  return
  end
```

Returns the index of the value found.

Program

```
/*************************************************************/
/*                                                           */
/*    main: Binary Search                                    */
/*                                                           */
/*************************************************************/
/*                                                           */
/*    Defined constants:                                     */
/*        ARSIZE          -  the size of the array           */
/*                                                           */
/*    Input Variables:                                       */
/*        array           - the sorted array of data values  */
/*        value           -  value to be found               */
/*        location        -  location of the value found     */
/*                                                           */
/*    Output Variables:                                      */
/*        value           -  value to be found               */
/*        location        -  location of the value found     */
/*        array[location] - the sorted array of data         */
/*                          values                           */
/*                                                           */
/*    Functions called:                                      */
/*        funcbinary  - binary search function               */
/*                                                           */
/*************************************************************/

#include <stdio.h>
#define ARSIZE  5

int funcbinary(float [ ], float);
```

```
int main( )
{
    float  array[ARSIZE], value;
    int  i, location;
    int  first = 0;
    int  last = ARSIZE - 1;
    printf("Enter the sorted array:\n");
    for (i = 0; i < ARSIZE; i++)
        scanf("%f", &array[i]);

    printf("Enter the value to be found:\n");
    scanf("%f", &value);

    location = funcbinary(array,value);
    if(location >= 0)
        printf("%4.1f is found in position %d\n",
                array[location], location + 1);
    else
        printf("%4.1f is not found:\n", value);
    return 0;
}

/***********************************************************/
/*                                                         */
/*    funcbinary: Binary Search                            */
/*                                                         */
/***********************************************************/
/*                                                         */
/*    Input Parameters:                                    */
/*       array1[ARSIZE]     - the array of values to be    */
/*                            searched                     */
/*       value1             - value to be found            */
/*                                                         */
/*    Return variables:                                    */
/*       position - location of the value found            */
/*                                                         */
/***********************************************************/

int funcbinary(float array1[ ],float value1)
{
    int position = -1, middle, first = 0, last = ARSIZE;
```

```
    while(first <= last && position == -1)
    {
        middle = (first + last) / 2;
        if(array1[middle] > value1)
            last = middle - 1;
        else if(array1[middle] < value1)
            first = middle + 1;
        else
            position = middle;
    }
    return  position;
}
```

Input and Output

```
================
Enter the sorted array:
1.2 3.5 6.7 8.6 9.8

Enter the value to be found:
3.5

 3.5 is found in position 2

Enter the sorted array:
1.2 3.5 6.7 8.6 9.8

Enter the value to be found:
4.6

 4.6 is not found
```

7.6.7 Inventory of an Engineering Sales Company

Problem Calculate the total value of the inventory of a sales company.

Method Input three arrays consisting of 5 digit part numbers, number of units of each part, and the unit cost of each part from a data file. Compute the total cost for all units of each part and store it in an array. Compute the total units and the total cost of all parts.

Pseudocode

```
main:
   call funcinput1( )
   call funcinput2( )
   call funccomput( )
   call functotunits( )
   call functotcost( )
   call funcoutput( )
   stop

funcinput1:
   for each part
      Input the 5 digit part id, number of units, unit cost
   end for
   return

funccomput:
   for each part id
      tot-unit-cost ← units * unit cost
   end for
   return

functotunits:
   total_units ← 0
   for each part id
      tot_units ← tot_units + units
   end for
   return
```

functotcost:

total_cost ← 0
for each part id
  tot_cost ← tot_cost + total_unit_cost
end for
return

funcoutput:

for each part id
  output the 5 digit part id, number of units, unit cost, total unit cost
end for
output the total units and total cost
return

Program

```
/*********************************************************/
/*                                                       */
/*    main: Inventory of an Engineering Company          */
/*                                                       */
/*********************************************************/
/*                                                       */
/*    Defined Constants:                                 */
/*        NUMPRTS    -  number of different parts        */
/*                                                       */
/*    Input Variables:                                   */
/*        partid     -  identification of each part      */
/*        partunits  - number of units of each part      */
/*        unitcost   - cost of each part                 */
/*                                                       */
/*    Computed Variables:                                */
/*        unitscost  - cost of total units of each part  */
/*        totalunits -  total units of all parts         */
/*        totalcost  - total cost of inventory           */
/*                                                       */
/*    Output Variables:                                  */
/*        partid     -  identification of each part      */
/*        partunits  - number of units of each part      */
/*        unitcost   - cost of each part                 */
/*        unitscost  - cost of total units of each part  */
/*        totalunits -  total units of all parts         */
```

```
/*        totalcost    - total cost of inventory          */
/*                                                        */
/*    Functions Called:                                   */
/*        funcinput( )     - function to input the data   */
/*        funccomput( )    - function to compute total    */
/*                           units cost of each part      */
/*        functotunits( ) - function to compute total     */
/*                           units of all parts           */
/*        functotcost( )   - function to compute the      */
/*                           total cost of all parts      */
/*        funcoutput( )    - function to output the data  */
/*                                                        */
/*********************************************************/
#include <stdio.h>

#define NUMPRTS  5

void funcinput(int [ ], float [ ], int [ ], int);
void funccomput(int [ ], float [ ], float [ ], int);
int  functotunits(int [ ], int);
float functotcost(float [ ], int);
void funcoutput(int [ ],int [ ],float [ ],float [ ],
                int, float, int);

int main( )
{
    int totalunits, partid[NUMPRTS], partunits[NUMPRTS];
    float totalcost, unitcost[NUMPRTS], unitscost[NUMPRTS];

    funcinput(partid, unitcost, partunits, NUMPRTS);
    funccomput(partunits, unitcost, unitscost, NUMPRTS);
    totalunits = functotunits(partunits, NUMPRTS);
    totalcost = functotcost(unitscost,NUMPRTS);
    funcoutput(partid,partunits,unitcost,unitscost,
               totalunits, totalcost,NUMPRTS);

    return 0;
}

/*********************************************************/
/*                                                       */
/*    funcinput: Input Parts and Costs from a Data File  */
/*                                                       */
/*********************************************************/
```

```
/*                                                          */
/*    Input Variables:                                      */
/*       partid1[n]   - part identification                 */
/*       unitcost1[n] - cost of each unit                   */
/*       n            - number of parts                     */
/*                                                          */
/*    Output Parameters:                                    */
/*       partid1[n]   - part identification                 */
/*       unitcost1[n] - cost of each unit                   */
/*       partunits1   - number of part units                */
/*                                                          */
/*    Data files used:                                      */
/*       filein1.dat  - part identification and             */
/*                      cost of each unit                   */
/*                                                          */
/************************************************************/
void funcinput(int partid1[ ], float unitcost1[ ], int partunits1[ ],
int n)
{
   FILE  *inptr1;
   int i;

   inptr1 = fopen("filein.dat","r");

   for(i = 0; i < n; i++)
   {
      fscanf(inptr1,"%d %f %d", &partid1[i],&unitcost1[i],
             &partunits1[i]);
   }
   fclose(inptr1);
   return;
}

/************************************************************/
/*                                                          */
/*    funccomput: Computes the Unit's Cost                  */
/*                                                          */
/************************************************************/
/*                                                          */
/*    Input Parameters:                                     */
/*       partunits1[n] - number of units                    */
/*       unitcost1[n]  - cost of each unit                  */
/*       n             - number of parts                    */
/*                                                          */
/*    Computed Variables:                                   */
/*       unitscost1[n] - total cost of each part            */
/*                                                          */
```

```
/*    Output Parameters:                                        */
/*        unitscost1[n] - cost of each unit                     */
/*                                                              */
/****************************************************************/
void funccomput(int partunits1[ ], float unitcost1[ ],
                float unitscost1[ ],int n)
{
   int  i;

   for(i = 0; i < n; i++)
   {
      unitscost1[i] = partunits1[i] * unitcost1[i];
   }
   return;
}

/****************************************************************/
/*                                                              */
/*    functotunits: Compute Total Units of All Parts            */
/*                                                              */
/****************************************************************/
/*                                                              */
/*    Input Parameters:                                         */
/*        partunits1[n] - number of units                       */
/*        n             - number of parts                       */
/*                                                              */
/*    Computed Variables:                                       */
/*        totalunits    - total units of all parts              */
/*                                                              */
/*    Returned Variables:                                       */
/*        totalunits    - total units of all parts              */
/*                                                              */
/****************************************************************/
int functotunits(int partunits1[ ],int n)
{
   int  i, totalunits = 0;

   for(i = 0; i < n; i++)
      totalunits += partunits1[i];
   return totalunits;
}

/****************************************************************/
/*                                                              */
/*    functotcost: Compute Total Cost of All Parts              */
```

```
/*                                                          */
/************************************************************/
/*                                                          */
/*    Input Parameters:                                     */
/*        unitcost1[n] - cost of each unit                  */
/*        n            - number of parts                    */
/*                                                          */
/*    Computed Variables:                                   */
/*        totalcost    - total cost of all parts            */
/*                                                          */
/*    Returned Variables:                                   */
/*        totalcost    - total units of all parts           */
/*                                                          */
/************************************************************/

float functotcost(float unitscost1[ ], int n)
{
    int  i;
    float totalcost = 0.0;

    for(i = 0; i < n; i++)
    {
        totalcost += unitscost1[i];
    }
    return totalcost;
}

/************************************************************/
/*                                                          */
/*    funcoutput: Output Data to a Data File                */
/*                                                          */
/************************************************************/
/*                                                          */
/*    Input Parameters:                                     */
/*        partid1[n]    - part identification               */
/*        partunits1[n] - number of units                   */
/*        unitcost1[n]  - cost of each unit                 */
/*        unitscost2[n] - total cost of each part           */
/*        totalunits1   - total units of all parts          */
/*        totalcost1    - total cost of all parts           */
/*        n             - number of parts                   */
/*                                                          */
/*    Output Variables:                                     */
/*        partid1[n]    - part identification               */
/*        partunits1[n] - number of units                   */
```

```
/*        unitcost1[n]  - cost of each unit                    */
/*        unitscost2[n] - total cost of each part              */
/*        totalcost     - total cost of all parts              */
/*        totalunits1   - total units of all parts             */
/*                                                             */
/*   Data files used:                                          */
/*        fileout.dat   - output the inventory table           */
/*                                                             */
/**************************************************************/
void funcoutput(int partid1[ ],int partunits1[ ],
                float unitcost1[ ],float unitscost2[ ],
                int totalunits1, float totalcost1, int n)
{
    FILE  *outptr;
    int i;

    outptr = fopen("fileout.dat", "w");
    for(i = 0; i < n; i++)
    {
        fprintf(outptr,"%2d  %5d  %3f  %5.2f  %8.2f\n",
                i, partid1[i],partunits1[i],unitcost1[i],
                unitscost2[i]);
    }
    fprintf(outptr,"\nTotalunits: %5d    Totalcost: %8.2f\n",
            totalunits1, totalcost1);
    fclose(outptr);

    return;
}
```

```
INPUT DATA FILE: "filein.dat"
65478       18     2.56
75396       25     3.67
89352       16     1.25
97169       45     4.86
99578       29     6.54

OUTPUT DATA FILE: "fileout.dat"
 0   65478   18     2.56        46.08
 1   75396   25     3.67        91.75
 2   89352   16     1.25        20.00
 3   97169   45     4.86       218.70
 4   99578   29     6.54       189.66

Totalunits:   133    Totalcost:   566.19
```

Chapter Summary

A one-dimensional array is a data type derived from the basic data types `int`, `float`, `double`, or `char`. One-dimensional arrays are used to store large amounts of data in the form of lists when the data is being processed more than once or is not being processed in the order it is provided. In science and engineering applications one-dimensional arrays are used to store vectors. The general form of the declaration of one-dimensional arrays in C is as follows:

data-type array-name[number of elements];

For example:

```
int  value[5];
```

Notice that the data type of the array is `int`, the array-name is `value`, and the number of elements is 5. The effect of this declaration is simply to allocate five storage cells for the array `value` and each storage cell is allocated four bytes of storage because the type is `int`. C uses zero-origin subscripting so the five elements are stored as `value[0],...,value[4]`.

Data can be stored in array elements in three different ways:

- initialize the array when it is declared
- assign data values to each individual element using assignment statements
- input the data values using the input function `scanf()` or `fscanf()`

The input and output of arrays may be conveniently implemented by using a `for` loop that indexes the array elements.

Initialization is as follows:

```
int  i, a[5];
for (i = 0; i < 5; i++)
    a[i] = 0;
```

or `int  a[5] = {0, 0, 0, 0, 0};`

or `a[0] = 0; a[1] = 0; a[2] = 0; a[3] = 0; a[4] = 0;`

Input is as follows:

```
for (i = 0; i < 5; i++)
    scanf("%d", &a[i]);
```

Output is as follows:

```
for (i = 0; i < 5; i++)
    printf("%d\n", a[i]);
```

All of the arithmetic and logic operations performed on individual variables may be performed on the elements of an array. Arithmetic and logic operations may be performed on array elements accessed either randomly by using an explicit index or sequentially by using a for loop index. Small amounts of data to be sorted or searched can be stored in an array. If the data has been sorted the fast binary search can be used.

One-dimensional arrays are passed to a function by passing the array name. When an array is passed to the function by array name, the function knows the starting address of the array. When the array values are changed in the function, the changes will be reflected in the arguments passed in the calling function.

```
#define ARSIZE  10    /* defined constant */
void  func(int [ ]); /* function prototype */
int  array[ARSIZE];   /* array declaration */
func(array, ARSIZE); /* function call passing array name and size */

void func(int arr[ ], int n) /* function header */
```

Array elements may be passed to the function by explicitly specifying the indexes of the elements. In passing the elements to the function they may be passed by value or by address and are treated as though they were ordinary variables. The following shows an element of the array passed by value to the function using an explicit index:

```
#define ARSIZE  10                      /* compiler constant */
void  funccomput(int, int);             /* function prototype */
int  i,  a[ARSIZE] = { 2, 3, 4, 5, 6}; /* array declaration and
                                           initialization */
funccomput(a[4]);     /* function call, passing array element */
void funccomput(int  x)                 /* function header */
{
   .........
   return;
}
```

The array element a[4] is passed by value. If the value of the parameter in the function is changed the change will not be reflected in the argument in the calling function.

```
#define ARSIZE  10
void  funccomput( int *);               /* function prototype */
int  i,  a[5] = { 2, 3, 4, 5, 6};  /* array declaration and
                                          initialization */
funccomput(&a[4]);                      /* function call */
void funccomput(int  *x)                /* function header and body */
{
 . . .
   return;
}
```

Here the array element a[4] is passed by address and picked up by a pointer variable. If the value of the parameter in the function is changed the change will be reflected in the argument in the calling function.

Exercises

1. Write a program to input 100 values into an array a[100]. Compute the count, sum, and average of positive numbers and the count, sum, and average of negative numbers. Output the array, ten numbers per row, the count, the sum, and the average of the positive and negative numbers.
2. Write a program to generate 500 numbers in the range of 1 to 20 using the random number generator. Count the number of times each number occurs in this set and print the numbers and their frequencies. Use an array to store the numbers.
3. Write a program to generate the Cartesian coordinates from polar coordinates for a circle with radius r and the angle θ in the increments of 5°. Store the x and y coordinate values in two one-dimensional arrays. The formula for the conversion of polar coordinates to Cartesian coordinates is as follows:

   $x = r \cos \theta$

   $y = r \sin \theta$

4. Write a program to compute the tip speed of a propeller having diameter *d* as input for various speeds *s*, measured in revolutions per minute. Let $s = 50, 100, 150,\ldots, 1000$. Store the tip speed of the propeller in a table and print the table. The formula for computing the radial velocity in feet per second is as follows:

$$\omega = \frac{2\pi s}{60} \quad v = \frac{\omega d}{2}$$

where *d* is the propeller diameter in ft.
   s is the tip speed in revolutions per minute
   ω is the radial velocity in radians per minute
   v is the velocity per minute

5. Write a program to record the temperature and pressure values in a scientific experiment and store the data in two one-dimensional arrays, then identify the extreme values of pressure and temperature. The array size is 20.

6. Write a program to store survey measurements of height above a base line at every 10 feet of land over a 500 foot terrain and store the measured values in an array. Compute the approximate cubic feet of soil to be removed to dig a level trench five feet wide and six feet deep at the lowest measured point as the reference depth. Use the trapezoidal approximation formula.

7. A farmer raises pigs on a farm and keeps the weight data for 20 pigs in a computer. Write a program to input the five character alphanumeric ID and the weight data and sort the IDs in descending order by the corresponding weights.

8. Write a program to find the mode that is the number that occurs most often in a list of 100 data values.

CHAPTER 8

Multidimensional Arrays

Objective

To process data in the form of rows and columns representing tables, determinants, and matrices. Also, to process data in more than two dimensions as multidimensional arrays.

Homogeneous tabular data in the form of rows and columns is stored in two-dimensional arrays. Points in a two-dimensional space-coordinate system represented as *f*(*x*, *y*) may be stored either as two one-dimensional arrays `x[ ]` and `y[ ]` or as a two-dimensional array `pt[ ][ ]`. Variables representing values at grid points on a plane would be stored in a two-dimensional array. If the values are not evenly spaced, a three-dimensional array would be needed to store the values and their locations. If points are situated in three-dimensional space and also in time, then their locations must be stored in a four-dimensional array. There are many scientific and engineering applications in which variables are represented in two-dimensional space dependent on time. Functions that are dependent on two-dimensional space are represented as *f*(*x*, *y*). Functions that are dependent on two-dimensional space and time are represented as *f*(*x*, *y*, *t*).

Functions that are dependent on three-dimensional space only are represented as $f(x, y, z)$. Functions that are dependent on three-dimensional space and time are represented as $f(x, y, z, t)$. Two-dimensional arrays can store a table of values of a single variable type, or a set of vectors of a single type. A three-dimensional array can store a three-dimensional matrix or a set of two-dimensional tables, all of the same data type.

In scientific computing, for example in the two-dimensional modeling of fluid flow or stress analysis, we use two-dimensional arrays; and in three-dimensional modeling we use three-dimensional arrays. If the flow is time-dependent we use three- and four-dimensional arrays for two-dimensional and three-dimensional modeling problems, respectively.

8.1 Introduction to Two-Dimensional Arrays

Data in the form of rows and columns is two-dimensional. For example, the average rain gauge measurements in four cities in three months may be recorded and stored in the form of a table.

	CITY 1	CITY 2	CITY 3	CITY 4
MONTH 1	8.5	6.2	9.3	7.2
MONTH 2	12.5	9.8	7.2	8.4
MONTH 3	3.2	4.2	6.4	2.5

Each data value can be uniquely identified by its row and its column. This data may be collectively named “rain,” and the mathematical notation for any single element of the arrangement is given by

$$\text{rain}_{i,j} \qquad i = 1, 2, 3, \text{ and } j = 1, 2, 3, 4$$

where i is the row subscript (MONTH), and
j is the column subscript (CITY).

The components of $\text{rain}_{i,j}$ are as follows:

	COLUMN 1	COLUMN 2	COLUMN 3	COLUMN 4
ROW 1	$\text{rain}_{1,1}$	$\text{rain}_{1,2}$	$\text{rain}_{1,3}$	$\text{rain}_{1,4}$
ROW 2	$\text{rain}_{2,1}$	$\text{rain}_{2,2}$	$\text{rain}_{2,3}$	$\text{rain}_{2,4}$
ROW 3	$\text{rain}_{3,1}$	$\text{rain}_{3,2}$	$\text{rain}_{3,3}$	$\text{rain}_{3,4}$

The first subscript is called the row subscript because it is the same for all the elements in a row, and the second subscript is called the column subscript because it is the same for all the elements in a column. The second, or column, subscript varies on the row to indicate the column position of each element in a row. The row subscript varies on the column to indicate the row position of each element in a column.

The elements of a two-dimensional array can be accessed sequentially in two ways: either as row elements or as column elements. To access the elements of two-dimensional arrays by rows, an outer `for` loop is used for the row index and an inner `for` loop is used for the column index. To access the elements of two-dimensional arrays by columns, the outer `for` loop index must be the column index and the inner `for` loop index must be the row index.

Sequential Access by Rows

```
for each row i
   for each element of the row
      access rain_{i, j}
   end for
end for
```

Sequential Access by Columns

```
for each column j
   for each element of the column
      access rain_{i, j}
   end for
end for
```

> *Programming Hint:* Vary the column subscript to access the elements by rows, and the row subscript to access the elements by columns.

In C notation the index starts at zero instead of at one. The elements of a two-dimensional array a in C are identified as follows:

	column0	column1	column2	column3
row0	a[0,0]	a[0,1]	a[0,2]	a[0,3]
row1	a[1,0]	a[1,1]	a[1,2]	a[1,3]
row2	a[2,0]	a[2,1]	a[2,2]	a[2,3]

In C, the index gives the offset from the beginning of the row or column. Because of this, each index starts at zero.

8.1.1 Declaration Statement

A declaration statement is used to specify the data type, name, and size of an array. The data type of the array may be `int`, `float`, `double`, or `char`. The name of the array is subject to the rules of identifier names and does not include the subscript. The size of the array specifies the maximum number of rows and the maximum number of columns. The general form of the declaration statement for a two-dimensional array is as follows:

datatype name[# of rows][# of columns];

for example:

```
int a[4][5];
```

Two dimensional arrays may be declared with the row size and column size specified by defined constants so that the program is more generic. The following code shows this type of generic declaration.

```
#define  IMAX   4
#define  JMAX   5
int   a[IMAX][JMAX];
```

The elements of the fourth row of the array can be accessed as follows:

```
for(j = 0; j < JMAX; j++)
   ..a[3][j]..                /* refers to the fourth row */
```

The elements of the third column of the array can be accessed as follows:

```
for(i = 0; i < IMAX; i++)
    ...a[i][2]...         /* refers to the third column */
```

All of the elements of the array can be accessed by rows as follows:

```
for(i = 0; i < IMAX; i++)
{
     for(j = 0; j < JMAX; j++)
     {
      ...a[i][j]...
     }
}
```

All of the elements of the array can be accessed by columns as follows:

```
for(j = 0; j < JMAX; j++)
{
    for(i = 0; i < IMAX; i++)
    {
     ...a[i][j]...
    }
}
```

A single element of the array can be accessed as follows:

```
a[2][3]    /* refers to the element in the third row and the fourth
              column */
```

8.1.2 Storage Allocation

The storage for the array is determined when an array declaration statement is compiled. The number of storage cells needed is the product of the number of rows and the number of columns specified in the declaration. The size of each storage cell is determined by the data type of the array. This is compile-time storage and once storage is allocated during the loading of the program, the storage is dedicated to the array until the program terminates. If the array is too small, the defined constants that specify the size of the array need to be changed and the program must be recompiled after the change. Since storage is one-dimensional and sequential in order, the array elements are allocated sequential storage. In C the elements of a two-dimensional array are stored sequentially in row-major order, meaning that they are stored by rows.

The storage arrangement shown in this example uses the array subscript, also called the array indices.

Array declaration: `int a[3][4];`

Array elements:

```
a[0][0]  a[0][1]  a[0][2]  a[0][3]
a[1][0]  a[1][1]  a[1][2]  a[1][3]
a[2][0]  a[2][1]  a[2][2]  a[2][3]
```

Storage allocation:

row0	a[0][0]
	a[0][1]
	a[0][2]
	a[0][3]
row1	a[1][0]
	a[1][1]
	a[1][2]
	a[1][3]
row2	a[2][0]
	a[2][1]
	a[2][2]
	a[2][3]

Notice that the elements of row0 are stored first followed by row1 and then by row2. The elements of each row are stored in ascending order by column index. In this case the column subscript changes more rapidly than the row subscript. Because of this, arrays may be processed most efficiently by rows.

8.1.3 Array Initialization

Initialization of an array provides values for the elements of the array at the time the array is declared. There are other ways of providing values to the elements of the array: through explicit assignment, assignment inside a for loop, and through input. The following examples show the initialization of a two-dimensional array.

```
int a[3][4] = {1, 4, 2, 7, 5, 9, 6, 10, 12, 15, 1, 18};
```

The values are assigned and stored in row-major order.

a[0][0], a[0][1], a[0][2], and a[0][3] are assigned the values 1, 4, 2, and 7 — row0

a[1][0], a[1][1], a[1][2], and a[1][3] are assigned the values 5, 9, 6, and 10 — row1 a[2][0], a[2][1], a[2][2], and a[2][3] are assigned the values 12, 15, 1, and 18 row2

Notice that there are 12 elements and there are 12 values. The number of values specified is exactly the same as the number of elements. If the number of values specified is less than the number of elements, zeroes are substituted for the rest of the elements. If the number of values specified is more than the number of elements then an error occurs.

Programming Error: Do not specify more values than the number of elements declared for the array.

There is another form of initialization, that is, the rows can be explicitly specified using braces as follows:

```
int a[3][4] = {{1,4,2,7},{5,9,6,10},{12,15,1,18}};
```

If the number of elements specified in any row is less than the declared number of elements in each row, zeroes are substituted for the rest of the elements in that row. If the number of elements specified in any row is more than the declared size of the row, an error will occur. And if fewer rows are given values than are declared, the extra rows are filled with zeroes.

If the initial values are all the same, say for example 1.0, there are two ways to initialize such an array. One way is to specify the values in the declaration as follows:

```
float a[3][4] = {1.0, 1.0, 1.0, 1.0, 1.0, 1.0, 1.0, 1.0, 1.0, 1.0,
1.0, 1.0};
```

This is not an efficient method of initialization for large arrays. Large arrays may be initialized using nested for loops and assignment statements. The following code shows initialization of large arrays.

```
#define IMAX  100
#define JMAX  200
int main( )
{
    float  a[IMAX][JMAX];
    int  i, j;
```

```
    for(i = 0; i < IMAX; i++)
    {
        for(j = 0; j < JMAX; j++)
        {
            a[i][j] = 1.0;
        }
    }
    return 0;
}
```

Two-dimensional arrays may also be initialized by an explicit assignment. The following code shows such an assignment of values to the elements of the array.

```
float  a[3][4];

a[0][0] = 2.5;
a[0][1] = 6.3;
       ....
a[2][2] = 16.8;
a[2][3] = 12.6;
```

This is not an efficient way to initialize two-dimensional arrays as it is not practical with large arrays.

> *Programming Hint:* For large arrays, use nested `for` loops to initialize array elements having the same initial value.

For large size arrays initialization during declaration and also by an explicit assignment is not practical unless they are being initialized to zero or a scalar value. To initialize such arrays use an input statement as shown in the next section.

> *Programming Hint:* To store data in large size arrays use an input statement.

Arrays do not have to be processed by rows or by columns. For example, in a square array the diagonal elements may be set to a certain value, the lower triangle elements set to a different value, and the upper triangle elements set to a third value.

```
#define  IMAX  4
#define  JMAX  4
```

```
int main( )
{
    float  value[IMAX][JMAX];
    int  i, j;

    for(i = 0; i < IMAX; i++)
    {
        for(j = 0; j < JMAX; j++)
        {
            if(i == j)
                value[i][j] = 2.0;
            else if(i > j)
                value[i][j] = 4.0;
            else
                value[i][j] = 8.0;
        }
    }

    return 0;
}
```

The values assigned to the array are:

```
2.0    8.0    8.0    8.0
4.0    2.0    8.0    8.0
4.0    4.0    2.0    8.0
4.0    4.0    4.0    2.0
```

Notice that all the major diagonal elements are set to a value of 2.0, the lower triangle elements are set to 4.0, and the upper triangle elements are set to 8.0.

8.1.4 Review Questions

1. Indicate whether the following statements are true or false.
   a. In C, two-dimensional arrays are stored in column order.
   b. To process two-dimensional arrays by rows, the outer loop index must be the row index.
   c. To process two-dimensional arrays by columns, the inner loop index must be the column index.
   d. To access a specific element of a two-dimensional array, an explicit index of such an element must be specified.

2. Write the declaration statements for the following arrays:
   a. float $a_{i,j}$ $i = 0, 9$ $j = 0, 19$
   b. integer $x_{i,j}$ $i = 0, 19$ $j = 0, 39$
   c. double $w_{i,j}$ $i = 0, 49$ $j = 0, 199$
   d. double $w_{i,j}$ and $q_{i,j}$ $i = 0, 99$ $j = 0, 199$
3. Show the storage and indices for the following array:

   ```
   float  c[2][3];
   ```

4. Write the nested for loops to process the following array by rows using array indices:

   ```
   float  x[10][20];
   ```

5. Write the nested for loops to process the following array by columns using array indices:

   ```
   double  q[300][400];
   ```

6. Show the storage for each of the following declarations:
   a. `int a[2][3] = {1, 1, 1};`
   b. `int b[2][3] ={{1}, {1}};`

8.2 Input of Two-Dimensional Arrays

Input of data into two-dimensional arrays may be accomplished by using array indices. Nested for loops may be used to index the elements of the array to input the data values into two-dimensional arrays. Other methods of inputting values into an array will be presented in Chapter 10.

8.2.1 Standard Input

It is efficient to input data into a two-dimensional array in row order, because the storage is allocated in row order. The following example shows the input of data into a two-dimensional array by rows.

Input Data Arranged in Rows

```
28.5    46.3    57.9    72.6
14.3    15.7    31.4    19.4
48.9    13.9    90.6    57.8
```

Standard Input by Rows This data is entered from the keyboard as shown by rows. The following program shows the code for standard input:

```
#include <stdio.h>
#define  IMAX  3
#define  JMAX  4

int main( )
{
    float  values[IMAX][JMAX];
    int  i, j;

    for(i = 0; i < IMAX; i++)
    {
        for(j = 0; j < JMAX; j++)
        {
            scanf("%f", &values[i][j]);
        }
    }

    return 0;
}
```

8.2.2 Input from a Data File

In scientific computing, the data is normally stored in a data file.

myfilein.dat

3 4 28.5 46.3 57.9 72.6 14.3 15.7 31.4 19.4 48.9 13.9 90.6 57.8

Input by Rows from a "myfilein.dat" Data File This data is arranged in rows in data file "myfilein.dat". The input of this data using indices and for loops is as follows:

```
#include <stdio.h>
#define  IMAX  3
#define  JMAX  4
FILE  *inptr;

int main( )
{
    float  values[IMAX][JMAX];        /* maximum space allocated */
```

```
    int  i, j, n, m;
    inptr = fopen("myfilein.dat", "r");
    fscanf(inptr, "%d  %d", &n, &m);        /* actual space input */
    if(n <= IMAX && m <= JMAX)
    {
        for(i = 0; i < n; i++)
        {
            for(j = 0; j < m; j++)
            {
                fscanf(inptr,"%f", &values[i][j]);
            }
        }
    }
    else
    {
        printf("Array storage space insufficient");
    }
    fclose(inptr);
    return 0;
}
```

8.2.3 Review Questions

1. Write the code to input the following integer numbers from the keyboard into a two-dimensional array. Assume the data is to be input by columns into `int arr[3][4]`. Show how the data is stored in memory.

   Input data:
   5 8 12 16 19 16 14 18 20 35 10 11

2. Write the code to input the following real numbers from a data file into a two-dimensional array `arr`. Assume the data is stored in the file by rows. Check for the end of file and print an error message if there are fewer than 12 values.

   Input data:
   28.25 12.65 18.97 26.12
   56.87 67.32 45.87 12.87
   25.89 98.88 13.76 57.03

8.3 Output of Two-Dimensional Arrays

The output of two-dimensional arrays is generally in the form of rows and columns. Nested `for` loops may be used to print the tables and matrices in rows and columns. The following pieces of code show the output of two-dimensional arrays using array indices.

8.3.1 Standard Output

The following storage and the code show the output of a two-dimensional array.

Assume the values in storage are as follows:

row0	a[0][0]	28.5
	a[0][1]	46.3
	a[0][2]	57.9
	a[0][3]	72.6
row1	a[1][0]	14.3
	a[1][1]	15.7
	a[1][2]	31.4
	a[1][3]	19.4
row2	a[2][0]	48.9
	a[2][1]	13.9
	a[2][2]	90.6
	a[2][3]	57.8

The data values from the storage are output to the monitor.

```
#include <stdio.h>
#define  IMAX  3
#define  JMAX  4

int main( )
{
    float  values[IMAX][JMAX];
    int  i, j;
    . . .
    for(i = 0; i < IMAX; i++)
    {
        for(j = 0; j < JMAX; j++)
        {
            printf("%4.1f    ", values[i][j]);
        }
```

```
        printf("\n");
    }

    return 0;
}
```

The output to a monitor from this code is as follows:

```
28.5   46.3   57.9   72.6
14.3   15.7   31.4   19.4
48.9   13.9   90.6   57.8
```

Notice that the array is output in row and column format with spaces between the columns. For readability, the `newline` character (\n) is output after every row.

8.3.2 Output to a Data File

In many scientific applications the data generated by computations or entered from a keyboard needs to be saved for further computations, analysis, and design. The data values of two-dimensional arrays from the storage may be saved by writing to a data file. The following program shows two-dimensional array data saved by rows in a data file `"myfileout.dat"`.

```
#include <stdio.h>
#define  IMAX  3
#define  JMAX  4
FILE *outptr;

int main( )
{
    float  values[IMAX][JMAX] = {{28.5, 46.3, 57.9, 72.6},
                                 {14.3, 15.7, 31.4, 19.4},
                                 {48.9, 13.9, 90.6, 57.8}};
    int  i, j;

    outptr = fopen("myfileout.dat", "w");

    for(i = 0; i < IMAX; i++)
    {
        for(j = 0; j < JMAX; j++)
        {
            fprintf(outptr,"%5.2f  ",
                              values[i][j]);
        }
    }
    fclose(outptr);

    return 0;
}
```

Notice that no `newline` character is included in the output. The data written to the data file `"myfileout.dat"` is as follows:

	index	
row0	a[0][0]	28.5
	a[0][1]	46.3
	a[0][2]	57.9
	a[0][3]	72.6
row1	a[1][0]	14.3
	a[1][1]	15.7
	a[1][2]	31.4
	a[1][3]	19.4
row2	a[2][0]	48.9
	a[2][1]	13.9
	a[2][2]	90.6
	a[2][3]	57.8

8.3.3 Review Questions

1. Write the code segment to output the following two-dimensional real array of size 3 by 4 from storage. Output the data in row and column format with 10 spaces between each element of the array and each row on a new line.

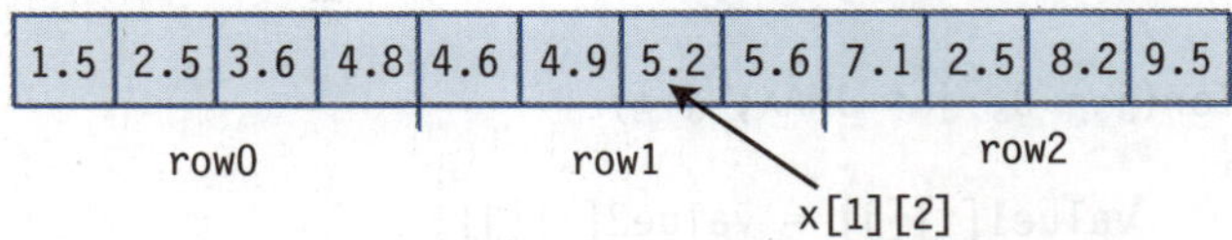

2. Write the code segment to output double precision numbers with row and column labels such as the following. The numbers should have two spaces between them.

	1	2	3	4	5	6
1	18.65254	15.63564	16.87678	14.45567	18.83967	16.56125
2	11.29262	18.90178	17.11987	14.55114	11.97225	78.09776
3	23.45667	56.76789	89.32923	56.73456	24.56310	27.87809
4	98.80768	67.09456	4.67890	56.76876	78.97546	17.56381

3. Write the code segment to output a two-dimensional array `velocity[40][60]` to a file in row order, preceded by the dimensions of the array.

8.4 Manipulation of Arrays

In C it is not possible to perform the arithmetic operations of addition, subtraction, multiplication, and division on arrays by array name. These operations must be performed element-by-element using nested `for` loops for indexing the elements of the array. Also, assignment of one array to another array must be element-by-element, not by array name.

8.4.1 Array Assignment

The following example shows the assignment of a two-dimensional array `value2` to another two-dimensional array `value1`.

```
#define  IMAX  3
#define  JMAX  4

int main( )
{
    float  value1[IMAX][JMAX], value2[IMAX][JMAX];
    int  i, j;
    . . .
    for(i = 0; i < IMAX; i++)
    {
        for(j = 0; j < JMAX; j++)
        {
            value1[i][j] = value2[i][j];
        }
    }

    return 0;
}
```

Before

value1				**value2**			
uuuu	uuuu	uuuu	uuuu	12.34	15.34	19.90	18.67
uuuu	uuuu	uuuu	uuuu	10.90	12.65	18.67	14.78
uuuu	uuuu	uuuu	uuuu	56.23	76.45	19.81	67.23

After

value1				value2			
12.34	15.34	19.90	18.67	12.34	15.34	19.90	18.67
10.90	12.65	18.67	14.78	10.90	12.65	18.67	14.78
56.23	76.45	19.81	67.23	56.23	76.45	19.81	67.23

Notice that the values of the elements of the array value2 are assigned to the elements of the array value1 element-by-element in row order. This is the most efficient order for processing the arrays. Notice also that the arrays must be the same size and shape. The contents of the elements of array value2 do not change.

A specific row of one array may be assigned to a specific row of another array. For example the code to assign the third row of array value2 to the second row of array value1 is as follows:

```
#define  IMAX  10
#define  JMAX  20

int main( )
{
   float value1[IMAX][JMAX], value2[IMAX][JMAX];
   int  i, j;

   . . .

   for(j = 0; j < JMAX; j++)
   {
         value1[1][j] = value2[2][j];
   }

   return 0;
}
```

Before

value1				value2			
uuuu	uuuu	uuuu	uuuu	12.34	15.34	19.90	18.67
uuuu	uuuu	uuuu	uuuu	10.90	12.65	18.67	14.78
uuuu	uuuu	uuuu	uuuu	11.25	13.07	19.81	10.56

After

value1				value2			
uuuu	uuuu	uuuu	uuuu	12.34	15.34	19.90	18.67
11.25	13.04	19.81	10.56	10.90	12.65	18.67	14.78
uuuu	uuuu	uuuu	uuuu	11.25	13.07	19.81	10.56

Notice that the values of the third row from array `value2` are copied to the second row of array `value1`, replacing the original values.

A specific column of one array may be assigned to a specific column of another array. For example, the code to assign the fourth column of array `value2` to the second column of array `value1` is as follows:

```
#define  IMAX  3
#define  JMAX  4

int main( )
{
   float value1[IMAX][JMAX], value2[IMAX][JMAX];
   int  i, j;
   for(i = 0; i < IMAX; i++)
   {
      value1[i][1] = value2[i][3];
   }
   return 0;
}
```

Before

value1				**value2**			
uuuu	uuuu	uuuu	uuuu	12.34	15.34	19.90	18.67
uuuu	uuuu	uuuu	uuuu	10.90	12.65	18.67	14.78
uuuu	uuuu	uuuu	uuuu	11.25	13.07	19.81	10.56

After

value1				**value2**			
uuuu	18.67	uuuu	uuuu	12.34	15.34	19.90	18.67
uuuu	14.78	uuuu	uuuu	10.90	12.65	18.67	14.78
uuuu	10.56	uuuu	uuuu	11.25	13.07	19.81	10.56

Notice that the values of the fourth column from array `value2` are copied to the second column of array `value1`, replacing the original values.

8.4.2 Array Arithmetic

The arithmetic operations of addition, subtraction, multiplication, and division applied to arrays are performed element-by-element using nested `for` loops. The arrays must be of the same size and shape. The following example shows the addition operation.

Addition:

```
#include <stdio.h>
#define  IMAX  3
#define  JMAX  4

int main( )
{
    int  a[IMAX][JMAX], b[IMAX][JMAX], c[IMAX][JMAX];
    int  i, j;
    . . .
    for(i = 0; i < IMAX; i++)
    {
        for(j = 0; j < JMAX; j++)
        {
            c[i][j] = a[i][j] + b[i][j];
        }
    }
    return 0;
}
```

```
          a                        b                        c
 12   16   18   24       2   3   4   8       14   19   22   32
 13   20   40   28       7   9   6   3       20   29   46   31
 18   16   24   50       6   3   8   5       24   19   32   55
```

Notice that array `a` is added to array `b` element-by-element and the result is assigned and stored in array `c`. Subtraction, multiplication, and division operations are similar.

8.4.3 Matrix Operations

The addition and subtraction operations defined on mathematical matrices are the same as array arithmetic, which is carried out element-by-element, but matrix multiplication is a special operation. Two matrices of the same size and shape may be added or subtracted element-by-element. Matrix transpose, inverse, and multiplication are uniquely defined basic operations in matrix algebra. The following examples show arithmetic operations on matrices.

```
#define  IMAX  3
#define  JMAX  5

int  a[IMAX][JMAX], b[IMAX][JMAX], c[IMAX][JMAX];
int  i, j, k;
```

Initial Values:

Matrix a | Matrix b

$$\begin{bmatrix} 4 & 2 & 3 & 1 & 0 \\ 5 & 6 & 4 & 8 & 9 \\ 9 & 3 & 7 & 2 & 8 \end{bmatrix} \begin{bmatrix} 9 & 2 & 5 & 3 & 1 \\ 7 & 4 & 3 & 9 & 6 \\ 5 & 9 & 2 & 4 & 7 \end{bmatrix}$$

Addition:

$c = a + b$ is implemented as:

```
for(i = 0; i < IMAX; i++)
{
    for(j = 0; j < JMAX; j++)
    {
        c[i][j] = a[i][j] + b[i][j];
    }
}
```

Matrix a | Matrix b | Matrix c

$$\begin{bmatrix} 4 & 2 & 3 & 1 & 0 \\ 5 & 6 & 4 & 8 & 9 \\ 9 & 3 & 7 & 2 & 8 \end{bmatrix} \begin{bmatrix} 9 & 2 & 5 & 3 & 1 \\ 7 & 4 & 3 & 9 & 6 \\ 5 & 9 & 2 & 4 & 7 \end{bmatrix} \begin{bmatrix} 13 & 4 & 8 & 4 & 1 \\ 12 & 10 & 7 & 17 & 15 \\ 14 & 12 & 9 & 6 & 15 \end{bmatrix}$$

Subtraction:

$c = a - b$ is implemented as:

```
for(i = 0; i < IMAX; i++)
{
    for(j = 0; j < JMAX; j++)
    {
        c[i][j] = a[i][j] - b[i][j];
    }
}
```

$$\text{Matrix a} \quad \begin{bmatrix} 4 & 2 & 3 & 1 & 0 \\ 5 & 6 & 4 & 8 & 9 \\ 9 & 3 & 7 & 2 & 8 \end{bmatrix} \quad \text{Matrix b} \quad \begin{bmatrix} 9 & 2 & 5 & 3 & 1 \\ 7 & 4 & 3 & 9 & 6 \\ 5 & 9 & 2 & 4 & 7 \end{bmatrix} \quad \text{Matrix c} \quad \begin{bmatrix} -5 & 0 & -2 & -2 & -1 \\ -2 & 2 & 1 & -1 & 3 \\ 4 & -6 & 5 & -2 & 1 \end{bmatrix}$$

These operations are performed element-by-element.

Matrix Transpose:

Interchanging the rows and columns of a matrix is called a matrix transpose. The following code shows the matrix transpose.

```
#define  IMAX  3
#define  JMAX  5

int main( )
{
    int a[IMAX][JMAX], b[JMAX][IMAX];
    int i, j;
    .  .  .
    for(i = 0; i < IMAX; i++)
    {
        for(j = 0; j < JMAX; j++)
        {
             b[j][i] = a[i][j];
        }
    }
return 0;
}
```

Before:

$$\text{Matrix } a \quad \begin{bmatrix} 4 & 2 & 3 & 1 & 0 \\ 5 & 6 & 4 & 8 & 9 \\ 9 & 3 & 7 & 2 & 8 \end{bmatrix}$$

After:

Matrix b

$$\begin{bmatrix} 4 & 5 & 9 \\ 2 & 6 & 3 \\ 3 & 4 & 7 \\ 1 & 8 & 2 \\ 0 & 9 & 8 \end{bmatrix}$$

Notice that the rows of matrix *a* are transposed to columns of matrix *b*. Matrix *b* has the same size as matrix *a,* but a different shape.

Matrix Multiplication:

Matrix multiplication is not carried out by the multiplication of corresponding elements. It is an inner product of row and column vectors. If two matrices are to be multiplied, the number of columns of the left matrix must be equal to the number of rows of the right matrix. The size of the resulting matrix is equal to the number of rows of the left matrix and the number of columns of the right matrix.

$$x_{i,j} = \sum_{k=1}^{kmax} y_{i,k} z_{k,j}$$

This product is shown in the following matrices:

$$y = \begin{bmatrix} y_{00} & y_{01} & y_{02} \\ y_{10} & y_{11} & y_{12} \end{bmatrix} \quad z = \begin{bmatrix} z_{00} & z_{01} \\ z_{10} & z_{11} \\ z_{20} & z_{21} \end{bmatrix}$$

$$x = \begin{bmatrix} y_{00}z_{00} + y_{01}z_{10} + y_{02}z_{20} & y_{00}z_{01} + y_{01}z_{11} + y_{02}z_{21} \\ y_{10}z_{00} + y_{11}z_{10} + y_{12}z_{20} & y_{10}z_{01} + y_{11}z_{11} + y_{12}z_{21} \end{bmatrix}$$

Notice in this case matrix y is 2×3 and matrix z is 3×2. The number of columns of matrix y is three and the number of rows of matrix z is three, therefore they can be multiplied. The size of the resulting matrix x is 2×2, because the number of rows of y is two and the number of columns of z is two.

The following program shows the multiplication of two matrices: $x = y * z$

```
#include <stdio.h>
#define IMAX   3
#define JMAX   5
#define   KMAX     4
int main( )
{
    int i, j, k, sum;
    int  x[IMAX][JMAX], y[IMAX][KMAX], z[KMAX][JMAX];
    . . .
    for(i = 0; i < IMAX; i++)
    {
        for(j = 0; j < JMAX; j++)
        {
            sum = 0.0;
            for(k = 0; k < KMAX; k++)
            {
                sum = sum + y[i][k] * z[k][j];
            }
            z[i][j] = sum;
        }
    }
    return 0;
}
```

This is a standard algorithm for matrix multiplication that is used in solving a system of equations. Matrix multiplication is also used in the geometric transformations of computer graphics such as translation, rotation, and scaling.

8.4.4 Review Questions

1. Indicate whether the following statements are true or false.
   a. In C a two-dimensional array may be assigned to another two-dimensional array of the same size by name.
   b. In C a row of a two-dimensional array may be assigned to a row of another two-dimensional array by using a `for` loop.
   c. Arithmetic operations on two-dimensional arrays may be performed by array name.

d. Two matrices of any size may be multiplied.

2. Write code to prove or disprove the statements of Question 1.
3. Given the following two-dimensional arrays x and y, show the result of each of the following operations.

array x

```
2.5  4.2  5.2  6.4
4.2  2.6  1.2  9.8
3.5  8.5  5.9  5.3
1.3  2.1  3.2  4.8
```

array y

```
3.6  5.8  1.5  6.3
4.3  2.4  4.5  5.7
5.3  6.7  3.4  2.9
3.6  9.1  7.8  6.9
```

a.
```
for(i = 0; i < 4; i++)
    x[2][i] = y[i][1];
```

b.
```
for(i = 0; i < 4; i++)
    x[i][3] = y[i][1] + y[i][2];
```

c.
```
for(i = 0; i < 4; i++)
    x[i][3] = y[i][1] + y[3][i];
```

d.
```
for(i = 0; i < 4; i++)
    for(j = 0; j < 4; j++)
        x[i][j] = 2 * y[i][j] + 5.5;
```

4. Given the two-dimensional integer array `x[4][5]`, write the code to perform the following operations.
   a. To compute the sum of each row and store the sum in the corresponding element of a one-dimensional array.
   b. To compute the sum of each column and store the sum in the corresponding element of a one-dimensional array.
   c. To compute the sum of all the elements of the array.
   d. To output the rows, columns, row sums by the side of rows, column sums under the columns, and the total sum of all the elements under the row sums in the same line as the column sums.
5. Given the square matrix `x[5][5]`, write the code segments to perform the following operations.
   a. To compute the sum of the major diagonal.
   b. To compute the sum of the minor diagonal.
   c. To compute the sum of the elements in the upper triangular matrix.
   d. To compute the sum of the elements in the lower triangular matrix.

8.5 Passing Arrays to Functions

A two-dimensional array is passed to a function as an argument by array name. The value of the name of the array is actually an address so the location of the array is passed to the function. In the function prototype the data type of the array and the square brackets for the first dimension without the row size and the second square bracket with the number of columns specified must be provided. The array name in the function prototype is optional.

8.5.1 Passing Fixed Size Arrays

The fixed size arrays are passed to the functions by array name. The following examples show the function prototype with the array parameters for fixed size arrays.

```
#define IMAX  3
#define JMAX  4

void  func(int  [ ][JMAX]);    /* one form of function prototype */
```

It is necessary to have the number of columns specified in the function prototype and the function header, because the way the computer locates the address of any element in the array requires the number of columns. The number of elements in each row is the number of columns. The address of any element of the array is equal to the number of full rows preceding the row in which the element is located multiplied by the number of columns plus the position in the row of the element under consideration.

Address of any element = number of full rows * JMAX + column index of the element under consideration. Where JMAX is the number of columns.

```
arr[i][j] is in position i * JMAX + j
```

> *Programming Warning:* To compute the address, the number of columns is required. The number of columns must be specified in both the prototype and the function header parameters.

For example, the element `x[1][2]` is located after one full row and two more elements. In an array declared as `x[3][4]`, the element `x[1][2]` is located after 1 * 4 + 2 other elements.

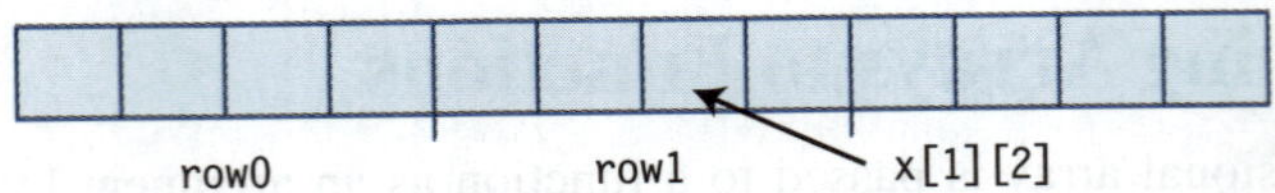

The following program shows the passing of two-dimensional arrays as arguments and parameters to functions that input, add, and output them.

```
#include <stdio.h>
#define  IMAX  3
#define  JMAX  4

void funcinput (int  [ ][ JMAX]);
void funcadd(int [ ][ JMAX], int  [ ][JMAX], int  [ ][JMAX]);
void funcoutput(int  [ ][ JMAX]);

int main( )
{
    int  a[IMAX][JMAX], b[IMAX][JMAX], c[IMAX][JMAX];

    funcinput(a);
    funcinput(b);
    funcadd(a , b , c);
    printf("Array a:\n\n");
    funcoutput(a);
    printf("Array b:\n\n");
    funcoutput(b);
    printf("Array c:\n\n");
    funcoutput(c);

    return 0;
}

void funcinput (int  arr[ ][ JMAX])
{
    int  i , j;

    for(i = 0; i < IMAX; i++)
    {
        for(j = 0; j < JMAX; j++)
        {
            scanf("%d", &arr[i][j]); /* assume IMAX *JMAX values are */
                                     /* found for each array */
        }
    }
    return;
}
```

```
void funcadd(int  a2[ ][ JMAX],  int  b2[ ][JMAX],
          int  c2[ ][JMAX ])
{
    int i , j;

    for(i = 0; i < IMAX; i++)
    {
        for(j = 0; j < JMAX; j++)
        {
            c2[i][j] = a2[i][j] + b2[i][j];
        }
    }
    return;
}
void funcoutput(int  arr[ ][ JMAX])
{
    int  i , j;

    for(i = 0; i < IMAX; i++)
    {
        for(j = 0; j < JMAX; j++)
        {
             printf("%d    ", arr[i][j]);
        }
        printf("\n");
    }
    return;
}
```

Notice that the storage for the arrays a, b, and c is allocated in the main function where they are declared. Storage must be allocated in the main function if it is to be available to all the subfunctions. Arrays a and b are passed one at a time to the function funcinput( ) by array name in separate calls to the function. The input values found by the function funcinput( ) are stored in array a and array b. The arrays a, b, and c are passed to the funcadd( ) to add a and b element-by-element and store the sums in elements of array c. All three arrays are passed by name. The arrays a, b, and c are passed one at a time to the funcoutput( ) to print them.

8.5.2 Passing Array Elements

Two-dimensional arrays may be passed to functions element-by-element. Passing elements of a two-dimensional array to a function may be either by value or by address. The following examples show the passing of two-dimensional array elements by value and by address.

```
#include <stdio.h>
#define  IMAX  3
#define  JMAX  4

void  funcadd(int,  int, int *);

int main( )
{
    int  a[IMAX][JMAX], b[IMAX][JMAX], c[IMAX][JMAX];
    int i, j, x, y;

    . . .

    for(i = 0; i < IMAX; i++)
    {
        for(j = 0; j< JMAX; j++)
        {
            funcadd(a[i][j] , b[i,j], &c[i][j]);
        }
    }

    . . .

void funcadd(int a1, int b1, int *c1)
{
    *c1 = a1 + b1;
    return;

}
```

The arrays a and b cannot be passed by value. But by passing their elements by value, the arrays are protected against inadvertent change in the function. The elements of array c are passed by address as array c is to receive the result of the addition.

8.5.3 Review Questions

1. Indicate whether the following statements are true or false.
   a. In C, two-dimensional arrays may be passed to a function by name.
   b. Passing a two-dimensional array by name means passing the two-dimensional array by value.
   c. In the prototype of the function with array parameters, the second dimension of any two-dimensional array must be specified.

   d. A two-dimensional array passed to a function may be manipulated by rows and columns in the function.
   e. Two-dimensional arrays may be passed to a function element-by-element either by value or by address if they are to be to manipulated in the function.
2. Write code to prove or disprove each statement in Question 1.
3. Write a function to recive an array of pressure values and identify the maximum value of the pressure in each row and output the array and the maximum value of each row at the end of each row.
4. Write a `main` function and the following other functions:
   a. Write a function to input the temperature measurements in cooling towers arranged in 10 rows and 5 columns.
   b. Write a function to determine the average temperature in each of the 10 rows and in each of the 5 columns.
   c. Write a function to output the rows and columns and the average temperatures in each row and in each column. The row averages must be printed at the end of each row and the column averages must be printed at the end of each column.

8.6 Higher-Dimensional Arrays

In science and engineering, mathematical modeling of physical problems for simulation and design is very common. Often problems involve three dimensions and sometimes even four dimensions. Problems having three-dimensional geometry require three-dimensional arrays. Three-dimensional problems such as airflow over an airfoil, wave propagation in solid and liquid media, vibration of three-dimensional objects, and stress analysis in three-dimensional structures dealing with three space variables and, in some cases, a time variable require four dimensions.

8.6.1 Declaration and Storage Allocation

In C a three-dimensional array may be declared as planes, rows, and columns. The general form of the declaration is:

```
data type array-name[number of planes][number of rows]
                    [number of columns];
```

In each plane the corresponding row and column elements will have the same row and column index. In C the lower index defaults to zero. The plane index varies from zero to the number of planes minus one. The row index varies from zero to the number of rows minus one. The column index varies from zero to the number of columns minus one. The following example shows the declaration and storage allocation for a three-dimensional array.

```
float x[5][3][4];
```

The array x has five planes, three rows, and four columns. This array is indexed as follows:

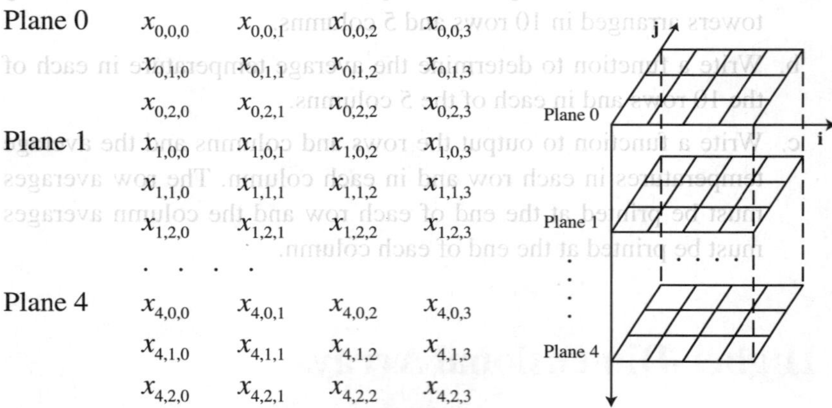

The following depicts storage allocation. This shows only the first two planes, the plane indexed zero and the plane indexed one.

In a similar fashion, a four-dimensional array might be defined as x(volume, page, row, column) or as velocity(x, y, z, t) and a five-dimensional array as x(edition, volume, page, row, column). In general, an n-dimensional array is defined as $x(k_1, k_2, \ldots, k_n)$ and processed varying k_1 the most slowly and k_n the most rapidly.

Element	Plane/Row
x[0][0][0]	Plane 0, Row 0
x[0][0][1]	
x[0][0][2]	
x[0][0][3]	
x[0][1][0]	Plane 0, Row 1
x[0][1][1]	
x[0][1][2]	
x[0][1][3]	
x[0][2][0]	Plane 0, Row 2
x[0][2][1]	
x[0][2][2]	
x[0][2][3]	
x[1][0][0]	Plane 1, Row 0
x[1][0][1]	
x[1][0][2]	
x[1][0][3]	
x[1][1][0]	Plane 1, Row 1
x[1][1][1]	
x[1][1][2]	
x[1][1][3]	
x[1][2][0]	Plane 1, Row 2
x[1][2][1]	
x[1][2][2]	
x[1][2][3]	

etc.,

In order to calculate the position of an element in a three-dimensional array, the computer must know the number of planes that precede it and the size of the plane and therefore must know the number of rows and columns in a plane. Because of this, when a three-dimensional array is passed to a function, the function declaration and header must specify the number of rows and columns expected.

8.6.2 Input of Three-Dimensional Arrays

Three nested `for` loops are required to input data into a three-dimensional array using array indices and the array pointer. The outer `for` loop must be the plane loop, the next inner `for` loop must be the row loop, and the innermost `for` loop must be the column loop. The following code shows the input of data into a three-dimensional array.

Input Using Array Index

```
#define  KMAX  5
#define  IMAX  3
#define  JMAX  4

float  x[KMAX][IMAX][JMAX];
int  i,  j,  k;

for(k = 0; k < KMAX; k++)
{
    for(i = 0; i < IMAX; i++)
    {
        for(j = 0; j < JMAX; j++)
        {
            scanf("%f", &x[k][i][j]);
        }
    }
}
```

In general, an *n*-dimensional array would be input as as follows:

```
#define  NNMAX   4
.   .   .   .   .   .   .   .
#define  N3MAX  5
#define  N2MAX  3
#define  N1MAX  4

float  x[NNMAX]   .   .   .   [N2MAX][N1MAX];
int  n1,  n2,  n3,   .   .   .   . ,nn;
for(nn = 0; nn < NNMAX; k++)
{

    .   .   .   .   .
    for(n3 = 0; n3 < N3MAX; n3++)
    {
        for(n2 = 0; n2 < N2MAX; n2++)
```

```
            {
                for(n1 = 0; n1 < N1MAX; n1++)
                {
                    scanf("%f", &x[nn]. . . [n3][n2][n1]);
                }
            }
        }
        . . .
}
```

8.6.3 Output of Three-Dimensional Arrays

To output data from a three-dimensional array using index variables requires three nested `for` loops. The outer `for` loop must be the plane loop, the next inner `for` loop must be the row loop, and the innermost `for` loop must be the column loop. The following code shows the output of a three-dimensional array with blanks separating each set of rows and columns.

Output Using Array Index

```
#define  KMAX  5
#define  IMAX  3
#define  JMAX  4

float  x[KMAX][IMAX][JMAX];
int  i,  j,  k;
for(k = 0; k < KMAX; k++)
{
    printf("page no: %d\n", k);
    for(i = 0; i < IMAX; i++)
    {
        for(j = 0; j < JMAX; j++)
        {
            printf("%f    ", x[k][i][j]);
        }
        printf("\n");
    }
    printf("\n\n");
}
```

8.6.4 Manipulation of Three-Dimensional Arrays

Multidimensional arrays may be used in assignment statements and arithmetic operations. These arrays are processed most efficiently in the order in which they are stored in the memory. They are stored in the order of planes, rows, and columns.

Array Assignment The following code shows the assignment of a scalar value of 5.8 to each of the elements of a three-dimensional array.

```
#define  KMAX  3
#define  IMAX  4
#define  JMAX  5

int main( )
{
    float  x[KMAX][IMAX][JMAX];
    int  i,  j,  k;

    for(k = 0; k < KMAX; k++)
    {
        for(i = 0; i < IMAX; i++)
        {
            for(j = 0; j < JMAX; j++)
            {
                x[k][i][j] = 5.8;
            }
        }
    }

    return 0;
}
```

The following code shows the assignment of array y to array x.

```
#define  KMAX  3
#define  IMAX  4
#define  JMAX  5

int main( )
{
    float  x[KMAX][IMAX][JMAX], y[KMAX][IMAX][JMAX];
    int  i,  j,  k;

    for(k = 0; k < KMAX; k++)
    {
        for(i = 0; i < IMAX; i++)
        {
            for(j = 0; j < JMAX; j++)
            {
```

```
                x[k][i][j] = y[k][i][j];
            }
        }
    }

    return 0;
}
```

In this case array y is copied into array x. The contents of array x change, but the contents of array y remain unchanged.

Array Arithmetic

Arithmetic operations such as addition, subtraction, multiplication, and division may be performed on three-dimensional arrays element-by-element.

```
#define  KMAX  3
#define  IMAX  4
#define  JMAX  5

int main( )
{
    float  x[KMAX][IMAX][JMAX], y[KMAX][IMAX][JMAX];
    float  z[KMAX][IMAX][JMAX];
    int    i,  j,  k;
    for(k = 0; k < KMAX; k++)
    {
        for(i = 0; i < IMAX; i++)
        {
            for(j = 0; j < JMAX; j++)
            {
                z[k][i][j] = x[k][i][j] + y[k][i][j];
            }
        }
    }

    return 0;
}
```

Array x is added to array y and the result is stored in array z. Similarly other arithmetic operations may be performed.

Because multidimensional arrays quickly become very large, they are usually stored in a file and input and processed one plane at a time.

8.6.5 Review Questions

1. Indicate whether the following statements are true or false.
   a. The storage for three-dimensional arrays is allocated in column order.
   b. The storage for three-dimensional arrays is allocated in row order.
   c. In three-dimensional arrays the first index is the row index.
   d. In three-dimensional arrays the middle index is the plane index.
   e. Three-dimensional arrays may be manipulated most efficiently by plane, then by row, and then by column order.
2. Write the declaration statements for the following indexed variables and give the size of each array.
   a. Real variable $x_{i,j,k}$ where $i = 1, 20$; $j = 1, 50$; and $k = 1, 100$.
   b. Integer variable $y_{i,j,k}$ where $i = 1, 200$; $j = 1, 500$; and $k = 1, 100$.
   c. Double variable $z_{i,j,k}$ where $i = 1, 10$; $j = 1, 10$; and $k = 1, 20$.
3. Write a `main` program and the following functions:
   a. Function to input a three-dimensional array `n[2][2][2]`.
   b. Function to multiply every element of the first plane by 10.0 and the next plane by 20.0.
   c. Function to output the three-dimensional array with each plane on a separate page.

8.7 Sample Programs

These sample programs have been compiled and linked with the library routines required to produce the executable code. The C code, the input, and the output are presented.

8.7.1 Drag Force

Drag force is the resistance a body offers when it is exposed to the flow of air. Drag force is computed when engineers design automobiles, airplanes, speed boats, and so on.

Problem Construct a table showing how the drag force on the end of a circular cylinder varies with the diameter of the cylinder and the velocity of the air. Let the diameter vary from one to five feet in increments of one foot, and the velocity of air vary from 60 ft/sec to 100 ft/sec in increments of 10 ft/sec. This example shows the initialization of a two-dimensional array by computation, and the output of the array.

Data

The density of air is 2.33×10^{-3} slug/ft^3

The drag coefficient is assumed to be 0.3

Method The magnitude of the drag force is determined by the following equation:

$$F_D = \tfrac{1}{2} \rho A v^2 C_D$$

Where ρ is the density of air in slug/ft^3,

A (ft^2) is the projected area of the cylinder facing the air flow,

v is the velocity of air flow on the cylinder in ft/sec, and

C_D is the drag coefficient.

The drag coefficient C_D is assumed to be 0.3.

Pseudocode

```
main:
   funcdragforce( )
   funcoutput( )
stop

fundragforce:
   for each diameter
      for each velocity
         calculate dragforce
      end for
   end for
end

funcoutput:
   for each diameter
```

```
      for each velocity
         output dragforce
      end for
   end for
end
```

Program

```
/*******************************************************/
/*                                                     */
/*    main: Computation of the Drag Force on a Cylinder */
/*                                                     */
/*******************************************************/
/*                                                     */
/*    Constants:                                       */
/*       airdensity = 2.33 x 10-3 slug/ft3             */
/*       coeffdrag  = 0.3                              */
/*                                                     */
/*    Input Variables:                                 */
/*       diameter[IMAX]    - cylinder diameter         */
/*       velocity [JMAX]   - velocity of air           */
/*                                                     */
/*    Computed Variables:                              */
/*       drgfrce[IMAX][JMAX]- drag force               */
/*                                                     */
/*    Output Variables:                                */
/*       diameter[IMAX]      - cylinder diameter       */
/*       velocity[JMAX]      - velocity of air         */
/*       drgfrce[IMAX][JMAX]- drag force               */
/*                                                     */
/*    Functions Called:                                */
/*       funcdrgfrce( ) - drag force                   */
/*       funcoutput( )  -  output the drag force       */
/*                                                     */
/*******************************************************/

#include <stdio.h>

#define  IMAX  5
#define  JMAX  5

void funcdragforce(float diameter[ ], float velocity[ ],
                   float drgfrce[ ][JMAX]);
```

```
void funcoutput(float diameter[ ], float velocity[ ],
                float drgfrce[ ][JMAX]);

int main( )
{

    float diameter[IMAX], velocity [JMAX];
    float drgfrce[IMAX][JMAX];

    funcdragforce(diameter, velocity, drgfrce);
    funcoutput(diameter, velocity, drgfrce);

    return 0;
}
/*********************************************************/
/*                                                       */
/*    funcdragforce:  Compute the Drag Force             */
/*                                                       */
/*********************************************************/
/*                                                       */
/*    Constants:                                         */
/*        density = 2.33 x 10^-3 slug/ft3 density of air */
/*        coeffdrag = 0.3      coefficient of drag       */
/*                                                       */
/*    Computed Variables:                                */
/*       drgfrec[IMAX][JMAX] - drag force                */
/*                                                       */
/*    Output Parameters:                                 */
/*        diameter[IMAX]      - cylinder diameter        */
/*        velocity[JMAX]      - velocity of air          */
/*        drgforce[IMAX][JMAX]- drag force               */
/*                                                       */
/*                                                       */
/*********************************************************/
void funcdragforce(float diameter[ ], float velocity[ ],
                   float drgforce[ ][JMAX])
{

    int i, j;
    float area;
    const float PI = 3.141593;
    const float airdensity = 2.33E-03;
    const float coeffdrag  = 0.3;
    velocity[0] = 60.0;
    for(j = 1; j < IMAX; j++)
```

```
    {
       velocity[j] = velocity[j - 1] + 10.0;
    }
    for(i = 0; i < IMAX; i++)
    {
       diameter[i] = i + 1.0;
       area = (PI *diameter[i] * diameter[i])/ 4.0;

       for(j = 0; j < JMAX; j++)
       {
          drgforce[i][j] = (0.5)* airdensity * area *
          velocity[j] * velocity[j] * coeffdrag;
       }

    }

    return;
}

/*****************************************************************/
/*                                                               */
/*    funcoutput: Output the Results                             */
/*                                                               */
/*****************************************************************/
/*                                                               */
/*    Input Parameters:                                          */
/*       diameter[IMAX]         - cylinder diameter              */
/*       velocity[JMAX]         - velocity of air                */
/*       drgforce[IMAX][JMAX]   - drag force                     */
/*                                                               */
/*****************************************************************/
void funcoutput(float diameter[ ], float velocity[ ],
                float drgforce[ ][JMAX])
{
    int  i, j;

    printf("Diameter:");
    for(i = 0; i < IMAX; i++)
    {
       printf("%8.2f   ", diameter[i]);
    }
    printf("\n\nVelocity:\n");
    for(j = 0; j < JMAX; j++)
    {
       printf("  %3.0f", velocity[j]);
```

```
        for(i = 0; i < IMAX; i++)
        {
           printf("%8.3f   ",drgforce[i][j]);
        }
        printf("\n");
    }

    return;
}
```

Output

```
Diameter:     1.00         2.00         3.00         4.00         5.00

Velocity:
   60    .988         3.953        8.894       15.811       24.705
   70   1.345         5.380       12.105       21.521       33.626
   80   1.757         7.027       15.811       28.108       43.919
   90   2.223         8.894       20.011       35.575       55.586
  100   2.745        10.980       24.705       43.919       68.624
```

8.7.2 Saddle Point

Problem Write a program to locate saddle points of an array of data recorded for elevations in the mountains. The elevation of a mountain pass forms a saddle point in the array. This example processes a two-dimensional array by rows and by columns.

Method A saddle point is an element in an array of elevation data that is the maximum in its row and minimum in its column, or the minimum in its row and the maximum in its column. Note that this assumes there is a single maximum and a single minimum in each row and column.

Data Input values for elevations.

Pseudocode

```
Input the data into a two-dimensional array
   For each column
      Find the maximum and the minimum in the column and their locations
   End for
   For each row
```

Find the maximum and the minimum in the row and their locations
End for
For each row
Check the row maximum to see whether it is also a column minimum
If so, print the position
Check the row minimum to see whether it is also a column maximum.
If so, print the position
End for
Stop

Program

```
/*********************************************************************/
/*                                                                   */
/*       Locate the Saddle Point in an Array                         */
/*                                                                   */
/*********************************************************************/
/*    Input Variables:                                               */
/*        elevation[IMAX][JMAX]- values of elevation                 */
/*                                                                   */
/*    Computed Variables:                                            */
/*        rowmax - maximum elevation in row                          */
/*        rowmin - minimum elevation in row                          */
/*        colmax - maximum elevation in column                       */
/*        colmin       - minimum elevation in column                 */
/*        jrmax[IMAX]   - location of rowmax                         */
/*        jrmin[IMAX]- location of rowmin                            */
/*        icmax[JMAX]- location of colmax                            */
/*        icmin[JMAX]   - location of colmin                         */
/*                                                                   */
/*********************************************************************/
#include<stdio.h>
#define IMAX 5
#define JMAX 4

FILE  *inptr;

int main( )
{
    float  elevation[IMAX][JMAX];
    float  rowmax, rowmin, colmax, colmin;
    int    jrmax[IMAX], jrmin[IMAX], icmax[JMAX],icmin[JMAX];
```

```
    int  i, j;

    inptr = fopen("elevation.dat", "r");

    printf("INPUT a %d x %d array from a data file:\n\n", IMAX, JMAX);
    for(i = 0; i < IMAX; i++)
        for(j = 0; j < JMAX; j++)
            fscanf(inptr, "%f",&elevation[i][j]);

    for(i = 0; i < IMAX; i++)  /* check each elevation to see how it */
    {                          /* compares with the row and column */
        rowmax = elevation[i][0];
        rowmin = rowmax;
        jrmax[i] = 0;
        jrmin[i] = 0;

        for(j = 0; j < JMAX; j++)
        {
            if(rowmax < elevation[i][j])
            {
                rowmax = elevation[i][j];
                jrmax[i] = j;
            }
            if(rowmin > elevation[i][j])
            {
                rowmin = elevation[i][j];
                jrmin[i] = j;
            }
        }
    }
for(j = 0; j < JMAX; j++)
{
    colmax = elevation[0][j];
    colmin = colmax;
    icmax[j] = 0;
    icmin[j] = 0;
for(i = 1; i < JMAX; i++)
{
    if(colmax < elevation[i][j])
    {
        colmax = elevation[i][j];
        icmax[j] = i;
    }
    if(colmin > elevation[i][j])
```

```
                {
                    colmin = elevation[i][j];
                    icmin[j] = i;
                }
            }
        }

        /*  compare the maximums and the minimums to find the
            saddle point  */

        printf("OUTPUT\n\n");

        printf("                     Saddle points\n");
        printf("             row      column    elevation\n");
        for(i = 0; i < IMAX; i++)
        {
            j = jrmax[i];
            if(icmin[j] == i)
                printf("           %d          %d       %5.2f\n",
                        i, j, elevation[i][j]);
            j = jrmin[i];
            if(icmax[j] == i)
                printf("           %d          %d       %5.2f\n",
                        i, j, elevation[i][j]);
        }

        return 0;
    }
```

```
INPUT a 5 x 5 Array from a Data File:

3.0  3.0  4.0  2.0
3.0  4.0  5.0  6.0
4.0  5.0  6.0  7.0
5.0  6.0  7.0  8.0
6.0  7.0  8.0  9.0


OUTPUT

Saddle points

          row      column   elevation

          0          3        4.00
          4          0        5.00
```

8.7.3 Computation of Pressure

Problem Compute the pressure at each point and the average pressure over a rectangular area at the bottom of the sea floor for the construction of an oil rig platform. The input to the program is the depth measurements in feet at grid points over a 400-foot by 500-foot rectangular area. The depth measurements are recorded at 50-foot intervals and stored in a file `"depth.dat"`. This example reads a two-dimensional array from a file and processes individual elements.

Method Input the depth measurements (8 rows and 10 columns) and store them in an array `depth[8][10]`. The formula is derived in Section 6.4.2.

The formula for the computation of pressure is given by:

$$p = \rho g h$$

Where

p is the pressure (pounds per square inch),
ρ is the mass density of water (mass per unit volume),
g is the gravitational acceleration (ft/sec^2), and
h is the depth of water in feet.

where $\rho g = 0.4333$
$p = 0.4333 * h$ (lbf/inch^2)

Data Values of depth input from a data file

Pseudocode

```
main:
  input the data
  output the data labeled
  for each grid point
    calculate the pressure
  calculate the average pressure
  output the pressure
  output the average pressure
stop
```

```
funcinput:
   for each grid point
         input depth
end
```



```
funcpressure:
   for each grid point
         pressure = 0.4333 * depth
end

avgpressure:
   sumpressure = 0.0
   for each grid point
      sum the pressure
   calculate the average pressure
end

funcoutput:
   output the pressure by rows
   output the average pressure
end
```

Program

```
/*****************************************************************/
/*                                                               */
/*    main: Computation of Pressure at Sea Floor                 */
/*                                                               */
/*****************************************************************/
/*    Input Variables:                                           */
/*        depth[IMAX][JMAX]- depth of water at sea floor         */
/*                                                               */
/*    Computed Variables:                                        */
/*        pressure[IMAX][JMAX]- computed pressure at sea         */
/*                              floor                            */
/*        averagepressure  -  average pressure                   */
/*                                                               */
/*    Output Variables:                                          */
/*        depth[IMAX][JMAX]- depth of water at sea floor         */
/*        pressure[IMAX][JMAX]- computed pressure at sea         */
/*                              floor                            */
/*        averagepressure  -  average pressure                   */
/*                                                               */
/*    Functions Called:                                          */
/*        funcinput       - input depth values into array        */
/*        funcpressure    -  compute the pressure                */
/*        funcavgpressure  -  compute average pressure           */
/*        funcoutput      - output the arrays                    */
/*                                                               */
/*****************************************************************/
#include <stdio.h>

#define  IMAX  8
#define  JMAX  10

void  funcinput(float depth1[ ][JMAX]);
void  funcpressure(float depth1[ ][JMAX], float presssure[ ][JMAX]);
float funcavgpressure(float pressure[ ][JMAX]);
void  funcoutput(float array1[ ][JMAX]);

int main( )
{

    float depth[IMAX][JMAX];
    float pressure[IMAX][JMAX], averagepressure;
```

```
    funcinput(depth);

    printf("Measured Depths\n");
    funcoutput(depth);
    funcpressure(depth, pressure);
    printf("Computed Pressure\n");
    funcoutput(pressure);
    averagepressure = funcavgpressure(pressure);
    printf("Average Pressure: %6.2f\n", averagepressure);

    return 0;
}

/*******************************************************/
/*                                                     */
/*    funcinput: Input the Measured Values of the      */
/*               Depth in Feet                         */
/*                                                     */
/*******************************************************/
/*                                                     */
/*    Output Parameters:                               */
/*        depth1[ ][JMAX] - measured depth of water    */
/*                          in feet                    */
/*                                                     */
/*    Input Variables:                                 */
/*        depth1[ ][JMAX] - measured depth of water    */
/*                          in feet                    */
/*                                                     */
/*******************************************************/
void funcinput(float depth1[ ][JMAX])
{
    FILE  *inptr;
    int  i, j;

    inptr = fopen("depth.dat", "r");

    for(i = 0; i < IMAX; i++)
        for(j = 0; j < JMAX; j++)
            fscanf(inptr,"%f", &depth1[i][j]);

    fclose(inptr);

    return;
}
```

```
/********************************************************/
/*                                                      */
/*    funcpressure: Compute the Pressure in Pounds      */
/*                  per Square Inch                     */
/*                                                      */
/********************************************************/
/*                                                      */
/*    Input Parameters:                                 */
/*        pressure1[ ][JMAX] - pressure of water in     */
/*                             pounds per square inch   */
/*                                                      */
/*    Computed Variables:                               */
/*        pressure1[ ][JMAX] - pressure of water in     */
/*                             pounds per square inch   */
/*                                                      */
/*    Output Parameters:                                */
/*        pressure1[ ][JMAX] - pressure of water in     */
/*                             pounds per square inch   */
/*                                                      */
/********************************************************/
void  funcpressure(float depth1[ ][JMAX], float pressure1[ ][JMAX])
{
    int  i, j;

    for(i = 0; i < IMAX; i++)
        for(j = 0; j < JMAX; j++)
            pressure1[i][j] = 0.4333 * depth1[i][j];

    return;
}

/********************************************************/
/*                                                      */
/*    funcavgpressure: Compute the Average Pressure     */
/*                     in Pounds per Square Inch        */
/*                                                      */
/********************************************************/
/*                                                      */
/*    Input Parameters:                                 */
/*        pressure1[ ][JMAX] - pressure of water in     */
/*                             pounds per square inch   */
/*                                                      */
/*    Returned Variables:                               */
/*        averagpressure1  -  average pressure in pounds */
/*                            per square inch           */
/********************************************************/
```

```
float  funcavgpressure(float pressure1[ ][JMAX])
{
    int  i, j;
    float sumpressure1 = 0.0;
    float average_pressure = 0;

    for(i = 0; i < IMAX; i++)
        for(j = 0; j < JMAX; j++)
            sumpressure1 += pressure1[i][j];

    average_pressure = (sumpressure1 / (IMAX * JMAX));
    return average_pressure;

    return;
}

/*********************************************************/
/*                                                       */
/*   Function: funcoutput( )                             */
/*      Output the Depth and Pressure                    */
/*                                                       */
/*********************************************************/
/*                                                       */
/*   Input Parameters:                                   */
/*      array1[ ][JMAX] - dummy array replaced by the    */
/*                        depth and pressure arrays      */
/*                                                       */
/*   Output Variables:                                   */
/*       array[ ][JMAX] - dummy array replaced by the    */
/*                        depth and pressure arrays      */
/*                                                       */
/*********************************************************/
void  funcoutput(float  array1[ ][JMAX])
{
    int  i, j;

    for(i = 0; i < IMAX; i++)
    {
        for(j = 0; j < JMAX; j++)
        {
            printf("%6.2f    ", array1[i][j]);
        }
        printf("\n");
    }
```

```
    return;
}
```

Input: "depth.dat"

```
10       20       30       40 . . .
50       80       100      120 . . .
90       320      420      500 . . .
. . .    . . .    . . .    . . .
```

Output:

```
Measured Depths
 10.00     20.00     30.00     40.00 . . .
 50.00     80.00    100.00    120.00 . . .
 90.00    320.00    420.00    500.00 . . .
 . . .
Computed Pressure
  4.33      8.67     13.00     17.33 . . .
 21.67     34.66     43.33     52.00 . . .
 39.00    138.66    181.99    216.65 . . .
 . . .
Average Pressure:  64.27
```

8.7.4 Geometric Transformations

In computer graphics, points, lines, and polygons are translated from one position to another, and lines and polygons are rotated and scaled. These types of operations are sufficient to change the position, the orientation, and the size of the objects that are displayed. These are called geometric transformations. Transformations in two-dimensions are carried out by multiplying three-by-three square matrices. Transformations in three-dimensions are carried out by multiplying four-by-four square matrices. This example shows the development of a small library of useful functions.

Translation of a Line

Problem Translate a line segment between the coordinate points $L(x1, y1)$ and $L(x2, y2)$, an x distance t_x, and a y distance t_y.

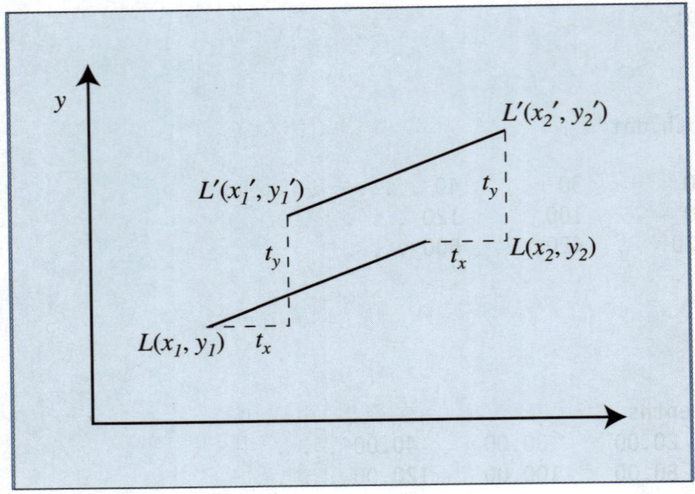

Method Input the translation matrix

$$T\left(t_x, t_y\right) = \begin{bmatrix} 1 & 0 & t_x \\ 0 & 1 & t_y \\ 0 & 0 & 1 \end{bmatrix}$$

Where t_x is the translation in the *x*-coordinate direction, and
t_y is the translation in the *y*-coordinate direction.

Input the coordinates of the line.

$$L(x_1, y_1)\ L(x_2, y_2)$$

$$L = \begin{bmatrix} x_1 & x_2 \\ y_1 & y_2 \\ 1 & 1 \end{bmatrix}$$

Multiply the translation matrix and the coordinates of the line.

$$L' = T(t_x, t_y) * L$$

$$\begin{bmatrix} x_1' & x_2' \\ y_1' & y_2' \\ 1 & 1 \end{bmatrix} = \begin{bmatrix} 1 & 0 & t_x \\ 0 & 1 & t_y \\ 0 & 0 & 1 \end{bmatrix} * \begin{bmatrix} x_1 & x_2 \\ y_1 & y_2 \\ 1 & 1 \end{bmatrix}$$

Where L' is the matrix for the translated line segment between points (x_1', y_1') and (x_2', y_2').

Data

Translation matrix

$$\begin{bmatrix} 1 & 0 & t_x \\ 0 & 1 & t_y \\ 0 & 0 & 1 \end{bmatrix}$$

Coordinate matrix: `oldline`

$$\begin{bmatrix} x_1 & x_2 \\ y_1 & y_2 \\ 1 & 1 \end{bmatrix}$$

Pseudocode

main:

input the translation matrix
input the coordinate matrix
funcmultiply
output the newline matrix.

stop

functransmat:

input translation values and set up the translation matrix

end

funcinput:

input the line segment coordinates and set up the coordinate matrix

end

funcmultiply:

multiply the translation matrix and the line coordinate matrix

end

funcoutput:

output the line coordinates

end

Program

```
/*********************************************************/
/*                                                       */
/*   main: Translation of a Line Segment in an x-y Plane */
/*                                                       */
/*********************************************************/
/*                                                       */
/*    Input Variables:                                   */
/*       transmat[3][3]   - translation matrix           */
/*       oldline[3][2] - coordinate points of line       */
/*                                                       */
/*    Computed Variables:                                */
/*       newline[3][2] - translated coordinate points    */
/*                       of line                         */
/*                                                       */
/*    Output Variables:                                  */
/*       oldline[3][2] - old coordinate points of line   */
/*       newline[3][2] - new coordinate points of line   */
/*                                                       */
/*    Functions called:                                  */
/*       funcmultiply  -  multiplication of the          */
/*                        coordinate and                 */
/*                        transformation matrix          */
/*                                                       */
/*********************************************************/
#include <stdio.h>
#define IMAX 3
```

```
#define JMAX 2
#define KMAX 3

void functransmat(float  [ ][IMAX]);
void funcinputline(float [ ][JMAX]);
void funcmultiply( float [ ] [IMAX], float [ ] [JMAX],
                   float [ ][JMAX]);
void funcoutput(float [ ][JMAX]);

int main( )
{
    float  transmat[IMAX][IMAX] = {0.0};
    float oldline[IMAX][JMAX],newline[IMAX][JMAX];

    functransmat(transmat);
    funcinputline(oldline);
    funcmultiply(transmat, oldline, newline);

    printf("\nOutput of old coordinate points: x1 y1,");
    printf(" x2 y2\n\n");
    funcoutput(oldline);
    printf("\nOutput of new coordinate points: x1 y1,");
    printf(" x2 y2\n\n");
    funcoutput(newline);

    return 0;
}

/*******************************************************/
/*                                                     */
/*    functramsmat: Set Up the Translation Matrix      */
/*                                                     */
/*******************************************************/
/*                                                     */
/*    local variables:                                 */
/*        tx – translation value of the x coordinate   */
/*        ty – translation value of the y coordinate   */
/*                                                     */
/*    Output Variables:                                */
/*        transmit[ ][IMAX] –  translation matrix      */
/*                                                     */
/*                                                     */
/*******************************************************/
void functransmat(float  transmat1[ ][IMAX])
{
    float tx, ty;
```

```
    printf("Input the translation values tx and ty:\n");
    scanf("%f  %f",&tx, &ty);

    transmat1[0][0] = 1.0;
    transmat1[0][2] = tx;
    transmat1[1][1] = 1.0;
    transmat1[1][2] = ty;
    transmat1[2][2] = 1.0;

    return;
}

/*********************************************************/
/*                                                       */
/*   funcinputline: Input the Coordinates of the Line    */
/*                                                       */
/*********************************************************/
/*                                                       */
/*   local variables:                                    */
/*       i,j - variables to index the for loop           */
/*                                                       */
/*   Output Variables:                                   */
/*       oldline[ ][JMAX] - line coordinate points       */
/*                                                       */
/*********************************************************/
void funcinputline(float  oldline1[ ][JMAX])
{
    int i, j;

    printf("\nInput the coordinate points x1 y1, x2 y2:\n");

    for(j = 0; j < JMAX; j++)
    {
        for(i = 0; i < IMAX-1; i++)
        {
            scanf("%f",&oldline1[i][j]);
        }
        oldline1[IMAX-1][j] = 1.0;
    }

    return;
}

/*********************************************************/
/*                                                       */
/*   funcmultiply - This Function Multiplies the         */
```

```
/*                  Coordinate Matrix and                   */
/*                  the Transformation Matrix               */
/*                                                          */
/**********************************************************/
/*                                                          */
/*    Input parameters:                                     */
/*        transmat1[IMAX]- transformation matrix            */
/*        oldline[IMAX]  - the coordinates of old line      */
/*                                                          */
/*    Computed Variables:                                   */
/*        newline[IMAX] - translated coordinates of new     */
/*                        line                              */
/*                                                          */
/*    Output Variables:                                     */
/*        newline[JMAX] - new coordinates of line           */
/*                                                          */
/*                                                          */
/**********************************************************/
void funcmultiply( float transmat1[ ] [IMAX], float oldline1[ ] [JMAX],
                   float newline1[ ][JMAX])
{
    int i, j, k;
    for(i = 0; i < IMAX; i++)
    {
        for(j = 0; j < JMAX; j++)
        {
            newline1[i][j] = 0.0;
            for(k = 0; k < KMAX; k++)
            {
                newline1[i][j] += transmat1[i][k] * oldline1[k][j];
            }
        }
    }

    return;
}

/**********************************************************/
/*                                                          */
/*    funcoutput: Output the Line Coordinates               */
/*                                                          */
/**********************************************************/
/*                                                          */
/*    local variables:                                      */
```

```
/*       i,j - variables to index the for loop           */
/*                                                       */
/*    Output Variables:                                  */
/*       linecoord[ ][JMAX] -  line coordinate points    */
/*                                                       */
/*******************************************************/
void funcoutput(float  linecoord[ ][JMAX])
{
   int i, j;

   for(j = 0; j < JMAX; j++)
   {
      printf( "POINT %d: ( ", j+1 );
      for(i = 0; i < IMAX - 1; i++)
      {
         printf("%4.2f  ",linecoord[i][j]);
      }
      printf(" )\n");
   }
   return;
}
```

Input and Output

```
Input the translation values tx and ty:
2.0 3.0

Input the coordinate points x1 y1, x2 y2:
1.5 2.5
2.5 4.5

Output of old coordinate points: x1 y1, x2 y2

POINT 1: ( 1.50  2.50 )
POINT 2: ( 2.50  4.50 )

Output of new coordinate points: x1 y1, x2 y2

POINT 1: ( 3.50  5.50 )
POINT 2: ( 4.50  7.50 )
```

Note that this program is used by engineers and scientists to do computer graphics. The function funcmultiply is a standard matrix multiplication function that can be used for rotation of lines, scaling of lines, and also for translation, rotation, and scaling of polygons. This multiplication function may also be used for composite transformations such as translation and rotation, or translation and scaling, or translation, rotation, and scaling.

Rotation of a Line

Problem Rotate a line with the coordinate point $L(x_1, y_1)$ and $L(x_2, y_2)$ around the origin by an angle θ to $L'(x_1, y_1)$ and $L'(x_2, y_2)$.

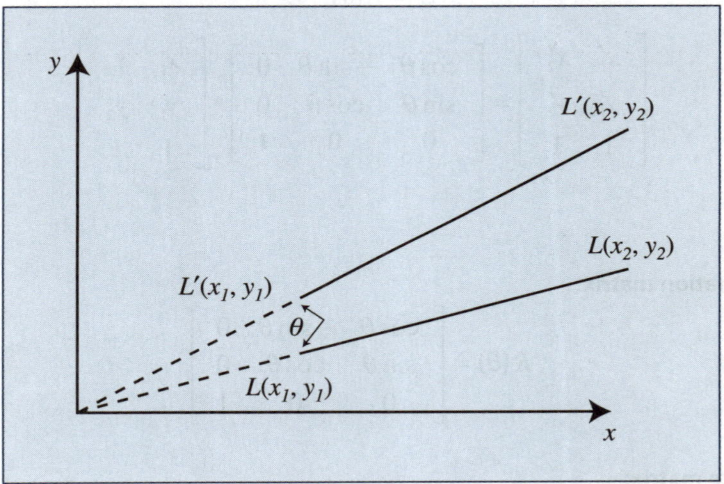

Method

Input the rotation angle.

Calculate the rotation matrix.

$$R(\theta) = \begin{bmatrix} \cos\theta & -\sin\theta & 0 \\ \sin\theta & \cos\theta & 0 \\ 0 & 0 & 1 \end{bmatrix}$$

Where $R(\theta)$ is the rotation matrix and θ is the counterclockwise rotation angle of the line.

Input the coordinates of the line.

$$L = (x_1, y_1)\ (x_2, y_2)$$

Set up the coordinate matrix.

$$L = \begin{bmatrix} x_1 & x_2 \\ y_1 & y_2 \\ 1 & 1 \end{bmatrix}$$

Multiply the translation matrix and the coordinate matrix.

$$L' = R(\theta) * L$$

$$\begin{bmatrix} x_1' & x_2' \\ y_1' & y_2' \\ 1 & 1 \end{bmatrix} = \begin{bmatrix} \cos\theta & -\sin\theta & 0 \\ \sin\theta & \cos\theta & 0 \\ 0 & 0 & 1 \end{bmatrix} * \begin{bmatrix} x_1 & x_2 \\ y_1 & y_2 \\ 1 & 1 \end{bmatrix}$$

Data

Transformation matrix:

$$R(\theta) = \begin{bmatrix} \cos\theta & -\sin\theta & 0 \\ \sin\theta & \cos\theta & 0 \\ 0 & 0 & 1 \end{bmatrix}$$

Coordinate matrix:

$$L = \begin{bmatrix} x_1 & x_2 \\ y_1 & y_2 \\ 1 & 1 \end{bmatrix}$$

Pseudocode

```
main:
   funcrotate
   funcinput
   funcmultiply
   funcoutput
stop

funcrotate:
   input the rotation angle and set up the rotation matrix
end
```

funcinput:
  input the line coordinates matrix
end

funcmultiply:
  multiply the rotation matrix and the line coordinates matrix
end

funcoutput:
  output the line coordinates
end

Notice that the functions `funcinput`, `funcmultiply`, and `funcoutput` are already available in the line translation program. You do not need to write those functions. You can use them from the line translation code. The only function you need to write is the `funcrotatemat`, which sets up the line rotation matrix.

Program

```
/*******************************************************/
/*                                                     */
/*    main: Rotation of a Line Segment in an x-y Plane */
/*                                                     */
/*******************************************************/
/*                                                     */
/*    Input Variables:                                 */
/*        theta - angle of rotation                    */
/*        oldline[3][2] - coordinate points of line    */
/*                                                     */
/*    Computed Variables:                              */
/*        newline[3][2] - rotated coordinate points    */
/*                        of line                      */
/*                                                     */
/*    Output Variables:                                */
/*        oldline[3][2] - old coordinate points of line */
/*        newline[3][2] - new coordinate points of line */
/*                                                     */
/*******************************************************/
```

```
#include <stdio.h>
#include <math.h>
#define IMAX 3
#define JMAX 2
#define KMAX 3

void funcrotate(float [ ] [IMAX]);

int main( )
{
    float  angle, theta, rotation[IMAX][IMAX]= {0.0};
    float  oldline[IMAX][JMAX],newline[IMAX][JMAX];

    funcinputline(oldline);  /* same as before */

    oldline[2][0] = 0;
    oldline[2][1] = 0;
    funcrotate(rotation);
    funcmultiply(rotation, oldline, newline);     /* same as before */
    printf("Output of old coordinates points x1 y1,");
    printf("x2 y2:\n\n");
    funcoutput(oldline);     /* same as before */
    printf("Output of new coordinates points x1 y1,");
    printf("x2 y2:\n\n");
    funcoutput(newline);     /* same as before */

    return 0;
}

/*********************************************************/
/*                                                       */
/*   funcrotate: Set Up the Rotation Matrix              */
/*                                                       */
/*********************************************************/
/*                                                       */
/*  Defined constants:                                   */
/*       PI =  3.141593                                  */
/*                                                       */
/*   local variables:                                    */
/*       theta - rotation angle                          */
/*                                                       */
/*   Output Variables:                                   */
/*       rotatemat1[ ][IMAX] - translation matrix        */
/*                                                       */
/*********************************************************/
```

```
void funcrotate(float rotatemat1[ ][IMAX])
{
    const  float  PI = 3.141593;
    float  angle, theta;
    printf("Input the angle of rotation (degrees):\n");
    scanf("%f",&angle);

    theta = (PI /180.0) * angle;
    rotatemat1[0][0] = cos(theta);
    rotatemat1[0][1] = -sin(theta);
    rotatemat1[1][0] = sin(theta);
    rotatemat1[1][1] = cos(theta);
    rotatemat1[2][2] = 1.0;

    return;
}
```

Input and Output

```
Input the coordinate points x1 y1, x2 y2:
1.50   2.50
2.50   4.50

Input the angle of rotation (degrees):
10.0

Output of old coordinates points x1 y1,x2 y2:

POINT 1: ( 1.50  2.50 )
POINT 2: ( 2.50  4.50 )

Output of new coordinates points x1 y1,x2 y2:

POINT 1: ( 1.04  2.72 )
POINT 2: ( 1.68  4.87 )
```

Notice that the multiplication matrix `funcmultiply` is used from the translation of the line program with the argument of the translation matrix replaced by the rotation matrix.

Scaling of a Line

Problem Scale a line between the coordinate points $L(x_1, y_1)$ and $L(x_2, y_2)$ by a factor of s_x in the x direction and s_y in the y direction.

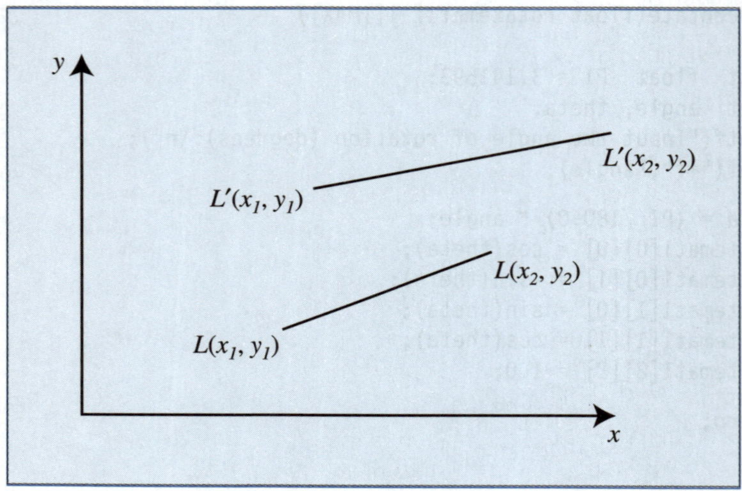

Method Set up the scaling matrix.

$$S\left(s_x, s_y\right) = \begin{bmatrix} s_x & 0 & 0 \\ 0 & s_y & 0 \\ 0 & 0 & 1 \end{bmatrix}$$

Where s_x is the scaling factor of the x coordinate, and
s_y is the scaling factor of the y coordinate.

Input the coordinates of the line.
Setup up the coordinate matrix.

$$L = \begin{bmatrix} x_1 & x_2 \\ y_1 & y_2 \\ 1 & 1 \end{bmatrix}$$

Multiply the scaling matrix and the coordinate matrix.

$$L' = S(s_x, s_y) * L$$

$$\begin{bmatrix} x_1' & x_2' \\ y_1' & y_2' \\ 1 & 1 \end{bmatrix} = \begin{bmatrix} s_x & 0 & 0 \\ 0 & s_y & 0 \\ 0 & 0 & 1 \end{bmatrix} * \begin{bmatrix} x_1 & x_2 \\ y_1 & y_2 \\ 1 & 1 \end{bmatrix}$$

Data

Scaling matrix:

$$S = \begin{bmatrix} s_x & 0 & 0 \\ 0 & s_y & 0 \\ 0 & 0 & 1 \end{bmatrix}$$

Coordinate matrix:

$$L = \begin{bmatrix} x_1 & x_2 \\ y_1 & y_2 \\ 1 & 1 \end{bmatrix}$$

Pseudocode

```
main
   Input the scaling matrix
   Input the coordinate matrix
   Multiplication of the scaling matrix and coordinate matrix
   Output the transformed coordinate matrix
Stop
```

Program

```
/****************************************************/
/*                                                  */
/*    Scaling of a Line Segment in an x-y Plane     */
/*                                                  */
/****************************************************/
/*                                                  */
/*    Input Variables:                              */
/*        sx - scale in x coordinates               */
/*        sy - scale in y coordinates               */
/*        oldline[3][2] - coordinate points of line */
/*                                                  */
/*    Computed Variables:                           */
/*        newline[3][2] - translated coordinate points */
/*                        of line                   */
/*                                                  */
/*    Output Variables:                             */
/*        oldline[3][2] - old coordinate points of line */
/*        newline[3][2] - new coordinate points of line */
/*                                                  */
/****************************************************/
#include <stdio.h>
#define IMAX 3
#define JMAX 2
#define KMAX 3

void funcscalemat(float scalemat1[ ][IMAX]);
void funcinputline(float [ ][JMAX]);
void funcmultiply( float [ ] [IMAX], float [ ] [JMAX],
                   float [ ][JMAX]);
void funcoutput(float [ ][JMAX]);

int main( )
{
    int  i, j, k;
    float sx, sy, scalemat[IMAX][IMAX]= {0.0},
          oldline[IMAX][JMAX],newline[IMAX][JMAX];

    funcscalemat(scalemat);
    funcinputline(oldline);             /* same as before */
    funcmultiply(scalemat, oldline, newline);    /* same as before */
```

```
    printf("\nOutput of old coordinate points: x1 y1,");
    printf(" x2 y2\n\n");

    funcoutput(oldline);                    /* same as before */

    printf("\nOutput of new coordinate points: x1 y1,");
    printf(" x2 y2\n\n");

    funcoutput(newline);                   /* same as before */

    return 0;
}

/*********************************************************/
/*                                                       */
/*    funcscalemat: Set Up the Scaling Matrix            */
/*                                                       */
/*********************************************************/
/*                                                       */
/*    local variables:                                   */
/*        sx - scaling factor for x coordinates          */
/*        sy - scaling factor for y coordinates          */
/*                                                       */
/*    Output Variables:                                  */
/*        scalemat1[ ][IMAX] - scaling matrix            */
/*                                                       */
/*                                                       */
/*********************************************************/
void funcscalemat(float scalemat1[ ][IMAX])
{
    float sx, sy;

    printf("Input x and y coordinate scaling factors:\n");
    scanf("%f  %f",&sx, &sy);

    scalemat1[0][0] = sx;
    scalemat1[1][1] = sy;
    scalemat1[2][2] = 1.0;

    return;
}
```

Input and Output

```
Input x and y coordinate scaling factors:
2.0     2.0

Input the coordinate points x1 y1, x2 y2:
1.5     2.5
2.5     4.5

Output of old coordinate points: x1 y1, x2 y2

POINT 1: ( 1.50  2.50 )
POINT 2: ( 2.50  4.50 )

Output of new coordinate points: x1 y1, x2 y2

POINT 1: ( 3.00  5.00 )
POINT 2: ( 5.00  9.00 )
```

8.7.5 Inventory of Cars in the XYZ Dealership

Problem The XYZ car dealership has five car lots at different locations. Each car lot carries six different models. Data for the car lots is arranged as five rows with six columns representing the models. Computerize the inventory. Assume that the cost per car may differ by lot as well as by model. Note that it is not necessary for each lot to carry all models.

Method

Input the number of cars of each model on each lot (by rows) from a data file.
Input the unit cost of each model on each lot (by rows) from a data file.
Compute the cost by store and by model.
Compute the total inventory and the cost for each store and each model.
Compute the total number of cars in the dealership.
Compute the total cost of all cars in the dealership.
Output the results.

Data

Data values for the number of cars and the number of each model in each lot from a data file.

Data values for the cost of each car in each lot and in each model from a data file.

Pseudocode

```
main:
  input models and cost per lot
  calculate value of inventory per lot and per model
  calculate the size and value of inventory for each lot
  calculate the size and inventory for each model
  print the inventory tables
stop

funcinput:
  input the number of cars per model per lot
  input the cost of each model per lot
end

funccost:
  calculate the total cost per model per lot
end

funcinventory:
  calculate the overall total cars and value per model and also per lot
end

functotunits:
  calculate the overall number of cars
end

functotcost:
  calculate the overall cost
end
```

funcoutput:

for each lot and model

output the number of cars

output the total number of cars per lot

output the total number of cars per model

output the overall total number of cars in inventory

output the value of cars

output the total value of cars per lot

output the total value of cars per model

output the overall total value of the inventory

end

Program

```
/*************************************************************************/
/*                                                                       */
/*    main: Inventory of the XYZ Car Dealership                          */
/*                                                                       */
/*************************************************************************/
/*                                                                       */
/*    Input Variables:                                                   */
/*      numcars[IMAX][JMAX]  - number of cars of each model in each      */
/*      store                                                            */
/*      carprice[IMAX][JMAX] - cost of each model in each store          */
/*                                                                       */
/*                                                                       */
/*    Computed Variables:                                                */
/*      totcostcars[IMAX][JMAX]- total cost of cars of each model in     */
/*      each store                                                       */
/*                                                                       */
/*      totstorecars[IMAX] - number of cars in each store                */
/*      totmodelcars[JMAX] - number of cars of each model                */
/*      totstorecost[IMAX] - cost of all cars in each store              */
/*      totmodelcost[JMAX] - cost of all cars of each model              */
/*      totcarsinvent      - total number of all cars in inventory       */
/*      totcostinvent      - total cost of all cars in inventory         */
/*                                                                       */
/*    Output Variables:                                                  */
/*      numcars[IMAX][JMAX]- number of cars of each model in each store */
/*      carprice[IMAX][JMAX] - cost of each model in each store          */
```

```
/*      totstorecars[IMAX] – number of cars in each store           */
/*      totmodelcars[JMAX] – number of cars of each model           */
/*      totstorecost[IMAX] – cost of all cars in each store         */
/*      totmodelcost[JMAX] – cost of all cars of each model         */
/*      totcarsinvent      – total number of all cars in inventory  */
/*      totcostinvent      – total cost of all cars in inventory    */
/*                                                                  */
/*    Functions Called:                                             */
/*      funcinput( )– input the number of cars of each model in each */
/*                    store and the cost per model                  */
/*      funccost( ) – calculate the total cost of cars of each model */
/*                    and in each store                             */
/*      funcinventunits( ) – calculate the number of cars in each store*/
/*                           and the number of cars in each model   */
/*      funcinventcost – calculate tcost of cars in each store      */
/*                       and the cost of cars in each model         */
/*      functotunits( )– calculate the total number of cars         */
/*                       in inventory                               */
/*      functotcost( ) – calculate the total cost of all cars       */
/*                       in inventory                               */
/*      funcoutput( )  – output the number of cars in each store and */
/*                       of each model                              */
/*                     – output the total cost of cars in each store */
/*                       and of each model                          */
/*                     – output the total cars in each store and    */
/*                       of each model                              */
/*                     – output total cars in inventory and total   */
/*                       cost of all cars in inventory              */
/*                                                                  */
/*******************************************************************/

#include <stdio.h>

#define  IMAX  5
#define  JMAX  4

void funcinput(int [ ][JMAX], float [ ][JMAX]);
void funccost(int [ ][JMAX], float [ ][JMAX], float [ ][JMAX]);
void funcinventunits(int [ ][JMAX], int [ ], int [ ]);
void funcinventcost(float  [ ][JMAX], float [ ], float [ ]);
int functotunits(int [ ]);
float functotcost(float [ ]);
void funcoutput(int [ ][JMAX], float [ ][JMAX], int [ ], int [ ],
                float [ ], float [ ],int, float, float[ ][JMAX] );
```

```
int main( )
{
    int  numcars[IMAX][JMAX], totstorecars[IMAX],
         totmodelcars[JMAX], totcarsinvent;
    float carprice[IMAX][JMAX], totcostcars[IMAX][JMAX],
          totstorecost[IMAX], totmodelcost[JMAX], totcostinvent;

    funcinput(numcars, carprice);
    funccost(numcars, carprice, totcostcars);
    funcinventunits(numcars, totstorecars, totmodelcars);

    funcinventcost(totcostcars, totstorecost, totmodelcost);

    totcarsinvent = functotunits(totstorecars);
    totcostinvent = functotcost(totstorecost);
    funcoutput(numcars, carprice, totstorecars, totmodelcars,
               totstorecost, totmodelcost, totcarsinvent,
                totcostinvent, totcostcars);

    return 0;
}
/***************************************************************/
/*                                                             */
/*   funcinput: Input the Number of Cars of Each Model         */
/*              and the Price                                  */
/*                                                             */
/***************************************************************/
/*                                                             */
/*   Output Parameters:                                        */
/*     carunits1[IMAX][JMAX]- number of cars of each model in each */
/*     store                                                   */
/*                                                             */
/*     carunitcost[IMAX][JMAX] - cost of each model in each store */
/*                                                             */
/*                                                             */
/*   Input Variables:                                          */
/*     carunits1[ ][JMAX] - number of cars of each model in each */
/*     store                                                   */
/*     carunitcost[ ][JMAX])- price of each model in each store */
/*                                                             */
/***************************************************************/

void funcinput(int carunits1[ ][JMAX], float carunitcost [ ][JMAX])
{
    int i, j;
```

```
    FILE *inptr;
    inptr = fopen("cardatain.dat", "r");

    for(i = 0; i < IMAX; i++)
        for(j = 0; j < JMAX; j++)
            fscanf(inptr,"%d",&carunits1[i][j]);

    fclose(inptr);

    inptr = fopen("carpricedatain.dat", "r");
    for(i = 0; i < IMAX; i++)
        for(j = 0; j < JMAX; j++)
            fscanf(inptr,"%f",&carunitcost[i][j]);

    fclose(inptr);
    return;
}


/*****************************************************************/
/*                                                               */
/*   funccost: Compute the Cost of All Cars of Each Store        */
/*             and Each Model                                    */
/*                                                               */
/*****************************************************************/
/*                                                               */
/*   Input Parameters:                                           */
/*     carunits1[IMAX][JMAX]- number of cars of each model in each */
/*     store                                                     */
/*                                                               */
/*     carunitcost1[IMAX][JMAX] - cost of each model in each store */
/*                                                               */
/*                                                               */
/*   Computed Variables:                                         */
/*     totcostcars1[IMAX][JMAX]- total cost of cars of each model */
/*                               in each store                   */
/*                                                               */
/*   Output Parameters:                                          */
/*     totcostcars1[IMAX][JMAX]- total cost of cars of each model */
/*                                      in each store            */
/*                                                               */
/*****************************************************************/
void funccost(int numcars1 [ ][JMAX],
              float carunitcost1[ ][JMAX],
              float totcostcars1[ ][JMAX])
```

```
{
    int  i, j;

    for(i = 0; i < IMAX; i++)
        for(j = 0; j < JMAX; j++)
            totcostcars1[i][j] = numcars1[i][j]* carunitcost1[i][j];
    return;
}


/***********************************************************************/
/*                                                                     */
/*    funinventunits: Compute the Number of Cars in Each               */
/*                    Store and of Each Model                          */
/*                                                                     */
/***********************************************************************/
/*                                                                     */
/*  Input Parameters:                                                  */
/*      carunits1[ ][JMAX]- number of cars of each model in each       */
/*      store                                                          */
/*                                                                     */
/*  Computed Variables:                                                */
/*      totstorecars1[ ] - number of cars in each store                */
/*      totmodelcars1[ ] - number of cars of each model                */
/*                                                                     */
/*  Output Parameters:                                                 */
/*      totstorecars1[ ] - number of cars in each store                */
/*      totmodelcars1[ ] - number of cars of each model                */
/*                                                                     */
/***********************************************************************/
void funcinventunits(int carunits1[ ][JMAX],int totstorecars1[ ],
                     int totmodelcars1[ ])
{
    int  i, j;

    for(i = 0; i < IMAX; i++)
    {
        totstorecars1[i] = 0;
        for(j = 0; j < JMAX; j++)
        {
            totstorecars1[i] += carunits1 [i][j];
        }
    }
```

```
    for(j = 0; j < JMAX; j++)
    {
        totmodelcars1[j] = 0;
        for(i = 0; i < IMAX; i++)
        {
            totmodelcars1[j] += carunits1[i][j];
        }
    }

    return;
}


/*****************************************************************/
/*                                                               */
/*   funinventcost: Compute the Cost of All Cars in Each Store and */
/*   All Cars of Each Model                                      */
/*                                                               */
/*                                                               */
/*****************************************************************/
/*                                                               */
/*  Input Parameters:                                            */
/*      totcostcars1[ ][JMAX] - total cost of cars of each store and */
/*                              each model                       */
/*                                                               */
/*                                                               */
/*  Computed Variables:                                          */
/*      totstorecost1[ ] - cost of all cars in each store        */
/*      totmodelcost1[ ] - cost of all cars of each model        */
/*                                                               */
/*  Output Parameters:                                           */
/*      totstorecost1[ ] - cost of all cars in each store        */
/*      totmodelcost1[ ] - cost of all cars of each model        */
/*                                                               */
/*****************************************************************/
void funcinventcost(float costcars1[ ][JMAX], float totstorecost1 [ ],
                    float totmodelcost1[ ])
{
    int  i, j;

    for(i = 0; i < IMAX; i++)
    {
        totstorecost1[i] = 0.0;
```

```
        for(j = 0; j < JMAX; j++)
        {
            totstorecost1[i] += costcars1[i][j];
        }
    }

    for(j = 0; j < JMAX; j++)
    {
        totmodelcost1[j] = 0.0;
        for(i = 0; i < IMAX; i++)
        {
            totmodelcost1[j] += costcars1[i][j];
        }
    }

    return;
}
/*******************************************************************/
/*                                                                 */
/*   functotunits: Compute the Total Number of Cars of All Models */
/*                 in All Stores                                   */
/*                                                                 */
/*******************************************************************/
/*                                                                 */
/*   Input Parameters:                                             */
/*     totstorecars1[ ] - number of cars in each store             */
/*                                                                 */
/*   Returned Variables:                                           */
/*     totcarsinvent1  - total number of cars in inventory         */
/*                                                                 */
/*******************************************************************/
int functotunits(int totstorecars1[ ])
{
    int  i;
    int totcarsinvent1 = 0;

    for(i = 0; i < IMAX; i++)
        totcarsinvent1 += totstorecars1[i];

    return totcarsinvent1;
}
```

```
/*****************************************************************/
/*                                                               */
/*    functotcost: Compute the Total Cost of All Cars of All Models */
/*    in All Stores                                              */
/*                                                               */
/*                                                               */
/*****************************************************************/
/*                                                               */
/*    Input Parameters:                                          */
/*        totstorecost1[ ] - cost of cars in each store          */
/*                                                               */
/*    Returned Variables:                                        */
/*      totcostinvent1 - total cost of all cars in inventory     */
/*                                                               */
/*****************************************************************/
float functotcost(float totstorecost1[ ])
{
    int  i;
    float  totcostinvent1 = 0;

    for(i = 0; i < IMAX; i++)
        totcostinvent1 += totstorecost1[i];

    return totcostinvent1;
}


/*****************************************************************/
/*                                                               */
/*   funcoutput: Output of the Cars of Each Model in Each Store  */
/*               Total Cars in Each Store and Each Model,        */
/*               Total Number of Cars in All Stores and          */
/*               Total Number of Cars of All Models, and Overall */
/*               Value of All Cars                               */
/*                                                               */
/*                                                               */
/*****************************************************************/
/*                                                               */
/*    Input Parameters:                                          */
/*      carunits1[ ][JMAX]- number of cars in each store and model   */
/*      totcostcars1[ ][JMAX]- total cost of cars of each store and  */
/*                             in all models                     */
/*      totstorecars1[ ] - number of cars in each store          */
/*      totmodelcars1[ ] - number of cars of each model          */
/*      totstorecost1[ ] - cost of all cars in each store        */
/*      totmodelcost1[ ] - cost of all cars of each model        */
```

```
/*      totcarsinvent1   - total number of cars in inventory         */
/*      totcostinvent1 - total cost of cars in inventory             */
/*                                                                   */
/*    Output Variables:                                              */
/*      carubits1[ ][JMAX]- number of cars of each model in each     */
/*      store                                                        */
/*      totcostcars1[ ][JMAX]- total cost of cars of each model in   */
/*      each store                                                   */
/*                                                                   */
/*      totstorecars1[ ] - number of cars in each store              */
/*      totmodelcars1[ ] - number of cars of each model              */
/*      totstorecost1[ ] - cost of all cars in each store            */
/*      totmodelcost1[ ] - cost of all cars of each model            */
/*      totcarsinvent1   - total number of cars in inventory         */
/*      totcostinvent1 - total cost of cars in inventory             */
/*                                                                   */
/*******************************************************************/
void funcoutput(int numcars1[ ][JMAX], float costcars1[ ]
      [JMAX], int totstorecars1[ ],int totmodelcars1[ ],
      float totstorecost1[ ], float totmodelcost1[ ],
      int totcarsinvent1, float totcostinvent1,
         float totcostcars1[ ][JMAX])
{
    int i, j;

    FILE  *outptr;
    outptr = fopen("cardataout.dat", "w");

    fprintf(outptr,"NUMBER OF CAR UNITS IN EACH STORE");
    fprintf(outptr," AND MODEL:\n\n");

    fprintf(outptr,"            Model 1    Model 2    ");
    fprintf(outptr,"Model 3    Model 4    Store total\n\n");

    for(i = 0; i < IMAX; i++)
    {
        fprintf(outptr,"Store %2d", i + 1);
        for(j = 0; j < JMAX; j++)
        {
            fprintf(outptr,"%10d",numcars1[i][j]);
        }
        fprintf(outptr,"%12d\n",totstorecars1[i]);
    }
```

```
    fprintf(outptr,"\nModel total");
    for(j = 0; j < JMAX; j++)
        fprintf(outptr,"%10d",totmodelcars1[j]);
    fprintf(outptr,"%12d\n", totcarsinvent1);

    fprintf(outptr,"\n\n\nCOST OF CAR UNITS IN EACH");
    fprintf(outptr," STORE AND MODEL:\n\n");
    fprintf(outptr,"            Model 1    Model 2     ");
    fprintf(outptr,"Model 3     Model 4\n");

    for(i = 0; i < IMAX; i++)
    {
        fprintf(outptr,"\nStore %2d", i + 1);
        for(j = 0; j < JMAX; j++)
        {
            fprintf(outptr,"%12.2f",costcars1[i][j]);

        }
    }

    fprintf(outptr,"\n\n\nTOTAL COST OF CARS OF EACH MODEL IN EACH");
    fprintf(outptr," STORE:\n\n");
    fprintf(outptr,"            Model 1    Model 2     ");
    fprintf(outptr,"Model 3     Model 4 Store Total\n\n");

    for(i = 0; i < IMAX; i++)
    {
        fprintf(outptr,"Store %2d", i + 1);
        for(j = 0; j < JMAX; j++)
        {
            fprintf(outptr,"%12.2f",totcostcars1[i][j]);

        }
        fprintf(outptr,"%12.2f\n",totstorecost1[i]);
    }

    fprintf(outptr,"\nModel total");
    for(j = 0; j < JMAX; j++)
        fprintf(outptr,"%12.2f",totmodelcost1[j]);
    fprintf(outptr,"%12.2f\n", totcostinvent1);

    fclose(outptr);

    return;
}
```

Input: "cardatain.dat"

```
6   5   3   2
4   3   5   6
8   2   4   5
9   2   3   4
3   2   3   4
```

Input: "carpricedatain.dat"

```
12500    9800    11250   18650
11950    10050   10998   17890
11860    10040   10650   18060
12540    10100   11050   17400
120780   10025   10860   16980
```

Output: "cardataout.dat"

```
NUMBER OF CAR UNITS IN EACH STORE AND MODEL:

              Model 1    Model 2     Model 3     Model 4   Store Total

Store 1          6          5           3           2          16
Store 2          4          3           5           6          18
Store 3          8          2           4           5          19
Store 4          9          2           3           4          18
Store 5          3          2           3           4          12

Model total     30         14          18          21          83

COST OF CAR UNITS IN EACH STORE AND MODEL:

              Model 1    Model 2     Model 3     Model 4

Store 1       12500.00    9800.00    11250.00    18650.00
Store 2       11950.00   10050.00    10998.00    17890.00
Store 3       11860.00   10040.00    10650.00    18060.00
Store 4       12540.00   10100.00    11050.00    17400.00
Store 5      120780.00   10025.00    10860.00    16980.00

TOTAL COST OF CARS OF EACH MODEL IN EACH STORE:

              Model 1    Model 2     Model 3     Model:4   Store total

Store 1       75000.00   49000.00    33750.00    37300.00   195050.00
Store 2       47800.00   30150.00    54990.00   107340.00   240280.00
Store 3       94880.00   20080.00    42600.00    90300.00   247860.00
Store 4      112860.00   20200.00    33150.00    69600.00   235810.00
```

```
Store 5       362340.00  20050.00   32580.00    67920.00   482890.00
Model total  692880.00 139480.00  197070.00  372460.00   1401890.00
```

Chapter Summary

Two-dimensional arrays are used for storing tabular data in rows and columns. Two-dimensional matrices in scientific computing result from the modeling of two-dimensional problems. Storage for arrays is allocated by declaring an array explicitly. The declaration consists of data type, array name, and the number of rows and columns. The general form of a declaration is as follows:

data-type array-name[number of rows][number of columns];

The row index varies from zero to one less than the number of rows and the column index varies from zero to one less than the number of columns. Small two-dimensional arrays may be initialized at the time of declaration. Large arrays are initialized to nonzero values using `for` loops. Two-dimensional arrays can be processed using either an array index or an array pointer.

Arithmetic operations may be performed on ordinary two-dimensional tables. Row and column manipulations must be performed on ordinary tabular data element-by-element. Mathematical matrix operations may be performed on two-dimensional arrays of appropriate sizes.

Two-dimensional arrays may be passed to functions. In a function prototype the first dimension may be a default, but the second dimension must be specified even though the array name is optional. In the function header the first dimension is optional and the second dimension must be specified, as must the array name. A function returns an array through its argument list.

Arrays with more than two-dimensions are multidimensional. In the storage of multidimensional arrays the first index is the slowest varying index and the last index is the the fastest varying index. For three-dimensional arrays the first index is the plane index, the second index is the row index, and the third index is the column index. Input/output and manipulation of three-dimensional arrays is an extension of two-dimensional arrays with an additional `for` loop for the plane index.

Exercises

1. Write a program to input a two-dimensional array. Compute the average of the elements of each row and store the row averages in a one-dimensional

array. Compute the average of the elements of each column and store the column averages in a one-dimensional array. Output the array with the row averages in a column to the right of the rows and the column averages under the columns.

2. Write a program to compute the rotation of a point $p(x, y, z, 1)$ around the origin in three-dimensional space. The rotation angle around the x-axis is θ_x, around the y-axis is θ_y, and around the z-axis is θ_z. These angles are input to the program. Compute a single rotation matrix, R = Zrot * (Yrot *Xrot), which has the effect of performing the rotation around the x-axis, then around the y-axis, and then around the z-axis. For each point, print its original location and its location after the composite rotation.

$$x\text{-rotation} = \begin{bmatrix} 1 & 0 & 0 & 0 \\ 0 & \cos\theta_x & -\sin\theta_x & 0 \\ 0 & \sin\theta_x & \cos\theta_x & 0 \\ 0 & 0 & 0 & 1 \end{bmatrix}$$

$$y\text{-rotation} = \begin{bmatrix} \cos\theta_y & 0 & -\sin\theta_y & 0 \\ 0 & 1 & 0 & 0 \\ \sin\theta_y & 0 & \cos\theta_y & 0 \\ 0 & 0 & 0 & 1 \end{bmatrix}$$

$$z\text{-rotation} = \begin{bmatrix} \cos\theta_z & -\sin\theta_z & 0 & 0 \\ \sin\theta_z & \cos\theta_z & 0 & 0 \\ 0 & 0 & 1 & 0 \\ 0 & 0 & 0 & 1 \end{bmatrix}$$

These matrices are in a homogeneous coordinate system.

3. Write a program to input different diameters in inches of a set of pipes in a two-dimensional arrangement of five rows and six columns. Given the velocity v in feet/sec of the flow, compute the flow rate in the pipes, and print the table of diameters and the table of the flow rates.

$$q = a * v$$

Where $a = \dfrac{\pi d^2}{4}$

d is the diameter (ft),

a is the cross-sectional area of the pipe (sqft),

v is the velocity (ft/sec), and

q is the flow rate (cft/sec).

4. Write a program to input the load on equally spaced load-bearing rectangular steel columns arranged in a grid. Given the compression stress of 6000 psi. Compute the dimensions of the columns given the depth d, which is 0.8 times the width w of the cross sectional area of each column.

   stress = load/area

   area = load/stress

   area = width * depth

   depth = 0.8 * width

   Output the load array and column dimension array.

5. A grid has been projected on a surface in order to model it. A 7 × 5 array `a` of elevations at the grid points is stored in a file in row-major order. Write a program that generates a 13 × 9 array `b` of approximate elevations on a half grid by averaging the surrounding points of `a`.

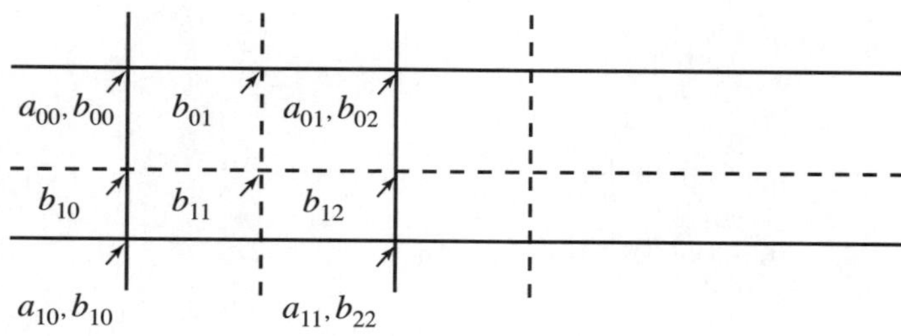

   Use the formula

$$b_{ij} = (a_{i/2\ j/2} + a_{(i+1)/2\ j/2} + a_{i/2(j+1)/2} + a_{(i+1)/2\ (j+1)/2})/4$$

   Print the elevations for the two grids, spacing the elements of `a` twice as far apart as the elements of `b`, so that they can be compared.

6. Write a program that reads daily maximum and minimum temperatures for January from a data file. Store the temperatures in a 2-dimensional array where the first column contains the minimum, the second column contains the maximum, and the third column is an average of the other two. Determine the maximum and minimum temperatures for the month. Count the number of days the minimum was within 10° of the lowest temperature, and the number of days the maximum was within 10° of the highest temperature.

CHAPTER 9

Characters and Strings

Objectives

To learn to define, use, and manipulate character data and character strings.

Character data storage and manipulation is a powerful feature of the C programming language. There are many software application programs such as word processors, spreadsheets, and multimedia, as well as database tools developed using character and string data and manipulation features. Scientists and engineers use character strings in creating formulas, drawing graphics, and developing software. In general wherever text is required; for example, names of people, floor plans, animals, cars, planes, machines, or machine parts, strings may be used. The common operations performed on strings are concatenation, comparison, copying, extracting substrings, and locating substrings. More complex data manipulation operations include sorting a list of unsorted strings and searching for specific strings in a list of sorted strings.

9.1 Introduction to Character Data

In C, there is no string data type. The string data type is derived from the basic data type char and the derived array data type. However, an array of characters is not the same as a string.

A variable of type char has just enough storage to store a single character. A character literal is a single character within single quotation marks. A variable of type char can be used to store a simple code. For example:

```
char  unit;

unit = 'F';    /* for Fahrenheit */
..........
unit = 'C';    /* for Centigrade */
```

Most codes and ID's require more than one character. In mailing addresses, two characters are used to identify a state and five characters are used to identify a zip code. They could be stored in character arrays as follows.

```
char state[2], zip[5];
```

Numbers such as zip codes, which are used for identification purposes and are not used in arithmetic, should be stored as arrays of type char, rather than as integers.

9.1.1 Declaration of Character Data

In C, a character array is declared using the basic data type char and the derived data type array. An example general declaration of a character array is as follows:

```
char  chararray[n];
```

Notice that the data type is char, the name of the array is chararray, and n is the number of elements. The following example shows the declaration and allocation of storage for a character array that can hold 10 characters.

```
char  chararray[10];

chararray[0]  = 'a';
chararray[1]  = 'x';
chararray[2]  = 'c';
chararray[3]  = 'b';
chararray[4]  = 'l';
chararray[5]  = 'k';
chararray[6]  = 'm';
```

```
chararray[7] = 'd';
chararray[8] = 'g';
chararray[9] = 'f';
```

The preceding characters are stored as follows:

a	x	c	b	l	k	m	d	g	f

Notice that 10 characters are stored in this array `chararray`. As with any array these characters can only be accessed individually.

9.1.2 Initialization of Character Data

Since most character data is stored in arrays of type `char`, initialization is similar to that of other types of arrays. An array can be initialized by explicit assignment of values to its elements as in the previous example. An array can be initialized in the array declaration as shown in the following:

```
char  mystate [2] = {'C', 'A'};
char myzip [5] = { '9', '2', '3', '1', '2'};
```

Notice that the number of literals must match the number of elements in the array. If too few literals are specified, the rest of the array is filled with blank characters. Notice also that a number being stored in a `char` array must be specified as individual digits.

If values in an *x*, *y* coordinate system are to be plotted, a graph can be set up for $0 \le x \le 50$, $0 \le y \le 50$ by declaring a two-dimensional `char` array of 51 rows and 51 columns, and initializing it to all blank characters except for horizontal lines in row 0 and vertical lines in column 0 for the *x*- and *y*-axis, respectively.

```
#include <stdio.h>

int main( )
{
   char  graph[51][51];
   int  x, y;

   for(x = 1; x < 51; x++)
   {
      for(y = 1; y < 51; y++)
```

```
        {
            graph [y][x] = ' ';
        }
    }

    for(x = 1; x < 51; x++)
    {
        graph[0][x] = '-';
    }

    for(y = 1; y < 51; y++)
    {
        graph [y][0] = '|';
    }

    graph[0][0] = '+';

    return 0;
}
```

If this is printed, starting with row 50 and ending with row 0, it has the appearance of the following graphic:

An equation $y = f(x)$ can then be graphed for integer values of x in the range 0–50 by calling a function f and rounding the results, checking that they are also in the range 0–50, and putting a character in the position x, y.

```
#include <stdio.h>
int main( )
{
    char  graph[51][51];
    int  x, y;

    for(x = 0; x < 51; x++)
    {
        y = f(x) + 0.5;    /* round f(x) */
        if(0 <= y && y <= 50)
        {
            graph[y][x] = '*';
        }
```

```
    }
    return 0;
}
```

Empirical data could be plotted by rounding values for both *x* and *y* and checking that they are within range.

```
#include <stdio.h>
int main( )
{
    char graph[51][51];
    float measx, measy;
    int i, j, k;

    for(k = 0; k < n; k++)   /* n sets of measurements */
    {
        scanf("%f  %f", &measx, &measy);
        i = measx + 0.5;
        j = measy + 0.5;
        if(0 <= i && 0 <= j && i <= 50 && j <= 50)
        {
            graph[j][i] = '*';
        }
    }
    return 0;
}
```

Note that array indices must be non-negative integers. It is important that the indices be within the array bounds or there can be unpredictable side-effects. The computer does not check for array bounds errors.

9.1.3 Input/Output of Character Data

In C, the standard input and output functions `scanf()` and `printf()` may be used to input and output character arrays. When input function `scanf()` is used, input comes from the keyboard. When the output function `printf()` is used, the characters are displayed on the monitor. Characters may be input from a data file by using `fscanf()` and characters may be output to a data file using `fprintf()`. These are general input and output functions in the header file `stdio.h`. The standard input and output functions `scanf()`, `fscanf()`, `printf()`, and `fprintf()` may have a variable number of arguments. These are the same functions that are used for input and output of numeric data as discussed in Chapter 3.

Use of `scanf()` and `printf()` Functions Character data may be entered from a keyboard or may be read from a data file using the `scanf()` or `fscanf()` functions, respectively.

When character data is input using the `scanf()` function the control field is `"%nc"`, where `n` is the number of characters. The following code shows the input of a character array from the keyboard. When reading the input characters, `scanf()` ignores any leading blanks and starts reading with the first nonblank character entered. The `scanf()` function reads the input characters including embedded and trailing blanks until the required number of characters have been read. The following sample code shows the input and output of character arrays.

```
#include <stdio.h>

int main( )
{
    char  name[20];

    printf("Enter the name:\n");
    scanf("%15c\n", name);
    printf("The name entered is: %15c\n", name);

    return 0;
}
```

The input and output of this code is as follows:

```
Enter the name: JOHNNY APPLESEED
The name entered is: JOHNNY APPLESEE
```

In the input statement there is no need to specify the address operator `"&"` in front of the `char` array `name`, because `name` is the address of the array. Notice that 15 characters are read, which may include the new line feed `'\n'` or trailing blanks. Since 15 characters have been specified, 15 characters will be read including embedded or trailing blanks and control characters. If more than 15 characters are entered, only 15 characters are read because of the specification `"%15c"` in the control field. Thus, the rest of the characters entered are ignored. Since 16 characters are entered, the character `"D"` is ignored.

The characters are stored as follows:

name

J	O	H	N	N	Y		A	P	P	L	E	S	E	E					
0	1	2	3	4	5	6	7	8	9	10	11	12	13	14	15	16	17	18	19

Notice that with a character array, the entire array can be input or output by just using the array name and using a field width that matches the number of elements in the array. The preceding code is a shorthand version of the following code that reads characters into an array one-by-one.

```
#include <stdio.h>

int main( )
{
   char  name[15];
   int k;

   printf("Enter the name:\n");
   for (k = 0 ; k < 15; k++)
   {
      scanf("%c", &name[k]);
   }
   printf("\nThe string entered is:");
   for (k = 0 ; k < 15; k++)
   {
      printf("%c", name[k]);
   }

   printf("\n");

   return 0;
}
```

When initializing char arrays either through input or within repetition structures, as with any array, it is important that the index remain within bounds.

9.1.4 Review Questions

1. Write an input statement to input the following characters using the `scanf()` function with the `"%c"` control field. Assume the maximum array length of 50 characters.

   Electronic Computers
   Nuclear Reactions
   Atomic Weight
   Molecular Formula

2. Show how the input characters in Question 1 are stored in computer memory.

3. Write C code to print the character arrays stored in Question 2, left-justified.
4. Write C code to print the characters stored in Question 2, right-justified.

9.2 Introduction to Strings

A string constant in C is zero or more characters including blanks, enclosed between two double quotes. For example "axcmn" and "x5+*mc" are string constants. If there are no characters between double quotation marks (""), it is a null string. String constants are used in every input/output statement that has a format, but they can also be stored in character arrays and given names. A string stored in a character array differs from character data stored in a character array in that a string is treated as a single value, must be shorter than the declared size of the array, and must be followed by a special character known as the null terminating character ('\0').

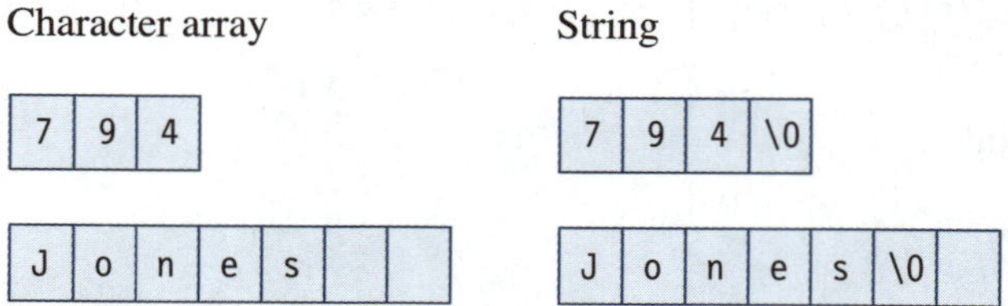

String variables can be initialized when they are declared, either by specifying the individual elements of the variable, or by using a string constant.

Character array	**String**
`char IDnum[3] = {'7','9','4'};`	`char ID[4] = {'7','9','4','\0'};` or `char ID[4] = "794";`

`char name[8] = {'J','o','n','e','s'};`	`char strname[8] =`
	`{'J','o','n','e','s','\0'};`
	or `char strname[8] = "Jones";`

Here IDnum and name are character arrays. Initializing them places the characters in the array, left-justified with blanks filled on the right. ID and strname are strings. If they are initialized character-by-character, the null terminating character must be stored following the final character of the string. If they are initialized using the value of a string constant, then the null terminating character is automatically stored. `IDnum` used all of its positions for storage. `ID` needed to be declared large enough to hold any name stored in it and the null terminating character. As a string, `strname` needed to be declared one larger than any name stored in it. The presence of the null terminating character in a `char` array is what distinguishes between a character array and a string.

9.2.1 Declaration and Initialization of Strings

Declaration A string is stored in an array of data type `char`. The declaration statement to allocate the storage for a string is as follows:

```
char  strname[20];
```

The data type is `char`, the string name is `strname`, and it is an array with 20 storage locations to hold 19 characters plus the null terminating character.

A string array is undefined until a string is stored in it. There are three different ways of defining a string array.

- Initialization at the time of declaration
- Assignment of characters to each individual array location
- Input into the string array

> *Programming Warning:* Make sure that enough storage space is allocated to store a string and a null terminating character.

Initialization Any string constant may be assigned to a string array when it is declared. The following examples show the declaration and initialization of strings.

```
char  strname[10]  =  "computers";
```

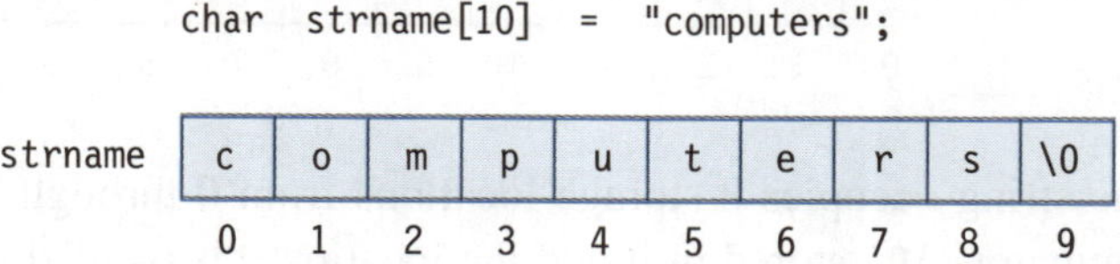

Notice that the number of characters assigned to `strname` is 9 and they are stored in locations 0 through 8. The null terminating character is automatically stored in location 9. In this case the number of characters stored, including the null terminating character, fits the storage exactly. There are two other cases to consider; if the string constant assigned is longer than the number of storage locations or if the string constant assigned is shorter than the number of storage locations.

For example if the string assigned is longer than the number of storage locations allocated the string is stored as follows:

```
char  strname[10]  =  "ELECTRONICS";
```

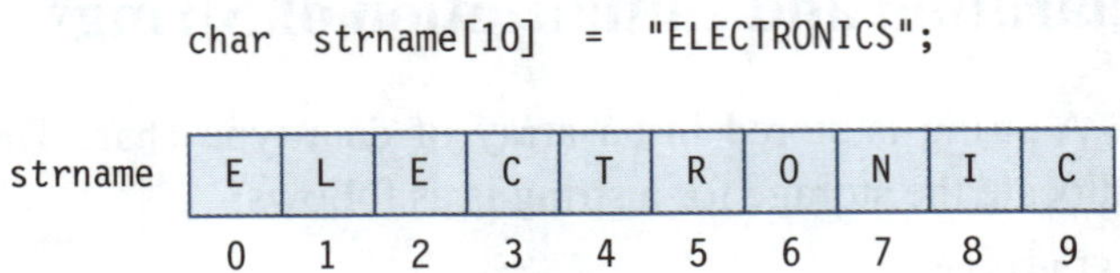

Notice that `S`, which is the last character in the string assigned to string array `strname`, is not stored and the array is not a character string because there is no storage location to store the null terminating character `'\0'`. It is simply an array of individual characters, which can be handled like any array, but may not be manipulated as a string. When such a situation occurs the compiler may give a warning because there is memory overflow that may cause side effects.

> *Programming Warning:* Make sure to allocate enough storage to store all of the characters of the string and the null terminating character so there is no memory overflow, which may cause side effects.

If the string assigned is shorter than the number of storage locations the string is stored as follows:

```
char  strname[10]  =  "ELECTRON";
```

strname	E	L	E	C	T	R	O	N	\0	\0
	0	1	2	3	4	5	6	7	8	9

Notice that the string occupies 8 storage locations from 0 through 7. Location 8 has a null terminator `'\0'` stored in it and the location 9 is padded with the same null terminating character `'\0'`.

Character Assignment Individual characters may be assigned to a string either in the declaration statement itself or separately after the declaration by assigning individual characters to each element of the string explicitly. Such a character array is a character string only if the null character is in the array. The following examples show such an assignment.

Explicit Assignment

```
char  strname[10];

strname[0] = 'C';
strname[1] = 'O';
strname[2] = 'M';
strname[3] = 'P';
strname[4] = 'U';
strname[5] = 'T';
strname[6] = 'E';
strname[7] = 'R';
strname[8] = 'S';
strname[9] = '\0';
```

The string is stored as follows:

strname

C	O	M	P	U	T	E	R	S	\0
0	1	2	3	4	5	6	7	8	9

Notice that each character is assigned explicitly to each individual element of the character string array `strname`. Also the null terminator must be explicitly assigned to the element following the assignment of the last character.

Since strings are stored as character arrays, an assignment statement such as `str = strname` does not copy the value of the string contained in `strname`. If `str` and `strname` are both array names then they are both address constants and cannot be used on the left side of an assignment. One string must be copied element-by-element to the other string.

The following code shows the output of character strings.

```
#include <stdio.h>

int main( )
{
```

```
    char name1[15] = "Washington";
    char name2[15] = "Adams";

    printf("The first string is: %s\n", name1);
    printf("The second string is: %s\n", name2);

    return 0;
}
```

The output from this program is as follows:

```
The first string is: Washington
The second string is: Adams
```

The first declaration gives the array name `name1` to the string `"Washington"`, which is then printed. The second declaration gives the array name `name2` to the string `"Adams"`, which is then printed.

Note that when string literals are stored as character string arrays either the string literal is assigned to the array during the array declaration or the string must be input into the array using input statements.

String variables may be defined through the input. There are several library functions to input and output string data. Input and output of strings is presented in the following sections.

A string is a particular type of character array. Since strings are created as one-dimensional arrays, lists of strings are two-dimensional arrays. The general form of the declaration is as follows:

```
char string_name[number of actual characters + 1];  /* one string */

char string_arr[# of strings][# of characters + 1]; /* list of strings */
```

Notice that `char` is the basic data type, `string_name` is the identifier of the string, and `number of actual characters + 1` is the size of the array. In C, a string must always terminate with a null terminating character `'\0'`, otherwise it will not be a string. The dimension must have one additional space to store the null terminating character `'\0'`. For example, consider the meaning of the following declaration:

```
char  strarr[3][10];
```

`char` indicates that it is a character data type, `strarr` is the identifier to store the character data, 10 (9 + 1) is the size of each string, which includes the location for the null terminating character `'\0'`. This means nine characters may actually be stored in each string of `strarr` and the tenth character is `'\0'`. If the actual number of characters exceeds nine then the null terminator is not stored and the characters stored in the array will not be recognized as strings. If fewer than nine characters are stored in the array then the null character immediately follows the last character. The array has space to store three strings.

The storage allocated for string variable `strname` is 30 storage locations; one for each character for each of the three strings as shown:

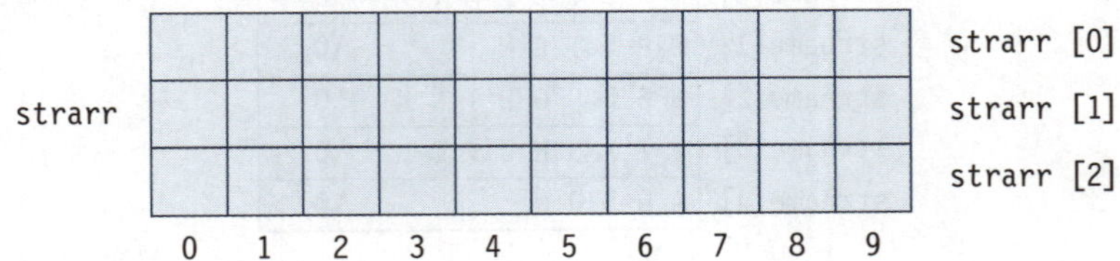

The string variable storage is indexed as follows:

```
strname[0][0]
strname[0][1]
strname[0][2]
.............
strname[2][8]
strname[2][9]
```

Notice that the second array index varies from 0 to 9, which means there are 10 storage locations allocated for each string. The name of the array is the address of the array and it is a constant (as it is for any array we have considered so far).

9.2.2 Storage of String Arrays

Strings may be stored in a fixed-size array using compile-time memory allocation. A set of strings of similar length may be stored as a two-dimensional array. Strings may also be stored using dynamic storage. This will be discussed in Chapter 10.

When a set of strings are to be stored and manipulated using two-dimensional arrays, the storage allocated for each string is of equal length. This method of storage allocation is efficient when strings vary only slightly in length. Such arrays are called *smooth arrays*, because the storage allocated for each string is of the same length. The following code shows the declaration of smooth arrays.

```
char  strname[5][10];
```

There are 5 strings with 10 storage locations allocated for each string. The first index indicates the number of strings and the second index indicates the number of characters in each string. Each string is stored in a single row of the array.

Assume the elements of the array `strname` are as follows: `strname[0]`, `strname[1],...,` `strname[4]`. The strings are referenced by using the first index.

The storage allocation is as follows:

	← 10 →
strname[0]	A X B C L N M T \0
strname[1]	P R S T L M \0
strname[2]	G G B C G H T N K \0
strname[3]	W Z X G N U V C L \0
strname[4]	A D S D N \0

Using the String Array Index The following code shows the input and output of arrays of strings using the array index.

```
#include <stdio.h>
#define  NUMSTR  5
#define  STRLNG  10

int main( )
{
   int  i;
   char strname[NUMSTR][STRLNG];

   printf("Input the strings:\n");
   for(i = 0; i < NUMSTR; i++)
   {
      scanf("%10c", strname[i]);
      strname[i][9] = '\0';
   }
   printf("\nOutput of strings:\n");
   for(i = 0; i < NUMSTR; i++)
   {
      printf("%10c\n", strname[i]);
   }

   return 0;
}
```

```
Input the strings:
AXBCLNMT        /* blank fill to 9 characters */
PRSTLM
GGBCGHTNK
```

```
WZXGNUVCL
ADSDN

Output of strings:
AXBCLNMT
PRSTLM
GGBCGHTNK
WZXGNUVCL
ADSDN
```

The array `strname` is two-dimensional, therefore each row can be used to store a string. Only the row index is needed to identify a string. For instance, `strname[0]` is the first string, `strname[1]` is the second string, and so forth.

In these codes using the array index, the input character strings contain nine characters and a line feed character. The nine characters are stored in locations zero through eight and the new line character `'\n'` is stored in the tenth location. The reason for this is that when the `scanf()` function is used for string input, the entire string and the new line character must be read, otherwise the results are unpredictable. The input statement `"%10c"` is used to read the strings, all of which must be nine characters long followed by a new line. A terminator is written to replace the new line character so that these are recognizable as strings. In Section 9.7, a sample program is coded and executed to show the application of such smooth arrays. Strings of unequal length can also be stored in a smooth array. However, each string must then be scanned to replace the new line character `'\n'` with the string terminator `'\0'`.

9.2.3 Input/Output of Character Strings

Character strings may be input and output using the `scanf()` and `printf()` function with a `"%s"` string control field. The following example shows this.

```
#include <stdio.h>
int main( )
{
    char  strname[15];

    printf("Enter the string:\n");

    scanf("%s", strname);

    printf("\nThe string entered is: %s\n", strname);

    return 0;
}
```

In this example the input and output of this program is as follows:

```
Enter the string
xxyyklmn

The string entered is: xxyyklmn
```

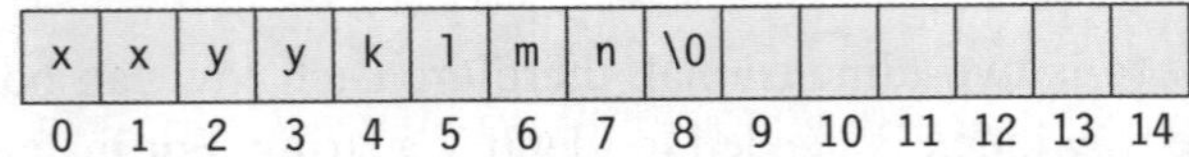

There is no need to specify the number of characters to be entered when a "%s" control field specification is used. The input function "%s" will read all the characters that are entered up to the first blank or the first control character. However, the storage must be large enough that overflow does not occur. There is no need to specify the null terminator when control field "%s" is used for the input of character strings as it is automatically stored after the last valid character. Strings with embedded blanks cannot be read using a "%s" control field.

The following example shows the input of a character string with an embedded blank space.

```
#include <stdio.h>
int main( )
{
    char  strname[15];

    printf("Enter the string:\n");

    scanf("%s", strname);

    printf("\nThe string entered is: %s\n", strname);

    return 0;
}
```

The input and output of this program is as follows:

```
Enter the string
xxyyklmn pnk

The string entered is:
xxyyklmn
```

The string is stored as follows:

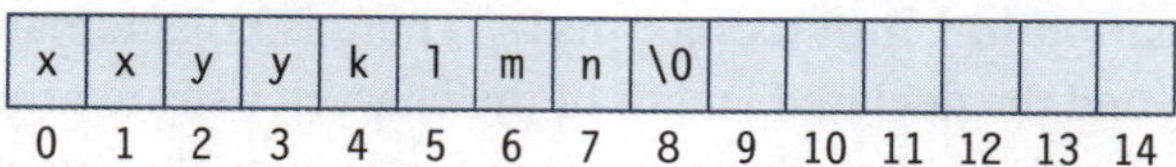

Notice that with the "%s" control field, the computer reads the characters up to the blank space, the tab, or the new line character. The null terminator is stored in the place of the blank or control character. Also notice that in the first example the string does not have a blank character. In the second example the string has a blank character. The "%s" specification only reads the characters in the string up to the blank space.

> *Program warning:* The storage must be large enough to hold the longest string. C will not check the array size. If the string entered is larger than the storage allocated, it will write the string beyond the allocated storage.

The following example shows the input and output of two character strings.

```
#include <stdio.h>

int main( )
{
    char  string1[10], string2[20];

    printf("Enter two strings:\n");
    scanf("%s   %s", string1, string2);

    printf("\nThe output is as follows\n");
    printf("string1: %s                string2: %s\n",
           string1, string2);

    return 0;
}
```

The strings are entered as follows:

```
Enter two strings:

   AAXBBCL MMPKKLN
```

or
```
   AAXBBCL
   MMPKKLN
```

```
The output is as follows:
string1: AAXBBCL          string2: MMPKKLN
```

Width Specification in Input using "%ns" There is no automatic protection for overwriting beyond the declared length of the character string array. If the array is declared to be of size 15 then there is space for 14 actual characters and a space for the null terminator. If more than 14 characters are entered, the extra characters will be written to the storage and the results will be unpredictable. To protect against this, the user may specify the control field to be "%14s". This prevents the computer from picking up more than 14 characters. With this control field specification of "%14s", if the user attempts to enter more than 14 characters the extra characters will be interpreted as belonging to another character string.

The following example shows the input and the storage using "%ns".

```
#include <stdio.h>
int main( )
{
    char  strname[15];
    printf("Enter a string:\n");
    scanf("%14s", strname);
    printf("\nThe string entered is:%s\n", strname);
    return 0;
}
```

The input and output from this program is as follows:

```
Enter a string:
xxyyklmnprstqh

The string entered is: xxyyklmnprstqh
```

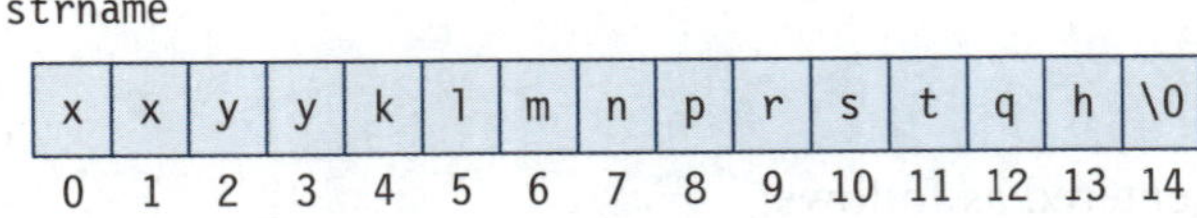

Notice that the string has 14 characters and they are stored in the storage of `strname`.

If the input string is:

```
kkllmpmfrtgqwelas
```

strname

k	k	l	l	m	p	m	f	r	t	g	q	w	e	\0
0	1	2	3	4	5	6	7	8	9	10	11	12	13	14

Notice that only 14 characters are stored and the rest of the input string "las" is ignored. This is to safeguard the storage without writing to an area that does not belong to the string array.

In both the examples presented there are no embedded blank spaces. The following example shows the input string with embedded blank spaces.

If the input string is:

```
kkllmp frtgqwelas
```

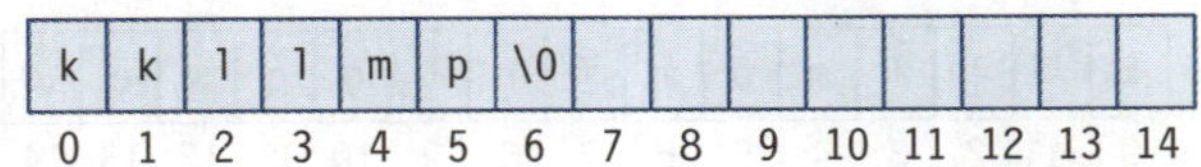

Notice that the string is read only up to the blank space and the rest of the input string is ignored.

> *Programming Warning:* Always give the maximum string size when using the "%ns" format specification.

Input from a Data File Data can be input from a data file instead of being entered from the keyboard. The input file pointer must be declared and the file must be opened for input. The function `fscanf()` is used for file input. The following program code shows file input:

```
#include <stdio.h>

FILE  *inptr;

int main(  )
{
```

```
    char  strname[15];
    inptr = fopen("stringin.dat", "r");

    fscanf(inptr, "%14s", strname);

    fclose(inptr);

    return 0;
}
```

Data file:stringin.dat

inptr ⟶ kkllmpmfrtgqwe

Notice that the data is read from the data file "stringin.dat" instead of being entered from the keyboard. The control field is specified as "%14s" to limit the number of characters read.

The string is stored as follows:

strname

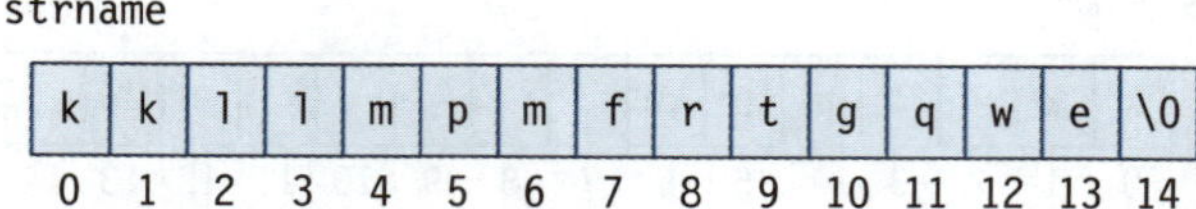

Output Using the `printf()` Function String output may be displayed on the monitor or may be written to a data file using the `printf()` or `fprintf()` function, respectively.

`printf()` with `"%s"` The output function `printf()` can be used to print strings. The control field "%s" may be used to print the strings. With the control field "%s", the string in storage is printed left justified excluding the null terminator. The following examples show the output using the `printf()` function.

The string `strname` in storage is as follows:

strname

x	x	y	y	k	l	m	n	\0	\0	\0	\0	\0	\0	\0
0	1	2	3	4	5	6	7	8	9	10	11	12	13	14

The following output statement prints the string `strname`.

```
#include<stdio.h>
int main( )
{
    char  strname[20]= "xxyyklmn";

    printf("%s\n", strname);

    return 0;
}
```

The output from this program is as follows:

```
xxyyklmn
```

Notice that the null terminating character is not printed. The characters up to the null terminating character are printed.

A string containing blank spaces may be printed using the "%s" format control field. The following string in the storage is printed as follows:

strname

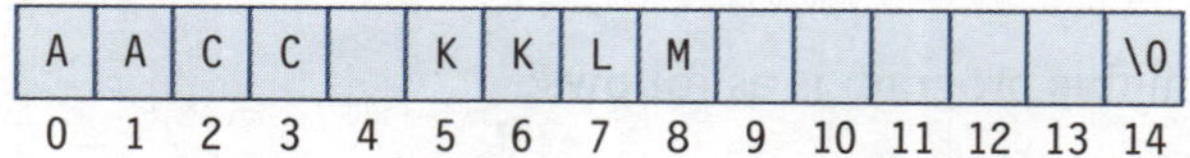


```
char  strname[15] = "AACC KKLM     ";
printf("%s", strname);
```

The output is as follows:

```
AACC KKLM
```

The string `strname` has a blank space between the character C and the character K, and also there are five trailing blank spaces in the string literal. Notice that there is no specification of the number of characters to be printed in the control field "%s". The entire string is printed with blank spaces up to the null terminating character.

Width Specification in Output Using "%ns" The length of the string to be printed may be specified in the control field as "%ns", where n is the number of characters to be printed. The default output control string is "%s". Consider the following storage and print statements using the control string "%ns" in the output statement.

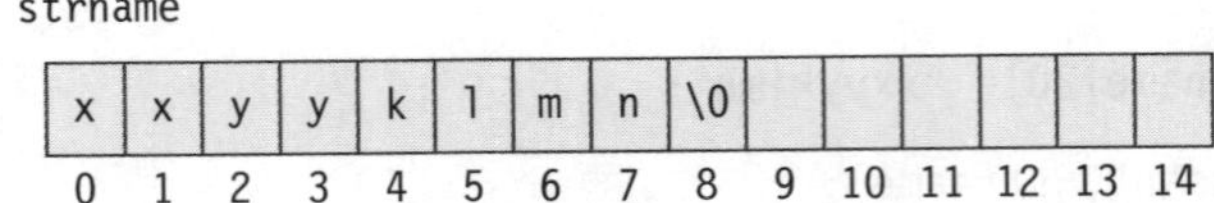


```
#include <stdio.h>
int main( )
{
    char strname[15] = "xxyyklmn";

    printf("The string is: %s\n", strname);
    printf("The string is: %8s\n", strname);
    printf("The string is: %5s\n", strname);
    printf("The string is: %12s\n", strname);
    printf("The string is: %-12s\n", strname);

    return 0;
}
```

The output from this program is as follows:

```
The string is: xxyyklmn
The string is: xxyyklmn
The string is: xxyyklmn
The string is:     xxyyklmn
The string is: xxyyklmn
```

Notice in the first case with the control field "%s", the entire string up to the null terminating character is printed. In the second case with the control field "%8s", the printable characters of the string are printed, because there are only eight printable characters of the string so the field width of eight is sufficient. In the third case the control field, "%5s", is not sufficient to print eight characters, but C provides the necessary field width to print the entire string. In the fourth case the control field is "%12s", which is more than required to print eight characters. The printable characters are printed right-justified with four spaces to the left. In the last case the control field is "%-12s". This left-justifies the output of the string within the field width of 12. The blank spaces appear to the right of the string.

Using "%s" without a field width specification also left-justifies the string, however it does not provide for spaces before the next output.

Input/Output of Strings (*String I/O*) There are functions in the C library `stdio.h` header file specifically designed for the input and output of character strings. These functions are `gets()` and `fgets()` for input, and `puts()` and `fputs()` for output of character strings. These functions differ from the `scanf()` and `printf()` functions in that the string input and output (string I/O) functions only handle a single string or array of strings. These string I/O functions have fixed numbers of arguments, whereas `scanf()` and `printf()` have variable numbers of arguments.

Input of Strings The special functions available for the input of character strings in the C library `stdio.h` are `gets()` and `fgets()`.

Input Function `gets()` To input a character string from a keyboard, the `gets()` function is used. The general form of the `gets()` function is as follows:

```
gets(strname);
```

Where `strname` is a character string variable name. This function reads characters into the string variable `strname` until the new line character `'\n'` is entered. The character `'\n'` is not stored, but instead the function stores the null terminator `'\0'` in its place. The following example shows the code, the input, and the storage of a character string entered from a keyboard.

```
char  strname[15];

gets(strname);
```

The input string is " `hard disk`" with one leading blank in the front.

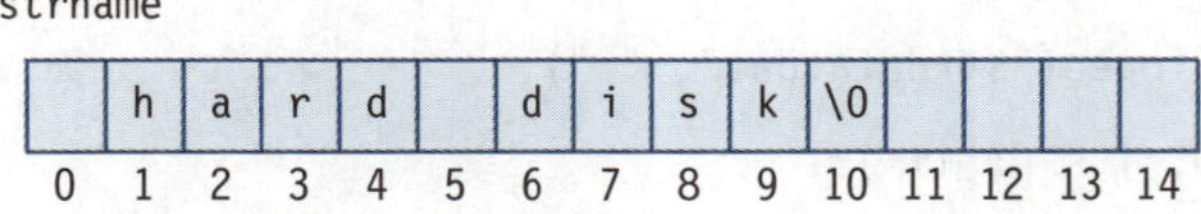

Notice that the string " hard disk" is stored with a null terminator at the end and the new line character is not stored. Unlike the `scanf()` function, which ignores any leading blanks, the `gets()` function reads the leading blanks, because it reads everything up to, and including, the line feed character.

> *Program Warning:* The input character string must not exceed the declared length of the string but must provide space for the null terminator. If the array exceeds the array bounds, the results may be unpredictable.

Input Function `fgets()` The input function `fgets()` is used to input strings from a data file. The `fgets()` function has three arguments. The general form of the function is as follows:

```
fgets(strname, strleng, infptr);
```

where `strname` is the string variable name,

`strleng` is the string length including the null terminator, and

`infptr` is the input file pointer.

The function `fgets()` reads the number of characters specified by the `strleng` field and stores them in the variable `strname` until the new line character or end-of-file (EOF) is encountered. The null terminator is automatically stored at the end of the string. If `fgets()` encounters the EOF, it is not stored. If the string has a new line character '\n', it is automatically stored preceding the null terminator. The following example shows the code and the input string.

```
#include <stdio.h>
#define  STRLENG  14

FILE  *infptr;

int main( )
{
    char  strname[STRLENG + 1];
    int i;

    infptr = fopen("strdata.dat", "r");

    for(i = 0; i < 4; i++)
    {
        fgets( strname, STRLENG, infptr);
    }
```

```
fclose( infptr );
return 0;
}
```

strdata.dat

```
ABXCLMKN\nXCNOPK\nLKRFTYGGHHIIJJKK\n
```

first string read	ABXCLMKN\n
second string read	XCNOPK\n
third string read	LKRFTYGGHHIIJJ
fourth string read	KK\n

Output of Strings There are special functions available exclusively for the output of strings in the C library `stdio.h`. These output functions are `puts()` and `fputs()`.

Function puts() The `puts()` function has only one argument, which is the string name. This function displays a string excluding the null terminator. This function also activates the `newline` character `'\n'`, so that any further output will be on the next line. The following example shows the output of a string stored in `strname`.

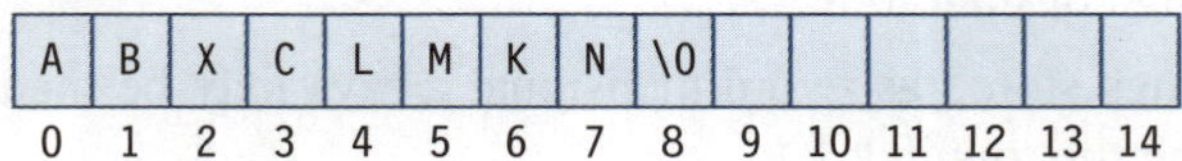


```
puts(strname);
puts(strname);
puts(strname);
```

The output is:

```
ABXCLMKN
ABXCLMKN
ABXCLMKN
```

Notice that there is no `newline` character specified in the output statement. The `puts()` function automatically shifts to a `newline` after output.

Function `fputs()` The `fputs()` function is used to write character strings to a data file. This function has two arguments, the first argument is the string name and the second argument is the output file pointer. The `fputs()` function writes the string into the data file excluding the null terminator. The `fputs()` function does not add a `newline` character to the end of the line. The general form of the function is:

```
fputs(strname, outptr);
```

Where `strname` is the string name and `outptr` is the output file pointer. The function arguments must be specified in that order.

9.2.4 Review Questions

1. Indicate whether the following statements are true or false.
   a. A string constant must be enclosed within single quotes.
   b. A string is a data type derived from the basic data type `char` and the derived data type array.
   c. Strings may be stored in two-dimensional arrays.
   d. Strings with large variability in their lengths may be efficiently stored in two-dimensional arrays.
   e. A string must have a null terminator at the end for it to be a character string.
   f. A string array may be initialized when it is declared by assigning a string constant to it.
   g. Strings stored as two-dimensional arrays may be manipulated by using the row index.
   h. The column index may be used to access a specific character in a particular indexed string.
   i. When a string array is initialized with a string constant when it is declared, a null terminator is automatically stored at the end of the string in storage.
   j. When individual characters are assigned to a string array, a null terminator must be explicitly assigned at the end.
   k. Input function `scanf()` may be used to input strings using either a control field of `"%c"` or `"%s"`.
   l. When control field `"%c"` is used in the `scanf()` input function the null terminator is automatically stored in the storage along with the string.

m. When control field `"%s"` is used in the `scanf()` input function the null terminator is not stored in the storage along with the string.

n. To control the number of characters in input using the `scanf()` function using the control field `"%s"`, one can specify the number of characters in the control string as `"%ns"` where `n` is the number of characters.

o. Output function `printf()` uses the control string `"%s"` to output the string. When the string is printed the null terminating character is not printed.

p. When control field `"%ns"` is used, the `n` characters of the string are printed left-justified within the field width of `n` positions.

q. When control field `"%-ns"` is used, the `n` characters of the string are printed right-justified within the field width of `n` positions.

r. The string input function `gets()` stores the line feed character `'\n'` along with the string.

s. The string input function `fgets()` inputs data from a data file and stores the new line character `'\n'` preceding the null terminator.

t. The string output function `fputs()` outputs data to a data file but does not insert a termination character.

2. Declare and initialize a string array by assigning individual characters of the following string constant:

   Amazon River

3. Write an input statement to input the following string using the `scanf()` function with the `"%ns"` control field. Assume the maximum string length of 50 characters including the null terminator.

   Atomic Weight

4. Write an output statement to print the string shown in Question 3.

5. Write a statement using the `fgets()` function to input the following strings from a data file `"string.dat"` into `str[3][20]`. Also show how the strings are stored.

   Computer Associates
   Communication Medium
   Electronic Media

6. Write statements using the `puts()` function to output strings stored in Question 5 with the third one double-spaced.
7. Write an output statement to print the strings stored in Question 5, right-justified.
8. Write an output statement to print the strings stored in Question 5, left-justified.

9.3 Strings and Functions

Strings are passed to a function by address, because they are stored as arrays. Arrays of strings declared as two-dimensional arrays are passed to functions the same way as numeric two-dimensional arrays are passed. These concepts are presented in the following sections.

9.3.1 Passing Strings to Functions

Character string arrays of any dimension may be passed to functions. The following code passes a single string to a function that prints it.

```
#include <stdio.h>
#define STRLNG  20

void funcoutput( char  [ ]);

int main(  )
{
    char  strname[STRLNG] = "CONSTANTINOPLE";

    funcoutput(strname);

    return 0;

}

void  funcoutput(char  strname1[ ])
{
    printf("String: %s\n", strname1);

    return;
}
```

The output from this code is as follows:

```
String: CONSTANTINOPLE
```

This string can be printed in a function that does not know either the length of the string or the size of the array because a null terminator identifies the end of the string.

An array of strings may be passed to a function as a two-dimensional array. The following code indicates how an array of strings is passed to a function.

```
#include <stdio.h>

#define NUMSTR  5
#define STRLNG  10

void  funcinput( char  [ ] [STRLNG] );
void  funcoutput( char  [ ] [STRLNG] );

int main( )
{
   char  strname[NUMSTR][STRLNG];

   funcinput(strname);
   funcoutput(strname);

   return 0;
}

void  funcinput( char  strname1[ ][STRLNG] )
{
   int  i;

   for(i = 0; i < NUMSTR; i++)
      gets(strname1[i]);

   return;
}

void  funcoutput( char  strname2[ ] [STRLNG] )
{
   int  i;

   for(i = 0; i < NUMSTR; i++)
   {
      puts(strname2[i]);
   }

   return;
}
```

Input Data:

```
AAAAAAAAA
XXXXXX
YY  YY  Y
PP KKKLLL
CCCCCCCCC
```

Output Data:

```
AAAAAAAAA
XXXXXX
YY  YY  Y
PP KKKLLL
CCCCCCCCC
```

In this program notice that the input function `fgets()` reads each string including the new line character `'\n'` and stores it in the storage allocated for an element of the string array `strname`. The `'\n'` is then replaced with `'\0'`. Also notice that the string I/O uses the name of the string array with the first dimension identifying the string. The string length STRLNG must be included in the function declarations and headers in order to determine where each string begins.

9.3.2 Review Questions

1. Indicate whether the following statements are true or false.
   a. A string may be passed to a function as a two-dimensional array.
   b. When an array of strings is passed to a function the second dimension is optional.
   c. When a string is passed to a function, only the characters preceding the null terminator are passed.
2. Write a function to input the following strings from the keyboard into a two-dimensional array. Show the function call.

   Computing Machinery
   Thunder Storms
   Forming Tools
   Earth-Moving Machinery
   XYZ Trucking Company

9.4 String Library Functions

In C there are no operators to manipulate strings because string is not a basic data type. However, C has a rich library of string manipulation functions. They are in the `string.h` library. This library must be included in the program in order to use these functions. The statement `#include <string.h>` will provide access to all of the string functions. The functions are used for the common operations of joining strings to build longer strings, comparing strings, copying strings, extracting substrings from strings, and extracting characters from strings. String functions are used to implement string operations in application software such as word processors, spreadsheets, and databases. A list of string functions are presented in Appendix B.

9.4.1 String Assignment

Because strings are stored as arrays, the value of one string cannot be copied to a different variable by an assignment. To assign a string variable to another string variable in such a way that there are two string variables with the same value, it is necessary to use the string copying function `strcpy`.

```
char  strname1[10] = "XXAABCL";
char  strname2[10];
```

Unless the `strcpy` function is used, `strname1` must be copied to `strname2`, element-by-element if `strname1` and `strname2` are to have the same values.

9.4.2 String Copy (strcpy)

The string copy function is used to copy a string value from one string variable to another string variable. There are two forms of the string copy function, one form with two arguments and another with three arguments.

First Form of the Function with Two Arguments The following code shows the use of the string copy function. This function can be used to assign the value of one string variable to another. It can also be used to replace partial strings.

```
char  strng1[ ] = "Storage Technology Today";
char  strng2[ ] = "Most Advanced";
```

Strings before Copy:

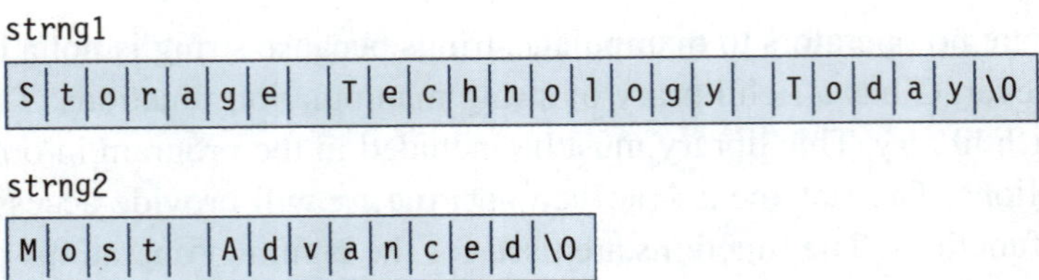

The string copy function is coded as follows:

```
strcpy( strngl, strng2);
printf("strngl: %s\n", strngl);
printf("strng2: %s\n", strng2);
```

The output after copy is as follows:

```
strngl: Most Advanced
strng2: Most Advanced
```

Strings after Copy:

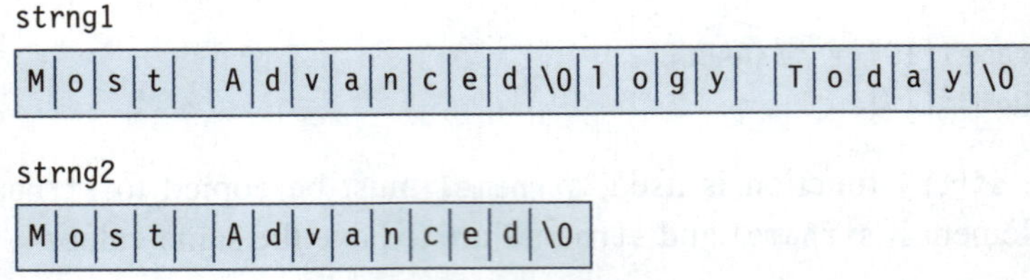

Notice that strng2 is copied into strngl. In doing this, make sure that the storage for strngl has enough storage to store the copied value. Also notice that when strng2 is copied into strngl the null terminator is also copied, which marks the end of the string. The characters beyond the null terminator in strngl cannot be accessed as a string after copying strng2 to strngl. Those characters are only accessible element-by-element.

Second Form of the Function with Three Arguments The second form of the string copy function has three arguments. The third argument specifies the number of characters to be copied. The use of such a function is as follows:

```
char  strngl[ ] = "Storage Technology Today";
char  strng2[ ] = "Most Advanced";
```

Strings before Copy:

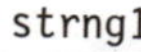

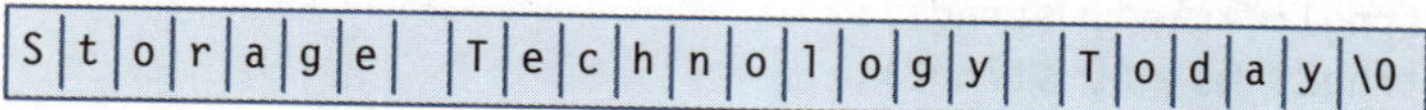

strng2

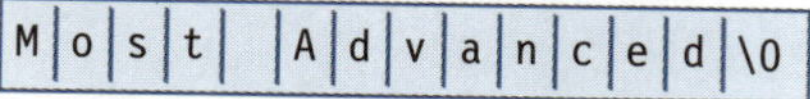

The string copy function is coded as follows:

```
strncpy( strng1, strng2, 4);
printf("strng1: %s\n", strng1);
printf("strng2: %s\n", strng2);
```

The output after copy is as follows:

```
strng1: Mostage Technology Today
strng2: Most Advanced
```

Strings after Copy:

strng1

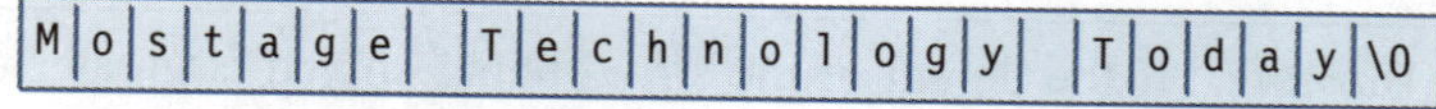

strng2

M o s t   A d v a n c e d \0

Notice that only the first four characters `"Most"` of `strng2` are copied into `strng1` and the rest of the characters in `strng1` are retained including the null terminator. If only part of `strng2` is copied, as in this example, then the null terminating character is not copied.

Strings before Copy:

strng1

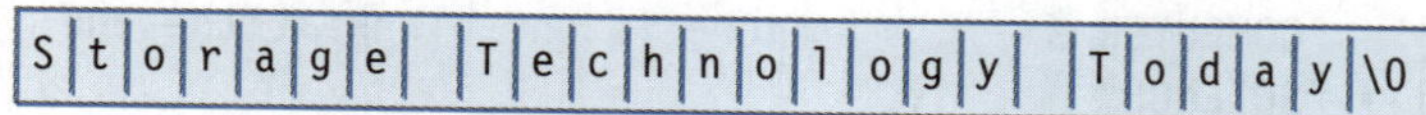

strng2

M o s t   A d v a n c e d \0

The string copy function is coded as follows:

```
strncpy( strng1, strng2, 15);
printf("strng1: %s\n", strng1);
printf("strng2: %s\n", strng2);
```

The output after copy is as follows:

```
strng1: Most Advanced
strng2: Most Advanced
```

Since the third argument is greater than the non-null terminating characters of `strng2`, the null character is copied along with the other characters.

Strings after Copy:

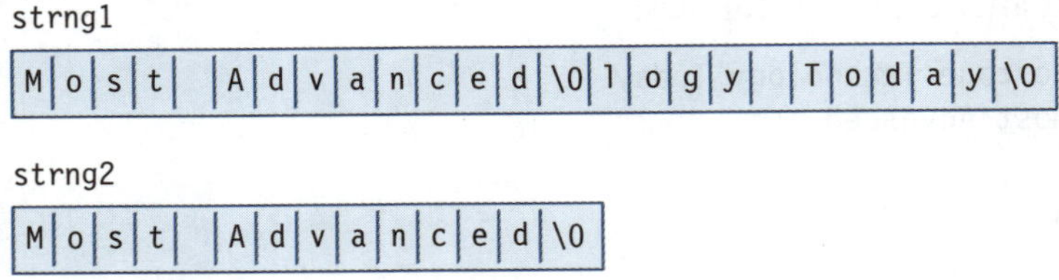

> *Program Warning:* If the length of the string being copied is greater than the size of the space it is copied to, the result may be unpredictable.

9.4.3 String Concatenation (`strcat`)

Joining two or more strings to build longer strings is called concatenation. This is a common operation used to construct sentences from words, paragraphs from sentences, pages from paragraphs, and so on. There are several operations in word processors where word, sentences, and paragraphs can be cut from one part of the text and can be pasted to another part of the text. There are two forms of the concatenation function, one with two arguments and one with three arguments. The following examples show the use of the string concatenation function.

```
strng1[20] = "COMPUTER "     /*  there is one blank at the end */
strng2[15] = "SCIENCE"
```

First Form of the Function with Two Arguments The general form is as follows:

```
strcat(strng1, strng2);
```

where strcat is the function name, strng1 is the first argument, and strng2 is the second argument. When this function is executed the entire string, strng2, is concatenated to the string value in strng1 and the resulting string is stored in strng1. For this operation to succeed, strng1 must have enough storage to store the concatenated string.

Strings before Concatenation:

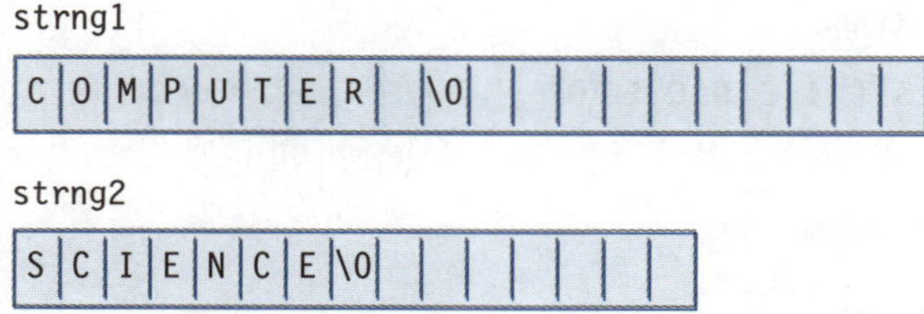

Strings after Concatenation:

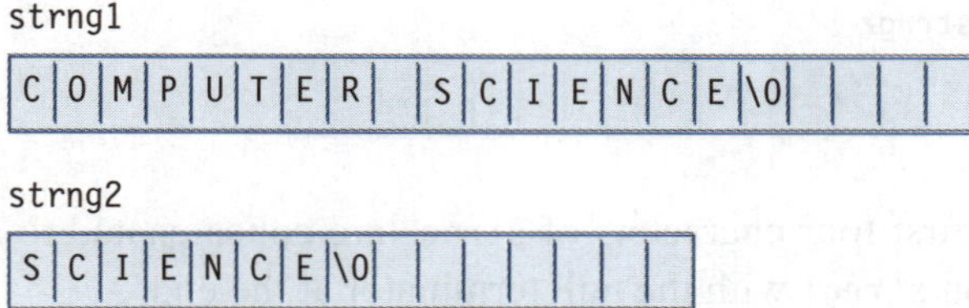

Notice that when strng2 is concatenated to strng1, the value of strng2, including the null terminator, is copied into strng1 beginning at the position of the null terminator in strng1.

Second Form of the Function with Three Arguments The general form is as follows:

```
strncat(strng1, strng2, n);
```

where strncat is the function name, strng1 is the first argument, strng2 is the second argument, and n is the third argument, which is an integer. When this function is executed the first n characters of strng2 are concatenated to strng1 and the resulting string is stored in strng1. Again the string variable strng1 must have enough storage to store the concatenated string. The null terminating character is automatically placed at the end of the concatenated string.

```
strncat(strng1, strng2, 4);
```

The first four characters of strng2 are concatenated to the value in strng1 and the resulting string is stored in strng1.

Strings before Concatenation:

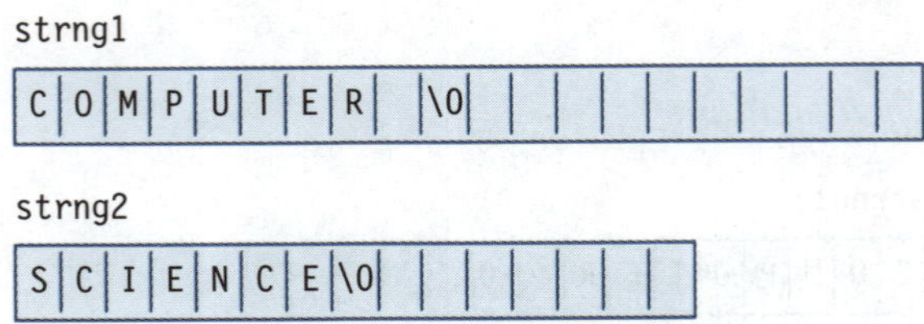

Strings after Concatenation:

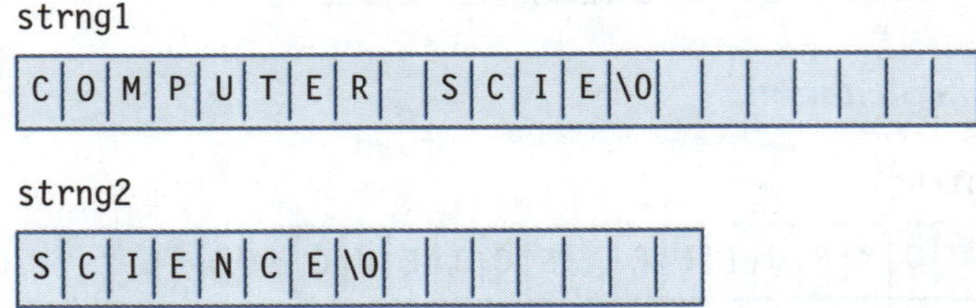

Notice that the first four characters of strng2 are concatenated to strng1 and the result is stored in strng1 with the null terminator at the end.

The following code concatenates four words to construct a sentence.

```
#include <stdio.h>
#include <string.h>
#define STRLNG  80

int main( )
{
    char  result[STRLNG] = "";
    char  word[STRLNG] ;
    int  i;
    for(i = 0; i < 4; i++)
    {
        gets(word);
        strcat(result, word);
        strcat(result, " ");
        printf("\n%s\n\n", result);
    }
}
```

Input and Output

`Computers`	input
`Computers`	result
`are`	input
`Computers are`	result
`electronic`	input
`Computers are electronic`	result
`machines.`	input
`Computers are electronic machines.`	final result

Input strings and concatenated strings are shown alternately with a carriage return. At the beginning, the result contains a null string. The final resulting string is "`Computers are electronic machines.`" The blank space must be included either at the end or at the beginning of each string to leave a space between the words in constructing sentences. This program may be generalized to concatenate any number of words to construct sentences.

9.4.4 String Comparison

In C, the characters are represented in the internal machine code by numbers, which are chosen so that A < B < C < D, the capital letters precede the lower case letters, and so on. Most computers use either the ASCII or the EBCDIC code. Thus, character strings can be compared for identity, variance, or alphabetical ordering by comparing their numeric representations. This is done using the string comparison functions found in the `string.h` library. There are two string comparison functions: `strcmp()` and `strncmp()`.

The `strcmp()` function has two arguments and returns an integer as follows:

```
int k;
k = strcmp(strng1, strng2);
```

In this case, the character strings `strng1` and `strng2` are compared character-by-character. When unequal characters are found the order of the two strings is determined. Based on the order of the two strings the comparison generates the following results:

$k > 0$	positive number	`strng1` after `strng2`
$k = 0$	positive number	`strng1` identical to `strng2`
$k < 0$	negative number	`strng1` before `strng2`

The following example shows the use of the `strcmp()` function:

```
int k;
srtng1[ ] = "comparison";
strng2[ ] = "communication";

k = strcmp(strng1, strng2);
```

strng1

c	o	m	p	a	r	i	s	o	n	\0

strng2

c	o	m	m	u	n	i	c	a	t	i	o	n	\0

Characters in `strng1` and `strng2` are compared character-by-character. In the fourth position `m` and `p` are unequal, and the numerical code for `p` is greater than the numerical code for `m`, which identifies `strng1` as after `strng2`. This comparison generates a number greater than zero, because `strng1` alphabetically follows `strng2`. The programmer may test the result of this comparison and execute a statement or statements as follows:

```
if(strcmp(strng1, strng2) > 0)
    statement1;
else
    statement2;
```

In this case since `strng1` is alphabetically later than `strng2`, `statement1` is executed.

This may also be implemented in another way by declaring an integer variable and assigning the result of the string comparison to this integer variable. The following code shows such an implementation.

```
int  c;
c = strcmp(strng1, strng2);
if(c > 0)
    statement1;
else
    statement2;
```

Since `strng1` is greater than `strng2`, the string comparison generates a number greater than zero and assigns that number to c and the relational expression `c > 0` is true in this case, therefore `statement1` is executed.

Sometimes only the first few characters in a string need to be compared, such as comparing dates in the form mm/dd/yyyy for month only. To take care of such cases there is another form of the string compare function. This function has three arguments. The following example shows the use of such a function.

```
srtngl[ ] = "comparison";
strng2[ ] = "communication";

k = strncmp(strngl, strng2, n);
```

strngl

c	o	m	p	a	r	i	s	o	n	\0

strng2

c	o	m	m	u	n	i	c	a	t	i	o	n	\0

Where n is the number of characters from the beginning of strng2 to be compared with strngl. If n is specified as 5 the string compare function is as follows:

```
strngl[ ] = "comparison"
strng2[ ] = "communication"

k = strncmp(strngl, strng2, 5);
```

In this case only the first five characters of strng2, which is "commu" are compared with the first five characters of strngl, which is "compa" to determine the relative magnitudes of strngl and strng2. Since the first three characters are the same in both strings and the fourth character is different and unequal, this is sufficient to determine the relative order of the strings. In this case character p in position four of strngl is greater than character m in position four of strng2, which determines that strngl alphabetically follows strng2. The function returns the positive value 4, to indicate where the strings differ.

If two strings differ in that one is longer than the other string as in the following example:

```
stringl[] = "add";
string[] = "addition";
```

then

```
k = strcmp(stringl, string2);
```

The function returns a negative value −4, as stringl precedes string2 alphabetically and they differ in the fourth position.

The string compare functions are used to compare strings in string sorting algorithms. String comparison is also used in searching a list of strings. Searching algorithms such as sequential search and binary search require the use of string comparison functions when the data consists of strings.

9.4.5 String Length (`strlen`) and Other String Functions (`strstr`, `strchr`, and `strrchr`)

There is a function that returns the length of a string. This function is `strlen`. There are functions that search for substrings in strings or search for specific characters in strings. These functions are `strstr`, `strchr`, and `strrchr`.

Function: `strlen` This function is commonly used to determine the length of a string. This is a single argument function. The argument may be a string variable or a string literal. The function `strlen` returns an integer that is the count of the number of characters in the string including embedded blanks and excluding the null terminator. The following code shows the use of this function.

```
#include <stdio.h>
#include <string.h>
int main( )
{
   char  strname1[20] = "COMPUTERS";
   char  strname2[20] = "GOLD LEAFLET";
   int   n;

   n = strlen(strname1);
   printf("The number of characters in strname1 is: %d\n", n);

   n = strlen(strname2);
   printf("The number of characters in strname2 is: %d\n", n);

   n = strlen("ELECTRONIC MACHINES");
   printf("The number of characters in string literal is: %d\n"
         , n);

   return 0;
}
```

The output is as follows:

```
The number of characters in strname1 is: 9
The number of characters in strname2 is: 12
The number of characters in string literal is: 19
```

Function: strstr The function strstr searches for substrings in strings. The following code shows the use of this function.

```
#include <stdio.h>
#include <string.h>

int main( )
{
   char  strname1[40] = "Computers are electronic machines";
   printf("strstr string is: %s\n", strstr(strname1, "elect"));
   printf("strstr string is: %s\n", strstr(strname1, "eletn"));

   return 0;
}
```

The output is as follows:

```
strstr string is: electronic machines
strstr string is:
```

Notice that the function strstr locates the substring "elect" in the string strname1 and returns all the characters beginning with the substring "elect" to the end of the string strname1. If there is no match the function returns null. Since there is no match in the second function for substring "eletn" the function strstr returns a null. The substring function strstr simply means "string in string." It locates the last occurrence of the substring in the string.

Function: strchr This string function searches for the first occurrence of a character in a string. The following code shows the use of this function.

```
#include <stdio.h>
#include <string.h>

int main( )
{
   char  strname1[40] = "Computers are electronic machines";

   printf("strchrstring is: %s\n", strchr(strname1, 'c'));
   printf("strchrstring is: %s\n", strchr(strname1, 'k'));

   return 0;
}
```

The output is as follows:

```
strchrstring is: ctronic machines
strchrstring is:
```

Notice that the first occurrence of character 'c' is in the word "electronic" because the "c" in "Computers" is capitalized. In the output, the string returned starts with the first occurrence of the character 'c' and continues to the end of the string. If the character is not present in the string, which is the case with the character 'k', the function strchr returns a null string.

Function: strrchr This function searches for the rightmost or last occurrence of a specified character in the string and returns the rest of the string. The following code shows the use of this function.

```
#include <stdio.h>
#include <string.h>

int main( )
{
char  strname1[40] = "Computers are electronic machines";

printf("strrchr string is: %s\n", strrchr(strname1, 'c'));
printf("strrchr string is: %s\n", strrchr(strname1, 'k'));

return 0;
}
```

The output is as follows:

```
strrchr string is: chines
strrchr string is:
```

Notice that the string returned is "chines", which is the string starting from the last occurrence of the character 'c' to the end of the string strname1. If the character is not in the string the function strrchr returns a null string.

9.4.6 Review Questions

1. Indicate whether the following statements are true or false.
   a. There are no operators in C to manipulate character strings.
   b. All string concatenation functions have three arguments.
   c. Two strings cannot be compared using a relational operator to generate a logical value.
   d. String comparison functions must be used to compare two strings to generate a value > 0, = 0, or < 0.
   e. The string copy function has two forms, one with two arguments and the other with three arguments.

f. In the function `strstr`, if the string is not found inside another string the function returns a null value.

g. In the function `strchr`, if the character is found, the position of the character is returned.

2. Write the code to concatenate the following strings to form a sentence.

   Germany
   is
   in
   Europe

3. Compare the following strings and show the logical value generated for the first string to be greater than the second string, the first string to be less than the second string, and the first string to be equal to the second string.

   computers *and* compute
   Value Line *and* limited value
   constant *and* concern
   Collaboration *and* Collaborator

4. Copy `str2` to `str1` and show what is in the storage before and after the copy.

a.
```
str1[ ] = "Vanlines used for transportation";
str2[ ] = "valentines day";
```
b.
```
str1[ ] = "computers";
str2[ ] = "electrons";
```
c.
```
str1[ ] = "communications";
str2[ ] = "electronic communications";
```

9.5 Sample Programs

These programs show the storage and manipulation of strings. These programs also show the sorting and searching operations performed on string arrays. The results are presented along with the code.

9.5.1 Creating a List of Names from a File

A list of names is stored in a file. Make a copy of the file, temporarily storing the names in an array.

Problem Write a program to input and store a list of names in an array, then output them.

Method

Declare an array for strings.

Use a function to input strings from a file into the array.

Use another function to write the strings to a second file.

Pseudocode

```
main:
  funcinput( )
  funcoutput( )
stop

funcinput:
  for each string
    input the string
  end for
  return
end

funcoutput:
  for each string
    output the string
  end for
  return
end
```

Program

```
/*********************************************************/
/*                                                       */
```

```
/*       main: Input and Store Strings                     */
/*                                                         */
/***********************************************************/
/*                                                         */
/*    Input Variables:                                     */
/*       name[NUM][STRLNG] - list of names                 */
/*                                                         */
/*    Output Variables:                                    */
/*       name[NUM][STRLNG] - list of names                 */
/*                                                         */
/*    Functions Called:                                    */
/*       funcinput( ) -  function to input names           */
/*       funcoutput( ) -  function to output names         */
/*                                                         */
/***********************************************************/

#include <stdio.h>
#include <string.h>

#define  NUM     10
#define  STRLNG  40

void  funcinput(char  [ ][STRLNG]);
void  funcoutput(char  [ ][STRLNG]);

int main( )
{
   char  name[NUM][STRLNG];

   funcinput(name);
   funcoutput(name);

   return 0;
}

/***********************************************************/
/*                                                         */
/*       funcinput - Input Strings                         */
/*                                                         */
/***********************************************************/
/*                                                         */
/*    Input Parameters:                                    */
/*       strname1[NUM][STRLNG] - array storage             */
/*                                                         */
/*    Output Parameters:          - list of names          */
/*       name[NUM][STRLNG]                                 */
```

```
/*    Data Files used:                                          */
/*       strinfile.dat  - input data file                       */
/*                                                              */
/****************************************************************/

void funcinput(char name1[ ][STRLNG])
{
    FILE  *inptr;
    int i;

    inptr = fopen("strinfile.dat", "r");

    for(i = 0; i < NUM; i++)
       fgets(name1[i], STRLNG, inptr);

    fclose(inptr);

    return;
}
/****************************************************************/
/*                                                              */
/*       funcoutput - Output the Character Strings              */
/*                                                              */
/****************************************************************/
/*                                                              */
/*    Input Parameters:                                         */
/*       strname[NUMS]{STRLNG] - list of names                  */
/*                                                              */
/*    Data Files used:                                          */
/*       stroutfile.dat  - output data file                     */
/*                                                              */
/****************************************************************/

void funcoutput(char  name1[][STRLNG])
{
    FILE  *outptr;
    int i;

    outptr = fopen("stroutfile.dat", "w");

    for(i = 0; i < NUM; i++)
       fputs(name1[i], outptr);

    fclose(outptr);

    return;
}
```

Input Strings

```
INDUSTRIAL CONSULTANTS
CHRISTMAS HOLIDAYS
THANKSGIVING HOLIDAY
INDEPENDENCE DAY
COMMUNICATIONS
LIONS CLUB
VALUE LINE
WALL STREET
SPRING BREAK
NEW YEARS EVE
```

Output Strings

```
INDUSTRIAL CONSULTANTS
CHRISTMAS HOLIDAYS
THANKSGIVING HOLIDAY
INDEPENDENCE DAY
COMMUNICATIONS
LIONS CLUB
VALUE LINE
WALL STREET
SPRING BREAK
NEW YEARS EVE
```

In this program every string is allocated 40 storage locations, which is specified in the second dimension of the string declaration. There is a large variation in the string lengths, hence wasted storage. In Chapter 10 we will show how to store character strings more efficiently.

9.5.2 Sorting a List of Names

Often there is a need for strings to be in alphanumeric order. In engineering applications the names of parts and part numbers of various machines such as machine shop machinery, airplanes, cars, farm equipment, and other engineering equipment may need to be stored in order.

Sorting Strings Stored as a List

Problem Write a program to sort the names stored in a list into alphabetical order. Print the unsorted and sorted names.

Method

Input the names into a list.
Output the unsorted names.
Sort the names in alphabetical order.
Output the sorted names.

Data

Input 11 names.

Pseudocode

```
main:
   call funcinput
   call funcsort
   call funcoutput
stop

funcinput:
   for each name
      input the name
   end for
   return
end

funcsort:
   for each name i
      for each name j   j > i
         if ( name j should be followed by name i)
            swap the names
         end if
      end for
   end for
end
```

funcoutput:
for each name
output the name
end for
return
end

Program

```
/**********************************************************/
/*                                                        */
/*    main: Sort the String in Alphabetical Order         */
/*                                                        */
/**********************************************************/
/*                                                        */
/*    Input Variables:                                    */
/*        name[NUMSTR][STRLNG] - list of names            */
/*                                                        */
/*    Output Variables:                                   */
/*        name[NUMSTR][STRLNG] - list of names            */
/*                                                        */
/*    Functions Called:                                   */
/*        funcinput - function to input the data          */
/*        funcsort  - function to sort the data           */
/*        funcout   - function to output the data         */
/*                                                        */
/*                                                        */
/*    Data Files Used:                                    */
/*        out.datsort - output data file                  */
/*                                                        */
/**********************************************************/

#include <stdio.h>
#include <string.h>

#define  NUMSTR  11
#define  STRLNG  40

void  funcinput(char [ ][STRLNG]);
void  funcsort(char  [ ][STRLNG]);
void  funcoutput(char [ ][STRLNG]);

FILE  *outptr;
```

```
int main( )
{
    char  strname[NUMSTR][STRLNG];

    printf("Unsorted names:\n\n");
    funcinput(strname);
    funcsort(strname);
    outptr = fopen("sortout.dat","w");
    printf("\nSorted names:\n\n");
    funcoutput(strname);

    return 0;
}
/*********************************************************************/
/*                                                                   */
/*   funcinput:  Input Strings into a List                           */
/*                                                                   */
/*********************************************************************/
/*                                                                   */
/*   Input Parameters:                                               */
/*       strname1[NUMSTR][STRLNG] - storage space                    */
/*                                                                   */
/*   Output Parameters:                                              */
/*       strname1[NUMSTR][STRLNG] - list of names                    */
/*                                                                   */
/*   Data Files Used:                                                */
/*       sortin.dat - input data file                                */
/*                                                                   */
/*********************************************************************/

void funcinput(char  strname1[ ][STRLNG])
{
    FILE  *inptr;
    int  i;

    inptr = fopen("sortin.dat", "r");

    for(i = 0; i < NUMSTR; i++)
    {
        fgets(strname1[i], STRLNG, inptr);
        printf("%s\n", strname1[i]);
    }

    fclose(inptr);

    return;
}
```

```
/***************************************************************/
/*                                                             */
/*    funcsort:  Sort Strings in a List                        */
/*                                                             */
/***************************************************************/
/*                                                             */
/*    Input Parameters:                                        */
/*       strname1[NUMSTR][STRLNG] - list of names              */
/*                                                             */
/*    Output Parameters:                                       */
/*       strname1[NUMSTR][STRLNG] - sorted list                */
/*                                                             */
/*                                                             */
/*                                                             */
/*                                                             */
/***************************************************************/
void funcsort( char  name1[ ][STRLNG])
{
   int  i, j;
   char  tempname[STRLNG];

   for(i = 0; i < NUMSTR - 1; i++)
  {
      for(j = i + 1; j < NUMSTR; j++)
      {
         if(strcmp(name1[i], name1[j]) > 0)
         {
            strcpy(tempname , name1[i]);
            strcpy(name1[i] , name1[j]);
            strcpy(name1[j] , tempname);
         }
      }
   }

   return;
}

/***************************************************************/
/*                                                             */
/*    funcoutput: Output the List of Strings                   */
/*                                                             */
/***************************************************************/
/*                                                             */
```

```
/*    Input Parameters:                                          */
/*       name1[NUMSTR][STRLNG] – list of names                   */
/*                                                                */
/*****************************************************************/
void funcoutput(char  name1[ ][STRLNG])
{
   int i;

   for(i = 0; i < NUMSTR; i++)
   {
      fputs(name1[i], outptr);
      printf(%s\n", name1[i]);
   }

   return;
}
```

Output

```
Unsorted names:

piston rings
bolts
nuts
clamps
valves
gaskets
oil pan
clutch
oil pump
water pump
oil

Sorted names:

bolts
clamps
clutch
gaskets
nuts
oil
oil pan
oil pump
piston rings
valves
water pump
```

9.5.3 Sequential Search of Parts List

In many engineering applications it may be necessary to search for part names, material types, components to assemble a machine part, materials for construction of a building, and so on. The method of search depends on whether or not the list is sorted. The search algorithms presented are linear search and binary search. The list to be searched must be sorted for the binary search.

Linear Search In the linear search we search for a particular part ID in a list of IDs. If the list contains the string, the search stops. If the ID is not contained in the list, then the entire list must be searched if the list has not been sorted. This program returns the position of the ID in the list or a negative number if the ID was not found.

Problem Write a program to search for IDs in a sorted list.

Method

Input the IDs from a data file.
Search for each ID wanted.
Stop.

Data Four IDs to be found and an inventory list.

Pseudocode

```
main:
  Input the sorted inventory list of IDs from a data file
  Input the number of IDs to be found
  For each ID wanted
     call funcinput
     For each ID to be found
         call funcsearch
          if found
              output ID, message, location
          else
              output ID, message
    End for
  End for
stop
```

```
funcinput:
   for each ID
      input ID from a file to a list
   end for
end

funcsearch:
   for each ID wanted
      position = −1
      for each IDj until ID found
         if ( IDj = search ID)
            save position
         end if
      end for
   end for
end
```

Program

```
/***********************************************************/
/*                                                         */
/*    main:  Search for a String in a Sorted List          */
/*                                                         */
/***********************************************************/
/*                                                         */
/*    Input Variables:                                     */
/*       ID[NUMSTR][STRLNG]  - list of ID's                */
/*                                                         */
/*    Output Variables:                                    */
/*       position            - location of the ID found    */
/*       IDS[STRLNG]         - ID found                    */
/*                                                         */
/*    Functions Called:                                    */
/*       funcinput  - function to input data               */
/*       funcsearch - function to search for the strings   */
/*                                                         */
/***********************************************************/

#include <stdio.h>
#include <string.h>

#define  NUMSTR  10
#define  STRLNG  8
```

```
void  funcinput(char [ ][STRLNG]);
int funcsearch(char [ ][STRLNG], char [], int);

FILE *ptrsr;
int main( )
{
    char  ID[NUMSTR][STRLNG];
    char  IDS[STRLNG];
    int numwanted, i, location;

    ptrsr = fopen("filesrchin.dat", "r");

    funcinput(ID);

    fscanf(ptrsr, "%d ", &numwanted);

    for(i = 0; i < numwanted; i++)
    {
        fscanf(ptrsr, "%7c", IDS);
        IDS[6] = '\0';

        location = funcsearch( ID, IDS, NUMSTR);

        if(location >= 0)
            printf("\n%s  is found in position:%4d\n", IDS, location +
                 1);
        else
            printf("\n%s is not found.\n", IDS);
    }

    return 0;
}
/************************************************************/
/*                                                          */
/*    funcinput: Input Sorted Names                         */
/*                                                          */
/************************************************************/
/*                                                          */
/*    Input Parameters:                                     */
/*        strname1[NUMSTR][STRLNG] - empty list             */
/*                                                          */
/*    Output Parameters:                                    */
/*        strname1[NUMSTR][STRLNG] - list of names          */
/*                                                          */
/*    Data Files:                                           */
/*        sortin.dat - input data file                      */
/*                                                          */
/************************************************************/
```

```
void funcinput(char  strname1[ ][STRLNG])
{
    FILE  *inptr;
    int  i;

    inptr = fopen("sortin.dat", "r");

    for(i = 0; i < NUMSTR; i++)
    {
        fgets(strname1[i], STRLNG, inptr);
    }

    fclose(inptr);

    return;
}

/***********************************************************/
/*                                                         */
/*   funcsearch:  Search the Strings in a Sorted List      */
/*                                                         */
/***********************************************************/
/*                                                         */
/*   Input Parameters:                                     */
/*       ID1[NUMSTR][STRLNG] - list of sorted names        */
/*       ID[STRLNG]          - string wanted               */
/*                                                         */
/*   Output Parameters:                                    */
/*       location            - location in list            */
/*                                                         */
/*                                                         */
/*                                                         */
/*                                                         */
/***********************************************************/

int funcsearch(char  ID1[ ][STRLNG],char ID[])
{
    int i, location = -1;
    for(i = 0; i < NUMSTR; i++)
    {
        if(strncmp(ID1[i],ID,strlen(ID)) == 0)
        {
            location = i;
            i = NUMSTR;
        }
    }

    return location;
}
```

Input File: "sortin.dat"

```
ABC245
BCX376
FDC245
IJH980
MKS567
RPM745
SFM289
SRK190
TML398
TEB278
```

Input File: "filesrchin.dat"

```
4
AXB367
FDC245
MKX675
TML398
```

Output:

```
AXB367 is not found

FDC245  is found in position:  3

MKX675 is not found

TML398  is found in position:  9
```

Chapter Summary

Strings in C are derived from the basic data type char. Strings are stored as arrays where each character of the string is stored as an element of the array. A string differs from an array of type char in that a string is always shorter than the size of the array it is stored in, and is followed by the null terminating character '\0'. String literals are enclosed in double quotation marks, for example "MARKET" is a string literal. A string with no characters enclosed between double quotation marks, for example "" is called a null string. Strings are declared as follows:

```
char  strname[10];
```

In this declaration statement, char is the basic character data type, strname is the string array name, and the number 10 in square brackets is the number of character locations allocated to store nine characters and the null terminating character.

Strings may be stored in the array strname either by initialization, or by assignment of individual characters, or as input from the keyboard or a data file. Initialization may be done at the time of declaration as follows:

```
char  strname[20] = "corner stone";
```

The string "corner stone" is stored with a null terminator '\0' at the end. The only way to assign a new value to a string is to use the library function strcpy or to assign individual characters to the array elements.

String elements may be assigned as individual characters as follows:

```
char  strname[20];
strname[0] = 'c';
strname[1] = 'o';
strname[2] = 'r';
strname[3] = 'n';
strname[4] = 'e';
strname[5] = 'r';
strname[6] = ' ';
strname[7] = 's';
strname[8] = 't';
strname[9] = 'o';
strname[10] = 'n';
strname[11] = 'e';
strname[12] = '\0';
```

Notice that one character is stored in each element location and an explicit null terminator is stored. Also, a blank ' ' is an actual character.

Input and output of strings may be accomplished by using formatted input and output scanf(), printf(), fscanf(), and fprintf() functions with the format control strings "%c" or "%s" for input and "%s" for output. There are special string I/O functions in C that are preformatted with fixed arguments. These functions are gets(), puts(), fgets(), and fputs().

For string manipulations there are no operators, but there is a rich collection of library functions contained in the header file <string.h>. These library functions are used for concatenating strings, comparing strings, copying strings, extraction of substrings, and searching for characters in strings.

Exercises

1. Write a `main` program and the following functions:

   A function to input the parts codes, the parts count, and the unit price for each of 20 parts, where the parts codes are character strings.

   A function to compute the inventory value for each part.

   A function to compute the total value of inventory.

   A function to output the part code, number of units, unit price, and total value of each part type in the form of a table. Also, output the total count of all parts and the grand total value of all parts.

2. Write a program to read words from a data file, stopping when a period is found. Print the list of words and concatenate them to form a sentence ending with a period.

3. Write a function that counts the non-overlapping occurrences of a substring in a string.

4. Write a program to plot the curve $f(x) = x^2 - 5x + 10$, $0 \leq x \leq t$. Use the character `'+'` to plot the curve.

5. Write a function to merge two sorted files of names and write the names to a new file, eliminating duplicates.

CHAPTER 10

Pointers and Dynamic Storage

Objectives

Understand the concept of pointer variables and their use in the manipulation of data and the dynamic allocation of storage space for data.

In the chapter on arrays, we saw that the array name has the address of the array as its value. Also the address operator "&" has been introduced and used in calls to system and user input functions so that the input data could be placed directly in the program variables. Now it is time to introduce a form of variables designed to have addresses as their values; these are the pointers. In C, data may be manipulated by using pointers whose values are the memory addresses of the data. Pointers are also used to implement the dynamic use of storage, allocating memory from free storage for various data structures such as arrays and strings whose size is not known in advance.

10.1 Concept of a Pointer

A pointer is a type of variable whose value is a memory address. A pointer variable is like any other variable except that it is used exclusively for storing memory addresses. A pointer variable is always allocated four bytes of storage, because the memory address stored in a pointer variable is an unsigned integer and may be a large number. The symbol "*" is used to indicate that a variable has an address as its value. A pointer variable can only "point to" a regular variable of a single data type.

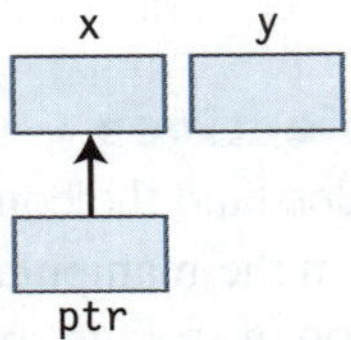


```
int x, y;        /* integer variable */
int *ptr;        /* pointer to an integer variable */
x = 256;         /* value of x is a number */
ptr = &x;        /* value of ptr is an address */
y = *ptr;        /* ptr is dereferenced to assign the value 256 to y */
*ptr = 37;       /* ptr is dereferenced to obtain an address in order to
                    store 37 in x*/
```

A pointer variable is declared as a pointer to the data type of the variable for which it is used. This is important because, when a pointer is used to access storage, the amount of storage accessed is based on the data type of the variable to which the pointer is pointing. The memory address of any type of variable may be assigned to an appropriate pointer variable by using an address operator "&". The symbol "*", which identifies `*aptr` as a pointer variable is interpreted differently on the left side and the right side of an assignment statement. On the left side, the value of the pointer variable is taken as the address of the memory location where the value from the right side is to be stored. In an assignment statement, the L-value (value on the left of the "=") is always an address. The R-value (on the right of the "=") is taken as the address where a data value is to be found and the data value is picked up. In both cases, as an L-value and as an R-value, the pointer is said to be dereferenced.

10.1.1 Pointers and Pointer Variables

There are as many data types of pointers as there are data types of variables. The built-in-data types of the variables are int, float, double, and char. The corresponding data types of pointer variables are int *, float *, double *, and char *. A pointer variable is declared as the same data type as the variable it will be pointing to, followed by an asterisk. A pointer variable that points to a character string is of data type char *. A pointer variable that points to an array is of the same data type as the array.

The general form of the declaration of a pointer variable is as follows:

```
data-type  *varptr;
```

```
where data-type      /* data type of the pointer variable, meaning  */
                     /* that it is a pointer to variables of the type */
                     /* data type */
      varptr         /* pointer variable name */
```

The following examples show the declaration and definition of pointer variables pointing to the data types int, float, double, and char.

```
int value1;                 int intarr[10];
int *ptrvalue1;             int *ptrintarr;

float value2;               float floatarr[15][27];
float *ptrvalue2;           float *ptrfloatarr;

double value3;              double dblarr[5];
double *ptrvalue3;          double *ptrdblarr;

char value4;                char str[40];
char *ptrvalue4;            char *ptrstr;
```

Storage of addresses in these pointer variables is shown in Figure 10.1.

Pointers to arrays and character strings will be discussed in Sections 10.3–10.5.

Notice that the pointer variables ptrvalue1, ptrvalue2, ptrvalue3, and ptrvalue4 are declared to be pointers to the data types of the variables value1, value2, value3, and value4, respectively. A pointer variable must be defined before using it. A pointer variable is defined by assigning the address of a variable

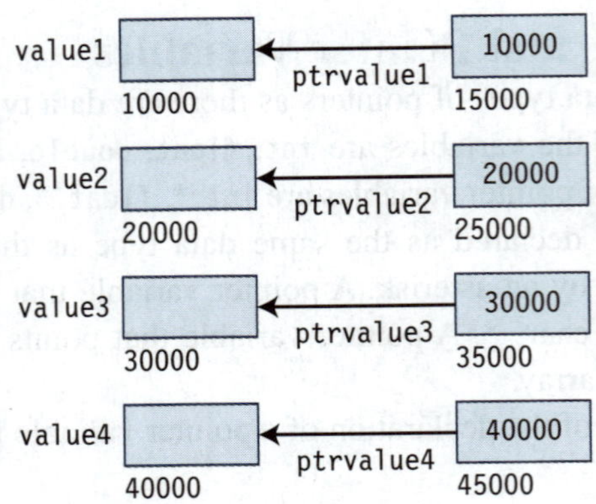

Figure 10.1 Variables and their pointers

of the right data type to the pointer. The following assignments define the pointer variables for the corresponding variables of `value1`, `value2`, `value3`, and `value4`.

```
ptrvalue1 = &value1;
ptrvalue2 = &value2;
ptrvalue3 = &value3;
ptrvalue4 = &value4;
```

The memory locations may be accessed by using the variables `value1`, `value2`, `value3`, and `value4` or dereferencing the pointers `ptrvalue1`, `ptrvalue2`, `ptrvalue3`, and `ptrvalue4`. The following code shows the declaration of the variables and the pointers, and the assignment of the memory addresses of the variables to the pointers. Then the assignment of values to variables can be either through variable names or through the pointers.

```
     int  value1;
     int  *ptrvalue1;
     ptrvalue1 = &value1;
     value1 = 458;
or   *ptrvalue1 = 458;

     float  value2;
     float  *ptrvalue2;
     ptrvalue2 = &value1;
     value2 = 645.89;
or   *ptrvalue2 = 645.89;
```

```
    double  value3;
    double  *ptrvalue3;
    ptrvalue3 = &value3;
    value3 = 84.9765;
or  *ptrvalue3 = 84.9765;

    char  value4;
    char  *ptrvalue4;
    ptrvalue4 = &value4;
    value4 = 'A';
or  *ptrvalue4 = 'A';
```

Notice that Figure 10.2 shows that the values are stored in the variables by assigning values to the variables `value1`, `value2`, `value3`, and `value4`, or through their pointers `ptrvalue1`, `ptrvalue2`, `ptrvalue3`, and `ptrvalue4`.

The values stored in the variables `value1`, `value2`, `value3`, and `value4`, may be accessed and printed as follows:

```
printf("Values using variable names: %d  %f  %f  %c\n",
    value1, value2, value3, value4);
```

or

```
printf("Values using pointers: %d    %f    %f    %c\n",
   *ptrvalue1, *ptrvalue2, *ptrvalue3, *ptrvalue4);
```

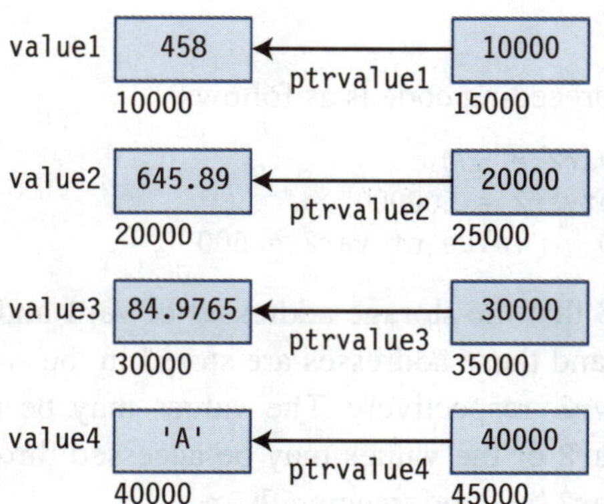

Figure 10.2 Variables, pointers, and the storage of values

The output is as follows:

```
Values using variable names: 450  645.890000    84.976500   A
Values using pointers: 450  645.890000    84.976500   A
```

Notice that the pointer variables must be dereferenced to access the values from the memory locations of the variables `value1`, `value2`, `value3`, and `value4`.

The following simple program shows the use of pointers to access data.

```
#include <stdio.h>

int main( )
{
    int var1, var2;          /* variable declaration:   var1 and var2 */
    int *ptvar1, *ptvar2; /* pointer variable declaration:   ptvar1,
                             ptvar2 */

    ptvar1 = &var1;          /* storing the address of var1 in pointer
                                variable ptvar1 */
    ptvar2 = &var2;          /* storing the address of var2 in pointer
                                variable ptvar2 */

    var1 = 100;              /* value of 100 is stored in variable var1 */
    var2 = 500;              /* value of 500 is stored in variable var2 */

    printf("var1 = %d    var2 = %d\n", var1, var2);
    printf("ptvar1 = %d    ptvar2 = %d\n",     ptvar1, ptvar2);
    printf("value of var1= %d     value of var2 = %d\n",
            *ptvar1, *ptvar2);

    return 0;
}
```

The output from the preceding code is as follows

```
var1 = 100          var2 = 500
ptvar1 = 10000      ptvar2 = 50000
value of var1 = 100     value of var2 = 500
```

Notice in Figure 10.3 that the storage addresses of `var1` and `var2` are 10,000 and 50,000, respectively and these addresses are stored in the storage of pointer variables `ptvar1` and `ptvr2`, respectively. The values may be accessed through the variables `var1` and `var2` or the values may be accessed through the pointer variables `ptvar1` and `ptvar2` by dereferencing them.

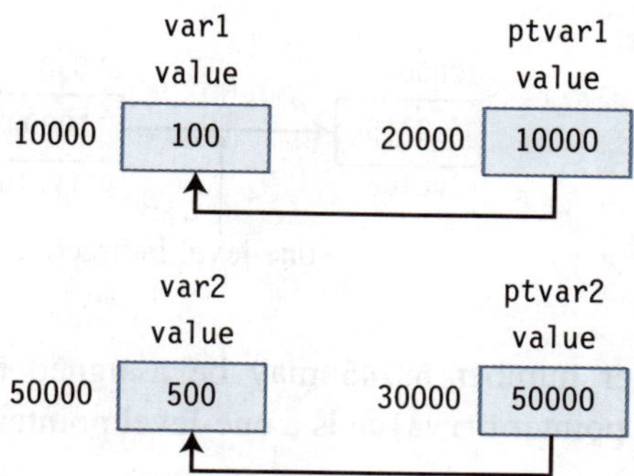

Figure 10.3 Variables and pointer variables

Since pointer variables are variables, they can point to different variables at different times, but they must always point to variables of the same data type.

In the following code:

```
int x, y;
int *ptr;

x = 312;
y = -74;
ptr = &x;
printf("%d  ", *ptr);
ptr = &y;
printf("%d", *ptr);
```

the output is: `312 -74`

The pointer variable `ptr` is first assigned the address of `x` so that it points to the value `312` stored in `x`. And then it is assigned the address of `y` so that it points to the value `-74` stored in `y`.

10.1.2 One Level and Multilevel Indirection

The value stored in a variable may be accessed using its name or its memory address. Accessing a variable using its pointer is called one level indirection. The following example shows code of one-level indirection.

One-Level Indirection

```
int  value;
int  *ptrvalue;

ptrvalue = &value;
*ptrvalue = 68745;
```

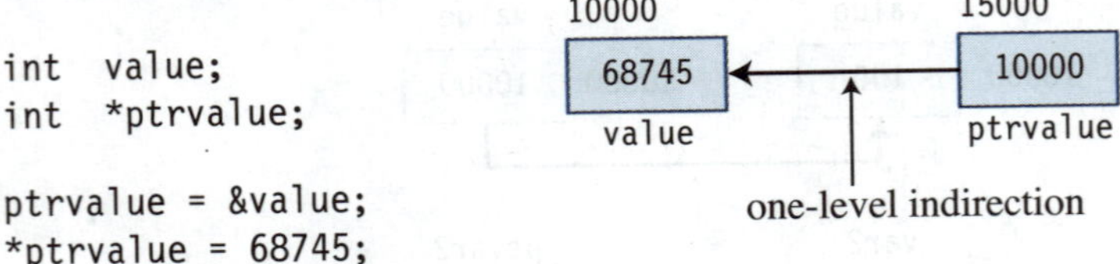

Notice that the integer number 68745 may be assigned by dereferencing the pointer ptrvalue. The pointer ptrvalue is a one-level pointer.

Multilevel Indirection A pointer variable may point to any value except a constant. A pointer variable may even point to another pointer. This means that a pointer variable may point indirectly to an ordinary variable.

ptra → ptrx → x;

This is called multilevel indirection. The storage of a variable may be accessed by using multilevel pointers. The following code shows the declaration of multilevel pointers and storage access using multilevel pointers.

```
int  value;

int  *ptrvalue1,  **ptrvalue2,  ***ptrvalue3;
```

Here ptrvalue1 can only point to a variable of type int, ptrvalue2 can only point to a variable of type int *, and ptrvalue3 can only point to a variable of type int **.

The following example shows the organization of multilevel pointers.

```
ptrvalue1 = &value;
ptrvalue2 = &ptrvalue1;
ptrvalue3 = &ptrvalue2;
```

Notice that the addresses of the variables must be assigned to the pointer variables before a value may be accessed through the pointer variables ptrvalue1, ptrvalue2, and ptrvalue3.

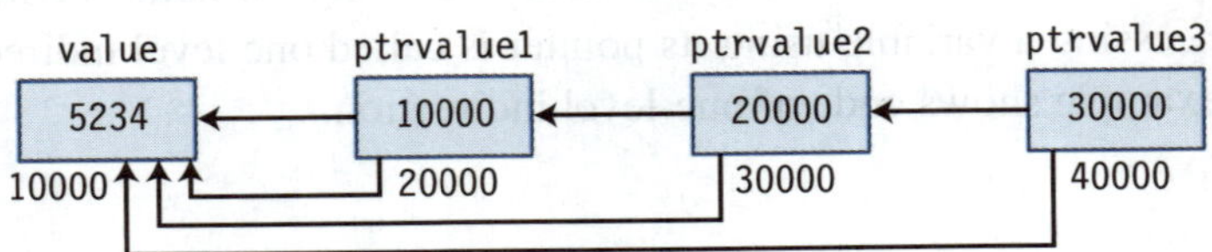

The integer number 5234 stored in the variable value may be accessed using any of the pointers ptrvalue1, ptrvalue2, or ptrvalue3. The following print statements show the addresses and values of the variables.

```
printf("The address of the variable value: %u \n", &value);
printf("The contents of the variable value: %d \n", value);
printf("The address of the pointer ptrvalue1:%u \n", &ptrvalue1);
printf("The contents of the pointer ptrvalue1:%u \n", ptrvalue1);
printf("The address of the pointer ptrvalue2:%u \n", &ptrvalue2);
printf("The contents of the pointer ptrvalue2:%u \n", ptrvalue2);
printf("The address of the pointer ptrvalue3:%u \n", &ptrvalue3);
printf("The contents of the pointer ptrvalue3:%u \n", ptrvalue3);
```

The output is as follows:

```
The address of the variable value: 10000
The contents of the variable value: 5234
The address of the pointer ptrvalue1: 20000
The contents of the pointer ptrvalue1: 10000
The address of the pointer ptrvalue2: 30000
The contents of the pointer ptrvalue2: 20000
The address of the pointer ptrvalue3: 40000
The contents of the pointer ptrvalue3: 30000
```

Notice that "%u" used in the output control string is the control specification for the output of unsigned integers.

The contents of the variable value may be accessed using pointers ptrvalul, ptrvalue2, and ptrvalue3 as follows:

```
printf("The contents of the variable value:%d \n", value);
printf("The contents of value by pointer ptrvalue1:%d \n", *ptrvalue1);
printf("The contents of value by pointer ptrvalue2:%d \n", **ptrvalue2);
printf("The contents of value by pointer ptrvalue3:%d \n",***ptrvalue3);
```

The output is as follows:

```
The contents of the variable value: 5234
The contents of value by pointer ptrvalue1: 5234
The contents of value by pointer ptrvalue2: 5234
The contents of value by pointer ptrvalue3: 5234
```

The integer value 5234 printed by using the variable value is by direct access. The value 5234 printed using ptrvalue1 uses one-level indirection. The value 5234 printed using `ptrvalue2` uses two levels of indirection. The value 5234 printed using `ptrvalue3` uses three levels of indirection.

10.1.3 Review Questions

1. Indicate whether the following statements are true or false.
   a. A pointer variable must be declared specific to the data type of the variable whose address will be assigned to it.
   b. A pointer has as its value a signed integer that is allocated four bytes of storage.
   c. To assign the address of a variable to a pointer variable an address operator must be used.
   d. To access the contents of a variable through a pointer variable, the pointer variable must be assigned the memory address of the variable first, and then the pointer must be dereferenced.
   e. A pointer variable has no data type of its own.
   f. A pointer variable must contain an unsigned integer so it cannot point to a character string.
2. What is printed in the following code segments?
   a.
```
int x;
int  *xptr;
xptr = &x;

x = 3950;
printf("%u\n", xptr);
printf("%d\n", x);
printf("%d\n", *xptr);
```

xptr: 80000 [56000] → x: 56000 [3950]

   b.
```
int x;
int *xptr1, **xptr2;
xptr1 = &x;
xptr2 = &xptr1;
x = 8550;
printf("%d\n", xptr1);
printf("%d\n", x);
printf("%d\n", *xptr1);
printf("%d\n", *xptr2);
printf("%d\n", x);
printf("%d\n", **xptr2);
```

x: 4000 [8550] ← xptr1: 5000 [4000] ← xptr2: 6000 [5000]

10.2 Address and Pointer Arithmetic

Arithmetic operations must not be performed on addresses using pointer variables as operands unless one operand is a pointer variable that points to an array and the other operand is either an integer or a pointer to the same array. Then addition or subtraction can sometimes be performed. Since a pointer is a memory address, it cannot be misused to access unauthorized memory locations. The memory system has protection mechanisms built into it to protect it from unauthorized access. Programmers must be careful when performing arithmetic operations on array pointer variables to make sure not to access a memory location outside the array the pointer variable accesses.

10.2.1 Arithmetic Operations on Pointers

There are rules to follow in performing arithmetic operations on pointer and pointer variables.

Yes: A pointer can be subtracted from another pointer.

For example: If `ptr1` and `ptr2` are two pointers, `(ptr1 - ptr2)` is a legal operation. However, it is meaningless unless the two pointers point to elements of the same array. The parentheses are necessary as pointer arithmetic is not associative.

This type of operation gives the offset between two pointers and should only be used when `ptr1` and `ptr2` point to different elements of the same array.

The difference between the two pointers will give the number of cells between the two pointers. This is a meaningful operation in manipulating arrays.

Yes: A scalar constant can be added to a pointer variable.

For example: If `ptr` is a pointer variable, `(ptr + 25)` is a legal operation. This offsets the pointer `ptr` by `25` cells of the data type to which the pointer `ptr` points. The result is meaningless unless it points to an element of the same array. The parentheses are necessary as pointer arithmetic is not associative.

No: A scalar constant cannot be assigned to a pointer variable.

For example, if ptr is a pointer variable, an assignment such as (ptr = 2895) is an illegal operation. The computer reserves the right to assign memory addresses.

No: A pointer cannot be added to another pointer.

For example, if ptr1 and ptr2 are two pointers, the operation (ptr1 + ptr2) is illegal. The sum of two addresses is meaningless.

No: A pointer cannot be divided by another pointer.

For example, if ptr1 and ptr2 are two pointers, (ptr1 / ptr2) is an illegal operation. The quotient of two addresses is meaningless.

No: A pointer cannot be multiplied by another pointer.

For example: If ptr1 and ptr2 are two pointers, (ptr1 * ptr2) is an illegal operation. The product of two addresses is meaningless.

> *Program Warning:* Use pointer variables carefully. Do not access unauthorized memory locations.

10.2.2 Dereferencing of Pointers

```
int arr[5];
int *ptrarr;
ptrarr = arr; /* assigns address of arr to ptrarr */

arr[2] = 7;
or ptrarr[2] = 7;
```

The value of the array name arr is already an address so as an R-value, it can be stored directly in ptrarr without the address operator "&". Then the array name and the pointer both have the address of the array. The difference is that the array name is a constant and cannot be changed, while the pointer is a variable. When a pointer variable has the array address as its value, it does not need to be dereferenced but can be used the same way the array name is used.

```
arr[2] /* is the element offset by 2 from the beginning of the array */
ptrarr[2] /* is the element offset by 2 from the beginning of the same
             array */
```

Pointer variables must be dereferenced when they are used in place of ordinary variables for instance.

```
int  x;
int  *ptr;

...= x;             or   ...= *ptr;
x = ...             or   *ptr = ....

printf("%d", x);    or   printf("%d", *ptr);
func(x);            or   func(*ptr); call by value
```

Pointer variables are not dereferenced when they are used in context where the address operator "&" would be used with an ordinary variable, for example.

```
int  x;
int  *ptr;

scanf("%d", &x);    or   scanf("%d", ptr);
  ..= &x;           or   ..= ptr;
```

Pointer variables are also dereferenced when they point to arrays, but they are used subscripted or in array arithmetic just as array names are, for instance.

```
int  arr[10];
int  *ptr;

arr[6] = ..         or   ptr[6] = ....;
..= arr[6];         or   ..=  ptr[6];
```

10.2.3 Review Questions

1. Indicate whether the following statements are true or false.
   a. A pointer variable must not be assigned a scalar constant.
   b. A pointer variable can be added to another pointer variable.
   c. A pointer variable can be subtracted from another pointer variable.
   d. A pointer variable can be used to change the address of an array.
   e. Two pointer variables can point to the same variable.
2. Write code to prove or disprove the statements of Question 1.

10.3 Pointers and Arrays

Since an array name is an address constant, the array name may be used as an array pointer to access the array. Once the beginning address of the array is known, then it is relatively simple to access and manipulate the elements of the array sequentially through a pointer variable. This is true for numeric and character data stored in one-dimensional and multidimensional arrays.

10.3.1 One-Dimensional Arrays

An array name is an address constant, as shown below. An array name may be assigned to a pointer variable and the elements of the array may be accessed sequentially or randomly using the pointer variable. The following code shows the declaration of an array `ar`, an array pointer `arptr`, and an assignment of the array name to a pointer variable `arptr = ar`.

```
int  ar[10];
int  *arptr;

arptr = ar;
```

Assuming that the address of the array `ar` is 1000, the storage is allocated as follows:

	←4 bytes→		
ar[0]		1000	← address of the array ar is the value of ar
ar[1]		1004	
ar[2]		1008	
ar[3]		1012	
ar[4]		1016	
ar[5]		1020	
ar[6]		1024	
ar[7]		1028	
ar[8]		1032	
ar[9]		1036	

Notice that the address of the first element of the array starts at the byte location 1000 and the address of each of the other elements is four bytes higher. The addresses of the other elements for the example shown are as follows:

`ar + 0` or `aptr + 0` is 1000 or `&ar[0]` is 1000

`ar + 1` or `aptr + 1` is 1004 `&ar[1]` is 1004

ar + 2 or aptr + 2 is 1008	&ar[2] is 1008
ar + 3 or aptr + 3 is 1012	&ar[3] is 1012
ar + 4 or aptr + 4 is 1016	&ar[4] is 1016
ar + 5 or aptr + 5 is 1020	&ar[5] is 1020
ar + 6 or aptr + 6 is 1024	&ar[6] is 1024
ar + 7 or aptr + 7 is 1028	&ar[7] is 1028
ar + 8 or aptr + 8 is 1032	&ar[8] is 1032
ar + 9 or aptr + 9 is 1036	&ar[9] is 1036

If the array name is incremented by one, the address is incremented by the cell size of each element. Notice that the address is incremented by four because for the int data type each cell is allocated four bytes of storage. The cell size increments for each of the data types are shown as follows:

DATA TYPE	CELL SIZE
int	4 bytes short int or short is 2 bytes
float	4 bytes
double	8 bytes
char	1 byte

The following code and output shows the array address for the array ar as shown.

```
#include <stdio.h>
int main( )
{
    int ar[10];
    int *arptr;

    arptr = ar;

    printf("Address using the array name: %u\n", ar);
    printf("Address of the first element: %u\n", &ar[0]);
    printf("Address using the pointer variable: %u\n", arptr);
    return 0;
}
```

The output is as follows:

```
Address using the array name: 1000
Address of the first element: 1000
Address using the pointer variable: 1000
```

Notice that ar is the name of the array and as it is a constant it cannot be changed. The name of the array ar may be stored in a pointer variable arptr of the data type of the array it points to. The pointer variable arptr may be changed by incrementing it or by decrementing it to access the array elements.

The following code and output shows the value of the first element of the array ar.

```
ar[0] = 57;
arptr = ar;
printf("value using the array name: %d\n", *ar);
printf("value using the first element: %d\n", ar[0]);
printf("value using the pointer variable: %d\n", *(arptr + 0));
printf("value using the pointer variable: %d\n", arptr[0]);
```

The output in each case is 57.

The following code and output show the value of the last element of the array ar.

```
ar[9] = -43;
arptr = ar;
printf("value using the array name: %d\n", *(ar + 9));
printf("value using the last element: %d\n", ar[9]);
printf("value using the pointer variable: %d\n", *(arptr + 9));
printf("value using the pointer variable: %d\n", arptr[9]);
arptr = arptr + 9;
printf("Value using the pointer variable: %d\n", *arptr);
```

The output in each case is -43.

Input/Output Using an Array Pointer The following examples show input and output using address arithmetic for the data type int. The array name, being an address constant, is itself a pointer and can be used to input the data into an array. The array pointer for each element must be dereferenced to output the array.

Input/Output of Integer Numbers The storage of integer numbers using the array name ar is as follows:

ar + 0	45
ar + 1	56
ar + 2	76
ar + 3	93
ar + 4	15

Standard Input/Output

```
#include <stdio.h>
int main( )
{
    int  i, ar[5];

    printf("Input the elements of the array:\n");

    for(i = 0; i < 5; i++)
    {
        scanf("%d", (ar + i));  /* (ar + i) is an address */
    }
    printf("Output the elements of the array:\n");

    for(i = 0; i < 5; i++)
    {
        printf("%d     ", *(ar + i));
    }

    return 0;
}
```

The data is entered from the terminal keyboard and stored in the memory allocated for the array and output as follows:

```
Input the elements of the array:
45   56   76   93   15
Output the elements of the array:
45   56   76   93   15
```

The previous example locates elements of an array giving the offset, a starting value of zero for the beginning of the array, then incrementing the offset. The pointer variable can be incremented instead, as in the following example.

```
#include <stdio.h>
int main( )
{
    int i, ar[5];
    int  * arptr;

    printf("Input the elements of the array:\n");
    arptr = ar;
    for(i = 0; i < 5; i++)
    {
        scanf("%d", arptr);
        arptr++;
    }
```

```
    printf("Output the elements of the array:\n");
    arptr = ar;
    for(i = 0; i < 5; i++)
    {
        printf("%d    ", *arptr);
        arptr++;
    }

    return 0;
}
```

Notice that the elements of the array are accessed sequentially by incrementing the pointer variable `arptr`. To access them a second time for output, the pointer must be reset back to the beginning of the array.

Manipulation Using Array Offset The elements of a one-dimensional array may be manipulated by using an array pointer. The elements of the array can be accessed individually by specifying the pointer of a specific element or they can be accessed sequentially starting from a pointer to the first element of an array or starting from a pointer to the last element of the array.

Array Assignment The values of the elements of an array can be copied from one array to another array using array arithmetic within a `for` loop. The index of the `for` loop may be used as an offset. Incrementing the pointer by one increments the address by the number of bytes allocated for each cell of the data type of the array. When numeric arrays are copied, if the data type of the source and the destination array do not match a data type, conversion will occur. The following code shows the assignment of array `a` to array `b` using the array name and an offset.

```
#include <stdio.h>
int main( )
{
    int  i;
    float a[5], b[5];

    for(i = 0; i < 5; i++)
    {
        *(b + i) = *(a + i);
    }

    return 0;
}
```

The values contained in the arrays a and b before the assignment and after the assignment are as follows:

Before

	a		b
a + 0	12.75	b + 0	uuuuuu
a + 1	18.34	b + 1	uuuuuu
a + 2	9.85	b + 2	uuuuuu
a + 3	23.78	b + 3	uuuuuu
a + 4	16.96	b + 4	uuuuuu

After

	a		b
a + 0	12.75	b + 0	12.75
a + 1	18.34	b + 1	18.34
a + 2	9.85	b + 2	9.85
a + 3	23.78	b + 3	23.78
a + 4	16.96	b + 4	16.96

Notice that the address must be dereferenced to access the contents of the elements of the arrays and must also be dereferenced to obtain storage for the value being copied. Rather than using an offset, the pointer variables could have been incremented as in the following example.

The array a can be copied into array b in reverse order by using address offset. The address must be dereferenced. The following code shows such a copy.

```
#include <stdio.h>

int main( )
{
    int  i, j;
    float a[5], b[5];
    float  *ptra, *ptrb;

    ptra = a;
    ptrb = &b[4];

    for(i = 0; i < 5; i++)
    {
        *bptr = *aptr;
        aptr++;
```

```
        bptr--;
    }
    return 0;
}
```

Before

a[0]	12.75	b[0]	uuuuuu
a[1]	18.34	b[1]	uuuuuu
a[2]	9.85	b[2]	uuuuuu
a[3]	23.78	b[3]	uuuuuu
a[4]	16.96	b[4]	uuuuuu

After

a + 0	12.75	b + 0	16.96
a + 1	18.34	b + 1	23.78
a + 2	9.85	b + 2	9.85
a + 3	23.78	b + 3	18.34
a + 4	16.96	b + 4	12.75

Notice that the elements of array a are copied into array b in the reverse order.

Arithmetic Operations Using Array Offset Arithmetic operations such as addition, subtraction, multiplication, and division may be performed using array offset. The following program code shows the addition operation using array offset.

```
#include <stdio.h>
int main( )
{
    int ar[5] = {5, 8, 4, 6, 12};
    int br[5] = {4, 9, 2, 3, 15};
    int i,  cr[5];

    for (i = 0; i < 5; i++)
    {
        *(cr + i) = *(ar + i) + *(br + i);
    }

    printf("The elements of array cr are: ");
    for (i = 0; i < 5; i++)
    {
        printf("%d    ", *(cr+i));
    }
```

```
    return 0;
}
```

The output is as follows:

```
The elements of array cr are: 9    17    6    9    27
```

Notice that the elements of the array ar are added to the elements of the array br element-by-element and the result is stored in the array cr. Similarly other arithmetic operations may be performed using array offsets.

10.3.2 Increment and Decrement Operations

Increment and decrement operations on pointers can be used in manipulating numeric arrays and character string arrays without using subscripts. Array pointers to one-dimensional and multidimensional arrays can be incremented to access the elements of the array sequentially from the beginning of the array. The array elements can be accessed sequentially from the end of the array by decrementing the array pointer by one from the end of the array. The increment and decrement operators and operations were presented in Chapter 2. The following code shows the increment operation for a pointer to a string.

```
#include <stdio.h>

int main( )
{
    char  strname[10] = "ELECTRON";
    char  *strptr;
    int  i;

    strptr = strname;

    for(i = 0; i < 8; i++)
    {
        printf("%c ", *strptr);
        strptr++;

    }

    return 0;
}
```

The output is as follows:

```
E L E C T R O N
```

Note that the array name `strname` cannot be used in the way `strptr` is used to scan the array, because the array name is a constant and cannot be changed.

> *Program Warning:* If an array name is assigned to a pointer variable, and if the pointer variable is incremented, it no longer points to the beginning of the array; the pointer must be reset to point to the beginning of the array.

10.3.3 Two-Dimensional Arrays

Two-dimensional arrays are stored by rows in sequential memory locations. The beginning memory location at which an array starts in memory is stored in the array name as its value.

An array name can be used with an offset to process a two-dimensional array. The following example shows array offsets and the storage for the array.

Assume the array address starts at location 1000. Then the addresses of the elements are incremented by four because the `int` data type is allocated a cell size of four bytes. But if there are four columns, the addresses of the rows are incremented by 16 because the four elements of each row require 16 bytes of storage. The address of the first row is `a + 0`, the address of the second row is `a + 1`, and the address of the third row is `a + 2`. The addresses corresponding to these rows are 1000, 1016, and 1032.

	Index	Address	Row addresses
Array pointer a →	a[0][0]	**1000**	**a + 0**
row 0	a[0][1]	1004	
	a[0][2]	1008	
	a[0][3]	1012	
	a[1][0]	**1016**	**a + 1**
row 1	a[1][1]	1020	
	a[1][2]	1024	
	a[1][3]	1028	
	a[2][0]	**1032**	**a + 2**
row 2	a[2][1]	1036	
	a[2][2]	1040	
	a[2][3]	1044	

The address of the first row is a + 0, which is 1000.

The addresses of the elements of row0 are given as follows:

```
(*(a + 0) + 0)    1000
(*(a + 0) + 1)    1004
(*(a + 0) + 2)    1008
(*(a + 0) + 3)    1012
```

The addresses of the elements of row1 are given as follows:

```
(*(a + 1) + 0)    1016
(*(a + 1) + 1)    1020
(*(a + 1) + 2)    1024
(*(a + 1) + 3)    1028
```

The addresses of the elements of row2 are given as follows:

```
(*(a + 2) + 0)    1032
(*(a + 2) + 1)    1036
(*(a + 2) + 2)    1040
(*(a + 2) + 3)    1044
```

Notice that the row address indicates the beginning of the row. To get to the addresses of the elements of the row, the row address must be dereferenced and the element offset added.

To access the contents of the storage of an element of the array using an array address with row and column offsets, it must be dereferenced again. The following example shows the *double dereferencing* of two-dimensional arrays.

The contents of the elements of row0 are given as follows:

```
*(*(a + 0) + 0)
*(*(a + 0) + 1)
*(*(a + 0) + 2)
*(*(a + 0) + 3)
```

The contents of the elements of row1 are given as follows:

```
*(*(a + 1) + 0)
*(*(a + 1) + 1)
*(*(a + 1) + 2)
*(*(a + 1) + 3)
```

The contents of the elements of row2 are given as follows:

```
*(*(a + 2) + 0)
*(*(a + 2) + 1)
*(*(a + 2) + 2)
*(*(a + 2) + 3)
```

Input/Output by Array Offset Input/output of the data values into the storage allocated for two-dimensional arrays can be accomplished using nested `for` loops and array offsets. The array name indicates the beginning address of an array. It is efficient to input the data into a two-dimensional array in row order, because the storage is allocated in row order. The output may be displayed by row and column format. The following example shows the input/output of data by rows.

Input Data

```
28.5     46.3     57.9     72.6
14.3     15.7     31.4     19.4
48.9     13.9     90.6     57.8
```

The values are stored as follows:

Row	Element	Value	Address	Pointer
row0	a[0][0]	28.5	**1000**	**a + 0**
	a[0][1]	46.3	1004	
	a[0][2]	57.9	1008	
	a[0][3]	72.6	1012	
row1	a[1][0]	14.3	**1016**	**a + 1**
	a[1][1]	15.7	1020	
	a[1][2]	31.4	1024	
	a[1][3]	19.4	1028	
row2	a[2][0]	48.9	**1032**	**a + 2**
	a[2][1]	13.9	1036	
	a[2][2]	90.6	1040	
	a[2][3]	57.8	1044	

This data is entered from the input device keyboard, as it is shown by rows, and output is displayed on the monitor, which is a standard output device. The code to input and output this data using array offset is as follows.

Nested for loops are used to increment the array pointer by rows and by columns.

```
#include <stdio.h>
#define  IMAX  3
#define  JMAX  4
int main( )
{
    float  values[IMAX][JMAX];
    int  i, j;
    for(i = 0; i < IMAX; i++)
    {
        for(j = 0; j < JMAX; j++)
        {
          scanf("%f", (*(values + i) + j));
        }
    }
    for(i = 0; i < IMAX; i++)
    {
        for(j = 0; j < JMAX; j++)
        {
            printf("%5.2f    ", *(*(values + i) +j));
        }
        printf("\n");
    }

    return 0;
}
```

As the computer does not check array bounds, if an array is stored in row-major order, an array pointer and a single for loop can be used to input or output all elements of the array sequentially as in the following:

```
float values[IMAX][JMAX];
float *ptr, valuesend, i;
```

```
ptr = values;
valuesend = IMAX * JMAX;
for(i = 0; i < valuesend; i++)
    scanf("%f", *(ptr + i));
ptr = values;
for(i = 0; i < valuesend; i++)
    printf("%5.2f    \n", *(*(ptr+i)));
```

Pointer variables have unsigned integers as their values, so they can be used for loop control. Note however, that this does not provide any line control for printing or displaying a two-dimensional array by rows.

Dereferencing of Pointers to Arrays To access the contents of a memory location to which a pointer is pointing, the pointer must be dereferenced. For example if `ptr` is a pointer pointing to a memory location, then to access the contents of that memory location `*ptr` must be used. The `*ptr` will access the contents of the memory location, which may be used for computation or for output. When dealing with numeric and character string arrays, each cell of the array may be accessed by dereferencing and then either incrementing or decrementing the pointer.

Dereferencing and Incrementing a Pointer The following code shows the dereferencing and incrementing of an array pointer. The code also shows the effect of pre-increment or post-increment. The order of precedence of the dereferencing and increment operators is from right to left.

```
int  numbers[10] = {12,25,67,85,90,72,94,86,9,18};
```

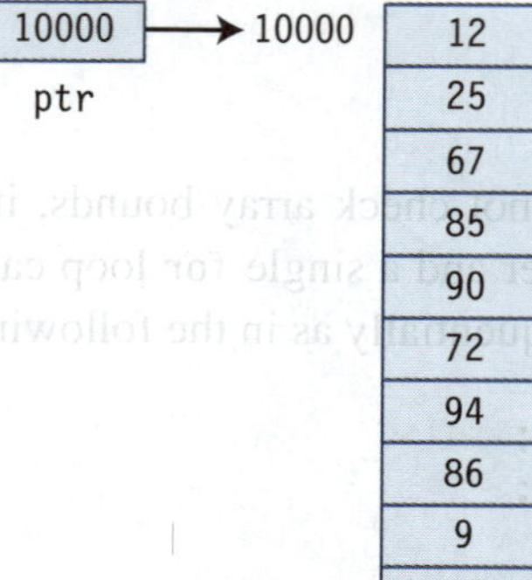

```
#include <stdio.h>
int main( )
{
    int  numbers[10] = {12,25,67,85,90,72,94,86,9,18};
    int  *ptr;

    ptr = numbers;
    printf("The address printed is: %d\n", ptr);
    printf("The number printed is: %d\n", *ptr);
    printf("The number printed is: %d\n", *++ptr);
    printf("The number printed is: %d\n", ++*ptr);
    printf("The number printed is: %d\n", *ptr++);
    printf("The number printed is: %d\n", *ptr);
    printf("The number printed is: %d\n", *++ptr);

    return 0;
}
```

`*++ptr` is the same as `*(++ptr)`

`++*ptr` is the same as `++(*ptr)`

`*ptr++` is the same as `*(ptr++)`

The output is as follows:

```
The address printed is: 10000
The number printed is: 12    /* pointer is used */
The number printed is: 25    /* pointer is incremented then used */
The number printed is: 26    /* array element is incremented */
The number printed is: 26    /* pointer is used then incremented */
The number printed is: 67    /* pointer is used */
The number printed is: 85    /* pointer is incremented then used */
```

Notice that the address of the numeric array is printed as 10000 in the first print statement. In the second print statement the number 12 is printed by *ptr, which is simply dereferencing the first memory location. In the third print statement the pointer is incremented and then dereferenced, which prints number 25. In the next print statement the pointer is dereferenced, which points to the location containing the number 25 and the value 25 is incremented by 1 so that 26 is printed. The number 26 replaces the number 25 in memory. In the next statement, the number 26 is printed, having been changed from 25, and the post-increment is not effective in that print statement. In the print statement `*ptr++`, the increment occurs after number `26` is printed. In the next statement, number `67` is printed because of the post-increment in the previous print statement. In the last statement the pointer is incremented and the number `85` is printed.

10.3.4 Review Questions

1. Indicate whether the following statements are True or False.
   a. An array name is an address variable.
   b. The address of an array is found as either the array name or the explicit address of the first element of the array.
   c. The elements of a one-dimensional array may be accessed by dereferencing the array name since it is a pointer.
   d. The elements of a two-dimensional array may be accessed by dereferencing the offset address only once.
   e. To input data to an array using a pointer variable, the name of the array may be used to specify the address of the array elements.
   f. Arithmetic operations may be performed by using an array name without dereferencing the name.
   g. An array can be copied by assigning the address to a pointer variable.
2. Write the code to input and output the data into the following one-dimensional array by using the pointer variables.

```
int a[10], *ptra;
```

3. Write the code to input and output the data into the following two-dimensional array by using the array names plus offsets.

```
float b[20][20]
```

10.4 Dynamic Storage and Arrays

Dynamic storage is simply storage that is allocated while a program is executing. It is allocated from the available part of computer memory after the program determines how much storage is needed. Storage that is declared in a program is called static storage. It is allocated before the program is executed. When the size of an array is not known in advance, or storage is at a minimum so space must be reused, the function `calloc()` from the `stdlib.h` library may be used to allocate dynamic storage and assign an array pointer to it. The function `calloc()` allocates a block of storage until it is released by the `free()` function or the program terminates. The `calloc()` function is passed arguments telling it how many data cells are needed, and what their size is, in bytes. The address returned by the `calloc()` function must be converted to the declared data type of the pointer to which the address is assigned.

10.4.1 One-Dimensional Arrays

Dynamic storage for a one-dimensional array is allocated as follows:

```
int *xptr;
xptr = (int *) calloc (5, sizeof(int));
```

This call on `calloc()` asks for five data cells of four bytes each. The address that is returned is converted to data type `int *`.

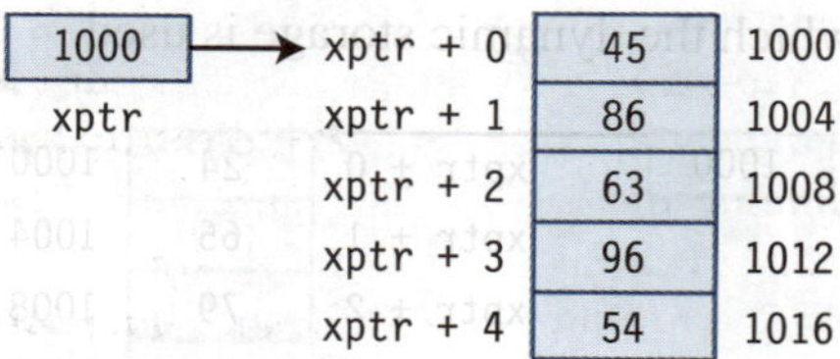

The following code shows the dynamic storage allocation and prints the address of each element of the array.

```
#include <stdio.h>
#include <stdlib.h>
int main( )
{
    int  i, *arptr, arsize;

    scanf("%d", &arsize);

    arptr = (int *)calloc(arsize, sizeof(int));

    printf("The memory addresses are: ");
    for(i = 0; i < arsize; i++)
    {
        printf("%d    ", arptr);
        arptr++;
    }

    return 0;
}
```

The output is as follows:

```
The memory addresses are: 1000    1004    1008    1012    1016
```

The function `calloc()` is in the `<stdlib.h>` standard library, which must be included. The call to the function `calloc()` tells it how many array elements to allocate and the size of each element. It does not tell it the data types of the elements so the pointer returned by `calloc()` must be cast to a pointer to integers.

Notice that `arptr` is a pointer variable of type `int *`. The storage location of a block of storage is assigned and stored in `arptr`. Each cell of this block of storage is four bytes long. The pointer `arptr` contains the beginning address, or the first cell address, of this particular piece of dynamic storage.

Standard Input/Output The following example shows input and output using the dynamic storage allocation function. The storage is allocated during execution and the beginning address of the storage is assigned to a pointer variable of the specific data type for which the dynamic storage is used.

xptr		Value	Address
1000	xptr + 0	24	1000
	xptr + 1	65	1004
	xptr + 2	79	1008
	xptr + 3	94	1012
	xptr + 4	98	1016

If the array size is five then five cells of the storage size of the `int` data type are allocated and the address of the storage is assigned to the pointer variable `xptr`. The following code shows the dynamic storage allocation and the input into and output from an array using a dynamic pointer.

```
#include <stdlib.h>

int main( )
{
    int  i, *xptr, SIZE;

    scanf("%d", &SIZE);
    xptr = (int *) calloc(SIZE, sizeof(int));

    for(i = 0; i < SIZE; i++)
    {
        scanf("%d", xptr);
        xptr++;
    }
```

```
    xptr = xptr - SIZE;
        printf("The array output is:\n");
    for(i = 0; i < SIZE; i++)
    {
        printf("%d.  %d   ", i + 1,*xptr);
        xptr++;
    }

    return 0;
}
```

The data is entered from a terminal keyboard. The first number entered is the size of the array, the number of data values to be entered. The storage is allocated and the data values are entered and stored in the storage allocated using the dynamic storage pointer `xptr`. The output is displayed on the monitor. The data entered is as follows:

```
5   45   86   63   96   54
```

The array output is:

```
1.  45   2.  86   3.  63   4.  96   5.  54
```

Notice that the memory address of the storage allocated is stored in the dynamic pointer variable `xptr`. Any time the dynamic pointer is incremented by one the address is incremented by the number of bytes allocated for the storage cell of the data type specified for the dynamic pointer. At the end of the `for` loop the pointer variable `xptr` no longer points to the beginning of the array. It can be reset back to the beginning address using `xptr = xptr - size`. The dynamic pointer must point to the beginning of the array before the output loop.

Free Statement The memory allocated by the dynamic memory allocation function `calloc()` can be deallocated or freed by using the `free()` function. The general form of the function is as follows:

```
free(aptr);
```

where `aptr` is the pointer to the dynamic storage. Once the `free` statement is executed the pointer `aptr` is disconnected from the memory and becomes undefined. The memory will be deallocated or freed. This allows the space to be reused for another large array. If dynamic storage is allocated with a loop, or local to a function, the storage should be freed before a new block of storage is assigned to the pointer. Otherwise the program has storage that cannot be accessed.

Array Assignment The values stored in one dynamic array may be copied into another dynamic array. A for loop may be used to copy one array to another array one element at a time. When numeric arrays are copied, if the data type of the source and the destination array do not match, a proper data type conversion within the rules of the C language will occur. The following code shows the assignment of one array to another array using dynamic pointers.

```
#include <stdlib.h>
#define ARMAX  5

int main( )
{
    int i;
    float    *aptr,  *bptr;
    aptr= (float*) calloc(ARMAX, sizeof(float));
    bptr = (float *) calloc(ARMAX, sizeof(float));

    *(aptr + 0) = 12.75;
    *(aptr + 1) = 18.34;
    *(aptr + 2) = 9.85;
    *(aptr + 3) = 23.78;
    *(aptr + 4) = 16.96;
    for(i = 0 ; i < ARMAX; i++)
    {
       *bptr++ = *aptr++;
    }
    bptr = bptr – ARMAX;
    aptr = aptr – ARMAX;

    return 0;
}
```

The values contained in the dynamic arrays with pointers aptr and bptr before and after the assignment is as follows:

Before

aptr + 0	12.75	bptr + 0	uuuuuu
aptr + 1	18.34	bptr + 1	uuuuuu
aptr + 2	9.85	bptr + 2	uuuuuu
aptr + 3	23.78	bptr + 3	uuuuuu
aptr + 4	16.96	bptr + 4	uuuuuu

After

aptr + 0	12.75	bptr + 0	12.75
aptr + 1	18.34	bptr + 1	18.34
aptr + 2	9.85	bptr + 2	9.85
aptr + 3	23.78	bptr + 3	23.78
aptr + 4	16.96	bptr + 4	16.96

If two copies of a single array are needed, the array must be copied element-by-element. The assignment statement `bptr = aptr` cannot be used as it results in two pointers to a single array and loses the block of storage assigned to `bptr`.

10.4.2 Two-Dimensional Arrays

Dynamic storage for two-dimensional arrays may be allocated using the dynamic storage allocation function `calloc()` from the standard library. A block of storage is allocated from the free store. The block of storage is divided into the number of cells specified in the `calloc()` function argument. The storage address is assigned to a pointer, which is of the same data type as the data to be stored in the free storage allocated by the `calloc()` function. The `calloc()` function does not distinguish between one- and two-dimensional arrays. It simply allocates the amount of storage requested.

For an array `arry[IMAX] [JMAX]` the call to `calloc()` should have the form

```
calloc(IMAX * JMAX, sizeof(data type of arry));
```

The storage is allocated as follows:

```
#include <stdlib.h>
#define IMAX  3
#define JMAX  4

int main( )
{
    int  *arptr;       /* dynamic pointer declaration */

    arptr = (int *) calloc(IMAX * JMAX, sizeof(int));
    .   .
    return 0;
}
```

Storage allocation:

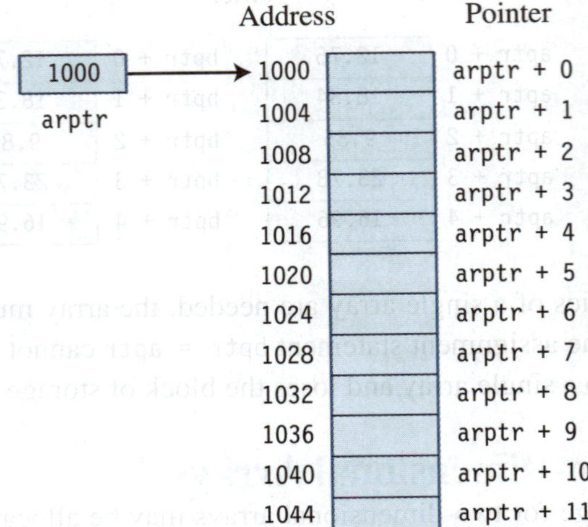

Notice in this case a block of storage is allocated. The block consists of `IMAX * JMAX` storage cells and the size of each cell is the number of bytes of the data type for which the dynamic storage is allocated. For `int` and `float` data types the cell size is four bytes, but for data type `double` the cell size is eight bytes. The dynamic pointer `arptr` points to the block of storage containing 12 storage cells of `int` data type where each cell is four bytes long. The input/output, assignment, and arithmetic operations may be performed on dynamic storage through the dynamic pointer `arptr`. The way the storage is handled in the program determines whether the array is one- or two-dimensional and which elements belong to the same row or the same column of the two-dimensional array.

If `aptr` points to the beginning of a block of dynamic storage that will hold 12 elements, then the storage can be interpreted as a 3 × 4 array as follows:

aptr + 0 aptr + 3
aptr + 4 aptr + 7
aptr + 8 aptr + 11

In this, the element $A_{2,3}$ has the address `aptr + JMAX * (i – 1) + (j – 1)` wherein `i` is 2 and `j` is 3 and `JMAX` is 4.

The same block of storage can be interpreted as a 4 × 3 array, a 2 × 6 array, or a 6 × 2 array. If the array is processed sequentially by rows, it is not necessary to calculate the addresses of the individual elements or distinguish between the rows. If the pointer is passed to a function, the function definition can structure it so as to use subscripts or row offsets. Storage can also be allocated in a function and the address returned to the calling routine.

Input/Output by Dynamic Pointer Input data values may be entered through the standard keyboard or from a data file. It is natural to input the data by rows into the dynamic storage to keep track of the row and column configuration of the data. Nested `for` loops are used to keep the row and column configuration of the block of storage allocated by using dynamic storage. The following data and the code show the use of dynamic storage to store two-dimensional arrays to input and output. When dynamic storage is being used, the size of the array may be part of the run-time data.

It is natural to enter data from a keyboard by rows and to display it on a monitor by rows. This can be done using a dynamic pointer. Nested `for` loops are used to increment the dynamic pointer. The code to input and output this data using a dynamic array pointer is as follows:

```
#include <stdio.h>
#include<stdlib.h>

int main( )
{
    float  *valptr, *arptr;
    int  i, j, IMAX, JMAX;
    scanf("%d  %d", &IMAX, &JMAX);

    arptr = (float *) calloc(IMAX * JMAX,
              sizeof(float));

    valptr = arptr;

    for(i = 0; i < IMAX; i++)
    {
        for(j = 0; j < JMAX; j++)
        {
            scanf("%f", valptr);
            valptr++;
        }
    }
```

```
    printf("Data Output to the Monitor\n\n");

    valptr = arptr;

    for(i = 0; i < IMAX; i++)
    {
        for(j = 0; j < JMAX; j++)
        {
            printf("%5.1f     ", *valptr);
            valptr++;
        }
        printf("\n");
    }

    return 0;
}
```

Input data:

```
3       4
28.5    46.3    57.9    72.6
14.3    15.7    31.4    19.4
48.9    13.9    90.6    57.8
```

The values are stored in dynamic storage as follows:

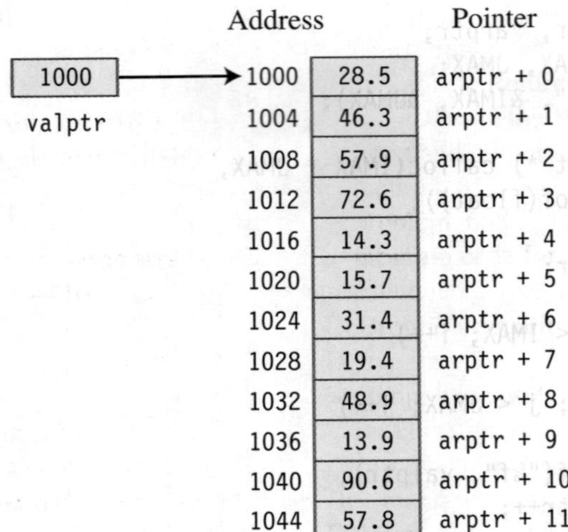

Data Output to the Monitor:

```
28.5    46.3    57.9    72.6
14.3    15.7    31.4    19.4
48.9    13.9    90.6    57.8
```

Notice that the dynamic pointer is incremented and dereferenced to access the contents of the storage cells without regard to the array structure. The structure is imposed by the use of nested `for` loops and the new line field specification.

Since dynamic storage does not have any implicit structure, it is possible to impose more than one structure on it. The 12 elements in the preceding example can be treated as a one-dimensional array of 12 elements to simplify the input and then as a two-dimensional array of three rows and four columns to make the output readable. It would even be possible to see it as three vectors of four elements each and assign the vector names as follows:

```
int *x, *y, *z;

x = arptr;
y = arptr + 4;

z = arptr + 8;
```

10.4.3 Review Questions

1. Indicate whether the following statements are true or false.
   a. The dynamic storage allocation functions are in the `stdlib.h` header file in C.
   b. To allocate a block of storage at the time of execution of the program, dynamic storage allocation functions are used.
   c. The pointer to the dynamic storage returned by `calloc()` must be cast to the data type it is pointing to.
   d. When a dynamic pointer is incremented by one, the address is incremented by the number of bytes of the data type it is pointing to.
   e. When a dynamic pointer is incremented, the address of the dynamic pointer variable will change.
2. Write the code to declare a dynamic pointer and allocate storage to store a one-dimensional array of 200 elements of data type `int`.

3. Write the code to declare a dynamic pointer and allocate storage to store a one-dimensional array of 80,000 elements of data type `float`.
4. Write a program to declare a dynamic pointer and allocate storage to store a two-dimensional array of 50 $\times$ 60 of data type `float`. Also write the code to input data to the dynamic array and output the data from the dynamic array.

10.5 Character Strings and Pointers

Character strings may be manipulated using pointers and dynamic pointers. Dynamic pointers are used when the character strings vary greatly in length. Storage for variable length strings may be allocated by using the `malloc()` function from the `stdlib.h` library header file.

The dynamic storage allocation function `malloc()` is a single-argument function, the argument being the number of bytes needed to store a single variable, whereas the dynamic storage allocation function `calloc()` is a two-argument function with the first argument being the number of storage cells and the second argument being the size of each storage cell. The function `malloc()` is generally used to allocate storage for strings.

10.5.1 Dynamic Storage of Character Strings

Smooth arrays are not efficient for storing strings, which vary greatly in their lengths. They should be allocated storage from the free store with their addresses assigned to a pointer variable of type `char`.

The following code shows the allocation of storage from free store by using the dynamic storage allocation function `malloc()`. In order to allocate exactly the right amount of storage for each string, the string must be input into a static `char` array of maximum size, the actual length of the string determined, the right amount of storage allocated using the dynamic storage allocation function `malloc()`, and the character string copied into it. To keep track of all of the strings, their pointers are stored in a character pointer array. The function `malloc()` is used rather than `calloc()` to store a character string because a character string may be manipulated as a unit.

```
#include <stdio.h>
#include <stdlib.h>
#include <string.h>
```

```
#define NUMSTR  4
#define STRLNG  80

int main( )
{
    int  i;
    char  strname[STRLNG];    /* an input buffer for the string */
    char  *strptr[NUMSTR];    /* an array of string pointers */

    printf("Input strings:\n");
    for(i= 0; i< NUMSTR; i++)
    {
        gets(strname);
        strptr[i] = (char *)malloc(strlen(strname) + 1);
        strcpy(strptr[i],strname);
    }

    printf("Output strings:\n");
    for(i= 0; i< NUMSTR; i++)
        puts(strptr[i]);

    return 0;
}
```

```
Input strings:
AAAAAAAA
BBBBBBBBBBBBBBB
EEEE
PPPPPPPPPPPPPPPPP

Output strings:
AAAAAAAAA
BBBBBBBBBBBBBBB
EEEE
PPPPPPPPPPPPPPPPP
```

Each time the dynamic storage allocation function `malloc()` is called, it allocates a single block of storage and returns its address, which is cast to datatype `char*` and stored in the pointer array. This function is in the library `stdlib.h`, which must be included as `#include <stdlib.h>`. The other functions, `strlen()` and `strcpy()`, are in the `string.h` library, which must be included as `#include <string.h>`.

Storage at the time the program terminates is allocated as follows:

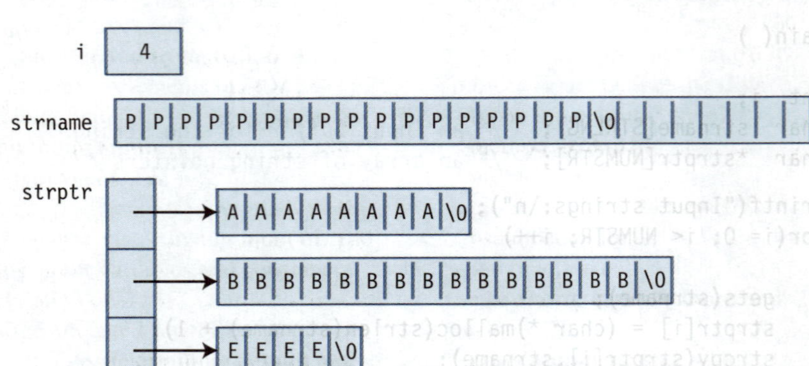

With a maximum string length of 80 characters it would take 320 bytes of memory to store these strings in a static array. Using dynamic arrays, 48 bytes are needed for the strings, 80 more for the buffer, and 16 for the pointer array for a total of 144 bytes.

10.5.2 Passing Strings to Functions as Dynamic Arrays

A character string stored in dynamic storage may be passed to a function using the dynamic pointer and the string may be printed in the function. The following code shows the output of such a string.

```
#include <stdio.h>

void  funcoutput( char  *);

int main( )
{
    char  strname[20] = "COMPUTATION";
    char  *chrptr;

    chrptr = (char *) malloc(strlen(strname) + 1);

    strcpy(chrptr, strname);
    funcoutput(chrptr);

         return 0;
}
```

```
void funcoutput(char  *strptr1)
{
    printf("String: %s\n", strptr1);
    return;
}
```

The output is as follows:

```
String: COMPUTATION
```

Notice that the dynamic storage is allocated using the function `malloc( )`. The string is copied from `strname` to the dynamic storage pointed to by the dynamic pointer `chrptr`. The dynamic string pointer is passed to the function and the string is printed in the function.

When several strings are being stored as dynamic arrays, their pointers are in a static array. The string pointer array may be passed to a function and the strings manipulated inside the function. The following code shows the input and output of dynamic character strings in an array.

```
#include <stdio.h>
#include <string.h>
#include <stdlib.h>

void funcinput(char *strptr1[ ], int NUMSTR);
void funcoutput(char  *strptr1[ ], int NUMSTR);

int main( )
{
    const int NUMSTR = 5;
    int  i;
    char  *strptr[NUMSTR];

    funcinput(strptr, NUMSTR);
    funcoutput(strptr, NUMSTR);

        return 0;
}

void funcinput(char *strptr1[ ], int NUMSTR)
{
    const int STRLNG = 80;
    int  i;
    char  strname[STRLNG];
```

```
    for(i = 0; i < NUMSTR; i++)
    {
        gets(strname);
        strptr1[i] = (char  *) malloc(strlen(strname+1));
        strcpy(strptr1[i], strname);
    }

    return;
}

void  funcoutput(char  *strptr1[ ], int NUMSTR)
{
    int  i;

    printf("\nOUTPUT STRING:\n");
    for(i = 0; i < NUMSTR; i++)
    {
        printf("%2d    ", strlen(strptr1[i]));
        puts(strptr1[i]);
        printf("\n");
    }

    return;
}
```

Input Data:

```
AAAXXXAAAAAA
XXX  YYYYPPPPPPPP
KPPKKK  KLLKKLLKKLL   KKKKK
LLLLLLL
BBBBKKBBBBBLLLBBBBBBBPPPBBBBBBB
```

Output Data:

```
OUTPUT STRING:
12    AAAXXXAAAAAA
17    XXX  YYYYPPPPPPPP
27    KPPKKK  KLLKKLLKKLL   KKKKK
 7    LLLLLLL
31    BBBBKKBBBBBLLLBBBBBBBPPPBBBBBBB
```

Notice that the input data contains strings with embedded blank spaces and since trailing blanks are ignored, the strings are of different lengths. The string input function `gets()` inputs strings from a data file up to and including the line feed character `'\n'` and stores them in `strname`, which has space for 80 characters. This is a temporary buffer to hold the variable length strings. The strings are copied into dynamic storage, which is allocated just large enough to hold each string. The address of each string is assigned to an element of the array of character string pointers. The dynamic storage allocation function `malloc()` is used to allocate storage from the free store to store each variable length string. The string copy function `strcpy` is used to copy each string from the buffer `strname` to the free storage allocated by the `malloc()` function. From this point on, the strings may be manipulated using the pointer array, which contains the addresses of the strings stored in free store.

10.5.3 Review Questions

1. Indicate whether the following statements are true or false.
   a. If there is not much variability in length of the character strings they may be stored in smooth arrays.
   b. To store strings with large variability in their length, dynamic storage should be used.
   c. The dynamic storage allocation function `malloc( )` may be used to allocate storage to store strings.

10.6 Sample Programs

These sample programs demonstrate the use of pointers for manipulating single variables and one- and two-dimensional arrays. Also, some of the programs presented in this section use dynamic storage for manipulation of one- and two-dimensional arrays and character strings.

10.6.1 Tensile Stress

Problem Create a table that shows stress in a rectangular steel bar with width *w*, thickness *t*, and length *l* subject to varying tensile loads. Ask the user for the range of loads and the increment.

Data

Input the cross-section dimensions.
Input the minimum load, maximum load, and increment size.

Method

Compute the cross-sectional area.
Compute the number of values in the table.

Allocate storage for the table.

Calculate the stress from the formula

$$\sigma = p/\text{area};$$

Where σ is the stress in pounds per square inch,

p is the load in pounds, and

area is the cross-sectional area of the bar subject to tensile load.

Output the load and the stress.

Pseudocode

```
input the cross sectional dimensions width w and thickness t
area = w * t
input load minimum and maximum and increment
table size = (loadmax – loadmin) / increment + 1
for load minimum to load maximum at requested increments
   stress = load / area
end
print the table
stop
```

Program

```
/*********************************************************/
/*                                                       */
/*    main: Computes the Stress in Rectangular Cross     */
/*          Section Steel Bar using Array Pointer        */
/*                                                       */
/*********************************************************/
/*                                                       */
/*    Defined Constants:                                 */
/*        -none-                                         */
/*                                                       */
/*    Input Variables:                                   */
/*        width   - cross sectional width of steel bar   */
/*        thick   - cross sectional thickness of steel bar*/
/*        minload - minimum load applied                 */
/*        maxload - maximum load applied                 */
/*        inc     - load increments                      */
/*                                                       */
```

```
/*    Computed Variables:                                        */
/*        area    - cross sectional area                         */
/*        stress  - stress in the column                         */
/*                                                               */
/*    Output Variables:                                          */
/*        load    - load on the column                           */
/*        stress  - tensile stress in pounds                     */
/*                  per square inch                              */
/*                                                               */
/*****************************************************************/

#include <stdio.h>

int main( )
{
    int i, n;
    float width, thick, area, minload, maxload, inc, stress;
    float *loadptr, *stressptr;

    scanf("%f  %f", &width, &thick);
    scanf("%f  %f  %f", &minload, &maxload, &inc);

    area = width * thick;

    n = (maxload - minload)/ inc + 1;

    loadptr = (float *) calloc(n, sizeof(float));
    stressptr = (float *) calloc(n, sizeof(float));

    for(i = 0; i < n; i++)
    {
        *loadptr = minload + i * inc;
        *stressptr = *loadptr / area;
        loadptr++;
        stressptr++;
    }

    loadptr -= n;
    stressptr -= n;

    for(i = 0; i < n; i++)
    {
        printf("%8.2f         %8.2f\n",*loadptr, *stressptr);
        loadptr++;
        stressptr++;
    }

    return 0;
}
```

Input

```
3 4
1000 10000 1000
```

Output

```
 1000.00         83.33
 2000.00        166.67
 3000.00        250.00
 4000.00        333.33
 5000.00        416.67
 6000.00        500.00
 7000.00        583.33
 8000.00        666.67
 9000.00        750.00
10000.00        833.33
```

10.6.2 Days of Above Average Temperature

This program uses an array pointer to manipulate a one-dimensional array.

Problem

Input the name of the month and display average temperatures for the month. Determine the number of days that the average temperature was above the monthly average.

Data

The name of the month.

Method

Input month name.

Look the month up in a table to find out how many days it has (ignore leap year).

Allocate space for the daily average temperatures.

Input average temperatures.

Compute the monthly average.

Print the monthly average.

Print the number of days above average.

Pseudocode

```
input month name
locate month name in an array of month names and get the number of days
allocate array storage
for each day
  input average temperature and store in an array
  add average temperature to sum
end

average = sum / ndays
output average

for each day
  compare the average temp to average
  counting those that are above average
end
output count
stop
```

Program

```
/***********************************************************/
/*                                                         */
/* main: Compute the Sum and Average Temperatures          */
/*       Using Array Pointer                               */
/*                                                         */
/***********************************************************/
/*                                                         */
/*    Defined Constants:                                   */
/*        -none-                                           */
/*                                                         */
/*    Input Variables:                                     */
/*        month[] - name of month                          */
/*        datacnt - number of numbers of type float        */
/*                                                         */
/*    Computed Variables:                                  */
/*        sum     - sum of numbers                         */
/*        average - average of numbers                     */
/*        ndays   - number of days in month                */
/*                                                         */
```

```
/*    Output Variables:                                     */
/*       count   - number of above average days             */
/*       sum     - sum of the numbers                       */
/*       average - average of numbers                       */
/*                                                          */
/*    function called:                                      */
/*       funcmonth - return number of days in the month     */
/************************************************************/

#include <stdio.h>
#include <stdlib.h>
#include <string.h>

int funcmonth(char []);

int main( )
{
    int i, ndays, count;
    char month[10];
    float sum, average;
    float *avgtemp;

    scanf("%s", month);

    ndays = funcmonth(month);

    avgtemp = (float *)calloc(ndays, sizeof(float));

    sum = 0.0;
    for(i = 0; i < ndays; i++)
    {
        scanf("%f", avgtemp);
        sum += *avgtemp;
        avgtemp++;
    }

    avgtemp = avgtemp - ndays;
    average = sum / ndays;
    printf("average temperature for %s is %8.2f\n", month, average);

    count = 0;
    for(i = 0; i < ndays; i++)
    {
        if(*avgtemp > average)
            count++;
        avgtemp++;
    }
```

```
   avgtemp = avgtemp - ndays;

   printf("%d days above average\n", count);

   return 0;
}

/*****************************************************************/
/*                                                               */
/*   funcmonth: Returns the Number of Days in the Month          */
/*                                                               */
/*****************************************************************/
/*                                                               */
/*   Input Parameters:                                           */
/*       datamonth   – name of month                             */
/*                                                               */
/*   Output Parameters:                                          */
/*       –none–                                                  */
/*                                                               */
/*   Local Variables:                                            */
/*       days[ ]       – number of days in each month            */
/*       month[ ][ ] – an array with name of each month          */
/*                                                               */
/*   Return Variables:                                           */
/*       ndays         – number of days in data month            */
/*                                                               */
/*****************************************************************/

int funcmonth(char datamonth[])
{
   int days[12] = {31, 28, 31, 30, 31, 30, 31, 31, 30, 31, 30, 31};
   char month [12][10] = {"January", "February", "March", "April",
                          "May", "June", "July", "August",
                          "September", "October", "November",
                           "December"};

   int k, ndays;

   for (k = 0; k < 12; k++)
      if(strncmp(month[k], datamonth, 3)== 0)
         ndays = days[k];

   return ndays;
}
```

Input

```
February
35
40
60
20
80
90
100
40
50
60
80
23
55
60
77
80
1
100
110
80
40
45
80
90
56
65
77
88
```

Output

```
average temperature for February is    63.64
14 days above average
```

10.6.3 Sorting Dynamically Stored Character Strings

Problem

Write a program to sort the strings stored in a dynamic storage in alphabetical order. Print the unsorted and sorted strings.

Method

Use buffer for input.

Allocate dynamic storage for each string.

Store the addresses of the strings in a pointer array variable.

Output the unsorted strings.

Sort the strings in alphabetical order, rearranging them by rearranging their pointers.

Output the sorted strings.

Data

Input 10 strings.

Pseudocode

```
main( )
  call funcinput
  call funcoutput
  call funcsort
  call funcoutput
stop

funcinput( )
  input the number of strings (at most 20)
  for each string
    input string into a buffer
    allocate dynamic storage
    assign the address to a pointer array element
    copy the string from the buffer to dynamic storage
  end for
  return
end

funcsort( )
  for each string i
    for each string j, j > i
```

```
            if ( string i is greater the string j)
               swap the string pointers
            end if
         end for
      end for
      return
   end

   funcoutput( )
      for each string
         output strings
      end for
      return
   end
```

Program

```
/**********************************************************/
/*                                                        */
/*   Sort the Character String in Alphabetical Order      */
/*                                                        */
/*                                                        */
/**********************************************************/
/*                                                        */
/*   Working Variables:                                   */
/*       *strptr[NUMSTR}  - character pointer array       */
/*                          to store pointers             */
/*                          to character strings          */
/*   Output Variables:                                    */
/*       *strptr[NUMSTR}  - character pointer array       */
/*                          to store dynamic pointers     */
/*                          to character strings          */
/*                                                        */
/*   Functions Called:                                    */
/*       funcinput  - function to input data              */
/*       funcsort   - function to sort the strings        */
/*       funcoutput - function to output strings          */
/*                                                        */
/*   Files Used:                                          */
/*       sortin.dat - input data file                     */
```

```
/*       sortout.dat - output data file                         */
/*                                                              */
/****************************************************************/

#include <stdio.h>
#include <string.h>

#define  MAXSTR  20

void  funcinput(int, char *strptr1[ ]);
void  funcsort(int, char  *strptr1[ ]);
void  funcoutput(int, char *strptr[ ]);

int main( )
{
   char  *strptr[MAXSTR];
   int numstr;

   scanf("%d", &numstr);
   if (numstr > MAXSTR)
       numstr = MAXSTR;

   printf("UNSORTED STRINGS\n");
   funcinput(numstr, strptr);
   funcsort(numstr, strptr);
   printf("\nSORTED STRINGS\n");
   funcoutput(numstr, strptr);

   return 0;
}

/****************************************************************/
/*                                                              */
/*    funcinput: Input Character Strings into Dynamic           */
/*               Strings and Store the Addresses in a           */
/*               Character Pointer Array                        */
/*                                                              */
/****************************************************************/
/*                                                              */
/*    Input Variables:                                          */
/*       strname1[STRLNG] - character string buffer             */
/*                                                              */
/*    Output Parameters:                                        */
/*       *strptr1[NUMSTR] - character pointer array             */
/*                                                              */
/****************************************************************/
```

```
void funcinput(int numstr, char *strptr1[ ])
{
    int const STRLNG = 80;
    int  i;
    char  strname[STRLNG];

    FILE *inptr;

    inptr = fopen("sortin.dat", "r");

    for(i = 0; i < numstr; i++)
    {
        fgets(strname , STRLNG, inptr);
        strptr1[i] = (char *) malloc(strlen(strname) + 1);
        strcpy(strptr1[i], strname);
        printf("%s\n", strname);
    }
    fclose(inptr);

    return;
}
/**********************************************************/
/*                                                        */
/*    funcsort: Sort the Character Strings                */
/*                                                        */
/**********************************************************/
/*                                                        */
/*    Input Parameters:                                   */
/*        strptr1[ ]- unsorted character string array     */
/*                    pointers                            */
/*                                                        */
/*    Output Parameters:                                  */
/*        strptr1[ ]- sorted character string array       */
/*                    pointers                            */
/*                                                        */
/**********************************************************/
void funcsort(int numstr, char  *strptr1[ ])
{
    int  i, j;
    char  *strtemp;

   for(i = 0; i < numstr - 1; i++)
   {
        for(j = i + 1; j < numstr; j++)
        {
            if(strcmp(strptr1[i], strptr1[j]) > 0)
```

```
            {
                strtemp = strptr1[i];
                strptr1[i]= strptr1[j];
                strptr1[j] = strtemp;
            }
        }
    }

    return;
}

/*********************************************************/
/*                                                       */
/*    funcoutput: Output the Character Strings           */
/*                                                       */
/*********************************************************/
/*                                                       */
/*    Input Parameters:                                  */
/*        strptr1[ ] - character string arrays           */
/*                                                       */
/*********************************************************/
void funcoutput(int numstr, char *strptr1[ ])
{
    FILE *outptr;
    int i;

    outptr = fopen("sortout.dat", "a");
    for(i = 0; i < numstr; i++)
    {
        fputs(strptr1[i], outptr);
        printf("%s\n", strptr1[i]);
    }

    fclose(outptr);
    return;
}
```

Input and Output

```
10

UNSORTED STRINGS
piston rings
bolts
nuts
```

```
clamps
valves
gaskets
oil pan
clutch
oil pump
water pump

SORTED STRINGS
bolts
clamps
clutch
gaskets
nuts
oil pan
oil pump
piston rings
valves
water pump
```

Chapter Summary

Pointers are very powerful features of the C language. The memory address of a variable may be assigned to a pointer variable of the same data type. The pointer variable containing the address of a variable may be used to access the storage of the variable. For example the following code shows the declaration of a variable, a pointer variable, and the memory access using the pointer variable.

```
int value;
int *ptrvalue;

ptrvalue = &value;
*ptrvalue = 57;
printf("%d", *ptrvalue);
```

Notice that `value` is a variable of type `int`, `ptrvalue` is a variable of type `int *`, and the address of `value` is assigned to the pointer variable `ptrvalue`. The integer number `57` is stored in the storage allocated for the variable `value` using the pointer `ptrvalue` by dereferencing `ptrvalue`. It is accessed the same way. Accessing the value contained in the storage of a variable through a pointer associated with the variable is called indirection. This method of accessing the memory location by the pointer to a variable is called one level of indirection.

One- and two-dimensional arrays may be accessed by using the array names in address arithmetic. For example the third element of array `stress[10]` may be accessed at the location `stress + 2` since the array name `stress` is the address of the array.

One- and two-dimensional arrays may be allocated dynamic storage using the `calloc()` function from the `stdlib.h` header file. Input/output and manipulation of one- and two-dimensional arrays may be accomplished by using array pointers to the block of dynamic storage. For example, for one-dimensional arrays a dynamic pointer is declared, a block of storage is allocated for an array, and the storage address of such storage is assigned to the pointer. The following code shows such a declaration and storage allocation for an array of integers.

```
int *arptr;

arptr = (int *) calloc(n, sizeof(int));
```

Now `arptr` will contain the address of a block of memory allocated by the `calloc()` function. Notice that the first argument is `n`, which means it allocates `n` cells of storage for the array. Each cell has enough bytes to store an integer. Dynamic storage allocation should be used when the amount of space needed is not known in advance.

Similarly for two dimensional arrays, dynamic starage is allocated by using the `calloc()` function. The following code shows such an allocation:

```
float *arptr;
. . .
arptr = ( float *) calloc( imax * jmax, sizeof(float));
```

A block of storage containing `imax * jmax` cells is allocated. This storage can hold a two-dimensional array of size `[imax] [jmax]`. In this case each cell contains four bytes of storage because the type of data stored in these cells is `float`.

Character strings may be stored in character string variables by declaring pointers. The following code shows the declaration of a pointer to a character string.

```
char *strname;
```

In this case `strname` is a character string pointer that will be assigned the address of storage where the string is stored. In this declaration, storage is set up to store an address in `strname`.

A character string pointer can point to a character string variable in static storage or to dynamically allocated storage.

A list of character strings of unknown size may be stored and processed by storing the address of each string in an array of pointers pointing to the character strings. Each string is allocated dynamic storage by using the dynamic storage allocation function `malloc()` from the `stdlib.h` header file. The address of such dynamic storage is stored in a pointer array of data type `char *`.

Exercises

1. Write a program using pointer variables and dynamic storage to input a list of real numbers of unknown length, sum and count all the positive numbers, and sum and count all the negative numbers. Output the sum and count of all the positive numbers and the sum and count of all the negative numbers. Assume the first number in the list is an integer indicating the length of the list.

2. Write a program and the following functions to compute the average rainfall for the year. Use an array to store pointers to the first day of each month and another array to store the number of days in each month.

   a. A function to input the average rainfall data of each day of the year into a one-dimensional array.

   b. A function to compute the average rainfall for the year or any month.

   c. A function to output the average rainfall for each month and the yearly average rainfall.

3. Write a program and the following functions to compute the average value for the following data values stored in a two-dimensional array. Pass the array by name and pick it up using a pointer variable.

   a. A function to input the data into a two-dimensional array.

   b. A function to compute the row averages and store them in a one-dimensional array.

   c. A function to compute the column averages and store them in a one-dimensional array.

   d. A function to compute the average of all the values in the array.

   e. A function to output the array, row averages, column averages, and the overall average.

4. Write a program and the following functions to compute the average value for the following data values stored in a two-dimensional array of unknown size.

   a. A function to input the data into a two-dimensional dynamic array.
   b. A function to compute the row averages and store them in a one-dimensional array.
   c. A function to compute the column averages and store them in a one-dimensional array.
   d. A function to compute the average of all the values in the array.
   e. A function to output the array, row averages, column averages, and the overall average.

5. Write a program and the following functions using dynamic storage to manipulate the character strings.

   a. A function to input an unknown number of character strings of unknown length (max 80) and store each string in dynamic storage.
   b. A function to output each character string and its corresponding length in terms of the number of characters.

   The program should begin by reading the number of character strings to be processed and allocating dynamic storage for the pointers.

CHAPTER 11

Structures

Objectives

A structure is a derived data type designed to group variables of different data types that are related as a unit called a record.

A structure in C is a derived data type derived from the built-in basic data types `int`, `float`, `double`, and `char`, and the derived data types: arrays, strings, and pointers. A structure data type groups related data items of different data types to form a cohesive unit called a record. In many engineering and scientific applications there are data records consisting of a group of related data items of different data types. For example a hardware component has an identification code that is a string, a component count that is an integer, and a cost that is a real number. A structure may be declared to group the related data items of a hardware component having an identification code, a component count, and a component cost. A variable of a structure data type may be declared just like the declaration of variables of built-in data types. The declaration of a structure and structure variables are presented in the following sections. Structure variables may be initialized, and the basic assignment operations may be performed on structure variables. Input/output, arithmetic, and logic operations may be performed on the members of the structure variables. Structure variables may be passed to a function by value or by pointer like variables of built-in basic data types. Whereas an array variable contains homogeneous data, a structure variable contains heterogeneous data.

11.1 Structures and Structure Variables

A structure is a block of code defining a set of related data items where each data item is declared with its data type and identifiers. The data type of each member of the structure is either `int`, `float`, `double`, `char`, array, string, pointer, or another structure variable. The structure declaration gives a name to a structure data type and to its members. Variables of a structure type are declared as instances of the structure. The following sections show the declaration of a structure and structure variables.

11.1.1 Declaration of Structures and Variables

A structure must be declared. A structure may be declared without a structure tag or with a structure tag. The general form of the structure declaration is as follows:

```
struct  tag
        {
          data items
        };
```

Where `struct` is a reserve word, the `tag` is a user-defined structure tag subject to the rules of identifiers, used as a name for the structure data type. A structure data type declaration has a list of structure members enclosed between two braces and ends with a semicolon.

When a structure is declared with a structure tag, a storage template is set up to store instances of the data members of the structure. The programmer has a choice either to declare the structure variables along with the structure declaration or the structure variables may be declared by using the structure tag in a separate declaration statement after the structure declaration.

When a structure is declared without a structure tag, in which case the storage template to store the data members of the structure is not set up, the structure variables must be declared with the structure declaration. Every structure declaration defines a new data type for the programmer's convenience.

The following examples show the declaration of a structure without and with the structure tag and also show the declaration of structure variables. The first example shows the hardware components to build a mechanical gadget. The data items consist of a component identification code, the number of units, the unit cost of the component, and the total cost of all the units.

Declaration of a structure without a structure tag is as follows:

```
struct
       {
           char     partname[10];
           int      count;
           float    unitcost;
           float    totalcost;
       }part1, part2, part3;
```

Storage is allocated when an unnamed structure is declared along with the structure variables.

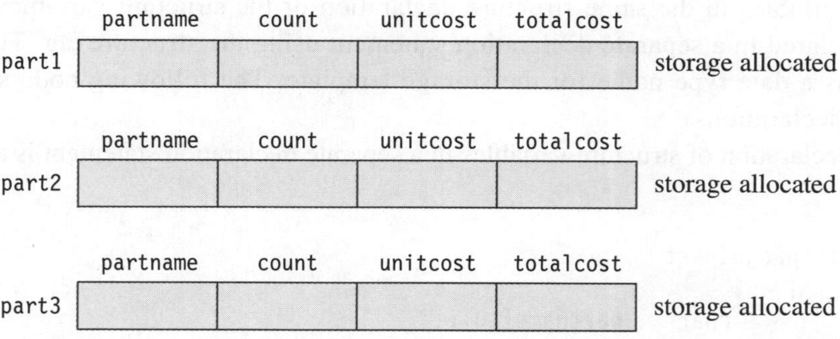

Notice that the structure variables part1, part2, and part3 are declared with the structure declaration. In this case the programmer has no choice because there is no structure tag to use to declare the variables in a separate statement. A storage template is not set up because there is no tag. In this case the storage is directly allocated to the members of the structure variables part1, part2, and part3 when the structure is declared. This is perfectly valid as long as you declare the variables in the structure declaration itself.

Declaration of a structure with a structure tag is as follows:

```
struct  gadgetpart
        {
            char    partname[10];
            int     count;
            float   unitcost;
            float   totalcost;
        };
```

In this case only a storage template is set up to allocate storage to the data items of the structure variables when such variables are declared.

```
 partname    count    unitcost   totalcost
+----------+--------+----------+----------+
|          |        |          |          |   storage not allocated
+----------+--------+----------+----------+
```

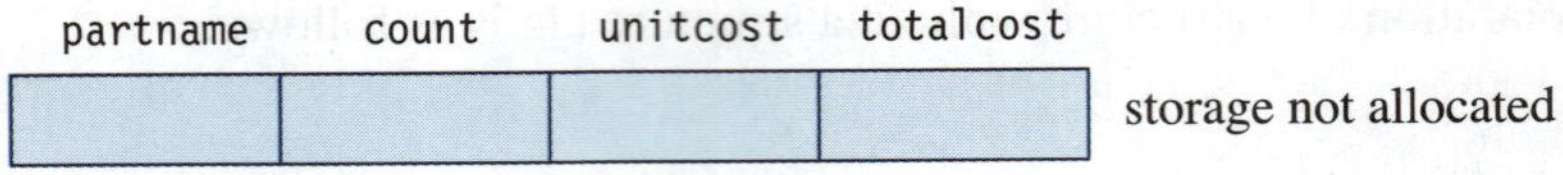

Notice that in this case the structure variables need not be declared in the structure declaration, because there is a structure tag. Since the structure declaration has a structure tag, a storage template is set up. When structure variables are declared, the storage is allocated to the data items of the structure variables according to the structure storage template. Since the structure declaration has a structure tag the programmer has the choice to declare the structure variables in the same structure declaration or the structure variables may be declared in a separate declaration statement using the structure tag. The tag acts as a data type name for the storage template. The following code shows such declarations.

Declaration of structure variables in a separate declaration statement is as follows:

```
struct  gadgetpart
        {
             char    partname[10];
             int     count;
             float   unitcost;
             float   totalcost;
        };
struct gadgetpart part1, part2, part3;
```

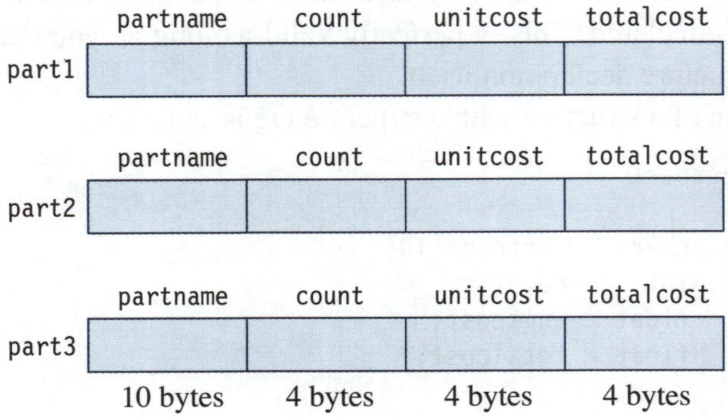

```
          partname     count    unitcost   totalcost
        +-----------+----------+----------+----------+
part1   |           |          |          |          |
        +-----------+----------+----------+----------+

          partname     count    unitcost   totalcost
        +-----------+----------+----------+----------+
part2   |           |          |          |          |
        +-----------+----------+----------+----------+

          partname     count    unitcost   totalcost
        +-----------+----------+----------+----------+
part3   |           |          |          |          |
        +-----------+----------+----------+----------+
          10 bytes    4 bytes    4 bytes    4 bytes
```

In this declaration struct is the reserved word and gadgetpart is the programmers defined structure tag. It is the name of the new data type. The members of the structure are partname (a character string that is an array of data type char), count (the number of part units of data type int), unitcost (the cost of each part of data type float), and totalcost (the cost of all parts of data type float). The structure members are enclosed between two curly braces and the declaration is terminated by a semicolon. This declaration sets up the storage template.

Notice that the template is set up for total storage of 22 bytes to store the data items of the structure. The structure's storage template provides storage for structure variable members with 10 bytes for partname, 4 bytes for count, 4 bytes for unitcost, and 4 bytes for totalcost. When structure variables are declared for this structure gadgetpart the total number of bytes allocated for each variable is 22. The storage is allocated only when variables of the type gadgetpart are declared. As with array names, the name of a structure variable has the address of the beginning of the structure instance as its value. Also like arrays, a structure variable is an address constant.

11.1.2 Declaration of Arrays of Structure Variables

Just as arrays may be members of structures, structures may be elements of arrays. A structure must be declared first to set up a storage template to allocate storage for the elements of the array. As it was stated before, structure variables may be declared with the structure declaration or in a separate statement provided the structure declaration has a structure tag to identify the new data type. The declaration of an array of structure variables may be included in the structure declaration itself as follows:

```
struct    gadgetpart
          {
               char     partname[10];
               int      numparts;
               float    unitcost;
               float    totcost;
          }parts[10];
```

Notice that the array parts[10] included in the structure declaration itself, is an array of 10 instances of the structure. In this case the tag name gadgetpart is optional, and the declaration without the structure tag is as follows:

```
struct
          {
               char     partname[10];
               int      county;
```

```
        float    unitcost;
        float    totcost;
    }parts[10];
```

These two declarations are equivalent. In both cases the array variable `parts[10]` is an array of 10 elements of the same heterogeneous data type. When the structure tag is not specified, the array must be declared with the structure declaration, because no storage template is set up.

When the structure has been given a data type name, the array may be declared in a separate declaration statement after the structure is declared. The following code shows the declaration of structure variables in a separate statement.

```
struct   gadgetpart
    {
        char     partname[10];
        int      count;
        float    unitcost;
        float    totalcost;
    };

struct gadgetpart  parts[10];
```

Notice that the structure is declared first, and the array is declared in a separate statement following the structure declaration. To declare structure variables in a separate statement as shown, the structure tag must be included in the structure declaration.

The storage allocated for the structure array variable `parts[10]` is as follows:

	partname ↓ 10 bytes	count ↓ 4 bytes	unitcost ↓ 4 bytes	totalcost ↓ 4 bytes
parts[0]				
parts[1]				
parts[3]				
parts[4]				
.				
.				
parts[9]				

Once an array variable is allocated storage, the values for the members may be stored and manipulated just like single variables. The members of the structure variables may be accessed by using either a member operator or by using the structure variable pointer. Arrays of structures are manipulated in the same way.

11.1.3 Structure Member and Pointer Operators

The members of a structure variable must be accessed to initialize them before they can be used in other ways. A structure variable member may be initialized when declared, or through an assignment statement, or by data input. The following demonstrates the use of the member operator and structure variable pointer to access the structure members.

Structure Member Operator The members of a structure variable can be accessed by using a member operator (.). The following code shows the use of the member operator.

```
struct   gadgetpart
         {
              char     partname[10];
              int      count;
              float    unitcost;
              float    totalcost;
         };

struct gadgetpart part;

part.partname
part.count
part.unitcost
part.totalcost
```

The storage is allocated as follows:

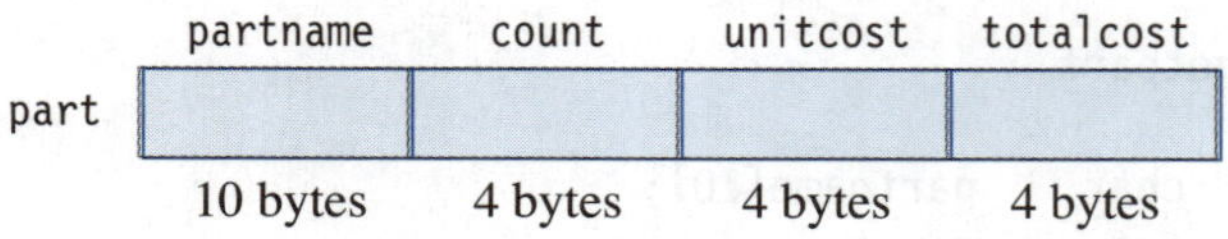

	partname	count	unitcost	totalcost
part				
	10 bytes	4 bytes	4 bytes	4 bytes

Notice that the variable name is followed by the member operator followed by the name of the structure member. Each one of these `part.partname`, `part.count`, `part.unitcost`, and `part.totalcost` is used like a single variable. The only difference is that each of the structure members is identified as belonging to structure variable part.

The following example shows the use of a member operator to assign values to the structure variable members.

```
strcpy(part.partname,"bolt");
part.count = 20;
part.unitcost = 0.25;
part.totalcost = part.count * part.unitcost;
```

Notice that in each of these assignment statements the left-hand side consists of members of the structure variable part with a member operator (.). Since name is a character string array, a string cannot be assigned directly to it; instead the string copy function strcpy is used to copy the string "bolt" to the string member partname. The members count, unitcost, and totalcost are numeric; they are assigned numeric values using assignment statements.

The values are stored as follows:

part.partname	part.count	part.unitcost	part.totalcost
bolt	20	0.25	5.00
10 bytes	4 bytes	4 bytes	4 bytes

A structure variable may also be initialized at the time it is declared as follows:

```
struct gadgetpart part1 = {"bolt", 20, .25, 5.0};
```

Structure Variable Pointer A pointer to a structure variable contains the memory address of the storage allocated to it. The value of the pointer is the address of the first byte of the storage allocated to the structure variable. Structure variables and structure pointers may both be declared following the structure declaration. The following code shows the declaration of structure variables and a structure pointer.

Structure declaration:

```
struct    gadgetpart
          {
               char    partname[10];
               int     count;
               float   unitcost;
               float   totalcost;
          };
```

Structure variable declaration:

```
struct gadgetpart part1, part2, part3, part4[10];
```

Structure pointer declaration:

```
struct gadgetpart  *ptr1, *ptr2, *ptr3, *ptr4;
```

Where ptr1, ptr2, ptr3, and ptr4 are pointers to structure variables of datatype gadgetpart. The addresses of the structure variables part1, part2, part3, and part4[10] may be assigned to the structure pointers ptr1, ptr2, ptr3, and ptr4, respectively. The following code shows the assignment of the structure variable part1 address to pointer ptr1.

```
ptr1 = &part1;
```

The storage and the pointer access of the storage of the structure variable part1 is as follows:

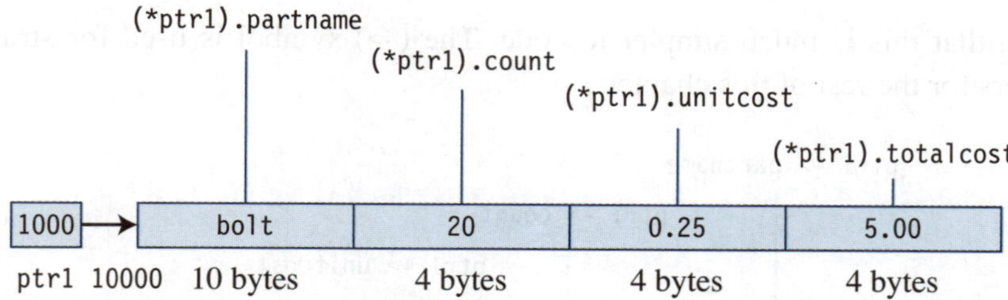

Notice that ptr1 points to the structure, therefore structure members of structure variable part1 may be accessed using ptr1. For example, the address stored in ptr1 is 1000.

To access the members of the structure variable part1 using the pointer ptr1, the pointer must be dereferenced first and then the member operator used.

As the member operator (.) has higher precedence than the dereference operator (*), and the structure variable pointer must be dereferenced first and then the member operator must be applied, parentheses must be used to indicate the order of precedence of the dereference operator and the member operator.

The code to implement this is as follows:

```
(*ptr1).partname
(*ptr1).count
(*ptr1).unitcost
(*ptr1).totalcost
```

This is cumbersome to code and is also error prone. In C a special symbol called a *member dereference operator* (->), which is a hyphen followed by the greater than symbol without any space between them, is provided to simplify the notation. The preceding expressions may be coded using the operator (->) as follows:

```
ptr1 -> partname
ptr1 -> count
ptr1 -> unitcost
ptr1 -> totalcost
```

The following example shows the use of the member dereference operator to assign values to the members of the structure variable.

```
strcpy(ptr1 -> partname,"nut");
ptr1 -> count = 20;
ptr1 -> unitcost = 0.25;
ptr1 -> totalcost = ptr1 -> count * ptr1 -> unitcost;
```

Notice that this is much simpler to code. The (->) symbol is used for structure pointers for the rest of this chapter.

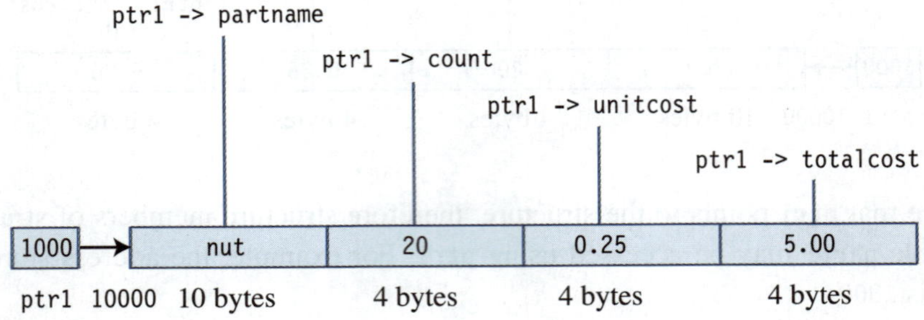

Notice that the character string is copied into `partname`, and values for the numeric variables `count`, `unitcost`, and `totalcost` are assigned using assignment statements.

Members that Are Pointer Variables Pointers, arrays, and structures may be members of structure variables. The following structures describe the properties of a square and of the circles that can be inscribed within it and circumscribed around it.

```
struct Circle
       {
          float diam;
          float area;
       };

struct Square
     {
        float  side;
        float  area;
        struct Circle innercircle;
        struct Circle outercircle;
     };
```

Given the length of the side of a square, an instance of the structure `Square` can be defined. The length of the side of the square can be used to determine the area of the square and the two instances of the structure `Circle`, one of which describes the circle inscribed in the square and the other of which describes a circle circumscribed around the square. The code would be as follows:

```
int main( )
{
   const float PI = 3.141593;
   struct Square box;
   float x, s;

   scanf("%f", &x);
   box.side = x;
   box.area = x * x;
   box.innercircle.diam = x;
   box.innercircle.area = PI * x * x / 4.0;
   s = sqrt(2.0 * x * x);
   box.outercircle.diam = s;
   box.outercircle.area = PI * s * s / 4.0;

   return 0;
}
```

If instead of declaring two members of the structure `Square` as `Circle`, they were declared as pointers to circles, the declaration of a `Square` and definition of an instance of a `square` would require the definition of two instances of a `Circle` as follows:

```
struct Circle
      {
          float  diam;
          float area;
      };

struct Square
      {
            float  side;
            float  area;
            Circle *innercircle;
            Circle *outercircle;
      };

int main( )
{
    const float PI = 3.141593;
    struct Square box;
    struct Circle in, out;
    float x, s;

    scanf("%f", &x);
    box.side = x;
    box.area = x * x;
    in.diam = x;
    in.area = PI * x * x / 4.0;
    box.innercircle = &in;
    s = sqrt(2.0 * x * x);
    out.diam = s;
    out.area = PI * s * s / 4.0;
    box.outercircle = &out;

    return;
}
```

If the area of a circle inscribed in the `Square` box is to be printed, it can be accessed as

```
(*(box.innercircle).area)    or      box.innercircle -> area
```

Members That Are Arrays A structure may have members that are arrays of any data type other than the data type defined by the structure. For example, the following structure contains an array of real numbers and a character array that will contain a character string.

```
struct Polygon
    {
        char  name[20];  /* name of a particular type of polygon */
        int   n;         /* number of vertices */
        float point[10][2]; /* coordinates of the vertices of the
                               polygon */
    };
```

Instances of type `Polygon` would be declared as follows.

```
struct Polygon triangle = {"triangle", 3}, hexagon = {"hexagon", 6};
```

Because the variables are initialized when they are defined, the coordinates of the vertices are initialized to 0.0. The values of the coordinates can be supplied as input data. Once they have values, the *x* and *y* coordinates of the three vertices of the triangle can be accessed as:

```
x1 = triangle.point[0][0];
y1 = triangle.point[0][1];
x2 = triangle.point[1][0];
y2 = triangle.point[1][1];
x3 = triangle.point[2][0];
y3 = triangle.point[2][1];
```

As arrays may be of any data type, it is possible to declare arrays of structures, which themselves contain arrays, for example,

```
struct Line
    {
        float p1[2]; /* coordinates of one endpoint of a line */
        float p2[2]; /* coordinates of the other endpoint of a line */
};

. . .
struct  Line triangle[3]; /* declare a triangle as having three sides */
```

Then `triangle[0]` is one side of the triangle; `triangle[1]` is another side, and `triangle[2]` is the third side. The sides must, of course, share endpoints or the name `triangle` is misleading. For example the following defines an actual triangle.

```
triangle[0].p1[0] = 3.5;   triangle[0].p1[1] = 5.2;     /* point(3.5, 5.2) */
triangle[0].p2[0] = 14.6;  triangle[0].p2[1]= 8.9;     /* point(14.6,8.9) */
triangle[1].p1[0] = 3.5;   triangle[1].p1[1] = 5.2;    /* point(3.5,5.2) */
```

```
triangle[1].p2[0] = 6.2;   triangle[1].p2[1] = 10.0;  /* point(6.2,10.0) */
triangle[2].p1[0] = 6.2;   triangle[2].p1[1] = 10.0;  /* point(6.25,10.0)*/
triangle[2].p1[0] = 14.6;  triangle[0].p1[1] = 8.9;   /* point(14.6,8.9) */
```

Each of the sides shares an endpoint with each of the other sides. Notice that a subscript must be used for each element of the array `triangle` and then a subscript must be used for each element of the arrays `p1` and `p2`.

11.1.4 Definition of Structure Variables

Structure variables must be defined before they are used. This simply means the structure variable members must have values before they are manipulated. There are four different ways the members of a structure variable can be defined.

1. By initializing the members of a structure variable when the structure and variable are declared.
2. By initializing the members of a structure variable when it is declared using a named structure data type.
3. By explicit assignment of values to the members of a structure variable after it is declared using assignment statements and `strcpy`.
4. By data input to the members of a structure variable.

Initialization of Structure Variables Structure variables may be initialized in several ways. One way is to initialize the structure variable in a declaration of both the structure and the structure variable. The following code shows such an initialization.

```
struct   gadgetpart
         {
               char    partname[10];
               int     count;
               float   unitcost;
               float   totalcost;
         }part = {"bolt", 20, 0.25, 0.00};
```

Notice that the structure data type and the structure variable `part` are declared and the structure variable `part` is initialized. The member `partname` has the string value `"bolt"`, the member `count` has the value 20, the member `unitcost` has the value 0.25, and the member totalcost is initialized to a value of 0.00. The structure variable part is now defined and can be used in computation and output.

Another way is to declare the structure first and then initialize a structure variable in the declaration of the structure variable. The following code shows such an initialization.

```
struct   gadgetpart
         {
              char    partname[10];
              int     count;
              float   unitcost;
              float   totalcost;
         };

struct gadgetpart part = {"bolt", 20, 0.25, 0.00};
```

When an array of structures is declared, the elements of the array may be initialized in the same way as a regular numeric array. The following code shows the initialization of an array.

```
struct   gadgetpart
         {
              char    partname[10];
              int     numparts;
              float   partunitcost;
              float   totcost;
         };

struct gadgetpart parts[3] = {{"bolt", 20, 0.25, 0.00},
                              {"nut", 20, 0.15, 0.00},
                              {"shaft", 40,1.50, 0.00}};
```

Notice that there are three elements in the array parts[0], parts[1], and parts[2] and each element is initialized to the values shown in three separate braces.

The values are assigned to parts[0] as follows:

parts[0].partname is assigned the string "bolt"

parts[0].numparts is assigned the value 20

parts[0].partunitcost is assigned the value 0.25

parts[0].totcost is assigned the value 0.00

Similarly the other initialized values are assigned to array elements `parts[1]` and `parts[2]`.

Note that the values specified in the braces are stored in the members of the elements of the array `parts[3]` in the order in which the structure members are specified in the structure declaration.

If only a few values are specified in the initialization they are assigned in the order in which the members are specified in the structure declaration. The remaining members are automatically initialized to zero or an empty string depending on the member type. The following code shows such an initialization.

```
struct   gadgetpart
         {
               char    partname[10];
               int     count;
               float   unitcost;
               float   totalcost;
         };

struct gadgetpart part = {"bolt", 20};
```

Notice that in this case there are only two values specified, but there are four members in the structure declaration, the first two members are initialized as specified and the last two members are initialized to zero.

Also, notice that in all initialization statements shown so far there is no need to specify explicitly the members along with the structure variables, because the members are implicit to the variable type used in the initialization.

Assignment of Values to Variables Values may be assigned to structure members using assignment statements. The following example shows such an assignment. The values may be assigned using either the member operator or by using the structure variable pointer.

```
struct   gadgetpart
         {
               char    partname[10];
               int     count;
               float   unitcost;
               float   totalcost;
         };

struct gadgetpart part, *partptr;
```

Assignment Using Member Operator

```
strcpy( part.partname,"bolt");
part.count = 20;
part.unitcost = 0.25;
part.totalcost = part.count * part.unitcost; /* totalcost is calculated */
```

Assignment Using Structure Variable Pointer

```
strcpy( partptr -> partname,"bolt");
partptr -> count = 20;
partptr -> unitcost = 0.25;
partptr -> totalcost = partptr -> count * partptr -> unitcost;
```

Notice that the first set of assignment statements assigns values using only the member operator. The second set of assignment statements assigns values using the structure pointer with the member dereference operator.

Also notice that the value of `part.totalcost` is computed and the result is assigned. Also by using the pointer the value `partptr -> totalcost` is computed and the result is assigned. The input data into the structure variables is discussed in Section 11.2.

Assignment of One Structure to Another Once `part1` has been declared and defined as being a structure variable of the derived data type `gadgetpart`, if `part2` has been declared to be a variable of the same data type, the values of `part1` can be assigned to the members of `part2` by the assignment statement:

```
part2 = part1;
```

This type of assignment statement is unique for structures and cannot be used for arrays or strings unless they are also structures.

11.1.5 Review Questions

1. Indicate whether the following statements are true or false.
   a. A particular structure is a derived data type derived from the basic and derived data types.
   b. When a structure is declared without a structure tag, a storage template is set up to allocate storage for the structure variables.
   c. When a structure is declared without a tag, the structure variables must be declared in the structure declaration statement itself.

d. When a structure is declared with a structure tag the programmer has a choice of declaring the structure variables in the structure declaration itself or in a separate statement using the structure tag.

e. Structure variables may be initialized in the structure declaration statement itself.

f. Structure variables may be assigned values by using assignment statements.

g. Structure variable members may be assigned values by computations.

h. Structure variables may be elements of an array.

i. Structure variables are manipulated by using the member operator.

j. Structure variables may not be manipulated by using the structure variable pointers.

2. Write a structure declaration statement to declare the following related items. Name the new data type and declare two variables of that type.

   Employee Name
   Employee ID
   Weekly Hours Worked
   Hourly Wages
   Gross Pay
   Deductions
   Net Pay

3. Write a declaration statement to initialize a structure variable of the type described in Question 2 to the following values.

   Name: John Johnson
   ID: EMP3456
   Weekly Hours: 48 with 8 hours overtime
   Hourly Wages: 18.60

   Show the calculation steps for other members.

4. For the structure that you declared in Question 2, assign the values given in Question 3 using a structure pointer.

11.2 Manipulation of Structures

Variables of a structure data type may be manipulated just like the variables of the basic data types, array data types, and character data types. Input and output operations, arithmetic, and logic operations may be performed on structure variables.

11.2.1 Input/Output of Structure Variables

Input to a structure variable may be accomplished by entering the data values into the members of the structure variable from a keyboard or from a data file. We can input and output to structure variable members of data type `int`, `float`, `double`, `char`, arrays, and strings. The following examples show the input and output of structure variables whose members are of the basic data types.

Input Using Member Operator The following example shows the input to a structure variable.

```
#include <stdio.h>

struct record
        {
          int   part_num;
          int   num_part_units;
          float part_unitcost;
          float part_total_cost;
        };


int main( )
{
    struct record auto_part;

    scanf("%d  %d  %f", &auto_part.part_num,
    &auto_part.num_part_units, &auto_part.part_unitcost);

    auto_part.part_total_cost = auto_part.num_part_units *
                  auto_part.part_unitcost;
```

```
    printf("%d    %d    %6.2f    ", auto_part.part_num,
            auto_part.num_part_units,
            auto_part.part_unitcost);

    printf("total_cost=%8.2f\n",
            auto_part.part_total_cost);

    return 0;
}
```

Notice that the structure members `part_num`, `num_part_units`, `part_unitcost`, and `total_cost` of the structure variables are accessed using the structure member operator (.) The member operator has higher precedence than the address operator so no parentheses are needed.

Input Using Structure Pointers The following example shows the input to a structure variable using a pointer and the structure member dereference operator.

```
#include <stdio.h>

struct record
    {
        int   part_num;
        int   num_part_units;
        float part_unit_cost;
        float total_cost;
    };

int main( )
{
    struct record auto_part, *auto_partptr;
    auto_partptr = &auto_part;

    scanf("%d  %d  %f", &auto_partptr -> part_num,
          &auto_partptr -> num_part_units,
          &auto_partptr -> part_unit_cost);

    auto_partptr -> total_cost = (auto_partptr ->
         num_part_units)*(auto_partptr-> part_unit_cost);

    printf("%d    %d    %6.2f \n", auto_partptr ->
          part_num, auto_partptr ->num_part_units,
          auto_partptr -> part_unit_cost);

          printf("total_cost = %8.2f\n", auto_partptr ->
              total_cost);
```

```
    return 0;
}
```

Notice that the structure members part_num, num_part_units, part_unit_cost, and total_cost of the structure variables are accessed using the structure member dereference operator (->), because the auto-partptr is a pointer to the structure variable auto_part whose address was assigned to the auto_partptr in the statement auto_partptr = &auto_part.

The following example shows the input and output of structure variables of data type int, float, char, arrays, and character strings. This program uses the member operator (.).

```
#include <stdio.h>

    struct strec
            {
                char    stid[6];    /* student id */
                char    name[20];   /* student name */
                int     score[4];   /* test score */
                float   sum;        /* total score */
                float   average;    /* average score */
                char    ltgrd;      /* letter grade */
            };

FILE *inptr;

int main( )
{
    struct strec  record;
    int  i;

    inptr = fopen("stdata.dat", "r");

    while((fscanf(inptr, "%5c   %19c",
          record.stid, record.name)) != EOF)
    {
        for(i = 0; i < 4; i++)
          fscanf(inptr,"  %d ", &record.score[i]);

        record.stid[5]  = '\0';
        record.name[19]  = '\0';
        record.sum = 0;
        for(i = 0; i < 4; i++)
        {
          record.sum += record.score[i];
```

```
        }
        record.average = record.sum / 4.0;

       if(record.average >= 90.0)
          record.ltgrd = 'A';
       else if(record.average >= 80.0)
          record.ltgrd = 'B';
       else if(record.average >= 70.0)
          record.ltgrd = 'C';
       else if(record.average >= 60.0)
          record.ltgrd = 'D';
       else
          record.ltgrd = 'F';

       printf("%s    %s",
          record.stid, record.name);
       for( i = 0 ; i < 4; i++)
          printf("     %d    ", record.score[i]);
       printf("     %5.2f     %c\n\n",
          record.average, record.ltgrd);
    }
    return 0;
}
```

The following example shows the input and output of structure variables of data type `int`, `float`, `char`, arrays, and character strings. This program uses a pointer to the structure variable and the member dereference operator (->).

```
#include <stdio.h>

struct strec
     {
         char    stid[6];
         char    name[20];
         int     score[4];
         float   sum;
         float   average;
         char    ltgrd;
     };

FILE *inptr;

int main( )
{
    struct strec  record, *stptr;
```

```
    int  i;

    stptr = &record;
    inptr = fopen("stdata.dat", "r");

    while((fscanf(inptr, "%5c     %19c",
           stptr -> stid, stptr -> name))
                          != EOF)
    {
        for(i = 0; i < 4; i++)
           fscanf(inptr,"  %d ", &stptr -> score[i]);

        stptr -> stid[5] = '\0';
        stptr -> name[19] = '\0';

        stptr -> sum = 0;
        for(i = 0; i < 4; i++)
        {
           stptr -> sum += stptr -> score[i];
        }
        stptr->average = stptr-> sum / 4.0;

        if(stptr ->average >= 90.0)
           stptr ->ltgrd = 'A';
        else if(stptr -> average >= 80.0)
           stptr -> ltgrd = 'B';
        else if(stptr -> average >= 70.0)
           stptr -> ltgrd = 'C';
        else if(stptr -> average >= 60.0)
           stptr -> ltgrd = 'D';
        else
           stptr -> ltgrd = 'F';

        printf("%s     %s",stptr -> stid, stptr -> name);
        for( i = 0 ; i < 4; i++)
        {
           printf("    %d  ", stptr -> score[i]);
        }
        printf("      %5.2f      %c\n\n",
                  stptr -> average, stptr -> ltgrd);
    }

    return 0;
}
```

Assignment of Structure Variables An assignment operator (=) may be used to assign the value of one structure variable to another structure variable. A structure variable may be assigned to another structure variable provided that the two structure variables are of the structure data type; the same data members of the same data type. An assignment statement when executed simply copies the values from the members of one structure variable to the members of the other structure variable. The following example shows the assignment of one structure variable to another structure variable of the same type having the same structure members with the same data types.

```
#include <stdio.h>
#include <string.h>

struct parts
        {
            char   *part_name;
            char   *part_id;
            int     num_units;
            float   unit_cost;
            float   total_cost;
        };

int main( )
{
    struct parts part1;

    part1.part_name = "pulley";
    part1.part_id = "ply1254";
    part1.num_units = 50;
    part1.unit_cost = 2.50;
    part1.total_cost = part1.num_units * part1.unit_cost;
    printf("\n%s %s %d  %82f   %8.2f\n", part1.part_name, part1.part_id,
          part1.num_units, part1.unit_cost, part1.total_cost;

    return 0;
}
```

```
OUTPUT

pulley    ply1254    50       2.50       125.00
```

Assign structure variable part1 to structure variable part2 as follows:

```
part2 = part1;
```

This will copy the members of structure variable part1 to members of structure variable part2. This is a valid assignment statement because the assignment operator is defined for structures.

This is equivalent to the assignment of each member of part1 to each member of part2 explicitly as follows:

```
strcpy(part2.part_name,part1.part_name);
strcpy(part2.part_id,part1.part_id);
part2.num_units = part1.num_units;
part2.unit_cost = part1.unit_cost;
part2.total_cost = part1.total_cost;
```

Notice that each member of structure variable part1 is copied to the corresponding member of structure variable part2. Assignment of individual members is useful when structure variables have some members alike and other members different and there is a need to copy specific members from one structure variable to specific members of another structure variable.

```
y = x;
```

x and y are two separate arrays that contain the same values.

```
struct charstring
       {
          char name[20];
       }name1 = {"Joseph"}, name2;

name2 = name1; /* copies name1 to name2 */
```

Note, structures provide a way to use the assignment operator with arrays and character strings.

```
struct array
       {
          int number[5];
       };

struct array x = {1, 2, 3, 4, 5}, y;

y = x;  /* copies array x to array y */
```

11.2.2 Arithmetic on Structure Variables

Arithmetic operations such as addition, subtraction, multiplication, and division may be performed on appropriate members of structure variables. The arithmetic operations are performed on the members of the structure member by using either the structure member operator or the structure pointer. The following example shows arithmetic operations on structure variables.

Using the Structure Member Operator

```
struct      tagname
      {
          int    a;
          float  b;
          float  c;
      };


struct tagname  var1, var2, var3;

var1.a = 20;
var1.b = 12.5;
var1.c = var1.a * var1.b;

var2.a = 40;
var2.b = 25.0;
var2. c = var2.a * var2.b;
```

Addition of two structures:

```
var3.a = var1.a + var2.a;
var3.b = var1.b + var2.b;
var3.c = var1.c + var2.c;
```

Notice that the addition operations are performed on the members of the structure. The addition of two structure variables is implemented using the addition of corresponding members of the structure as shown. Similarly, other arithmetic operations such as subtraction, multiplication, division, and exponentiation may be performed on structure variables using structure member operators.

Using the Structure Pointer Dereference Operator

```
struct      tagname
      {
          int    a;
          float  b;
          float  c;
      };
```

```
struct tagname  var1, var2, var3, *ptr1, *ptr2, *ptr3;
ptr1 = &var1;
ptr2 = &var2;
ptr3 = &var3;
ptr1 -> a = 20;
ptr1 -> b = 12.5;
ptr1 -> c = ptr1 ->a * ptr1 ->b;
ptr2 -> a = 40;
ptr2 -> b = 25.0;
ptr2 -> c = ptr2 -> a * ptr2 -> b;
```

Addition of two structures:

```
ptr3 -> a = ptr1 -> a + ptr2 -> a;
ptr3 -> b = ptr1 -> b + ptr2 -> b;
ptr3 -> c = ptr1 -> c + ptr2 -> c;
```

Notice that the dereference operator is used to access the members of the structure using the structure variable pointer. Similarly, other arithmetic operations may be performed on the structure variables.

11.2.3 The typedef Statement and its Usage

The `typedef` statement lets the programmer provide a synonym for either user-defined or the basic data types. The `typedef` is used when the structure is declared or after the structure is declared. The following code shows the declaration of structure variables by use of the `typedef` construct.

```
typedef struct record
                {
                    char   name[20];
                    int    hours;
                    float  hourly_rate;
                    float  gross;
                    float  net;
                } RECORD;
```

or

```
struct record
     {
         char   name[20];
         int    hours;
         float  hourly_rate;
         float  gross;
         float  net;
     };
typedef struct record RECORD;
```

Both forms are valid and RECORD is the synonym for record, the structure tag of the structure.

The structure variables may be declared using the typedef name RECORD as follows:

```
RECORD record1, record2, record[5];
```

The structure variables are record1, record2, and a structure variable array with five elements is record[5]. The short name RECORD is used to define the structure variables instead of struct record. This is a compact form to provide a data type name for the structure. It is required in order to pass structures to functions and return them. This use of typedef is shown in the next section.

11.2.4 Review Questions

1. Indicate whether the following statements are true or false.
   a. Input into a structure variable is effectively input into the individual members of the structure.
   b. Data input and output may be done using either the structure member operator or by using a pointer dereference operator.
   c. The assignment of values to structure variables is accomplished by using the structure member operator or a structure pointer dereference operator.
   d. A structure variable may be assigned to another structure variable provided both structure variables have the same structure data type.
2. Write an input statement to input data to the members of the structure variable colm1.

```
struct  stlcolumn     /* steel column data */
        {
             int    numcolumns;
             float  diameter;
             float  length;
        };

struct stlcolumn  colm1;
```

3. Write an output statement to output the data members of the structure variable colm1.

```
struct  stlcolumn
        {
            int    nuncolumns;
            float  diameter;
            float  length;
        };

struct stlcolumn  colm1;
```

4. Write a `typedef` statement for the following structure and declare two single variables and a one-dimensional array using the `typdef` name.

```
struct strength
       {
            float  load;
            float  diameter;
            float  length;
            float  stress;
            float  strain;
       };
```

5. Declare a structure type vector to hold any size vector of up to 10 elements, where the number of elements is part of the structure.

11.3 Structures and Functions

A structure variable may be passed to a function in the same way a scalar variable of a basic data type is passed, by value or by pointer. A function can return a variable of structure data type. If a function is returning a structure variable, the return data type in the function prototype and in the function header must be a structure data type. When structure variables are passed to a function as arguments, the parameters in the function prototype and in the function header must be of the same structure data type. In the function prototype the variable names for the parameters are optional, but in the function header of the function definition, variable names must be specified for the function parameters. When structures are passed between functions, the `typedef` statement must be used. The following sections show the passing of structures to functions by value and by pointer.

11.3.1 Passing Structure Variables by Value

Structure variables are passed by value simply by naming the variables in the function call.

For example, consider the following structure:

```
#include <stdio.h>

struct cylinder
      {
           float radius;
           float length;
           float section;
           float volume;
      };
typedef struct cylinder CYLINDER;

void funcoutput(CYLINDER);

int main( )
{
    CYLINDER can;
    const float PI = 3.141593;

    scanf("%f  %f", &can.radius, &can.length);
    can.section = PI * can.radius * can.radius;
    can.volume = can.length * can.section;
    funcoutput(can);

    return 0;
}

void funcoutput(CYLINDER can1)
{
    printf("Radius: %f\n", can1.radius);
    printf("Length: %f\n", can1.length);
    printf("Section: %f\n", can1.section);
    printf("Volume: %f\n", can1.volume);

    return;
}
```

Notice that the function passes the `CYLINDER` variable `can` to the function by value. In C, variables of all named data types are passed by value or by pointer. The function `funcoutput` receives the structure by value and the structure variable `can1` in the function header is used to access the members of a copy of the `CYLINDER` variable `can` defined in the `main` function.

The following sample program shows the passing of several structure variables by value. This program computes the stress and strain in a steel column subject to compression load in pounds. The modulus of elasticity for steel is given as $E = 30 \times 10^6$ psi.

```
#include <stdio.h>

struct  column
        {
             float  diameter;
             float  compload;
             float  stress;
             float  strain;
        };

typedef struct column COLUMN;

float   fnstress(COLUMN);
double  fnstrain(COLUMN);
void    fnoutput( COLUMN);

int main( )
{
    struct column steelcolm;

    scanf("%f  %f", &steelcolm.diameter,&steelcolm.compload);

    steelcolm.stress = fnstress(steelcolm);
    steelcolm.strain = fnstrain(steelcolm);
    fnoutput(steelcolm);

    return 0;
}
float  fnstress(COLUMN steelcolumn1)
{
    const float PI = 3.141593;

    float area, tempstress;

    area = (PI * steelcolumn1.diameter * steelcolumn1.diameter)/
             4.0;

    tempstress = steelcolumn1.compload / area;

    return tempstress;
}


double  fnstrain(COLUMN steelcolm1)
{
    const float E = 30000000.00;

    double tempstrain;

    tempstrain = steelcolm1.stress / E;
```

```
    return tempstrain;
}
void fnoutput(COLUMN steelcolm1)
{
    printf("Stress = %10.4f    strain = %20.10f\n",
          steelcolm1.stress, steelcolm1.strain);

    return;
}
```

Notice that there are three functions. The first function, `fnstress`, computes the stress in the steel column and returns it to the `main` program, then the second function `fnstrain` is invoked to compute the strain. After the strain is computed it is returned to the `main` program. The third function `fnoutput` is invoked to print the values for stress and strain. These values cannot be stored directly by the functions because `steelcolm` has been passed by value. One problem with passing structure variables by value is that temporary storage is created for each variable, passed to the function. For large structures this is an inefficient use of time and space. However, it protects the variables against inadvertent changes in the function.

Arrays differ from all other data types in that they cannot be passed to a function by value and cannot be returned from a function. Because of this, it is simpler to use a function to change values in an argument that is an array than in any other type of argument. At the same time, this makes arrays vulnerable to inadvertent changes in functions. If it is more important to protect the values in an array than it is to be able to change them, say the values are experimental data that cannot easily be replaced, or values in a database that are only supposed to be altered by the database administrator, then an array data type can be declared as follows:

```
struct array
      {
         float elem[100];
      };

typedef struct array Array
.  .  .
     Array  x, y, z;
```

Here `x`, `y`, and `z` are arrays of the same shape, size, and data type, each allocated sufficient storage for 100 real numbers. If a function is to be used to add arrays `x` and `y` element-by-element and place the sums in the corresponding positions in `z` that is, `z[k] = x[k] + y[k]`, then the following function and function call can be used.

```
Array funcadd(Array, Array)
. . .
    Array x, y, z;
. . .
    z = funcadd(x, y);
. . .

Array funcadd(Array a, Array b)
{
    Array c;
    int k;

    for(k = 0; k < 100; k++)
        c.elem[k] = a.elem[k] + b.elem[k];

    return c;
}
```

Structures are passed to functions by value and also returned by value. Therefore, in this example, array `a.elem` is a value in a copy of array `x` and array `b.elem` is a value in a copy of array `y`. By returning the value of `c` and storing it in `z`, the array `z` holds the sum of arrays `x` and `y`.

11.3.2 Returning Structure Variables

Structure variables are treated in C in the same way scalar variables are treated in the operations of assignments, and passing to and from functions. A structure variable has as its value the entire instance of the structure, that is, the set of values of members that make up the structure. When one structure variable is assigned to another variable of the same structure, corresponding member values are copied from one variable to the other. When a structure variable is used as an argument to a function, space is allocated for a dummy parameter of the same type, and the corresponding member values are copied from the argument to the dummy parameter. When a function is declared to be of structure type, the function must contain a local variable of that type that can be returned. Then on return, the corresponding member values are copied from the local variable to a receiving variable in the calling function. This is shown in the following example.

```
#include <stdio.h>

struct project
    {
        char idnum[5];    /* project id */
```

```
            char  name[20];   /* name of director */
            int   date;       /* completion target date */
            float cost;       /* projected cost */
        };

typedef struct project Project;
Project funcupdate(Project); /* declares function that updates a
                                project */

int main( )
{
    . . .
    Project aquifer;          /* declaration of project */
    . . .
    aquifer = funcupdate(aquifer);
    . . .
    return 0;
}
Project funcupdate(Project currproj)
{
    . . .
    currproj.name = .  .  .   /*update project information */
    currproj.date = .  .  .
    currproj.cost =  .  .  .
    return currproj;
}
```

In the main function, a variable of type Project is declared. Values for Project aquifer are obtained and Project aquifer is sent as an argument to funcupdate. Space has been allocated for the local variable currproj of type Project, which is the parameter of the function definition. The values of the members of aquifer are copied to the corresponding members of currproj. The fields that need to be updated are given new values. Since structures are passed by value, this does not change the values in aquifer. The updated values are returned in the return statement and assigned to the variable aquifer. This avoids the use of the pointer that would be necessary if the address of aquifer were passed to the function.

11.3.3 Passing Structure Variables by Pointer

Structure variables may be passed to a function by pointer. As with any variable of a named data type, this address is necessary for direct input. Whenever the members of a structure variable are altered within a function, the altered values are passed back to the calling function through the pointer to the structure variable. This is not possible if the structure variable is passed by value.

The following sample program shows the passing of structure variables by pointer to an input function and computation functions. This program computes the stress and strain in a steel column subject to a compression load. The modulus of elasticity for steel is given as $E = 30 \times 10^6$ psi.

```
#include <stdio.h>

struct column
      {
         float  diameter;
         float  compload;
         float  stress;
         float  strain;
      };

typedef struct column COLUMN;

void  fninput(COLUMN *);
void  fnstress(COLUMN *);
void  fnstrain(COLUMN *);
void  fnoutput( COLUMN);

int main( )
{
   COLUMN steelcolm;

   fninput(&steelcolm);
   fnstress(&steelcolm);
   fnstrain(&steelcolm);
   fnoutput(steelcolm);

   return 0;
}

void fninput(COLUMN *steelcolm1)
{
   scanf("%f  %f", &steelcolm1 -> diameter,
         &steelcolm1 -> compload);
   return;
}

void  fnstress(COLUMN  *steelcolm1)
{
   const float PI = 3.141593;
```

```
    float area;

    area = (PI * steelcolm1 -> diameter *
            steelcolm1 -> diameter)/ 4.0;

    steelcolm1 -> stress = steelcolm1 -> compload / area;

    return;
}

void  fnstrain(COLUMN  *steelcolm1)
{
    const float E = 30000000.00;

    steelcolm1 -> strain = steelcolm1 -> stress / E;

    return;
}

void fnoutput(COLUMN steelcolm1)
{
    printf("Stress = %10.4f    strain = %20.10f\n",
            steelcolm1.stress, steelcolm1.strain);

    return;
}
```

Notice that the structure variable steelcolm is passed to all the functions except the output function by pointer. The input function inputs the diameter and compload directly into the variable steelcolm. The member stress of the COLUMN variable passed to the function is changed in the function fnstress. The member strain of the COLUMN variable passed to the function fnstrain is changed in the function. The changes in stress and strain of the structure variable members are reflected in the calling program variable steelcolm because the parameter provided the function with the address of the structure.

Another example that uses structure pointers is the inventory of certain parts:

```
#include <stdio.h>

typedef struct record
        {
            int    part_num;
            int    num_part_units;
            float  part_unit_cost;
            float  total_cost;
        }RECORD;
```

```
void  fninput(RECORD *);
void  fncompute(RECORD *);
void  fnoutput(RECORD);

int main( )
{
    RECORD auto_part;

    fninput(&auto_part);
    fncompute(&auto_part);
    fnoutput(auto_part);

    return 0;
}

void  fninput(RECORD *auto_part1)
{

    scanf("%d  %d  %f", &auto_part1 -> part_num,
          &auto_part1 -> num_part_units,
          &auto_part1 -> part_unit_cost);
    return;
}

void  fncompute(RECORD *auto_part1)
{

    auto_part1 -> total cost = auto_part1 ->
    num_part_units * auto_part1-> part_unit_cost;
    return;
}

void  fnoutput(RECORD auto_part1)
{

    printf("%d    %d    %6.2f \n", auto_part1.part_num,
    auto_part1.num_part_units,
    auto_part1.part_unit_cost);
    printf("total cost = %8.2f\n", auto_part1.total_cost);

    return;
}
```

Notice that the structure variable auto_part is passed to the functions fninput and fncompute by pointer because the input from the function needs to be passed back to the calling function main and the computed values of the structure members in the function `fncompute` need to be passed back to the `main` function. Since the function `fnoutput` does not make any changes to the structure members, the structure variable may be passed by value to output the structure members.

11.3.4 Review Questions

1. Indicate whether the following statements are true or false.
   a. A structure variable may be passed to a function by value or by pointer.
   b. If a structure variable is passed to a function by value and the structure variable members are to be altered in the function, they are not reflected in the calling function.
   c. When a function inputs the values for a structure variable, one way to send such input values to the calling program is through the structure pointer.
   d. Structure variables must be passed to a function by pointer if such variables are to be altered in the function and returned to the calling program as parameters.
   e. Structure members may be passed individually to a function and if they are altered in the function they must be returned to the calling function by pointer.
   f. In a function, when a structure member is used for the calculation of a value, the value may be returned to the calling function through the return statement, and the value returned may be assigned to a variable declared in the calling program.
   g. When structure members are altered in a function they cannot be returned to the calling function.
2. Given the code to declare and initialize a structure and structure variable for a closed circular cylinder of diameter 8.5 inches and length of 12.0 inches as shown, write a function to compute the surface area and the volume of the cylinder. Pass the structure variable by value. Return the updated structure to the `main` function.

   Write a function to print the surface area and the volume.

```
struct  volume
        {
            float  diameter;
```

```
        float  length;
        float  surfarea;
        float  volume;
    }cylinder = {8.5, 12.0, 0.0, 0.0};
```

3. Write the code and use the structure declared and initialized in Question 2. Pass the structure variable members `diameter` and `length` to the functions `funcsurfarea` and `fnvolume` to compute the values of the surface area and the volume and return the values through the functions. Return statements to the `main` function and store the values returned in the local variables declared in the `main` function to hold the surface area and the volume of the cylinder. Output the surface area and the volume.

11.4 Nested and Self-Referential Structures

C has the capability to declare and define nested and self-referential structures. Nested structures are structures nested inside other structures. The detailed implementation of such structures is provided in the next section. Self-referential structures are structures where one or more of the structure members are pointers to the same structure data type. The self-referential structures have many applications in data structures, particularly in the implementation of linked lists and trees. Using dynamic storage, they make it possible to store data of unknown size.

11.4.1 Nested Structures

Nesting one structure inside another structure simply means that one structure may be a member of another structure. A structure can be declared having a structure of a different and previously declared type as a member. The structure that is nested within another structure as a member must be declared before declaring the structure block in which it is to be nested. For example, if structure ABC is to be nested inside structure XYZ, then structure ABC must be declared before the structure XYZ is declared. The following examples show the declaration and manipulation of nested structures.

```
struct load
    {
        char   loadtype[4];
```

```
        char   materials[15];
    };
typedef struct load LOAD;

struct forces
    {
        LOAD  type;
        float diameter;
        float length;
        float load;
        float stress;
    };
typedef struct forces FORCES;


FORCES compforce, tensforce, shearforce;
```

Notice that a variable of the structure data type LOAD is a member of the structure data type FORCES. An instance of LOAD is nested inside the declaration of FORCES. The declarations of the structures must be in the following order: the structure LOAD must be declared first and the structure FORCES must be declared later. The structure variable of the structure of the data type LOAD is type, which is a member of each instance of the structure data type FORCES. The structure variables of the data type FORCES are compforce, tensforce, and shearforce.

The following program shows the input, computation, and output of this nested structure. This code shows two ways of handling nested structures, through the use of the member operator and the through use of the structure pointer dereference operator.

The following code shows the use of the member operator with nested structures.

```
#include <stdio.h>

struct load
    {
        char   loadtype[5];
        char   materials[15];
    };
typedef struct load LOAD;

struct forces
    {
        LOAD type;
```

```
          float  diameter;
          float  length;
          float  load;
          float  stress;
     };

typedef struct forces FORCES;

int main( )
{
     const float PI = 3.141593;
     FORCES  compforce;
     float area;

     scanf("%4c     %14c", compforce.type.loadtype,
          compforce.type.materials);
     scanf("%f  %f  %f", &compforce.diameter,
          &compforce.length, &compforce.load);

     compforce.type.loadtype[4] = '\0';
     compforce.type.materials[14]= '\0';

     area = ( PI * compforce.diameter *
            compforce.diameter)/ 4.0;

     compforce.stress = compforce.load / area;

     printf("%s  %s  %5.2f   %5.2f   %10.2f   %10.2f",
     compforce.type.loadtype,compforce.type.materials,
     compforce.diameter, compforce.length, compforce.load,
     compforce.stress);

     return 0;
}
```

In this code `type` is a member of `struct forces` where `type` is a structure variable of the data type `LOAD`. To access a member of the `LOAD` variable `type` from the variables of the type `FORCES`, the member operator must be used twice as shown in the code. For example, to access the member `materials` of the member structure `LOAD` of the `FORCES` variable `compforce`, you must first access the structure member `type` and then access the structure member `materials` using the member operator twice as follows: `comforce.type.materials`. Similarly the tensile forces and shear forces may be implemented.

The following code shows the use of a pointer with member dereference operator to nested structures.

```
#include <stdio.h>

struct members
      {
          char  loadtype[5];
          char  materials[15];
      };

struct forces
      {
          struct members *type;
          float  diameter;
          float  length;
          float  load;
          float  stress;
      };


int main( )
{
    const float PI = 3.141593;
    struct  forces  *ptcompforce;
    float area;

    ptcompforce = (struct forces *)malloc(sizeof(struct
                                   forces));

    scanf("%4c   %14c", ptcompforce->type->loadtype,
          ptcompforce->type->materials);
    scanf("%f  %f  %f", &ptcompforce->diameter,
          &ptcompforce->length, &ptcompforce->load);

    ptcompforce->type->loadtype[4]  = '\0';
    ptcompforce->type->materials[14]= '\0';

    area = ( PI * ptcompforce->diameter *
            ptcompforce->diameter)/ 4.0;

    ptcompforce->stress = ptcompforce->load / area;

    printf("%s  %s  %5.2f   %5.2f   %10.2f    %10.2f",
    ptcompforce->type->loadtype,
    ptcompforce->type->materials,
    ptcompforce->diameter, ptcompforce->length,
```

```
    ptcompforce->load, ptcompforce->stress);
    . . .
    free(ptcompforce);

    return 0;
}
```

Notice that when structure variable pointers are used they must be dereferenced twice to access the members of the nested structures. In this case `ptcompforce -> type -> loadtype` is dereferenced twice to access the `loadtype` member, which is a member of the nested structure. Also notice that the members of the nesting structure need to be dereferenced only once as `ptcompforce -> diameter` because `diameter` is the member of the nesting structure.

11.4.2 Self-Referential Structures

A self-referential structure is a structure where one or more of its members are pointer members. The pointers point to variables of the same structure and are primarily used for data structures in the form of linked lists with one or more links or pointers linking or pointing to the data members of the structure. The declaration and implementation of a self-referential structure is shown as follows:

```
struct datalist
      {
          char  partid[7];
          char partname[20];
          struct datalist *numptrs;
      };
```

The storage for this structure is allocated as follows:

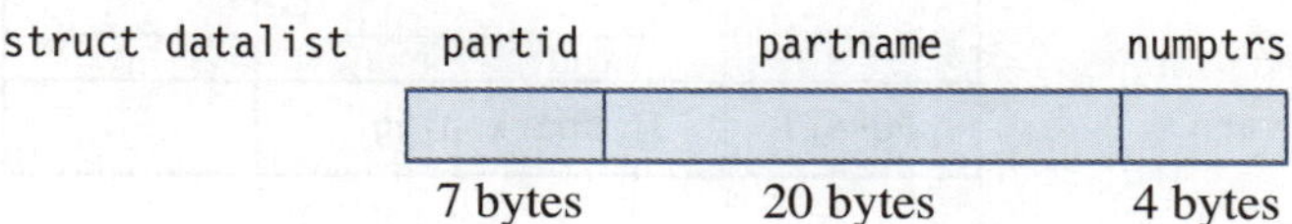

Notice that the structure member `partid` is a character string of 7 bytes, the structure member `partname` is also a character string of 20 bytes, and the structure member `numptrs` (which is a pointer member) is usually 4 bytes long unless otherwise specified. This can be implemented as a linked list to logically order the list by `partid`. The following diagram shows the ordering and the code will follow.

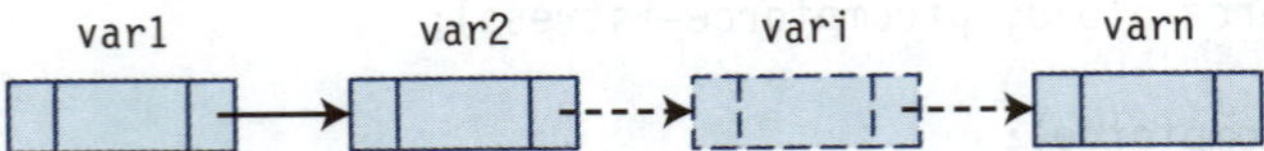

This is the logical order of the list with each structure `datalist` variable pointing to the next variable in the order of the `partid`.

```
struct datalist var1, var2,....,vari,   ....varn;

strcpy(var1.partid, "XYZ453");
strcpy(var1.partid, "crank shaft");
var1.numptrs = &var2;

strcpy(var2.partid, "XPY576");
strcpy(var2.partid, "brake disk");
var2.numptrs = &var3;

strcpy(var3.partid, "KLM 987");
strcpy(var3.partid, "radiator");
var3.numptrs = &var4;

. . .

varn.numptrs = 0;      /* assign the null pointer */
```

The linked list for this data is created as follows:

header: 1000

	partid	partname	numptrs
var1 1000	XYZ453	crank shaft	1031
var2 1031	XPY576	brake disk	1062
var3 1062	KLM987	radiator	1093
var4 1093	-----	----------	-----
varn	PQR471	spark plug	0

Notice that the header points to the first structure variable address 1000 of `var1`. The pointer member of `var1` points to the address 1031 of the structure variable `var2`, and so on. This shows the implementation of the linked list using the self-referential structures. It provides a useful way of ordering items in an array of structures without actually rearranging them. It can also be used with an unknown number of structures and dynamic storage allocation.

11.4.3 Review Questions

1. Indicate whether the following statements are true or false.
   a. A structure may be nested inside another structure.
   b. A structure nested inside a structure must be declared before the structure it is nested into.
   c. Nested structures may not be manipulated using the structure pointers.
   d. At least one member of a self-referential structure must be a pointer.
   e. A self-referential structure may have more than one pointer member.
   f. Other members of a self-referential structure may be nonpointer members.
2. Declare a nested structure where the first structure members are the student ID and name, the second structure in which the first structure is nested has members to hold four test scores, the average, and the letter grade. Write a function to output the student ID, name, four test scores, average, and the letter grade.
3. Write a self-referential structure for a bank customer. The members are the customer name, account number, home address, and pointer member pointing to the next customer name in an alphabetical list.

11.5 Union and Enumeration Data Types

Union and enumerated data types are similar to structures in their declaration. Unions are used for customizing the storage to store only the member of the union that is currently accessed. An enumerated data type provides a name for a set of user-given data values. Union is very effective in optimizing storage if the members of the union are large size arrays where one array member is active at a time. This is very useful in scientific computing when we have large size one-dimensional and multidimensional arrays.

11.5.1 Declaration of Union and Union Variables

The declaration of a union is the same as that of a structure except that the word "structure" is replaced by the word "union." A union has members of different data types; only one of which exists at any one time. A union variable may be allocated storage only for the active data member; unlike structure variables that are allocated storage for all of the members. This is to optimize the storage requirements by reusing the same storage space for different variables. The following code shows the declaration of a union.

```
union datavalues
          {
               int  counter;
               float value;
               double  balance;
          };
```

In this declaration `union` is the keyword and `datavalues` is the tag. The data members of the union are `counter`, `value`, and `balance`. The data types of these union members are `int`, `float`, and `double`. This uses the same eight bytes of storage either for a counter, or for a real value, or for a balance.

The union variables are declared as follows:

```
union datavalues value1, value2;
```

Notice that the union variables are `value1` and `value2`. These variables may have integer, real, or double-precision values depending on which member is referenced.

11.5.2 Operations on Unions

The union variables `value1` and `value2` have data members `counter`, `value`, and `balance`.

An integer may be assigned to the data member `counter` of union variable `value1` as follows:

```
value1.counter = 100;
```

Also a floating-point number 895.75 may be assigned to the member `value` of the union variable `value1` as follows:

```
value1.value = 895.75;
```

Only one member of a union variable is assigned storage at any one time. The assignment of 895.75 to union member `value` will clear the storage assigned to the union variable member `counter`. The integer number 100 assigned to the member counter of the union variable `value1.counter` is now unavailable for access. At this point only 895.75, which is stored in `value1.value` is available for access. The maximum storage allocated to a union variable is based on the largest number of bytes required for a data member declared in the union. In this case the member balance is allocated eight bytes of storage because its data type is double.

In engineering and scientific applications arrays are very common data structures. Unions are very useful for solving problems with large arrays when storage optimization is required. The following example of a union and union variable shows such an application.

```
union fluid
      {
          float  pressure[100][200];
          float velocity[100][200];
          float  density[1000][200];
      };
```

The declaration of union variables as arrays;

```
union fluid airflow[500];
```

Notice that the members of the union `pressure` is an array of 100 rows and 200 columns, which is 20,000 elements, the array `velocity` is an array of 100 rows and 200 columns, which is 20,000 elements, and density is an array of 100 rows and 200 columns, which is 20,000 elements. The union member `pressure` array, which is a member of the union variable `airflow[0]`, is assigned a value of 230 psi for the first row as follows:

```
airflow[0].pressure[0][0]  = 230;
airflow[0].pressure[0][1]  = 230;
---------------------------------
airflow[0].pressure[0][199]  = 230;
```

Notice that the storage is used only for the member `pressure` of the union array elements `airflow[0]` through `airflow[99]`.

Now if values are assigned to the union member `velocity`, the storage is used for the union variable `airflow[0].velocity[0][0]`, `velocity[0][1],...,velocity[0][199]`, and so on. Then the values for the union member `pressure` will not exist. The maximum storage is used for the union member `density` because it has 200,000 elements and it requires a storage for all the elements of the union variable `airflow[500]`, which is 1 million locations of four bytes each. When the storage is used for the member `density` the values stored previously for the members `pressure` and `velocity` no longer exist.

11.5.3 Enumeration Data Type

Enumerated data types are data types whose data values are specified by the user. The general form of the enumerated data type declaration is as follows:

```
enum  colors{ value1, value2, value3};
```

`enum` is the key word and `colors` is an optional tag, which is followed by the left curly bracket, followed by data values, followed by the right curly bracket, and ending with a semicolon.

For example, for an RGB color screen we can specify the data values as red, green, and blue using an enumerated data type as follows:

```
enum colors{ red, green, blue };
```

The user-defined data type is `enum colors` and the possible data values are `red`, `green`, and `blue`.

The declaration of variables for the enumerated data type is similar to the variables of structure and union types. The following declaration shows the data type `enum` for different colors.

```
enum colors color1, color2, color3;
```

The values assigned to the enumeration variables `color1`, `color2`, and `color3` must be one of the values specified in the `enum colors` declaration statement where the values for colors are specified.

For example,

```
color1 = red;
```

or

```
color2 = blue;
```

This is very useful when the programmer knows the finite set of data values that he can use for some variables.

The storage for `enum` data type is not allocated when the `enum` type is declared. When variables are declared and assigned values, the storage is allocated. In the declaration statement

```
enum colors{ red, green, blue };
```

an integer is associated with each of the data values specified. The first data value specified is assigned the integer zero by default, the second value one, and the third value two. One can also explicitly assign integer values to the data values specified as follows:

```
enum colors{ red = 5, green = 50, blue };
```

`red` is assigned `5`, `green` is assigned `50`, and `blue` is automatically assigned `51`, one more than `green`. The data values may be accessed by the assigned integer values.

11.5.4 Review Questions

1. Indicate whether the following statements are true or false.
   a. A value may be assigned to only one of the members of the union variable.
   b. When a value is assigned to a second member of the union variable, the value assigned to the first member of the union variable is erased.
   c. Enumerated data types are useful if only a finite set of values may be assigned to a variable.
2. Define the following enumerated data types:
   a. The months of the year.
   b. Acceptable ways of writing the name of the country.
   c. Permissible subscript values for the array `a[10]`.

11.6 Sample Programs

These sample programs demonstrate the declaration of structures and structure variables. Input/output and arithmetic operations are performed on structure variables. Manipulation of structure variables in functions is by passing a value or a pointer.

11.6.1 Parts Table

Problem Compute the total cost of each part and the total cost of all the parts in stock given the part code, part name, the number of units of each part, and the unit cost of each part. This program demonstrates the use of structures to hold records.

Method

Declare the structure.

Declare the structure variable.

For each part:

Input the data from a data file.

Compute the total cost of each part.

Output the input data and the total cost of each part.

Calculate the total cost of all parts.

Pseudocode

```
main:
  for each part
    input the partid, partname, partunits, partunitcost
    compute the total cost for each part
    output the partid, partname, partunits, partunitcost, partstotalcost
    compute the total cost of all parts
  end for
    output the total cost of all parts
stop
```

Program

```
/**********************************************************/
/*                                                        */
/* main: Compute the Total Cost of Each Part and          */
/*       the Total Cost of All Parts                      */
/*                                                        */
/**********************************************************/
/*                                                        */
/*    Defined Constants:                                  */
/*        -none-                                          */
/*                                                        */
/*    Input Variables:                                    */
/*        partid    - part identification number          */
/*        partname  - part name                           */
/*        partunits - number of units of each part        */
/*        unitcost  - cost of each part units             */
/*                                                        */
/*    Computed Variables:                                 */
/*        costunits - cost of each part units             */
```

```
/*        costtotal - total cost of all units               */
/*                                                          */
/*    Output Variables:                                     */
/*        partid        - part identification number        */
/*        partname      - part name                         */
/*        partunits     - number of units of each part      */
/*        partunitcost  - cost of each part units           */
/*        parttotalcost - total cost of each part           */
/*        totpartscost  - total cost of all units           */
/*                                                          */
/*    Files Used:                                           */
/*        "inventin.dat"  - input data file                 */
/*        "inventout.dat" - output data file                */
/*                                                          */
/*    Functions Called:                                     */
/*        -none-                                            */
/*                                                          */
/***********************************************************/

#include <stdio.h>
struct  recinvnt
        {
             char  partid[8];
             char  partname[12];
             int   partunits;
             float partunitcost;
             float parttotalcost;
             float totpartscost;
        };

FILE  *inptr, *outptr;

#define NUMREC 5

int main( )
{
   int  i;
   struct recinvnt   record;

   record.totpartscost = 0;
   inptr = fopen("inventin.dat", "r");
   outptr = fopen("inventout.dat","w");

   for(i = 0; i < NUMREC; i++ )
   {
      fscanf(inptr,"%7c %12c   %d  %f ", record.partid,
```

```
        record.partname,&record.partunits,
        &record.partunitcost);
    record.partid[7] = '\0';
    record.partname[11] ='\0';
    record. parttotalcost= record.partunits * record.partunitcost ;
    record.totpartscost += record. parttotalcost;
    fprintf(outptr,"%s    %s    %5d   %7.3f    %8.2f\n",
            record.partid,record.partname,record.partunits,
            record.partunitcost, record.parttotalcost);


    fprintf(outptr,\n""The total value of the parts inventory is:");
    fptrintf(outptr,"  %10.2f\n", record.totpartscost);

    fclose( inptr );
    fclose( outptr );

    return 0;
}
```

Sample Input File: inventin.dat

```
BOL0534    bolt           10000    1.25
HYM0333    hammer         500      4.75
CS09276    crank_case     25       230.85
TYR0324    tie_rods       128      95.86
WID0542    wind_shield    50       165.00
```

Output: inventout.dat

```
BOL0534    bolt            10000      1.250      12500.00
HYM0333    hammer            500      4.750       2375.00
CS09276    crank_case         25    230.850       5771.25
TYR0324    tie_rods          128     95.860      12270.08
WID0542    wind_shield        50    165.000       8250.00

The total value of the parts inventory is:   41166.33
```

11.6.2 Calculation of the Cost of Painting a Cubicle

Problem Compute the total surface area of a cubicle with length l, width w, and height h. The cost to paint one square foot is \$2.50. Calculate the total cost to paint the four walls of the cubicle. Output the dimensions of the cubicle, the surface area of the four walls to be painted, and the total cost to paint the four walls. This program demonstrates the passing of structures to functions.

Method

Declare the structure.
Declare the structure variable.
For each cubicle:
- Input the dimensions of the cubicle from a data file.
- Compute the surface area of four walls to be painted.
- Compute the total cost to paint.
- Output the dimensions of the cubicle, surface area of walls to be painted, and the total cost to paint the cubicle.

Data

Length, width, height, and cost per square foot.

Pseudocode

```
main:
   for each cubicle
      funinput( )
      funcompute( )
      funoutput( )
   end for
stop

funinput( )
   input length, width, height
end

funcompute( )
   wallarea = 2 * length * height + 2 * width * height
   paintcost = wallarea * costpersqft
end

funoutput( )
   output length, width, height
   outout wallarea
    output paintcost
end
```

Program

```
/**********************************************************/
/*                                                        */
/* main: Compute the Surface Area of a Cubicle and the    */
/*      Cost to Paint the Four Walls                      */
/*                                                        */
/**********************************************************/
/*                                                        */
/*    Defined Constants:                                  */
/*    COSTSQFT    = $2.50                                 */
/*                                                        */
/*    Input Structure Members:                            */
/*        length - floor length                           */
/*        width  - floor width                            */
/*        height - height of cubicle                      */
/*                                                        */
/*    Computed Structure Members:                         */
/*        wallarea  - area of four walls of cubicle       */
/*        paintcost - cost to paint four walls            */
/*                                                        */
/*    Output Structure Members:                           */
/*        length - floor length                           */
/*        width  - floor width                            */
/*        height - height of cubicle                      */
/*        wallarea  - area of four walls of cubicle       */
/*        paintcost - cost to paint four walls            */
/*                                                        */
/*    Functions called:                                   */
/*         funinput( )  -  function to input data         */
/*         funcompute( )- function to compute            */
/*         funoutput( )- function to output the data      */
/*                                                        */
/**********************************************************/

#include <stdio.h>

#define COSTSQFT  2.50
#define ENTRIES 4

typedef struct cubicle
        {
```

```
            float  length;
            float  width;
            float  height;
            float  areawall;
            float  paintcost;
        }CUBICLE;

void funinput(CUBICLE [ ]);
void funcompute(CUBICLE [ ]);
void funoutput(CUBICLE [ ]);

int main()
{
    CUBICLE room[ENTRIES];

    funinput(room);
    funcompute(room);
    funoutput(room);

    return 0;
}
/*********************************************************/
/*                                                       */
/*     Function to Input the Structure Variable          */
/*                                                       */
/*********************************************************/
/*                                                       */
/*    Output Parameters:                                 */
/*        room1  - structure variable                    */
/*                                                       */
/*                                                       */
/*    Called by:                                         */
/*        main                                           */
/*                                                       */
/*    Files used:                                        */
/*        "infile.dat" - input data file                 */
/*                                                       */
/*********************************************************/
void funinput(CUBICLE  room1[ ])
{
    FILE *inptr;
    int  i;
```

```
    inptr = fopen("infile.dat", "r");
    for(i = 0; i < ENTRIES; i++)
    {
        fscanf(inptr,"%f  %f  %f", &room1[i].length,
              &room1[i].width,&room1[i].height);
    }

    fclose( inptr );
    return;
}

/**********************************************************/
/*                                                        */
/*          Function Computes the Structure Members       */
/*                                                        */
/**********************************************************/
/*                                                        */
/*    Input/Output Parameters:                            */
/*       room1  -  structure variable                     */
/*                                                        */
/*    Called by:                                          */
/*       main                                             */
/*                                                        */
/**********************************************************/
void funcompute(CUBICLE *room1)
{
    int i = 0;

    for( i = 0; i < ENTRIES; i++ )
    {
        room1[i].areawall = 2 * ( room1[i].length * room1[i].height
                              + room1[i].width * room1[i].height);
        room1[i].paintcost = room1[i].areawall * COSTSQFT;
    }

    return;
}

/**********************************************************/
/*                                                        */
/*   Function to Output the Structure Variable            */
/*                                                        */
/**********************************************************/
/*                                                        */
/*    Input Parameters:                                   */
```

```
/*        room1     - the structure variable               */
/*                                                          */
/*    Called by:                                            */
/*        main                                              */
/*                                                          */
/*    Files used:                                           */
/*        outfile.dat - output data file                    */
/*                                                          */
/***********************************************************/
void funoutput(CUBICLE  room1[])
{
    FILE *outptr;
    int i;
    outptr = fopen("outfile.dat", "w");

    for( i = 0; i < ENTRIES; i++ )
    {
        fprintf(outptr,"Room: %d\n", i+1);
        fprintf(outptr,
                "length: %5.2f  width: %5.2f  height: %5.2f\n\n",
                room1[i].length, room1[i].width, room1[i].height);
        fprintf(outptr,"total wall area: %6.2f\n\n",
                room1[i].areawall);
        fprintf(outptr,"cost to paint walls: %6.2f\n",
                room1[i].paintcost);
        fprintf(outptr,"\n\n");
    }

    fclose( outptr );
    return;
}
```

Input and Output

```
Input data file: "infile.dat"
20.5 16.5 10.0
30.6 25.4  8.0
45.5 30.0  9.5
16.5  12.8 8.0

Output data file: "outfile.dat"
Room: 1
length: 20.50  width: 16.50  height: 10.00
```

```
total wall area: 740.00

cost to paint walls: 1850.00

Room: 2
length: 30.60  width: 25.40  height:  8.00

total wall area: 896.00

cost to paint walls: 2240.00

Room: 3
length: 45.50  width: 30.00  height:  9.50

total wall area: 1434.50

cost to paint walls: 3586.25

Room: 4
length: 16.50  width: 12.80  height:  8.00

total wall area: 468.80

cost to paint walls: 1172.00
```

Chapter Summary

A structure is a derived data type used to store and manipulate related data in the form of a heterogeneous record. A structure is declared with or without a tag to set up a template for storage to be allocated. The tag functions as a data type name uniquely assigned to the structure. Once the structure is declared then the structure variables may be declared to allocate storage for the members of a structure variable. The general form of the structure declaration is as follows:

```
struct tagname
      {
          structure data members;
      };
```

The declaration of structure variables is as follows:

```
struct tagname  variable1, variable2,..., variablen;
```

Once the structure variables are declared, the storage is allocated to them based on the structure declaration template.

Values for the data members of the structure variables may be defined by initialization, by assignment, through input, or through computation. The data members of the structure variables may be accessed by using either a member operator, which is a dot (.) or by dereference and member operator (->) using a structure variable pointer. All arithmetic operations may be performed on the numeric members of the structure variables.

A synonym may be defined for a structure data type using the typedef construct. This is done as follows:

```
typedef struct student_record
      {
            .
         structure members;
            .
      }STUDENT;
```

In this case STUDENT is the synonym for struct student_record. Structure variables may be declared using the synonym STUDENT instead of struct student_record. The following example shows such a declaration.

```
struct student_record var1, var2;
```

is equivalent to

```
STUDENT  var1, var2;
```

Where var1 and var2 are structure variables.

The values of a structure variable may be assigned to another structure variable if the two structure variables have the same data type; otherwise the assignment must be member-by-member.

Structure variables may be passed to a function by value or by pointer. A structure variable may be returned from a function through the return statement or through argument and parameters.

A structure may be nested inside another structure. The nested structure must be declared first and the structure in which it is nested must be declared next.

A structure member may be a pointer to a variable of the same structure data type. Such structures are called self-referential structures. They are very useful for implementing linked lists.

A union is a construct used for optimizing the use of storage. In this construct only one member of the union is active and is allocated storage. Enumeration is used for data that can only have a small set of values, for example the name of each month, primary colors, etc.

Exercises

1. Write a C program using the following structure to describe the axis of a cylinder, a circular cross-section, and the cylinder. Compute the area of the circular cross-section, the surface area of the cylinder, and the volume of the cylinder, given the length of the axis, and the radius.

```
struct shape
        {
                float line;
                float radius;
                float areacircle;
                float areacylinder;
                float volumecylinder;
        };
```

2. Write a C program using the following structure to hold the compression load p and the diameter d of a column of length l. Compute the compression stress and the strain in the column. Output the load, diameter, stress, and strain with proper format.

```
struct strength
        {
                float p;
                float d;
                float stress;
                float strain;
        };
```

Use the following formulas to compute the stress and strain.

area = $(\pi d^2)/4$

stress = p/area

strain = stress/E

where E is the modulus of elasticity, which is 30×10^6 psi for steel.

3. Write a program to compute the weekly pay for 10 machine shop workers with a 6 character ID, a 20 character name, the hours worked, and the hourly rate of pay. Compute the gross pay with 25% deductions from the gross pay for the net pay. Output the ID, name, hours worked, hourly rate of pay, gross pay, deductions, and net pay. The overtime pay rate over 40 hours is 1.5 times the hourly rate of pay. Organize the data by employee.

4. Write a program to compute the inventory for three car lots with five different car models. Each model has a certain number of cars with a cost for each car. Compute the total cost of all cars of each model. Also compute the total number of cars for all of the models and also compute the total cost of all the cars of all of the models. The input consists of a 20-character model name, the number of cars of each model, and the price for each car for each of the models. Output the model name, cost of each car, total cost of all cars of each model, the total number of cars of all of the models, and the total cost of all cars of all of the models. Organize the data by model for each lot.

APPENDIX A

Nonprintable ASCII Characters

Dec	Hex	Oct	Bin	Character
0	0	0	0000000	NUL—Binary Zero
1	1	1	0000001	SOH—Start of Header
2	2	2	0000010	STX—Start of Text
3	3	3	0000011	ETX—End of Text
4	4	4	0000100	EOT—End Of Transmission
5	5	5	0000101	ENQ—Enquiry
6	6	6	0000110	ACK—Acknowledge
7	7	7	0000111	BELL—Bell
8	8	10	0001000	BS—Backspace
9	9	11	0001001	HT—Horizontal Tab
10	a	12	0001010	LF—Line Feed or Newline
11	b	13	0001011	VT—Vertical Tabulation
12	c	14	0001100	FF—Form Feed
13	d	15	0001101	CR—Carriage Return
14	e	16	0001110	SO—Shift Out
15	f	17	0001111	SI—Shift In
16	10	20	0010000	DLE—Data Link Escape
17	11	21	0010001	DC1—Device Control 1
18	12	22	0010010	DC2—Device Control 2

Dec	Hex	Oct	Bin	Character
19	13	23	0010011	DC3—Device Control 3
20	14	24	0010100	DC4—Device Control 4
21	15	25	0010101	NAC—Negative Acknowledgment
22	16	26	0010110	SYN—Synchronization
23	17	27	0010111	ETB—End of Text Block
24	18	30	0011000	CAN—Cancel
25	19	31	0011001	EM—End of Medium
26	1a	32	0011010	SUB—Substitute
27	1b	33	0011011	ESC—Escape
28	1c	34	0011100	FS—File Separator
29	1d	35	0011101	GS—Group Separator
30	1e	36	0011110	RS—Record Separator
31	1f	37	0011111	US—Unit Separator
127	7f	177	1111111	DEL—Delete

Printable ASCII Characters

Dec	Hex	Oct	Bin	Character
32	20	40	0100000	SP—Space
33	21	41	0100001	!
34	22	42	0100010	“
35	23	43	0100011	#
36	24	44	0100100	$
37	25	45	0100101	%
38	26	46	0100110	&
39	27	47	0100111	‘
40	28	50	0101000	(
41	29	51	0101001	)
42	2a	52	0101010	*
43	2b	53	0101011	+
44	2c	54	0101100	,
45	2d	55	0101101	-

Dec	Hex	Oct	Bin	Character
46	2e	56	0101110	.
47	2f	57	0101111	/
48	30	60	0110000	0
49	31	61	0110001	1
50	32	62	0110010	2
51	33	63	0110011	3
52	34	64	0110100	4
53	35	65	0110101	5
54	36	66	0110110	6
55	37	67	0110111	7
56	38	70	0111000	8
57	39	71	0111001	9
57	3a	72	0111010	:
59	3b	73	0111011	;
60	3c	74	0111100	<
61	3d	75	0111101	=
62	3e	76	0111110	>
63	3f	77	0111111	?
64	40	100	1000000	@
65	41	101	1000001	A
66	42	102	1000010	B
67	43	103	1000011	C
68	44	104	1000100	D
69	45	105	1000101	E
70	46	106	1000110	F
71	47	107	1000111	G
72	48	110	1001000	H
73	49	111	1001001	I
74	4a	112	1001010	J
75	4b	113	1001011	K
76	4c	114	1001100	L

Dec	Hex	Oct	Bin	Character
77	4d	115	1001101	M
78	4e	116	1001110	N
79	4f	117	1001111	O
80	50	120	1010000	P
81	51	121	1010001	Q
82	52	122	1010010	R
83	53	123	1010011	S
84	54	124	1010100	T
85	55	125	1010101	U
86	56	126	1010110	V
87	57	127	1010111	W
88	58	130	1011000	X
89	59	131	1011001	Y
90	5a	132	1011010	Z
91	5b	133	1011011	[
92	5c	134	1011100	\
93	5d	135	1011101	]
94	5e	136	1011110	^
95	5f	137	1011111	_
96	60	140	1011000	‘
97	61	141	1100001	a
98	62	142	1100010	b
99	63	143	1100011	c
100	64	144	1100100	d
101	65	145	1100101	e
102	66	146	1100110	f
103	67	147	1100111	g
104	68	150	1101000	h
105	69	151	1101001	i
106	6a	152	1101010	j
107	6b	153	1101011	k

Dec	Hex	Oct	Bin	Character
108	6c	154	1101100	l
109	6d	155	1101101	m
110	6e	156	1101110	n
111	6f	157	1101111	o
112	70	160	1110000	p
113	71	161	1110001	q
114	72	162	1110010	r
115	73	163	1110011	s
116	74	164	1110100	t
117	75	165	1110101	u
118	76	166	1110110	v
119	77	167	1110111	w
120	78	170	1111000	x
121	79	171	1111001	y
122	7a	172	1111010	z
123	7b	173	1111011	{
124	7c	174	1111100	|
125	7d	175	1111101	}
126	7e	176	1111110	~

APPENDIX B

This appendix contains the most commonly used input/output functions, mathematical functions, string functions, and memory management functions. To access these functions provided in the C language, the header files containing these functions must be linked to the program by the `#include` directive. For example to include all of the input/output functions the include directive is `#include <stdio.h>` and to include mathematical functions the directive is `#include <math.h>`, and so on.

Input and Output Functions Input and output is performed by using input and output functions built into the C language. The prototypes of these functions are contained in a header file called `stdio.h` (an abbreviation meaning "standard input/output"). For the program to have access to these functions the programmer must include the `stdio.h` header file in the program by writing the following statement:

```
#include <stdio.h>
```

Where the `.h` extension means that `stdio.h` is a header file. Also note that all system header files must be included between two angle brackets.

The input and output functions from the C library header file `stdio.h` can be grouped into two distinct groups: format driven functions and data driven functions.

Format Driven Functions These functions are input and output functions with a variable number of arguments and corresponding format control fields. These functions are:

`scanf()` and `printf()`	for standard external input and output of all data types
`fscanf()` and `fprintf()`	for file (storage device) input and output for all data types

When these functions are called within the program the arguments are specified within the parentheses. The detailed syntax and how to use these functions is presented in Chapter 3.

Data Driven Functions These functions are input and output functions with a fixed number of arguments and preformatted control fields. These functions are:

`getchar()` and `putchar()`	for standard input and output of characters
`fgetc()` and `fputc()`	for file input and output of characters
`gets()` and `puts()`	for standard input and output of strings
`fgets()` and `fputs()`	for file input and output of strings
`fread()` and `fwrite()`	for file input and output of machine-readable data
`sscanf()` and `sprintf()`	for internal input and output for data conversion between character type data and numeric type data

The detailed syntax and use of some of these functions is presented in Chapters 3 and 9.

Mathematical Functions The header file containing the prototypes of the mathematical functions is `math.h`. To use the mathematical functions, the header file must be included by writing the `#include` statement as follows:

```
#include <math.h>
```

This library contains the following groups of functions.

Commonly used trigonometric functions:

`acos()`	arccosine
`asin()`	arcsine
`atan()`	arctangent
`cos()`	cosine
`sin()`	sine
`tan()`	tangent
`sinh()`	hyperbolic sine
`tanh()`	hyperbolic tangent

String conversion functions:

`atoi()`	string to `int`
`atof()`	string to `float`
`atol()`	string to `long int`

Algorithmic functions:

`log()`	$\log_e x$
`log10()`	$\log_{10} x$

Exponential function:

`exp()`	e^x

Absolute value functions:

`abs()`	absolute value of an integer
`labs()`	absolute value of a long `int`
`fabs()`	absolute value of a `float`

Power function for exponentiation:

`pow()`	a^b

Random number generator:

`rand()`	random number
`srand()`	initialize the random number generator

Floor and ceiling functions:

`ceil()`	ceiling round up
`floor()`	floor round down

Square root function:

`sqrt()`	square root

The detailed syntax and the use of a few of these functions are presented in the text.

Character String Functions In C there are no built-in operators to manipulate character strings. Character strings may be manipulated only by using library functions. To use the string manipulation functions one must include the `string.h` file as follows:

```
#include <string.h>
```

There are several functions to manipulate the strings. These are listed as follows:
String concatenation functions:

`strcat()`	two arguments: appends one string to another
`strncat()`	three arguments: appends part of one string to another

String comparison functions:

`strcmp()`	two arguments: logical comparison of two strings
`strncmp()`	three arguments: logical comparison of first *n* characters of two strings

String copy functions:

`strcpy()`	two arguments: copies one string into another string
`strncpy()`	three arguments: copies *n* characters of one string into another string

String length function:

`strlen()`	one argument: determines the length of the string

Character search and substring functions:

`strchr()`	finds leftmost occurrence of character in string
`strrchr()`	finds rightmost occurrence of character in string
`strstr()`	finds substring

The detailed syntax and the implementation of string functions are presented in Chapter 9.

Memory Allocation Functions There are dynamic memory allocation functions in the header file `stdlib.h`. To use these functions you must include the header file as follows:

```
#include <stdlib.h>
```

The memory allocation functions are:

`malloc()`	allocates memory cells for a string
`calloc()`	allocates memory cells for an array or structure
`realloc()`	reallocates multiple memory cells from free store
`free()`	frees the storage allocated by `malloc()`, `calloc()`, or `realloc()`

These functions are presented in Chapter 10.

APPENDIX C

Answers To Review Questions

Chapter 1

Section 1.1.4

1. hardware, software
2. input/output devices, memory devices, central processing unit
3. machine code or object code
4. arithmetic, logic
5. control
6. central processing
7. character
8. magnetic tape, magnetic disk
9. application
10. arithmetic and logic unit (ALU), control unit (CU)
11. operating
12. firmware

Section 1.2.4

1. subproblems
2. A lower level module describes a subfunction of the higher level module that invokes it.
3. false

Section 1.3.6

1. An algorithm is a procedure consisting of a number of precisely defined steps for solving a problem.
2. A program is a sequence of unambiguous, executable instructions written in a computer language.
3. Top-down design methodology begins with a general specification of an algorithm, then separates it into logical parts at ever more detailed levels.
4. If the design is validated at each stage, it should not be necessary to start over.
5. An assignment statement copies a value into the memory location of a variable.
6. tape, disk, print, display, plot, device control
7. input/output, move, arithmetic, control, logic
8. character
9. input data
10. output data
11. internal
12. checking that the data values are appropriate
13. to describe the steps to be carried out by the computer in a semiformal verbal/mathematical form
14. to describe the functional analysis of the algorithm
15. to describe the flow of control and types of operations involved in the algorithm
16. so that it is understandable, easy to read, and attractive

17. so that correct answers are produced within a reasonable time
18. to switch between sets of instructions depending on the logical comparison of data values

Section 1.4.6

1. A compiler converts source code to object code, checking for errors in grammar, spelling, and punctuation.
2. A linker links object code to modules from the system library.
3. source
4. object
5. A loader stores the executable program into memory.
6. program coding: logic errors
   program compilation: grammatical and spelling errors
   program execution: overflow, arithmetic errors, etc.
7. to help users use the program, to help programmers modify the program
8. debugging
9. to make sure the program detects erroneous data

Section 1.5.3

1. Several users have access to the computer at the same time.
2. The operating system schedules and controls program execution.
3. Several programs are in memory at the same time and take turns being executed.
4. CPU
5. to automatically control equipment
6. Interactive programming: a human user interacts with the processing.
   Real-time processing: a piece of equipment interacts with the processing.
7. When programming for batch processing, input and output data are stored in files on a magnetic storage device.

Chapter 2

Section 2.1.4

1. a. false
   b. true
   c. false
   d. true
   e. true
   f. false
2. a. sequence, selection, repetition
   b. typed
   c. arrays, character strings, structures
   d. functions
   e. main

Section 2.2.6

1. a. true
   b. false
   c. true
   d. false
   e. false
   f. true
   g. true
2. a.
```
int iter, counter;
int i, j, k;
int max, min, ival, imax, jmax;
```
   b.
```
int maxcount = 50, icount = 20, kvalue = 100;
```
   c.
```
float balance, energy, power, voltage, current, acidity,
phvalue;
```
   d.
```
double atomic_number, refractive_index, specific_gravity,
density;
```

e. `char code, basic_colors, student_status, depth_code;`

f. `const int THREE = 3;`

```
const char PLUS = '+';
const float  E = 30.0E06; /* psi */
const float GRAVITY = 32.0; /* ft/sec sq */
```

or `const float GRAVITY = 9.80665; /* m/sec sq */`

3. a. `int, float, double, char`

   b. `array, string, structure`

Section 2.3.9

1. a. true
   b. false
   c. true
   d. false
   e. true
   f. true
   g. true
2. a. $x + y / z + w * p$
   b. $(x + y) / w + r - s$
   c. $8.0 * (a + b) / (6.0 * f) - k * n$
   d. $-a + b * c * (-d) * g$
   e. $(1.0 / 3.0) * b * h + 0.25 * k * n$
3. a. 19
   b. 3
   c. 17
   d. 1
   e. 12
4. a. 6.423076
   b. 3.961538
   c. 14.8

d. 1.466666

e. 12.1

5. a. $(w + x) / (y + 2.0) + x * t$

b. $a * x + b * x - c * x + d$

c. $(a + b + c) / (d + e - (f + g) /(l + j))$

d. volume = length * width * height

e. force = mass * acceleration

6. a. −13

b. 105

c. 27

d. 60.0

e. −38.5

7. a. `p = ( m * R * t)/ v;`

b. `p1 = (p2 * v2) / v1;`

c. `m = (p * v) / (R * t);`

d. `r = pow((double) (a / (4.0 * 3.141593)), (double) 0.5);`
or `r = sqrt((a/(4.0 * 3.141593));`

e. `m = (2.0 * a) / (r * r);`

f. `p = rho * R * 100;`

g. `h = (f * l * v) / ( d * d * G);`

h. `z = k * pow((double) (2.0 * g * l * pow((double) h, (double) 1.5)), (double) 0.5);`
or `z = k * sqrt(2.0 * g * l * h * sqrt(h));`

i. `r = 1.0 / (1.0 / r1 + 1.0 / r2 + 1.0 / r3 + 1.0 / r4 + 1.0/ r5);`

Section 2.4.4

1. a. true

b. true

c. true

d. false

e. true

f. true

g. true

h. false

2. a. `/* , */`

   b. `int main( )`

   c. `;`

   d. `int addsub( )`

   e. `/* I am learning C programming fundamentals in this chapter. */`

Chapter 3

Section 3.1.4

1. a. true

   b. false

   c. false

   d. true

   e. true

2. a.
```
scanf("%d  %d  %f   %f    %f", &ID_num, &count, &cost,
&weight, &average);
```
   b.
```
scanf("%f  %f  %f  %f  %f  %f  %f", &Sun, &Mon, &Tue,
&Wed, &Thu, &Fri, &Sat);
```
   c.
```
scanf("%5.1f %5.1f %d", &val1, &val2, &val3);
```
3. a.
```
printf("radius = %f  diameter = %f", rad, diam);
```
   b.
```
printf("%f\n%f\n%f\n%f\n%f\n    \n%f", item1, item2,
item3, item4, item5, total);
```
   c.
```
printf("%f  %f  %f", x, y, z);
```
4. a. `%d`

   b. `%f`

c. %d

d. %d

e. %d

Section 3.2.5

1. a. true

   b. true

   c. false

   d. false

   e. false

   f. false

   g. true

   h. true

   i. false

2. a.
   ```
   fscanf(inptr, "%d  %d  %d  %d  %d", &value1, &const1,
   &pressure, &velocity, &projection);
   ```
   b.
   ```
   fscanf(inptr,"%f  %f  %f  %f", &minval, &variance1,
   &stress, &load);
   ```
3. a.
   ```
   fprintf( outptr, %d %d %d %d %d", value1, const1,
   pressure, velocity, projection);
   ```
   b.
   ```
   fprintf(outptr, "%f  %f  %f %f", minval, variance1,
   stress, load);
   ```
4.
   ```
   FILE inptr;
   inptr = fopen("coord.dat", "r");
   fscanf(inptr,"%f %f %f %f %f %f", &x1, &y1, &z1, &x2, &y2,
   &z2);
   ```

Section 3.3.3

1. a. true

   b. false

   c. false

   d. true

e. false

f. false

g. true

h. false

i. true

j. true

k. false

l. true

2. a. i. 2352256789876543−2350

```
scanf("%5d%4d%7d%5d", &num1, &num2, &num3, &num4);
```

ii. 2352256789876543−2350

```
scanf("%5d  %4d  %7d  %5d", &num1, &num2, &num3, &num4);
```

iii. 23522   5678   9876543   −2350

```
scanf("%5d%4d%7d%5d", &num1, &num2, &num3, &num4);
```

iv. 23522 5678 9876543 −2350

```
scanf("%7d  %7d  %7d  %7d", &num1, &num2, &num3, &num4);
```

b. i. 123.456–432.76987.0980.0345

```
scanf("%7f%7f%7f%6f", &val1, &val2, &val3, &val4);
```

ii. 123.456–432.76987.0980.0345

```
scanf("%7f  %7f  %7f  %6f", &val1, &val2, &val3, &val4);
```

iii. 123.456   −432.76   987.098   0.0345

```
scanf("%7f%7f%7f%6f", &val1, &val2, &val3, &val4);
```

iv. 123.456 −432.76 987.098 0.0345

```
scanf("%7f  %7f  %7f  %7f", &val1, &val2, &val3, &val4);
&num4);
```

3. a. i.

```
printf("%5d\n  %4d\n  %7d\n  %5d", num1, num2, num3,
num4);
```

23522

5678

9876543

−2350

ii. `printf("%7d\n  %7d\n  %7d\n  %7d", num1, num2, num3, num4);`

```
  23522
   5678
9876543
  -2350
```

iii. `printf("%10d\n  %10d\n  %10d\n  %10d", num1, num2, num3, num4);`

```
     23522
      5678
   9876543
     -2350
```

b. i. `printf("%7.3f\n  %7.2f\n  %7.3f\n  %6.4f", val1, val2, val3, val4);`

```
123.456
-432.76
987.098
0.0345
```

ii. `printf("%7.3f\n  %7.2f\n  %7.3f\n  %7.4f", val1, val2, val3, val4);`

```
123.456
-432.76
987.098
0.0345
```

iii. `printf("%9.4f\n  %9.4f\n  %9.4f\n  %9.4f", val1, val2, val3, val4);`

```
 123.4560
-432.7600
 987.0980
   0.0345
```

Section 3.4.4

1. a. true
   b. false
   c. false
   d. false
   e. true
   f. true
2. a.
```
FILE *outptr;
char ch;
outptr = fopen("chfileout.dat","w");
while((ch = getchar( )) != '\n')
    fprintf(outptr, "%c",ch);
```
   b.
```
FILE *inptr;
char ch;
inptr = fopen("chfilein.dat","r");
fscanf(inptr, "%c",&ch);
while(ch  != '\n')
{
     putchar(ch);
     fscanf(inptr, "%c",&ch);
}
```
3.
```
scanf("%2d %c %2d  %2d  %c  %2d",&hr1,&ch1,
    %min1,&hr2,&ch2,&min2);
time1 = 60 * hr1 + min1;
time2 = 60 *hr2 + min2;
elapsed_time = time2 – time1;
```
4.
```
inptr = fopen("myfilein.dat", "r");
outptr = fopen("myfileout.dat", "w");
fscanf(inptr, "%c", &ch);
while(ch != '\n')
{
    fprintf(ouptr, "%c", ch);
    fscanf(inptr, "%c", &ch);
}
```

Chapter 4

Section 4.1.3

1. a. false
   b. true
   c. true
   d. true
   e. false
   f. true
   g. true
   h. true
   i. false
2. a. true
   b. true
   c. true
   d. true
   e. true
3. a. true
   b. true
   c. false
   d. true
4. a. true
   b. true
   c. true
   d. true

Section 4.2.4

1. a. false
   b. true
   c. true

d. false

e. true

f. true

g. true

2.
```
if(c1)
{
    if(c2)
        stmt3;
    else
        stmt2;
}
else
    stmt1;
```

3. a.

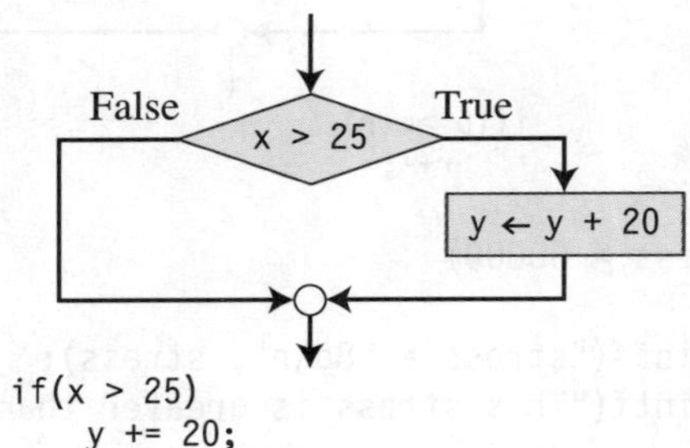

b.

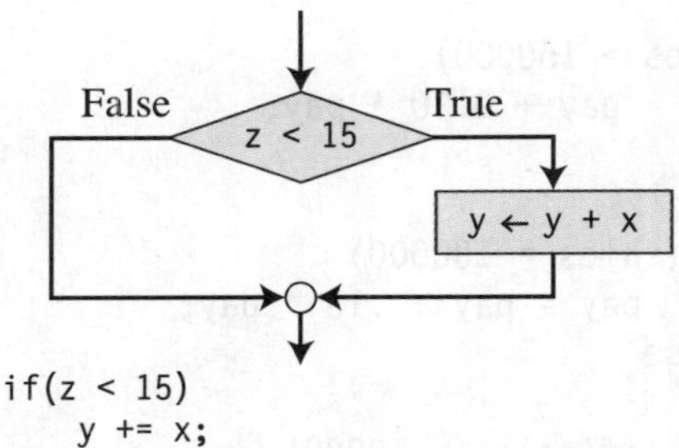

c.

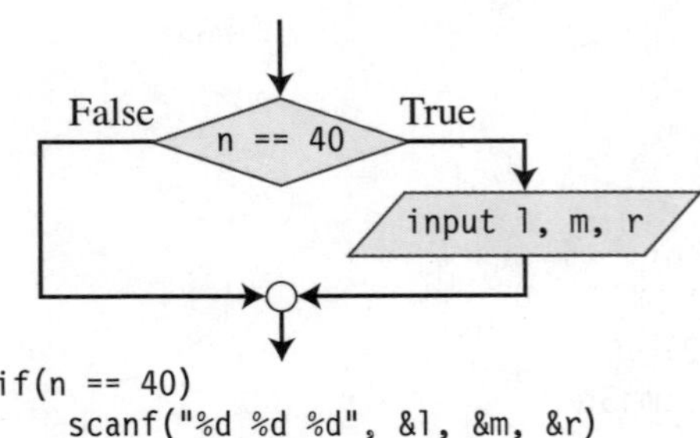


```
if(n == 40)
   scanf("%d %d %d", &l, &m, &r)
```

d.

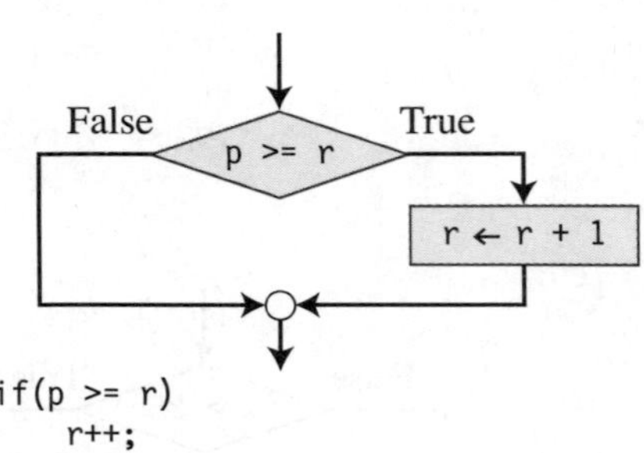


```
if(p >= r)
   r++;
```

4. a.
```
if(stress > 50000)
{
    printf("stress = %8d\n", stress);
    printf("This stress is greater than 50,000\n");
}
```

b.
```
if(sales > 10000)
   pay = pay + 0.05 * pay;
```

c.
```
if(sales > 150000)
   pay = pay + 0.20 * pay;
else
{
    if(sales > 100000)
        pay = pay + .15 * pay;
    else
    {
        if(sales > 50000)
            pay = pay + .10 * pay;
    }
}
```

5. a.
```
if(a == 0)
   printf("not a quadratic equation\n");
else
{
   d = b * b - 4.0 * a * c;
   if(d < 0.0)
      printf("Roots are complex");
   else
   {
      x1 = (-b + sqrt(d) / (2.0 * a));
      x2 = (-b - sqrt(d) / (2.0 * a));
      printf("Roots are:  %f and %f", x1, x2);
   }
```

b.
```
if(sales >= 100000)
   comm = 0.25 * sales;
else
   comm = 0.15 * sales;
printf("Sales = %d    commission = %10.2f", sales, comm);
```

c.
```
s = 0.5 * (a + b + c);
area = sqrt( s * (s - a) * (s - b) * (s - c));
printf("Sides are %f  %f  %f   Area is %f", a, b, c, area);
if(c * c == a * a + b * b)
   printf("This is a right triangle.");
```

Section 4.3.4

1. a. true
   b. true
   c. true
   d. true
   e. true
   f. true
2. a. should not be a semicolon at the end.
   b. loop will not execute as termination condition is false.
   c. loop will not terminate as termination condition is larger than initial value and index *i* is being decremented.
   d. "," where there should be a ";".

e. nested inner and outer loops use the same index variable.

f. nested inner and outer loops use the same index variable.

3. a. Inside `for` loop $i = 0$

   Inside `for` loop $i = 1$

   Inside `for` loop $i = 2$

   Inside `for` loop $i = 3$

   Outside `for` loop $i = 4$

   b. $i = 5$

   $i = 4$

   $i = 3$

   $i = 2$

   $i = 1$

   Outside `for` loop $i = 0$

   c. Inside loop $i = 0$

   Inside loop $i = 1$

   Inside loop $i = 2$

   Inside loop $i = 3$

   Outside loop $i = 4$

   Sum = 6

4. a. $i = 0 \quad j = 0$

   $i = 0 \quad j = 1$

   $i = 0 \quad j = 2$

   $i = 1 \quad j = 0$

   $i = 1 \quad j = 1$

   $i = 1 \quad j = 2$

   b. $i = 0$

   $j = 0$

   $j = 1$

   $j = 2$

   Outside $j = 3$

   $i = 1$

$j = 0$

$j = 1$

$j = 2$

Outside $j = 3$

Outside $i = 2$

Section 4.4.3

1. a. true
   b. false
   c. true
   d. false
2. 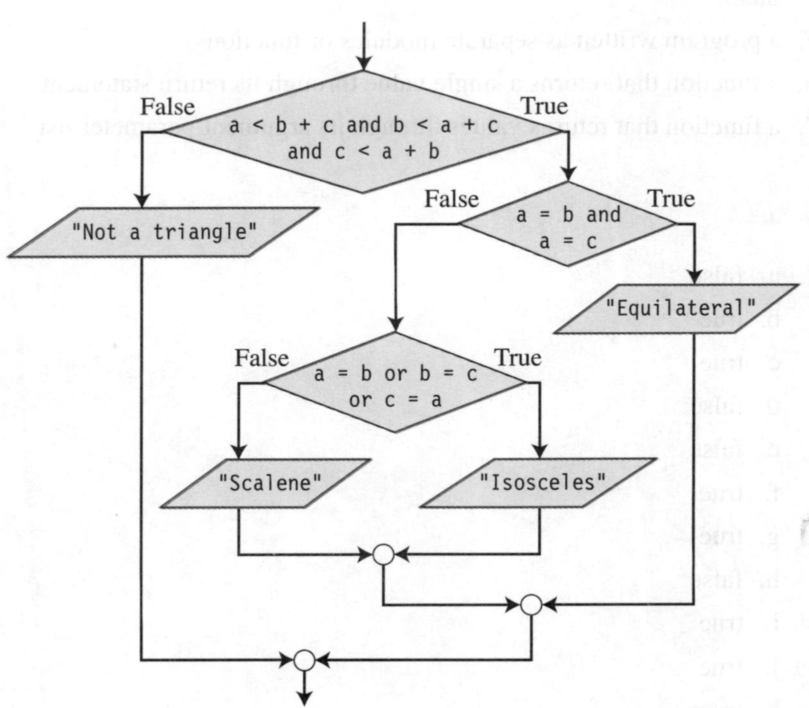

Chapter 5

Section 5.1.3

1. a. true
   b. false
   c. true
   d. true
   e. false
   f. false
2. a functional description of the program
3. They are independent.
4. Lower level modules represent subfunctions of the module above them.
5. a program written as separate modules or functions
6. a function that returns a single value through its return statement
7. a function that returns values through its argument/parameter list

Section 5.2.5

1. a. false
   b. true
   c. true
   d. false
   e. false
   f. true
   g. true
   h. false
   i. true
   j. true
   k. true
   l. false

2. a. `float funcmanipulate(int, int, float);`
   b. `float funcmanipulate(int var1, int var2, float var3);`
   c. `void funccompute(double, double, int);`
   d. `void funccompute(double var1, double var2, int var3);`
3. a. terminating semicolon is missing.
   data types of parameters are missing.
   terminating semicolon and the return data type are missing.
   b. terminating semicolon should not be present.
   data types of parameters are missing.
   return data type is missing.
   c. `main` can call `func1`, which is global and `func2`, which is local
   `func2` can call `func1`, which is global
   d. `main` can only call `func2`, which is local
   `func2` can call `func1`, which is global to it.
4. Order of execution
   starts at `Main`
   `Function1`
   returns to `Main`
   `Function2`
   `Function5`
   returns to `Function2`
   `Function6`
   returns to `Function2`
   returns to `Main`
   `Function3`
   returns to `Main`
   `Function4`
   `Function7`
   `Function5`
   returns to `Function7`

Function6

returns to Function7

returns to Function4

Function8

returns to Function4

returns to Main

terminates at Main

Scope of functions is:

Function1, Function2, Function3, and Function4 must be global to or local to Main.

Function5 and Function6 must be global to Function2 and Function7.

Function7 and Function8 must be global to or local to Function4.

Section 5.3.3

1. a. true
   b. true
   c. true
   d. true
   e. true
   f. true
   g. true
   h. true
2. a. `int func(int, int, int);`
   b. `float func(float *, float *, float *);`
3. a. `int funclargest(int, int, int);`

```
int funclargest(int n1, int n2, int n3)
{
    int max;
    max = n1;
    if(max < n2)
        max = n2;
```

```
   if(max < n3)
      max = n3;
   return max;
}
```

b. `void funcminmax( int, int, int, int *, int *);`

```
void funcminmax( int a, int b, int c, int *min, int *max);
{
     *min = a;
     *max = a;
     if(*min > b)
       *min = b;
     if(*max < b)
       *max = b;
     if(*min > c)
       *min = c;
     if(*max < c)
       *max = c;
     return;
}
```

Section 5.4.3

1. a. true
   b. true
   c. true
   d. true
   e. true
   f. true
   g. true
   h. true
   i. false
2. a. `int main( )`

```
{
     void funcgettriangle(int *, int *, int *);
       int a, b, c;
       funcgettriangle(&a, &b, &c);
       . . .
}
```

```
void funcgettriangle(int *s1, int *s2, int *s3)
{
    scanf("%d  %d  %d", s1, s2, s3);
    return;
}
```

b.
```
void funcweeksales(int *id, float *sales)
{
    scanf("%d  %f", id, sales);
    return;
}
```

c.
```
void funcoutput(int  id, float sales, float comm)
{
    printf("Salesman:  %5d    Sales:  %10.2f    Commission:
           %10.2f", id, sales, comm.);
    return;
}
```

Section 5.5.3

1. a. true

   b. true

   c. true

2.
```
void funcFibonacci(int a, int b, int n, int count)
{
    if (a==0)
   {
        count = 0;
        b = 1;
   }
   printf("%d", b);
   count++;
   if(count < n)
      funcFibonacci(b, a + b, n, count);
   return;
}
```

3.
```
int funccomb(int n, int k)
{
   int comb;
   if(n == 1 || k == 1)
      comb = 1;
```

```
    else if(n > 1 && k > 1 && k <= n)
       comb = funccomb(n - 1, k - 1) + funccomb(n - 1, k);
    else
       printf("error in data");

    return comb;
}
```

Chapter 6

Section 6.1.4

1. a. true
   b. true
   c. true
   d. false
   e. true
2. a. $x = 5$
   $x = 15$
   $x = 25$
   $x = 30$
   $x = 50$
   b. In `main` $x = 10$
   In `main` $x = 25$
   In `func1` $x = 25$
   In `func1` $x = 35$
   In `func1` $x = 5$
   In `func1` $x = 45$
   In `main` $x = 55$
3. In `func1` local `a` has not been given a value.
   In `func1` local `c` has neither been declared nor given a value.
   In `func2`, `b` is not accessible as it is local to `main`.
   In the header of `func2` there should be an integer parameter.

Section 6.2.5

1. a. true
   b. false
   c. false
   d. false
   e. true
   f. true
   g. true
   h. true
2. a. $x = 135$ in `func1`
   $a = 10$ $b = 12.500000$ $c = 125.000000$
   $x = 5$
   b. $x = 27$
   $a = 10$ $b = 12.500000$ $c = 32.000000$
   $x = 27$
   $x = 43$
   $c = 54.500000$
   c. $a = 2$
   $b = 15$
   $a = 4$
   $b = 15$
   $a = 6$
   $c = 15$
   $a = 8$
   $c = 15$

Section 6.3.2

1. a. false
   b. true
   c. false

d. false

e. true

f. false

2. In `main` $x = 10$

   In `func1` $x = 15$

   In `main` $x = 20$

3. In `main` $y = 15$

   In `main` $x = 10$

   In `func1` $x = 15$

   In `func1` $y = 30$

   In `main` $x = 20$

   In `main` $y = 50$

Chapter 7

Section 7.1.4

1. a. false

   b. false

   c. false

   d. false

   e. true

   f. false

   g. true

2. a. OK as 0 is the lowest possible subscript

   b. subscript out of bounds as only values 0–4 may be used

   c. only one subscript may be used

   d. OK as *j*/2 evaluates to 4

   e. *x* may not be both an array and a scalar variable

   f. OK as relation expression evaluates to 0 or 1

3. a.
```
float x[100];
int x[10];
double value[200];
```

b.

x		y		w	
x[0]		y[0]		w[0]	
x[1]		y[1]		w[1]	
x[2]		y[2]		w[2]	
x[3]		y[3]		w[3]	
x[4]		y[4]		w[4]	
				w[5]	
				w[6]	
				w[7]	
				w[8]	
				w[9]	

c.
```
int  a[5] = {2, 5, 7, 1, 3};
float  x[5] = {6.4, 5.8, 3.2, 4.9, 2.4};
double  y[5] = {1.2245, 18.493827, 12456965.};
```

a		x		y	
a[0]	2	x[0]	6.4	y[0]	1.2245
a[1]	5	x[1]	5.8	y[1]	18.493827
a[2]	7	x[2]	3.2	y[2]	12456965.0
a[3]	1	x[3]	4.9	y[3]	0.0
a[4]	3	x[4]	2.5	y[4]	0.0

Section 7.2.3

1. a. true

   b. false

2.
```
FILE *inptr;
inptr = fopen("filearrayin.dat", "r");
for(i = 0; i < 5; i++)
    fscanf(inptr, "%d", &a[i]);
```

3.
```
for(i = 4; i > 0; i--)
    scanf( "%f", &a[i]);
```

4.
```
for(i = 0; i < 5; i++)
    scanf("%d  %d", &x[i], &y[i]);
```

Section 7.3.3

1. a. true
   b. true
   c. true
   d. true
2. a.

0	23
1	43
2	65
3	67
4	87

   b.

4	87
3	67
2	65
1	43
0	23

3. a.

0	23	86
1	43	67
2	65	43
3	67	65
4	87	59

   b.

173	154	130	152	146
153	134	110	132	126
151	132	108	130	124
129	110	86	108	102
109	90	66	88	82

4.
```
printf("element");
for(i = 0; i < 5; i++)
    printf("%d         ", i);
printf("\na        ");
for(i = 0; i < 5; i++)
    printf("%d         ",a[ i]);
printf("\nb        ");
for(i = 0; i < 5; i++)
    printf("%6.3f        ", b[i]);
```

5.
```
printf("element   array a   array b\n");
for(i = 0; i < 5; i++)
    printf("%d. %11d %12.3f\n", a[i], b[i]);
```

Section 7.4.3

1. a. false
   b. false
   c. true
   d. true
2. a.

a	*b*
0	45
10	55
21	66
31	76
42	87

   b.

a	*b*
7	35
8	40
12	60
8	40
14	70

3. a.

a	*b*
3	18
6	36
7	42
8	336
348	14616

3. a. *a* is 1   2   1   1   6
   b. *b* is 6.25   3.2   1.7   1.3   0.75
   c. *a* is 18   15   8   6   26
   d. *a* is −6   2   1   1   23

Section 7.5.3

1. a. false
   b. false
   c. true
   d. true
   e. false
   f. true

2.
```
void funcmult(int a[ ], int b[ ], int c[ ], int n)
{
    int  k;
    for(k = 0; k < n; k++)
        c[k] = a[k] * b[k];
    return;
}
```

3.
```
float funcsum(float x[ ], int n)
{
    int  k;
    float  sum = 0;
    for(k = 0; k < n; k++)
        sum += x[k];
    return  sum;
}
```

4.
```
int  main( )
{
    const int  ARRSIZE = 5;
    int x[ARRSIZE], y[ARRSIZE];
    for(k = 0; k < ARRSIZE; k++)
        if(funcequal(x[k], y[k])
            printf("%d and %d are equal\n",x[k], y[k]);
    return  0;
}
```

Chapter 8

Section 8.1.4

1. a. false

   b. true

   c. false

   d. true

2. a. `float  x[10][20];`

   b. `int  x[20][40];`

   c. `double  w[50][200];`

   d. `double  w[100][200], q[100][200];`

3.

c[0][0]
c[0][1]
c[0][2]
c[1][0]
c[1][1]
c[1][2]

4.
```
for(i = 0; i < 10; i++)
    for(j = 0; j < 20; j++)
    {
        ...
        x[i][j]
        ...
    }
```

5.
```
for(j = 0; j < 400; j++)
    for(i = 0; i < 300; i++)
    {
        ...
        q[i][j]
        ...
    }
```

6. a.

a[0][0]	1
a[0][1]	1
a[0][2]	1
a[1][0]	0
a[1][1]	0
a[1][2]	0

b.

b[0][0]	1
b[0][1]	0
b[0][2]	0
b[1][0]	1
b[1][1]	0
b[1][2]	0

Section 8.2.3

1.
```
#define ROWS 3
#define COLS  4
.  .  .
    int  arr[ROWS][COLS], i, j;
    for(j = 0; j < COLS; j++)
        for(i = 0; i < ROWS; i++)
            scanf("%d" , &arr[i][j]);
```

a[0][0]	5
a[0][1]	16
a[0][2]	14
a[0][3]	35
a[1][0]	8
a[1][1]	19
a[1][2]	18
a[1][3]	10
a[2][0]	12
a[2][1]	16
a[2][2]	20
a[2][3]	11

2.
```
count = 0;
for(i = 0; i < 3; i++)
   for(j = 0; j < 4; j++)
      if(fscanf(inptr, "%f", &arr[i][j]) == EOF)
      {
         i = 3;
         j = 4;
      }
      else
        count++;
if(count < 12)
   printf("data missing");
```

Section 8.3.3

1.
```
for(i = 0; i < 3; i++)
 {
     for(j = 0; j < 4; j++)
     {
         printf("%14.1f ", a[i][j]);
     }
     printf("\n");
 }
```

2.
```
printf("     ");
for(j = 0; j < 6; j++)
   {
      printf("%8d", j + 1);
   }
```

```
printf("\n");

for(i = 0; i < 4; i++)
{
    printf("%2d", i);
    for(j = 0; j < 6; j++)
    {
        printf("%8.5f", arr[i][j]);
    }
    printf("\n");
    }
```

3.
```
#define IMAX  40
#define JMAX  60
. . .
    fprintf(outptr, "%d  %d", IMAX, JMAX);
    for(i = 0; i < IMAX; i++)
        for(j = 0; j < JMAX; j++)
            fprintf(outptr, "%d", arr[i][j]);
```

Section 8.4.4

1. a. false
   b. true
   c. false
   d. false
2. a.
```
int  a[2][3] = {1, 2, 3, 4, 5, 6}, b[2][3] = {10, 20, 30,
40, 50, 60};
a = b;  /* this statement should cause an error */
for( i = 0; i < 2; i++)
    printf("%d %d %d\n",a[i][0], a[i][1], a[i][2]);
```
   b.
```
int  a[2][3] = {1, 2, 3, 4, 5, 6}, b[2][3] = {10, 20, 30,
40, 50, 60};
for( j = 0; j < 3; j++) /* this should run correctly */
    a[1][j] = b[2][j];
for( i = 0; i < 2; i++)
    printf("%d %d %d\n",a[i][0], a[i][1], a[i][2]);
```

c.
```
int  a[2][3] = {1, 2, 3, 4, 5, 6}, b[2][3] = {10, 20, 30,
40, 50, 60};
a = a + b; /* this statement should cause an error */
for( i = 0; i < 2; i++)
   printf("%d %d %d\n",a[i][0], a[i][1], a[i][2]);
```

d.
```
int  a[2][3] = {1, 2, 3, 4, 5, 6}, b[2][3] = {10, 20, 30,
40, 50, 60};
int sum, i, j, k;
for( i = 0; i < 3; i++)
{
   for(j = 0; j < 3; j++)
   {
      sum = 0;
      for(k = 0; k < 3; k++)
         sum += a[i][k] * b[k][j];  /* index will go out of bounds */
      c[i][j] = sum;
   }
}
for( i = 0; i < 3; i++)
{
   for(j = 0; j < 3; j++)
      printf("%d %d %d\n",a[i][0], a[i][1], a[i][2]);
   printf("\n");
}
```

3. a. array x

2.5	4.2	5.2	6.4
4.2	2.6	1.2	7.8
5.8	2.4	6.7	9.1
1.3	2.1	3.2	4.8

b. array x

2.5	4.2	5.2	7.3
4.2	2.6	1.2	6.9
3.5	8.5	5.9	10.1
1.3	2.1	3.2	16.9

c. array x

2.5	4.2	5.2	9.4
4.2	2.6	1.2	11.5
3.5	8.5	5.9	14.5
1.3	2.1	3.2	16.0

d. array x

12.7	17.1	8.5	18.1
14.1	10.3	14.5	16.9
16.1	18.9	12.3	11.3
12.7	23.7	21.1	19.3

4. a.
```
for( i = 0; i < 4; i++)
{
    temp = 0;
    for(j = 0; j < 5; j++)
        temp += x[i][j];
    rowsum[i] = temp;
}
```

b.
```
for(j = 0; j < 5; j++)
{
    temp = 0;
    for(i = 0; i < 4; i++)
        temp += x[i][j];
    colsum[j] = temp;
}
```

c.
```
sum = 0;
for(i = 0; i < 4; i++)
    for(j = 0; j < 5; j++)
        sum += x[i][j];
```

d.
```
for(i = 0; i < 4; i++)
{
    for(j = 0; j < 5; j++)
    {
        printf("%10d ",x[i][j]);
    }
    printf("%10d\n", rowsum[i]);
}
for(j =0; j < 5; j++)
{
    printf("%10d", colsum[j]);
}
printf("%10d\n", sum);
```

5. a.
```
majorsum = 0;
for(k = 0; k < 5; k++)
    majorsum += x[k][k];
```

b.
```
minorsum = 0;
for(k = 0; k < 5; k++)
    minorsum += x[k][4 - k];
```

c.
```
uppersum = 0;
for(i = 0; i < 5; i++)
    for(j = i + 1; j < 5; j++)
        uppersum += x[i][j];
```

d.
```
lowersum = 0;
for(i = 0; i < 5; i++)
    for(j = 0; j < i; j++)
        lowersum += x[i][j];
```

Section 8.5.3

1. a. true
   b. false
   c. true
   d. true
   e. true
2. a.
```
func(int a, n, m);
. . .
void func(int a[][JMAX], n, m) /* this should run correctly */
{
    int i, j;
    for(i = 0; i < n; i++)
        for(j = 0; j < m j++)
            printf("%d", a[i][j]);
    return;
}
```

b.
```
arr[0][0] = 3;
func(arr);
printf("%d" , arr[0][0]); /* this should print original value */
                          /* if it is passed by value */
```

```
void func(int arr[  ][JMAX])
{
    arr[0][0] = 25;
    return;
}
```

c.
```
func(int [ ] [JMAX]); /* this should cause an error */
```

d.
```
void func(int arr[ ][JMAX], n, m) /* this should run correctly */
{
    int  row1sum = 0, col1sum = 0, i , j;
    for(j = 0; j < m; j++)
        row1sum += arr[0][j];
    for(i = 0;i < n; i++)
        col1sum += arr[i][0];
    return;
}
```

e.
```
printf("%d", arr[2][3]);
func(arr[2][3], &arr[2][3]);
printf("%d", arr[2][3]);
. . .
void func(int a, int *b) /* this should cause an error */
{
    printf("%d %d \n", a, *b);
    a = 10;
    *b = 20;
    printf("%d %d \n", a, *b);
    return;
}
```

3.
```
void funcmax(float pressure[  ][JMAX], n, m)
{
    float  rowmax[IMAX] = 0.0, max;
    for(i = 0; i < m; i++)
    {
        max = 0.0;
        for(j = 0;j < n; j++)
            if(max < pressure[i][j])
                max = pressure[i][j];
        rowmax[i] = max;
```

```
    }
    for(i = 0; i < n; i++)
    {
        for(j = 0; j < m; j++)
            printf("%f ", pressure[i][j]);
        printf("%f\n", rowmax[i]);
    }
```

4.
```
#define  IMAX  10
#define  JMAX  5
```

a.
```
int main()
{
   float temperature[IMAX]{JMAX];
   float rowavg[IMAX], colavg[JMAX];
   funcin(temperature);
   funcavg(temperature, rowavg, colavg);
   functout(temperature, rowavg, colavg);

   return 0;
}
void funcin(float temp[ ][JMAX])
{
    int  i, j;
    for(i = 0; i < IMAX; i++)
        for(j = 0; j < JMAX; j++)
            scanf("%f", &temp[i][j]);
    return;
}
```

b.
```
void funcavg(float temp[ ][JMAX], float rowavg[ ], float
colavg[ ])
{
    int  i, j;

    for(i = 0; i < IMAX; i++)
    {
        rowavg[i] = 0.0;
        for(j = 0;j < JMAX; j++)
            rowavg[i] += temp[i][j];
    }
    rowavg[i] = rowavg[i]/JMAX;

    for(j = 0; j < JMAX; j++)
```

```
    {
        colavg[j] = 0.0;
        for(i = 0; i < IMAX; i++)
            colavg[j] += temp[i][j];
    }
        colavg[j] = colavg[j]/IMAX;

    return;
}
```

c.
```
void funcout(float temp[ ][JMAX], float rowavg[ ], float
colavg[ ])
{
    int  i, j;

    for(i = 0; i < IMAX; i++)
    {
        for(j = 0; j < JMAX; j++)
        {
            printf("%f        ", temp[i][j]};
        }
        printf("%f        \n ", rowavg[i]);
    }
    for(j = 0; j < JMAX; j++)
    {
        printf("%f        ", colavg[j]);
    }

    return;
}
```

Section 8.6.5

1. a. false
   b. false
   c. false
   d. false
   e. true
2. a. `float x[20][50][100];     /* contains 100,000 numbers */`
   b. `int y[200][500][100];     /* contains 10,000,000 numbers */`

c. `double z[10][10][20];    /* contains 2,000 numbers */`

3.
```
#include <stdio.h>
#define IMAX 2
#define JMAX 2
#define KMAX 2
void funcin(float [ ] [IMAX][JMAX]);
void funccomp(float [ ] [IMAX][JMAX]);
void funcout(float [ ] [IMAX][JMAX]);

   int main( )
   {
      float  arr[KMAX][IMAX][JMAX];
      funcin(arr);
      funccomp(arr);
      funcout(arr);

      return 0;
   }

   void funcin(float arr[ ][IMAX][JMAX])
   {
      int k, i, j;
      for(k = 0; k < KMAX; k++)
         for(i = 0; i < IMAX; i++)
            for(j = 0; j < JMAX; j++)
               scanf("%f", &arr[k][i][j]);

   return;
}

void funccomp(float a[ ] [IMAX][JMAX])
{
   int  i, j;
   for(i = 0; i < IMAX; i++)
      for(j = 0; j < JMAX; j++)
      {
          a[0][i][j] = 10.0 * a[0][i][j];
          a[1][i][j] = 20.0 * a[1][i][j];
      }

   return;
}
```

```
void funcout(float arr[ ] [IMAX][JMAX])
{
    int k, i, j;
    for(k = 0; k < KMAX; k++)
    {
        for(i = 0; i < IMAX; i++)
        {
            for(j = 0; j < JMAX; j++)
                printf("%f", arr[k][i][j]);
               printf("\n");
        }
        printf("\f");
    }

    return;
}
```

Chapter 9

Section 9.1.4

1. `scanf("%21c\n", str);` will input any of the strings.
2.
```
|E|l|e|c|t|r|o|n|i|c| |C|o|m|p|u|t|e|r|s| |
|N|u|c|l|e|a|r| |R|e|a|c|t|o|r|s| |
|A|t|o|m|i|c| |W|e|i|g|h|t| |
|M|o|l|e|c|u|l|a|r| |F|o|r|m|u|l|a| |
```
3. `printf("%s\n", str);` will print any of the strings left-justified.
4. `printf("%-s\n", str);` will print any of the strings right-justified.

Section 9.2.4

1. a. false
   b. true
   c. true
   d. false
   e. true
   f. true
   g. true

h. true

i. true

j. true

k. true

l. false

m. false

n. true

o. true

p. true

q. true

r. false

s. false

t. true

2. `char river[13] = {'A', 'm', 'a', 'z', 'o', 'n', ' ', 'R', 'i', 'v', 'e', 'r', '\0'};`

3. `scanf("%50s", name);`

4. `printf("%s\n", name);`

5.
```
#define STRLNG  20
#define NUMSTR  3
for(k = 0; k < NUMSTR; k++)
     fgets(strname[k], STRLNG-1, inptr);
```

C	o	m	p	u	t	e	r		A	s	s	o	c	i	a	t	e	s	\0
C	o	m	m	u	n	i	c	a	t	i	o	n		M	e	d	i	a	\0
E	l	e	c	t	r	o	n	i	c		M	e	d	i	a	\0			

6.
```
for(k = 0; k < 2; k++)
     puts(strname[k]);
puts("\n ");
puts(strname[2]);
```

7.
```
for(k = 0; k < 3; k++)
     printf("%25s"\n,strname[k]);
```

8.
```
for(k = 0; k < 3; k++)
     printf("%-25s\",strname[k]);
```

Section 9.3.2

1. a. false

   b. false

   c. false

2.
```
#define NUMSTR 5
#define LENGTH 80

void funcgetlist(char [ ] [LENGTH]);

int main( )
{
    . . .
    funcgetlist(strn);
    . . .
    return 0;
}

void funcgetlist(char strname1[ ][LENGTH])
{
    int  k;
    for(k = 0; k < 3; k++)
        gets(strname1[k]);

    return
}
```

Section 9.4.6

1. a. true

   b. false

   c. true

   d. true

   e. true

   f. true

   g. false

2.
```
char sentence[80];
strcpy(sentence, "Germany ");
strcat(sentence, "is " );
strcat(sentence, "in ");
strcat(sentence, "Europe.");
```

3. a. 1 0 0
   b. 1 0 0
   c. 1 0 0
   d. 0 1 0
4. a. `strcpy(str1, str2);`

```
before str1: vanlines used for transportation\0
       str2: valentines day\0
after  str1: valentines day\0 or transportation\0
       str2: valentines day\0
```

   b. `strcpy(str1, str2);`

```
before str1: computers\0
       str2: electrons\0
after  str1: electrons\0
       str2: electrons\0
```

   c. error as `str2` is too long

Chapter 10

Section 10.1.3

1. a. true
   b. false
   c. true
   d. true
   e. false
   f. false
2. a. 56000
   3950
   3950

   b. 4000
   8550
   8550
   4000
   8550
   8550

Section 10.2.3

1. a. true
   b. false
   c. true
   d. false
   e. true
2. a.
```
int  *ptr;
ptr = 2; /* causes an error */
```
   b.
```
int  *ptr1, *ptr2, *ptr3;
int  x[5] = {1, 2, 3, 4, 5};
ptr1 = x;
ptr2 = x;
ptr3 = ptr1 + ptr2; /* causes an error */
```
   c.
```
int  *ptr1, *ptr2, *ptr3;
int  x[5] = {1, 2, 3, 4, 5};
ptr1 = x;
ptr2 = x;
ptr3 = ptr1 - ptr2; /* permissible but to use ptr3 */
```
   d.
```
int  a[3], b[3];/* would cause an error */
int *ptra;
ptra = a;
b = ptra;
a = a + ptra; /* causes an error */
```
   e.
```
int  x;
int *ptr1, *ptr2;
ptr1 = &x;
ptr2 = &x;
```

Section 10.3.4

1. a. false
   b. true
   c. true
   d. false

e. true

f. false

g. false

2.
```
ptr = a;
for(k = 0; k <10; k++)
{
    scanf("%d", ptra);
    ptra++;
}
ptra = a;
for(k = 0; k <10; k++)
{
    printf("%d", *ptra);
    ptra++;
}
```

3.
```
for(k = 0; k < 400; k++)
    scanf("%f", b + k);
for(k = 0; k < 400; k++)
{
    printf("%f",  *(b + k));
    if(20 * (k / 20) == k)
        printf("%\n");
}
```

Section 10.4.3

1. a. true

   b. true

   c. true

   d. true

   e. false

2.
```
int  *ptr;
ptr = (int *) calloc(200, sizeof(int));
```

3.
```
float  *ptr;
ptr = (float *) calloc(80000, sizeof(float));
```

4.
```
float  *ptr;
ptr = (float *) calloc(50 * 60, sizeof(float));
for(k = 0; k < 3000; k++)
{
    scanf("%f", ptr);
    ptr++;
}
ptr = ptr - 3000;
for(k = 0; k < 3000; k++)
{
    printf("%f", *ptr);
    ptr++;
}
```

Section 10.5.3

1. a. true
   b. true
   c. true

Chapter 11

Section 11.1.5

1. a. true
   b. false
   c. true
   d. true
   e. true
   f. true
   g. true
   h. true
   i. true
   j. false
2.
```
struct employee
{
    char name[20];
```

```
      char id[7];
      float  hours;
      float  wages;
      float  gross;
      float  deductions;
      float  net;
   }clerk, janitor;
```

3.
```
struct employee security = {"John Johnson", "EMP3456", 48.0,
                            18.60, 0.0, .20};

security.gross  = security.hours * security.wages;
if(hours > 40)
   security.gross += (security.hours – 40) * security.wages / 2.0;
security.deductions = 0.2 * security.gross;
security.net = security.gross – security.deductions;
```

4.
```
struct employee, security, *emptr;
emptr = &security;

strcpy(emptr -> name, "John Johnson");
srtcpy(emptr -> id, "EMP3456");
emptr -> hours = 48.0;
emptr -> wages = 18.0;
emptr ->gross = emptr -> hours * emptr -> wages;
if(hours > 40)
   empttr -> gross += (emptr -> gross – 40.0) * emptr -> wages / 2.0;
emptr -> deductions = 0.2 * emptr -> gross;
emptr -> net = emptr -> gross – emptr -> deductions;
```

Section 11.2.4

1. a. true
   b. true
   c. true
   d. true
2. `scanf(%d      %f      %f",   &colm1.numcolumns,   &colm1.diameter, &colm1.length);`
3. `printf(%d      %f      %f\n",   colm1.numcolumns,   colm1.diameter, colm1.length);`

4. ```
typedef struct strength
             {
                 float load;
                 float diameter;
                 float length;
                 float stress;
                 float strain;
             }COLUMN;

          COLUMN col1, col2, colarr[10];
```

5. ```
struct vector
{
    int size;
    float values[10];
}
```

Section 11.3.4

1. a. true
   b. true
   c. false
   d. true
   e. true
   f. true
   g. false
2. ```
struct volume funccomp(struct volume cyl1)
{
    const float PI = 3.141593;
    cyl1.surfarea = 2 * (PI * cyl1.diameter * cyl1.diameter) /
                           4.0 + PI * cyl1.diameter * cyl1.length;
    cyl1.volume = PI * (cyl1.diameter * cyl1.diameter) / 4.0 *
                          cyl1.length;

     return cyl1;
}
```
```

```
void funcoutput(struct volume cyl1)
{
    printf("Surface area: %5.2f  Volume: %5.2f\n",
            cyl1.surfarea, cyl1.volume);

    return;
}
```

3.
```
cylinder.surfarea = funcsurfacearea(cylinder.diameter,
cylinder.length);
cylinder.volume = funcvolume(cylinder.diameter / 2.0,
cylinder.length);
.  .  .
float funcsurfacearea(float  diam, float  length)
{
    const  float PI = 3.141593;
    return (2 * (PI * diam * diam)/ 4.0) + PI * diam * length;
}

float funcvolume(float radius, float.  length)
{
    const float PI = 3.141593;
    return (PI * radius * radius * length);
}
```

Section 11.4.3

1. a. true
   b. true
   c. false
   d. true
   e. true
   f. true
2.
```
struct student
      {
         char id[5];
         char  name[20];
      };
```

```
struct record
       {
          struct student stu;
          float  testgrade[4];
          float  average;
          char lettergrd;
       };

struct record student;

void funcoutput(struct record student1)
{
    int  i;
    printf("%s    %s" , student1.stu.id, student1.stu.name):
    for(i = 0; i < 4; i++)
        printf("%6.2f      ", student1.testgrade[i]);
    printf("%6.2f     ", student1.average);
    printf ("%c", student1.lettergrd);

    return;
}
```

3.
```
struct customer
{
    char  name[20];
    char  acct[10];
    char  addr[40];
    struct customer *next;
};
```

Section 11.5.4

1. a. true
   b. true
   c. true
2. a. `enum months{Jan, Feb, Mar, April, May, June, July, Aug, Sept, Oct, Nov, Dec};`
   b. `enum country{United States of America, United States, USA, US};`
   c. `enum index{0, 1, 2, 3, 4, 5, 6, 7, 8, 9};`

APPENDIX D

Order of Precedence of Operators from Highest to Lowest

Description	Operator	Associate from
Function `expr`	`( )`	
Array `expr`	`[ ]`	
`struct` indirection	`->`	left to right
`struct` member	`.`	
Increment/decrement	++ –	
One's complement	`~`	
Unary not	`!`	
Address	`&`	right to left
Dereference	`*`	
Cast	`(data type)`	
Unary plus/minus	`+ -`	
Size in bytes	`sizeof`	
Multiplication, division, and Modulus	`* / %`	
Addition, subtraction	`+ -`	
Shift left/right	`<< >>`	left to right
Comparisons	`< <= > >= = = !=`	

<table>
<tr><th>Description</th><th>Operator</th><th>Associate from</th></tr>
<tr><td>Bitwise and</td><td>&</td><td></td></tr>
<tr><td>Bitwise inclusive or</td><td>|</td><td></td></tr>
<tr><td>Bitwise exclusive or</td><td>^</td><td></td></tr>
<tr><td>Logical and</td><td>&&</td><td></td></tr>
<tr><td>Logical or</td><td>||</td><td></td></tr>
<tr><td>Conditional</td><td>? :</td><td>right to left</td></tr>
<tr><td>Assignment</td><td>= %= += -+ *= /=
> >= < <= &= ^= |=</td><td></td></tr>
<tr><td>Comma</td><td>,</td><td>left to right</td></tr>
</table>

Index

Italicized page locators indicate a figure; tables are noted with a *t*

M

K

L

M

X